THE UNIVERSITY OF
WINCHESTER

Martial Rose Library
Tel: 01962 827306

HENRY THE YOUNG KING, 1155–1183

HENRY the YOUNG KING
1155–1183

MATTHEW STRICKLAND

YALE UNIVERSITY PRESS
NEW HAVEN AND LONDON

For information about this and other Yale University Press publications, please contact:
U.S. Office: sales.press@yale.edu   yalebooks.com
Europe Office: sales@yaleup.co.uk   yalebooks.co.uk

Typeset in Adobe Caslon Pro by IDSUK (DataConnection) Ltd
Printed in Great Britain by Gomer Press Ltd, Llandysul, Ceredigion, Wales

Library of Congress Cataloging-in-Publication Data

Names: Strickland, Matthew, 1962- author.
Title: Henry the Young King, 1155-1183 / Matthew Strickland.
Description: New Haven : Yale University Press, 2016.
LCCN 2016009450 | ISBN 9780300215519 (cl : alk. paper)
LCSH: Henry, King of England, 1155-1183. | Great Britain—Kings and rulers—
    Biography. | Henry II, King of England, 1133–1189—Family. | Great Britain—
    History—Henry II, 1154-1189.
Classification: LCC DA206 .S77 2016 | DDC 942.03/1092—dc23
LC record available at http://lccn.loc.gov/2016009450

A catalogue record for this book is available from the British Library.

10 9 8 7 6 5 4 3 2 1

For Debra

Contents

Illustrations

Maps

Preface

'A KING WITHOUT A realm is at a loss for something to do: at such a loss was the noble and gracious Young King.'[1] Thus the poet Jordan Fantosme, writing for the Plantagenet court soon after the great war of 1173–74 which had pitted Henry II against his own son, Henry 'the Young King', encapsulated the paradox that lies at the heart of this study. Young Henry was the first – and last – king of England since the Norman Conquest to be crowned in the lifetime of his father. The desire to have his son created as an anointed king had been a driving factor in Henry II's policies from at least 1162, and in 1170 he had pushed through his son's coronation by the archbishop of York in highly contentious circumstances, which would lead, unwittingly but directly, to the murder of Thomas Becket only six months later. Yet despite the enormous significance he had attached to his son's regal status, Henry II never felt able to grant his eldest son direct rule of any of the Angevin lands. The resulting tension between young Henry's royal rank and his lack of effective power was, as Jordan Fantosme recognized, the root cause of his rebellion in 1173, which shook the Angevin empire to its core. This book is a study of the life of young Henry, not only principal heir to Henry II and titular co-ruler of the heartlands of the great Plantagenet dominions, but also one of the most charismatic and celebrated chivalric figures of later twelfth-century Europe. It is also the story of an experiment in associative kingship that failed catastrophically, and of a king without a kingdom.

The book adopts a chronological framework, but the examination of the nature of Angevin kingship, of associated rulership, of warfare and of rebellion runs as binding thread throughout. It falls naturally into three parts. The first examines young Henry's early life, from the extraordinary circumstances of his marriage, when aged only five to the still younger Margaret, daughter of Louis VII, through his brief but influential period in the household of Thomas

Becket, to his coronation in 1170 and regency of England until 1172, a regency plunged into crisis by the return of Archbishop Thomas from exile, then fatefully overshadowed by Becket's murder and its consequences. The second part comprises an analysis of the causes, course and consequences of the great war of 1173–74, which came close to unseating his father, the Old King, and profoundly affected subsequent relations between father and son, particularly in the years between 1175 and 1177, when fears of renewed war were never distant. The third traces the period of comparative stability from 1178 to 1182, marked by young Henry's prominent participation in the tournament circuit and his significant role in the military and diplomatic efforts of the Angevins to keep the balance of power in northern France. It then turns to the collapse of this entente in the bitter war of 1183 which resulted from young Henry's attempt to wrest Aquitaine from his brother Richard, but which again plunged much of the Angevin empire into turmoil, and only ended with the Young King's premature death from disease on campaign. It concludes with an examination of his death, commemoration and legacy.

In the preface to his own chronicle, the Winchester monk and historian Richard of Devizes explained to his friend Robert, the work's recipient, that he would commence his account a little earlier than they had agreed, and begin from the accession of Richard I in 1189. 'And because I could not hope to unravel the whole story', he noted, 'I have undertaken only the latter part of it. Why, and how, and when the father crowned his son; how much and what manner of things they accomplished; whose lands they invaded and when and to what extent; and to what end each came; all this I have left to those who want to bring forth bigger things.'[2] I should no doubt have done likewise. Richard's wisdom in declining to embark on the dauntingly large subject of Henry II and his family became increasingly clear as this work progressed, and Devizes himself would surely have appreciated Manuel Rojas' jest that it was taking so long to write the book that the Young King was becoming the Old King.

Nevertheless, one of the great dividends of undertaking this study of the young Henry has been the pleasure of engaging with a large number of scholars who have generously shared their very diverse expertise in and beyond 'l'espace Plantagenêt'. I have been greatly helped by a number of friends and colleagues, and here I would like to thank Adrian Ailes, Bill Aird, Stuart Airlie, Richard Allen, Martin Aurell, David Bates, Rob Bartlett, Matthew Bennett, Maïté Billoré, Colette Bowie, Dauvit Broun, David Carpenter, Jo Cerda, Stephen Church, Michael Clanchy, Laura Cleaver, David Crouch, Archie Duncan, Katy Dutton, Peter Edbury, John France, Daniel Gerrard, John Gillingham, Judith Green, Sandy Heslop, John Hudson, Jitske Jasperse, Edmund King, Henry Mayr-Harting, Ralph Moffat, Alheydis Plassmann,

Daniel Power, Manuel Rojas, David Sherlock, Ian Short, Jim Simpson, Roger Smith, Michael Staunton, Keith Stringer, Liesbeth van Houts, Colin Veach, Nicholas Vincent, Bjorn Weiler and Bill Zajac.

Deserving of special thanks are Stephen Church and the anonymous reader for Yale University Press (who betrayed a particularly in-depth knowledge of the Pipe Rolls and of equine matters), as well as Stephen Marritt, Andrew Roach and Manuel Rojas, all of whom read through early drafts of the book, saved me from numerous errors and made many helpful comments. John Gillingham likewise kindly read a later draft, and the resulting book is much the stronger for his valuable input. It has equally benefited very considerably from Dan Powers expertise on Normandy and its aristocracy, while I am also grateful to Michael Staunton for advice both on Thomas Becket and on historical writing in the later twelfth century. Nicholas Vincent helpfully provided me with a copy of the as yet unpublished Angevin *Acta*, and both he and David Crouch have been generous with references and in sharing unpublished research and materials. Judith Everard kindly sent me her Itinerary of Henry II ahead of its publication in the Angevin *Acta*.

My thanks are due to Heather McCallum, Melissa Bond and Rachael Lonsdale at Yale University Press for steering the book through to completion with patience and good-natured forbearance, and to Beth Humphries whose careful copy-editing has saved me from numerous stylistic infelicities.

The writing of this book was made possible by an Arts and Humanities Research Council matching study leave grant, and the sabbatical leave given to me by the College of Arts at the University of Glasgow. I would also like to thank the Master and Fellows of Fitzwilliam College Cambridge for a Visiting Fellowship, which permitted me to research and write in such stimulating and convivial circumstances. It was while working as a doctoral student with the late Sir James Holt, then the Master of Fitzwilliam College, that I first began to develop my interest in the Young King. This is a fitting place to acknowledge my great debt to Jim Holt as a teacher and mentor, as well as to the late Marjorie Chibnall, who always took a keen interest in my research and whose work has been an important influence on it. To Michael Prestwich I owe an equally important debt.

My warm thanks are due to Paul Strickland and Caroline Rose, and to Mike, Tom and Claire Strickland for their encouragement and unfailing welcome in deepest Norfolk, which Jordan Fantosme himself knew to be the best county 'between here and Montpellier'. My greatest thanks are to my wife, Debra Strickland. Not only have I benefited throughout from her knowledge as a medieval art historian and from her editorial expertise, but she has also been a constant source of advice, help, and inspiration. This book could not have been written without her untiring support, and it is dedicated to her with love.

A Note on Terms and Currency

I N THE TWELFTH CENTURY, the word 'prince' (*princeps*) could be used in a general sense to refer to a ruler, as in Gerald of Wales' work *De principis instructione*. It had not yet, however, become adopted as a formal title or rank for cadets of the English royal family, so that to speak of 'Prince Henry' would be anachronistic. In this book the term prince is applied to young Henry before his coronation in 1170 simply as a term of convenience for denoting a royal son. Contemporaries would have afforded him the title *Dominus*, while the term used by chroniclers and in governmental records such as the Pipe Rolls to refer to young Henry before 1170 was usually simply *filius regis*, and after 1170, *rex filius regis* or *rex junior*.

The name Ralph of Diss has been used here for the chronicler traditionally referred to as Ralph de Diceto. It has long been thought probable that 'Diceto' was Diss in Norfolk, but Professor Dauvit Broun has recently shown beyond doubt that this is certainly correct.[1]

A number of different currencies were in circulation concurrently in the Angevin lands, though the coinage itself principally comprised the silver penny or denier. In England, a pound sterling comprised 240 silver pennies (known as sterlings or esterlins), with twelve pennies in a shilling and twenty shillings in the pound. The mark, which existed only as a unit of account and not as an actual coin, was two-thirds of a pound or 160 pennies. In Normandy and Anjou, the main currency was the *livre angevin* (equivalent to the *livre tournois*) with four *livres angevins* being the equivalent value of one pound sterling.[2]

Abbreviations

AM	*Annales monastici*, ed. H. R. Luard, 4 vols (Rolls Series, London, 1864–1869)
ANS	*Anglo-Norman Studies*
Bosham	*Vita Sancti Thomae archiepiscopi et martyris, auctore Herberto de Boseham*, in *Materials for the History of Thomas Becket, Archbishop of Canterbury*, ed. J. C. Robertson and J. B. Sheppard, 7 vols (Rolls Series, London, 1875–1885), III
CCM	*Cahiers de civilisation médiévale*
CDF	*Calendar of Documents Preserved in France, vol. 1, 918–1206*, ed. J. H. Round (London, 1899)
Chronicles of the Reigns of Stephen, Henry II and Richard I	*Chronicles of the Reigns of Stephen, Henry II and Richard I*, ed. R. H. Howlett, 4 vols (Rolls Series, London, 1884–1889)
Chroniques des comtes d'Anjou	*Chroniques des comtes d'Anjou et des seigneurs d'Amboise*, ed. L. Halphen and R. Poupardin (Paris, 1913)
Continuatio Beccensis	*Continuatio Beccensis*, in *Chronicles of the Reigns of Stephen, Henry II and Richard I*, ed. R. H. Howlett, 4 vols (Rolls Series, London, 1884–1889), IV
Councils and Synods	*Councils and Synods, with other Documents Relating to the English Church, I, AD 871–1204*, ed. D. Whitelock, M. Brett and C. N. L. Brooke, 2 vols (Oxford, 1981)

CTB	*The Correspondence of Thomas Becket, Archbishop of Canterbury, 1162–1170,* ed. and trans. A. J. Duggan, 2 vols (Oxford, 2000)
De principis	*De principis instructione liber*, ed. G. Warner, in *Giraldi Cambrensis Opera*, ed. J. S. Brewer, F. Dimock and G. Warner, 8 vols (Rolls Series, London, 1861–1891), VIII
Dialogus	*Dialogus de Scaccario and the Constitutio Domus Regis*, ed. and trans. E. Amt and S. Church (Oxford, 2007)
Diceto	*Opera Historica: The Historical Works of Master Ralph de Diceto, Dean of London*, ed. W. Stubbs, 2 vols (Rolls Series, London, 1876)
Draco Normannicus	Stephen of Rouen, *Draco Normannicus*, in *Chronicles of the Reigns of Stephen, Henry II and Richard I*, II
EEA	*English Episcopal Acta*
EHD	*English Historical Documents, II, 1042–1189,* ed. D. C. Douglas (2nd edn, Oxford, 1961)
EHR	*English Historical Review*
Eleanor of Aquitaine. Lord and Lady	*Eleanor of Aquitaine. Lord and Lady*, ed. B. Wheeler and J. C. Parsons (New York, 2003)
Expugnatio	*Expugnatio Hibernica: The Conquest of Ireland, by Giraldus Cambrensis*, ed. and trans. A. B. Scott and F. X. Martin (Dublin, 1978)
Eyton	R. W. Eyton, *The Court, Household and Itinerary of Henry II* (London, 1878)
FitzStephen	William FitzStephen, *Vita sancti Thomae Cantuarensis archiepiscopi et martyris, Materials for the History of Thomas Becket, Archbishop of Canterbury*, ed. J. C. Robertson, and J. B. Sheppard, 7 vols (Rolls Series, London, 1875–1885), III
Foedera	*Foedera, conventiones, litterae,* I, part i, ed. T. Rymer, A. Clarke, F. Holbrooke and J. Caley (London, 1816)
Foundation of Walden	*The Book of the Foundation of Walden Monastery*, ed. and trans. D. Greenway and L. Watkiss (Oxford, 1999)

Gerald, *Opera*	*Giraldi Cambrensis Opera*, ed. J. S. Brewer, F. Dimock and G. Warner, 8 vols (Rolls Series, London, 1861–1891)
Gervase	*The Historical Works of Gervase of Canterbury*, ed. W. Stubbs, 2 vols (Rolls Series, London, 1879–1880)
Gervase, *Otia imperialia*	Gervase of Tilbury, *Otia imperialia*, ed. and trans. S. E. Banks and J. W. Binns (Oxford, 2002)
Gesta regum	William of Malmesbury, *Gesta regum Anglorum*, ed. and trans. R. B. Mynors, R. M. Thomson and M. Winterbottom, 2 vols (Oxford, 1998–1999)
Gesta Stephani	*Gesta Stephani*, ed. and trans. K. R. Potter and R. H. C. Davis (Oxford 1976, reprinted 2004)
GH	*Gesta regis Henrici secundi Benedicti abbatis: The Chronicle of the Reigns of Henry II and Richard I, AD 1169–1192*, ed. W. Stubbs, 2 vols (Rolls Series, London, 1867)
Gilbert of Mons	*La Chronique de Giselbert de Mons*, ed. L. Vanderkindere (Brussels, 1904), trans. L. Napran, *Gilbert of Mons, Chronicle of Hainault* (Woodbridge, 2005)
Gouiran	*L'Amour et la guerre. L'oeuvre de Bertran de Born*, ed. G. Gouiran, 2 vols (Aix-en-Provence, 1985)
Guernes	*La Vie de Saint Thomas le Martyr par Guernes de Pont-Sainte-Maxence: poème historique du XIIe siècle (1172–1174)*, ed. E. Wahlberg (Lund, 1922); trans. I. Short, *A Life of Thomas Becket in Verse* (Toronto, 2013)
Henry II. New Interpretations	*Henry II. New Interpretations*, ed. C. Harper-Bill and N. Vincent (Woodbridge, 2007)
HGM	*L'Histoire de Guillaume le Maréchal, comte de Striguil et de Pembroke, régent d'Angleterre de 1216 à 1219: poème français*, ed. P. Meyer, 3 vols (Société de l'Histoire de France, Paris, 1891–1901)

HH	Henry of Huntingdon, *Historia Anglorum*, ed. and trans. D. Greenway (Oxford, 1996)
Histoire des ducs	*Histoire des ducs de Normandie et des rois d'Angleterre*, ed. F. Michel (Paris, 1840)
History of the Counts of Guisnes	*Lamberti Ardensis historia comitum Ghisnensium*, ed. J. Heller, *MGH, Scriptores*, XXIV (1879); trans. L. Shopkow, *Lambert of Ardres, The History of the Counts of Guisnes and Lords of Ardres* (Philadelphia, 2007)
History of the King's Works	*The History of the King's Works*, ed. H. M. Colvin et al., 8 vols (London, HMSO, 1963–1982)
Howden	*Chronica magistri Rogeri de Hoveden*, ed. W. Stubbs, 4 vols (Rolls Series, London, 1868–1871)
HWM	*History of William Marshal*, ed. A. J. Holden, with English translation by S. Gregory and historical notes by D. Crouch, 3 vols (Anglo-Norman Text Society, London, 2002–2006)
JF	*Jordan Fantosme's Chronicle*, ed. and trans. R. C. Johnston (1981)
JMH	*Journal of Medieval History*
JW	*The Chronicle of John of Worcester*, ed. and trans. R. R. Darlington and P. McGurk, 3 vols (Oxford, 1995–)
Letters and Charters of Henry II	*The Letters and Charters of Henry II King of England (1154–1189)*, ed. N. Vincent et al., 5 vols (Oxford, forthcoming)
LJS	*The Letters of John of Salisbury*, ed. and trans. W. J. Millor, H. E. Butler and C. N. L. Brooke, 2 vols (Oxford, 1979, 1986)
Map	Walter Map, *De nugis curialium*, ed. and trans. M. R. James, revised by C. N. L. Brooke and R. A. B. Mynors (Oxford, 1983)
Matthew Paris, *Historia Anglorum*	*Matthaei Parisiensis monachi sancti Albani, historia Anglorum*, ed. F. Madden, 3 vols (Rolls Series, London, 1865–1869)
Melrose	*The Chronicle of Melrose*, ed. A. O. Anderson and M. O. Anderson (London, 1936)

MGH SRG	*Monumenta Germaniae Historica. Scriptores rerum Germanicarum in usum Scholarum*
MGH SS	*Monumenta Germaniae Historica. Scriptores*
MTB	*Materials for the History of Thomas Becket, Archbishop of Canterbury*, ed. J. C. Robertson and J. B. Sheppard, 7 vols (London, Rolls Series, 1875–1885)
Northamptonshire Charters	*Facsimiles of Early Charters from Northamptonshire*, ed. F. M. Stenton (London, 1930)
ODNB	*Oxford Dictionary of National Biography*
Orderic	*The Ecclesiastical History of Orderic Vitalis*, ed. M. Chibnall, 6 vols (Oxford, 1969–1980)
Padern	*The Poems of the Troubadour Bertran de Born*, ed. W. D. Padern, T. Sankovitch and P. Stablein (Berkeley, 1986)
PL	*Patrologia Latina*
Plantagenêts et Capétiens	*Plantagenêts et Capétiens: confrontations et héritages*, ed. M. Aurell and N.-Y. Tonnerre (Turnhout, 2006)
PR	*The Great Rolls of the Pipe of the Reign of Henry the Second*, 5th to 34th years, 30 vols (Pipe Roll Society, 1884–1925)
Ralph Niger, *Chronicle*	*Radulphi Nigri Chronica,* ed. R. Anstruther (London, 1851)
Recueil	*Recueil des actes de Henri II*, ed. L. Delisle and E. Berger, 4 vols (Paris, 1909–1917)
RHF	*Recueil des historiens des Gaules et de la France*, ed. M. Bouquet et al., 24 vols (Paris, 1869–1904)
Rigord	Rigord, *Histoire de Philippe Auguste*, ed. É. Charpentier, G. Pon and Y. Chauvin (Paris, 2006)
RRAN	*Regesta regum Anglo-Normannorum*, ed. H. W. C. Davis, H. A. Cronne and R. H. C. Davis, 4 vols (Oxford, 1913–1969)

RRS, I	*Regesta regum Scottorum, I. The Acts of Malcolm IV, King of Scots 1153–1165*, ed. G. W. S. Barrow (Edinburgh, 1960)
RRS, II	*Regesta regum Scottorum, II. The Acts of William I, King of Scots, 1165–1214*, ed. G. W. S. Barrow (Edinburgh, 1971)
Smith, *'Acta'*	R. J. Smith, 'Henry II's Heir: The *Acta* and Seal of Henry the Young King, 1170–1183', *EHR*, 116 (2001), 297–326
Staunton, *Lives*	*The Lives of Thomas Becket* (Manchester, 2001)
Torigni	*The Chronicle of Robert of Torigni*, in *Chronicles of the Reigns of Stephen, Henry II and Richard I*, ed. R. Howlett, 4 vols (Rolls Series, London, 1884–1889), IV
Torigni, ed. Delisle	*Chronique de Robert de Torigni*, ed. L. Delisle, 2 vols (Rouen, 1872–1873)
TRHS	*Transactions of the Royal Historical Society*
Vigeois	Geoffrey of Vigeois, *Chronica*, ed. P. Labbe, *Novae bibliothecae manuscriptorum et librorum rerum Aquitanicarum*, 2 vols (Paris, 1657), II
Vita Galfridi	Gerald of Wales, *De vita Galfridi archiepiscopi Eboracensis*, in *Giraldi Cambrensis Opera*, ed. J. S. Brewer, F. Dimock and G. Warner, 8 vols (Rolls Series, London, 1861–1891), IV
Wace, *Roman de Rou*	*Wace's Roman de Rou*, trans. G. S. Burgess, with the text of A. J. Holden and notes by G. S. Burgess and E. M. C. van Houts (St Helier, Jersey, 2002)
William of Canterbury	William of Canterbury, *Vita et passio et miracula Sancti Thomae, auctore Willelmo, monacho Cantuariensi*, in *Materials for the History of Thomas Becket, Archbishop of Canterbury*, ed. J. C. Robertson and J. B. Sheppard, 7 vols (Rolls Series, London, 1875–1885), I
William of Tyre	William of Tyre, *Chronique*, ed. R. B. C. Huygens, 2 vols (Corpus Christianorum. Continuatio medievalis, 63–63a, Turnhout, 1986)

WN	William of Newburgh, *Historia rerum Anglicarum*, in *Chronicles of the Reigns of Stephen, Henry II and Richard I*, ed. R. Howlett, 4 vols (Rolls Series, London, 1884–1889), I and II
Writing Medieval Biography	*Writing Medieval Biography, 750–1250. Essays in Honour of Professor Frank Barlow*, ed. D. Bates, J. Crick and S. Hamilton (Woodbridge, 2006)

CHAPTER I

A Forgotten King?

You would have been king of the noble and emperor of the brave, lord, if
you had lived longer, for you had gained the name Young King; you were
indeed the guide and father of youth. And hauberks and swords, and beautiful buckram, helmets and gonfalons, pourpoint and lappets and joy and
love have nobody to maintain them or bring them back. They will follow
you; like all mighty, honourable deeds, they will disappear with you.
– Bertran de Born, *Mon chan fenis ab dol et ab maltraire*[1]

IN EARLY JUNE 1183, Henry III, king of England, lay dying in the little town
of Martel in the Quercy.[2] Gathered around him in the humble house of a
blacksmith were some of the greatest nobles of France, his recent allies in a
bitter and still ongoing war against his own brother and father which had
devastated much of Aquitaine by fire and sword. Finally, on 11 June, after days
of being racked by acute fever brought on by dysentery, the Young King – *li res
jovens, li giemble reis, l res joves* or *rex junior*, as he was better known to his
contemporaries – breathed his last, aged only twenty-eight.[3] Of all the
Plantagenet kings, the young Henry remains the least known. His effigy is not
at the abbey of Fontevraud among the famous tomb sculptures of Henry II,
Eleanor and Richard the Lionheart for he died before Fontevraud became
established as the principal Angevin mausoleum.[4] Instead, he was buried in
Rouen cathedral with his ducal ancestors. There, however, his tomb fared less
well, and little remains of his original monument.[5] The stylized images of
young Henry on the few surviving examples of his great seal are badly worn,
and as he struck no independent coinage, no silver pennies or deniers carry his
depiction. He and his wife Margaret may be represented by the finely sculp-
tured heads of a young king and queen in the early thirteenth-century portal
of the church of Candes-Saint-Martin, close to Fontevraud, but there are few

if any contemporary images extant of a man once famed for his striking good looks, charm and knightly prowess.[6]

Yet his life, though short, had been a remarkable one. The eldest surviving son of Henry II, he was chief heir to the Angevin empire, one of the greatest agglomerations of territories seen since the days of Charlemagne.[7] In 1170 he had been anointed king, the first heir to be crowned in the lifetime of his father in England since 796. For thirteen years, England was to have two kings. Yet within three years of his coronation the young Henry was at the head of a powerful coalition of rebel nobles and external enemies leagued against his father, precipitating a bitter two-year war which marked the gravest crisis of Henry II's reign. Reconciled with his father after his failed rebellion, the Young King had by the late 1170s become an international celebrity, fêted for his feats of arms in the tournament circuit of northern France and renowned as an open-handed patron of knights. After a decade of uneasy peace, however, and still with no territories to call his own, he had answered the call of the nobles of Aquitaine, chafing under the iron-fisted rule of his younger brother Richard, to be their duke. His campaign had come close to wresting the duchy from Richard when young Henry was seized by his fatal illness. Healing miracles were reported at his tomb and he was hailed by some as a saint – the only Angevin ruler ever to have been so regarded.

Handsome, athletic and with a winning character, young Henry was seen by many as the embodiment of chivalry and as possessing the virtues of an ideal prince. One of his chaplains, Gervase of Tilbury, described him thus:

> He was tall in stature, and distinguished in appearance; his face expressed merriment and mature judgment in due measure; fair among the children of men, he was courteous and cheerful. Gracious to all, he was loved by all; amiable to all, he was incapable of making an enemy. He was matchless in warfare, and as he surpassed all others in the grace of his person, so he outstripped them all in valour, cordiality, and the outstanding graciousness of his manner, in his generosity and in his true integrity. In short, in this man, God assembled every kind of goodness and virtue, and the gifts which fortune usually bestows on single individuals of special distinction, she exerted herself to give all together and in richer measure to this man, so as to make him worthy of all commendation.[8]

Gervase, writing as he was for young Henry's nephew Emperor Otto IV, was doubtless guilty of flattering hyperbole. To those closer to Henry II, the younger Henry appeared more as a reckless and divisive ingrate who had stirred up unmerited and illicit war against a doting father. Nevertheless, the

Young King's untimely death had been marked by an outpouring of grief. The Limousin castellan and troubadour Bertran de Born, who had been an ally in the young Henry's war in Aquitaine in 1183, spoke for many of the nobility and especially for the younger, often landless knights, known collectively as the *juvenes* or 'youth', when he hailed him as 'the head and father of Youth (*de joven*)', 'the best king who ever bore a shield, the most audacious, the best tourneyer', whose equal was unknown before or since Roland.[9] Another *planh* or lament noted that at his death Merit and Youth (*Pretz e Jovens*) had been left grieving, for death had robbed the world of 'the best knight that ever was in all the world (*il melhor chavalier as tout al mon*)', 'the most valiant of the worthy (*lo plus valens dels pros*)', beside whom 'the most generous were mean'.[10] So too the author of the *History of William Marshal*, the long Anglo-Norman poem celebrating the life of the knight who had begun his remarkable career as young Henry's tutor in arms, complained that the Young King's death had 'changed chivalry into inactivity and idleness. Generosity (*largesce*) became an orphan, and the world was deprived of light by what Fortune had destroyed.'[11]

Nor were such sentiments restricted to the lords and knights who had been particular beneficiaries of the Young King's patronage. Ecclesiastical chroniclers throughout the Angevin territories mourned his passing and praised his qualities.[12] Robert of Torigni, the abbot of the great Norman abbey of Mont Saint-Michel, noted that the death of 'the young king, our dearest lord', was 'the occasion to us of deepest grief', not only because he was Henry II's son, but also 'because he was of the most handsome countenance, of the most pleasing manners, and the most free handed in his liberality of all the individuals with whom we have been acquainted'.[13] In Anjou, a monk of the great abbey of Saint-Aubin in Angers could write that young Henry's death 'was lamented by nearly all the world', while to a chronicler at Waverley abbey he was 'King Henry the Third, the illustrious man of wonderful qualities'.[14] In the 1220s, young Henry was regarded as a role model for a new generation of rulers, held up to his two royal nephews, Otto IV of Germany and King John's son Henry, as the mirror of knighthood and chivalry.

Yet, perhaps ironically, it was in the wake of the coronation of the latter on 28 October 1216 that the title of Henry III began no longer to be applied to his uncle the Young King, but to the new Henry. By the time Matthew Paris painted his famous depictions of the series of English kings from 1066 onwards in his *Historia Anglorum*, *c*.1250–55, he could portray the Young King, labelled as 'Henricus Iunior', crowned and clean shaven, but in bust only and in a small arch between the seated figures of Henry II and Richard I. Here his raised hand points up to Richard, as his successor, labelled as 'rex sextus' following the Norman Conquest, while Henry II is labelled 'rex quintus'.[15] The Bermondsey annals, a compilation of earlier materials brought together around 1433, recorded the belief that 'this King Henry is not numbered in the numbering of kings because he was injuriously crowned by Roger, archbishop of York, while the blessed Thomas, archbishop of Canterbury was in exile for the cause of justice'.[16] This is unlikely to have been contemporary reasoning behind the transference of regnal title, which may have been a gradual process and more probably reflected the growing assumption that the Young King should be passed over in regnal numbering because he had predeceased his father and not reigned alone.[17]

As he lost the title of Henry III, so too in time voices of approbation began to fade. Young Henry's great reputation as the epitome of chivalry would come to be eclipsed by the fame of his younger brother Richard, the towering figure of the Third Crusade, who was becoming the stuff of legend even before his death in 1199. The process was gradual: in the later thirteenth century an anonymous interpolator of the Old French crusade history known as *La Chronique d'Ernoul* could hail young Henry as 'the greatest hearted prince born of a king that ever was since the time of Judas Maccabeus', and noted that he was called 'the Lion'.[18] Yet equally by the 1260s, the anonymous French poet known as the Minstrel of Rheims could present a remarkably garbled account of the Young King's career and even mistakenly call him 'Curtmantle' – 'Short cloak' – the epithet given by contemporaries to his father Henry II.[19] An independent tradition, seemingly drawn from the semi-fictitious Provençal biographies (*vidas*) and commentaries (*razos*) attached to the poetry of Bertran de Born, saw young Henry appearing in the *Novellino*, a late thirteenth-century collection of Italian tales, in which he was celebrated as a prince of such generosity that he beggared himself, turning a blind eye to thefts from him by the needy: one *Novelle* even tells the story of how, hard pressed by his creditors, the Young King mortgaged his soul to the Devil, but was redeemed by his father, who paid off his debts.[20] Yet in such tales he has been transformed into an anonymous archetype known only as 'lo giovane re d'Inghilterra', while Bertran de Born gains increasing prominence as a malevolent Svengali, whose scheming tutelage sets the prince and his father at odds.[21] It is thus that Dante knew him simply as the *re giovane*, when soon after 1300 the poet placed Bertran de Born in his *Inferno* among the sowers of discord, his head for ever severed from his body for maliciously stirring up war between father and son and parting those who should have been closely knit.[22]

It was not literary echoes, however, that most powerfully shaped posterity's perception of the young Henry, but rather a more hostile and enduring tradition. Of the very few extant narrative sources to be written in later twelfth-century Aquitaine, the most significant is the chronicle of Geoffrey of Vigeois, monk of the abbey of St Martial's, Limoges, then abbot of Vigeois (1170–84), who had witnessed the Young King strip his abbey of St Martial of its treasures to pay his mercenaries and bring a devastating war into Geoffrey's beloved Limousin.[23] Still more significantly, his leading role in the war of 1173–74 against his father, followed by the circumstances of his death while in rebellion, once again led to a damning verdict on him by contemporary writers in the orbit of the Angevin court, and it is their profoundly negative legacy that has influenced the assessment of the Young King by the great majority of historians ever since. In recording the Young King's untimely death, chroniclers such as Roger of Howden, Walter Map and Gerald of Wales reflected a sensitivity to Henry II's deep grief at the death of his son, as well as the sorrow felt by the court at the loss of so promising a young man, whose popularity they well understood. Nevertheless, with the expectation that the young Henry would succeed to his father removed – and with it the need for circumspection in any condemnation of the heir – they and subsequent writers were free to be fiercely critical of a son who had risen not once but twice against his own father. To these *curiales*, young Henry was not only a deeply ungrateful son, but a rebel and parricide, a second Absalom, who had abused his father's love and trust until he was finally struck down by the avenging hand of God.[24] Walter Map, a royal clerk and one of the great *literati* of the Angevin court, had accompanied Henry II on his expedition to suppress the rebellion in Aquitaine in 1183. In happier days, he had been involved in young Henry's education and clearly held the prince in affection, describing him as 'a man full of grace and favour. Rich, noble, loveable, eloquent, handsome, gallant, every way attractive, a little lower than the angels'.[25] Yet in a powerful passage written in the royal camp as Henry II's army continued the siege of Limoges and only weeks after young Henry's death at Martel, Map wrote bitterly: 'Truly he left nothing unprobed, no stone unturned; he befouled the whole world with his treasons, a prodigy of unfaith and prodigal of ill, a limpid spring of wickedness, the attractive tinder of villainy, a lovely place of sin ... the originator of the heresy of traitors ... a false son to his father ... the peaceful king'.[26] To Ralph of Diss, the learned dean of St Paul's, young Henry's death offered a salutary moral lesson, 'leaving for the approval of the wise the opinion that sons who rise up against fathers to whom they owe everything that they are and everything from which they live, and by whose goods they expect to be enriched, are worthy only of being disinherited'.[27]

The Young King's premature death, moreover, meant that it was his brother Richard – his bitter enemy in the war of 1183 – who inherited Henry II's great empire.[28] As a result, chroniclers might shape or reshape their depictions of young Henry to suit the times. Gerald of Wales, who joined the Angevin court in 1184, had included a lengthy paean for young Henry in his *Topographica Hibernica*, written between 1186 and 1188 when Henry II still reigned and with his patronage very much in mind. In this, he extolled young Henry as 'an honour of all honour, the beauty and ornament of the city and of the world, the splendour, glory, light and highest honour in war, a Julius Caesar in genius, in valour a Hector, an Achilles in strength, an Augustus in conduct, a Paris in beauty'. His only fault was that 'of ingratitude, and the affliction which he brought to the best of fathers'.[29] Yet in his *Expugnatio Hibernica*, written during the late 1180s and dedicated soon after Henry II's death on 6 July 1189 to Richard 'noble count of Poitou, duke of Normandy and ruler of England in the near future', Gerald included a polished literary comparison of Richard with the Young King.[30] With a clear view to pleasing the new king, Gerald noted that Richard

> was second to his illustrious brother in age only, and not in virtue. For although they sprang from the same stock, they were of different manners and pursuits, yet each deserved glorious praise and eternal memory. Both were of noble stature, somewhat more than of middle height, and of beauty worthy of an empire. In activity and greatness of mind they were nearly equal, but very unlike in their ways of showing their virtues. Henry was praised for his lenity and liberality, Richard was remarkable for his severity of manner and firmness of purpose. The former was commendable for the sweetness, the latter for the gravity of his manner. For the former, an easy-going nature demanded praise, for the latter, constancy. The former was remarkable for his mercy, the latter for his justice. The former was the refuge of the wretched and of evil doers, the latter was their punishment. The former was the shield of the bad, the latter their destroyer. Again, the one was addicted to martial games, the other to serious pursuits. The one was attached to foreigners, the other more to his own subjects. The one was beloved by all, the other only by the good. The one coveted the world by the greatness of his mind, the other, not without success, sought the authority that was his by right. But why should I specify each of their various quali-ties? Neither the present age nor any period of antiquity calls to mind two so great and yet so different men as the sons of one ruler.[31]

This superficially even-handed contrast, however, was a thinly veiled critique of the Young King for taking up the cause of the nobles of Aquitaine against Richard in 1183, for these are 'the wretched', 'the evil doers', 'the bad' and the 'foreigners', while Richard's harsh rule, which had caused the rebellion, is exon-erated by Gerald, both here and in an ensuing encomium, as firm and just government. The Young Henry may have been generous, likeable and easy-going, but these, Gerald implies, were not the qualities demanded by real rulers; in contrast to Richard's zealous engagement in the serious business of governing Aquitaine, the Young King's sporting activities reflected his essential frivolity.

Unlike Rigord of St Denis, who could style himself 'cronographus regis Francorum', Roger of Howden appears not to have been an 'official' historiographer of the Angevin court, but as a royal clerk, justice and diplomat with access to royal archives he was often well informed and his *Gesta regis Henrici*, begun in 1170 and thereafter largely written up year by year until 1192, constitutes the single most important chronicle for the career of the Young King.[32] Yet Roger had soon been alienated by young Henry's leading role in the rebellion of 1173–74, then further outraged in 1176 at the young Henry's harsh treatment of his vice-chancellor, Adam of Churchdown, a member of the clerical circle of Archbishop Roger of York with which Howden had close connections.[33] His animus towards the Young King reached its climax in his reportage of young Henry's last war in Aquitaine in 1183 and of his last days and death. When in the mid 1190s Roger reworked the *Gesta* into his larger but substantially revised *Chronica*, he used the opportunity to adapt his picture of the Young King. The *Gesta's* contemporary account had noted the involvement of both Queen Eleanor and Richard, as count of Poitou, in the rebellion of 1173–74, yet in the *Chronica* mention of both was dropped, and blame instead heaped solely upon young Henry:

> For this one of the king's sons was lost to all reason and feeling. He abandoned an innocent man, persecuted his father, usurped power, attacked the realm; he alone was to blame, setting a whole army against his father. 'One madman makes many others'. For he thirsted for the blood of his father, for the death of his progenitor.[34]

Similarly, in the *Gesta* Howden had reported the acts of oppression Richard was alleged to have committed against the barons of Aquitaine, but these were removed from the *Chronica*, where it was noted instead that the rebels allied to the Young King 'inflicted much harm on Count Richard'.[35] Howden's revision of his account of the Young King's death was more complex, but as revealing. In the *Gesta*, he had briefly described the Young King's death from fever at Martel, reported Henry II's intense grief, then put a speech into the Old King's mouth addressed to his army besieging Limoges in which Henry stresses how God has saved him from near-destruction by being avenged on the sins of his son. Accordingly, though the king laments the death of one so handsome and talented, 'it is preferable to be glad of his death, rather than to grieve', and better instead that his men should turn their efforts to defeating the Young King's allies, who were bent on destroying his father.[36] In the *Chronica* Howden gives a much fuller account, apparently drawn from eyewitnesses, of the Young King's death and his seemly acts of penitence.[37] King Henry's speech is omitted, and instead Roger adds his own condemnation:

> O how dreadful a thing it is for sons to persecute a father! For it is not opposing sword nor enemy hand that takes up the father's injury, but fever that retaliates, and flux of the bowels, with excoriation of the intestines, avenges. With the son laid prostrate, all return to the father. All are over-joyed, all rejoice: the father alone bewails his son. Why, glorious father, do you bewail him? He was no son of yours who could commit such violence against your fatherly affection. This defence of you has brought security for fathers and checked the audacity of parricides. Wanting to introduce parricide into this world, it was his deserts to perish by a severe retribution, for just as He avenges the tribulations of the righteous, so the Judge of all minds sometimes punishes the persecutions of the wicked.[38]

When Howden penned this, Henry II had been dead for some years. While the sentiments expressed may very well reflect Roger's own, his reworking of the narratives concerning the Young King strongly implies that he expected Richard, or at least those close to the king, to see his work, at a time when issues of propaganda and the projection of the royal image were very much to the fore.[39] Howden, moreover, came to regard the Young King's death as punishment both for his own misdeeds and for the failings of his father, not least Henry II's failure to counter the growing threat of heresy by not permitting the burning of heretics within his lands.[40] Roger records how a certain Walter, servant of Eustace, abbot of Flaye, told Henry II of a vision in which a heavenly voice had commanded the king, 'In the name of Christ, annihilate and destroy', and threatening the death of his sons if he did not obey. Henry II, however, did not understand the vision, took no action, and as a result first young Henry, then Geoffrey, died.[41]

Nor was Howden alone in depicting the Young King's fate as part of a larger narrative of providential retribution on Henry II. Thomas Becket's clerk and hagiographer Herbert of Bosham recounted how the tearful archbishop had told Herbert of his prophetic dream, in which he had foretold the death of young Henry (who as a child had been Becket's ward) as the result of God's anger at Henry II's persecution of the Church and of Thomas himself.[42] It was, however, Gerald of Wales who set the Young King within a still darker and more distorting picture of Henry II and his family in his *De principis instruc-tione*, a work begun in the 1190s but not completed until 1218, by which time Gerald was seeking the favour of the Capetians. By then deeply embittered by his failure to gain the ecclesiastical preferment he believed he deserved, Gerald sought to portray the Angevins as a uniquely dysfunctional family. As he has Count Geoffrey of Brittany say, 'It is our own basic nature, planted in us as if by hereditary right from both our close and our distant ancestors, that none of us should love the other, but that always brother should fight against brother, and son against father'.[43] Henry II himself is depicted as a king who moved from excessive love for his children to deep hatred of them, for 'this had been the perverse nature of King Henry, that, with all his power, he excited and perpetuated quarrels between his sons, hoping from their discord to gain peace and quietness for himself'.[44] This inbred hostility was, argued Gerald, the result of a corrupted lineage; not only was Henry II's marriage to Eleanor 'adulterous', but Henry's own father Geoffrey le Bel had, he alleged, had sexual relations with her, while Eleanor's own infidelities to both Louis VII and Henry II were notorious. The dynasty was thus a blighted and doomed one. The Young King's rebellions, moreover, were part of a morality tale on a grand scale.[45] Henry II, rising to the heights of power and fortune through divine favour but then turning from God through sin, tyranny and persecution of the Church, compelled God to chastise him, especially by the rebellion of the Young King. For a time Henry's penance and humility over Becket's death regained divine favour, allowing him to defeat his enemies, but he again lapsed into evil ways, and, despite ignoring repeated warnings, was destroyed by the successive rebellions of his children. Gerald could thus regard young Henry as a *flagellum Dei*, a tool of divine vengeance against Henry II, but at the same time condemn his 'monstrous ingratitude' in rebelling against his father.[46] Gerald readily acknowledged the Young King's qualities and martial reputa-tion, but now such virtues served only as a poignant *vanitas*, highlighting the fragility and emptiness of worldly fame and heightening the tragedy of his untimely end.

The depiction of the Young King by Gerald of Wales, Howden and other chroniclers has had a profound and long-lasting influence. Historians of Henry II, Eleanor, Richard the Lionheart, Thomas Becket and William Marshal have all touched on the Young King where his life intersected with those of their principals, yet their gaze has usually been brief and their verdicts almost always harsh. They echo the chroniclers' condemnation of young Henry's acts of rebel-lion against his father, seen both as morally reprehensible and as demonstrating a want of responsibility and political acumen.[47] The tone was set early. Bishop Stubbs deprecated young Henry's filial disobedience, but struggled to explain the apparent paradox of his evident popularity: 'that wicked son in whom, although we see little else than unreasonable and perfidious disobedience, his contemporaries saw so much that was attractive and charming, that his popularity was one of the wonders of his age'.[48] Such a view was endorsed by Kate Norgate in her influential history of the Angevins: 'From the day of his crowning to the day of his death, not one deed is recorded of him save deeds of the meanest ingratitude, selfishness, cowardliness and treachery'.[49] For Norgate, young Henry lacked the true qualities of either the Angevin or the Norman, and appeared the antithesis of her hero Richard the Lionheart. Even his acknowledged virtues could not compare with those of Richard: 'Richard's generosity and graciousness were of a higher type than young Henry's; they were displayed only when they were deserved', while the Young King's 'careless, easy, shallow disposition' contrasted with the latter's 'energetic temperament'.[50] Like Stubbs, she found his contemporary popularity bewildering, while 'the attraction exercised by him over a man so far his superior as William Marshal, is well-nigh incomprehensible'.[51] Her condemnation was repeated almost verbatim by Olin Moore, author of the first dedicated study in English of the Young King, who dismissed expressions of praise upon his death as mere self-serving flattery of courtiers or attempts by Henry II's critics to cast him in a more negative light in comparison with his son's alleged qualities.[52]

More recent historians, while not displaying the moral outrage of Stubbs and Norgate at the young Henry's filial impiety, have remained critical. It was perhaps inevitable that for Lewis Warren, the pre-eminent biographer of Henry II, the Young King fell far short of his great father, whose reign he did so much to trouble. Warren recognized young Henry's personal charm and winning character, yet still dismissed him as 'shallow, vain, careless, empty headed, incompetent, improvident and irresponsible'.[53] In a typically vivid character sketch, he encapsulates what has remained the prevailing verdict:

> The Young Henry was the only member of the family who was popular in his own day. It is also true that he was also the only one who gave no evidence of political sagacity, military skill, or even ordinary intelligence, but such, after all, are not looked for in a fairytale prince, and the young Henry had all the trappings of a hero of romance or aubade. He was tall, handsome, gay, and splendidly improvident. He had the sort of charm that makes even gross irresponsibility seem nothing more than the mischievousness of a lively boy.[54]

Even David Crouch, the historian who has best captured young Henry's glamorous stardom and importance in the tournament circuit of northern France, sees his as 'a wasted young life', and implicitly has found this 'feather-brained lord devoted entirely to military pleasures' wanting when compared to his tutor-in-arms, the great William Marshal.[55] What kind of king young Henry would have made had he outlived Henry II and enjoyed sole rule of the heartlands of the Angevin empire can only remain conjecture. But we might reflect that had William Marshal died in 1183, before he had been propelled into increasing political prominence by the final crises of Henry II's reign, he would have been remembered, if at all, merely as an outstanding but ruthlessly acquisitive prizefighter with a talent for self-promotion and self-preservation, not as the commander or senior statesman that he came to be in his later years.

That such predominantly negative judgements of young Henry have remained largely unchallenged is in part due to the paucity of studies devoted to the Young King, in contrast to the much more extensive scholarship focusing on his brothers Richard and John, as well as on Henry II and Eleanor of Aquitaine.[56] C. E. Hodgson's 'Jung Heinrich, König von England', a 1906 German doctoral dissertation, has long remained the most detailed historical study, while the only dedicated work in English, O. H. Moore's *The Young King Henry Plantagenet 1155–1183 in History, Literature and Tradition*, deals briefly with his career and, as its title suggests, is primarily concerned with his literary *Nachleben*.[57] Since these early studies, various aspects of his career have been examined further, as they are in Anne Duggan's important re-dating of the papal mandate authorizing the young Henry's coronation by the archbishop of York, Thomas Jones' analysis of the war of 1173–74, and Ralph Turner's work on the households of Henry II's sons and the upbringing of royal children.[58] An important milestone was reached in 2001 with Roger Smith's analysis of the Young King's status as associate king as revealed by his seal and charters, accompanied by a calendar of his surviving *acta*.[59] Nevertheless, it is striking that despite a renaissance in Angevin studies within Anglo-French scholarship, the most recent dedicated study of the Young King has been Valter Leonardo Puccetti's *Un fantasma letterario. Il «Re Giovane» del Novellino*, a masterly exploration of the genesis of the character and qualities of young Henry as they appear in the *Novellino*, which sheds much light on his ideological and cultural milieu.[60]

A new analysis of the life of the young Henry and his developing role in the politics and culture of the Angevin empire thus needs little justification. To study the career of the Young King is to go to the heart of the critical issues of succession, delegation of power and the division of the Plantagenet lands. Likewise, important light can be shed on conceptions of Angevin kingship and of co-rulership by tracing plans for young Henry's coronation, mooted as early as 1161, Henry II's reasons for wishing to crown his son, the precedents on which he drew and the coronation's place in the bitter struggle between Henry II and Thomas Becket.[61] The dominant image, moreover, of the Young King as a frivolous sporting playboy can be challenged as misleading in many ways. Young Henry jointly presided with his father over secular and ecclesiastical councils from the age of seven, was trained for future rule in his boyhood, and between 1170 and 1172 acted as regent of England. There is not the slightest evidence that he lacked 'even ordinary intelligence'; indeed, Walter Map may have been among his tutors, he was noted for his eloquence and courtliness, and is known to have retained *eruditi* such as Ralph Niger and Gervase of Tilbury among his household. Nor was avid participation in the tournament in any way incompatible with the serious business of rule, as is amply demonstrated by the careers of two of the tournament's other greatest patrons and habitués in the later twelfth century, Henry the Liberal, count of Champagne, and Philip, count of Flanders, who was to become a chivalric mentor to the Young King. Indeed, by the second half of the twelfth century, the tournament had become an integral aspect of noble culture, and an increasingly important mechanism for the projection of princely power, wealth and influence, which young Henry was to exploit to the full. If, moreover, the Young King devoted so much of his energies between 1176 and 1182 to the tournament circuit of northern France it was because he was denied the opportunity, which he had consistently requested, of ruling one of the constituent territories of the Angevin dominions. For at the root of the developing tensions with his father from 1173 was not his lack of interest in government, but quite the opposite: a pressing desire to assume the position which his coronation had heralded yet which was being withheld from him.

The Young King's resulting rebellion may have shocked contemporaries as 'unnatural', yet it stood in a long tradition of conflict between ruling fathers and their eldest sons, at the heart of which lay fundamental but often contentious issues of succession and territorial division. If a charge of ingratitude is appropriate in such circumstances, then his brothers Richard, Geoffrey and John were equally guilty, for all rebelled against their father, and both Geoffrey and Richard in turn would also ally with the king of France. That they did so, however, points less to any supposed moral failings of young Henry or his siblings than to systemic problems between a dynast and his heirs.[62] Young Henry's rebellion was nevertheless of singular importance. Never before had a king of England had to contend with a rebellious son who was an anointed sovereign in his own right, nor would any thereafter. Accordingly, an examination of how the Young King's royal status related to the causes of the war of 1173–74, its conduct, the terms of peace that ended it, and the long and fragile process of reconciliation that followed, lies at the heart of this study.

Beyond the familiar generic difficulties of writing the biography of medieval secular figures, a number of peculiar challenges confront the historian
attempting to examine the Young King's life and career.[63] Young Henry did
not live long enough to receive his own *Gesta* or *Historia*. Rather, as we have
seen, his rebellions ensured that from 1173 onwards he was viewed by several
of the principal writers at Henry II's court at best with ambivalence and at
worst with outright hostility. Nor, despite the glittering circle of *literati* at
Henry II's court, did any contemporary compose a Life of either Henry II or
Eleanor, in which the young Henry might have been expected to feature with
a degree of prominence.[64] The chronicle material for the first sixteen years of
Henry II's reign, and hence for the childhood and much of the adolescence of
young Henry, is particularly thin, with Robert of Torigni's chronicle standing
in near isolation. Yet though Torigni was an intimate of the royal family, his
brief, annalistic style contrasts markedly with the more detailed and richly
anecdotal writings of earlier Anglo-Norman historians such as Orderic Vitalis
and William of Malmesbury, while the decision of the witty and acerbic
Winchester monk Richard of Devizes not to begin his history of 'the confused
house of Oedipus', as he called the Angevins, before 1189 can only be
lamented.[65] Even after 1170, the young Henry appears intermittently and
often only fleetingly in the more detailed narratives of Roger of Howden and
Ralph of Diss, the 'administrative historians' associated with Henry II's court.[66]
As was also the case with Richard and Geoffrey, Howden usually referred to
the Young King's movements in any detail only when the young Henry was
with Henry II or when Roger had access to reports sent by the king's sons. His
account of the period between May 1175 and Easter 1176, for example, when
father and son remained together almost constantly, provides an exceptionally
full record of the Young King's itinerary. By contrast, however, Roger records
the Young King's independent activities on the continent laconically, if at all,
except when they directly involved Henry II. Thus, for instance, although the
Gesta is often the sole source to mention the expeditions undertaken by the
Young King in Aquitaine and Berry in the later 1170s, the bare record makes
it hard to gain anything but an impressionistic view of what must have been
large-scale military operations, or to gauge young Henry's role as commander
and warrior in them.

 Charters, writs and other records can be used to offset the partisan and
often distorting lens of chroniclers. Yet whereas some 3,000 *acta* of Henry II
have been identified, only thirty-two of the Young King's are extant.[67] The
majority of these, moreover, are homologues, confirmations of his father's
grants issued in near identical form and language, reflecting the Young King's
lack of a landed endowment with which to make his own grants.[68] Destruction

of some was deliberate: few if any of the Young King's charters issued during his period of rebellion in 1173–74 survive, for when the war ended, Henry II demanded that any such charters were surrendered to him, whereupon they were almost certainly destroyed.[69] Perhaps surprisingly, given his extensive contacts with them, the Young King appears rarely if at all in the known charters of his two principal allies, Louis VII and Count Philip of Flanders, while he witnesses very few of his father's *acta*. Few as they are, however, the witness lists to the Young King's own surviving *acta* provide an important glimpse of the extent to which his father's men guided young Henry's affairs before 1173 and of the composition of the Young King's household, particularly after 1175.[70]

The paucity of such charter evidence can, however, be supplemented by a range of other sources. The letters of John of Salisbury, and the voluminous correspondence of Becket and his supporters, focused though they are on the archbishop's struggle with Henry II, nevertheless provide valuable glimpses of young Henry. A brief shaft of light provided by the biographers of Becket falls on the prince in the early 1160s, when he became the chancellor's ward and played a prominent role in presiding over the installation of Thomas as archbishop of Canterbury, and again still more brightly in the critical years of 1169–70, as the dispute over his coronation and his subsequent position as regent drew him ever more deeply into his father's conflict with Becket.[71] Despite the tragic outcome, moreover, the picture drawn of the young Henry by Becket's biographers was almost wholly positive, and his early act of penance and veneration at Thomas' shrine in 1172 won him the approbation of Canterbury's own chroniclers. It is, however, secular texts that afford the fullest and most valuable perspectives on the Young King. Of particular importance is Jordan Fantosme's remarkable poem concerning the war of 1173–74, written shortly after the establishment of peace between young Henry and his father.[72] Little is known of Jordan, but he was probably a clerk of the bishop of Winchester and master of the cathedral schools, which would have placed him close to Henry II's trusted *familiaris*, Richard of Ilchester, who had been elected to the bishopric of Winchester in 1173. Jordan's focus on events in northern England, his intimate knowledge of the court of William the Lion and his praise of William's younger brother David – who is held up to the Young King as a model of correct conduct – suggest that he may have played a role in Anglo-Scottish diplomacy. The nature and purpose of his *Chronicle*, as it is traditionally but misleadingly called, has been variously interpreted, though it is unquestionably a *pièce d'occasion*, celebrating the bravery and loyalty of those lords who had stood by Henry II during the war.[73] Yet, crucially, it is written without hindsight of young Henry's death and in the full expectation that he would in due course succeed his father. It thus displays a careful polit-ical balance, censuring young Henry for the folly of rebellion, while at the same time pointing out to Henry II that he must bear a degree of blame for giving his son a royal title but without any real power. Jordan's poem provides both a vivid and detailed account of the war itself and a precious glimpse of the Angevin court in its aftermath, attempting to heal wounds through a process of reconciliation and political rehabilitation.

In stark contrast, the poems of Bertran de Born relating to the war of 1183 had as their stated purpose to inflame war in Aquitaine between the nobles and Richard, and to stir the Young King to action in their support.[74] As the Provençal *vida* (a semi-fictional biographical introduction) prefacing his verses put it, Bertran was 'a good knight, and a good fighter and a good squire of ladies, and a good troubadour, and wise and well spoken, knowing how to deal with bad and good – and all this time he was at war with his neighbours'.[75] His poems are not without interpretative difficulties: they can only be dated approximately, so that their chronological arrangement remains a matter of (sometimes differing) editorial choice, while their highly allusive nature, including references to leading figures by a *senhal* or enigmatic pseudonym, has resulted in a plurality of interpretation. Nevertheless, even the small number of poems relating to the Young King provide a vivid reflection of the political climate in Aquitaine in 1182–83 and of the outlook of the lesser nobility of Aquitaine who looked to young Henry as their liberator.

The single most important vernacular text relating to the Young King remains the *History of William Marshal*, composed some time between 1224 and 1229 by John, a trouvère, for William Marshal's eldest son William, and probably written in the Marshal lands of Gloucestershire and Gwent, centred on Chepstow.[76] Though it dates from some forty years after young Henry's death and is clearly influenced by romance and *chansons*, the poem draws directly on the Marshal's own reminiscences, as well as other materials and testimony, such as that of the Marshal's former household knight John d'Earley.[77] The poet's account of the Marshal's life is partisan, self-justificatory, and highly selective in the events it describes, yet it provides an intimate and unmatched view of William's service in young Henry's household between 1170 and 1183, of the nature of the tournament in the 1160s and 1170s, and of the Young King's prominent role in the tournament circuit of northern France. Although it is particularly coloured by its attempts to justify and explain away the Marshal's quarrel with young Henry in 1182 and his expul-sion from the Young King's *mesnie* or household, the *History's* depiction of the Young King nevertheless remains a highly positive one, reflecting the close bond between the two men, as well as the esteem and deep affection in which

many of the Marshal's contemporaries held the king. Like the shattered frag-
ments of a once great stained-glass window, these sources, even when pieced
together, afford only partial and haphazard traces of the Young King. Imperfect
and impressionistic though it often is, such evidence allows a different vision
of the young Henry, and of a king whose status and actions played a fundamental role in the fortunes of the Angevin empire.

CHAPTER 2

Born in the Purple

EARLY CHILDHOOD AND INFANT MARRIAGE,
1155–1160

> Like as arrows in the hand of the giant, even so are the young children.
> Happy is the man that hath his quiver full of them; they shall not be
> ashamed when they speak with their enemies in the gate.
>
> – Psalm 127:4–5, *Nisi Dominus*

ELEANOR OF AQUITAINE was already pregnant with her second son when on 19 December 1154 she was crowned, together with her husband Henry II, at Westminster Abbey by Archbishop Theobald of Canterbury.[1] It was a time of great hope and expectation.[2] At last, King Stephen's troubled reign and the bitter civil war, when men 'said openly that Christ and his saints were asleep', were over.[3] Even before his coronation, Abbot Ailred of Rievaulx had told Henry that 'not without merit does everyone proclaim you the glory of the Angevins, the protector of the Normans, the hope of the English, and the ornament of the Aquitanians'.[4] The new king, 'the most energetic of young men', was just twenty-one, but he was already a seasoned military commander, a forceful leader and, as William of Newburgh later noted, 'at his very outset he bore the appearance of a great prince'.[5] His marriage to Eleanor in May 1152, only eight weeks after her divorce from King Louis of France, had made him ruler of her vast and wealthy duchy of Aquitaine. It also gave him a wife who bore him that most essential of things for a medieval ruler and dynast – sons. There had been a number of reasons for Louis' divorce from Eleanor: the marriage had long been a stormy one, and Eleanor famously was said to have complained that Louis was more of a monk than a king.[6] Rumours of her infidelity with her uncle Raymond of Antioch during the Second Crusade may have been unfounded, but they had been as persistent as they were scandalous.[7] The marriage was eventually annulled on the technical grounds of consanguinity, but what had ultimately forced Louis into a separation which cost the house of Capet control over one-third of France was the couple's failure to produce a male heir.[8] Henry and Eleanor were to have no such difficulties, and in 1153 the duchess had given birth to William, the first of eight children.[9] In London on 28 February 1155, their second son, Henry, was born to now royal parents.[10] He was the first of the line of the counts of Anjou to be 'born in the purple', and this distinction as the son of an anointed king of England would come profoundly to shape his expectations and perception of his status.

According to Robert of Torigni, abbot of Mont Saint-Michel, who enjoyed a close relationship with the royal family, William had been named after Eleanor's dynasty.[11] Her father and grandfather had been called William, as had many of the earlier dukes of Aquitaine and counts of Poitou. But their second-born was named after his paternal great-grandfather Henry I, a conscious invocation of the most powerful of the Anglo-Norman kings, 'the famous King Henry, the Lion of Justice', who as Walter Map wrote was 'not so much emperor or king as father of England'.[12] In 1156, Henry II decreed that the laws of his grandfather were to be inviolably observed throughout the kingdom, and as he grew, the young prince Henry was to become increasingly aware of the profound influence upon his father of the figure of Henry I as a touchstone of kingship, good governance and regalian right.[13] Latin and vernacular histories of Henry I had been produced, while John of Salisbury, writing in 1159, noted that stories of Henry I's great victory at Brémule over Louis VI in 1119 were so familiar that they needed no repetition.[14] The magnificence of Henry I's court and his use of royal ceremonial as a manifesta-tion of power and authority were strong influences on the Plantagenet court from 1154.[15] As a young man, Henry II had styled himself 'Henry, son of the daughter of King Henry', and it was as this king's grandson that John hailed Henry II himself as 'destined ... to be the greatest king of the whole age among the British lands, as well as the most fortunate duke of the Normans and Aquitanians, surpassing all others not only in power and wealth but also in the splendour of his virtues'.[16] In his two namesakes, the infant Henry thus had before him formidable exemplars of kingship.[17]

The child was baptized by Richard de Belmeis, bishop of London, whose great cathedral church of St Paul's dominated the city of London.[18] The city, noted Thomas Becket's clerk and biographer William FitzStephen, 'as historians have shown, is a much older city than Rome, for though it derives from the same Trojan ancestors, it was founded by Brutus before Rome was founded by Romulus and Remus'. It had been distinguished by being the birthplace of Thomas, but, adds FitzStephen, among the kings and conquerors which it had produced, 'in modern times also London has given birth to illustrious and noble monarchs', most notably the Empress Matilda and 'Henry III' – the young Henry.[19]

Young Henry's birth had been timely indeed, for his elder brother William was sickly. When at Wallingford on 3 April 1155, Henry II commanded the barons assembled in a general council to swear fealty to William 'for the kingdom of England' as his firstborn, they also promised that if William died prematurely, they would recognize his brother Henry.[20] The site for this act of recognition was not accidental. The great fortress of Wallingford, guarding a vital crossing of the Thames, had been a key Angevin stronghold throughout the long civil war and had seen much bitter fighting.[21] But it was also here that in 1153, King Stephen and Duke Henry had been compelled by the magnates to step back from a bloody pitched battle and instead negotiate a lasting settlement.[22] A place indelibly associated with civil strife now witnessed a promise of lasting peace in the recognition of the heirs to a new king.

Though in 1154 Henry II had faced no overt challenge for the throne, his designation of William and Henry was a necessary precaution against the claims of potential rivals.[23] The Treaty of Winchester had passed over King Stephen's surviving son William of Blois, and although he had received a substantial landed endowment with the hand of the Warenne heiress, Henry held him in suspicion, as his subsequent treatment of the earl was to show.[24] There was also, moreover, the very real threat still posed by Henry II's own younger brothers, Geoffrey and William. On the sudden death from fever of their father Count Geoffrey in September 1151, Henry, who had already been invested with the duchy of Normandy the year previously, had moved swiftly to take control of Anjou as well.[25] His brother Geoffrey, however, who was his junior by just one year, claimed that he had been bequeathed the county of Anjou as his father's dying wish.[26] In 1152 he had risen in open rebellion with the all too ready assistance of King Louis VII of France and a powerful coalition of Henry's enemies. Geoffrey's defection had been made more serious by the fact that it occurred at a time when Henry was still heavily engaged in his war with King Stephen for the throne of England. Henry had nevertheless been able to contain Geoffrey's revolt in Anjou, and by making a separate agreement with him had detached him from Louis and the coalition.[27] But Henry can have been under no illusions about the fragility of this accord, while his brother's ambitions went even beyond control of Anjou: in 1152, Geoffrey, when only sixteen, had attempted to kidnap the recently divorced Eleanor of Aquitaine as she travelled from the Île-de-France to Poitiers, in order to marry her himself.[28]

The brothers' enmity, however, was no anomaly, and reflected the harsh realities of power in the territorial principalities of twelfth-century France. Their father, Count Geoffrey, had himself refused to give Maine to his younger brother Helias once he had subdued Normandy, and after suppressing Helias' revolt in 1145, had imprisoned him until his death.[29] In the previous century a fierce war had erupted between Geoffrey the Bearded, nephew and successor of Count Geoffrey Martel, and his younger brother Fulk le Réchin who, having vanquished him, took his brother's place as count in 1067 and kept Geoffrey imprisoned at Chinon for twenty years.[30] Stories of similar strife could be found not just in the earlier history of the house of Anjou, but in those of several of its rival dynasties, not least in Normandy.[31] Duke Richard III faced rebellion by his younger brother Robert, and it was even rumoured that he had been poisoned by him, while fraternal conflict had been prominent during the reign of William Rufus in England and his brother Robert Curthose in the Norman duchy. In 1155, it had been but twenty years since Duke Robert of Normandy had died in captivity after languishing in the custody of his younger brother Henry I since his defeat at Tinchebray in 1106.[32] Nor were the Capetians immune from such rivalry; in 1149, Louis VII's younger brother Robert, count of Dreux, who had returned from the Second Crusade before the king, having quarrelled violently with him, was at the centre of a dangerous plot, which at the least aimed to unseat the regent, Abbot Suger, even if contemporary fears that he planned to overthrow Louis himself were exaggerated.[33]

Henry II's youngest brother, William FitzEmpress, also known as William 'Longsword', had been left neither lands nor castles by their father, but as the careers of Henry I of England or of King David I of Scotland amply testified, it was unwise to underestimate the ambition of a landless youngest brother.[34] It was thus no coincidence that in the September following the recognition of Henry's sons by the nobles of England at Wallingford, one of the chief matters discussed by a great council at Winchester was the possible conquest of Ireland, which Henry II intended to bestow on William. Not for the last time, however, William's expectations were disappointed when the scheme was shelved, in part because of the opposition of their mother, the Empress Matilda.[35] Nevertheless, Henry II ensured that his youngest brother received extensive estates in England, and by 1156 William held lands in nine counties, mostly concentrated in Kent, Essex, Norfolk and Suffolk.[36] When in that year their brother Geoffrey again took up arms in revolt, having rejected terms offered by Henry, William remained loyal and accompanied the king on his campaigns to reduce Geoffrey's castles in Anjou, including the siege of the great fortress of Chinon.[37] Geoffrey submitted, was allowed to keep one of his Angevin castles, Loudun, and was granted an annual revenue of £1,000 from England and 2,000 livres angevins.[38] Soon afterwards, however, an opportunity came to secure for him a more tangible endowment. The citizens of Nantes ejected Hoel, son of Duke Conan III of Brittany, and invited Geoffrey to be their count. Henry readily assented to a move which, to some extent at least, recompensed his disaffected brother and also extended Angevin power to a major commercial entrepôt at the mouth of the Loire.[39] Henry II's own struggle with his brother Geoffrey nevertheless epitomized three of the central themes that would dominate the young prince Henry's life: his father's refusal to relinquish control of any part of his paternal inheritance, the hostility between brothers over the division of their father's lands, and the ruthless exploitation by the king of France of disputes within the Angevin family.

The wisdom of having the magnates recognize the infant Henry at Wallingford was all too quickly revealed when his brother William, as feared, succumbed to illness and 'passed away like the morning dew without staying for the sun's warmth', aged only three.[40] On 2 December 1156, he was buried at Henry I's royal foundation at Reading, at the feet of his great-grandfather, whose magnificent tomb stood before the high altar.[41] It is probable that Queen Eleanor's admission to the confraternity of Reading abbey was in response to her benefactions to the monks on behalf of her firstborn son, and it was at the queen's request that Henry II issued a confirmation to Hurley priory, for the soul of William.[42] Young Henry thus became chief heir to his father, a king who, as William of Newburgh noted, 'possessed the dignity of more extensive empire than any other who had hitherto reigned in England, for it extended from the further boundary of Scotland to the Pyrenean mountains'.[43]

During his early childhood, young Henry remained in the care of his mother Eleanor and her immediate household, as was customary. While relations between royal or noble parents and their offspring have sometimes been characterized as emotionally distant, Eleanor appears to have had considerable affection for her children and as a well-educated woman and patron in her own right, it seems likely that she took a keen interest in their education and upbringing.[44] Nevertheless, the queen's direct involvement in their rearing was limited by the significant role she played in affairs of state, particularly during Henry's frequent absences, despite her near-continuous pregnancies.[45] Instead, the child's daily care was entrusted to a wet-nurse, who would have been the most immediate and consistent source of female love in his early years.[46] A masculine presence was provided by a master (*magister*), Mainard, who was assigned to young Henry as early as 1156.[47] Despite his title, Mainard was not necessarily a cleric, or even a teacher. His appearance in Henry's first year suggests that his role, at least initially, was supervisory rather than primarily educational, with responsibility, still probably within the queen's household, for the care, discipline and protection of the king's son.[48] He was to remain Henry's *magister* until at least 1159, and his role appears to have been similar to that of the *nutricii* who were appointed to help raise the children of Fulk V and Geoffrey le Bel.[49] Eleanor's household as queen contained some trusted servants from her own duchy of Aquitaine, and it may have been in these early years, rather than as an adult, that young Henry became conversant with the *langue d'oc*, as well as with the Anglo-Norman French that would have been his principal language.[50] It is likely that he also had contact with his maternal grandmother, the redoubtable Empress Matilda, during visits to the duchy's capital, and the favoured royal residence close by at Quevilly.[51] Though she had ostensibly retired from active politics to the priory of Notre-Dame-du-Pré, opposite Rouen on the south bank of the Seine, she continued to advise her son Henry II until her death in 1167, and played an important role as peace-maker between her two eldest sons.[52] It was in her honour that Henry and Eleanor's third child, born in June 1156, was named Matilda.[53]

From his earliest years, young Henry experienced the itinerant nature of his royal parents' government. In the summer of 1156, Eleanor and her children crossed to Normandy to join Henry II before journeying south on a great progress through the duchy of Aquitaine.[54] The family celebrated Christmas at Bordeaux, but in February 1157 young Henry returned with Queen Eleanor and his sister via Southampton to London.[55] Henry II's was a cross-Channel empire, and these early voyages in the royal galley or *esnecca* were to be young Henry's first taste of numerous Channel crossings.[56] These were routine enough – an estate in Kent was even held for the service of holding the king's head when he was seasick – but were nonetheless fraught with danger of ship-wreck.[57] The disaster of the White Ship, in which Henry I's only legitimate son, William Aetheling, was drowned with many of the royal court following the vessel's wreck off Barfleur in 1120, had been both a dynastic and a national catastrophe, still etched in men's minds: 'No ship that ever sailed', wrote William of Malmesbury, 'brought England such disaster, none was so well known the wide world over.'[58] In 1131, Henry I himself had been caught in such a violent storm when crossing the Channel that he had vowed to remit the heavy land tax known as Danegeld for seven years.[59] It was little wonder then that on occasion Henry II himself would send to the abbey of Reading for its greatest relic, the hand of St James, to invoke the saint's protection before boarding ship, and he was careful to choose important holy days, espe-cially the feast days of the Virgin, or their vigils, for crossings of the Channel.[60] Similar fears of wreck would trouble his eldest son. One of the miracle stories relating to Thomas Becket compiled by William of Canterbury relates how, some time after 1170, the young Henry was detained at Barfleur by severe weather while waiting to cross to England. Accordingly, he requested Rotrou, archbishop of Rouen, to consecrate an altar to St Thomas in the church of St Saviour's in Barfleur. The next day, the winds subsided and the sea, hitherto

impassable for fifteen days, could be navigated. The place itself soon became a
site of miracles, where many blind and lame were cured.[61] No doubt the Young
King knew all too well the fate of William Aetheling, but his anxieties had
been fuelled by a more recent maritime catastrophe: in March 1170 a great
tempest in the Channel had damaged and scattered the king's ships, sinking a
large transport vessel with 400 souls on board, including many members of
Henry II's household.[62] The danger always remained, and in 1177 young
Henry's chancellor, Geoffrey, provost of Beverley, was to be drowned with
around 300 others when their ship was wrecked by storms when crossing from
England to Normandy.[63]

Between February 1157 and late 1158, Eleanor and her children remained
in southern England, chiefly itinerating between Winchester, Salisbury and
London.[64] The queen's mobility, however, was increasingly constrained by her
latest pregnancy, and at Oxford, on 8 September 1157, she gave birth to
Richard.[65] For King Henry, Richard's birth must have been the cause of great
relief; he once more had two sons, and thus another heir should child mortality
again rob him of his elder son. But in August 1157 it had been Henry II's own
life that was threatened. The king had returned to England at Easter to defuse
mounting tensions between Earl Hugh Bigod and Stephen's son William of
Blois, which posed a serious threat to the stability of East Anglia and perhaps
even to the kingdom itself.[66] He had then launched a major campaign to
subdue the ascendant Welsh ruler Owain of Gwynedd, but Henry and a group
of his men had been cut off by a Welsh ambush. For a terrible moment, it was
believed that he had been slain, but Henry had recovered the situation and
pressed home the campaign until Owain submitted.[67] Had he been killed,
young Henry would have become king as a child of two, and a long regency
would have spelt great uncertainty for a kingdom still barely pacified after the
years of civil war. It may well have been with this contingency in mind that
Henry had entrusted his queen and family to the protection of Archbishop
Theobald of Canterbury and Thomas Becket, his chancellor and intimate
friend.[68] As it was, Henry concluded a triumphal year, in which he reasserted
his authority over the magnates of England, the king of Scots, and the Welsh
princes, by a great crown-wearing at Lincoln, where the court feasted on
venison brought from the king's forests as far apart as Worcestershire,
Nottinghamshire and Essex.[69] The death of his turbulent brother Geoffrey in
July 1158 removed a long-standing danger, while in September that year
Eleanor gave birth to another son, also named Geoffrey, after Henry II's father
Count Geoffrey le Bel.[70]

When Henry II again crossed to Normandy in August 1158, the young
prince Henry remained with his mother and his younger siblings at

Winchester.[71] Though London was rapidly becoming the greatest commercial centre in England, the cross-Channel nature of the Anglo-Norman and Angevin kings' domains had ensured the continuing vitality and significance of the former capital of Wessex, strategically located within easy reach of the ports of embarkation at Portsmouth and Southampton. The Exchequer was now permanently based at the royal palace of Westminster, but the royal castle at Winchester, built by William the Conqueror in the south-west corner of the city, remained the principal treasury of the kingdom and it was here that the royal regalia was kept, as well as the Domesday Book, that great and unprecedented survey of wealth and tenure.[72] Henry II was to spend consider-able sums throughout his reign on the castle and royal apartments within, and young Henry would come to know it well.[73] The city itself, an 'urbs nobilissima', had been ravaged by fire during the siege of 1141, when St Mary's abbey, Hyde abbey and more than forty churches had been burned, and war damage must still have been visible in the 1150s.[74] But the peace and economic stability ushered in by Henry II's accession enabled a period of rebuilding and growth, and there were signs too that old political scars were healing. In 1155, Henry of Blois, the bishop of Winchester and King Stephen's brother, had fled the kingdom without Henry II's permission to take refuge at Cluny, leaving his castles to be demolished by the king. By late 1158, however, the bishop had returned to the king's peace, and to his episcopal city, where he very likely had contact with Eleanor and the royal family. Winchester was to be a principal residence for the queen's household, but she also travelled between other major sites such as Salisbury and Sherborne.[75]

Something of the domestic life of the young Henry can be glimpsed in this period. His master, Mainard, was assisted in the care of the prince by royal administrators such as Hugh de Gundeville, who had charge of some of his expenses.[76] Hugh had been a constable in the household of Henry II's uncle, Robert of Gloucester, then of his son Earl William, before moving into the royal service.[77] Holding estates in Dorset, Hampshire and Gloucestershire, he farmed the royal manor of King's Somborne in Hampshire, and many of his duties related to the king's affairs in Winchester, including maintenance of the royal family.[78] Hugh is found purchasing horses for the king, and as a constable it is likely that he oversaw the young Henry's first training in horsemanship. As with all nobles, this began early; a famous Carolingian proverb ran that unless a boy could ride by seven he was fit only to be a clerk, and Charlemagne's son Louis the Pious was noted to have been a skilled rider by that age.[79] Similarly, in 1159–60, the prince was in the care of William FitzAldelin, another rising *curialis* or 'man of the court', who appears a little later as one of the king's marshals.[80] Training in arms also began early, with scaled-down weapons and even armour being provided to accustom youths to their usage; the Pipe Roll for 1160 records among the queen's expenditure payment for 'boys' shields'.[81] The rolls also reveal the kind of expensive luxuries enjoyed by the queen and her family, including pepper, cumin, cinnamon and almonds, as well as incense.[82] At Salisbury in November 1158, young Henry may have been taken ill, for the Pipe Rolls record payment of 100 shillings to Girard, the boy's doctor.[83] The ever-present reality of child mortality was reflected in the confirmation of a charter of Henry II in favour of the abbey of Saint-Sauveur-le-Vicomte, given at Westminster some time between 1155 and 1158, before his return to France, for the souls not only of his parents and grandfather, Henry I, but 'for the health of my young children'.[84] The young prince was strong enough to cross over to Normandy with Eleanor in December, but by then, the king had already begun to plan for his son's future marriage.[85]

Betrothal and Marriage

Henry II's relations with the French king Louis VII had been strained long before he succeeded to the throne of England.[86] Geoffrey of Anjou's marriage to Henry I's daughter Matilda had confronted Louis with the grave threat of the unification of Anjou and the Anglo-Norman realm. Although Stephen's *coup d'état* in 1135 had prevented the immediate realization of such an alliance, his failure successfully to defend Normandy after 1137 had allowed Geoffrey of Anjou steadily to reduce Normandy to his control. Rouen fell to the Angevins in 1144, and the following year Louis was forced to recognize Geoffrey as duke of Normandy, though he demanded the great fortress of Gisors and part of the Norman Vexin as his price.[87] In 1151, Louis had extracted more of this vital border county from Henry in return for the Capetian king's recognition of his succession to the duchy by the acceptance of the duke's homage. Yet Louis could not realistically expect his powerful neighbour readily to accept so significant a diminution of his territory for long. Nevertheless, in his attempts to regain his lost possessions Henry initially chose his preferred path of diplomacy rather than a policy of open aggression against Louis.

Thus it was that in August 1158, following the death of his brother Geoffrey, Henry II took the opportunity to establish more peaceful relations with the French king. He had already sent his chancellor Thomas Becket to France that spring to open negotiations about the marriage of the young Henry to Margaret, Louis' daughter by his second wife, Constance, the daughter of Alfonso VII of Castile. The boy was now only three and Margaret herself not yet fully a year old, but it was common practice for royal children to be betrothed at such a tender age. Becket arrived in Paris in great magnificence at the head of a huge and gorgeously apparelled retinue, intending 'to display and lavish the opulence of England's luxury'.[88] Exploiting the successful negotiations carried out by Becket, the two kings met on the river Epte between Gisors and Neufmarché to discuss the proposed marriage. King Louis was anxious to secure peace: though he had exploited first the war between Stephen and the Angevins, then the rebellion of Geoffrey Plantagenet with some success, a policy of direct military confrontation with Henry II had proved unwise. Louis, moreover, was profoundly concerned about the succession to the throne of France. His two daughters by his first marriage to Eleanor of Aquitaine, Marie and Alice, had respectively been married to Henry, count of Champagne, and his brother Theobald V, count of Blois, thereby forging a strong bond with the house of Blois-Champagne. Yet the continuity of the Capetian dynasty in the direct male line was still in danger. The political price of the divorce from Eleanor had been heavy: not only had the duchy of Aquitaine reverted to Eleanor, but by her marriage to Henry II it had come under the control of Louis' Angevin rival, thereby enormously increasing his power and prestige. Yet Louis' new wife, Constance of Castile, had borne him only daughters, Margaret and Alice. His agreement to Margaret's marriage to young Henry has thus been regarded as potentially 'a dynastic safety net', but for the Capetians the prospects were scarcely propitious.[89] If Louis was to die, there were a number of potential claimants, including the sons of his sister Constance and Raymond of Toulouse, or perhaps Henry, count of Champagne, the husband of his eldest daughter, Marie.[90] Alternatively, the marriage of young Henry and Margaret offered the possibility that the Angevins might absorb the house of Capet. Louis cannot have relished either eventuality, and must have hoped that since the actual union of Henry and Margaret would be a distant prospect because of their very young age, he might yet have a son by Constance.

There was, moreover, a potential benefit for the king of France. The strategic value of the Vexin made it all too clear that Henry would seek to obtain its restoration as soon as he could, by force if need be. Accordingly, Louis agreed to make Margaret's dowry the Vexin, with its key castles of Gisors, Neaufles and Châteauneuf-sur-Epte. It was further agreed that if young Henry died Margaret was to marry another of Henry II's sons, under the same terms.[91] To Louis, the move seemed an astute piece of diplomacy; he thereby asserted the Capetians' legal claim to the Vexin while at the same time holding out to Henry the prospect of its return to de facto Plantagenet control, but seemingly not for many years. In addition, Henry II settled a handsome dower on Margaret. In Normandy, she was to hold the city of Avranches, two castles,

200 *livres angevins* in revenue from the duchy, and the dues from 200 knights'
fees. In England, she was also to receive the city of Lincoln, £1,000 of revenue,
and dues from 300 knights' fees.[92] For Henry, this was a small price for what
seemed a sure way of eventually recovering the strategically vital territory
of the Vexin, and even held out the hope – however distant – that he would
obtain the throne of France for the Plantagenets by marriage. After all, it
had been by marriage, not the sword, that in one extraordinary year, 1128,
his grandfather Fulk V had obtained the kingdom of Jerusalem for himself
through the hand of Queen Melisende, and succession to the Anglo-Norman
realm for his son Geoffrey by his marriage to the Empress Matilda.[93] And it
had been the failure of the male line of the kings of Aragon that in 1137 had
permitted Count Ramón Berenguer of Barcelona to obtain the kingdom by
marriage to Ramiro's daughter Petronella.[94] More immediately, Henry II was
anxious to obtain Louis' sanction for a campaign in Brittany against Conan IV,
who had seized the county of Nantes on the death of Geoffrey Plantagenet in
July 1158.

Contemporaries regarded the proposed marriage agreement as an important move towards peace after the hostilities of the previous decades. When
Henry II visited Louis again in September 1158, a great diplomatic effort was
made on both sides to extend courtesies and honours.[95] Having allowed Becket
to exhibit the wealth he could command, Henry's visit was deliberately low
key, as he sought to retain Louis' support for his actions against the Bretons.
Henry was greeted 'with inestimable honour' by Louis, his queen and by nobles
of the kingdom. In his turn, Henry graciously declined the king's offer to have
him met by a procession at every church in Paris, but gave alms and behaved
'magnificently and liberally towards everyone, especially the churches and
Christ's poor'.[96] It was in such a honeymoon atmosphere that Henry was able
to take back with him the infant Margaret on his return to Normandy. It was
a diplomatic triumph of the highest order – and one the French would come
bitterly to regret.[97] The harsh reality of Margaret's separation from her parents
at such an early age, and her de facto position as a hostage were an accepted
part of aristocratic life.[98] Henry II entrusted her to the safekeeping of Robert
de Neufmarché, the seneschal of Normandy and one of Henry's most trusted
fideles, 'to guard and rear her (*ad custodiendum et nutriendum*)'. On Robert's
death, however, she was probably transferred to Queen Eleanor's household,
where she certainly was by 1164.[99]

In November 1158, Henry reciprocated Louis' hospitality and accompanied his lord on a tour of some of Normandy's most important churches,
including Mont Saint-Michel and Bec.[100] The two kings' amicable relations,
however, were not to last long. The seeds of conflict lay in Henry II's attempt

in 1159 to make good Eleanor of Aquitaine's claims on the great principality of Toulouse.[101] Henry embarked on the fiscal and military preparations for probably the largest army he was ever to lead, while to lay his ground he forged an alliance with Ramón Berenguer, count of Barcelona. The count's daughter was to be betrothed to Henry II's second son Richard, who already had been assigned Aquitaine as his inheritance.[102] Louis was greatly alarmed by Henry's actions. If Henry succeeded in annexing Toulouse he would control the trade routes from the Mediterranean to the Atlantic, and from central France down to the Pyrenees; both his wealth and his political influence would be enormously increased. Count Raymond of Toulouse, moreover, was married to Louis' sister Constance. Despite a series of parleys, Louis was unable to deter Henry from leading his great host, mustered at Poitiers for Midsummer's Day, 24 June, into Raymond's territories. Initially, all went well. Cahors was taken, and much of the count's lands were overrun. The great city of Toulouse itself resolutely held out, but after three months' blockade Raymond's position was beginning to look desperate. Yet in a bold move, which Henry had completely failed to anticipate, King Louis suddenly entered Toulouse itself to aid his brother-in-law and defend his sister Constance.[103] Thomas Becket urged Henry to press home the siege despite Louis' presence, yet Henry baulked 'out of foolish superstition and regard for the counsel of others'; he would not attack the city if his lord, the king of France, remained inside.[104] It was a critical moment, and one that sharply revealed both the reality of Henry's scruples about injuring Louis' person and the potential disadvantages he might thus face as a vassal of the Capetian king.[105] With his army now succumbing to disease, Henry II withdrew from Toulouse and returned north, leaving Becket to secure the occupation of Cahors and the Quercy.[106] The failure of the Toulouse expedition was a major reverse for Henry, breaking a remarkable run of political and military successes, and it could not but sour relations with Louis: 'On account of this,' noted Ralph of Diss, 'the two kings were made enemies.'[107] Henry's earlier attempts to draw Louis from Toulouse by diversionary attacks on the Île-de-France had not only been unsuccessful, but had resulted in counter-attacks against Normandy. After continuing hostilities in the Vexin, the two kings resumed negotiations, and in December 1159 a truce was arranged to last until 22 May 1160.[108]

Henry and his family kept Christmas of 1159 at Falaise, but the festivities were doubtless overshadowed by the outcome of the Toulouse expedition, and in late December Eleanor returned to England to act as regent, taking her children, while Henry remained in Normandy.[109] On expiry of the truce, Henry and Louis met again in May 1160 to reaffirm peace. The king of France recognized Henry's gains in the Quercy, including the town of Cahors, and the terms of the prospective marriage were finalized.[110] This was to take place after three years, and until then Louis was to retain control of the lands of the Vexin, but its castles were to be held by the Templars as a neutral party.[111] Should Margaret die in the interim, the Vexin would be restored to Louis' possession. If, however, the Church consented to an earlier marriage, Henry would take control of Margaret's dowry with immediate effect, and in such circumstances the Templars pledged to hand over the castles to Henry. Louis had good reason for believing this would not in fact occur; the marriage of infants was, after all, in clear contravention of canon law. Yet Henry II, impatient to regain control of the Vexin, had no intention of letting the potential advantages of the treaty slip away.

His opportunity soon came. In July 1160, Henry responded to the pressing issue of the papal schism by summoning his lay and ecclesiastical magnates to a great council at Neufmarché, while Louis likewise convened his nobles at Beauvais.[112] On the death of Hadrian IV in September 1159, the majority of the college of cardinals had elected as pope the distinguished canonist Cardinal Orlando Bandinelli, who took the name Alexander III. Three cardinals, however, championed Emperor Frederick Barbarossa's candidate Cardinal Octavian as Pope Victor IV, and imperial agents succeeded in forcing Alexander to flee Rome. In February 1160, moreover, Barbarossa had presided over a council composed primarily of German and Italian bishops at Pavia, which officially recognized Victor IV. Though both Henry and Louis were inclined to support Alexander, in line with the sympathies of their respective Churches, the uncertainties caused by the schism gave Henry a political advantage he was swift to exploit. Alexander had sent a papal legation to France, and Henry met with them at Beauvais in the course of his own discussions with Louis. As the price of his recognition of Alexander III, Henry succeeded in extracting from the legates a dispensation for the marriage of young Henry to his infant bride.[113] Almost certainly obtained without Louis' knowledge, this papal licence has been aptly described as 'a masterpiece of tortured logic and hypocritical self justification' on the part of the legates.[114] Such casuistry, however, was well worth Henry's support. Armed with the dispensation, Henry bided his time, but summoned Eleanor to bring their eldest son from England to Normandy so that young Henry would be on hand should there be occasion for the nuptials to take place.

In October, the two kings met once more to confirm a pact of peace, and young Henry performed homage to Louis for the duchy of Normandy.[115] In doing so, he was following an established pattern: Henry I had always refused to perform homage for the duchy, regarding it as an infringement of his royal dignity, but he had allowed his son William Aetheling to do so in 1120. Similarly, King Stephen withheld his homage to Louis VI for Normandy, but this was performed by his son Eustace in 1137.[116] Henry Plantagenet had performed homage to Louis VII for Normandy in 1151 when only a duke, but he did not do so again, once king of England, in Louis' lifetime.[117] He was, however, content for his eldest son to do so, as by accepting his homage Louis was publicly recognizing young Henry's right of succession to the duchy.

The catalyst for Henry II's implementation of his papal dispensation was to be of Louis' making. In September 1160, Louis' queen, Constance, died in childbirth, though her baby daughter Alice survived. Barely two weeks later Louis, desperate for a male heir, announced his plans to remarry.[118] Angevin observers regarded such haste as indecent, but it was Louis' choice of bride that incensed Henry II. His new wife was to be Adela, daughter of Theobald IV of Blois-Champagne and thus the sister of his own sons-in-law Count Henry of Champagne and Theobald V of Blois.[119] This not only strengthened Louis' alliance with the house of Blois but meant that the children produced by the union of Louis and Adela would fuse this bond still more strongly. The renewed prospect of such heirs for Louis, moreover, threatened to nullify Henry's more ambitious hopes for the long-term impact of young Henry's marriage to Margaret. With hindsight, it is easy to underestimate the threat still posed to Henry by the house of Blois, with whom first his father Count Geoffrey, then he himself, had struggled since 1135. It was true that both Stephen's sons were now dead; Eustace had died in 1153, while the younger, William, earl of Warenne and count of Boulogne, had died of sickness contracted on the Toulouse expedition in 1159. But Henry of Champagne and Theobald V of Blois were Stephen's nephews, who might yet press a claim to the throne of England, while their uncle Henry of Blois, the great prince-bishop of Winchester, still exercised considerable influence in the English Church. 'The English king,' noted the chronicler Lambert of Waterlos, 'having got wind of this marriage, and moved by anger, attempted to counter it by every means.'[120] Faced with such a coalition, Angevin recovery of the Vexin became a pressing strategic concern. With Louis' marriage set for 13 November 1160, Henry II struck back by having the two children married at Le Neubourg on 2 November, by Archbishop Hugh of Rouen in the presence of the papal legates Henry of Pisa and William of Pavia, even though bride and groom were, in Roger of Howden's words, but 'babes squalling in the cradle'.[121] In accordance with the letter of the treaty, the Templars thereupon surrendered to Henry II the great fortress of Gisors 'which he had long desired' and the other castles of the Vexin, which the king of England quickly had fortified and strongly garrisoned.[122] Thenceforth, Gisors was transformed by Henry II into one of the mightiest of castles on the Norman border, and the linchpin of the Vexin's defences.[123]

Louis' outrage was matched only by his impotence to prevent Henry's coup.[124] In theory, young Henry and Margaret were related within the fourth and fifth degrees of consanguinity, but Louis could not use this as an argument to seek annulment, as his own marriage to Adela would be in similar contravention.[125] He vented his rage by banishing the three Templar sureties from France, and joined with Theobald of Blois in fortifying the important castle of Chaumont, between Blois and Amboise.[126] But even in this show of force he was to be thwarted. By a lightning march so characteristic of his generalship, Henry II surprised Louis and Theobald, put them to flight, and after a brief siege, took Chaumont and a haul of prisoners.[127] Having strengthened Amboise and other fortresses on the frontier with Blois, a triumphant Henry kept Christmas of 1160 with Eleanor and his children at Le Mans. After further hostilities, peace was eventually restored between Louis and Henry, and ratified at Fréteval in October 1161.[128]

Young Henry now found himself married at the age of only five. Royal children were commonly betrothed at a tender age, but to be actually wed so young was highly unusual for a king's son and the heir apparent.[129] Of his younger brothers, Richard married at thirty-three, Geoffrey at twenty-two, and John at twenty-two or twenty-three.[130] Within aristocratic society of the twelfth century, moreover, marriage usually marked a crucial change in a man's status, heralding the transition from a *iuvenis*, a 'youth' in the technical sense of one not having his own lands or family, to a *vir*, who had his own household and lands.[131] Young Henry was denied such a rite of passage, a factor which undoubtedly contributed to the ambiguity of his status that was to dog his life from his coronation in 1170 onwards. Child brides were customarily kept separate from their husbands until an age deemed suitable for the marriage to be consummated, but it is probable that, as they were so young, the children were together in the queen's household until 1162, when young Henry was removed from it. Thereafter, it is unknown how often young Henry and Margaret met as children, nor when as adolescents they began to cohabit, though it is likely that they did so from 1170, when the prince was crowned aged fifteen, or at the latest in 1172, when Margaret was finally anointed and crowned queen. Ironically, though their lives coincided with a great flowering of both troubadour love lyric and courtly romance literature, epitomized in the works of Chrétien de Troyes and Marie de France, scant evidence survives of the emotional relationship between young Henry and his half-Castilian bride. The little that does nevertheless suggests that love developed within their marriage, for, following his death, Margaret seems to have remembered Henry with great affection.[132] Young Henry and Margaret are known to have had only one child, who died soon after being born prematurely in 1177.[133] Yet whereas his father's extramarital affairs were as numerous as they were notorious, young Henry is not known to have had any mistresses, or to have fathered any illegitimate children. This may simply reflect the dearth of sources, but if young Henry's continence was real, then it was unusual among men of his rank and power.

In the early 1160s, Henry II's *coup de main* appeared as a master stroke, emblematic of the political guile for which he was renowned. The vital territory of the Vexin had been regained, and Louis had been outwitted and humiliated in both diplomacy and war. The French view of the affair was graphically captured by John of Salisbury, who recounted to Thomas Becket a conversation he had had with King Louis on a visit to Paris in 1164. Earlier that year, John had gone to Salisbury to seek Queen Eleanor's permission to leave the kingdom, and had found little Margaret in Eleanor's household. John took greetings from Margaret to her father Louis, but when he gave the French king news of his daughter, Louis had sorrowfully replied

> that he would be very thankful if she had already been received by the angels in Paradise. 'By God's mercy', I rejoined, 'this will someday happen, but before that she will bring gladness to many peoples'. 'With God the thing is indeed possible', the king replied, 'but it is far more likely that she will be the cause of much mischief (*causa malorum*) in time to come'. In his mind's eye, her father is full of foreboding. God forbid it turns out for her as he fears. 'I scarce hope', he said, 'that any good can come of her'. The French fear our King, and hate him, but so far as they are concerned, he can sleep safe at night.[134]

Louis' fears doubtless focused on what might befall should young Henry and Margaret eventually have a male heir, and on the possibility that the Capetians might be subsumed by the seemingly unstoppable rise of the Plantagenets. But in August 1165, Louis finally gained a son when his third wife, Adela, gave birth to Philip; Gerald of Wales, then studying in Paris, later recalled the joyous celebrations with the ringing of bells and the lighting of innumerable tapers so that the city seemed on fire.[135] Nevertheless, the long-term consequences of the marriage of young Henry to Margaret were indeed to be profound, but very different from those envisioned by either Henry II or Louis. For although the manner and context of the union had severely damaged relations between Louis and Henry II, already badly strained by the Toulouse campaign, young Henry's marriage served to create a closer dynastic relationship between the Angevins and Capetians. This was to be reflected in a marked intensification of face-to-face meetings between the king of England and the king of France, but it would also increasingly draw the young Henry into the orbit of his father-in-law, whom he frequently visited in the Île-de-France.[136] In time, Louis' influence over him was to become one of the most powerful weapons in the French king's arsenal against Henry II. The recovery of the Vexin, moreover, had come at a price: Henry had recognized it as the dowry of a Capetian princess, and hence ultimately as the *de jure* possession of the kings of France.[137] During the Young King's lifetime, this was of little practical consequence, but the seeds had been sown of a lasting strife injurious to the Angevins, whose significance was to become apparent within months of young Henry's death in 1183.

CHAPTER 3

Rex Puer

CORONATION PLANS AND ASSOCIATIVE KINGSHIP,
1161–1163

A man who wants to be generous should never look to possessions or to the
value of his land. A knight, God protect me, will not rise to great heights if
he enquires of the value of corn; nor is he full of prowess, honour, or bravery
who does not, in folly or in wisdom, give and spend more than his land may
be worth.

> – Raoul de Hodenc, *The Romance of the Wings*, ll. 161–72[1]

In the Household of Thomas Becket

At their Easter court at Falaise in 1162, Henry II and Queen Eleanor entrusted
young Henry to the charge of the chancellor, Thomas Becket, 'to bring up and
instruct in good conduct and courtly ways'.[2] Thomas, moreover, was required
to take the prince to England, where he was to receive the homage and fealty
of the magnates.[3] Henry may perhaps have been in Becket's care for some time
before this, but seven was the customary age for noble boys to be removed from
the household of their mothers and sent for their upbringing to the masculine
world of a great royal or aristocratic court.[4] Henry II himself had left his
mother Matilda's household at this age in 1139 to enter that of his father
Count Geoffrey until 1142, when he was taken by his uncle Earl Robert of
Gloucester to Bristol to be educated with the children of other nobles, including
the earl's youngest son Roger. When in an angry interview in 1170 King Henry
upbraided Roger, by then bishop of Worcester, for failing to attend the Young
King's coronation, he reminded his cousin of how Earl Robert 'brought us up
together in his castle, and had us instructed in the first elements of good behaviour and learning'.[5]

Such fosterage had long been an integral element of aristocratic life.[6] Boys
might be sent away to the households of great ecclesiastics as well as lay

magnates, and honorial lords often brought up and trained the sons of their own vassals, kinsmen or those in their affinity.[7] The young William Marshal, for example, who in 1170 would become young Henry's tutor in arms and thenceforth one of his closest companions, was placed in the household of William de Tancarville, the chamberlain of Normandy, where it was hoped he would win 'reputation and honour'.[8] Those of higher birth might sometimes seek the patronage of one of the great territorial princes.[9] It was not uncommon, however, for fathers to rear their own sons in their courts, entrusting their day-to-day instruction to tutors, *nutricii* or other non-parental male guardians.[10] For the eldest sons of kings, considerations both of rank and of security often dictated that they were similarly educated in their royal father's own household rather than being sent away to the court of a foreign prince.[11] During Anglo-French negotiations in 1169, it was proposed that prince Henry's younger brother, the eleven-year-old Richard, should be sent to the household of King Louis of France for his education and training. This was, however, no more than a diplomatic ruse by Henry II to gain custody of Louis' daughter Alice, and he had never seriously contemplated placing Richard in Louis' charge.[12]

The king's own court held out the best hopes of potential advancement, and here Henry II's sons would have shared their upbringing with the scions of the greatest aristocratic families from both within and beyond the Angevin lands.[13] Some time between 1155 and 1159, for example, the English Pope Hadrian IV sent one of his young Italian protégés to Henry II's court for his education, which included training in hawking, hunting and arms.[14] Such fosterage created important bonds between the king and a younger generation of nobles, and, just as importantly, between the king's heir and his contemporaries among the aristocracy, who would in time become his vassals and supporters. The act of dubbing to knighthood and the bestowal of arms, which marked the completion of knightly apprenticeship and coming of age, forged powerful ties of loyalty.[15]

For Henry II to entrust his eldest son and heir to the household of his chancellor was striking testimony to the extraordinary position Thomas Becket had come to enjoy in the king's favour: indeed, such custody mirrored the role that Lanfranc, archbishop of Canterbury, had played in the upbringing of William the Conqueror's son William Rufus and thus may even have been an intimation of further greatness for Becket.[16] Thomas was already a familiar figure to the young prince, for he had been closely linked to Henry II's government from the outset of his reign. Rising to prominence in the service of Archbishop Theobald of Canterbury, Thomas had been made archdeacon of Canterbury in October of 1154, and at Christmas that same year, shortly after Henry II's coronation, the influence of Archbishop Theobald, Henry, bishop of Winchester and other leading ecclesiastics had secured him the key office of royal chancellor, 'considered second in rank in the realm only to the king'.[17] Astute, hard-working and ruthlessly ambitious, Thomas had quickly become a leading counsellor.[18] Though Becket's biographers no doubt over-stressed Henry II's reliance on Thomas, his vital role in the royal administration is amply confirmed by the number of royal charters to which he attested.[19] Becket's position as leading minister was closely analogous to that of his counterpart and firm friend Robert of Aire (d. 1174), the chancellor and *familiaris* of Count Philip of Flanders, and to that of Stephen of Garlande (d. 1150), chancellor and seneschal at the Capetian court; all three were prominent examples of a class of highly able but low-born men, who as clerics rose fast through royal service in the developing royal administrations of the twelfth century.[20]

Yet what set Becket apart from these contemporaries was his remarkable intimacy with the king. 'Never in Christian times were there two greater friends, more of one mind,' noted William FitzStephen.[21] Accordingly, those who sought advancement or to gain access to the king needed first to woo the chancellor, and many were eager to exploit the honour and advantages of having their sons also brought up in Becket's household: 'Magnates of the kingdom of England and of neighbouring kingdoms placed their children in the chancellor's service, and he grounded them in honest education and doctrine, and when they had received the belt of knighthood he sent some back with honour to their fathers and family, and retained others.'[22] So it was, noted FitzStephen, that 'the king himself, his lord, commended his son, the heir to the kingdom, to his training, and the chancellor kept him with him among the many nobles' sons of similar age, and their appropriate attendants, masters and servants according to rank'.[23] The guardianship of young Henry was not only a great honour for Becket but also a mark of the mutual affection between the two men, and Thomas is said to have jokingly referred to young Henry as his adopted son.[24]

As the king fully realized, moreover, it also placed Becket in a position of enormous power should Henry II himself fall prey to disease or war, as had so nearly occurred during the Welsh campaign in 1157. In this eventuality, Becket could hope to play a key role in the regency government until young Henry's still distant majority.[25] Such a position would not be uncontested, but direct control of the king's heir, together with custody of the Tower of London, gave the chancellor a powerful advantage. Now one of the richest men in the kingdom, Becket had already exploited his high office and wealth to establish himself as the lord of a wide affinity.[26] As FitzStephen notes, 'countless nobles and knights gave homage to the chancellor, and he, saving fidelity to the lord king, received and cherished them with extraordinary patronage as his own men . . .'[27] The status of the royal chancellor customarily required an appropriate display of wealth and largesse, but Becket indulged the *arriviste*'s taste for magnificence to the full.[28] 'Thomas was a magnificent clerk and lived in great splendour,' noted Guernes of Pont-Sainte-Maxence. 'Henry the rich king who owns so much of the world did not live in greater – this is no exaggeration'.[29] While such a lifestyle attracted the criticism of some of Becket's clerical contemporaries, his own clerk William FitzStephen makes little attempt to hide his delight in Thomas' extravagance, providing a precious glimpse of the lifestyle of the great:

> The chancellor's house and table were open to the needs of any visitors to the king's court of whatever rank . . . Hardly a day did he dine without earls and barons as his guests. He ordered his floors to be covered every day with new straw or hay in the winter, fresh bulrushes or leaves in the summer, so that the multitude of knights, who could not all fit on stalls, could find a clean and pleasant space, and leave their precious clothes and beautiful shirts unsoiled. His house glittered with gold and silver vases, and abounded in precious food and drink, so that if a certain food was known for its rarity, no price would deter his ministers from buying it.[30]

The young prince Henry thus became part of a glittering court, famed for its opulence and conspicuous consumption, as well as for the élan of the chancellor's military household. For the boy, Thomas' lifestyle was a dazzling example of lordly pomp and magnificence, accompanied by two of the mainsprings of good lordship, largesse and *franchise* – the open-handed and great-hearted conduct expected of a nobleman.[31] 'Hardly a day went by,' noted FitzStephen, 'when he did not make a gift of horses, birds, clothes, gold or silver wares or money . . . the chancellor had such a gift for giving, that he found love and favour throughout the Latin world.'[32]

Given Becket's prominence in public affairs, first as chancellor then as archbishop, his direct contact with the prince while still in his household must have been limited, and his instruction, whether in letters, courtly manners or other necessary accomplishments, would of necessity have been delegated to tutors. Equally, Henry was too young to have had any serious engagement with members of the brilliant intellectual circle of clerks surrounding Thomas. Nevertheless, Becket himself provided young Henry with a role model of a knightly commander and warrior. Thomas' own path to greatness had been through the clerical household of Archbishop Theobald, but once in the king's service Becket strove to cut a chivalric figure. On Thomas' elevation to the primacy in 1162, his rival Gilbert Foliot sourly jested that the king had done a marvellous thing in turning a worldly man and a knight into an archbishop.[33] In reality, as a clerk in minor orders, Becket could not be knighted himself, but he undoubtedly relished his own role as a 'father of knights' and bestowed the arms of knighthood upon his young protégés.[34] Moreover, he effectively transformed the chancellorship into a great military, as well as administrative office. On the Toulouse campaign in 1159 he had led an impressive retinue, which FitzStephen claimed numbered 700 knights. During hostilities with Louis VII in the Vexin in 1161 Thomas fielded a still more powerful contingent, swelled by large numbers of stipendiary knights, who each received 'three shillings to take care of horses and squires, and all these knights sat at the chancellor's table'.[35] Becket himself even engaged one of the leading French knights, Enguerrand de Trie, in single combat, unhorsing him and taking his destrier as booty.[36]

Whether young Henry, who was in Normandy at the time, witnessed this feat of arms is unknown, but in a world in which the numbers in a lord's following and the level of wages paid to his knights directly proclaimed his own status and dignity, the size and extravagance of Becket's retinue, even when archbishop, was to remain an important exemplar for the prince.[37] Something of the impression created on the young Henry by the chancellor's household may perhaps be glimpsed through the earlier reminiscences of the chronicler Henry of Huntingdon, who was raised in the household of Robert Bloet, the great prince-bishop of Lincoln and formerly William Rufus' chancellor, who 'was looked upon as everyone's father and god'.[38] As an old man, the archdeacon recalled how:

> when, throughout my boyhood, adolescence and young manhood, I saw the glory of Robert, our bishop – I mean his handsome knights, noble young men, his horses of great price, his golden and gilded vessels, the number of courses at dinner, the splendour of those who waited upon him, the purple garments and satins – I thought nothing could be more blessed.[39]

By contrast, Henry II, it has been said, 'in appearance . . . might easily have been mistaken for one of his own huntsmen'.[40] Nevertheless, it would be a mistake to underestimate the wealth, ceremony and dignity of Henry II's own court, about which Becket's biographers or indeed other chroniclers writing of the 1150s and 1160s say little: it is only from a casual mention by Robert of Torigni, for instance, that we hear of the rich gifts including gold, silks, horses and camels that were presented to Henry II by a great embassy from the Muslim king of Valencia in 1162.[41] The surviving financial records reveal that Henry II's court enjoyed a sumptuous material culture, with expensive clothing and rich plate, while Walter Map could remark in passing that the king 'is always robed in precious stuffs, as is right'.[42] His court had a highly developed protocol, which, at least by the 1180s, was probably regulated by a king of arms.[43] Yet it is hard not to see the influence of Thomas on the younger Henry's extravagant display once he became king. In the later 1170s, during his prominent participation in the tournament circuit of northern France, the Young King himself would attract large numbers of knights into his own *mesnie* by offering prodigally high wages, and in 1182 a key element in the renewed settlement with his father was that Henry II should provide him with the revenue to keep 100 knights in his household: outside times of war, this was a very high number even for a royal *familia* and was ruinously expensive.[44] Indeed, from the 1170s, young Henry would come to fulfil a role closely analogous role to that of Chancellor Thomas as the showcase for Angevin wealth and splendour.

When Henry II sent his son to England with Becket in April 1162 it was on a dual mission. Archbishop Theobald had died on 18 April 1161, and, although he delayed an immediate appointment and enjoyed the revenues of the vacant see, Henry was determined that his chancellor and friend should become the new archbishop of Canterbury.[45] This had probably also been the wish of Theobald himself, and in 1162 Cardinal Henry of Pisa had joined with King Henry in urging Thomas to accept the post of archbishop.[46] Becket was, or so his biographers insisted, most reluctant, sensing an inevitable conflict with his lord, but he eventually was persuaded.[47] Henry II's most eminent biographer, W. L. Warren, has argued that Henry had pressed the archbishopric upon him as a means of rewarding Becket for his past services, but also of moving him aside, for the failure of the Toulouse expedition had shaken Henry's confidence in Becket's judgement, and his influence with the king was already in decline by 1162: Becket's increasing intransigence as archbishop was thus a reaction to his removal from Henry's inner counsels.[48] Yet such a view is hard to reconcile with Henry's great anger at Becket's resignation of the chancellorship soon after his elevation to the archbishopric, and with the key role the king had evidently envisaged for Thomas in a regency government in conjunction with his eldest son.

From at least the summer of 1161, Henry II had been giving thought to the coronation of young Henry. In June of that year, during the vacancy at Canterbury following Theobald's death, he had secured a mandate from Pope Alexander III, *Quantum per carissimum*, which was addressed to Roger, archbishop of York, granting him permission to carry out coronations and instructing him to crown young Henry whenever the king should wish it.[49] Yet whatever Henry's intentions when he obtained these instruments, by the summer of 1162 he was determined that his son would be crowned by Thomas, the new archbishop of Canterbury. Certain evidence of Henry II's intent was his purchase, recorded in the Pipe Rolls, of over £38 worth of gold from the London financier William Cade for the making of a crown and regalia for his son's coronation.[50] Such a crowning in the lifetime of a ruler would be unprecedented in post-Conquest England. Why then did Henry wish to have his son raised to regal dignity at such a young age, and at a time when Henry II's own position seemed so unshakably strong? To answer this central question it is necessary to examine the nature of anticipatory succession, the precedents which informed Henry II, and his own perceptions of Angevin kingship in the early years of his reign.

Anticipatory Succession: Motives and Precedents

The practice of anticipatory succession, marked by the coronation of an heir during the ruler's lifetime, had long been established in many European royal dynasties. The first Carolingian kings, Pepin and Charlemagne, had used the anointing of their sons as kings by the pope as a means of validating a new dynasty and securing its succession.[51] In the absence of blood right to rule, consecration had long served as a powerful act of legitimization. In the Old Testament itself, unction had been used not only to consecrate new kings but to validate the substitution of one ruler for another: when Saul was set aside as king of Israel, the priest Samuel in turn anointed the new ruler, David, whose authority was hallowed and legitimized as the 'christus Domini'.[52] As a mechanism to strengthen the position of a newly established dynasty, anticipatory association had been equally vital to the consolidation of early Ottonian power,[53] and still more so to that of the Capetians.[54]

In 987, Hugh Capet had displaced Louis V, the last Carolingian king of West Frankia, but as his dynasty had no hereditary right to the throne, he had engineered by sleight of hand the consecration of his son Robert II only a few months after his own coronation.[55] In turn, Robert the Pious (r. 996–1031) had his eldest son Hugh crowned in 1017, and on his death his younger brother Henry became associate ruler in 1026. Henry assumed sole kingship on his father's death in 1031, but in 1059 he had his seven-year-old son Philip crowned. Thereafter, though they had effectively suppressed any move to make the kingship elective beyond the formality of the approval of noble assemblies and their acclamation at the coronation itself, the Capetian dynasty faced no serious challenge to its right to succeed to the throne of France.[56] They continued, however, to use anticipatory succession in a variety of circumstances, most notably to secure the succession of an eldest son when challenged by a younger brother or half-brothers, to confirm the succession of a younger son on the sudden death of an older brother already so associated, or to associate a son with the rule of a royal father who was ailing or incapacitated.[57] Louis VI 'the Fat' (r. 1108–37) had been crowned and anointed at Orléans in 1108 only after the death of his father Philip I (r. 1060–1108), but from *c*.1100 he had increasingly taken over the effective running of the kingdom, and had been styled *rex designatus*.[58]

There can be little doubt that Henry II's desire to have young Henry crowned in 1162 owed much to Capetian practice. Nevertheless, Louis VII's own lack of sons before the birth of Philip in 1165 meant that it was his own coronation as a boy in 1131 that remained the most immediate precedent.[59] Louis VI's eldest legitimate son Philip, born in 1116, had been associated with his kingship as *rex designatus* from 1121, and was crowned at Rheims in 1129.[60] In 1131, however, after he was killed in a riding accident Louis VI's second son, Louis, was quickly crowned by Pope Innocent II at Rheims.[61] Though these circumstances were far more urgent than those of 1162 for young Henry, the coronation of the future Louis VII as a child – as with the earlier example of Philip I – indicates that for the young Henry to be crowned at the age of seven was not exceptional, and that seven was considered the minimum age for such a coronation.[62] Thereafter, Louis appeared in his father's charters as *Ludovicus rex junior* until he succeeded his father as sole ruler in 1137, and it would similarly be as *Henricus rex junior* that the Young King was often styled after his eventual coronation in 1170.[63]

Henry II, however, was equally cognizant of contemporary imperial Byzantine and German practice, as well as the use of anticipatory succession in kingdoms with more direct links to his own.[64] In the Latin kingdom of Jerusalem, anticipatory coronation had been used to counter the potentially dangerous circumstances first of a female heir, then of a minority, and then of the terminal illness of the ruling king. Melisende, eldest daughter and heir of Baldwin II, was crowned as his co-ruler in 1128, and succeeded him in 1131.[65] Soon after the death of her husband Fulk, Henry II's grandfather, she had their son Baldwin III crowned as her co-ruler on Christmas Day 1143.[66] And when in 1183 the kingdom of Jerusalem faced an imminent succession crisis with the rapidly deteriorating condition of the leper king, Baldwin IV, his nephew Baldwin V was crowned and anointed as his co-ruler, even though he was only five years old.[67] Likewise, in the Norman kingdom of Sicily, King Roger II had his son William crowned and anointed as a 'rex consors regni' by the archbishop of Palermo at Easter 1151.[68]

In the kingdom of England, however, the practice of crowning a son in the lifetime of his father had few precedents.[69] In the early Anglo-Saxon kingdoms, it had been common for kings to associate younger brothers or sons as co-rulers, and the practice was still visible in later ninth-century Wessex. Yet as far as can be seen, there was no ceremony of consecration of associate rulers, even after the kings of Wessex had succeeded in becoming kings of England during the tenth century. Seemingly, the only pre-Conquest instance occurred in 787, when Offa, the great king of the Mercians (r. 757–96) and overlord of much of England, had his son Ecgfrith consecrated as king, almost certainly in imitation of recent Carolingian practice.[70] The event was closely linked to a legatine visitation and Offa's creation of an archbishopric at Lichfield, intended as a counter to a hostile archbishop of Canterbury and Kentish resistance to Offa's authority. It had as its primary purpose, however, the overriding of existing customs of succession, whereby a number of eligible members of the royal kindred were held to be throne-worthy.[71] When on Offa's death in 796 Ecgfrith became sole ruler, it was 'the first time that a son had succeeded his father in Mercia for many generations'.[72] Nevertheless, despite the potential inherent in the consecration of associate rulers for the development of a more patrilineal model of succession, it was not an example followed by subsequent Anglo-Saxon kings before 1066.

Nor in post-Conquest England before the reign of King Stephen did Anglo-Norman kings adopt the practice of crowning their chosen successors in their own lifetime. William the Conqueror had designated his eldest son Robert as his heir to the duchy of Normandy, but his original intentions regarding succession to the kingdom of England are hard if not impossible to ascertain: if William had ever contemplated associating Robert with his kingship in the Capetian manner, the latter's repeated rebellions put paid to any such plans and resulted in the king's final deathbed bequest of England to his second son, the childless William Rufus.[73] Rufus' youngest brother and successor, Henry I, had only one legitimate son, William, to whom Orderic Vitalis accords the Anglo-Saxon title of 'Aetheling' or 'prince'. He had been recognized as Henry's heir at the age of twelve, when 'all the free men of England and Normandy' performed homage to him.[74] Following the death of Queen Matilda in 1118, her role as regent during Henry I's absences from the kingdom was assumed by William, aided by Bishop Roger of Salisbury and other of Henry I's leading *curiales* – a precedent of which Henry II was no doubt well aware.[75] There is no evidence that William was anointed king, but in 1119 he attested a charter of Henry I issued at Rouen in 1119 as 'Dei gratia rex designatus', and in describing events in 1120 the well-informed York chronicler Hugh the Chantor calls William 'rex et dux iam designatus'.[76] In 1120, Louis VI had finally recognized William Aetheling as his father's heir to Normandy, and one chronicler speaks of him as 'rex Normananglorum futurus'.[77] William's demise soon afterwards, however, in the wreck of the White Ship makes it impossible to know how far, if at all, Henry I intended to associate him as co-ruler in the actual governance of the duchy.[78]

The title 'heir and king designate (*heres et rex designatus*)' was also adopted before 1144 by Henry, only son of King David I of Scotland.[79] Though this has been seen as a direct emulation of Capetian practice, the close relationship between David and his brother-in-law Henry I makes it more probable that in this case the immediate influence was the example of William Aetheling.[80] Associated with his father's rule from *c.*1128, when he was aged about thirteen, Henry subsequently participated in the joint governance of the 'Scoto-Northumbrian realm' which David had carved out in the northern counties at the expense of King Stephen.[81] On Henry's premature death, his eldest son, Malcolm, though only a young child, was associated with his rule by King David. A striking image of this condominium is furnished by the illuminated initial of Malcolm's grant to Kelso abbey, in which the beardless young Malcolm sits crowned, enthroned and holding a sceptre beside his venerable grandfather, who himself holds a drawn sword to symbolize his superior authority.[82]

It was, however, the exigencies of a bitter civil war that led King Stephen to go beyond the insular tradition of designating an heir by attempting to have his own son Eustace crowned in his own lifetime. Such a move, which had strong support among the magnates at Stephen's court, was intended to secure the house of Blois on the throne of England and to counter the growing significance of the young Henry FitzEmpress, in whom the Angevins' hopes of an eventual succession now principally lay.[83] Eustace, who had performed homage to Louis VII for Normandy in 1137,[84] was knighted by his father in 1147 and advanced to comital rank.[85] Stephen, however, regarded it as essential to gain papal support for Eustace's coronation. For while Innocent II had confirmed Stephen's own claim to the throne, the question of succession was fiercely disputed by the Angevins, who equally pressed hard Henry's claims at the Curia. It was for precisely this reason that the pope refused to endorse Eustace's coronation, for by agreeing to it, the papacy would effectively be pronouncing on the issue of succession and the outcome of the civil war, which it refused to do. Instead, it resorted to diplomatic temporizing. When as early as 1143 approaches had been made to Celestine II, the pope had written to Archbishop Theobald, 'forbidding him to allow any change (*innovatio*) to be made in the kingdom of England in the matter of the crown, for that matter was in dispute and so any claim for the transfer to the right was to be refused'.[86] This policy was followed by his successors Lucius II and Eugenius III, and when in 1151 Henry Murdac, archbishop of York, made a sustained effort to persuade the latter to crown Eustace, he met with no success.[87] The failure to secure Eustace's coronation was a body blow to the fortunes of the house of Blois. While Eustace lived, he had continued to prove a formidable opponent to Henry Plantagenet, but on his death in 1153 it had been papal hostility that in large measure had led Stephen to abandon any attempt to have his second son William acknowledged as his heir.[88]

These events go far to explain Henry II's eagerness to have his own son Henry crowned when still a child. A king's designation of his successor and the performance of homage by the nobility to that heir could not guarantee the succession: Henry I had gone to great pains to compel the magnates of the Anglo-Norman *regnum* to swear homage and fealty to his daughter Matilda as his heir, yet this had not prevented Stephen's *coup d'état* in 1135. The civil war that raged between 1139 and 1153, and the shifting fortunes of the contenders for the crown, not least in 1141 following the capture of King Stephen at Lincoln, had constantly foregrounded the issue of succession and its uncertainties.[89] By 1162 there was no longer any immediate challenge to the throne, for William of Blois had died in 1159, the year after Henry's disaffected brother Geoffrey, even though the house of Blois-Chartres still remained a dangerous force to be reckoned with and was now bound to the Capetian king by close ties of marriage. The coronation of his heir would be both a wise precaution and a potent symbol of the success of the Angevin dynasty where his bitter rival Stephen had failed. Within the Plantagenet family itself, the coronation would make the succession to Henry II unambiguous and secure young Henry's place as future ruler of England.

Son of a King: Authority, Status and Plantagenet Kingship

Henry II's desire to have his son crowned reflected his concerns not simply for his dynasty's security but also for its status. While Eustace had advanced his claims to the throne of England as the son of a consecrated king, it remained an uncomfortable fact that Henry II, though the grandson of a king of England through his maternal line, was only the son of a count. Henry, by adopting the title 'FitzEmpress', stressed his mother's imperial status, but in so doing could not but draw attention to Geoffrey le Bel's lesser rank. Matilda's own title, moreover, was little more than honorary after the death of her first husband, Emperor Henry V, in 1125 while still more importantly, she had never been crowned and anointed as queen of England.[90] If to her supporters she could be titled 'the Lady of the English (*domina Anglorum*)', Stephen's charter confirming the Treaty of Winchester with Duke Henry Plantagenet in 1153 could refer to Matilda merely – and dismissively – as 'the mother of the duke'.[91] Matilda's status had suffered still further in the bitter propaganda war waged, especially at the Curia, between churchmen supporting the rival causes of Stephen and the Empress: Stephen's advocates had argued that as Henry I's wife Matilda had previously been a nun, their marriage was invalid and that by implication the Empress herself was illegitimate.[92]

Hostile contemporaries were quick to play on this perceived weakness, particularly after the deterioration in relations between Henry and Becket. William FitzStephen, who was probably an eyewitness, recounts a telling exchange at Angers in 1166, when Henry II gave an audience to some of Becket's clerks. One of these, the aristocratic and haughty Herbert of Bosham, upbraiding the king for adopting 'evil customs' which oppressed the Church, compared his actions with those of Frederick Barbarossa and further offended Henry by referring to Frederick merely as king, not as emperor. Henry, who had acknowledged the special imperial dignity of Frederick in an embassy of 1157, repaid the insult by alluding to the fact that as canon law forbade priests from marrying, their offspring were deemed illegitimate and as such were themselves barred from the priesthood. As he remarked angrily: 'For shame! It's come to a pretty pass when this son of a priest can upset my kingdom and disturb my peace'. 'Not I,' boldly retorted Herbert, 'nor am I the son of a priest, for I was born before my father became one. Just as you can't be the son of a king if your father wasn't one.'[93] A later anecdote reported by Matthew Paris tells of how, at the great banquet following young Henry's coronation at Westminster in 1170, Henry II personally served his son at table, to emphasize his new regal status. This moved the archbishop of York to comment to the young Henry how extraordinary it was to be waited on by a king, only to receive the reply, 'It is no disgrace for the son of a mere duke to serve the son of a king.'[94] A reflection of Matthew's deep hostility to Henry II for his opposition to St Thomas, the story is undoubtedly apocryphal. Yet it contains a grain of truth: young prince Henry must have been well aware of his privileged and novel status in the Angevin dynasty as the son of a king, and perhaps too of his father's own insecurities regarding his royal rank.

Henry II has been characterized as a king 'indifferent to rank and impatient of pomp, careless of his appearance, and disdaining the trappings of monarchy', whose practical, workaday dress reflected his ceaseless activity.[95] Such a picture, however, is misleading, for Henry II was acutely conscious of the importance of the symbolism of royal power, while his court may well have witnessed a new and heightened emphasis on courtliness and protocol precisely to counter doubts as to his regal status.[96] His wish to crown his son in and after 1162 was a continuation of his sustained efforts from 1154 to restore the authority and dignity of a kingship that had been severely damaged by a long civil war, and one which had even seen a reigning monarch defeated, captured and imprisoned in 1141. Consequently, Henry's plans in 1162 should be understood within the wider context of the great significance he had attached to crown-wearing ceremonies in the first years of his reign. Henry had spent from January 1156 to April 1157 on the continent, where he had suppressed the serious rebellion by his brother Geoffrey in Anjou, and had returned in time to quell potentially very dangerous unrest in East Anglia by forcing both Stephen's son William de Warenne and Earl Hugh Bigod to yield a number of key castles.[97] It was thus a major reassertion of his kingly authority when in May 1157, 'in the second month after his return across the sea', Henry wore his crown at Pentecost at Bury St Edmunds before a large assembly of prelates, magnates 'and a crowd of common people'.[98] Bury was an unprecedented site for a great council and crown-wearing, chosen not only to overawe both Warenne and Bigod but to reaffirm the close ties between the king and the great abbey of St Edmund.[99] At Christmas that same year, Henry again held a second crown-wearing, this time at Lincoln, following his imposition of over-lordship within the British Isles; his campaign against Owain of Gwynedd had nearly cost him his life, but had ended in the submission of the Welsh princes, while King Malcolm IV had been forced to yield the northern counties, lost to the English crown under Stephen, together with the great fortresses of Carlisle, Newcastle and Bamburgh, and had become Henry's man. Lincoln had been carefully chosen for its symbolism, for it was outside the walls that King Stephen had been defeated and captured in 1141 by Henry's uncle Robert of Gloucester.[100]

Then, in what was evidently envisaged as a fitting and dramatic climax to the year's extraordinary activity, and perhaps even to the whole period of his successful restoration of peace and royal authority since his coronation in December 1154, Henry and Eleanor wore their crowns at Easter at Worcester. This was another site that was unusual for a crown-wearing, its choice dictated by Henry's desire to assert his authority in the marches.[101] Yet there was to be a more striking dimension to the Worcester crown-wearing. As Roger of Howden noted, 'when they came to the offering, they took off their crowns and offered them up on the altar, vowing to God that never in their lives would they be crowned with any others'.[102] It was not unknown for crowns to be granted as votive offerings: the great crown worn by Henry at his first corona-tion in December 1154, for example, was gifted by his mother, the Empress, to the monastery of Bec.[103] Equally, royal oblations could subsequently be redeemed from the altar by gifts of money.[104] Nevertheless, there is no direct evidence for Henry II holding any further crown-wearing ceremonies until considerably later in his reign, when the impact of Becket's murder and his son's rebellion may well have compelled him to consciously reinforce his own royal dignity through ceremony, just as in 1172 he had adopted the style *Dei gratia* in his charters in the wake of Becket's murder and the settlement with the papacy. Reflecting an earlier tradition of insular historiography in which the study of symbolism and ritual had not yet found a significant place, Kate Norgate dismissed the incident at Worcester as stemming from 'nothing more than Henry's impatience of court pageantry'.[105] Both Roger of Howden and Ralph of Diss, however, were surely far closer to Henry's real motivation when they interpreted his actions at Worcester as a formal cessation of crown-wearing and thus a public and highly self-conscious gesture of royal humility.[106]

In this context, it is possible that as early as 1158 Henry II had already begun to envisage young Henry taking over the ceremonial dimensions of the kingship of England when he reached a suitable age. The Plantagenets themselves had attempted to use the eldest son's position to stress legitimacy and future unity beyond a time of existing conflict. Geoffrey le Bel's anomalous position as duke of Normandy, more in reality by conquest than in right of his wife, had led him to stress that he would step aside as soon as his son Henry was of age and that, in the interim, the latter would have a share in its governance.[107] Following King Stephen's capture at Lincoln in 1141, the Empress Matilda had begun to associate Henry's name with hers in her charters, while in the wake of her own ensuing political and military reverses, the Angevin party increasingly projected the youthful Henry Plantagenet as the legitimate heir, for whom Matilda and Geoffrey were but holding the Anglo-Norman *regnum* in trust till he came of age.[108]

What seems more certain is that Henry II intended the coronation of his eldest son in 1162 and Becket's elevation to the archbishopric of Canterbury to be the foundation of a regency government of England. Under young Henry's nominal rule, the kingdom's de facto administration would be in the hands of Thomas and the justiciars, operating in close communication with King Henry.[109] Such an arrangement would allow Henry II himself to concentrate his efforts on the consolidation and rule of his continental territories, where his political and military priorities – and his greatest challenges – firmly lay.[110] The ever-present threat of Capetian aggression and restless factions within regional aristocracies, particularly in Brittany and Aquitaine but also on the southern and eastern borders of Normandy, required the king's near-constant supervision. England, by contrast, with its well-developed structures of central and regional government – the Exchequer, the justiciars, the sheriffs, the shire and hundred courts – could be left under trusted deputies to run itself, save for intermittent crises such as insurrection in Wales, which called for Henry's personal intervention. Similarly, while a significant role in government may also have been envisaged for Queen Eleanor during those periods when she was in the kingdom, the vice-regency of young Henry would allow her to concentrate more of her efforts on the governance of Aquitaine on Henry II's behalf.[111]

Crucial to Henry II's conception of this regency was that the offices of chancellor and archbishop should be combined in the person of his trusted friend Thomas. Archbishops of Canterbury had long been among the king's most prominent advisors, but, as Ralph of Diss noted, King Henry was strongly influenced by imperial practice, whereby the archbishop of Mainz acted as arch-chancellor under the king in Germany, and the archbishop of Cologne did likewise in Italy under the emperor.[112] Hard-line reformers within the Church denounced the holding of secular office by ecclesiastics as uncanonical, but Dean Ralph (whose own bishop served as Henry II's treasurer) saw the uniting of the imperial seal and archiepiscopal staff in the hands of one man as beneficial to both the peace of the Church and the well-being of the empire.[113] Henry II had, moreover, or so he later claimed, obtained Pope Alexander's permission for Thomas to remain as chancellor when installed as archbishop.[114] There were in addition immediate precedents: the archbishop of Mainz had been chancellor to Conrad III (d. 1152), and Rainald of Dassel, Barbarossa's key advisor, continued to serve as chancellor after his promotion to the arch-bishopric of Cologne in 1159. Similarly at the Capetian court, Hugh of Champfleury had retained his office as chancellor, with papal encouragement, after his election to the bishopric of Soissons in 1159, and continued to hold both positions until 1172.[115] Henry thus sought to combine a practical solution to devolving government with the prestige of a chancellor-archbishop for the kingdom of England, whose immediate ruler was to be his son, crowned and anointed as king in his own right.

The Council of London and the Election and Consecration of Becket

As Thomas' biographer Edward Grim noted, Henry II ordered Becket to return to England in 1162 'especially to gain the fealty and subjection of all to his son, then to be crowned and sworn in as king'.[116] Young Henry, under the chancellor's guardianship, was sent on ahead, in order to receive the homage of the magnates.[117] Henry II seemingly had intended to follow soon after, to be in England for the feast of Pentecost on 27 May 1162.[118] Delayed by circum-stances or design, he instead sent an embassy headed by bishops Hilary of Chichester, Bartholomew of Exeter and Walter of Rochester with the abbot of Battle and the justiciar Richard de Lucy, to order the prior and convent of Christ Church, Canterbury, to proceed with the election of the archbishop.[119] Having elected Becket, though not without dissenting voices, Prior Wibert and a delegation of monks joined a great assembly, which had been summoned at London and was to include all the clergy of the southern province.[120] At this council, held on 23 May, young Henry received the homage and fealty of the English bishops, abbots and leading clergy, together with that of the lay magnates.[121] Thomas himself, as chancellor, was the first to perform this homage.[122] Strikingly, he made his accompanying oath to the young Henry 'saving his fealty to the king [Henry II] as long as he should live and should wish to reign over the kingdom'.[123] The clear implication was that following the impending coronation, Henry II might at some future stage wish to relax or even perhaps remit his direct authority in the kingdom.

Following the homage of the magnates, young Henry, as his father's representative, presided over the continuing process of Becket's election to the archbishopric, for Henry had granted his son 'unimpaired kingly power in all matters that concern the crown in this affair'.[124] In the refectory of Westminster abbey, the assembly approved the election, which was then officially published by Henry of Blois, the venerable bishop of Winchester and one of the most senior figures in the English Church.[125] Bishop Henry then formally presented young prince Henry with the petition of the clergy that Thomas should be chosen, asking for his 'assensus, favor et gratia', and to this the prince formally gave his consent 'with joy'.[126] As the late King Stephen's brother and a king-maker in his own right, Bishop Henry may well have reflected on the muta-bility of fortune, as he found himself having to propose the elevation of Thomas, the man who had played a leading role in securing papal prohibition of his nephew Eustace's coronation, to the son and heir of Henry Plantagenet, Stephen's opponent and nemesis.[127]

The young prince, 'the illustrious Henry, still a boy, the king's son and heir', played an equally prominent role at Thomas' consecration, which took place in Canterbury cathedral on 3 June 1162, only a day after Becket had been ordained priest by Bishop Walter of Rochester.[128] Henry, accompanied by the justiciar Richard de Lucy, personally led Becket to the church, which was thronged with an 'almost countless crowd of great men and nobles of the realm', and he presided as Henry of Winchester duly consecrated Thomas as archbishop.[129] Henry II's absence from both the election and consecration of an archbishop of Canterbury, and particularly that of his close friend and leading minister, was remarkable. Though it is possible that he sought to distance himself somewhat from an election which was undoubtedly more unpopular than Becket's biographers would admit, and which was clearly the result of overwhelming royal pressure, it is more likely that he sought to emphasize the position and honour of his son, and thereby to symbolize the new order he wished to establish in the kingdom.[130]

A Coronation Postponed

England now had a new primate. Yet the intended coronation of young Henry did not take place. It has been suggested that with the growing prospect of Becket's election, the bishops of the southern ecclesiastical province of England dissuaded Henry II from allowing Roger of York to go ahead with the coronation in line with the papal permissions obtained the year previously.[131] With a new metropolitan, Canterbury could retain its cherished – and jealously guarded – privilege of crowning the kings of England. Archbishop Roger, however, at once appealed to Rome for confirmation of York's ancient privileges of having his cross carried before him and of carrying out coronations. Accordingly, the pope issued a bull to this effect on 13 July 1162, at Montpellier. With both metropolitans claiming the right to crown the king's heir, Henry was forced to postpone the coronation of his son.[132] Not for the last time, the young Henry experienced the baleful effect of the bitter and long-standing rivalry between the archbishops of York and Canterbury.

Yet there was a much more immediate and still more contentious reason for the postponing of young Henry's coronation. For, once he had been consecrated as archbishop, Thomas promptly resigned the royal chancellorship. At what stage he decided to do so, or formally resigned, is uncertain. Becket's biographers, heavily influenced by their knowledge of the proceedings later brought against Thomas by Henry II in 1164, claimed that immediately prior to either his election or his consecration the young Henry had quitclaimed him of certain secular obligations.[133] They stress that the prince was fully authorized to make such a concession, acting on the authority of Henry II's letters from Normandy, and that his decision had been confirmed by Richard de Lucy and other of the king's ministers.[134] The resignation of the chancellorship may have been implicit in his request for such quittance, but Ralph of Diss linked it directly to his receipt of the pallium, with which he was invested at Canterbury on 10 August 1162.[135] Whatever the case, Thomas sent the great seal back to Henry II in Normandy. His reasons for so doing have been debated, but it was a course of action completely unforeseen by Henry II, who reacted with indignant fury.[136] The preparations for young Henry's coronations were postponed until further notice. In the wake of the heady atmosphere of Becket's own consecration, this postponement must have come as a puzzling anticlimax to the young prince, who in preparation had no doubt had been well schooled in the nature of the ceremony, his role in it, and the duties of the office. He also soon witnessed a remarkable transformation in his guardian: for while Thomas continued to keep a splendid court worthy of the primate, he now personally abandoned his former lavish, secular lifestyle, and was seen to 'put on the new man'.[137] Becket began to indulge in extensive almsgiving and, in imitation of Christ washing the feet of his disciples, he washed the feet of twelve paupers every day. His own diet became modest, and at meals the household knights were placed at the far end of the hall so as not to disturb the clergy, who were read to as they ate by Alexander Llewellyn, the archbishop's cross-bearer.[138] Nevertheless, as the king's son, young Henry was first among the noble youths of the archbishop's household to serve the archbishop at table every day, and Thomas would engage in joking conversations with him, keeping the boy close to him among the other diners.[139]

Henry II had intended to return to England in December 1162, having set his affairs in order and ensured that his castles in Normandy, Anjou, Aquitaine and 'even Gascony' were in a state of readiness.[140] But contrary winds had kept him in the duchy, and he and Eleanor accordingly held their Christmas court at Cherbourg.[141] On 25 January 1163, the king and queen, crossing from Barfleur, landed at Southampton.[142] Herbert of Bosham made much of the joyful reunion of the king with his son, and still more with Archbishop Thomas:

> The archbishop who, in the company of that distinguished boy Henry, the king's son and heir, had awaited his arrival for many days, immediately came to meet him. And when the archbishop was admitted to the king's lodgings with the king's son, Henry, the king and all his men came running to him and there was great joy and celebration throughout the whole court. The king and the archbishop threw themselves into mutual kisses and embraces, each trying to outdo the other in giving honour. So much so that it seemed that the king was not effusive enough, being entirely effusive towards the archbishop, and spread himself out into joy, now for the first time seeing his Thomas, once of the court, as archbishop.[143]

Others, however, had observed a noticeable cooling in King Henry's attitude to Becket: Thomas, according to Dean Ralph, 'was received with the kiss, but not into full favour, as was evident to all who were present by the king's turning his face away'.[144] To those who could read the early signs of royal *ira*, it was an ominous gesture. Further evidence of Henry's displeasure subsequently came when Becket was forced to resign the archdeaconry of Canterbury, which Henry proceeded to bestow on his trusted clerk, Geoffrey Ridel.[145]

The council of Woodstock in July witnessed a rapid deterioration in the relations between Henry II and the archbishop of Canterbury.[146] Becket successfully opposed the king's plans to pay a customary levy of two shillings on the hide (the principal unit of land assessment), known as the 'sheriff's aid', straight into the Exchequer, thereby transforming what had by custom been an increment given to the sheriff in recognition of his administrative labours into a direct royal tax.[147] More serious was the archbishop's prohibition, on the grounds of consanguinity, of Henry's plan to marry his younger brother, William FitzEmpress, to the countess Warenne, the widow of King Stephen's son William of Blois. Prior to this, the king had made generous provision for William, but the great Warenne inheritance and a comital rank would have been a fitting endowment for Henry's loyal sibling.[148] Stephen of Rouen believed that the disappointment of being denied this rich prize caused William's death in January 1164 from a broken heart, and that Henry II held Becket responsible.[149] Whatever its real cause, William's death was a source of grief to young Henry, for there seems to have been a particular bond of affection between uncle and nephew. Some of the earl's household subsequently took service with the prince and may well have been familiar to him before 1164, while in 1183 young Henry specified his wish to be buried in Rouen cathedral beside his uncle William.[150]

Responsibility for the growing tensions throughout 1163 between Archbishop Thomas and King Henry has been variously ascribed to Thomas' studied intransigence, as he sought to assert his new role as archbishop of Canterbury by mounting increasingly serious challenges to the king's authority, or, by those more sympathetic to Becket, to Henry, who reacted to the archbishop's quite proper, even courageous, stance with a vindictive desire to be revenged on his former friend.[151] What is certain is that Henry II regarded Becket's opposition to his policies as a deep betrayal of his trust and former favour, and the conflict resulted in an indefinite postponement of young Henry's coronation. For by now Henry was determined that Thomas should be denied the privilege of anointing his son. It was in the council at Westminster in October 1163 that the first major clash between king and archbishop occurred.[152] Concerned to address the problem of 'criminous clerks' – clerics who, through benefit of clergy, were escaping adequate punishment for serious crimes such as rape or murder – Henry II proposed that any cleric guilty of a serious offence should be first judged by an ecclesiastical court; once stripped of his holy orders, he should then be handed over to the secular authorities for condign punishment. Becket, however, argued that such an action punished a man twice for the same offence, and, still worse, represented an attack on the liberties of the Church.[153] In response to these objections, Henry demanded that Becket and the bishops acknowledge the royal customs that the king enjoyed in respect of the Church. Becket consented, but his insistence on a saving clause provoked the king's fury at what he deemed treacherous casuistry. Storming out of the council, Henry left London.[154] The next day, he removed his son from Becket's charge as a public demonstration of his anger and displeasure towards Thomas.[155]

As future king, nowhere was young Henry's involvement more significant than in matters directly touching royal authority and prerogative. As the conflict between Henry II and Becket intensified, young Henry could not but be drawn inexorably into the wider struggle it engendered between the crown and the Church. In late January 1164, the prince jointly presided with his father at the fateful council of Clarendon, held at the favoured royal palace close to Salisbury.[156] Following the confrontation at Westminster, Thomas had been pressured by a number of his episcopal colleagues, members of the nobility and a papal delegation to accept the royal customs without any qualification, being assured that Henry had no harmful intent towards the Church. Henry II, however, had insisted that because of the damage done to his honour by Thomas' initial refusal, the archbishop must make this acknowledgement publicly before the assembled clergy and magnates. Yet once the magnates had assembled at Clarendon, Thomas initially refused to acknowledge the royal customs. It was only after he and the bishops had been shut away for two days and had been repeatedly warned of the terrible consequences, both to the clergy and himself, if he did not do so, that Becket finally gave way, commanding that the bishops must likewise promise to uphold the royal customs 'in the word of truth'. There the dispute might have ended, but Henry II was determined to press home his advantage.[157] He had ordered a written record to be made of these customs, drawn up by the royal clerks with the advice of the 'older and wiser' nobles, which in sixteen clauses formed a 'record and declaration of a certain part of the customs, liberties and privileges of his ancestors, that is, of King Henry his grandfather, and of other things which ought to be observed and maintained in the realm'. This, the document was careful to note, was drawn up 'in the presence of the lord Henry, and of his father the lord king', for these were the inviolable rights of the crown, to be held by Henry II's heirs in perpetuity.[158] The text was then presented to the archbishop and his colleagues to confirm. It was a serious miscalculation on Henry's part, for it allowed Thomas and the bishops no room for manoeuvre. Faced with such an uncompromising statement of regalian rights, Becket equivocated, accepting the chirograph presented to him as a record, but refusing to set his seal to it. His ambiguous action, which was tantamount to accepting the king's demands, split the episcopate, who might well have been united behind him against so forthright an expression of royal authority, and led to a groundswell of resentment and anger against the archbishop.[159]

One of Thomas' last acts as archbishop before the final rupture with Henry II was to preside at a great ceremony, which young Henry probably attended, held in April 1164 to dedicate the royal abbey at Reading, 'in which Henry of divine memory . . . rests in a glorious mausoleum'.[160] Yet in the wake of the council of Clarendon, Henry II showed himself relentless in seeking Becket's downfall. After two failed attempts to escape from the kingdom to France to seek Pope Alexander III at Sens, Thomas was summoned to a council at Northampton in October, where he was arraigned on a number of charges. Accused of having failed to answer an earlier royal summons to court, he was condemned to forfeit all his moveable possessions. Even then, however, he faced royal demands to repay monies acquired when he was chancellor. When Bishop Henry of Winchester reminded the king that the young Henry and the chief justiciar had quitclaimed Thomas of all secular obligations at the time of his consecration, Henry II responded that they had exceeded their authority in so doing and that any such quittance was invalid.[161] The proceedings were conducted with increasing acrimony. The bishops were far from universal in their support for Thomas, and it was becoming all too clear that Henry II was implacable, at best aiming for the archbishop's resignation, and at worst his complete downfall. Realizing that all was lost, Becket left the council secretly and fled into exile, to be branded a traitor in his absence.[162]

The hagiographers of Becket afford only a glimpse of his relations with the prince before 1164, and knowledge of the archbishop's subsequent martyrdom strongly colour their depictions. Nevertheless, there seems to have been genuine affection between young Henry and his mentor. For young Henry, the increasingly bitter clash between his father and his former guardian cannot but have been a bewildering, even traumatic experience. Never before could he have seen the court in such turmoil. The council of Clarendon had been the scene of bitter discord, while at Northampton members of the lay nobility had uttered violent threats against Thomas in the king's name and the archbishop had left the court with cries of traitor ringing in his ears. The boy had witnessed at first hand a terrifying display of Henry II's royal *ira et malevolentia*, and his father's relentless destruction of his opponent.[163] The king would show himself equally ruthless towards Becket's relatives and clerks, several of whom must have been known to young Henry from his period under Thomas' guardianship but who now suffered exile and forfeiture.[164] From the height of power and influence, Thomas had utterly fallen from grace, a chilling example of the mutability of Fortune's wheel.

CHAPTER 4

Training for Kingship, 1163–1169

Who is able to count up the virtues with which the Lord enriched him? For the Lord made him to excel almost all men in this life in all decency of conduct and to have greater worth in the military arts. He was handsome of face, charming of speech, winsome and loveable.

– Roger of Howden, *Gesta Henrici Secundi*[1]

THOUGH THE DEEPENING quarrel with Thomas Becket had postponed plans for young Henry's coronation, Henry II had already taken pains clearly to associate his eldest son with his rule of the kingdom. After the celebration of his eighth birthday, the prince had probably attended the council at London in early March 1163, at which Gilbert Foliot was elected as bishop of London.[2] He was certainly with the royal entourage that travelled south to Canterbury, where the king and the archbishop celebrated Palm Sunday on 17 March, before moving on to Dover to meet Count Thierry of Flanders and his son Philip.[3] Here young Henry joined with his father in renewing the long-standing treaty between the kings of England and the counts of Flanders, who played a pivotal role in the power balance of northern France.[4] Though a vassal of the French king, Thierry had married Henry II's aunt Sibylla, and when in 1157 he had once again left for Jerusalem, he had associated Philip with his rule as count and placed his son and his lands under Henry's protection.[5] The new *conventio* closely followed the texts of the earlier agreements established between Henry I and the count of Flanders in 1101 and 1110,[6] but as Philip was now co-ruler with his father and prince Henry was associated with Henry II's rule, it differed in setting out its provisions in the joint names of both rulers and their eldest sons.[7] In return for a large annual payment, the counts pledged to bring 1,000 knights, each with three horses, 'to defend the kingdom of England against all men', saving the service they owed to King Louis, while, strikingly, the treaty envisaged that the younger Henry might summon the count of Flanders to his aid in his own right.[8] This was probably the prince's first meeting with Philip, twelve years his senior, who would come to have a strong influence on him as a patron in chivalry and as a future ally.

The summer of 1163 brought a more dramatic assertion of young Henry's position, this time as heir to the overlordship of Britain. On 1 July, he jointly presided over a great council at Woodstock, where Rhys of Deheubarth, Owain ap Gruffyd of Gwynedd and many of the other leading Welsh princes, as well as Malcolm IV, the young but sickly king of Scots, performed homage first to King Henry, then to his eldest son.[9] Their submission, however, had only been gained by Henry II's overawing power, and the council appears to have been a fraught one. The Welsh leaders were compelled to give hostages, as was Malcolm, including his brother David and some sons of his barons, 'in respect of keeping peace and for his castles which the king wished to have'.[10] As Malcolm had already yielded Carlisle and other key castles in Northumberland back in 1157, these fortresses were seemingly in lowland Scotland, and the demand for their custody was thus an unprecedented assertion of Angevin power.[11] Whether or not at Woodstock Henry II sought fundamentally to redefine the status of these rulers in order to emphasize their subordinate position and obligations as vassals is uncertain, but his high-handed conduct was soon to drive Malcolm into the arms of Louis VII, and to prompt a massive Welsh uprising in 1164, when 'all the Welsh of Gwynedd, Deheubarth and Powys with one accord cast off the Norman yoke'.[12]

More mundane business was also transacted at Woodstock, for it was probably on this occasion that young Henry attested, as 'Henricus filius Regis', a confirmation by his father of the grant by Robert, bishop of Bath, of the church of Banwell, Somerset, to the prior and convent of Bruton – a chance glimpse of what was undoubtedly becoming a commonplace activity of royal business for the prince.[13] Royal or comital children might attest charters at a very early age.[14] Evidence from Angevin comital charters indicates that when the count's son appeared at public ceremonies his guardian or *nutricius* would be present and might assist his ward in the verbal or ritual process of assent to charters, guiding his hand as he made his autograph cross or standing in as his representative in symbolic acts, such as the making of grants by placing a knife on the altar.[15] An eldest son's position as successor and thus future guarantor of charters of donation or confirmation made his attestation particularly important to the beneficiary.[16]

An Illustrious Inheritance

Few ceremonies, however, were as significant for his own perceptions of his kingly role as that attended by young Henry on 13 October 1163 at the 'famous and royal abbey of Westminster', when in the presence of King Henry and a great assembly, Archbishop Thomas – in one of his last acts before the final rift with Henry II – had solemnly translated the body of Edward the Confessor to a magnificent new shrine.[17] If Henry II had been contemplating the coronation of his son by at least 1162, the early 1160s had equally seen him striving to enhance the sacral nature and prestige of English kingship. In 1161, he had obtained the canonization of Edward the Confessor from Pope Alexander III, again succeeding where King Stephen had failed.[18] St Edward's crown, ring, sceptre and sandals, recovered when his tomb had been opened in 1102, were carefully preserved by the monks of Westminster as elements of the royal regalia.[19] Gaining added significance as the quarrel between Becket and Henry over royal and sacerdotal authority deepened, such a re-emphasis on holy and charismatic kingship was part of a wider reaction by European monarchies to the pretensions of the Gregorian reformers.[20] Only three years before the translation of Edward the Confessor, the bodies of the Three Kings had been appropriated by Frederick Barbarossa following his destruction of Milan and later, in 1164, they were brought with great ceremony to Cologne, where their relics became the focus of a burgeoning cult.[21] Henry II himself had been consulted by Frederick on the matter, and had also supported the efforts of the archbishop of Cologne, Rainald of Dassel, to secure the canonization of Charlemagne in December 1165.[22] Similarly, Ailred of Rievaulx could eulogize David I of Scotland (d. 1153), the Empress Matilda's uncle, as a 'sanctus rex', a pre-eminent exemplar of Christian kingship, while his grandson Malcolm IV, who in 1165 was laid to rest with him at the royal mausoleum of Dunfermline abbey, was likewise remembered as 'Christianissimus rex Scotorum', a 'piisimus rex', and 'an angel on earth'.[23] Young Henry can have been left in no doubt as to the sacred and solemn nature of the kingship to which he would be raised.

He was equally instructed in his illustrious royal pedigree. While the image of Edward shaped by Ailred of Rievaulx and the hagiographers of Westminster abbey as a wise, chaste and holy ruler blessed with thaumaturgical powers bore scant relation to the historical figure of the penultimate Anglo-Saxon king, the Confessor's canonization and translation gave the Plantagenet dynasty the lustre of a sainted royal ancestor, as well as stressing their descent from the great pre-Conquest kings of England.[24] In his *Vita Edwardi*, commissioned for the translation ceremony at Westminster, Ailred looked to Henry II as the cornerstone that bonded the Norman and English races in harmony, in whose reign ecclesiastics, nobles and knights of English stock could once more flourish.[25] Earlier, in his *Genealogia regum Anglorum*, written between Stephen's acceptance of Henry as his heir in 1153 and his coronation, Ailred had already made a strong connection between Henry II and the Old English monarchy. He traced Henry's distinguished genealogy via his grandmother Matilda, who was the daughter of St Margaret and had become Henry I's queen, back to the great Anglo-Saxon kings Edgar and Alfred and the early kings of Wessex, and their legendary ancestors – including Woden – and hence back to Noah himself.[26] In 1158, Bishop Henry of Winchester had given tangible expression to this link when, probably in Henry II's presence, he had the bodies of the Anglo-Saxon kings, as well as Winchester's saints, translated into a magnificent new setting in his cathedral church.[27] As the prince was no doubt reminded, in comparison with such an ancient and exalted pedigree, the Capetian kings of France were mere parvenus.[28]

As future overlord of Britain, moreover, young Henry could claim affinity with a ruler more illustrious and mighty than even Charlemagne. Geoffrey of Monmouth's *Historia Regum Britanniae*, completed *c.*1139, had transformed King Arthur from a magical figure of Welsh and Breton ballads to a supposedly historical ruler of all Britain who had conquered Gaul and defeated the Romans.[29] This hugely popular work was disseminated still more widely following its translation into Anglo-Norman verse around 1155 by the Jersey poet Wace, who is said to have presented a copy of his *Roman de Brut* to Queen Eleanor.[30] Although the extent of Henry II's patronage of subsequent Arthurian writers such as Chrétien de Troyes and Marie de France remains disputed, prince Henry undoubtedly grew up in court culture familiar with the 'material of Brittany'.[31] Geoffrey of Monmouth had modelled Arthur's court at Caerleon, with its magnificent crown-wearing ceremonies, on that of King Henry I, and both Henry II and his sons recognized the political kudos of associating their kingship with that of King Arthur.[32] Even in Normandy, the stories of Arthur could be used to attack the French, undermine the growing legend of Charlemagne, and vaunt the conquests of the king 'and his English' over them.[33]

Young Henry had, however, been made no less conscious of his great Norman forebears. An Anglo-French version of Ailred's *Life of St Edward*, written by an anonymous nun of Barking some time between 1163 and 1169, not only repeats Ailred's assertion that Henry II was, through 'la bone Mahalt', sprung from the English line of Edward himself and had thus united the English and Norman peoples, but also praises the Norman stock of Edward's mother, Emma, sister of Duke Richard II. The *Life* prays that the sons of 'the glorious King Henry' may be blessed with the wisdom and valour of their ducal ancestors, Count Robert, Richard the Good, and William the noble Bastard'.[34] In early 1162, before being sent to England in Becket's charge, prince Henry may well have been present at the solemn celebration at the great ducal abbey

of Fécamp on 11 March, when in the presence of King Henry II, Cardinal
Henry of Pisa and a great assembly of Norman clergy, the bodies of Dukes
Richard I and Richard II had been removed from their tombs and reburied in
a more fitting site in front of the altar of the Holy Trinity.[35] Certainly in
attendance was the poet and historian Wace, whom Henry II had commissioned to compose a history of his Norman ancestors, the *Roman de Rou*, which
incorporated the legendary history of these early dukes, cast in both a heroic
and a hagiographic mould. Its blend of fabliau, *chanson* and romance reflected
a body of oral tales which must have been familiar to Henry II and his sons,
while, significantly, both Wace and his successor Benoît of St Maure recast the
image of the early Norman dukes, depicting them as paragons of contemporary courtly and chivalric virtues.[36]

Young Henry was heir not only to such English and Norman identities but
also to those of the counts of Anjou and dukes of Aquitaine. Queen Eleanor
doubtless ensured that her children were familiarized with the great deeds of
her ducal ancestors, including those of her grandfather William IX, celebrated
as much as an accomplished poet as a warrior and crusader, and the prince may
well have listened to the performance of some of his witty, sometimes autobio-
graphical and often scurrilous songs in praise of the delights of love, as well
as of 'chivalry and pride'.[37] In Anjou, figures such as Fulk Nerra had already
passed into legend by the time that writers in the orbit of the Angevin comital
court, such as Thomas of Loches, chaplain and notary to both Fulk V and
Geoffrey le Bel, had begun to compile histories of the dynasty, while John of
Marmoutier's *Historia Gaufridi ducis,* composed in the 1170s, likewise drew on
a rich vein of oral anecdotes concerning the more recent deeds of young
Henry's grandfather. The *Historia* was very much a princely mirror for good
rulership, portraying Geoffrey both as an excellent knight and as a devout,
learned, just and merciful ruler.[38] The inscription surrounding the fine enamel
plaque associated with the tomb of Geoffrey himself in the cathedral of St
Julian in Le Mans closely echoes just such an image: the count is depicted not
as a mounted warrior but as a prince and defender of the Church, armed with
the sword of justice.[39] The cathedral and its saint held a special resonance for
the Angevins. As a young child, Geoffrey le Bel had been placed on the altar
of St Julian by his father Count Fulk when the latter was about to depart
for Jerusalem, and entrusted, along with the count's lands, to the saint's
special protection.[40] He and the Empress Matilda were married in the cathedral in 1128, and, in turn, Geoffrey V had his eldest son Henry Plantagenet
baptized in the cathedral and then presented him to St Julian, who became his
'advocate and patron'.[41] Whether or not Henry II had similarly presented the
young Henry to St Julian is unknown, but the prince almost certainly visited

Le Mans, said to have been the city Henry II held most dear, and seen the tomb of his illustrious grandfather.[42] It was powerful testimony to this bond and to the affection felt towards young Henry that when in 1183 the funeral cortège of the Young King rested for the night in the cathedral of St Julian, on its intended journey north to Rouen, the men of Le Mans seized his body and immediately buried it alongside the tomb of Geoffrey Le Bel.[43]

Lessons for Rule

Young Henry seems to have remained with his father until Henry II's departure for Normandy in the spring of 1165, when he was placed in the charge of a new *magister*, William FitzJohn.[44] William was a trusted royal administrator, who had served, among other functions, as an itinerant justice in Yorkshire and the West Country in 1159 and 1160, hearing pleas and investigating local officials.[45] He is named as a royal justice along with other 'wise men' of Henry II's court, and it is very likely that the young prince received instruction from him in the workings of government.[46] His tutelage in the 1160s occurred during a period of intensive effort on the part of the king and his agents in pursuing the consolidation of royal rights, the establishment of law and order and the enforcement of justice.[47] Together with the workings of royal justice and finance, the prince would also have been instructed in the ideology of the kingship he was to inherit, and few expounded this more zealously than the king's own ministers.[48] As the treasurer Richard FitzNeal later noted in his *Dialogue of the Exchequer*, the king's mission was 'to crush the rebels against peace and malcontents with all sorts of destruction, and to seal up in men's hearts every treasure of peace and loyalty'.[49] In times of peace, 'devout princes build churches, they feed and clothe Christ by giving alms to the poor, and they distribute money by practising other works of mercy'. And, he added, while rulers may gain glory in war, 'their greatest glory lies in those deeds whereby they gain a heavenly reward for a temporal price – a good bargain indeed'.[50]

During this time, young Henry came into more regular contact with some of Henry's most important administrators, including FitzNeal and Master Thomas Brown, the king's almoner and a key Exchequer official, Robert de Beaumont, earl of Leicester and the king's chief justiciar, and Richard of Ilchester, the archdeacon of Poitiers, another itinerant justice and leading figure at the Exchequer, who was said in the mid 1160s to have 'exercised the greatest power throughout England'.[51] William FitzAldelin, who had already been one of the prince's guardians in 1159–60, and who served as a marshal and royal justice, was also closely associated with young Henry.[52] Some of the prince's own household officers, such as Ailward, who appears variously as butler (*pincerna*) or chamberlain (*camerarius*), are glimpsed in the records, while the Pipe Rolls indicate that for much of 1165–66 the young Henry's itinerary was focused on southern England and major royal centres such as Winchester, the royal hunting lodge at Clarendon, and Sherborne, the magnificent palace-castle built by Bishop Roger of Salisbury.[53]

The issue of the younger Henry's own coronation was still very much alive. Writing in early 1164 to Thomas in exile in France, John of Salisbury reported the rumour that a papal visit to England was hoped for, and 'that the coronation of the king's son has been postponed that he may be blessed by the pope himself' in order to circumvent the archbishop's authority.[54] Nothing had come of such unrealistic plans, which can hardly have been condoned by Alexander III. Nevertheless, in a letter to Becket in early 1166, John, bishop of Poitiers, in referring to the costly failure of Henry II's major expedition against the Welsh in the previous summer, noted that 'they say that he [Henry II] often complains that he has been deprived of sound and reliable advice, and that he was more than usually disturbed by what happened to him in Wales, and is already thinking of the succession of his son (*iam de substitutione filii sui cogitet*). When I recently came to Tours, Hugh of Sainte Maure told me much about this matter very confidentially, which I have entrusted to the present messenger to repeat in your hearing only.'[55] Becket's supporters evidently already feared the possibility that Henry would seek a prelate other than Thomas to perform such a coronation. John's use of the term *substitutio* is striking, for it implied replacement rather than co-rule, a possibility that had been reflected in Thomas' oath as chancellor to the young Henry in 1162. The prominence in this matter of the Tourangeau noble Hugh of St Maure is particularly notable, for he was to be one of the leading figures in fomenting the rebellion against Henry II in 1173.[56] Becket was sufficiently alarmed by these rumours to persuade Alexander III to send a mandate, *Illius dignitatis*, to Archbishop Roger of York and all the English bishops, reaffirming Canterbury's prerogatives in the coronation and forbidding any other prelate to presume to crown the *novus rex*.[57]

Despite such concerns, Henry II himself appears to have made no active moves in regard to his son's coronation, though the great inquest into fiefs ordered by the king in early 1166, prior to his planned departure for the continent to quell a rebellion in Brittany, revealed his concern to reaffirm the nobility's loyalty. As the return of Roger, archbishop of York, stated, the king had required to know not only how many knights had been enfeoffed on his tenants-in-chief's estates before and also after 1135, but also the names of all those so enfeoffed, 'because you wish to know if there are any who have not yet done allegiance and whose names are not written in your roll, so that they may do you allegiance before the first Sunday in Lent'.[58] Though the majority of the extant returns, known collectively as the *Cartae Baronum*, do not include such information concerning homage, which presumably was returned separately, a small number refer to the performing of homage to both the younger Henry and the king. Thus a Northumbrian knight, Godfrey Baard, informed the king: 'Know that I hold of you three parts of a knight's fee, from which I am become your man and that of your son Henry'.[59] Similarly, the Norfolk knight, William of Colkirk, who owed but half a knight's service from his fee, noted that: 'I do not wish that my service is increased, for I do what I should do. I do homage to you, lord, and to my lord Henry your son, and I do service to your sheriffs.'[60] Terse though such comments are, they provide a revealing glimpse into the social range of those tenants-in-chief of the crown who, along with the great magnates of the realm, had performed the act of homage in 1162 by placing their hands within those of the young prince.[61]

Young Henry sailed to Normandy to join his father at Poitiers for Christmas 1166.[62] For the next two years, the prince's movements are unknown. The Norman Exchequer accounts have not survived for this period, but the English Pipe Rolls make no mention of him, suggesting that he spent much or all of his time on the continent.[63] These formative years of his early adolescence coincided with a period of turbulence and mounting resistance to Henry II not only in Aquitaine but in Brittany, where in 1166 Henry had deposed Count Conan and betrothed his third son Geoffrey to the count's infant daughter Constance. It is not impossible that the prince accompanied his father's armies in the campaigns of devastation which the king undertook in 1167 and 1168 against coalitions of rebel Breton and Aquitanian lords; Henry II himself had been only nine when he accompanied the relief force his uncle Robert of Gloucester brought from Normandy in November 1142 to aid the Empress then besieged in Oxford.[64] Yet the death in 1168 of the king's deputy Patrick of Salisbury in an ambush at the hands of the Lusignans, and the narrow escape of Queen Eleanor herself from capture, showed how perilous the situation was in Poitou:[65] Henry II may have thought it wiser to keep his eldest son in the comparative safety of Normandy.

Certainly it was the archbishop of Rouen, Rotrou, who in a letter composed for him by Peter of Blois *c.*1167/8 urged King Henry on behalf of his fellow bishops to provide his heir with suitable instruction:

> While the nature of other kings may be rude and deformed, yours, because
> it has been trained in letters, is provident in the administration of great

things, subtle in justice, cautious in precepts, and circumspect in counsel. Wherefore, all your bishops unanimously agree that Henry your son should be taught letters, so that he whom we regard as your heir may be the successor to your practical wisdom (*prudentia*) as well as to your kingdom.[66]

Young Henry's education was of such pressing concern to the episcopate as a body because, Rotrou went on to explain, learning was a vital prerequisite for good kingship:

For if the state is to be ruled, people united, castles maintained, machines of war built, ramparts kept repaired, defences maintained, or further, if the quiet of liberty, the cultivation of justice, reverence of laws, and the friendship of neighbours are encouraged, books teach all of these to perfection. A king without letters is a ship without oars or a bird without feathers.[67]

Writing in the following decade, John of Marmoutier put it more bluntly when he recounted the tale of how the French king Louis IV (936–54) had mocked Count Geoffrey Greygown of Anjou for singing anthems among the choristers at Tours, only to receive the cutting reply, 'Know, sire, that an unlettered king is a crowned ass.'[68] Apocryphal though the story was, a concern with education appears to have been a strong Angevin tradition: Fulk IV 'le Réchin', who ruled Anjou from 1068 to 1109, was even the author of a Latin chronicle of his family's history.[69] William of Conches, renowned as both a grammarian and a teacher of natural sciences, dedicated his *Dragmaticon philosophiae,* an exploration of natural philosophy, to Geoffrey le Bel, and cast it as a dialogue between the duke of Normandy and a philosopher.[70] It is unlikely that Henry II needed any prompting from the bishops to have his son suitably instructed, for Henry himself was acknowledged as having been particularly well educated for a layman.[71] As Peter of Blois famously wrote to a correspondent at the court of William II of Sicily: 'Your king is a good scholar, but ours is far better; with him there is school every day, constant conversation of the best scholars and discussions of questions.'[72]

Ironically, however, given the reputation of Henry II's court as an intellectual centre, the names of young Henry's tutors and details of his schooling are unknown. Nevertheless, at court he certainly came into contact with some of the leading intellectuals of the day, including Peter of Blois and Walter Map, products of the great schools of Paris and Tours.[73] Map, indeed, noted that young Henry had been 'educated by us and among us', and that he was 'ever "hanging on the lips of a speaker", seeking the company of his elders, looking for the gatherings of good men, making trial of all high deeds, never lazy, untiring in business, insatiably curious about all honourable arts, so much so that while he was no scholar (*cum non esset literatus*) – which I regret – he could copy (*transcribere*) any set of letters'.[74] This has sometimes been taken as implying that young Henry neglected study for his love of martial sports, but the term 'non literatus' did not imply illiteracy as such, but rather a lack of scholarly erudition and skill – from the point of view of clerks jealous of their learning – in writing Latin. Thus William of Tyre could note of Count Raymond of Antioch (d. 1149) that 'he cultivated letters, even though he was *illiteratus*'.[75] Basic literacy among the secular nobility was increasingly common during the twelfth century, and in a period in which royal bureaucracies were rapidly developing, a reading knowledge of Latin was a basic prerequisite for a ruler. The Young King would have been expected to understand the language in which records of government were written and in which the ecclesiastical assemblies he presided over were conducted.[76] His brother Richard's Latin grammar was said to be better than that of Hubert Walter, archbishop of Canterbury and royal chancellor, while John, who received an excellent schooling at Fontevraud abbey, 'was amongst the most highly educated secular men of his age'.[77] Unlike for John, however, no records are extant to reveal the books, whether in the vernacular or in Latin, which young Henry or members of his household may have owned, though clerks in his service such as Gervase of Tilbury clearly had access to a considerable variety of sacred and secular texts.[78]

Gaining the Accomplishments of the Court

If young Henry was not bookish, he was nonetheless highly accomplished in courtly speech and manners. As Walter Map remarked, he was 'richly endowed with eloquence and charm of address (*beatissimus eloquencia et affabilitate*)'.[79] His brother Geoffrey of Brittany was also noted as 'an excellent and eloquent knight, as much an heir to Ulysses as to Achilles', which strongly suggests that polished speech was an important element in the instruction of all Henry II's sons, and another family tradition: their grandfather Geoffrey le Bel had been praised for being 'most eloquent (*facundissimus*) among clerics and laymen'.[80] Refined manners were not only an indication of high birth and good breeding, but, as John of Salisbury explained, were an essential attribute for a ruler:

> he should be affable of speech, and generous in conferring benefits, and in his manners he should preserve the dignity of his authority unimpaired. A pleasant address and a gracious tongue will win for him the reputation for benignity . . . the reverence of subjects is a fit reward of dignity of manners.[81]

The court of Henry II, whom Map calls 'that treasure house of courtesy', was famed for the vibrancy of its intellectual circle and as a place of refined conduct.[82] It was not by chance that one of Henry's chaplains, Stephen of Fougères, who became bishop of Rennes, composed the earliest known vernacular French guide to courtesy and good manners, *Le Livre des manières*, as a guide for laymen.[83] For those with ambition and who sought the court as a place of advancement needed to master *curialitas*, among whose requirements were elegance of manners (*elegantia morum*), urbanity (*urbanitas*), and witty and sophisticated speech (*urbanissima facetiae*).[84] Gerald of Wales, for example, described William FitzAldelin, one of prince Henry's tutors and a man very much on the rise, as 'generous and courteous (*vir dapsilis et curialis*)', whose appearance 'was that of a generous and easy going man (*vir in facie liberalis et lenis*)'.[85] Young Henry had already received the very best instruction in *curialitas* in Becket's household, and his charming, affable manner was to strike many contemporaries. Gervase of Tilbury, a member of the Young King's court, noted of his lord that 'as he surpassed all others in the grace of his person, so he outstripped them all in valour, cordiality, and the outstanding graciousness of his manner (*morum insigni gracia*)', describing him as 'courteous and cheerful' and 'gracious (*graciosus*) to all'.[86]

The accomplishments ascribed to the prince find close echo in the description of the knight Folcon in the contemporary Provençal epic *Girart de Roussillon*: 'Lords, look at the best knight you have ever seen . . . he is brave and courtly and skilful, and noble and of a good lineage, eloquent, handsomely experienced in hunting and falconry: he knows how to play chess and backgammon, gaming and dicing. And his wealth was never denied to any, but each has as much as he wants . . .'[87] Hawking and hunting, the consuming passion of the medieval aristocracy, was to occupy much of young Henry's leisure time, both during and beyond his adolescence.[88] When in 1162 the prince had crossed from Normandy to England in the royal esnecca, falcons and goshawks had been transported with him.[89] These prized birds could be very costly; in 1170, for example, William de Havill received 24 shillings for two hawks purchased for 'the king, the king's son', and 20 shillings for one hawk for the king of Scots.[90] Huntsmen and falconers formed an important element within the royal household, while a number of serjeanty tenures were held for duties relating to hunting, including, for example, one which stipulated service with hawks and a greyhound between Michaelmas and Candlemas for when the king hunted herons.[91] It is likely that young Henry had accompanied Thomas Becket, his guardian, on hunting trips, while he would have also hunted regularly with his father, 'a great connoisseur of hounds and hawks', who earned the criticism of clerical observers for his immoderate love of the chase.[92] For in times of peace, sometimes even in those of war, the daily rhythm of the royal court, as well as its itinerary through the king's domains, was shaped by the insatiable addiction of the king and his companions to the hunt. In the late summer of 1169, for example, Henry II held a series of meetings with a papal delegation, headed by Gratian of Ostia and Vivian of Orvieto, which have been described as 'snatches of discussion squeezed in between hunting trips' as they followed the king while he itinerated around the duchy.[93] Doubtless the king intended this to emphasize how peripheral he regarded the matter of peace with Becket, yet in reporting these negotiations to Thomas an anonymous informant provides a valuable glimpse of what must have been a commonplace – the king and his son out hunting, each with his own entourage. While at Domfront, King Henry had returned from hunting and, late in the day, came to the legates' lodgings, greeting them 'with great honour and reverence and humility'. Just then, 'lord Henry, the king's son, came to the door of the lodging, and many young men with him, all blowing horns in the usual manner to announce the taking of a stag'. In a splendid courtly gesture already indicative of the charm and affability for which he would be renowned, young Henry presented the stag to the delegates.[94]

Yet for the nobility, hunting was more than recreation: it was vital training. Long before the development of the tournament, the hunt had been an essential mechanism of bonding within the warrior elite.[95] It developed the physical strength and endurance of young men and afforded training in horsemanship, agility in the saddle, riding at speed and the handling of weapons.[96] It was for good reason that Alfonso XI of Castile (1312–50) could later liken the chase to warfare, because 'one must be well horsed and well armed . . . be vigorous . . . suffer lack of good food . . . rise early . . . undergo heat and cold, and conceal one's fear'.[97] It exposed participants to very real danger; fatal shooting accidents were not uncommon, while the hazards of riding fast through the forest or falls from horseback claimed the lives of some, including young Henry's great-grandfather Fulk V of Anjou.[98] Hunting wild boar was especially perilous, but there were other dangers. In 1179, a hunting expedition near Compiègne almost proved fatal for the young Philip Augustus, then aged fourteen. Impetuously riding after a wild boar – or so the tale was later told – he had become separated from his entourage, and it was not until the following day that the boy, starving and terrified, was discovered by a charcoal burner and returned safely to his father. But the trauma and exhaustion led to the swift onset of a serious illness, which he was fortunate to survive.[99]

William FitzStephen gives a precious glimpse of other kinds of sporting activities that the prince and his companions would have engaged in when noting of the Londoners that 'on feast-days throughout the summer the young men indulge in the sport of archery, running, jumping, wrestling, slinging the stone, hurling the javelin beyond a mark and fighting with sword and buckler'.[100] Such activities accord closely with those listed in Gottfried von Strasbourg's *Tristan*, written *c.*1210, as among the youthful hero's accomplishments. He also 'learned to ride nimbly with shield and lance, to spur his mount skilfully on either flank, put it to the gallop with a wheel and give it free rein and urge it on with his knees, in strict accordance with the chivalric art'.[101] To hone just these skills, young Henry and his fellows would practise running at the quintain, described by Gerald of Wales as 'a strong shield hung securely to a beam, whereon aspirants for knighthood and stalwart youths mounted on galloping chargers may try their strength by breaking their lances or piercing the obstacle – this a prelude to the exercises of knighthood'. Gerald tells of his own delight in how, when passing through Arras at Pentecost, 1179, he had witnessed jousting at the quintain, which Count Philip of Flanders had had erected in the great town square, now crowded with spectators. From the balcony of his lodgings he saw 'the Count himself, and with him such a multitude of noble knights and barons, so many a fine horse galloping at the shield and so many lances broken, that, though he diligently watched each several thing, he could not sufficiently wonder at the whole'.[102]

As yet, Henry was still too young to participate in real tournaments, which would come to play so important a role in his later life. But William FitzStephen reveals that youths in their earlier adolescence who were not yet old enough to receive the belt of knighthood might engage in other forms of equestrian games. In London on every Sunday during Lent,

> after dinner a fresh swarm of young men go out into the fields on war-horses, steeds foremost in the contest, each of which is skilled and schooled to run in circles. From the gates there sallies forth a host of laymen, sons of the citizens, equipped with lances and shields, the younger ones with spears forked at the top, but with the steel point removed. They make a pretence at war, carry out field exercises and indulge in mimic combats. Thither too come many courtiers, when the king is in town, and from the households of the bishops, earls and barons come youths and adolescents, not yet girt with the belt of knighthood, for the pleasure of engaging in combat with each other ... their boy riders divide their ranks; some pursue those immediately in front of them, but fail to catch up with them; others overtake their fellows, force them to dismount and fly past them.[103]

Though less violent than the mêlée of the tournament itself, for which they provided a degree of basic training, such hastiludes or *behourds* were not without danger, and injuries were common. Nonetheless, remarked FitzStephen, 'theirs is an age greedy of glory, youth yearns for victory, and exercises itself in mock combats in order to carry itself more bravely in real battles'.[104]

The Vassal of King Louis: The Settlement of Montmirail, 1169

The necessity of such training for war was readily apparent, for in the years between 1166 and 1168 young Henry witnessed his father engaged in wide-spread and bitter warfare. Since his accession, Henry II had frequently been forced to take military action to quell disturbances in the borderlands where Brittany marched with Normandy and Anjou, but his move in 1166 to annex Brittany by the deposition of Conan, whose daughter was betrothed to Henry's third son Geoffrey, was fiercely resisted by elements of the Breton nobility.[105] Following the failure of Henry's major expedition of 1165, the Welsh, led by Rhys of Deheubarth and Owain of Gwynedd, had made a substantial recovery at the expense of the Anglo-Norman marcher lords.[106] Concurrently, in Aquitaine mounting discontent with Henry's attempts to impose a more direct and exploitative form of lordship in a region in which the nobility had enjoyed a substantial degree of autonomy had erupted into rebellion. King Louis, seeing his opportunity to weaken his Angevin opponent indirectly, had offered support to the insurgents, exploited Henry's continuing quarrel with the exiled Thomas Becket by granting him refuge at Sens, and in 1167 even raided into the Vexin in an attempt to force Henry to abandon a campaign to consolidate his authority in the Auvergne. Louis was worsted when Henry stormed and burned the great castle at Chaumont-sur-Epte, but the Breton and Aquitanian rebels continued to look to him for support, while they as well as Owain of Gwynedd and William the Lion of Scotland offered him their allegiance. Henry's response had been not to attack Louis directly, but to devastate the lands of his vassals on the frontiers of Normandy, including those of the counts of Ponthieu and Perche.[107] By the close of 1168, it was apparent to all that, despite Louis' efforts, Henry II had suppressed the insurrections in Brittany and Aquitaine and contained the attacks of the French, who now had little option but to come to a settlement.

Accordingly, on 6 January 1169, Henry II met with Louis at Montmirail in the county of Chartres near La Ferté-Bernard for a major peace summit, with the feast of the Epiphany carefully chosen for its royal symbolism. Its aim was to end the period of open hostilities between the two kings, to reconcile Henry with dissidents in Brittany and Poitou, and to stabilize dynastic rela-tions. For young Henry, the conference was to mark a crucial ratification of his position as Henry II's principal heir and define his own feudal relationship with Louis VII, his father-in-law and overlord. The talks had been brokered primarily, or so John of Salisbury believed, by Count Theobald of Blois and Bernard, a monk from the abbey of Grandmont, which Henry held in particular veneration, and it was hoped that the assembly would also afford an ideal forum for a final reconciliation between the king and Becket.[108] On the opening day, according to John of Salisbury, Henry II 'offered himself, his children, his lands, his resources, his treasures; placed all under his [Louis'] judgment, to use or abuse as he would, to hold, to seize, give to whom he would as he liked, with no conditions stipulated or attached'.[109] Writers favourable to Becket were eager to portray Henry II as a suppliant vassal recognizing the full authority of the Capetian king as his overlord, and to contrast the upright conduct of Louis, the *rex Christianissimus*, with the duplicity and bad faith of his Plantagenet rival.[110] Yet such studied, even exaggerated deference on Henry's part, which was a consistent feature of his dealings with Louis, was but a diplomatic tool and in 1169, as earlier, it masked the reality of the balance of power.[111]

The proceedings consisted of two distinct but closely related events: first, a settlement between the two kings themselves, then the performance of homage by young Henry and his brothers to Louis for their continental fiefs. Henry II had performed homage to Louis for the duchy of Normandy in 1151, but he had not done so again since becoming king of England.[112] In 1167, however, at a time of escalating hostilities, Louis had defied Henry, renouncing him as his man and returning his homage.[113] Such an act of *diffidatio* was more than just a formal declaration of war; it was an extreme step, designed to remove any restraint on military or political action imposed by the obligations binding lord and vassal, and, in theory, it allowed the lord to reclaim his fief by force from a contumacious erstwhile vassal. Yet as the recent warfare had once again painfully revealed, Louis was in no position to confiscate the duchy by force. Indeed, in such circumstances, Louis' defiance had only harmed his own position; of his own volition, he had dissolved the powerful ties of the lord–vassal relationship which had previously restrained the scope of Henry's actions against him, as events at Toulouse in 1159 had witnessed. In response to Louis' defiance, Henry II 'had often solemnly and publicly sworn that he would never again return to his homage and allegiance (*hominium*) to the most Christian king of France, so long as he lived'.[114] In his fiercely pro-Norman work the *Draco Normannicus*, Stephen of Rouen, a monk of Bec, made much of this reciprocal defiance by Henry, 'the indomitable lion spurning all yokes', and saw his rejection of French overlordship as the natural and indeed rightful consequence of the fact that Henry ruled a great empire, while Louis held a kingdom barely a third of Charlemagne's former realm.[115] Stephen went on to develop this theme, describing at length the replacement of the Merovingian 'rois fainéants' by Pepin, mayor of the palace, and his heirs.[116] The implication was clear: the Plantagenets were the new Carolingians, who should replace the weak and decadent Capetians.

It was fortunate for Louis VII that Henry II did not share Stephen's ambitions. Nevertheless, when at Montmirail the two kings made peace, Henry did not again perform homage to Louis. Instead, he returned to the allegiance he owed by his earlier homage in 1151, but did so by a handshake and the kiss of peace – gestures distinct from the ritual of placing the vassal's hands within those of the lord, an act central to the performance of homage itself.[117] Henry was careful to reserve his regal dignity and the Angevin principle was clear: homage to the king of France was acceptable before becoming king, but once crowned and anointed, kings of England did not perform homage to the kings of France. Should expediency require acts of submission, these were to be performed instead by the king's sons.

Henry's return to Louis' allegiance was an important concession. In return, what he sought – and obtained – was a very public recognition of his own family settlement, achieved by offering the homage of his sons to Louis for his continental fiefs. Montmirail represented not a case of homage being demanded by an overlord from a reluctant vassal, but of homage actively sought by Henry II as a formal recognition of his heirs' rights of inheritance.[118] For young Henry's succession would represent a highly significant transition in the status of Henry II's lands and mark an important step towards their unity and stability. Though customs of inheritance could vary within the territorial principalities of France, it was widely acknowledged that the eldest son would inherit the patrimony, that is the core territories which had previously passed to his father by inheritance, and which were generally regarded as indivisible. By contrast, there was greater freedom in the way a lord could bequeath acquisitions, those lands he had gained himself during his lifetime by marriage, purchase or conquest, and these might readily be granted as he chose to younger sons.[119] Yet whether a lord chose to divide his lands between sons or keep them united under one son, by the process of inheritance what had been acquisition in the earlier generation became patrimony in the next. Thus in 1151 Geoffrey V of Anjou had bequeathed his patrimony of Anjou and Maine to his eldest son Henry, along with his conquest of Normandy which he had claimed *iure uxoris*. Greater Anjou and Normandy were thus bound together as Henry II's inherited patrimony, which he in turn would bestow on young Henry, together with his acquisition of the kingdom of England. The combined territories of England, Normandy and Anjou now would become young Henry's indivisible patrimony, binding these three core elements of the Angevin 'empire' more firmly together.[120]

What made Louis amenable to the Angevin family settlement proposed at Montmirail was Henry's stipulation that Richard, as second son, was to inherit Aquitaine, while Geoffrey was to be assigned Brittany. Young Henry and Richard, moreover, were to perform homage directly to Louis, rather than to their father. Henry II was thus assuring the French king of at least a degree of future partition of his great assembly of lands. With good reason, Louis had been deeply concerned that if Henry chose to grant all or the majority of his lands to his eldest son, the Capetians would be confronted – and perhaps over-whelmed – by a Plantagenet rival possessing an unprecedented concentration of power.[121] These fears, which had long plagued Louis, had already been addressed by Henry in the terms of peace he had proposed to the French king in March 1168. According to John of Salisbury, King Henry had at that time offered

> to return to the French king's homage, to swear fealty before all in his own person and in public (*corporaliter et publice*) that he will serve him as his lord for the duchy of Normandy, as his predecessors as dukes used to serve the French kings. He was bound to hand over the counties of Anjou and Maine, and fealties pertaining to these dignities (*fidelitates procerum ad memoratos honores pertinentium*), to his son the lord Henry, who was to do homage and fealty to the French king against all men for them.[122]

Most significantly of all, these earlier terms continued by stipulating that 'the young Henry will owe nothing to his father or brothers save what they may deserve, or what natural affection dictates'. There was thus no saving clause, reserving prior homage and loyalty of the young Henry to his father, who was to receive from his son 'only what was owed by natural affection'.[123] Significantly, these terms had been offered by Henry, not demanded by Louis. The French king may indeed have grasped 'the value of his lordship over Henry's sons as a weapon for eating away at the English king's power', but the negotiations of 1168 reveal both that Henry was well aware of this, and that he believed it could be used to his own advantage.[124]

At Montmirail, the performance of homage by Henry II's sons to Louis was reserved for the second day of the conference, 7 January, to emphasize it as quite distinct from the reconciliation of Henry II and Louis. Young Henry had already performed homage to Louis for Normandy in October 1160, and hence well before his coronation originally intended for 1162.[125] Now at Montmirail, he performed homage and swore fealty to the French king for the counties of Anjou and Maine, though not the Touraine, which Henry II held *de jure* of Count Theobald of Blois.[126] In a departure from the earlier conces-sions proffered by Henry II, however, young Henry also performed homage to

Louis for Brittany. Though the Plantagenets thus acknowledged that Brittany was held as a fief of France, Louis' acceptance of young Henry's homage marked his recognition of the overlordship (*dominium*) which the dukes of Normandy had long claimed over it.[127] Young Henry would thus exercise a degree of authority over Brittany,[128] which the arrangement at Montmirail made clear that Geoffrey would hold as the vassal of his elder brother, and accordingly, at his father's command, he subsequently performed homage for Brittany not to Louis, but to young Henry.[129] Richard, by contrast, performed homage directly to the king of France for the county of Poitou, an arrangement fully sanctioned by Eleanor who still remained *de jure* duchess of Aquitaine.[130] Louis could thus be assured that under Richard's heirs Aquitaine would become independent from the ruler of the main Angevin territories. Further to strengthen his ties to the king of France, Richard was now betrothed to Alice, Louis' second daughter by Constance of Castile.[131] The obligation that Richard 'would take the French king's daughter to wife without a dowry', a condition proffered by Henry II in the earlier 1168 negotiations, was a major concession, undoubtedly intended to salve the injury caused by Henry II's coup in having young Henry and Margaret married as children in 1160.[132]

In early 1169 relations between Henry II and Louis appeared better than they had for nearly a decade. Even King Louis had been alienated by Becket's stubborn refusal to compromise and accept the peace offered to him by Henry II at Montmirail.[133] A second meeting was held between the two rulers at Tours, and by February, John of Salisbury could report that 'the kings have made a treaty with one another of mutual help against all men'.[134]

Henry, Seneschal of France

Young Henry himself played an important part in cementing this new entente. At Montmirail, Louis had granted his son-in-law the seneschalship of France, one of the greatest offices in the French royal household.[135] Among his most important functions, the seneschal played a key role in the coronation ceremonies and crown-wearings of the kings of France, while in war he led the vanguard of the royal host when the army moved against the enemy, and the rearguard as it withdrew. From at least the reign of Fulk V, the counts of Anjou had laid claim to this office as of ancient right, tradition asserting that this dignity, formerly known as the majoralty of the palace (*majoratum domus regiae*), had been given by King Robert the Pious to Geoffrey Greygown, count of Anjou (970–*c*.987), for his aid against Emperor Otto.[136] Even after becoming king of England, Henry II had exploited this claim. In 1158, as part of his embassy to France, Becket had obtained for him the grant of the seneschalship from Louis, and when later that year Henry led a campaign against his Breton opponents, he claimed it was by virtue of the authority vested in this office.[137] These events provide the most likely context for the composition of a tract, *De majoratu et senescalcia Franciae*, probably written by Hugh de Clers, a prominent Angevin *familiaris*, in which the origins and prerogatives of the office were set out at length.[138] Hugh, himself seneschal of La Flèche from *c.*1164 and a close advisor on Angevin affairs to Henry II, was still alive in 1170, and may well have played a role in instructing prince Henry on the functions of the office of the seneschal of France and its protocols.[139] For, following the summit at Montmirail, prince Henry travelled to his father-in-law's court to give tangible expression to his new office. At Paris on 2 February 1169, at the great feast to celebrate the Purification of the Virgin, young Henry personally served King Louis at table.[140] Regarded as a mark of high honour, such acts of personal service to a king or great lord were jealously guarded; the seneschalship was also claimed by Theobald of Blois, and young Henry's award of the office in 1169 may well have deepened the animosity of Theobald towards Henry II and his family.[141]

Shortly afterwards young Henry also performed homage to Louis' son and heir Philip, barely four years old.[142] The arrangements made at Montmirail were thus envisaged as extending to the next generation. Historians have been divided as to whether the acts of homage by the Angevins to the kings of France represented a fundamental weakness in Henry II's position: did such recognition of Capetian sovereignty within France represent a fatal flaw which hampered any attempt to create a lasting Plantagenet 'empire', or was it merely a pragmatic mechanism whereby Henry II sought to manipulate the nominal authority of the Capetians to secure ratification of his own dynastic schemes?[143] The true weakness, it has been plausibly argued, lay not in such acts of homage but in the conflicts which subsequently developed between Henry and his queen and their sons: had the Angevins remained united, issues of homage and subordinate status would have mattered little in reality.[144] The more negative implications of homage were certainly to become apparent soon after young Henry's death in 1183, when Henry II's position was weakened and his status as a vassal more relentlessly pressed by the new king, Philip Augustus. Yet in 1169, both the settlement at Montmirail and young Henry's willing assumption of the seneschalship of France reveal an unquestioning acceptance by the Angevins both of the legitimacy of Louis' overlordship over their continental domains, and of the primacy of the Capetians' status within France. Seeking further legitimation through tenure of a great office of the French crown was an act more consistent with the earlier outlook of the counts of Anjou than the aggressively independent stance of the dukes of Normandy.[145] Henry II may have been insistent on guarding his dignity as king of England, but tenure of the seneschalship proclaimed prince Henry's pre-eminence among the peers of France.

John of Salisbury noted of the settlement at Montmirail that 'in this distribution of honours the French reckon to lie the greatest hope for their kingdom; especially as they recalled with bitter sorrow that Henry, the king's son, had done homage for the whole inheritance (*pro omnibus*), when he and the king's daughter were betrothed'.[146] Remarkably, despite such misgivings, Louis nonetheless surrendered Alice into Henry's custody. He may well have been tricked into so doing in the expectation that he would receive Richard in exchange.[147] Henry II had made two visits to France soon after the summit at Montmirail, and in their wake probably brought Alice back with him.[148] But when in November Henry came to meet Louis at Saint-Denis, he put off handing Richard over as promised. Too late, Louis realized that he had been deceived again.[149] Little could he have suspected what a troubled future lay ahead for his daughter.[150]

Crusading Plans and Family Settlement

On 15 August 1169, Emperor Frederick Barbarossa had his own son Henry crowned as king of the Romans.[151] This was added stimulus for Henry II to delay no longer in his long-held plans to have young Henry crowned and anointed. Young Henry had already been acknowledged by the nobles of England and Normandy as Henry II's principal heir, but his coronation would be the climax to the dynastic settlement established at Montmirail and ensure a smooth process of succession in the event of Henry II's death. One other key factor appeared to drive Henry II's efforts, his stated desire – whether sincere or feigned – to undertake an expedition to the Holy Land.

Henry II ranked as one of the greatest kings in Western Europe, yet unlike Louis VII and Frederick Barbarossa, who had both participated in the Second Crusade, he himself had not yet fought in the defence of God's patrimony. To the dictates of honour and remission of sin urging such a *peregrinatio* were added Henry's close kinship with the kings of Jerusalem, a cadet branch of the Angevin house, which gave him a particular sense of responsibility for affairs in the Holy Land.[152] Ralph of Diss reflected Plantagenet sentiment in regarding Fulk V's election to the throne of Jerusalem – the throne of 'David the great king' – as a glorious achievement, which made the fame of his name shine widely throughout the world.[153] Angevin chroniclers similarly recorded the deeds of Fulk V's successors in the East with evident pride, but equally with mounting anxiety about the deteriorating fortunes of the crusader principalities.[154] Between

1162 and 1165 both Henry II and Louis had been the target of repeated letters from the king of Jerusalem, the Templars and other Frankish princes seeking aid, and a crusade may have been considered around 1163.[155] The catastrophic defeat of the Franks at Harim by the Muslim ruler Nur al-Din in 1164, which threatened the loss of Antioch, had led Pope Alexander III to reissue Eugenius III's great crusading encyclical *Quantum praedecessores* in January 1165.[156] Henry and Louis discussed plans for a crusade, and although mutual suspicion and ongoing hostility prevented them embarking on a joint expedition, the two kings had authorized a special tax in 1166 to aid the Holy Land.[157] The same year, Gilbert Foliot could inform the exiled Thomas Becket that King Henry II was anxious to go on crusade, and 'is hardly detained by the dearest ties of wife and children, and so many kingdoms that obey his rule, from taking up his cross . . .'[158]

Hostile contemporaries, particularly within the circle of Thomas Becket, were quick to dismiss Henry's promises to go on crusade merely as insincere and cynical diplomatic manoeuvring.[159] This view was still more vehemently expressed in the retrospective and embittered writings of Gerald of Wales, who saw Henry's eventual fall as punishment not only for Becket's death but also for his failure to aid the Holy Land in its time of greatest need.[160] Yet it is important not to judge Henry's crusading intentions in 1169–70 with hindsight, for the Young King's rebellion in 1173–74 was to mark a crucial political watershed that would profoundly affect Henry II's ability to undertake a crusade. If from the later 1170s Henry did indeed leave 'a sequence of false trails and broken promises' until his final assumption of the cross in 1188 following the fall of Jerusalem to Saladin, it was because fear of his sons' renewed disloyalty and of Capetian aggression rendered an expedition to the East all but impossible.[161] In 1173, in a response to an appeal by King Amalric for aid, Henry II told the king of Jerusalem that he would have set out already on an expedition to the East were it not for the outbreak of his sons' rebellion.[162]

By contrast, the settlement at Montmirail 'represented a considerable step towards the internal and external security of the Angevin lands'.[163] The intimate link between the settlement at Montmirail and Henry II's projected crusading plans is revealed by John of Salisbury's account of the peace talks that had preceded it in 1168. Henry II had told William aux Blanchesmains, then bishop elect of Chartres and an intimate counsellor of Louis, that he wished to undertake an expedition with the French king to the East.[164] 'Is it true what you say,' asked William, 'that you would like to go with him to Jerusalem?' To which Henry reportedly responded, 'I have never done anything more gladly – so long as my lord wishes it, and I am allowed to set my house

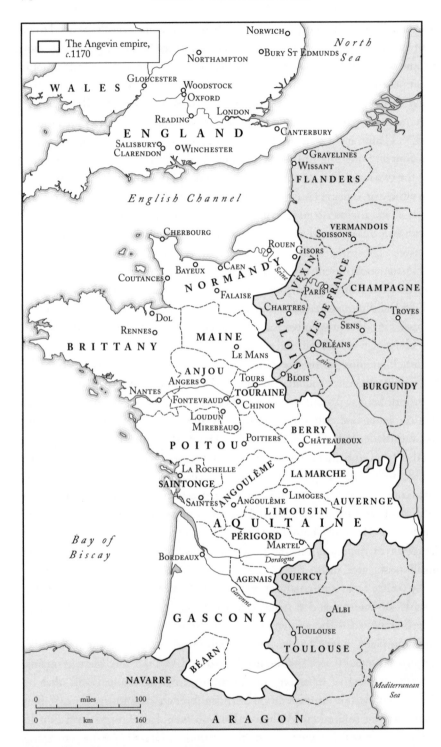

Map 1 The Angevin empire, *c.*1170

in order and make disposition for my children.'[165] Louis himself was said to be sceptical, but nevertheless was more inclined to make peace with Henry,[166] and his promise to join Henry on crusade removed the most pressing strategic threat posed to the Angevin lands in his absence.

By 1169, moreover, affairs in the East had taken a grave turn. Nur al-Din had already united the powerful principalities of Mosul, Aleppo and Damascus under his rule, placing the Frankish states under ever increasing military pressure. Between 1167 and 1169, Nur al-Din's general, Shirkuh, had engaged in a protracted struggle with Amalric, the able and energetic king of Jerusalem, for control of the moribund Fatimid caliphate of Egypt. The stakes were enormous: if Amalric succeeded in conquering Egypt and the Nile delta, its wealth and strategic importance would secure the crusader states indefinitely against resurgent Muslim aggression. But if it fell to Nur al-Din, the kingdom of Jerusalem would be all but surrounded and the balance of power decisively altered in Nur al-Din's favour.[167] By 1169, it had become clear that King Amalric had been thwarted in his attempts to conquer Egypt, but an expedition from the West might yet tip the strategic balance in favour of the kingdom of Jerusalem. The critical nature of the situation led to a major embassy by Frederick, archbishop of Tyre, and John, bishop of Banyas, to the kings and princes of the West, and the issuing on 20 July 1169 by Alexander III of a major crusading appeal, *Inter omnia*.[168] Henry II announced his intention to take the cross, and to depart for the East at Easter 1171.[169] His subsequent negotiations in 1170 to marry his youngest daughter Joanna to William II of Sicily equally suggested Henry's intention of securing an ally and a base for his forthcoming crusade.[170]

It is impossible to know to what extent Henry II was sincere in his intentions. Embarkation on crusade or a major military campaign was, however, a common catalyst for the formal recognition of heirs. In 1157, prior to his departure to the East, Thierry of Flanders had made his eldest son Philip, already associated in his rule, 'heir and count of all Flanders'.[171] In February 1170, young Henry turned fifteen, the age Geoffrey le Bel had been when invested with direct rule of Anjou on Fulk V's departure East to become king of Jerusalem.[172] If Henry II was to depart for the Holy Land, young Henry's coronation would itself be a crucial prerequisite: not only would many months of preparation be needed for so great an undertaking, but it would be essential to establish effective arrangements for the empire's governance in his absence. Should Henry himself die in the East, England would already be ruled by a crowned and anointed king. Yet even if he did not undertake such an expedition, his eldest son's coronation would set the seal on Henry II's dynastic plans by ensuring an undisputed succession to the throne.

CHAPTER 5

Novus Rex

THE CORONATION, 1170

And Samuel took a little vial of oil, and poured it upon his head, and kissed him, and said: Behold, the Lord hath anointed thee to be prince over his inheritance, and thou shalt deliver his people out of the hands of their enemies, that are round about them. And this shall be a sign unto thee, that God hath anointed thee to be prince.

– 1 Samuel 10:1

ONLY ONE IMPEDIMENT now stood in the way of young Henry's corona- tion. The archbishops of Canterbury had long claimed and jealously guarded the right to crown kings of England. Yet Archbishop Thomas, whose rift with the king had postponed the boy's intended coronation back in 1162, was still in exile after six long years of quarrel with Henry II. Although Becket had few supporters among the English episcopate, the improving political position of Alexander III in Italy, which made him less reliant on the Angevin king's goodwill, added to mounting international pressure on Henry to agree a settlement. Henry himself realized that peace had to be made with Becket, not least if his proposed expedition to the Holy Land was to depart at Easter 1171.[1] Alexander III had seen in the younger Henry himself a possible way out of the impasse caused by Henry II's continuing refusal to give Thomas the highly symbolic kiss of peace; in a mandate to William, archbishop of Sens, dated 19 January 1170, the pope ordered Henry II to restore Thomas and his followers, and the archbishop to submit to the king. If Henry II in person would not give Becket the kiss of peace, then young Henry could do so in his stead. The papal commissioners were to urge Becket to accept this element of the compromise, provided it did not endanger him or his followers.[2] Thomas was on the verge of accepting, but a planned reconciliation with Henry in Normandy was suddenly aborted by the king when he learned of the terms of peace to be brought by papal nuncios, and of the contents of letters obtained in February by Thomas' agents concerning the coronation of young Henry.[3] For on 24 February, Pope Alexander wrote to Thomas and all the English bishops forbidding them to crown and anoint the prince unless young Henry first took the coronation oath, which began with a promise to uphold the liberties of the Church and contained an explicit promise to abrogate all bad customs which had been introduced into the realm. The prince was to swear in particular to uphold the liberties of the church of Canterbury; and to release everyone from their oaths to observe the 'new customs' that Henry II had recently imposed upon them.[4] The pope, moreover, wrote to Archbishop Roger on 26 February, prohibiting him and all the bishops, on pain of losing their office and orders, from crowning young Henry while Becket was in exile as such an act would be in violation of the ancient privileges of Canterbury.[5]

In other circumstances, and with two men of different and less obdurate temperaments, the crowning and anointing of young Henry by Thomas, his old guardian, might have served as a fitting occasion for the reconciliation between king and prelate.[6] Indeed, Becket himself seems to have regarded young Henry's coronation as one of the best chances for gaining peace from Henry II, a fact which added yet greater vehemence to the defence of his prerogative as archbishop of Canterbury to perform the coronation.[7] Yet as an anonymous informant wrote to Thomas only days before the ceremony, the eventuality of the prince being crowned by York offered the frightening prospect of a new generation of hostility to the archbishop:

> What will you do, most unfortunate of men, if that which you have sighed for so long should be taken from you in a short space of time? If he who ought only to rule through you should be made king by the hand of another? Rather, what will you do if your enemy consecrates an enemy king for you, so that a much younger and stronger hand may rise against you in support of his father?[8]

The fear was a very real one, for Henry II still possessed the papal mandate, obtained in 1161 while the see of Canterbury was vacant, authorizing Archbishop Roger of York to crown his son. Roger, a long-standing opponent of Becket, was only too eager to contest the primacy of Canterbury and claim the dignity of coronation for his own metropolitan church.[9] He was also, moreover, a papal legate.[10] From the moment of his consecration, Thomas had shown himself fiercely defensive of the rights of the church of Canterbury, and Henry knew that for Roger to perform the coronation would be a grievous insult to Becket.[11] Yet the issue transcended personal animosity. For while Thomas regarded himself as the defender of the Church's liberties against royal tyranny and loudly proclaimed the precedence of *sacerdotium* over *regnum*, Henry II saw his opposition on the issue of criminous clerks and his vehement rejection of the Constitutions of Clarendon as a direct attack on royal rights which had been enjoyed by his grandfather Henry I and earlier monarchs. To permit Becket to undertake the coronation of the future ruler of the Angevin lands would be tantamount to admitting defeat and condoning papal interference in the coronation itself. He would not have the sacrality of the new king so tarnished.

For his part, Thomas, fully aware that the king might employ the earlier papal mandate to proceed without him, had instructed his agents at the papal Curia to obtain letters from the pope prohibiting the coronation from being undertaken by anyone save the archbishop of Canterbury himself. As he stressed in a letter to Roger, bishop of Worcester, in May 1170, Thomas was not against the coronation itself: 'indeed, if the lord king pleases,' he wrote, 'we are prepared to crown his son in accordance with the obligations of our office and to show due honour and respect to them both'. But he evidently feared that not only Roger of York, but also Gilbert Foliot or the bishop of Salisbury might usurp his right to do so, and, as he had heard, the bishop of Sées had boasted that he himself would perform the coronation if required.[12]

Henry responded by extracting an oath from all leading laymen, and a verbal promise from ecclesiastics, that they would not accept letters from Becket or the pope, or make any appeal to Rome without his permission. As early as Michaelmas 1169, an embargo had been placed on the English ports to prevent the arrival of any papal letters of prohibition, and harsh penalties were decreed for those attempting to deliver any such mandates, or for any clergy observing an interdict.[13] On returning to England, Henry held his Easter court of 1170 at Windsor, to which almost all the nobles and great men of England had been summoned, as well as King William of Scotland and his brother David.[14] The principal reason for their convocation soon became clear when shortly afterwards the great council met again at London to deliberate 'concerning the coronation of Henry his eldest son', while Roger archbishop of York, Hugh of Durham and other bishops were ordered to come to London for the ceremony.[15] The London council had other pressing but related business.[16] The king had been deeply concerned about the widespread abuses of his subjects by his sheriffs during his four-year absence on the continent, and he now ordered a great inquest. Throughout every shire, all men, noble, free or even villein, were made to swear on the Gospels that they would give truthful testament to a judicial eyre as to the nature and extent of the extortions made by the sheriffs and their men since the king had last crossed to Normandy in March 1166.[17] The day set for the reports of this commission of inquiry – the 'inquisitio mirabilis' which scrutizined the exactions of lordship in the counties in the minutest of detail – was to be 14 June, the day set for young Henry's coronation.[18] This conjuncture was no accident, but conveyed an important political message: Henry II's kingship, and now that of his son and heir, was concerned with upholding the law and good governance. The inquest was a tangible expression of the fulfilment of the oath taken at the coronation, which enjoined the enforcing of good laws and extirpation of the bad. In its wake, many of the sheriffs were dismissed and amerced, together with their bailiffs and officials.[19] This purge was a much-needed crackdown on the corruption and exactions of royal officials in the localities, though its extension to a far wider-ranging inquiry into the sums raised 'by judgment or without judgment' by all landholders and their officials from their lands and from each hundred and village was undoubtedly the cause of alarm and resentment that would store up trouble for the future.[20]

Despite Becket's issuing of a number of mandates forbidding the coronation, and his desperate attempts to smuggle papal letters of prohibition into the kingdom, Henry's cordon on the ports and his officials' vigilance ensured that these did not reach their intended recipients.[21] Becket later claimed that one of his agents had succeeded in placing such a prohibition into Archbishop Roger's hand the Saturday before the coronation, but Roger swore that he had never received or seen any such papal letters.[22] Henry II's cousin, Roger, bishop of Worcester, was forbidden by Queen Eleanor and the constable of Normandy, Richard du Hommet, from crossing the Channel to attend the coronation: officials had stopped him at Dieppe, for they 'had sure intelligence' that he would not allow the archbishop of York to crown young Henry 'while the archbishop of Canterbury, whose prerogative it was to crown kings, was still alive'.[23] Eleanor, who by 1170 was becoming increasingly distant from her husband, appears to have supported the coronation of her eldest son; the delegation of power to the young Henry could only strengthen her position, and would help pave the way for the investiture of Richard as count of Poitou and duke of Aquitaine.[24] Shortly before the day set for the coronation, young Henry was sent over from Normandy in the keeping of Richard of Ilchester, and bishops Henry of Bayeux and Froger of Sées.[25] Margaret and her household waited in readiness at Caen with Queen Eleanor to cross the Channel.[26] But in what appears to have been a calculated insult to Louis VII, Henry II decided that Margaret was not to be crowned alongside her husband, and ordered her to remain with Eleanor in Normandy.[27]

A Royal Knighting?

On Sunday 14 June 1170, the feast of St Basil, the magnates of the realm gath-ered at Westminster for the coronation of young Henry.[28] According to one of Thomas Becket's informants and Gervase of Canterbury, Henry II knighted his eldest son prior to the ceremony of coronation.[29] At fifteen, Henry could be considered relatively young to receive the arms of knighthood, although the age deemed suitable varied considerably and owed much to political circum-stances.[30] Dubbing to knighthood was one of the most important events in the life of a nobleman. It marked both coming of age and entry into an elite order of warriors, the order of knighthood, which, as Perceval is told by his tutor in arms in Chrétien de Troyes' *Conte du Graal*, 'is the highest order that God has set forth and ordained'.[31] Though knighting might take place on campaign, it frequently took place at court, and for the sons of kings or great nobles the bestowal of arms had long been regarded as a necessary preliminary to investi-ture.[32] King Stephen, for example, had bestowed knighthood on his eldest son Eustace around 1147 before endowing him with lands and the county of Boulogne, while in 1185 Henry II would make John a knight before intending to establish him as king in Ireland.[33] Following John's death in 1216 in the midst of a civil war, the magnates regarded it as proper to dub his son Henry as knight immediately before his coronation at Gloucester, even though he was only nine years old.[34]

By 1170, rituals for dubbing were well developed, and young Henry would have been familiar with the rich symbolism attached to them. The aspirant might spend the previous night in vigil in church, before taking a ritual bath of spiritual purification, reflecting the rite of baptism. Both John of Salisbury in his *Policraticus* and Stephen of Fougères in his *Livre de manières*, written in the 1170s, speak of the knight taking from the altar the sword with which he was to be belted, a ritual symbolizing his duty to uphold justice and defend the Church, widows, orphans and the poor.[35] The young man then had the sword belt girded on him and golden spurs attached to his feet; he pledged an oath of knighthood, and then received the *colée* or symbolic blow from the lord who was knighting him.

John of Marmoutier, writing in the later 1170s, gives a vivid picture of the ensuing ceremony when describing the knighting of young Henry's grandfa-ther Geoffrey le Bel by King Henry I at Rouen in 1128:

> On the great day, as was required by the custom for making knights, baths were prepared for use. The king had learned from his chamberlains that the Angevin [i.e. Geoffrey] and those who came with him had come from the

purification ceremony. He commanded that they be summoned before him. After having cleansed his body, and come from the purification of bathing, the noble offspring of the count of Anjou dressed in a linen undershirt, putting on a robe woven with gold and a surcoat of a rich purple hue: his stockings were of silk, and on his feet he wore shoes with little golden lions on them. His companions, who were to be knighted with him, were all clothed in linen and purple. He left his privy chamber and paraded in public, accompanied by his noble retinue. Their horses were led, arms carried to be distributed to each in turn, according to their need. The Angevin led a wonderfully ornamented Spanish horse, whose speed was said to be so great that birds in flight were far slower. He wore a matching hauberk made of double mail, in which no hole had been pierced by spear or dart. He was shod in iron shoes, also made from double mail. To his ankles were fastened golden spurs. A shield hung from his neck, on which were golden images of lioncels. On his head was placed a helmet, reflecting the lights of many precious gems, tempered in such a way that no sword could break or pierce it. He carried an ash spear with a point of Poitevin iron, and finally, a sword from the royal treasure, bearing an ancient inscription over which the superlative Wayland had sweated with much labour and application in the forge of the smiths.[36]

Though more than a little touched by epic and romance traditions, this description certainly reflected elements of contemporary practice in the 1170s, if not perhaps the 1120s. Yet how far young Henry's own knighting resembled such splendid events is unknown – if, indeed, he *was* knighted on this occasion. For the *History of William Marshal* makes the explicit but seemingly contradictory statement that the Young King was knighted in 1173 soon after the outbreak of his rebellion, and by none other than William Marshal. Though this latter story has been doubted, the *History* reiterates the claim when describing how at Gloucester in 1216 the magnates debated who should knight the child Henry III. They decided on the Marshal not only because of his pre-eminence and valour, but because he had already knighted one king. In knighting the Young King's nephew, Henry, William would thus, it notes, have dubbed two kings to knighthood.[37] Given the enormous importance of the act of dubbing in aristocratic society it is hard – though not impossible – to believe that the *History*, for all its evident bias, would dare to invent and foreground a story concerning so central and symbolic an event.[38]

There are further anomalies. Despite the fact that the knighting of the king's son was such a significant ceremony, often marked by great festivities, neither Roger of Howden, whose account is closely contemporaneous, nor

Ralph of Diss makes any mention of young Henry's knighting.[39] This is despite the fact that Roger was careful subsequently to record the dubbings of Henry II's other sons and had specifically noted King Henry II's dubbing of David, William the Lion's younger brother, at Windsor in April 1170.[40] As John of Marmoutier's account reveals, moreover, the knighting of the eldest son of a king or great lord often involved the subsequent dubbing of a number of his young companions.[41] In 1149, King David of Scotland had knighted Henry of Anjou together with Robert, earl of Hereford, 'and the sons of some men of birth', while the young Malcolm IV immediately followed up his own knighting by Henry II at Périgueux in 1159 by dubbing thirty of his young nobles who had accompanied him on the great expedition to Toulouse.[42] Yet there is no reference to such a group knighting of young Henry's noble companions. Nor did Henry II attempt to levy an aid for the knighting of his eldest son, though custom entitled him to it – in marked contrast to his concerted efforts to raise the aid towards the marriage of his eldest daughter Matilda in 1167.[43] The circumstances of the coronation itself, with Henry II seeking to steal a march on any attempt by Becket to thwart the ceremony, may perhaps account for such omissions, though it is clear that a great assembly of magnates had been summoned to Westminster. Certainly magnificent robes of green cloth, shoes, leggings and silk garments had been made for young Henry in 1170, costing the substantial sum of £9 15s., and these may have been intended for knighting as much as for the coronation.[44] It remains difficult to reconcile these conflicting accounts. It may be that Becket's informant and Gervase were mistaken, merely assuming that the ritual had taken place, but it is possible that young Henry may in fact have been knighted twice, first by his father on 14 June 1170, then again by William Marshal in 1173 at the outset of his rebellion as a gesture of defiance and of independence from his father.[45] If so, contemporaries would have appreciated the differing emphases of these rituals; the first was a ceremony of investiture of a prince by a king, the second a dubbing in the field of a new knight on his first real campaign by a warrior already famous for his prowess and chivalry. Whatever the case, young Henry was now to experience a still greater and far more profound transition than that from youth to knight, for the ensuing ceremony of coronation would transform him from the son of a king to an anointed monarch, hallowed and set apart by God.[46]

The Coronation of the Young King

Young Henry was solemnly crowned king in the presence 'of almost all the earls, barons and nobles of the kingdom' in the great abbey of Westminster, built by his ancestor Edward the Confessor and the site of royal inaugurations from the time of Harold II.[47] The coronation was attended by the majority of the English episcopate, including Hugh Puiset, bishop of Durham, Gilbert Foliot of London, Joscelin of Salisbury, Walter of Rochester, Richard of Chester and Bartholomew of Exeter, while of the Norman bishops Henry of Bayeux and Froger of Sées were also present.[48] After six long years of his quarrel with the king, Becket had few supporters remaining among the higher clergy in England. Some, indeed, notably Archbishop Roger of York and Gilbert Foliot, bishop of London, were openly hostile to him. Though as a body they were concerned to safeguard ecclesiastical liberties against perceived encroachments by the secular power, they realized the need for a modus vivendi with the king and had been placed in an invidious position by Thomas' stubborn refusal to compromise. Equally, there was little if any popular sympathy for the bruised rights of the rancorous archbishop of Canterbury, still in exile. As Roger of Howden noted, the ceremony took place 'with the great joy of the clergy and people'.[49]

Chroniclers nevertheless give few if any details of the coronation itself. Such ceremonies usually received brief notices in contemporary annals, whose authors either assumed knowledge of their particulars or were not privy to them. Despite its great political significance, for example, Henry II's own coronation in 1154 was recorded laconically.[50] In the case of the Young King, the reticence of chroniclers was increased by the grave embarrassment felt even by writers loyal to Henry II at the deliberate violation of Canterbury's prerogatives, while, crucially, most wrote with hindsight of the coronation's direct role in precipitating the events which resulted in Thomas' murder.[51] It is not until the accession of Richard I in 1189 that we possess the first detailed description of a medieval English coronation, provided by Roger of Howden, even though Roger was almost certainly also an eyewitness to the ceremony in June 1170.[52] Yet while some of the details of the ceremony of 1189 may have been innovations, it is likely that in its main outline it followed the coronations of 1154 and 1170, all three being conducted according to the version of the coronation *ordines* known as the Third Recension.[53] It is thus possible tentatively to reconstruct the principal elements of the Young King's coronation, even if some of its more distinctive features, such as the part played by Henry II himself, remain unknown.[54]

The solemnities began with a great procession of the clergy 'vested in silken copes, with the cross, torch bearers, censers and holy water going before them', who processed to the inner chamber of the adjacent royal palace of Westminster to receive the prince.[55] Flanked by Archbishop Roger and Bishop Hugh, young Henry was led in procession to the abbey church, walking on a rich woollen cloth that had been laid the whole way from the palace to the high altar, while the choir sang the anthem *Firmetur manus tua*, 'Let thy hand be strengthened, and thy right hand be exalted ...'[56] The crucifers, torch bearers and censors again led the solemn train, followed by the priors and abbots. Next came the bishops, while behind them came magnates each bearing elements of the regalia, including the rod and sceptre.[57] Next, three of the greatest laymen bore the swords of state, in their ornate golden sheaths.[58] A fine example of such a bearing sword, used for the imperial coronation of the Young King's nephew Otto IV in 1198, is extant, complete with its gold repoussé scabbard depicting great Old Testament kings, and with a verse from the *Laudes regiae* inscribed on its hilt – 'Christus vincit, Christus regnat, Christus imperat.'[59] It is probable that William the Lion, king of Scotland, bore the first sword, later identified as 'Curtana' or the 'sword of mercy with its blunted tip', and that he was placed by his royal rank in a position of pre-eminence between the two other sword bearers.[60] The presence at the ceremony not only of King William but of Godred, king of Man and the Isles, served to emphasize the imperial dimension of Plantagenet lordship within the British Isles.[61] It equally underlined the distinctive sacral nature of English kingship, for while the kings of Scots were invested according to long-established rituals, they were not as yet anointed as kings.[62] After the sword bearers, six earls and barons carried a chequered board or *scaccarium* on which lay other regalia and the royal robes, while they were followed by one of the most senior earls, carrying a great golden crown.[63] Finally, under a silken canopy, came young Henry himself, flanked by the archbishop of York and the bishop of Durham.

He and the two prelates prostrated themselves before the high altar while the *Te Deum Laudamus* was sung. Then the bishops raised him up and, touching the Gospel book and relics of the saints placed upon the altar, he swore the *tria praecepta* or threefold coronation oath.[64] The first of these was 'that he would keep peace, honour and duty towards God and holy Church and its customs all the days of his life'.[65] Next, he swore 'that he would exercise right justice and equity among the people committed to his charge', prohibit all depredations and injustice to all ranks of men, and, thirdly, that 'he would annul any evil laws and customs which might have been introduced into the realm, and make good laws and keep them without fraud or evil intent'.[66] The coronation oath formed a deeply significant element in the ceremony, for by it the king entered into a contract with his people and with the Church to rule as a just and lawful sovereign. Yet in the light of the long, bitter and still unresolved dispute over the Constitutions of Clarendon, young Henry's oath in 1170 acquired a still greater significance. Becket and the pope had feared that the wording might have been altered to the prejudice of the Church, perhaps to assert the 'new customs' that Henry II had claimed. Writing to Alexander later in 1170, however, Archbishop

Rotrou of Rouen assured him that the Young King had clearly sworn to observe all the rights of the Church, and Archbishop Roger likewise swore that young Henry had taken the customary oath, omitting nothing that ought to have been undertaken in the coronation of a king of England.[67]

After young Henry had made the oath came the *recognitio*, whereby one of the bishops asked the people if they were willing to submit to him as their ruler and obey his commands, to which they replied, 'We wish it and grant it so (*Volumus et concedimus*)'.[68] This reflected the element of election inherent in the king-making process. Kingship in England was less truly elective than in the empire, yet it was not nominal, as the circumstances of both King Stephen's accession in 1135 and the dramatic events of 1141 had so forcefully revealed. Blood right and designation by the previous ruler did not always guarantee a smooth succession, and the support of a majority of the nobility was essential.

It was only after these solemn promises had been made that the archbishop would proceed to the greatest and most sacred act, that of anointing.[69] After further prayers, in which the king was reminded of exemplars of good rulership from the Old Testament, his outer garments were removed, leaving him in his breeches and a shirt slit open at the shoulders. Then the archbishop of York first anointed his hands with holy oil, then his head, chest, shoulders and elbows.[70] As Becket had earlier reminded Henry II, 'kings are anointed in three places, on the head, on the breast, and on the arms, which signifies glory, wisdom and strength'.[71] Then, to hold in place and soak up the holy oil, the archbishop placed a consecrated linen cloth on the young king's head, and over this the royal cap.[72] By this act of anointing, young Henry was now hallowed, set apart and above other men as the *Christus Domini* – the anointed of the Lord. Following the ceremony, these consecrated garments were kept safely, for it was customary for kings to be buried in them, as young Henry was to be.[73]

During the bitter disputes of the Investiture Controversy and the assaults made on theocratic kingship by the reformed papacy from the later eleventh century, the nature of the holy oil used in the rite of coronation had become an important issue.[74] The papacy and its supporters sought to diminish the sacral element of royal anointing by substituting a less significant 'holy oil', known as the oil of catechumens, instead of the chrism; for anointing with chrism, used in the ordination of priests, implied that the ruler was a 'king-priest' in the mould of the Old Testament figure Melchizedek.[75] Some variants of English coronation *ordines* in the first part of the twelfth century may have mirrored this change, but at the coronation of Henry II in 1154, chrism was again used, doubtless reflecting his desire to restore the status and prerogatives of kingship as enjoyed by his grandfather.[76] His insistence on such matters was only strengthened by his own dispute with Becket, and it is possible that his clerical supporters knew of the polemical literature stressing royal sacrality that had been produced during the conflict over investiture between Henry I and Anselm.[77] One such tract, by 'Anonymous of York', had made far-reaching claims: 'The power of the king is the power of God, but it is God's through nature, the king's through grace, and whatever he does is not simply as a man, but as one who has been made God and Christ through grace ... No one by right ought to take precedence over the king, who is blessed with so many and such great sacraments ...'[78] It was by virtue of the sacrament of unction, noted Gilbert Foliot in his letter *Multiplicem nobis,* addressed to Thomas Becket in 1166, that the power to judge not just in secular affairs but even in certain ecclesiastical matters was claimed for the king.[79] While Gilbert did not necessarily concur with such a view, he nevertheless stressed the sacral qualities of kingship bestowed by anointing

> because holy unction sanctifies the king – for his hands are anointed for the purity of deeds, his elbows for the embrace of chastity, his chest for cleanliness of heart, his shoulders to bear labours for Christ, and the chrism poured on his head, so that like Christ (from whom the word *chrism* is derived) and consecrated through his name, he should always strive, through suitable government, to dispense those things lent to him – he is set apart from others, and considered not only a secular but also an ecclesiastical judge.[80]

It thus seems likely that the oil of chrism was used at young Henry's coronation, as it had been at his father's. That unction still bestowed a special power and aura upon the ruler is indicated by Peter of Blois, who, writing of Henry II, noted that 'there is something holy about serving the lord king, for the king is indeed holy and the anointed of the Lord'.[81] Referring to the practice whereby kings 'touched' victims of scrofula to heal them by virtue of their sacral power, Peter continued: 'The sacrament of unction at his coronation was not an empty gift. Its virtue, if there is anyone unaware of it or who calls it into question, will be most amply proved by the disappearance of the disease which attacks the groin and the cure of scrofulas.'[82] Henry I had reputedly touched for 'the king's evil', as scrofula was known, and although there is little evidence that either the young Henry or his father did likewise, Peter readily assumed their powers to do so.[83]

After the anointing, young Henry was clothed in a rich tunic and dalmatic before being invested with the regalia. In the ceremonies of 1154 and 1189, the new king first received 'the sword of the realm with which he was to repress evildoers against the Church', to which Becket referred when in 1166 he had reminded Henry of his duties as king:

> You should know that you are king by God's grace; in the first place, that you should rule yourself and shape your life according to the best practices so that the others might be inspired to better things by your example, according to the wise saying, 'The world is arranged in the king's image.' In the second place, that you should rule others, some by fining, others by punishing, both by the authority of the power which you received from the Church in the sacrament of unction and also by the office of the sword, which you bear to restrain those who do ill to the Church.[84]

Given Henry II's subsequent insistence on the Young King's royal status and their regal equality, it seems very likely that he too received the sword of justice during the service. Great golden spurs were attached to his feet, reflecting the permeation of a strong chivalric element into the coronation rituals during the twelfth century. The spurs also had a powerfully Christian meaning, for they symbolized the knight's swiftness to serve God.[85] Gold bracelets or armils were placed on his arms, his feet were shod in sandals worked with gold, while a rich royal mantle was placed over his shoulders, all elements added to the ceremony of the Third Recension to reaffirm royal status.[86] Then the prelates placed a great golden crown on the young king's head. It is likely that, as in the ceremony of 1189, two nobles were assigned to take its great weight from the monarch's head – a role that the Young King himself would later perform at the coronation of Philip Augustus at Rheims in 1180.[87] Further investiture with the ring, sceptre and rod followed, after which the king was blessed and led back to his throne, to sit in majesty while the choir chanted the *Te Deum*. Archbishop Roger then pronounced the prayer, *Sta et retine*, and conducted the ceremony of the Mass.[88] For the offertory, the two prelates again conducted young Henry to the altar, where he made the customary gift of one mark of pure gold.[89] At fifteen, Henry now found himself the crowned and anointed king of England.[90] Young, handsome and athletic, with piercing eyes and a pleasing countenance, he cut a fine figure, and to an admiring contemporary it seemed that all of nature's gifts had come together in him.[91] He was, noted the *History of William Marshal*, 'the most handsome prince in all the world, whether Christian or Saracen'.[92]

The Coronation Banquet

Following the coronation, the assembled nobles and clergy led the new king in procession back to the palace, where he removed the heavy crown and put on a lighter one. He was then escorted to the great hall of Westminster, built by William Rufus and described by the *Histoire des ducs* as 'une des plus riches sales del monde'.[93] Here a magnificent banquet was held; the royal plate had been transported from Woodstock to London, while more vessels had been gilded for the Young King's use.[94] As was customary, the new king sat with the higher clergy, the archbishop of York at his right. According to William of Canterbury, one of Becket's earliest biographers writing *c.*1173–74, Henry II served young Henry at table, to emphasize his son's regal dignity, and even 'protested that he himself was not king'.[95] Similarly, William FitzStephen claimed that Henry had forestalled an interdict by Thomas on England because, after his son's coronation, 'he was no longer king'.[96] In serving his son at table, Henry II may well have been stressing young Henry's equality as a crowned and anointed king, but it is scarcely credible that he in fact denied his own kingship. Nevertheless, such a view could be taken by continental chroniclers such as Gilbert of Mons.[97] Developing the trend already set by Becket's hagiographers, Matthew Paris' later story of the Young King's response that it was quite fitting for the son of a count to serve the son of a king demonstrates how easily the incident could be manipulated as a ready means of denigrating Henry II's authority.[98] An illustrated Anglo-Norman poem on the life of Becket, composed *c.*1220–40, depicts both the Young King's coronation and the ensuing banquet, at which Henry II offers a cup to his son. One of those seated at table holds a scroll bearing the inscription, 'Behold majesty too much bent low (*Ecce maiestas nimis inclinata*)', while the rubric repeats William of Canterbury's claim that Henry proclaimed himself not to be king.[99] By contrast, those chroniclers with close connections to the Angevin court, notably Roger of Howden, Ralph of Diss and Robert of Torigni, chose to omit all reference to Henry serving his son. That they may have regarded such a gesture as shocking and damaging to the king's dignity is suggested by a marginal poem added to one manuscript of Howden's *Chronica*: 'O heavy occurrence, miserable overthrow, singular pestilence! He who was once free now serves, he who was once rich goes begging. He who once reigned pre-eminent in hall now suffers exile.'[100]

This verse was penned with hindsight, well after the rebellion of 1173–74 and with knowledge of the Young King's subsequent disloyalty and death. Yet even in 1170, the coronation of a son in the lifetime of his father raised important issues concerning the respective authority of the two kings. The senior monarch not unnaturally might take steps to safeguard and proclaim his superior authority. In 1151, King Roger II of Sicily had his son William crowned, but before the consecration, the young man 'solemnly undertook in a public assembly at his father's precept that he would preserve peace and justice all his days, show reverence for the church of God, and throughout his father's life obey him as his lord. This undertaking he confirmed with an oath.'[101] If a similar oath preceded the Young King's coronation, it is not recorded. But the following day, 15 June 1170, when King William of Scotland and his brother David, followed by all the earls, barons and free tenants of the realm, became the men of the new young king, swearing allegiance (*ligantiam*) and fealty to him against all men, their oath explicitly saved their fealty to Henry the elder.[102] Looking back after the great rebellion, Jordan Fantosme stressed this fact at the very start of his poem, to implicitly criticize those who had supported young Henry against his father:

> Noble king of England with right bold countenance, do you not remember that when your son was crowned you made the king of Scotland do him homage, with his hands placed in your son's, without being false in his fealty to you? Then you said to them both: 'May God's curse fall on any who take their love and affection from you. [And you, William] stand by my son with your might and your aid against all the people in the world, save where my own overlordship is concerned (*salve ma seignurie*)!'[103]

The coronation of young Henry stressed his regal dignity, but few of those attending the great ceremony at Westminster can have doubted the superiority of Henry II's kingship, and his authority over his royal son.

Reverberations

The coronation united father and son in a moment of triumph for the Angevins. As Henry II must have expected, there was a storm of protest from Thomas and his supporters, and the archbishop swiftly wrote to Pope Alexander to make complaint and seek disciplinary measures. But the blow against Thomas had been struck, and he had been powerless to prevent the coronation. Robert of Torigni, the loyal abbot of Mont Saint-Michel, gives what was effectively the 'official' court stance on Becket's exclusion, noting pointedly that Thomas had, after all, now been absent in France continuously for over six years, and that many of the English bishops were present to dignify the occasion.[104] Though there were those who took it badly that York had performed the ceremony, he wrote, there was a clear and distinguished precedent for such an act: no less a king than William the Conqueror had been anointed and consecrated by Ealdred of York, that 'most religious man', while Stigand, the archbishop of Canterbury, was in England, but under excommunication by the pope.[105] In condemning the bishops for violating the prerogative of Canterbury, moreover, even voices of protest within the realm had to be careful not to impugn the position of the new monarch. Thus when, soon after the coronation, Henry confronted Roger of Worcester and accused him of acting treasonously in failing to attend his son's crowning, Roger retorted that he had been forbidden to leave Normandy by Queen Eleanor, and that 'the wrong was done when you ordered me to be present at the crowning, for it was unlawful and an offence to God; not because of who was crowned, but because of who did the crowning. If I had been there, I would not have allowed him [Archbishop Roger] to crown your son.'[106] Writing in late 1174, Guernes of Pont-Sainte-Maxence was keen to stress that the sacrality of the Young King was in no way diminished by the act of usurpation committed by the 'false trinity' of Roger of York, Gilbert of London and Jocelin of Salisbury, whom he roundly condemned:

> It was these three impostors who anointed the child – may God increase his years, his virtue and his honour! – but this was not within their competence; they acted like thieves. The words of consecration are no less valid for that, however, nor is the child any the less consecrated. May God grant him his love![107]

A more overtly hostile response came from King Louis, equally outraged by Henry II's decision not to have Margaret crowned with young Henry, which he regarded as a deliberate insult; as an informant had told Becket shortly before the coronation, she had been left 'as if repudiated . . . to the disgrace and contempt of her father'.[108] He vented his anger by attacking the Norman border, forcing Henry II swiftly to return to the duchy to see to its defences.[109] After mediation between the kings by Count Theobald of Blois, Henry II met with Louis himself at Vendôme, and in subsequent talks between La Ferté and Fréteval, he succeeded in placating Louis over Margaret's exclusion from the coronation and restoring peace.[110] This accord paved the way for a settlement with Thomas. Accordingly, on 22 July, king and archbishop met at Fréteval. The two men conversed apart on horseback: Henry's manner was notably conciliatory, and both studiously avoided the earlier issues of contention, especially the question of royal customs. Nevertheless, Becket protested about the coronation of young Henry, and the words given to him by FitzStephen reflect just how great a blow this had been to the primate:

> I am indebted and accountable to you as my king and worldly lord, saving honour to God and Holy Church, especially now when you have just recalled and admitted me to your peace and favour. But among all the individual evils which in your anger and resentment I have endured – proscription, plunder, my banishment and that of my people and whatever oppressions of the

church of Canterbury – there is one that disturbs me most, and which I neither can nor ought to leave untouched or uncorrected: that you had your son crowned by the archbishop of York in the province of Canterbury. You despoiled the church of Canterbury, the church which anointed you as king with the unction of God's mercy, of its privilege of consecrating kings. This among all its privileges it has considered particular, its own and special for a long time past, since first the blessed Augustine established the metropolitan see of Canterbury.[111]

To Becket's complaints, Henry replied that the coronation had been necessary for the *status regni*, and also claimed that the right to select the officiating prelate was one of his royal customs. As FitzStephen has him say: 'I have heard and been informed that one of the royal privileges of my realm is that if a king of England while still living wishes to appoint his son king, he is allowed to do so wherever and through whatever archbishop or bishop he pleases. My great-grandfather William, the conqueror of England, was consecrated and crowned at London by the archbishop of York, and my grandfather by the bishop of Hereford [*recte* London].'[112] Becket acknowledged this was true, but pointed out that these coronations had not been in prejudice to Canterbury's rights. For in 1066, the irregularities of Stigand meant that the see of Canterbury was effectively vacant, while in 1100 Anselm had been in exile, and because any delay in the coronation 'could have been very dangerous to the kingdom', the ceremony had been conducted by one of Canterbury's suffragans. Henry replied: 'That could well be true. What I said on the matter, I did not say against the church of Canterbury. It anointed me, and I wish its dignity to be safe in all circumstances.'[113] The king promised to allow Becket to crown both young Henry and his wife Margaret. He might also seek papal judgement concerning the infringement of Canterbury's right by the archbishop of York and the other English bishops. As a further act of conciliation, Henry II added that when he took the cross, as he had pledged to, he would entrust the Young King to Becket's care. How sincere Henry was in making such an offer cannot be known, but it recalled the happier days when young Henry had been under Becket's tutelage, and held out the prospect of giving Thomas a position of considerable power and influence, analogous to that enjoyed by Abbot Suger during Louis VII's absence on crusade. Becket, however, responded by saying he would not accept any secular office, but offered his counsel to young Henry.[114] The negotiations concluded by the king agreeing to the restoration of Becket and restitution of lands, churches and goods lost by the archbishop and his supporters.

In the wake of the war of 1173–74, Henry was said to have deeply regretted having his son crowned king.[115] Yet few if any of these troubles could have been foreseen in 1170.[116] If Henry II had made an error of judgement, it had not been in the act of having his son crowned as associate ruler, but rather in proceeding to hold his son's coronation in such highly contentious circumstances. Events, indeed, quickly demonstrated Henry II's foresight and wisdom in having his successor crowned and anointed. For only two months after the ceremony, around 10 August, Henry fell seriously ill with fever at La Motte-de-Ger, near Domfront.[117] Fearing that he was close to death, he restated the divisions of his lands among his sons which he had established at Montmirail the previous year.[118] The Young King was to receive the kingdom of England, Normandy, Anjou and Maine, Richard was to have the duchy of Aquitaine, and Geoffrey the county of Brittany.[119] King Henry entrusted John to the guardianship of the Young King, 'that he might advance and maintain him'.[120] He gave instructions that his body was to be buried at the abbey of Grandmont, near Limoges, of whose order he was so great a patron, but his nobles vehemently protested that this lacked the dignity that befitted his royal majesty.[121] For the rest of August and into September, Henry's life hung in the balance. Rumours even spread through the kingdom of France that he had died. No contemporary records the reaction of his eldest son, whether grief, trepidation or exultant expectation. But young Henry must have waited on tenterhooks for news of his father's condition: direct rule of the lion's share of Henry's great empire appeared imminent. Had Henry died in the late summer of 1170, there would have been no interregnum – always a time of disturbance and instability – as the division of his great empire between his sons had been carefully mapped out and to a degree implemented. Judged without hindsight, the Young King's coronation had been an astute and timely move.

But Henry II survived. By late September, he had convalesced sufficiently to undertake a pilgrimage to Rocamadour.[122] This shrine to the Virgin, perched high in the cliffs above the river Alzou in the Quercy, was a renowned site for healing, and Henry may have made the journey as part of his recuperation as much as to give thanks for his recovery.[123] Henry's entourage, however, was more like an army than an escort. As Robert of Torigni noted, the king 'gathered a great company of armed men, both horsemen and footsoldiers, since he was approaching the lands of enemies, and came to pray equipped as though for battle, doing harm to no-one, but providing generously for all, and especially for the poor, with alms'.[124] It was a show of armed might in Aquitaine, and the message was clear: the Old King was alive, vigorous, and firmly back in power. Young Henry would have to wait.

CHAPTER 6

The Regent and the Martyr, 1170–1172

For England in the course of time would
Have two kings – so Merlin sang – but one of these
Would kill his father in the mother's womb.
            – Anon., *The Long-Veiled Voice of the Prophet*[1]

WHEN HENRY II had sailed for Normandy in late June 1170, he left his newly crowned son as his regent in England.[2] The Young King was given power to exercise all 'rights and justices' through the authority of his own seal, which his father had had made for him, and which bore the title 'Henricus Rex Anglorum et Dux Normannorum et Comes Andegavorum'.[3] Henry II's own seal, like those of preceding Anglo-Norman kings of England, was double sided: on the obverse, the king was shown in majesty, with a drawn sword in his right hand, and in his left an orb topped by a cross upon which was a dove. On the reverse was an equestrian image depicting him as a fully armed knight, with sword and shield.[4] In marked contrast, the Young King's new seal was single-sided, depicting the king in majesty, holding not a sword but a sceptre in his right hand, and an orb, apparently topped with a cross, in his left.[5] The absence of the sword, symbolizing the power of justice, and of a reverse to the seal, might be interpreted as reflecting the lesser authority of the Young King.[6] Yet his seal was almost certainly modelled directly on those of the Capetian kings of France, and on that of his father-in-law Louis VII in particular.[7] Capetian royal seals were normally single-sided, and depicted the king seated in majesty, holding a sceptre topped with a fleur-de-lys contained within a lozenge-shaped frame in one hand, and a small rod topped with a fleur-de-lys in the other.[8] The absence of a drawn sword, or of an equestrian warrior image, from the iconography of the seals of Louis VII and Philip Augustus clearly did not symbolize any limitation in authority. Indeed, speaking of the coronation of Louis VI, Suger noted that the king received 'the sceptre and the rod that symbolize the defence of the churches and the poor'.[9] As there were no precedents for an English associate king, it may be that in practical terms, the adoption of a single-sided seal for the Young King was a simple but effective means of distinguishing the charters of young Henry from those of his father. In symbolic terms, the significant omission from the legend of the Young King's seal of the phrase *Dei gratia* could very well represent an attempt to distinguish between the authority of father and son, as Henry II's own seal had borne this from the outset of his reign.[10] Nevertheless, the conscious borrowing of a Capetian model, like associative kingship itself, reflects Henry II's aspirations for Angevin kingship far more than a concern to indicate his son's subordinate status.[11]

The scheme for co-rulership which Henry II had envisaged since at least 1162 was thus finally put into practice. To assist young Henry in the governance of the realm, Henry II selected a number of *tutores* for his son, drawn 'from the most proven men to be found throughout the realm'.[12] Most were experienced officials, appointed by and loyal to his father and it was they who had charge of the de facto running of the government. Prominent among these senior *curiales* were Geoffrey Ridel, archdeacon of Canterbury, and Richard of Ilchester, archdeacon of Poitiers.[13] Both men had begun their careers in the royal chancery under Thomas Becket, and on the latter's resignation of the office in 1162, Ridel had become acting chancellor. Subsequently, however, they had adhered firmly to the king and became the archbishop's implacable opponents. Becket referred to Geoffrey, who had argued Henry II's case against Becket at the papal Curia, as 'our archdevil', while Ilchester was a kinsman of Becket's long-standing enemy, Gilbert Foliot.[14]

In addition to the two archdeacons, young Henry was assisted by a number of other *familiares* of Henry II, including William de St John, William FitzAldelin, Hugh de Gundeville and Ralf FitzStephen, all of whom are named by William of Canterbury as the *tutores* attending the Young King at his court at Winchester in early December 1170.[15] William de St John, a leading royal official in Normandy, appears as the most frequent witness to the Young King's writs in his period as nominal regent from late June 1170 until late 1172.[16] William FitzAldelin and Hugh de Gundeville already had a well-established connection with young Henry, and in 1170, probably as a reward for earlier services to the queen and the royal children, Hugh was appointed sheriff of Hampshire.[17] Ralph FitzStephen, together with his brothers William and Stephen, were long-standing *familiares* of the king, and Ralph had a close role in the maintenance of the royal family.[18]

As in Queen Eleanor's earlier periods of regency, the government of the Young King intinerated between a number of principal royal sites, mostly in southern England or the Thames valley.[19] A charter of William de Mandeville, earl of Essex, recording an exchange of land with Roger FitzRichard, was drawn up at Winchester 'at the Exchequer, before the lord king Henry, son of King Henry the second, and his barons', probably in early December 1170.[20] Similarly, it was at Woodstock, a favourite royal residence and hunting lodge near Oxford, that William FitzRalph issued grants to the monks of Newport Pagnell and to the priory of Tickford 'in the presence of Henry, the son of King Henry, and his barons'.[21] Once business was complete, the Young King and his companions would have enjoyed the chase in the king's park and the extensive demesne forests of Woodstock, Cornbury and Wychwood.[22] At Salisbury castle, where Henry I's chancellor Roger of Salisbury had constructed a magnificent palace, young Henry ordered the sheriff of Wiltshire to construct new mews, while Bigod, one of the king's falconers, was paid the considerable sum of 72s. 11d. for keeping the king's hawks.[23]

Though only a small number of the administrative writs from this period in the Young King's career survive, they give a glimpse of the routine and often humdrum nature of government. Thus his mandates in favour of the great abbey of Bury St Edmunds require Hamo Peche to pay 25 shillings rent for his holding at Shelfhanger, Norfolk, to the abbey, while he commands the men of the soke of Brockford and Palgrave to render their due services to the monks.[24] Another writ commands Henry the Forester to make good a ditch in Holywell meadow, Oxford, lest a holding and the weir of the monks of St Frideswide's abbey suffer harm. The reeves and burgesses of Bedford are warned not to molest those coming to the fair held by the monks of Elsdow abbey, while the sheriff, bailiffs and reeves of Huntingdon are similarly instructed to safeguard the rights of the monks of Ramsey abbey at the fair of St Ives.[25] In addition to such business, the Young King confirmed grants made by his father, for example, that of a mill in Bedminster, Somerset, and the church of Ashleworth by Gloucester to the monks of St Augustine's abbey, Bristol.[26] In this, as in subsequent periods, the majority of the Young King's charters took the form of such confirmations, with the absence of his own grants being testimony to his lack of landed resources. Nevertheless, the beneficiaries clearly felt it worth the time and expense to obtain new versions of their charters from the new king, in order to further safeguard their possessions.

After Becket's consecration as archbishop of Canterbury, Henry II had suspended the office of chancellor within his own household. But that of his son was, at least nominally, a separate entity, and it was important that the man who held the Young King's seal, and thus effectively controlled the issue of his charters and writs, was trustworthy. The man chosen by Henry II was Richard Barre, who had trained in Roman law at the great university of Bologna.[27] A skilful diplomat, he was one of the king's 'clerici et familiares' at the Roman Curia from 1169, where his activities on Henry II's behalf gained him the special odium of Becket and his followers.[28] In January and February 1170 he had again been in Rome, very possibly in connection with the plans for the Young King's coronation.[29] The chancellor also had supervision of the king's chapel and its clerics, such as Walter of Coutances, who appears as one of the young Henry's chaplains in the early 1170s.[30] The post of royal chaplain was much sought after, for it was normally the assured route to higher promotion – an archdeaconry, or perhaps even a bishopric. The chapel itself was not a fixed structure, but an element of the household that accompanied the king on his travels, its liturgical vessels and vestments set up as required in the chapels of castles, other royal residences, or in the king's pavilion in the field.[31] The chapel (*capella*) of Earl William de Mandeville was described in 1189 as 'a fine chapel which was worthy of such a man, fully equipped with vestments, books, chalice, vessels, wine ewers and bowls of silver, all stored properly in strong boxes'.[32] On the move, these precious devotional objects were packed on to sumpter horses or carts, and William FitzStephen noted that on Thomas' great embassy to Paris in 1158 'the chancellor's chapel had its own wagon, as did the chamber, bursary and kitchen'.[33] The clerics who performed religious offices for the new king also acted as his secretariat, as did those of more mundane office; Wigain, a clerk of the kitchen, is found in the later 1170s keeping a record of knights captured in the tourney by the members of Henry's *mesnie*.[34]

As the Young King had no direct control over the mechanisms of finance, he had no separate treasurer. His chamberlain, Ailward, would have been responsible not only for the immediate domestic arrangements of the Young King's itinerant household, including his wardrobe and valuables, but also for his finances. His chamber, or household financial office, regulated the income of monies received from his father's exchequers at Westminster and Caen, and probably also from major castle treasuries such as Chinon when he travelled further south. The chamberlain, assisted by a number of clerks, would have accounted for household expenditure, and for the wages of the household officers, knights and servants of the *familia*.[35] Young Henry also had at least one usher (*hostarius*), William Blunt, whose functions included keeping order in the king's hall and ensuring its smooth functioning.[36] In Henry II's court, protocol and highly sensitive issues of precedence may well have been the responsibility of a 'king of arms', a leading herald, though no similar officer is visible in the Young King's service.[37] At some stage after the death of William FitzEmpress in 1164, Henry II had transferred a number of members of his late brother's household to that of his son, including a trusted serjeant,

Solomon, who had been William's dispenser (*dispensator*), while Roger Caperun, who had been William's chamberlain, later appears as one of young Henry's chamberlains (*camerarius meus*).[38]

In addition to his father's *familiares*, the Young King had a number of younger, aristocratic companions in his household. At least one of these, William Marshal, had also been selected by King Henry. Soon after his coronation in the summer of 1170, Henry II entrusted his son to the Marshal with orders to 'guard and instruct him' in the use of arms and in knightly accomplishments.[39] William was a younger son of the Wiltshire baron John Marshal, a prominent Angevin supporter during Stephen's reign.[40] In part, William's appointment to the Young King's household in 1170 may have reflected Henry II's gratitude for his father's past services, but it was primarily William's own prowess and loyalty which had recently brought him to the attention of Queen Eleanor. In 1168, William had accompanied his uncle Patrick, earl of Salisbury, to Poitou, then in turmoil as a result of the rebellion of the powerful Lusignan family. Geoffrey and Guy de Lusignan had ambushed Earl Patrick's retinue while escorting Queen Eleanor, but though taken unawares and not fully armed, the royal escort had put up a fierce resistance. Eleanor was brought to safety, but Earl Patrick was struck down from behind and slain, and William himself was wounded in the thigh while valiantly attempting to avenge his uncle.[41] Despite a period in captivity, he was fortunate enough to be ransomed by Eleanor, who, noted the author of the *History of William Marshal*, 'was a very worthy and courtly lady'. Impressed by the young man, she took him into her service, and gave him 'horses, arms, money and fine clothes'.[42] In claiming that already 'kings and queens, dukes and earls had a very high opinion of him', the *History* undoubtedly exaggerates the extent of the Marshal's reputation in the early 1170s. Nevertheless, his valour and skill in arms were already evident in both war and the tournament, and as one of the queen's household knights, William was probably already known to the young Henry.

The Marshal soon came to occupy a leading place among the Young King's own household knights, and in all of his lord's charters which he witnesses, William's name heads the list of the household, following on from those of barons or clergy.[43] In Henry II's court the chief military officer of the king was the constable, assisted by the marshal. The Young King, however, is not known to have had his own constable, and it is likely that William Marshal performed the role of the *magister militum* – commander of the knights – within his household. Henry II, who was an astute judge of men, may well have recognized in William a man who was, as the *History* insists, 'most brave and true' (*proz et leials*), but it may also be that the king viewed an individual drawn from the lesser ranks of the nobility as a more reliable choice than a companion of highest birth.[44] Certainly the majority of the knights known to have been in or connected to the Young King's household were men of comparatively modest status, and not scions of the great Anglo-Norman noble families. When or under what circumstances young Henry first met these knights bachelor is unknown, but the core group of his household (or *mesnie privée*) appears to have been established at least by early 1173, when Roger of Howden could list many of those who later attest his *acta* as being among the rebels who first left the Angevin territories for France with him in April of that year.[45] Several were Normans, including Adam d'Yquebeuf, who enjoyed prominence in the household and appears as William Marshal's main rival,[46] Robert de Tresgoz, from a family holding lands in the Cotentin and who served as one of the Young King's stewards, Thomas de Coulonces, also from the Cotentin, and Gerard Talbot, while William de Tinténiac was a Breton.[47] Others, such as Simon Marsh and probably Robert de Londres, were English.[48] That William Marshal's detractors in the household made play of the fact that he was English by birth provides a glimpse of competing identities and regional rivalries at work among the young men jockeying for position around the Young King. Nevertheless, the predominance of Normans and Anglo-Normans in young Henry's household reflected a similar pattern in the court of Henry II, and it is striking that the Young King had few if any companions from Anjou, Poitou or Aquitaine in his permanent household.[49]

Tellingly, however, these companions attest none of the Young King's *acta* during his period as regent from July 1170 up to November 1172. These were only witnessed by the *tutores* appointed by King Henry II, a clear indication that young Henry enjoyed little or no independent power.[50] Moreover, even though England now had a second king, much of the direction of the government still came directly from Henry II, via writs 'from across the sea (*de ultra mare*)' and by mandates carried by the royal *familiares* who regularly travelled to and from the king in his continental lands.[51] In reality, there was little difference from the situation before 1170, when the justiciars Robert, earl of Leicester, and Richard de Lucy had acted as vice-regents in the king's absence but were in constant receipt of his instructions.[52]

The Young King and Becket's Return to England

Of the numerous missives that must have been received by the Young King and his counsellors, only one, a writ issued by Henry II from Chinon around 30 September 1170, survives, preserved because of its place in the tragic final months of Thomas Becket's life.

Henry, king of England, to his son Henry, the king, greeting. Be it known to you that Thomas, archbishop of Canterbury, has made peace with me according to my will. I therefore command that he and his men shall have peace. You are to ensure that the archbishop and all his men, who left England for his sake, shall enjoy their possessions in peace and honour, as they held them three months before the archbishop withdrew from England. Moreover, you shall cause the senior and more important knights of the honour of Saltwood to appear before you, and by their oath you shall cause recognition to be made of what is there held in fee from the archbishop of Canterbury, and what this recognition shall declare to be within the fief of the archbishop you shall cause him to have.

– Witnessed by Rotrou, archbishop of Rouen, at Chinon[53]

Brief though this writ was, its context and content were highly significant. Since the agreement of peace between the archbishop and the king at Fréteval in July 1170, Becket had remained on the continent. He had refused Henry's offer to join the court immediately after the reconciliation and to return with the king, choosing instead to make his farewells and settle his affairs in France – a serious mistake, for the moment to seal a lasting peace was lost.[54] The lands of the archbishopric, moreover, which had been taken into royal control following his flight from England in 1164, still remained in the hands of a hostile group of men with a vested interest in delaying his return for as long as possible while they enjoyed the revenues from the archiepiscopal estates.[55] Though Henry II had sent writs to the justiciars and bishops, announcing the peace and commanding the restoration of the property of the archbishop and his men,[56] Ranulf de Broc, the custodian of the archbishopric and a long-standing enemy of Becket's, had, with others, merely intensified their exploitation of the estates, selling off the autumn harvest and livestock, and denuding the forests.[57] Henry II was rendered incapable of further intervention by his severe illness, while the Young King's advisors had evidently been in no hurry to enforce the restoration, for the archiepiscopal lands were still being accounted for at the Michaelmas session of the Exchequer.[58]

Becket still had not received the kiss of peace from Henry II and, perhaps with justification, felt alarmed at returning to England without it unless he was accompanied by the king. At Chaumont-sur-Loire, in what would prove their final meeting, amicable relations were seemingly resumed and Henry promised to meet Thomas later at Rouen, where he would either give him the kiss of peace or send Becket with Archbishop Rotrou to England, where he would receive it from the Young King.[59] It was shortly thereafter that Henry II had sent his son the writ ordering the restoration of the property of Thomas and his clerks, and commanding a jury of recognition to establish the extent of the archiepiscopal lands at Saltwood.[60] This manor was of particular significance, both because Thomas had not actually been in possession of Saltwood three months before his flight from England, and because its castle was the base of operations of Ranulf de Broc and his kinsmen, the Brokeis. The king's sealed writ had been carried to England by some of Thomas' most trusted clerks, led by Herbert of Bosham, who presented it and other letters to the Young King at Westminster on 5 October.[61] Herbert later wrote to Becket with a detailed report of their reception, which gives a rare glimpse into the workings of the Young King's court.[62] Initially, the lay officials of the see, William of Eynsford and William FitzNigel, whom the clerks had brought with them, had not dared to enter young Henry's presence – an indication of the fear generally felt at being associated with Thomas at this time. But Herbert, having taken counsel with William FitzAldelin and Ralph FitzStephen, two of the Young King's advisors more sympathetic to Thomas, 'boldly and diligently approached the king in his chamber (in camera sua)', bringing with him only Robert, sacrist of Canterbury.[63] Here he found young Henry attended by the two archdeacons Geoffrey Ridel and Richard of Ilchester, as well as by William de St John and many others, including Henry II's uncle Earl Reginald of Cornwall, who had played a notable role as an intermediary between Henry II and Thomas at the tempestuous council of Northampton.[64] The letters brought by the clerks were read out, then they withdrew while the Young King took counsel, particularly with the royal official Walter de Lisle.[65] The clerks were then readmitted, and Geoffrey Ridel, answering for the Young King, informed them that in order to have reliable knowledge of the state of the archbishop's manors, it would be necessary first to summon Ranulf de Broc and the other officials entrusted by the king with the archbishopric's lands, goods and incomes, and that, accordingly, the Young King had assigned the date of 15 October for a full execution of his father's mandate.[66] Troubled by this delay, Herbert and some of his companions approached the Young King as he was travelling from London to Windsor and greeted him in Thomas' name 'with all care and humility'. It was evident that his initial response at Westminster had been dictated by the dominating presence of his tutores. For now, as Herbert noted, 'he in fact replied graciously to us, and showed us a very much more lively countenance on the road than he had previously shown us in the presence of his justices'.[67]

It was eventually agreed that restoration of the archiepiscopal estates should take place at Martinmas, 11 November, but when shortly thereafter John of Salisbury arrived in England on Thomas' orders to assess the situation, he found that, although Becket's proctors had reoccupied some of the estates they had been driven out almost immediately by Ranulf de Broc and his men, while the lands had already been stripped bare and even the Christmas rents collected in advance.[68] John went to see the Young King, 'and was received with tolerable courtesy (*satis humane receptus*)', although his *custodes* made some threats, not believing Becket to be sincere in his desire for peace. Henry II had been drawn south to Berry by a renewed offensive by Louis VII, and had been unable to meet with Thomas at Rouen. Nevertheless, to Henry II's men in England, Thomas' long delay in France seemed suspicious, his grant of a papal legation ominous, and many, not least the prelates involved in the coronation but even the monks of Canterbury cathedral priory, feared that his return would bring reprisals.[69]

Even at this stage, however, there might have been a real possibility of a peaceful settlement, had Thomas been able to see the Young King in person and assuage any suspicions his enemies had played upon that he intended to invalidate the coronation or disturb the realm. Yet at this critical and highly sensitive juncture Becket made a fateful decision. Shortly before he embarked for England from Wissant, he sent a messenger, Osbern, to Dover where, around 29 November, he served papal letters on Archbishop Roger, and the bishops of London and Salisbury, commanding their suspension, together with that of Durham, Exeter, Chester, Rochester, St Asaph's and Llandaff, and renewing the excommunication of London, Salisbury and Geoffrey Ridel.[70] He was undoubtedly provoked into this action by receiving news that the archbishop of York and the bishops of London and Salisbury had been ordered to attend Henry II in Normandy, bringing with them representatives from all the vacant sees in England in order to hold elections, and that those so elected were to be sent directly to the pope for consecration, thereby completely circumventing the role of the archbishop of Canterbury.[71] Still worse, it was highly likely that prominent among those who would be elevated to bishoprics in this process would be Becket's most hated opponents, Geoffrey Ridel, Richard of Ilchester, Reginald of Salisbury and John, archdeacon of Oxford.[72] To Becket's defenders, the issuing of the papal sentences was an understandable reaction to enormous provocation, an act of desperation in an impossible situation; to his critics, it proved Thomas to be vengeful and incapable of compromise. Whatever the case, it was a profoundly misguided move: it seemed like deliberate aggression, flew in the face of the reconciliation brokered at Fréteval,[73] and, worse, once more appeared to cast doubt on the very validity of the Young King's coronation. The prelates were now being punished merely for obeying the king's orders. It was little wonder that the reaction in England was one of dismay and great anger. Those of the Young King's *tutores* who had warned of Becket's craft and hostile intentions now seemed wholly vindicated.

When Thomas himself landed on 1 December 1170, at Sandwich, he was immediately confronted by the sheriff of Kent, Gervase of Cornhill, who accused him of bringing fire and sword rather than peace into the kingdom, and of wanting to un-crown young Henry. Becket replied that, though it had been illegal, he was not questioning the coronation but only punishing the bishops for usurping the rights of Canterbury, a punishment, moreover, which he claimed had been authorized by King Henry.[74] When on the following day representatives of the archbishop of York and the others met with Becket at Canterbury, he refused to revoke the sentences as they requested, claiming that they had been imposed not by him, but by the pope, who alone could revoke them. As the episcopal clerks pointed out, however, as papal legate, Becket, who was the real author of the sentences, had the power to lift them, and they may have suggested that Becket had only obtained papal authorization for the sentences by falsely alleging that the bishops had made the young Henry swear to observe the Constitutions of Clarendon at his coronation.[75] Under pressure from the king's officials, Thomas offered the bishops conditional absolution, provided they offered satisfaction and took an oath to stand by the pope's judgement, an action that went contrary to the Constitutions. Though Salisbury and London were minded to accept, the hostile biographers of Becket allege that Archbishop Roger steadied them in their resistance to Thomas, and advised that they should inform young Henry that Becket intended to depose him, and that they themselves should set out to see King Henry II in Normandy.[76]

Only months into his co-rule of England, young Henry was thus confronted by a grave and unprecedented crisis to which his response, as Thomas and his enemies alike knew, would be pivotal. Realizing it was crucial to see his former ward face to face, Thomas set out to visit young Henry at Winchester, where he was preparing to hold his Christmas court.[77] There too he hoped to see his old ally, the venerable Bishop Henry of Winchester, now very old and blind, but a voice that would certainly urge reconciliation on the young ruler.[78] While the archbishop himself made a wary progress via Rochester to Southwark, he dispatched Richard, prior of Dover, as his messenger to the Young King requesting his permission to visit him 'as his king and his lord'.[79] As a sign of his affection and goodwill, Thomas sent with him three fine warhorses, a gift carefully calculated to appeal to the young man's chivalric enthusiasms. William FitzStephen, who had an eye for good horseflesh, describes with evident appreciation these 'three valuable destriers, of remarkable speed, elegant stature and beautiful appearance, which walked tall, lifting supple legs, flickering their ears and quivering their limbs, standing restlessly, clothed in flowered and multi-coloured trappers, which he had arranged to give as a new gift to his new lord'.[80]

Prior Richard was closely questioned by the Young King's *tutores* before being finally granted access to the king, to whom he delivered Becket's greetings and assurance that, whatever his detractors had said, the archbishop had in no way intended to invalidate the young king's coronation or aim at his disinheritance. His only complaint was that he himself, according to the prerogative of the archbishop of Canterbury, had not placed the diadem on the Young King's head.[81] The Young King thanked the prior, less on account of his current mission than for the hospitality he had shown in the past to Queen Eleanor, and to his sister Matilda, during the preparations for her marriage to Henry, duke of Saxony.[82] Uncertain as to whether to grant the archbishop's request for an audience, however, young Henry sought the advice of Geoffrey Ridel and Richard of Ilchester, who were then at Southampton waiting to cross to Normandy.[83] Of the two, Ridel was the most implacably opposed to Becket, and had much to lose from Thomas' restoration.[84] Thomas' biographers agree that it was Ridel who urged the Young King not to admit Becket to his presence, claiming that the primate was undoubtedly a traitor seeking to invalidate his coronation or even to disinherit and depose him.[85]

There was now an intense debate in young Henry's court about the best way to proceed, and Reginald of Cornwall urged him to admit Becket. But the young man was swayed by other counsel and sent Jocelin of Arundel, Thomas de Tournebu and Hugh de Gundeville to London, where Thomas was residing at the house of the bishop of Winchester in Southwark, to forbid the archbishop from approaching his court.[86] Jocelin informed Becket that, at the present time, it was not possible for the archbishop to speak with the Young King. He was to return to Canterbury and remain there, and not to travel through the cities and towns of the realm.[87] Becket was evidently surprised and shaken by this response, 'judging that such a statement was not in the young king's nature', and asked if by this he had placed the archbishop 'outside the communication and security of his peace'.[88] 'His orders are just as I said,' replied Jocelin.[89] According to William of Canterbury, Becket's response had been to ask if the Young King had defied him, referring to the act of *diffidatio* whereby the bond formed by homage between lord and man was formally revoked, and with it the protection of lordship removed from the erstwhile vassal.[90] This was not the case, but the embassy showed its hostility by refusing to take back any message from Thomas to young Henry, or to give escort to any of his clerks.

Returning to London, Becket learned that a ship bearing wine sent to him as a gift from Henry II had been attacked by Ranulf de Broc and some of the sailors killed or imprisoned. Thomas immediately sent Richard of Dover and the abbot of St Albans to the Young King, whom they found at Fordingbridge, hunting in the New Forest.[91] This time, he refused to see the messengers in person. He ordered restoration of the ship to Thomas, but his counsellors told the envoys that Thomas' other grievances, which they had presented, would not be addressed while the archbishop continued in his opposition.[92] Matters were not helped when a messenger, bringing venison as a gift from the Young King to his great-uncle Earl Reginald, recognized one of Thomas' clerks, William of Canterbury, who had been sent there to gather information; although the earl's men protested a case of mistaken identity, Reginald felt his position compromised sufficiently to dismiss William immediately, with a warning to Thomas and his clerks that they were in grave peril.[93]

Meanwhile, de Broc and his kinsmen, based in Saltwood castle, continued to harass the archbishop, poaching deer in his parks, stealing his hunting dogs and seizing a packhorse bearing supplies. On Christmas Day, Thomas retaliated; at the close of the service for the Nativity in the cathedral, he formally excommunicated all violators of the rights of the church of Canterbury and all 'fomentors of discord', naming Ranulf and his brother Robert de Broc in person, and pronounced the papal sentences against the bishops involved in the Young King's coronation. By then, however, these same prelates, Roger of York, Jocelin of Salisbury and Gilbert Foliot, together with Richard of Ilchester, had crossed the Channel and were already at Bur-le-Roi, where Henry II was holding his Christmas court in the company of Eleanor, Richard, Geoffrey and John.[94] The bishops were joined by William de Mandeville, who had been sent by the Young King to inform his father of the situation. The bishops made bitter complaint to the king, and according to FitzStephen, they also claimed that Becket 'was careering about the kingdom at the head of a strong force of armed men'. This twisted the fact that on his return to Canterbury from his abortive journey towards Winchester Becket had an escort of five armed knights to prevent attack.[95] But in the circumstances, it was not so impossible to believe that the man who as chancellor had commanded a powerful force of knights on the Toulouse expedition might have raised stipendiaries or drawn on the substantial knight service available from the archiepiscopal lands. Henry II fell into a paroxysm of rage, in which he uttered the fateful words, as reported by Edward Grim, 'What miserable drones and traitors have I nourished and promoted in my household, who let their lord be treated with such shameful contempt by a low-born clerk!'[96] He is said by William FitzStephen to have laid a series of charges before his barons against Thomas, among which 'that he had entered the kingdom like a tyrant; that he had suspended the archbishop of York and all his bishops and excommunicated others for their obedience to the king; that he had disturbed the whole realm' and that he intended to deprive his son of the crown.[97]

A royal deputation, headed by William de Mandeville, Saher de Quincy and Richard de Hommet, the constable of Normandy, made ready to cross to England, confront Thomas, and probably to arrest him. But stung by the king's reproach and eager to avenge him, a sworn group of four knights – Reginald FitzUrse, Hugh de Moreville, William de Tracy and Roger le Bret – had already secretly left the court and taken ship for England, with the intention of seizing Becket themselves.[98] Earl William and Saher, who were to cross to Southampton and first visit the Young King in Winchester, were detained by contrary winds at Barfleur, although Richard made the crossing safely. On reaching Winchester, he ordered Hugh de Gundeville and William FitzJohn to send a force of household knights to Canterbury to arrest the archbishop.[99] Significantly, William FitzStephen notes that Richard instructed them not to inform the Young King, which suggests that young Henry might well oppose such forceful measures against Thomas.[100]

The four knights, however, had already reached Canterbury.[101] Making the long ride from Bur-le-Roi to Wissant, the shortest and most direct crossing, they had landed at Dover on 28 December, and were welcomed at Saltwood castle by Ranulf de Broc. The next day, they headed for Canterbury with a contingent of knights provided and led by de Broc, who had helped them formulate a plan of operations and who was in many ways the chief author of the events which now unfolded. Finding Thomas in an inner chamber of the archiepiscopal palace, the four knights presented the king's grievances against him, and according to Benedict of Peterborough, Reginald FitzUrse, who acted as their spokesman, demanded in Henry II's name that Becket go to Winchester and give satisfaction to the Young King. Thomas responded that he was anxious to see young Henry, his new lord, but would not go if this meant standing trial, for he was guilty of no crime.[102] After an increasingly heated exchange, the knights declared Thomas to be under arrest, then left the hall to summon their retinue and to arm themselves. Becket's servants, however, barred the doors, and, as de Broc's men tried to break into the palace, Thomas was hurried by his clerks into what was hoped would be the safety of the cathedral. As night was falling, the four knights caught up with him in the north transept. Their intention had only been to arrest him, but in the scuffle that followed Becket fiercely resisted their attempts to remove him. Stinging insults were exchanged, and as mounting panic fuelled their exasperation, the knights finally struck him down.[103]

Reaction to the Murder of Becket

The Young King's ministers would have been among the first to learn the shocking news of Becket's murder on 29 December 1170, and word was at once sent to Henry II in Normandy.[104] According to William FitzStephen, young Henry grieved bitterly, but also expressed thanks to God that the knights' intentions had been kept secret from him, and that none of his own men had been involved: it was at least some small solace to him that the murder had taken place before Hugh de Gundeville and William FitzJohn had reached Canterbury.[105] It is very probable that young Henry was genuinely saddened by his old guardian's death, and his subsequent actions reveal what may have been a mounting sense of guilt for the part he had played, albeit unwittingly, in the archbishop's demise. By the time of the Young King's rebellion in the summer of 1173, he and his supporters were making effective capital out of Becket's martyrdom. Yet there is little to support the assertion that in the immediate aftermath of the murder he held his father responsible for Becket's death or that this was a fundamental cause of the rift between father and son.[106] Like that of Henry II, the Young King's reaction to Becket's killing may have shifted over time.[107] Initially at least, he may have concurred in the sentiments expressed in Henry II's letter to Pope Alexander, in which he accused Becket of breaking the terms of the peace of Fréteval, of deliberately bringing not peace but strife on his return to England, and, in so doing, of challenging Henry's kingdom and his crown.[108] By excommunicating the king's men, Thomas had been deliberately provocative, and 'not willing to accept such impudence, the excommunicates and others from England fell upon him and (I say it with grief) killed him'.[109] While Robert of Torigni had devoted considerable space in his chronicle to Henry II's devotion and almsgiving during his pilgrimage to Rocamadour in September 1170, he merely noted Becket's murder with a bland quatrain, closely followed by the report of the murder of Hamo, bishop of Léhon in Brittany, by his nephew: though highly regrettable, there was nothing special about Thomas' death.[110]

Such a stance, however, rapidly became untenable as the international outcry grew ever louder. Among Henry II's most vociferous critics were King Louis VII, Theobald of Blois and his brother William, archbishop of Sens, all of whom wrote to the pope demanding heavy penalties, while Sens himself laid Normandy, Anjou, Poitou and Brittany under an interdict, despite the appeal of Rotrou of Rouen and his colleagues.[111] Fearing his own excommunication and an interdict on England, Henry II dispatched a major delegation headed by Roger of Worcester, Giles of Evreux and Richard Barre, the Young King's chancellor, to the Curia to state the king's case and extricate him from the rising tide of contumely and blame.[112] The mission, which arrived in early March, received a hostile response, and eventually succeeded only in averting an interdict on Henry himself and his kingdom by conceding that although Henry had not ordered or wished for the archbishop's death, he was in no small measure responsible, and the ambassadors bound the king by oath to accept the pope's judgement on the matter.[113] Alexander III had been outraged by Becket's murder and authorized a papal commission to investigate Henry's role in the martyr's death and 'to observe his humility' before the pope would absolve him.[114] Around Easter 1171, the Young King's wife Margaret, who had still not been crowned as queen, crossed with her household from England to Normandy, and received 20 marks, as well as horses, sumpters and clothing for her retainers.[115] No source states the reason, but it may well have been in order to visit her father Louis and to convey assurances that both royal father and son were guiltless in Becket's murder.

A Perilous Absence: Henry II's Expedition to Ireland

Before the impending papal legation could arrive, Henry II had determined to undertake an expedition to Ireland, moved more, it has been argued, by political necessity than by his desire to delay making satisfaction to the Church.[116] Though he had contemplated the subjugation of Ireland as early as 1155, the scheme had long been postponed, and in 1169 the king had given permission for English marcher lords from south Wales to assist the exiled king of Leinster, Dermot McMurrough, to recover his lands. By 1170, these adventurers had taken the city of Dublin and the coastal towns of Wexford and Waterford, while in May 1171 Richard de Clare, who was married to Dermot's daughter, Eva, had inherited Leinster on Dermot's death. Their rapid success had alarmed Henry, and fearing lest they should carve out autonomous principalities beyond his dominions, he now determined to assert his authority directly over these English lords as well as over the native Irish rulers.[117] In their social habits and ecclesiastical traditions, the Irish were deemed backward and unorthodox by the standards of twelfth-century Europe. By using his overlordship to effect major reforms in the Irish Church, Henry might demonstrate his good faith and concern for the universal Church and thereby offset some of the mounting opprobrium for Thomas' death.

After holding a great council at Argentan in July 1171 to discuss plans for the campaign, Henry left for England on 3 August.[118] By early September, Henry's great army had set out for Pembrokeshire; sailing from Milford Haven, the king arrived at the head of a great fleet of 400 ships near Waterford on 18 October 1171.[119] A number of the Young King's leading *tutores* had accompanied Henry II to Ireland, notably Hugh de Gundeville and William FitzAldelin, who was to play a key role as a royal representative in Irish affairs from the outset of Henry's expedition.[120] Shortly before leaving the duchy, Henry II had summoned the Young King to join him in Normandy: the Old

King judged it expedient for there to a be a continuing royal Angevin presence in his continental lands, not least at a time when he had recently asserted control over Brittany and when international outrage at Becket's death had significantly increased the possibility of open hostilities by Louis VII.[121]

In Ireland, Henry II's expedition met with considerable success. He took the homage of the English lords, who surrendered the major towns and received their lands back as fiefs, while he also accepted the submission of the great majority of the Irish princes.[122] Letters were dispatched to the Young King in England, informing him of the king's safe crossing and reception, and it is probable that such newsletters advertising Henry II's achievements were circulated beyond the court.[123] In early November, an ecclesiastical council at Cashel proceeded to promulgate a series of measures aimed at the radical reform of the Irish Church, and recognized the overlordship of Henry II.[124] These decrees were swiftly sent to the papacy, with a request for papal confirmation of the possession of Ireland by Henry and his heirs.[125] But as late autumn turned to winter, the weather grew increasingly severe. Gales and rough seas made communications all but impossible, and Henry II was effectively cut off from his son, from England, and from his continental domains.[126]

Like Henry II's severe illness in 1170, these circumstances again highlighted the practical wisdom of the Young King's associative kingship as a guarantor of stability and security. With the effective governance of the kingdom remaining in the hands of the justiciar, Richard de Lucy,[127] young Henry's presence in the Norman duchy may have been an important factor in deterring French attack. As his title proclaimed, he was not only king of the English, but also duke of the Normans and count of the Angevins, and thus equally able to exercise authority in the Angevin continental lands.[128] A number of charters show him engaged in the administration of Normandy, assisted by his father's trusted ministers, including the two archdeacons. A confirmation by the Young King of a gift in favour of Montebourg abbey, issued at Bur-le-Roi during one of his stays in Normandy between 1171 and 1172, was witnessed by William de St John, Geoffrey Ridel, Richard of Ilchester and Reginald of Salisbury, as well as Hugh de Cressy, Richard de Camville, Reginald de Courtnay, William de Lanvalei and John, dean of Salisbury.[129] Likewise, in the record of a gift made by William d'Abouville to the abbey of St Stephen at Caen 'in the presence of the lord king Henry the younger', we again glimpse him at an important gathering of nobles and clergy, including William de St John and William de Courcy, the king's justices, and bishops Arnulf of Lisieux, Froger of Sées, Jocelin of Salisbury and many others.[130]

Not all of young Henry's time, however, was devoted to affairs of state. The History of William Marshal speaks only in vague terms about the period from the Marshal's entry into the Young King's household in 1170 until the crisis of 1173, but stresses how as a result of the Marshal's careful tutelage, young Henry's chivalric propensities flourished: 'He did much for him, and brought him on so, that as a result of what he had learned, the Young King's reputation increased, along with his eminence and the honour paid to him; he also acquired the quality of valour'. For the *History* claims it was at this time that he began to participate in the tournament circuit of northern France, and to engage in a life of knight-errantry:

> At that time, there was no war, so the Marshal took him through many a region, as a man who knew well how to steer him in the direction of places where tournaments were to be held. The Young King knew about the use of arms, as much as any young nobleman could be expected to know. The life of combat pleased him well, which was very pleasing for his tutor. He travelled far and wide, he spent lavishly, for he was aiming at those heights which a king, and a son of a king, should rise to, if he wishes to attain high eminence.[131]

In reality, given his role as regent in Henry II's absence, it would have been impossible for young Henry to have undertaken any kind of itinerant knightly adventuring in 1171–72. Here the *History* seems merely to be reverting, perhaps from a dearth of information, to a topos familiar from the Arthurian romances, and suspiciously gives no details of time or place. Nevertheless, during his residences in the duchy during this period, it would have been easy enough for the Young King to have attended one of the great tournaments already being held with increasing regularity in the borderlands of Normandy and France.[132] He was now of an age to undertake such martial sports: his near contemporary, Arnold lord of Ardres, participated in *bohorts* – a form of hastilude – 'and tournaments all over' before he entered the court of Philip of Flanders and was knighted by him.[133]

Young Henry and Margaret also spent time in southern England, based in Winchester, where Ailward his chamberlain is found purchasing robes for the king at the city's fairs.[134] Margaret was provided with the furnishings necessary for her own chapel: a pyx, two liturgical ewers, candlesticks, lamps and a thurible, all of silver, as well as an altar covering. That she shared her husband's itinerant lifestyle is reflected in the provision of a sumpter horse and chest for these, as well as a palfrey for her chaplain, William, while expensive 'robes for riding' were bought for Margaret herself.[135]

It was in Normandy, however, that Henry II's extended absence in Ireland gave the Young King the opportunity to make his own mark. At Christmas

1171, while his father was lavishly feasting the Irish kings at Dublin, young Henry had held his own court at Bur-le-Roi, a favoured royal residence near Bayeux. As Robert of Torigni noted, 'because he was holding his first court in Normandy, he wanted to have the festival celebrated in magnificent fashion. Bishops, abbots, counts and barons were there, and many gifts were given to many men.'[136] The kind of splendid feasting enjoyed on such great occasions is captured by Lambert of Ardres' description of a banquet in the hall of the castle at Ardres in 1178:

> [D]ishes innumerable to the point of extravagance were liberally set down and joyfully accepted and one wine after another – Cyprian, Megarian, spiced wine and claret – flowed into goblets . . . The servers and waiters, who were instructed and trained by the butlers . . . poured the precious wine of Auxerre into glasses and small vessels from flagons.[137]

Such a throng of nobles, leading clergy and their retinues had assembled at Bur-le-Roi that the palace was overflowing. As a humorous solution to this overcrowding, two of the leading royal officials, William de St John and William FitzHamon, the seneschal of Brittany, forbade any knight whose name was not William from dining in the chamber they were in. Even so, as Torigni notes, 'when they put the others out of the room, there remained a hundred and ten knights who were all named William, in addition to many others of the same name who ate in the hall (*in aula*) with the king'.[138] The joke about the great number of Williams may also have been an allusion to the rising popularity of William Marshal as the most prominent of the Young King's household knights, or a compliment to William FitzHamon, Henry II's main agent guiding young Geoffrey in Brittany.[139] The presence of Geoffrey himself was also a reminder of a recent Plantagenet triumph. Conan, duke of Brittany, had died earlier that year and Henry II had taken effective control of the duchy, which was to come to Geoffrey on his marriage to Conan's daughter Constance.[140] Young Henry seems to have been on consistently good relations with Geoffrey, and for the moment both could enjoy their position, temporarily free from their father's overbearing presence. Beyond the feasting and pleasantries, this Christmas court was an opportunity for young Henry to mix with the assembled nobility of Normandy and further afield, who readily saw in the open-handed and affable young man a very different figure from his father.

There were, however, more sinister matters afoot. The well-informed Ralph of Diss noted that it was while Henry II was in Ireland that at Eleanor's instigation, 'as it is said', her uncle Ralph of Faye and Hugh of St Maure, a

l in the Touraine, began to incite the Young King against his
d of Wales likewise believed that 'the conspiracy of nobles
rince, and of the sons against their father', occurred between
ure for Ireland and the arrival of the papal legates in Normandy
² There was a rising groundswell of discontent among many of
agnates. In the spring of 1171, Henry II had ordered a major
to the extent of royal lands and rights as they stood at Henry I's
as well as what lands, woods and other demesne had since been
is barons or knights. Amercements and confiscations soon
1, Torigni believed, had doubled the king's revenue from the
duchy.¹⁴³ Henry II's heavy-handed policies there had alienated more Norman
lords than he appears to have realized, and there can be little doubt that at
young Henry's Christmas court there had been whispers of a major rebellion
in the name of the new king.

Any open stirrings of revolt, however, were pre-empted by Henry II's
return. When some ships were finally able to reach Ireland in February 1172
they had brought news to the king of the arrival of the two papal legates in his
domains. He had made immediate attempts to leave, arriving at Wexford by
1 March, but storms delayed his sailing until 16 April. Henry had been away
from contact with his kingdom and other domains, noted Dean Ralph, for
twenty whole weeks.¹⁴⁴ Landing near St David's on 17 April, he moved with
the greatest haste to Portsmouth where the Young King was awaiting him with
ships, and together they immediately sailed for Barfleur.¹⁴⁵ 'Be it known to
you', wrote Henry II to Bishop Bartholomew of Exeter, 'that by God's grace I
landed in Normandy after a favourable voyage and found all my lands across
the sea established by God's favour in all peace and tranquillity, and my men
and faithful subjects, as was fitting, filled with the greatest joy at my coming.'¹⁴⁶
Henry's words, however, betrayed his anxieties. Gerald of Wales believed that,
together with news of the legates' arrival in Normandy, rumours had reached
Henry in Ireland that his sons were conspiring against him, 'and in this had
many accomplices among the nobles of England and France. Having heard
this, having uncovered malice towards himself so profound and in such an
unexpected quarter, the king sweated with anxiety on many counts'.¹⁴⁷ It may
be doubted, however, if Henry had such a clear idea either of the involvement
of his family or of the extent of the growing conspiracy.¹⁴⁸ On his return to
England, he felt able to exact a scutage, and also went ahead with an investigation into the resources of Normandy.¹⁴⁹

Nevertheless, his awareness of rising political tensions is graphically indicated in the sharp increase in spending on royal castles. Fortresses not only on
the borders but in the Midlands and East Anglia were brought to a state of

readiness, suggesting fear of insurrection. In 1170–71, the Pipe Rolls record a total of £1,237 spent on the repair and garrisoning of royal castles in England, in part stimulated by Henry's wish to strengthen the kingdom's defences while he was absent in Ireland, while in the following fiscal year of 1171–72, a similar sum, £1,223, was disbursed.[150] Only the figures for royal castles in England are known, but Henry also fortified and provisioned castles throughout his continental lands, almost certainly involving expenditure of a similar magnitude. A dark note, moreover, had been struck by the fact that Adam de Port, lord of the barony of Kington in Herefordshire, had been charged with plotting Henry II's death. His guilt seemed to be confirmed by his refusal to attend the *curia regis* when summoned, and he was outlawed and disseised of his lands, including Neufmarché.[151] Nothing more is known of the alleged plot, nor if young Henry, Eleanor or Louis were cognizant of it, but Adam was to reappear as an active partisan in the Young King's rebellion, fighting in the forces of William the Lion during the Scots' invasion of northern England in 1174.[152] Whatever lay behind the incident, it was indicative of mounting tension between elements of the nobility and Henry II. The Old King sensed danger, but it seems he did not yet suspect some of the nobles who would become the imminent rebellion's principal leaders.

On his return from Ireland, however, Henry II's most pressing concern was the issue of making satisfaction for Becket's murder. Once back in Normandy, he received the legates, Theodwin, cardinal priest of S. Vitale, and Albert, cardinal priest of S. Lozenzo, at Gorron on 16 May, where they exchanged the kiss of peace.[153] Next day, at the great monastery of Savigny, near Avranches, there was a stormy interview, where Henry found the legates 'hard and apparently unyielding', and angrily refused to accept the conditions they put forward.[154] After mediation by the Norman clergy, however, he agreed to a form of compurgation to demonstrate his innocence in Becket's murder, which was to take place at Avranches on Sunday 21 May. Around this time, young Henry accompanied his father to the great abbey of Mont Saint-Michel, where in the chapter house both he and Henry II confirmed a grant by Abbot Robert to William de St John.[155] Significantly, however, he appears not to have been present at Savigny: it may be that Henry II was intentionally keeping him at a remove, as a representative of Angevin kingship untainted by direct involvement in Becket's demise, until he knew the legates' intentions and had agreed on terms. Young Henry's importance in the proceedings, however, was soon demonstrated in fresh negotiations held on 19 May.[156] Now Henry insisted on his son's presence and consent before a final settlement could be achieved: the terms of peace with the Church went well beyond Henry's personal penance and touched the dignity and prerogatives of both kings.[157] Accordingly, the

Young King was quickly summoned to Avranches, where on 21 May, the Sunday before Ascension Day, outside the cathedral of St Andrew, Henry II publicly purged himself of active involvement in Becket's death. He swore on the Gospels 'that he had neither ordered nor willed the murder of the archbishop of Canterbury', but admitted that he had been the cause of Becket's death because his angry words had caused his men, 'without his knowledge, to avenge his wrongs'.[158]

He accordingly promised to accept 'with all humility and devotion' the penance imposed by the legates.[159] He was to pay for 200 knights to serve in the Holy Land against the infidel for a whole year, under the command of the Templars. If the pope should so order, he was to go in person on crusade to Spain 'to liberate that land from the infidel'.[160] He was to make full restitution to the church of Canterbury, restoring its lands and goods to their condition a year before the quarrel with Archbishop Thomas began, and likewise to reinstate any who had suffered through their support for the archbishop. In addition, fasting and almsgiving were imposed on him, though this was done privately, doubtless so as not to injure the king's majesty.[161] These provisions involved Henry's personal expiation for Becket's murder. Of equal concern to the Young King, however, was the settlement of the issue that had lain at the heart of the dispute with Becket. The legates insisted that Henry II 'abrogate in their entirety the perverse statutes of Clarendon and all evil customs which had been introduced into God's churches during his reign'. Similarly, those evil customs already existing before his accession 'were to be restricted in accordance with the mandate of the lord pope and the counsel of religious men'.[162] Henry II reportedly agreed cheerfully to all these conditions. Finally, 'in order that nothing might be left undone', Henry was led out of the church 'and there on his knees, but without removing his clothes or receiving lashes, he was absolved and led back into the church'.[163] At a further meeting at Caen on 30 May, Henry II publicly repeated the oath he had made at Avranches, and this was confirmed by the Young King, save for those stipulations pertaining to Henry II alone.[164] Young Henry 'swore in the hands of the lord cardinal Albert' to observe these conditions, including the renunciation of the 'new customs', and pledged 'that if the king his father should be prevented by death or any other cause from fulfilling his penance, he would himself perform it for him'.[165] Both father and son agreed not to withdraw their support from Alexander, provided he continued to treat both rulers as Catholic and Christian kings.[166]

The meeting at Caen had also been an occasion for re-establishing peace with Louis. It was agreed that his daughter Margaret would now be crowned alongside her husband, and the Young King and his wife crossed to

Southampton on 24 August.[167] For the moment at least, the threat of French aggression aiming to exploit Henry's profound political embarrassment over Becket's murder had been dissipated, and with it the external support on which any effective uprising within the Angevin lands depended.[168]

The Coronation of Queen Margaret and the Young King's Pilgrimage to Becket's Shrine

On 27 August, in the great cathedral church of St Swithun in Winchester, Archbishop Rotrou of Rouen placed the crown on the Young King's head, then proceeded to anoint, consecrate and crown Margaret as queen in full accordance with the English royal coronation *ordines,* to the acclamation of the assembled nobility.[169] Rich robes had been procured for the Young King, Margaret and Queen Eleanor, and though Henry II himself had deliberately remained in Normandy, a number of the king's swords were refurbished with gold, probably to serve as bearing swords in the ceremony.[170] It was an event of dual significance. Margaret at last became *regina Angliae,* though none doubted that it was Queen Eleanor who retained the authority and perquisites of the pre-eminent queen of England.[171] For young Henry, the ceremony was a crown-wearing, not a consecration, for he had already been anointed in July 1170.[172] Nevertheless, it was one intended to restore the fullness of majesty and remove any taint that had been caused by the bitter controversy surrounding his coronation and the tragic sequel of Becket's murder. Though it stemmed from very different circumstances from the magnificent crown-wearings held by King Stephen to wipe away the stain of his defeat at Lincoln and subsequent imprisonment, and by Richard the Lionheart following his release from Germany in 1194 to counter the ignominy of captivity, the ceremony at Winchester in August 1172 was similarly a confirmatory coronation.[173] As such, it had been carefully arranged in terms of place and persons involved to avoid the controversial aspects of the coronation of 1170.[174] It was deliberately held not at Westminster, inextricably linked to the rights of Canterbury to crown monarchs, but at Winchester, one of the other three traditional sites for royal crown-wearings and a major royal centre, while at the request of King Louis, Roger, archbishop of York, Gilbert Foliot of London and Jocelin of Salisbury were forbidden to attend.[175] Becket's death had left the see of Canterbury vacant, so the service was performed by Rotrou as a distinguished prelate acceptable to all parties, assisted by Giles of Evreux and, among Canterbury's suffragans, Roger of Worcester, Henry II's cousin.[176]

Following this great ceremony, the Young King's court, together with the bishops, abbots and clergy, moved to Windsor where he presided over an ecclesiastical council intending to elect Thomas' successor as archbishop.[177] The election of the archbishop of Canterbury was always a matter of the greatest political importance and of equal sensitivity. The monks of Christ Church, loudly asserting the canonical right of the chapter to a free election, put forward Prior Odo, who had been an opponent of Thomas, but, as always, the bishops asserted their own rights in the election.[178] The anonymous Canterbury monk who recorded the proceedings was impressed by the Young King and by his handling of the delicate situation, calling him 'kind-hearted, affable and strong in good conduct'. He would do nothing, Henry said, either to harm the rights of Canterbury or to go against the orders and wishes of his father; he would convey with goodwill all that he had heard to the king.[179] The Young King was learning the political art of delay. He therefore adjourned the assembly until 6 October, when he presided over a second great assembly of clergy and magnates at Windsor. Here, the Canterbury monks once more asserted the candidacy of Odo, but were asked to make an alternative choice, lest King Henry II disapprove of their first. When they refused to do so unless granted absolute freedom of election, the Young King, recognizing this would be contrary to his father's wishes, judged that the election should be conducted in the presence of the senior king, and commanded the electors from the Canterbury monks to meet in Normandy at King Henry's court on 30 November. He too would be present, for his father had commanded him to cross to the duchy.[180]

Between the two councils at Windsor, the Young King had undertaken a highly symbolic pilgrimage to Canterbury to the shrine of Thomas.[181] Despite initial uncertainties as to Becket's sanctity, not least among the monks of Canterbury, a cult of the murdered archbishop had sprung up with astonishing speed and vigour, and by the autumn of 1172 there had already been a flood of reported miracles.[182] Thomas had been buried in the Trinity chapel at the far eastern end of the cathedral's crypt, in a marble sarcophagus, around which had been built a stone covering, pierced by four circular openings through which pilgrims could touch the tomb.[183] Before this shrine, young Henry prostrated himself in tears. He lamented that with his father, he too had opposed Thomas for some time, and that he himself had by royal decree ordered the archbishop to remain in Canterbury on pain of death. Whatever he believed his father's role in Becket's murder to have been, the Young King realized that his own actions in refusing to see Thomas in late December had effectively sealed Becket's fate. Now at Canterbury, before the tomb of his old tutor, 'who had brought him up in childhood and who had especially loved him', he was overcome with feelings of guilt and remorse, and humbly begged pardon for the injuries that both he and his father had caused to the martyr.[184] He was then honourably received by the monks in procession, and 'made many gifts to God and promised many more'.[185] Young Henry's was thus the first royal pilgrimage to Thomas' shrine, antedating his father's famous penance at Becket's tomb in July 1174 by nearly two years. It was a gesture well received by the Canterbury monks: the anonymous recorder of his visit confidently asserted that as a result of his humility and contrition, St Thomas had remitted all his anger and vengefulness (*ira et vindicta*) towards the new king.[186]

CHAPTER 7

'A King Without a Kingdom'

THE SEEDS OF WAR, 1172–1173

After this crowning and after this transfer of power you took away from your son some of his authority, you thwarted his wishes so that he could not exercise power. Therein lay the seeds of a war without love. God's curse be on it![1]

– Jordan Fantosme

FOLLOWING HIS RETURN to England in late August 1172, the Young King had again resumed his position as regent of the kingdom, and when in early November Henry II ordered his son and Queen Margaret to join him in Normandy, young Henry did so most unwillingly.[2] He was at last consolidating his position in the kingdom, and his second coronation must have seemed a good omen for his father's granting of wider autonomy in the near future. Instead, Richard de Lucy, as chief justiciar, took over effective governance.[3] Though he could not know it, the Young King was never again to hold the regency of England.

His father required him to undertake a diplomatic visit to King Louis, who was very eager to see his daughter Margaret, and such an embassy would help to repair the damage done to Angevin–Capetian relations in the wake of the Becket affair. Louis, indeed, welcomed the couple with joy, giving them a fine reception.[4] Roger of Howden, however, believed Louis' motive to have been more sinister: 'from this', he noted, 'great harm came to the kingdom of England, and even to that of France'.[5] Doubtless the Capetian king was as charmed as were so many of his contemporaries by young Henry's winning and affable manner, while the Young King may in turn have had genuine affection for his father-in-law, a man of radically different temperament from Henry II.[6] Though not a great war leader, Louis was widely admired for his piety and justice, including by several of the Paris-schooled intellectuals at

Henry II's court, while his protection and support of the exiled Thomas Becket had won this *rex Christianissimus* much kudos and the fulsome praise of Becket's *eruditi*.[7] Yet the French king was also a shrewd politician, and a veteran at exploiting divisions among the Angevins themselves. He saw – as apparently Henry II as yet did not – that the Young King was a perfect means by which to attack his more powerful rival. It was easy enough for him to play on the young man's mounting frustrations. Louis counselled him that immediately on his return to Normandy he should ask his father to give him either the whole of Normandy or all of England, so that he might rule his own lands and maintain Margaret in the style appropriate for a king and queen. Louis was deftly using Margaret's anointing as a means for ratcheting up young Henry's expectations in order to divide the most powerful bloc within Henry II's empire – Normandy and England. Should his father not grant either of these territories, then young Henry should return with his wife to France.[8] The implication was clear: if the Young King was to receive what was rightfully his, Henry II had to be given an ultimatum, and the French crown was ready to support young Henry, with force if need be, should his father refuse. By now, Henry II was becoming anxious at the way events were developing, and recalled Henry and Margaret from the Capetian court. With Louis' leave, they obeyed Henry's summons, and in an evident gesture of goodwill, the elder king permitted them to hold held their own Christmas court at the ducal castle of Bonneville-sur-Touques in Normandy, while he and Queen Eleanor held theirs in Anjou at the great palace-fortress of Chinon.[9]

The Maurienne Match

After Christmas, Henry II summoned the Young King from Normandy to join him, and in late January 1173 they journeyed together to Montferrat in the Auvergne to settle important dynastic business.[10] Here, on 2 February, Henry held a great regional summit, attended by Raymond V of Toulouse, Gerard of Mâcon, count of Vienne, Alfonso II, king of Aragon, and Humbert, count of Maurienne.[11] To hold such a great assembly at Monferrat was in itself a major assertion of Angevin claims of lordship in a region long disputed with the Capetians.[12] But Henry was about to clinch a remarkable deal with Humbert, which the count himself had first put forward in 1171 in an attempt to gain Henry's protection both from his hostile neighbour, Count Raymond V, and from Emperor Frederick Barbarossa.[13] Its successful conclusion would transform the balance of power in south-east France and beyond. Though he had married three times, Count Humbert had found himself with no male heirs and only two daughters. Now a treaty was drawn up whereby

Henry's youngest son John, whom his father jokingly called 'Johans senz Terre' or 'Lackland', was to marry Humbert's eldest daughter and heiress, Alice, in return for the sum of 5,000 marks.[14] Should Humbert have no sons by his current wife, John was to inherit all the count's extensive lands, which included not just the county of Maurienne but a conglomeration of territories and lordships that straddled the Alps – effectively much of the region that would soon be known as Savoy.[15] Even if Humbert did succeed in producing a male heir – and all parties seem to have regarded this as very unlikely – then this son would receive only the small and relatively unimportant county of Maurienne itself, while John and Alice were to hold all the other territories.[16]

These rich and strategically important lands made a handsome territorial provision for Henry's youngest son, and also promised to extend Angevin influence to the south-east as far as the Val d'Aosta and Turin. Gerald of Wales was no doubt guilty of hostile exaggeration when he claimed that Henry's desire to secure the Maurienne match was a further step in fulfilling his ambition to gain the imperial throne itself, though others too thought Henry had designs on Italy, and Peter of Blois believed that the Italian opponents of Barbarossa had even offered him the kingdom.[17] Control of some of the Alpine passes would certainly greatly strengthen Henry's hand in any dealings with emperor and pope alike, and the seriousness of his intentions at least in this respect is revealed by the fact that Alice's dowry specifically included a number of key castles controlling certain of the major routes over the Alps.[18] More immediately, it bolstered Henry's authority in south-eastern France and afforded the opportunity to place decisive pressure on his long-standing opponent, the count of Toulouse.[19]

That Henry regarded the Maurienne match as a key element in his grand diplomacy is indicated by the fact that while he was at Montferrat he received Alfonso II, the king of Aragon, and Raymond of Toulouse. The two men were bitter rivals, so in an attempt to reconcile them and to establish a more general peace in the region Henry took them to Limoges, where he convened a great assembly.[20] In the presence of Queen Eleanor, young Henry and his brother Richard, and a great number of magnates, Henry II established peace between them.[21] The full significance of Henry's deal with Humbert, moreover, had been fully grasped by Count Raymond. Ever since Henry's great but unsuccessful expedition against Toulouse in 1159, relations between Raymond and Henry had been strained, if not outright hostile.[22] Now, however, on 25 February 1173, Raymond became the man not only of Henry II, but also of the Young King, as the heir to the headship of the Plantagenet family, and of Richard as count of Poitou.[23] He was to hold his county of Toulouse 'from them in fee and by hereditary right, for the service of coming to the summons of the king or the count of Poitou to aid him in his war' with 100 knights for forty days.[24] Clearly, the Maurienne match and the submission of Toulouse were intimately linked, for immediately after Raymond's submission, Henry II received custody of Alice of Maurienne.[25] Faced with the imminent prospect of Plantagenet control of eastern Provence, Raymond felt he had little choice but to make peace on the best terms he could, while Henry himself strove to indicate the benefits of his lordship by brokering peace with Aragon.[26]

As surety, Henry II was given custody of four of Humbert's castles, 'reputed to be the best fortified by man or nature'.[27] Only one detail remained to be decided. Not unnaturally, Count Humbert was anxious to know what provision Henry intended to make for his daughter's prospective husband. Henry replied that he would give John the castles of Chinon, Loudun and Mirebeau in Anjou, which earlier counts of Anjou had sometimes granted as an appanage to younger brothers or sons.[28] The Young King, however, took deep offence and vociferously objected to this offer. It was not that he had a personal grudge against John himself: he can have had little contact with his youngest sibling, now a child of barely six, who had been raised from early boyhood at the abbey of Fontevraud in Anjou.[29] The three castles, moreover, would in reality have remained in the Old King's control. Yet with Richard invested as count of Poitou and duke of Aquitaine, his second brother Geoffrey installed as duke of Brittany, and now his youngest brother endowed with a rich trans-Alpine domain, the Young King must have felt his position to be increasingly anomalous and unfair. In such circumstances, it deeply rankled that part of his future inheritance in Anjou was being granted to his young brother; far more importantly, John was being given these castles at a time when young Henry still had neither a realm nor even any demesne lands to call his own. He refused to countenance the proposed grant to John and responded by making an outright demand for either Normandy, England or Anjou to rule in his own right.[30] Henry's flat refusal was the final straw for the Young King; 'he declined to heed his father's wishes,' noted Roger of Howden, 'would not hear any talk of a peaceful settlement, and sought a suitable opportunity to withdraw from him'.[31] The Old King succeeded in finalizing the settlement with Humbert despite the younger Henry's protests, but an open rift had now developed between father and son.[32]

The Causes of Conflict

Conflict between fathers and sons was a widespread phenomenon in the political structures of medieval Europe.[33] Heirs reaching manhood and impatient for a share of power confronted fathers often still in their prime and unwilling to relinquish hard-won authority. In Anjou, for example, Fulk Nerra's son Geoffrey Martel had been involved in a serious quarrel with his father during the 1030s,[34] while Fulk le Réchin was opposed by his son Geoffrey Martel II in 1103.[35] Similarly in Normandy, a bitter dispute between William the Conqueror and his eldest son Robert Curthose had blighted the king's final decade and led to a fateful disruption of his plans for the succession to the Anglo-Norman realm. In open rebellion by 1079, Robert had gained the support of the king of France and inflicted a humiliating defeat on his father at the siege of Gerberoy. Despite a brief period of reconciliation, relations quickly broke down, and Robert was forced into exile until the Conqueror's death in 1087.[36]

After describing the Young King's desertion of his father in 1173, the learned Dean Ralph proceeded carefully to set out for the readers of his history numerous examples of earlier rebellious sons, drawn from the Old Testament and from the history of the Assyrian, Persian and other eastern empires, as well as from those of Rome and Byzantium. His catalogue also included many of the conflicts between rulers and their sons in the early medieval kingdoms of the west, including the Merovingian, Carolingian, Ottonian and Staufen dynasties, as well as more recent examples from Normandy, Anjou and Poitou.[37] Abbot Suger of St Denis had praised Louis VI for not upsetting 'his father's lordship over the kingdom by any sort of plot, as other young men customarily do', but the Capetians had not been been immune from such disputes.[38] That the French royal house, moreover, was less troubled than its Angevin rivals in the twelfth century by disputes between reigning kings and their sons was in part accidental. Louis VII, who acceded in 1137, had no sons until Philip's birth in 1165; the resulting age discrepancy between father and son ensured that Philip posed little threat to Louis' rule, and he only assumed the kingship after Louis' debilitating stroke in 1179.

The Young King's own confrontation with his father was in many ways closely analogous to that of Robert Curthose with William I a century earlier. Indeed, when writing his history of the Norman dukes for Henry II, the poet Wace evidently considered the conflict between King William and Robert still to be such a sensitive subject that he omitted all reference to it in his *Roman de Rou*, instead holding up Henry I's son William Aetheling as the model of a loyal son and virtuous prince.[39] Their quarrels stemmed from many of the same underlying tensions: a young man, who had been publicly recognized as the king's or duke's heir, was of age and ambitious to exercise some form of devolved rule, yet the father had refused to cede any authority to him, despite having both patrimony and extensive acquisitions within his control. Robert's frustrations had been fuelled by the fact that though he had been acknowledged by the magnates of Normandy before his father's expedition in 1066, and during his father's absence had been given a degree of authority in the duchy, reflected in his title as count, King William had subsequently resumed effective control of Normandy from 1067. Likewise robbed of inheriting Maine after the death of Margaret, its heiress to whom he had been betrothed, Robert had remained unmarried: without a wife or lands, he remained a 'youth' even into his thirties, unable to attain the status of a fully adult male or adequately to remunerate his companions.[40]

Young Henry, by contrast, was only eighteen in 1173, but despite being married to a daughter of the king of France he was still regarded as being under a form of tutelage, and had enjoyed nothing of his wife's dower. As Roger of Howden noted, 'he took it badly that his father did not wish to assign him any of his own lands where he could dwell with his queen'.[41] Not only had he received the homage and fealty of the magnates in 1162 and 1170, but he had been crowned and anointed a king of England. Such a dramatic elevation in status had naturally raised his expectation of devolved rule or active condominium. As William of Newburgh explained: 'When this prince grew to manhood, he desired to obtain the reality of kingship as well as the oath of allegiance and title of the same, at the least to reign jointly with his father.'[42] Contemporary charters, indeed, proclaimed exactly such co-rule. A deed issued on 18 February 1173 in the archbishop of York's court at Ripon was 'given in the nineteenth year of King Henry, grandson of Henry the Elder and in the third year of the reign of Henry the son of the same king'.[43]

Yet the reality was very different. Contemporaries recognized the anomalous position in which young Henry found himself, and even those unswervingly loyal to Henry II acknowledged that the Young King had been wronged. At the very outset of his poem, composed in the immediate aftermath of the great war of 1173–74, Jordan Fantosme summed up the paradoxical position of young Henry: 'A king without a kingdom is at a loss for something to do: at such a loss was the noble and gracious Young King'.[44] Referring to the coronation of 1170, Jordan boldly censures Henry II, implying that he must bear ultimate responsibility for the recent war: 'After this crowning and this transfer of power you took away from your son some of his authority, you thwarted his wishes so that he could not exercise power. Therein lay the seeds of a war with no love lost (*guerre senz amur*). God's curse be on it!'[45] Wace, in a preface added to the *Roman de Rou* in or shortly after 1174, similarly criticized a policy which could only lay the Young King open to the wiles of the Angevins' enemies: 'Through our new king, who cannot rule as king (*par nostre novel roi, qui roi ne peut regner*), they [the French] thought they could capture or lay waste the whole of Normandy; in order to do harm to the father, they gave the sons bad advice (*lez fils mesconseillierent*).'[46] If Henry was to crown his son, then he must give him the reality of authority to accompany this kingship.

The Young King's grievance at being denied any realm to rule directly was heightened by the fact that Angevin precedent and the practice of contemporary rulers alike afforded ready examples of the effective delegation of power to eldest sons by their fathers. Philip I of France (r. 1060–1108) had in his lifetime invested his son Louis (the future Louis VI) with the Vexin, Mantes and Pontoise.[47] In Anjou, Geoffrey Martel, son of Fulk le Réchin, had been associated in the government with his father from 1103 until his death in 1106, while Fulk V had associated Geoffrey le Bel with his rule.[48] In Flanders, Count Thierry had not only committed the rule of the county to his son Philip during his three visits to the Holy Land, but each time on his return had ruled jointly with his son.[49] In the empire, Frederick Barbarossa had had his eldest son Henry elected as king of the Romans in 1169, while earlier, in 1167, his younger son Frederick had been invested with the dukedom of Swabia, though both were still children.[50] Examples were equally ready to hand of rulers who, when they had augmented their rule by the acquisition of new territories, had given an eldest son lands and power. King Stephen had made his eldest son Eustace count in 1147 at the time of his knighting, possibly investing him with Boulogne.[51] King David of Scotland had granted his eldest son Henry co-rule of much of his greatly enlarged 'Scoto-Northumbrian realm': while David retained sole rule of 'Scotia', the heartlands of the kingdom of Scots between the Forth and the Spey, Earl Henry had exercised active condominium in Cumbria, Lothian and his earldom of Northumberland until his premature death in 1152.[52] In the Norman kingdom of Sicily – which like the Anglo-Norman *regnum* was an island kingdom with the extensive 'cross-channel' territories of Apulia and Calabria – King Roger II had made his eldest son Roger (d. 1148) duke of Apulia and increasingly from the later 1130s entrusted running of affairs on the mainland to him.[53] The example, however, which must have been foremost in the Young King's mind was that of Henry II himself, who when just eighteen had been granted rule of Normandy by his father Count Geoffrey in 1151, while the latter retained control of Anjou.

In the majority of these cases, the active association of sons in rule was a logical and pragmatic response to a ruler's expansion of his territorial power base, whether through marriage, inheritance, purchase or conquest. Direct governance of one or more such acquisitions provided valuable experience of rulership for sons, ensured the immediate presence of a member of the dynasty, and might act as a focus for regional loyalties. Concurrently, the father's status as superior was symbolized by his retaining direct control of the most prestigious element of his domains, whether ancestral lands or a kingdom. Crucially, by giving eldest sons not just titles but the real exercise of power, rulers such as Roger II, King Stephen and David I helped to ensure the loyalty of their sons and never had to face the consequences of creating deeply disaffected heirs. Yet despite setting so much store by the coronation of his eldest son, Henry II paradoxically baulked at conceding him direct territorial power.[54] It was one thing to designate the younger Henry heir to the patrimony, as he had at Montmirail in 1169, and to ensure his recognition as future overlord of the Angevin lands and their hegemony, but it was quite another to hand over any part of its heartlands. Henry II was in part guided by important strategic considerations: to grant Normandy to his eldest son would mean that the Old King would lose direct control of the vital link between England and his other continental domains, potentially – though by no means inevitably – hampering his effective rule. England, moreover, was the source of Henry II's greatest supply of revenue. As – if not more – powerful was the fear that any such grant would mean a diminution of his own status. Unlike Frederick Barbarossa, who could designate devolved rule to his sons Henry VI and Frederick yet continue to reign unchallenged as emperor, Henry II had no formal imperial authority – even if Guernes of Pont-Sainte-Maxence could refer to him in 1174 as 'king and emperor' (*reis e emperere*).[55] England was the source of his sovereign kingship, while by the same token Henry could scarcely give up direct control of Anjou, his own patrimony.[56]

Beyond such considerations, Henry, like William the Conqueror when faced with the request of Robert Curthose for a territory to rule, felt the dynast's profound reluctance to share power.[57] It was no coincidence that both rulers had come to power early and had not themselves experienced the frustrations endured by their own sons. If sons began to openly demand lands, moreover, such reluctance could only turn into outright refusal, for in such circumstances any concession would be seen as weakness, especially if sons had the backing of external opponents such as the king of France. As Jordan Fantosme noted of Henry's stance at the outset of the war in 1173, 'he would choose death rather than life before his son came to that power [the kingdom of England], so long as he could smite with sword and lance'.[58]

Such a view did not stand in isolation among rulers. How far Henry I would have faced pressure for devolved rule of England or Normandy from his only legitimate son William Aetheling as 'rex designatus' cannot be known, though the mounting threat of William Clito to Henry I's control of Normandy goes far to explain the apparent solidarity between father and son before Aetheling's premature death aged only seventeen in the wreck of the White Ship. More certain, however, is that despite having subsequently worked so hard to secure the allegiance of the Anglo-Norman barons to his daughter

Matilda and her Angevin husband, Geoffrey le Bel, it was Henry I himself who dealt their chances of securing the succession on his death a grave blow by refusing to countenance their establishment of effective power bases in England and Normandy during his own lifetime.[59] Indeed, a dispute over control of key castles had caused an open rift between the king and his son-in-law that was ongoing at the time of Henry I's death, giving Stephen another major advantage in his race for the throne.[60] Nor was young Henry alone in being an anointed king deprived of actual power by a parent jealous of retaining full control. In the Latin kingdom of Jerusalem, Fulk V's widow Queen Melisende had had her son Baldwin III crowned in 1143, but resisted his assumption of full kingship long after he had attained his majority in 1145. Baldwin's mounting frustration reached a climax in 1152, when he demanded that Fulcher, patriarch of Jerusalem, crown him in the church of the Holy Sepulchre without his mother being present. When Fulcher refused, the young man processed through the city adorned with a laurel wreath in place of the crown which had been withheld from him.[61]

Yet while queen mothers might retain a considerable degree of authority once their sons had assumed full rule, as the reigns of Richard I and Louis IX demonstrate, the investiture of an eldest son with significant powers in the lifetime of his father might pose a very real threat to that ruler's authority and become a potent rallying point for disaffected nobles.[62] If there were instances of sons loyally enjoying condominium with their fathers, there were also alarming examples of fathers being challenged, defeated and even deposed by sons impatient for rule. Henry II was all too well aware of the fate of Emperor Henry IV of Germany (1056–1106), who had faced an attempt by his son Henry, whom Otto of Freising refers to as 'Henry the Younger', to supplant him.[63] In 1105, the emperor had been captured and forced to surrender the imperial regalia, and, though he subsequently rallied his forces and defeated his son's army outside Liège, Henry IV died before he could fully regain power.[64] As Henry V, this rebellious son was to become the first husband of Matilda, Henry II's mother.[65] For the Old King, it was an uncomfortably close precedent.

'Gent jofne e salvage': Pressures from within the Household

The underlying tensions between father and son were exacerbated by pressure from others with vested interests. A young prince's household companions, hungry for lands or heiresses, were often all too eager to pressure their lord into making demands for territories from which they could be suitably rewarded. Orderic had laid much of the blame for Robert's bitter quarrel with his father on such companions, and has the Conqueror warn his son against the seditious *iuvenes* who urged him to make unjustified demands on his father for their own profit.[66] Similarly, in the late 1170s the newly knighted Arnold of Ardres quarrelled with his father, the count of Guines, over knights he retained in his household, especially one prominent advisor, Philip of Montgardin, who repeatedly 'urged Arnold to ask and beg his father for Ardres and the properties that belonged to him through his mother's side'.[67] That young Henry was similarly influenced by companions in his *mesnie* is indicated by the fact that in late February 1173 Henry II expelled some individuals he regarded as troublemakers from his son's household, especially Hasculf of St Hilaire 'and other young knights (*alios equites juniores*)'.[68] Henry's purge of his son's household, however, only served to underline the Young King's dependence and subordinate status, and to fuel his resentment.[69] In such circumstances, it was all too easy for young firebrands to urge force as a means of obtaining rights unjustly withheld. In 1173, Jordan Fantosme believed that at William the Lion's court it was just such 'young and untutored' knights (*ces chevaliers, gent jofne e salvage*) – youthful hotheads with little to lose and much to gain – who urged the Scottish king to go to war against Henry II in support of the Young King.[70]

Even though he himself was not dismissed in 1173, William Marshal was, as a leading figure in the Young King's *mesnie*, likely to have been among those relentlessly importuning young Henry for advancement. His propensity to continually badger for reward is strikingly illustrated some years later in a writ of Henry II promising William the honour of Châteauroux in return for his military support in 1188, with the king adding wryly that 'you have ever so often moaned to me that I have bestowed on you a small fee'.[71] The *History of William Marshal* naturally makes no mention of such actions, but disingenuously lays the blame for the quarrel between father and son on the malice of some of Henry II's own followers. 'These tale-bearers *(losengers)*, these vicious men, these base scoundrels', it claimed, had stirred the Old King up against some of young Henry's tutors, whom they accused of encouraging the Young King's ruinously lavish expenditure. Misled by them, Henry II supposedly instructed the Young King to 'make out as best he could, for never more would he use any of his resources to make generous gifts, since the life his son led was far too lavish'.[72] Amazed by his father's reaction, the Young King inclined to those 'who advised him to turn against his father, and to use force to reduce him, against his will, to doing all his son's desires and wishes'.[73] Though this story may perhaps reflect the view from within the Young King's *mesnie*, it was transparently an attempt to shift the blame for the ensuing rebellion from Young Henry – and from his closest *familiaris*, William Marshal.

William of Newburgh, by contrast, believed that young Henry felt his father was being too parsimonious: 'he was highly indignant because his father had but sparingly supplied him with money to meet the expenses of his royal state'.[74] It may be that Henry II and his son disagreed about what constituted a suitable income, and certainly the question of revenue and a young lord's propensity for reckless spending were common sources of tension between fathers and sons. In the late 1170s or early 1180s, Arnold of Ardres, reconciled with his father after a quarrel over his inheritance, now obeyed him, 'except that he is said to have had more knightly companions than his father, and to have made more lavish expenditures than the extent of his possessions demanded, since he persisted in giving larger gifts than his father's advice taught or recommended'. 'Indeed,' noted Lambert, 'he gave more than he owned or kept for himself.'[75] Nevertheless, Henry II was to show himself consistently generous in the subsequent financial settlements he would offer his son, and his attitude to the Young King's activities on the tourneying circuit between 1176 and 1182 strongly suggests that the Old King had little objection to his son's extravagant lifestyle and open-handed giving.

The issue at stake, however, was about far more than mere revenue: it was a matter of status, honour and authority.[76] In describing the quarrel of 1173, the chronicler of the *Brut y Tywysogion* recognized the wider problem:

> In the meantime, whilst the king of England, Henry the Elder was staying beyond the sea, Henry the Younger, his son, came to him to ask him what he might do or what he ought to do after his being ordained new king. For although he was king with many knights under him, yet he had no means by which he could reward them, unless he obtained it from his father. And that was in Lent. And his father replied that he would give him for expenses twenty pounds daily of the money of that land. And the son, when he heard that, said that he had never heard of a king being a paid servant, and that he would not be such.[77]

The *Brut* here closely echoes the words of the Young King himself in a letter of justification sent to Pope Alexander III shortly after the outbreak of the war against his father.[78] Setting out a range of grievances, young Henry complained that though he had been crowned, against his own will, by his father, Henry II had nonetheless withheld power from him. As a result, young Henry was unable to protect the oppressed and exercise justice. Henry II, moreover, had imposed his own counsellors on his son, and had even removed members of young Henry's household in whom he trusted.[79] Such actions had damaged the Young King's honour, for they had been carried out 'quasi in contemptum nostrum et ignominiam'.[80] 'We remain silent now as then,' he added, 'about how, having taken away all my jurisdiction, he made a mercenary of a king and of his own son (*de rege et filio stipendiarium faceret*).'[81] Here, the Young King's language is strikingly similar to the remark that Orderic Vitalis puts into the mouth of Robert Curthose during his bitter dispute with his father William the Conqueror, *c*.1078, which descended into open rebellion. When Robert's request to be given rule of Normandy under his father's lordship was refused, he angrily retorted:

> I am not prepared to be your hireling (*mercennarius tuus*) for ever. I want at long last to have property of my own, so that I can give proper wages to my own dependants (*famulantes*). I ask you therefore to grant me legal control of the duchy, so that, just as you rule over the kingdom of England, I, under your rule, may rule over the duchy of Normandy.[82]

For young Henry, the fact that a crowned and anointed king, married to the daughter of the king of France, was reduced to little more than a pensioner on his father's payroll was still more intolerable. It was, he said, 'shameful for a consecrated king to have to beg bread from others'.[83]

Beyond the ambitious young knights of his household, there were other, more dangerous forces at work to pit son against father. The summit of 1173, which marked so clear a demonstration of Henry II's power, and the Maurienne agreement that envisaged it extending yet further, was the catalyst to set in motion the conspiracy which had been gradually forming since 1171.[84] Howden recorded the belief that the Young King had been put up to making his demand for England, Normandy or Anjou by King Louis and those magnates who hated Henry II, and that the authors of the plot were Louis and, 'so it was said by certain people', Queen Eleanor and her uncle Ralph, lord of Faye-la-Vineuse in Anjou.[85] A Poitevin, Ralph had as seneschal of the Saintonge gained an evil reputation as an oppressor and despoiler of church lands, not least those of the monks of St Radegonde in Poitiers and the priory of Oléron.[86] As early as 1165, John, bishop of Poitiers, had warned the exiled Thomas Becket that he could expect no aid from Queen Eleanor, then based at Angers and acting as regent during the king's absence in England, 'since she relies entirely on Ralph de Faie'. And, he added darkly, 'every day many tendencies come to light which make it possible to believe that there is truth in the dishonourable tale we remember mentioning elsewhere'.[87] The Tours chronicler also names Hugh of Sainte-Maure as one who, together with Ralph, had stirred up Eleanor against Henry II.[88] Ralph appears in Henry II's treaty with Humbert of Maurienne as one of the guarantors for the king, so, like Eleanor, he was certainly on hand to fuel the Young King's sense of grievance.[89] As Matthew Paris later noted, Eleanor, Hugh and Ralph incited young Henry to rebellion by telling him, 'It is not fitting that a king, whosoever he may be, should be seen [as] unable to exercise in his kingdom the power he has a right to'.[90] Not only that, but as William of Newburgh believed, 'certain persons indeed whispered in his ear that he ought now by rights to reign alone, for at his coronation his father's reign had, as it were, ceased'.[91]

A Great Escape

It was Raymond V who warned Henry that his wife and sons were plotting against him. On the count's advice, Henry II left the town with a small escort, as if he was going hunting, but being careful to take his eldest son and his companions with him. He then headed swiftly for Normandy, sending orders to fortify his towns and castles.[92] By now, the Angevin court was riven with mutual suspicions. The Melrose Chronicle recorded the belief that the Old King had even considered keeping his son in confinement: 'The father had intended to capture his son, and to put him in a sure and close place of custody, so at least common report goes.'[93] That young Henry believed, or was encouraged to believe, that this was his father's plan makes his next move more explicable, for the situation was soon to change dramatically.

When the royal entourage reached the great fortress of Chinon, it halted for the night.[94] But, unbeknown to his father, the Young King had resolved to make a daring escape. Somehow, among the bustle of the court as it settled into its lodgings, he and his personal retinue managed to give the slip to Henry II's men and those of his own household appointed by his father. A version of the story which reached Wales told how the Young King had attempted to borrow money from the burgesses of Chinon but was thwarted by his father's agents, who secretly forbade the citizens to make a loan. Then, when some of his father's counsellors were sent 'to keep friendly watch lest his son should go anywhere thence', young Henry made merry with them till they were drunk on fine wine, before stealing away.[95] The excuse of carousing in the town with his companions would certainly have freed young Henry and his *mesnie* from the confines of the fortress. By whatever means it had been achieved, however, it was a bold escapade, binding together Henry and his young companions in a shared sense of danger and purpose. Riding hard through the night, and almost certainly taking spare horses with them, they crossed the Loire and headed due north, passing Le Mans and continuing on until they reached Alençon – a journey of nearly 100 miles. Here they could be assured of welcome, as Count John of Sées was to be one of young Henry's followers in the ensuing rebellion.[96]

Knowing that his father was bound to pursue him, the Young King could not tarry. The fact that he initially pressed on further into Normandy, striking north-west as far as Argentan, may suggest that his initial plan had been to head for the coast and thence to England, where some of his supporters were at this time.[97] Had they aimed from the start to reach the Île-de-France, or the friendly territory of the count of Blois, the fugitives could have taken a much more direct route by riding north-east towards Vendôme, and thence via Châteaudun to Chartres.[98] Any attempt to cross the Channel, however, risked the vagaries of wind and tide, and the Young King could not have been sure of the loyalty of sailors or of those guarding the ports of Normandy or England. A delay of only a day or so and all might be lost, for his father was hot on his heels. As soon as King Henry had learned of young Henry's flight, he set off in pursuit, taking only a small retinue and frequently changing horses. He reached Alençon the night the fugitives had gained Argentan, nearly twenty-five miles further north, but the Young King and his companions had kept this advantage by mounting again at cockcrow.[99] From Argentan they swung back south-east, riding via Mortagne, with the safe conduct of Rotrou, count of Perche, who may well have been in on the initial conspiracy.[100] From thence it was an easy stage to Chartres, where they knew Louis VII was in residence, and by night-fall they were safe within the Capetian heartlands.[101]

The Young King had escaped from his father's power. It soon became clear, however, that his precipitous flight had badly wrong-footed several of his fellow conspirators, who as yet were not prepared for open action against Henry II. Robert, earl of Leicester, had no time to garrison Breteuil, his principal Norman castle, and was forced to flee to France, abandoning it to Henry II's forces.[102] His English estates were confiscated, and their revenues accounted for at the Exchequer.[103] Similarly, his kinsman Robert, count of Meulan, quickly followed young Henry to France, also leaving his castles without garrisons, and the Old King moved swiftly to occupy them.[104] William de Tancarville found himself on the wrong side of the Channel, but somehow he managed to leave England and join the Young King's cause. Likewise Hugh, earl of Chester, was just returning from a pilgrimage to St James at Compostella, but immediately joined Young Henry in France, as did William Patrick senior, together with his three sons, 'and many others of lesser name'.[105] Clearly, these men regarded themselves as irrevocably committed to young Henry's rebellion: dissimulation was no longer an option. Once their defection was known, Henry II had their houses, parks and woods destroyed, both as punishment and as a warning to others contemplating similar desertion.[106] The most striking indication of the unplanned nature of the Young King's escape, however, is that he had not been able to send his wife Margaret to the safety of her father at the Capetian court. Instead, she now became Henry II's hostage in all but name, joining her sister Alice in the Old King's custody.[107] Only the knowledge that Henry II had got wind of the conspiracy, and a deep-seated fear that his father would indeed arrest and imprison him, can have led the Young King to set in motion so prematurely an insurrection that had been long in gestation but was not yet ripe for action.

A Household Divided

The Young King's flight had painfully exposed the divisions within his own household. He had left behind at Chinon those officials who had been his father's appointees, including his chancellor, Richard Barre, Ailward his chamberlain, his chaplain Walter of Coutances, William Blund, his usher, and a number of other retainers, together with his baggage train of wagons and sumpter horses carrying his equipment. These men now returned to Henry II, and Barre surrendered to him the Young King's great seal, which the Old King ordered to be securely guarded.[108] Yet in a gesture of magnanimity and in the hope of yet achieving a reconciliation with his son, Henry II ordered these *familiares* to return to his son, and sent with them precious gifts, including silver plate, fine horses and raiment.[109] Yet what young Henry desired was not such trappings, but real authority. He accordingly demanded of the men returning to him that they swear an oath of fidelity to him against his father. Hitherto, all acts of homage and fealty to young Henry before and after his coronation had been made, properly enough, with a saving clause reserving faith to his father. Now the two monarchs were at odds, however, the Young King was determined to extract an unconditional pledge of loyalty. It was a mark of his deep frustration, but it was not good lordship: it placed Richard Barre and his companions, who owed their posts to Henry II, in an impossible position. Henry II's own demands for absolute and unreserved allegiance from Becket's clerks after the archbishop's fall from grace in 1164 had created a similar crisis of loyalty.[110] Unsurprisingly, Richard Barre and his colleagues refused such an oath, whereupon the Young King dismissed them, and any others who would not swear, and they returned to Henry II's service.[111]

For these officials, placement in the household of the man who would soon himself be ruler of the Angevin empire had been a major opportunity, holding out the prospect of future promotion and influence. Now such hopes of preferment had been cut short by the rift between father and son. Conscious of this and realizing that Barre's support for his old master had cost him the favour of the Young King, Henry II rewarded him with the archdeaconry of Lisieux. The appointment of Walter of Coutances as archdeacon of Oxford was probably a similar compensation.[112] By contrast Solomon the serjeant, who had been transferred to young Henry's household from that of his uncle William FitzEmpress, joined the Young King in rebellion, as did Eudo and William FitzErneis, and Robert de Buissum, all of whom had attested Earl William's charters.[113]

Having failed to prevent his son's flight to France, Henry II's immediate reaction had been to ensure that the defences of Gisors, the strategic key to the Vexin, were in good order. He then toured the duchy's other frontier defences, strengthening and revictualling his castles.[114] The open and immediate defection of a number of important Norman lords to the Young King was a troubling signal of deep disaffection in the duchy, and Henry II knew that an attack by Louis on Normandy could only be a matter of time. In an adroit move, Henry entrusted the defence of Gisors to Earl Richard de Clare, known as 'Strongbow', whose successes in Ireland had prompted the royal expedition of 1171; he thereby placed experienced marcher warriors in this crucial frontier fortress, while concomitantly removing the opportunity for these men to foment rebellion in Ireland to cast off Henry II's newly consolidated lordship there.[115] Henry also was under no illusion about the probable impact of the actions of his eldest son on the stability of his other territories: he informed his castellans in Anjou, Brittany, Aquitaine and England of the situation, ordering them to strengthen their castles and be on their guard. No records survive for these measures on the continent, but in England the Pipe Rolls record expenditure on at least forty-four castles across the kingdom.[116]

'The Eagle of the Broken Covenant': The Role of Eleanor of Aquitaine

Despite these preparations, Henry failed to anticipate treachery much closer to home.[117] It is unclear to what extent, if at all, Henry had been aware of Eleanor's role in the intrigues against him before the summit at Limoges in February 1173, when he seemingly was first warned of his wife's complicity. Even then, however, he took no pre-emptive measures but left Eleanor behind in Aquitaine at liberty with their younger sons Richard and Geoffrey while he headed north from Limoges with the Young King. Past experience must have led him to regard Louis as the principal troublemaker, and as long as Henry had control of the Young King he may have judged Eleanor's position to be too weak to be a serious threat. If so, it was a serious miscalculation. William of Newburgh recorded the rumour that the Young King himself had secretly travelled to Aquitaine and, with Eleanor's connivance, brought Richard and Geoffrey back to the Capetian court, for he 'was taught by the French to believe that the men of Aquitaine might be won over more easily to his side through Richard, and the Bretons similarly through Geoffrey'.[118] It seems improbable, however, that

Louis would have risked young Henry's capture on so dangerous a mission or even that such a clandestine journey would have been feasible in the wake of his flight from Chinon. It is far more likely that, as Roger of Howden noted, it was Eleanor herself who sent Richard and Geoffrey to join their elder brother, once the Young King was safely at the Capetian court.[119]

Contemporaries were quick to see in the rebellious Eleanor 'the eagle of the broken covenant' foretold in the 'Prophecies of Merlin'.[120] It has been suggested that Eleanor's growing alienation from Henry after 1168 helped to detach her sons from him, so that by their adolescence 'they lacked any loyalty to Henry'.[121] This is possible, but in reality little is known about young Henry's relationship with his mother, either before or after the rebellion of 1173–74.[122] Nevertheless, both to sympathizers in Aquitaine and to more hostile observers at Henry II's court, it seemed evident that Eleanor wielded a decisive influence over her sons. Writing after her subsequent capture, Richard the Poitevin could lament: 'Tell me, two-headed eagle, where were you when your eaglets, fluttering from the nest, boldly unsheathed their talons against the King from the North? For it was you – so we hear – who urged them to bring their father down.'[123] Earlier, in a letter to the queen that seems to have been written very soon after the outbreak of the uprising, Archbishop Rotrou of Rouen deplored the fact that she had left her husband and had 'opened the way for the lord king's, and your own, children to rise up against their father ... You alone are now the guilty one, but your actions will result in ruin for all in the kingdom.'[124] Nevertheless, Rotrou assured her that an amnesty was still possible, and urged her to return to her lord and husband:

> So before worse befall, return with your sons to the husband whom you should live with and obey. If you do return to him, no suspicion will fall on either you or your sons. We are quite sure that the King will offer you affection and full and utter safety. Exhort your sons, I pray you, to be obedient and devoted to their father: he has been through so much anxiety on their behalf, so many difficult situations, so much labour ... You are one of our flock, as is your husband, but we cannot ignore the demands of justice: either you come back to your husband or we shall be obliged by canon law to lay upon you the censure of the Church. We say that reluctantly, but reluctantly, in tears and in anguish, we shall do it, if you fail to come to a better mind.[125]

Eleanor returned neither to Henry II, nor to the court of her ex-husband to join her sons, but remained in Aquitaine, assisted by Ralph de Faye, to orchestrate the rebellion.

The queen needed to steer a careful course between the competing ambitions of her sons: the sixteen-year-old Richard may himself have been deeply resentful of the Young King's acceptance of Raymond's homage for Toulouse. Where she could unite them in common cause against Henry II was in their shared frustration at being denied real power by their father. Only the year previously, Richard had been invested with the county of Poitou and the duchy of Aquitaine, but as yet enjoyed no actual rule.[126] Similarly, although Geoffrey had been betrothed to Constance since 1166, the marriage itself had not yet taken place, even though Duke Conan had died in 1171, while the duchy itself was still run by Henry II's agents, and Geoffrey's authority remained nominal. Not only that, but following Conan's demise Henry II had kept in his own hands the barony of Tréguier and the great honour of Richmond which Geoffrey could regard as his rightful inheritance.[127] Whatever other justifications the queen put forward for rebellion, Eleanor must have won Richard and Geoffrey over to the Young King's cause by promises of effective power.

Unlike the revolt of sons against their fathers, there were few precedents for queens actively fomenting insurrection against their own husbands.[128] Ralph of Diss was right in regarding Eleanor's deep involvement in the unfolding war as 'something great, new, and unheard of'. It was a disaster that had been ominously heralded by a great burst of thunder heard on Christmas night 1172, not only in Ireland and England but in the whole of France – a 'sudden, horrible phenomenon'.[129] Yet the reasons for Eleanor's deep hostility to her husband by the early 1170s remain elusive. Contemporary chroniclers clearly regarded the matter as a dangerous subject; if they mentioned her involvement at all, it was qualified as being reported as hearsay, and none ventured to proffer any explanation for Eleanor's active aggression.[130] The Melrose chronicler, for example, speaking of the Young King's flight, noted cautiously that 'it is said that he did this by the advice of his mother, but of this we are ignorant; let her see to it and let Him judge'.[131] Later legend would make much of Eleanor's deep hatred and jealousy of Rosamund Clifford, Henry II's beloved and beautiful mistress, but Jean Flori has warned against underplaying the reaction of noble women to their husband's infidelities, and suggests that Eleanor may have been genuinely afraid of being supplanted as queen.[132] Yet how far her resentment of Rosamund or of Henry II's earlier and numerous liaisons played a driving force in her rebellion is now impossible to recover.[133] It seems very likely that Eleanor felt personally alienated by Henry's unconcealed passion for Rosamund, but it would have been quite exceptional to have gone to war over her husband's infidelities. Nor was Eleanor herself above suspicion, being widely rumoured to have conducted her own adulterous affairs.[134]

It is more likely that the real source of tension between Eleanor and her husband was the governance and status of Aquitaine, where she may have felt that her authority was increasingly marginalized by Henry's assertion of power.[135] In the duchy itself, Eleanor was able to harness the growing fears of the seemingly inexorable expansion of Angevin power. During the earlier rebellion of 1168–69, the chronicler Richard the Poitevin had expressed joy at the assertion of Aquitaine's independence from the oppressive rule of Henry II: 'Be glad, Aquitaine! Rejoice, Poitou! For the King of the North's sceptre is departing from you!'[136] Gerald of Wales believed Eleanor to be plotting by 1172, but what may have galvanized her into drastic action was the recent concordat at Limoges, when Raymond V had performed homage for Toulouse not only to Henry II and to Richard, as duke of Aquitaine, but also to the Young King. Henry II had exercised authority in Aquitaine in right of his marriage to its duchess, and had in 1159 pressed Eleanor's claims, inherited from her grandmother Philippa, to the overlordship of Toulouse. Yet if now young Henry, as the future ruler of England, Normandy and Anjou, was in turn to claim hegemony over it, Eleanor may have feared that Aquitaine itself would be swallowed up in a greater Anglo-Norman empire.[137] Raymond's submission had certainly prompted Ermengard, the spirited countess of Narbonne, forthrightly to rebuke Louis VII for his failure to challenge Henry's dominance in the Midi, as he had done with some success in 1159. Sending him 'greetings and the courage of Charlemagne', she continued:

My fellow countrymen and I are much saddened to see our region, which the vigour of the kings of the Franks adorned with liberty, at risk – through your absence, not to say your fault – of coming under the dominion of a stranger, a foreigner who has not the smallest right over us. Do not be angered, my dear lord, by my bold words. If I speak thus, it is because I am a vassal especially devoted to your crown, and because I suffer extremely when I see its power declining. It is not only the loss of Toulouse that is involved, but that of our whole country from the Garonne to the Rhône, which our enemies boast they will subjugate.[138]

Though this criticism must have stung Louis, he knew it to be no more than the truth. Henry II had accepted the homage of Raymond of Toulouse in defiance of Louis' own claims of overlordship, as he himself angrily complained to Henry.[139] Young Henry's acceptance of Raymond's homage, moreover, went against the tenor of the Treaty of Montmirail, in which Louis had attempted to ensure the detachment of Aquitaine from direct Angevin lordship.[140] Capetian influence in the region seemed in full retreat, while that of Anjou seemed to have been increased still further by the Maurienne agreement.[141] The arch-bishop of Narbonne was being overly alarmist in warning Louis that Henry was even planning to invade France, but it was clear to Louis that a counterstroke against Plantagenet expansion was urgently needed, before it was too late.[142] Eleanor's desire to safeguard the autonomy of Aquitaine from the 'King of the North' thus dovetailed with the interests of her former husband. Henry II was a formidable opponent, commanding, as Wace noted, 'so much land and so many towns that he can make Louis and his men tremble'.[143] Yet the rift between him and his wife and sons, and the particular disaffection of Young Henry, gave Louis an unparalleled opportunity to break the power of the Angevin colossus.

Forging an Alliance

Louis VII had naturally welcomed the Young King and his brothers with open arms, and quickly convened a great council of his magnates at Paris.[144] To bind the allies in their undertaking against Henry II, Louis swore on the Gospels that he would aid the Young King and his brothers with all his power against their father, and support young Henry's war to gain the kingdom of England.[145] In turn, the Young King, Richard and Geoffrey swore that they would not withdraw from the king of France or make peace with their father without the consent of Louis and his barons. Having received this assurance on oath, the French nobles took the same oath as King Louis to uphold the sons in their war.[146] As was customary at such councils of war, boasts and high vaunts were made of actions that would bring Henry II low.[147]

An embassy sent by Henry II to treat for peace, headed by Archbishop Rotrou and Arnulf of Lisieux, met with an icy reception: the ambassadors reported that although Louis had listened to their delegation, he had refused to acknowledge King Henry's salutation.[148] Writing considerably later, but with access to good information on the events of 1173–74, William of Newburgh painted a dramatic scene of the French king's response:

> Having discovered his son's treachery and knowing whither he had fled, his father sent to the king of France certain eminent men who in pacific terms demanded the return of the son by paternal right, and promised that if anything should appear to require amendment in respect of his son, it should be speedily rectified with the advice of the French king. At these words, the king of France asked, 'Who is it that sends such a message to me?' They replied, 'The king of England'. 'It is false', he replied, 'behold! The king of England is here present, and he sends no message to me

through you. But even if you still call king the father who was formerly king of England, know that he, as king, is dead. And though he may still act as king, this shall be speedily remedied, for he resigned his kingdom to his son, as all the world bears witness.'[149]

As a member of a dynasty long accustomed to associative coronation, which did nothing to harm the authority of the reigning monarch, Louis knew this to be an outrageous claim. Yet it played upon the novelty of crowning an heir in the father's lifetime in England, and exploited real uncertainty about Henry II's subsequent position. Louis also set out his *casus belli* against Henry, which, he told the legation, antedated the Young King's arrival in Chartres: Henry had repeatedly broken sworn agreements; he had accepted the homage of Raymond of Toulouse; and the Angevin's attempts to stretch his power from the Rhône to the Alps had earned Louis the odium of his own subjects who had fallen under Henry's sway. They were now at war, and Louis would not make peace with Henry II without the consent of his sons or of Queen Eleanor.[150]

Louis had assembled a formidable coalition to aid the Young King.[151] Among the greatest French lords were his own brother Robert, count of Dreux, his brothers-in-law, Henry, count of Champagne, Theobald, count of Blois, and Stephen, count of Sancerre, together with Philip, count of Flanders, and his brother Matthew, count of Boulogne. The Young King's new allies were expecting major territorial concessions in return for their support.[152] As Henry II now had custody of the seal the Young King had received after his coronation in 1170, Louis had immediately ordered a new one to be made for him, and it was with this that young Henry now sealed charters making extensive grants.[153] He granted Theobald of Blois revenue of 500 *livres angevins*, the strategically important castle of Amboise, situated between Tours and Blois, and all the rights he claimed in the Touraine.[154] A nephew of King Stephen, Theobald had long been an enemy of Henry II, and his demands reflected the continuing struggle between the houses of Blois and Anjou for control of Tours and the central Loire valley.[155] The chroniclers record no grants by the Young King to Theobald's brother Henry of Champagne, who brought support primarily in his role as Louis VII's vassal, but the potential of his military resources had been revealed only the previous year in the *Feoda Campanie*, a survey of fiefs and of service owed to the count, probably modelled directly on Henry II's own 1172 inquest in Normandy.[156]

After Louis himself, young Henry's most powerful supporter was his kinsman Philip of Flanders, or 'Philip the Warrior', as Jordan Fantosme calls him.[157] His marriage to Elizabeth of Vermandois in 1164 had brought him control of that important county, while trade and the burgeoning urban economies of the Flemish towns made him one of the wealthiest of the territorial princes of France. Though Count Thierry had renewed the Anglo-Flemish treaty in 1163, Philip's support for the Angevins was more equivocal. He had played an important role as a mediator in the dispute with Becket, but by 1168 Philip had openly sided with Louis in his war against Henry II.[158] Now in 1173 he performed homage to the Young King and swore fealty to him, receiving in return a promise of the county of Kent, and its two principal castles of Rochester and Dover, which reflected the holdings acquired by William of Ypres, King Stephen's leading Flemish supporter.[159] In addition, Philip was to receive an annual sum of £1,000 from English revenues. As this was the sum stipulated in the earlier Anglo-Flemish treaties of 1101 and 1163, it seems likely that the Young King was attempting to renew this money fief in his capacity as king of England and thereby secure for himself the single most important source of stipendiary knights in north-west Europe. Philip, as William of Newburgh noted, was 'a man of great resources and boundless boastfulness by reason of his confidence in the countless and warlike people whom he governed'.[160]

Philip, moreover, controlled the key Channel ports of Wissant and Gravelines, from which an invasion of England might be launched.[161] In 1160, his brother Matthew had married King Stephen's daughter Matilda, who brought him not only the county of Boulogne, with control of its powerful fleet, but also the lands held by the counts in England and a strong claim to the county of Mortain.[162] The potential danger posed by the Boulonnais fleet had already been made plain in 1167 when, during the war between Henry and Louis, Count Matthew had threatened to invade England with a fleet carrying Flemish soldiers, in order to pursue his claims.[163] Though Henry II had promised the count a large money fief in return for quittance of these territorial claims, the Young King's rebellion presented Matthew with a great opportunity to press again his full demands: he performed homage to the younger Henry for his county of Boulogne, and was granted the county of Mortain in Normandy, the soke of Kirkton in Lindsey, and the honor of Eye.[164]

The Young King's messengers had also been soliciting the aid of William the Lion, king of Scots. When in 1157 Henry II had forced Malcolm IV to cede the northern counties of England, William the Lion had been compelled to give up the earldom of Northumberland, which he had inherited from his father, Earl Henry.[165] In compensation, Malcolm received back the earldom of Huntingdon and William was granted the substantial lordship of Tynedale, held as a fief from the English king.[166] William, however, remained aggrieved and a burning desire both to regain his father's earldom of Northumberland

and to rebuild David I's great 'Scotto-Northumbrian realm' became a dominant factor in his relationship with the Angevin kings.[167] By July 1168 he had
openly sided with Louis VII, offering him aid and hostages.[168] The appearance
of William and his younger brother David at the English court and at the
Young King's coronation suggests that by 1170 an entente with Henry II had
been established, but the deteriorating relationship between Henry II and his
son in 1173 and the formation of a powerful coalition of Angevin enemies was
an opportunity that William found hard to resist.[169] He was nevertheless reluctant to enter a war against this powerful southern neighbour without a prior
demand for the restoration of Cumbria and the earldom of Northumberland.[170]
Envoys sent to Henry II in Normandy, however, met with a flat refusal: Henry
would not grant William's demands in such circumstances, but rather would
wait to see if William acted loyally, thereby holding out the prospect of
restoring to him all or part of his lordship if he supported Henry II against his
son. Henry's attempt to divide the Scottish royal house by summoning Earl
David and offering him lands in return for his service did not succeed, but
William's bluff had been called.[171] In a bitterly divided council, a strong lobby
of younger knights prevailed in their demands for war over wiser heads such as
Bishop Ingelram of Glasgow and Waltheof, earl of Dunbar.[172] Messengers
were sent to Paris, to accept the Young King's offer and to request military aid
from Count Philip, who duly dispatched Flemish troops to assist King William
in a planned summer offensive.[173]

The Young King's Baronial Supporters

In addition to these powerful external allies, the Young King could count on
the ready support of disaffected elements within the regional aristocracies of
the Angevin lands. A number of nobles were already inveterate opponents of
Henry II. In Poitou, where memories of the bitter campaigns of 1167–68 were
still fresh, Guy and Geoffrey de Lusignan, Geoffrey de Rancon, William
count of Angoulême, and the lord of Parthenay were once more among the
leading rebels. They were now joined by a significant number of other leading
Poitevin lords, including Joscelin de Mauléon, Thomas of Coulonces, William
de Chauvigny, Charles de Rochefort and two of the greatest magnates of
northern Poitou, Peter de Montrabei, lord of Preuilly, and Robert de Blé, who
held the stronghold of Champigny-sur-Veude.[174] Some, however, remained
loyal to the Old King, notably Aimar viscount of Limoges, whose marriage to
Sarah, daughter of Earl Reginald of Cornwall, led him fully to expect a rich
inheritance.[175] Despite Eleanor's own deep involvement in fomenting rebellion, very little can be gleaned concerning the course of the risings further

south, though it has been argued that the Aquitanian nobility regarded the war as an opportunity more to prosecute local quarrels than to fight primarily for the Young King's cause.[176] In Brittany, disaffected elements of the nobility were rallied by Ralph of Fougères, a long-standing opponent of Plantagenet pretensions to control of the duchy, and Eudo de Porhoët, who claimed for himself the title of duke of Brittany, 'Dei gratia'.[177] Attacks from these groups threatened western Normandy, Anjou and the Saintonge, while in turn Brittany served as a refuge for rebels from Henry II's other continental territories.[178] In Maine, there had already been stirrings of revolt in 1166 and 1168, provoked in large part by Henry II's policy of appropriating key castles along the marches of Normandy, while some of the dissident Manceaux lords had links to the rebels in Brittany.[179] In the Touraine, there was a notable concentration of rebel castles in the valleys of the Vienne and Creuse.[180] Their proximity to Blois, the principal fortress of Henry II's enemy Count Theobald, rendered this flank of the Angevin heartlands vulnerable and might leave Tours itself – the strategic key of the central Loire – open to attack.[181]

Little is known of the pattern of rebellion within Anjou itself, but it has been suggested that Henry II's absences from the province, and the shift of the dynasty's political focus away from the comital heartland, had weakened ties of affiliation between the local nobility and the count; few Angevins profited from Henry's greater conglomeration of lands and powers, and only the office of seneschal provided an aristocracy primarily focused on local affairs with any serious contact with comital government and the wider concerns of the empire.[182] In Anjou itself, moreover, the power of the count was far more circumscribed than that enjoyed by Henry II as duke of Normandy or as king of England. Despite efforts to build up a loyal cadre of officials raised from more minor families, comital demesne remained dispersed, the efficacy of local administration was restricted to areas formed around key comital castles, and the local nobility remained stubbornly autonomous.[183] Henry had inherited a tradition of sporadic rebellions of influential castellan families, against which his father Geoffrey had contended with mixed success. These lords may have felt increasingly excluded by 'an extended kin-group at the heart of the Angevin administration' which dominated key positions in the county over several generations, while John of Marmoutier was doubtless voicing wider resentment when he complained of the rapacity and corruption of local prévôts or bailiffs and lesser comital officials.[184]

In Normandy, support for young Henry was particularly strong.[185] In part, the involvement of nobles on the duchy's eastern and south-eastern borderlands reflected pre-existing patterns of rebellion.[186] The counts of Eu and Aumale, where Normandy marched with the county of Ponthieu, and the lords of the Norman Vexin had long been caught between the competing ambitions of the Anglo-Norman king-dukes and the Capetian kings of France.[187] Accordingly, they had an equally long tradition of being mercurial in their allegiance, not least during the major rebellions against Henry I in favour of his nephew William Clito in 1118–19 and 1123–24.[188] Similarly, the Franco-Norman counts of Meulan ruled an extensive agglomeration of estates that straddled the border between Normandy and France, but in times of conflict their loyalties more often than not lay with the kings of France.[189] In 1173–74, among the Young King's most powerful supporters in eastern Normandy was Count Robert II of Meulan, lord of Pont Audemer and one of the greatest landholders in the French Vexin.[190] The counts of Evreux and of Alençon, and other lords holding powerful and compact lordships on the southern and south-eastern confines of the duchy, similarly had a long tradition of resistance to ducal authority.[191] Thus among the rebels in 1173–74 were John, count of Sées, who held 111 knights' fiefs and had fought against Henry II in 1168, Gilbert de Tillières and Galeran d'Ivry, as well as the lords of L'Aigle, Breteuil and Le Neubourg.[192]

Compared with these border areas, there is little evidence for open rebellion in 1173–74 in the Cotentin, where lords such as Richard du Hommet, constable of Normandy, Jordan Taisson, lord of Saint-Sauveur-le-Vicomte, and William Vernon, lord of Néhou, remained prominent supporters of Henry II.[193] Equally, while hostilities broke out in the valleys of the Seine, Avre and Eure, central Normandy remained largely quiescent, as it had done under Henry I.[194] This, however, may well have been more a reflection of the strength of Henry II's military position in these areas of the duchy than of genuine support for him. Indeed, the rebellion of 1173–74 was far more serious in Normandy than has often been allowed.[195] By 1173, Henry II had clearly alienated not only fractious border lords but a significant element of the leading nobles of the duchy, including two of the greatest cross-Channel magnates.[196] Robert III, earl of Leicester, had inherited the extensive Beaumont lands in England in 1168, but his sphere of political influence seems to have been primarily in Normandy. As lord of the honours of Breteuil and Pacy, and of the Grandmesnil lands in central Normandy through marriage to his wife Petronilla, he was one of the most powerful magnates in the duchy, holding some 121 knights' fiefs. Two of his sons, William and Robert, also partisans of the Young King, were associated with the household of Count Robert of Meulan, with whom Earl Robert had close ties.[197]

Of similar stature was Hugh, earl of Chester, who in addition to lands in Cheshire, the northern Welsh marches, extensive estates in the Midlands and lands in some twenty English shires also wielded great power in south-west

Normandy. Here he was viscount of the Avranchin, the Bessin and the Val de Vire, as well as lord of the honours of St Sever in the Cotentin, and Briquessart, his chief Norman seat, near Bayeux. He held the important castle of St James de Beuvron on the marches with Brittany, and was connected through marriage to the count of Evreux.[198] When war broke out, Hugh made the Norman–Breton border, rather than the northern Midlands, the base for his resistance to the Old King, and formed an alliance with Ralph of Fougères. As he had been returning from Compostella when the Young King fled to France, this may have been the only pragmatic option left to Hugh, but it may also reflect the wider strategic aims of the young Henry and his advisors, for the long-standing claims by the earls of Chester to Carlisle could well have caused conflict with William the Lion, whose support the allies could not afford to lose. Hugh was followed into revolt by several of his vassals from the Welsh marches, such as William of Rhuddlan, who with others was to be captured fighting for the earl at Dol in 1173.[199] Other leading Norman supporters of young Henry included William of Tancarville, chamberlain of Normandy and the former lord of William Marshal, who held ninety-four fiefs, and William FitzErneis.[200] In all, these and other significant Norman rebels commanded the service of around 550 of their own knights, and accounted for around 100 of the 750 fiefs owing military service to the duke recorded in the inquest of 1172, but the rebels doubtless included men of more modest stature.[201]

The role of Robert of Leicester was critical in transforming simmering discontent in England into pockets of open revolt. Here, however, fewer great lords came out openly in support of young Henry than in Normandy and the Angevins' other continental lands, though the Old King was constantly in fear of more widespread defection. The network of strongly garrisoned royal castles served as an effective deterrent in much of the country, and active rebellion was largely restricted to the Midlands, East Anglia and parts of Yorkshire. In addition to the earls of Leicester and Chester, the known rebels in England included two other earls, William Ferrers of Derby and Hugh Bigod of Norfolk, together with Hamo de Masci, Geoffrey de Cotentin, Thomas de Muschamp, Robert de Lundres and Roger de Mowbray.[202] Of these, the most powerful supporter of the Young King was Hugh Bigod, who by 1173 had already had a long and turbulent political career.[203] His lands made him the fifth-richest magnate in the kingdom, and with an extensive power base centred on his castles at Framlingham and Bungay in east Suffolk, he was to prove a vital part of the allies' plans to use East Anglia as an invasion point.[204]

Support for the Young King was not universal, however, and in Warren's words, 'there was not so much a tide of baronial opposition so much as a choppy sea'.[205] An indication of the extent of support the Old King could still command is provided by Howden's list of Henry's principal army commanders at Breteuil in August 1173, which included William de Mandeville, earl of Essex, one of the great cross-Channel magnates and a close confidant of the king, William, earl of Arundel, Richard du Hommet, the constable of Normandy, John count of Vendôme, Richard de Vernon, Richard FitzCount, son of Earl Robert of Gloucester, Jordan Taisson and Henry du Neubourg.[206] In addition, the king's illegitimate brother, Hamelin, earl Warenne, William earl of Gloucester and Richard FitzGilbert, who also held substantial holdings in the duchy, all remained loyal, and there is no record of William de Roumare, earl of Lincoln, being in the rebel camp.[207]

The Young King, moreover, gained little support among churchmen in the Angevin lands. Save for Hugh de Puiset, bishop of Durham, who as Jordan Fantosme noted was 'hand in glove' with William the Lion, the English episcopate remained firmly loyal to Henry II, while the alleged complicity of the abbot of Peterborough with the rebels appears exceptional among the heads of religious houses.[208] Norman ecclesiastics, led by Archbishop Rotrou, were similarly unswerving in their support for the Old King, with the important exception of Arnulf, bishop of Lisieux, for long one of Henry II's leading counsellors, but who, disaffected by his waning influence at court, appears to have been in secret correspondence with the Young King.[209]

Motives and Ambitions

Why did such men support the Young King? If a coherent manifesto of grievances was drawn up by those who took young Henry's side against his father, it has left no record. The Young King's letter to Alexander III justifying taking up arms against his father remains the only direct voice of the opposition, and while it implies injustice and misrule, its emphasis is primarily on Henry II's abuses against the Church and his persecution of Becket.[210] Unsurprisingly, chroniclers close to the court displayed little sympathy for the motives of the rebels, and Ralph of Diss, who offers the fullest explanation, saw little save self-interest and unfounded resentment towards Henry II's policies:

> These men, who for just and provable causes the king had condemned to forfeiture, joined the party of the son, not because they regarded his as the juster cause, but because the father, with a view to increasing the royal dignity, was trampling on the necks of the proud and haughty, overthrowing the suspected castles of the country, or bringing them under his own power; because he ordered or even compelled the persons who were occupying the properties belonging to his own house and to the exchequer to be content

with their own patrimony; because he condemned traitors to exile, punished robbers with death, terrified thieves with the gallows and mulcted the oppressors of the poor with the loss of their own money.[211]

Certainly many of those who came out in support of the Young King had suffered the loss of revenues or castles resulting from Henry II's acts of resumption, had been frustrated in claims to lands, or chafed against the impositions of Angevin government.[212] As early as 1154, Henry, while still only duke of Normandy, had attempted 'gradually and circumspectly' to restore ducal demesnes encroached upon by predatory lords during the troubles of Stephen's reign or alienated by his father Geoffrey to the Norman magnates as a necessary means of buying their support.[213] From his return north following the Toulouse expedition in late September 1159 to the spring of 1163, Henry had based himself primarily in Normandy, intent on strengthening his authority there.[214] Nobles had been forced to surrender ducal castles they had previously held as the king's custodians, while in 1161 Henry II had taken the castles of the count of Meulan and many other Norman magnates into his own hands and garrisoned them with his men.[215] Similarly, in 1162 one of the most influential Manceaux lords, Geoffrey of Mayenne, had been forced to surrender the castles of Gorron, Ambrières and Châteauneuf-sur-Colmont on the Maine–Anjou border, while in 1166 William Talvas had to yield Alençon and Roche-Mabille.[216] In England, royal resumption or appropriation of key fortresses had likewise occurred on a significant scale in the opening years of Henry's reign.[217] Richer de l'Aigle, for example, had lost the castle of Pevensey after 1154, and it is probable that he sought its restoration and the grant of other lands from the Young King as the price of his support.[218]

Rights and prerogatives had also been challenged. In 1163, an inquest 'by sworn testimony into the respective rights of the king and the barons to revenues and customary dues in Normandy' had been undertaken under Rotrou, then bishop of Evreux, and Rainald of St Valéry.[219] In England, the inquest of 1166 resulting in the *Cartae Baronum* had been followed in 1170 by the extension of the Inquest of Sheriffs into a far wider investigation of the activities and revenue collection of all landholders and their officials.[220] If this was not sweeping enough, the 1170 inquest had also made provision for careful inquiry into and recording of 'transgressions of the forest, and concerning those who have trespassed in his [King Henry's] forests and injured his stags and hinds and other wild beasts'.[221] The later 1160s had witnessed notoriously oppressive forest eyres, which had continued until the eve of the war.[222] Normandy likewise experienced an intensification of Angevin government through the major inquest in 1172 into the knight service owed to the duke, which may have provoked well-founded fears of increased royal demands for money or service.[223] Henry II's government was perceived as venal, rapacious and harsh. Writing in 1174 shortly after the end of the war, Wace lauded Henry II as a strong king but did not attempt to disguise the heavy-handed nature of his rule:

> People often talk of him and his courage, and of the evil doers he destroys, like birds trapped in a cage. No baron in his land owns so much property that, if he dares infringe the peace, whether in open country or in wood-land, he is not shamed through mutilation if he can be caught, or who does not leave his body or soul behind as a hostage.[224]

In a still more revealing passage, Guernes acknowledged that the king needed to rule his unruly subjects firmly for 'he has an insolent people to rule over', but urged Henry II in the wake of the war to seize the opportunity to reform: 'The advice I now give the king is to restore the rights and liberties of Holy Church, as he promised, cherish his noblemen, be moderate in justice, not to avenge a few game animals by taking a human life, to grant each individual their rights, to shun covetousness.'[225] Guernes' words find an echo in Gerald of Wales' account of how in the 1170s a Lincolnshire knight, Roger of Asterby, was commanded by St Peter and the archangel Gabriel to present King Henry with a series of commandments, including to adhere to his coronation oath, uphold the laws of the kingdom, not to put anyone to death without judgment, even if guilty, to ensure that inheritances were restored to their lawful owners, to give justice freely and without payment, and to expel the Jews after restoring bonds to their debtors.[226] The last demand was explained by Roger's own indebtedness to the financier Aaron of Lincoln, but his other points of griev-ance provide a valuable glimpse of the dissatisfaction of the local nobility with the abuses of Angevin government. Ralph Niger, who had suffered exile at the hands of Henry II and was subsequently attached to the Young King's house-hold, gave such a lengthy and damning indictment of Henry's misgovernment that the continuator of his chronicle felt obliged to offer an apology for so immoderate an attack upon a king.[227] There can be little doubt that such issues were being raised by Henry II's opponents in the years leading up to the outbreak of rebellion in 1173, and that they looked to the Young King to remedy them once he came to power.

Beyond the oppressive nature of Henry II's rule, many of the leading rebels felt excluded from the king's counsels and patronage. The alienation of nobles who felt ever more distanced from mechanisms of power by increasingly specialist bureaucracies was to be a widespread phenomenon in later twelfth-

and early thirteenth-century Europe, and the precocious development of Angevin government had been accompanied by growing resentment of the undue influence of such administrative experts.[228] The later 1160s had seen the deaths of a number of Henry II's key counsellors, as well as his mother the Empress Matilda, who together had been influential in shaping the nature of his early government, and thereafter the king was perceived as relying increasingly on a small group of *curiales*, notably men such as the two archdeacons, Geoffrey Ridel and Richard of Ilchester. Even the loyal Walter Map criticized Henry for cutting himself off from everyone but his closest friends.[229] The principal cause of Robert III of Leicester's support for the Young King is likely to have been resentment that he had never achieved the prominence in the king's counsels enjoyed by his father Robert, who had been justiciar and a pillar of Henry II's regime between 1154 and his death in 1168.[230] Though Henry II had granted the hereditary stewardship of England and Normandy to his father in 1153, Robert himself may well not have held this office.[231] Henry II made few grants in Normandy save to members of his own family, such as his brother William and his half-brother Hamelin de Warenne, who received lands in the duchy on his marriage of the Warenne heiress.[232] Unlike King Stephen, moreover, he created no new earldoms, refused to recognize the hereditary nature of most of them, allowed several to lapse and failed to win the close attachment of a number of his earls.[233] While there are evident methodological problems in using witness lists of charters as indices of a particular magnate's standing at court or his relationship with the king, it nonetheless remains striking that none of the leading Norman rebels in 1173–74 appear among the regular witnesses to Henry II's surviving charters.[234] These lords, together with the earls of Lincoln and Devon, apparently kept their distance from the court, while nobles from Poitou and Aquitaine were conspicuous by their absence.[235]

The difficulties posed by the general silence of the chroniclers regarding the individual grievances of young Henry's supporters is compounded by the fact that after the war was over Henry II demanded the surrender and destruction of all charters issued by the Young King following his flight to France, making it hard to recover the specific territorial ambitions of any but a handful of the most prominent rebels. William, Earl Ferrers, seemingly sought to gain the lands of Peverel, which had escheated to Henry II when William Peverel fled from England in 1155, while Hugh Bigod's support of the Young King appears to have been primarily venal, with young Henry promising his long-sought-after goals of the custody of Norwich castle and the honour of Eye.[236] There is little evidence for any attempts by Henry II to infringe on the extensive liberties enjoyed Hugh, earl of Chester, who had received the king's own cousin Bertrada de Montfort in marriage.[237] He had, however, succeeded his father, Ranulf II, in 1153 as a minor, thereby allowing the king to ignore the enormous territorial concessions Ranulf had demanded from Henry, when still duke, as the price of his support.[238] Hugh may also have shared his father's aspirations to increase still further his power in the north Midlands and Lincolnshire, something that Henry II was as keen to curb as Henry I and Stephen had been.[239] Something of Earl Hugh's independent spirit is glimpsed in the refuge he gave at Chester to two hermits whose wild claims respectively to be Harold II of England and Emperor Henry V of Germany might have stretched the credibility of all but the most gullible, but who nevertheless thereby called into question the legitimacy of Henry II's kingship.[240]

The disaffection of Roger de Mowbray provides a clearer example of why some lords might be so eager to support the Young King. Henry I had granted Nigel d'Aubigny, the re-founder of the Mowbray family, those lands in England forfeited by Robert I de Stuteville for supporting Robert Curthose. Early in Henry II's reign, an agreement was reached between Robert (III) de Stuteville and Roger (I) de Mowbray, by which Mowbray relinquished ten knights' fees and the important manor of Kirbymoorside. Beyond this, Mowbray felt his regional influence threatened by the rising power of the Stutevilles through royal service.[241] Robert III de Stuteville had become sheriff of York in 1170, and Mowbray had been denied his claim to the custody of the city's castle. Doubtless he now looked to the Young King to make good his claims. It was precisely this availability of two competing sources of authority, each granting claims of supporters against local rivals backing their opponents, that had created such chaos in the reign of King Stephen and made the outbreak of a war between royal father and royal son so potentially catastrophic.

Some of the Young King's leading supporters, such as Hugh of Chester, were young men, and Ralph of Diss noted that among those who deserted Henry II were some men he had brought up from childhood and on whom he had bestowed the belt of knighthood.[242] Yet the conflict of 1173–74 cannot be seen merely as a 'war of the generations'. In some cases, sons did indeed join the Young King's party while their fathers remained loyal to the Old King, a long-established tactic of the nobility in times of major rebellion or civil war to ensure that, whatever the outcome, the family fortunes would be safeguarded.[243] Yet equally, there were a number of fathers who supported the Young King together with their sons, such as William Patrick senior and his sons Robert and Engeram, all captured at Dol in August 1173, Robert de Mowbray with his sons Nigel and Robert, and Ralph of Fougères with his son Juhel.[244] Some of the leading rebels, moreover, were anything but *iuvenes*; Hugh Bigod, in his seventies, may have been exceptional, but Robert of Leicester was in his forties and Roger de Mowbray had fought as a young man against the Scots at the battle of the Standard back in 1138. Whatever their individual grievances, the Young King offered such disaffected lords a crucial figurehead around whom to rally. Debonair, affable and open-handed, he cut a very different figure from his irascible and overbearing father. For all those who had experienced the Old King's *ira et malevolentia*, or who had felt the weight of Angevin government too heavily, young Henry held out the prospect of change and a better future.

CHAPTER 8

'The Cubs of the Roaring Lion Shall Awaken'

THE OUTBREAK OF WAR, 1173

Henry's son strove to destroy his father; his boast is that he will bring him to St Denis conquered and captured in war – but the king, his father, has promised him something very different; declaring that he will see many a white, red and grey banner, many a lined shield, and many a splendid horse, and many a joust run against his enemies, before there is any question of his being routed and beaten in battle.

– Jordan Fantosme[1]

THE GATHERING STORM finally broke soon after Easter 1173. 'The son took up arms against his father,' noted Ralph of Diss, 'at just the time when everywhere Christians were laying down their arms in reverence for Easter. Dissensions of this sort cannot end happily.'[2] The unprecedented scale of the insurrection led Roger of Howden to pardonable exaggeration: 'The whole of the kingdom of France and the king, the son of the king of England, Richard his brother count of Poitou, and Geoffrey, count of Brittany, and nearly all the earls and barons of England, Normandy, Aquitaine, Anjou and Brittany, rose against the king of England the father, and laid waste his lands on every side with fire, sword and rapine; they also laid siege to his castles, and took them by storm, and there was no one to relieve them.'[3]

The allied leaders had conceived a coherent and ambitious strategy.[4] Normandy had to be wrested from Henry II's control, for it was the linchpin of the Plantagenet empire.[5] Placed between England and the Angevin heart-lands of Anjou, Maine and the Touraine, its strategic importance was reflected in the fact that King Henry either stayed in or passed through Normandy in all but four of his thirty-five years of rule, and it was from Rouen, second only to Westminster in its importance as an administrative centre of the Plantagenet lands, that the majority of Henry II's charters were issued.[6] By taking

Normandy, the allies would cut Henry's empire in half, and either isolate him in England or force him to retreat to the Angevin heartlands of the Loire. As long as Henry held Normandy he could receive essential supplies of men and, still more significantly, of money from England, while from Rouen he might strike out at any uprising or the penetration of the Norman border by the Young King and his supporters. This was to be a war fought on many fronts, but its most important theatre would be Normandy.[7]

To achieve this objective the allies planned a three-pronged attack on the duchy, with Rouen as their chief target.[8] While Henry II was forced to guard his extensive frontiers and face a number of local insurrections spread over his far-flung domains, the Young King and the allies had the advantage of being able to concentrate their forces against key points of the Norman frontier.[9] Ralph of Fougères and his Breton supporters, aided by Earl Hugh of Chester, would threaten the Avranchin and push eastwards. Young Henry together with Philip of Flanders would invade from the north-east, while Louis would attack further to the south in the valley of the Avre, where the fortress of Verneuil guarded an area devoid of natural defences.[10] By this means they avoided a direct attack on the Vexin, with its formidable chain of fortresses. Having broken through the duchy's border defences, they would advance in a pincer movement on Rouen, control of which would secure their hold on upper Normandy. It was a sound strategy, albeit one that Henry II could have readily foreseen: Louis had attacked Verneuil in 1153, and in the war of 1167–68 the French king and his allies had followed a similar plan.[11] Plans were laid for a number of risings in Aquitaine and Anjou, while an invasion by William the Lion of northern England would aim to join forces with a powerful concentration of rebel garrisons in the Midlands. Troops sent from Flanders would both assist the Scots and reinforce the uprising planned by Hugh Bigod in East Anglia. Even if Henry II did not lose control of England, these attacks would pin down men and resources and prevent him reinforcing his position in Normandy.

The allies' ultimate intentions had they succeeded in such a strategy are harder to ascertain. There were doubtless some in the coalition who would have relished the destruction of Henry II. Yet for all the high vaunts made at the council of war at St Denis, it seems unlikely that the Young King himself envisioned the complete downfall of his father. Writing soon after the war, Wace believed that 'if the French could realize their ambitions, the King of England would own nothing on this side of the Channel; if they could do so, they would send him back across it in disgrace'.[12] By contrast, Jordan Fantosme suggests that the aim was to force Henry II to cede to young Henry complete and independent control of England.[13] As he has Count Theobald tell King

Louis, 'He [Henry II] will find no safety anywhere, be it in open country or forest, if he does not restore to the Young King his rightful inheritance (*l'eritage*), the realm of England. If he is prepared to act wisely, you will let him keep Normandy, if your rage dies down.'[14] The Old King would thus have his holdings reduced to his patrimony of Anjou and Normandy, while his sons would assume autonomous rule in England, Aquitaine and Brittany. In either eventuality, Louis would succeed in dividing the constituent elements of the Plantagenet empire, with its continental lands held directly as his fiefs. By contrast, however, the great cross-Channel magnates cannot have wished for a division of realms under two rival rulers: confronted with just such a situation in 1087 and 1100, which threatened to weaken their power and place them in a grave political dilemma, many of the most powerful Norman lords had rebelled first against William Rufus then against Henry I in favour of Robert Curthose in an attempt to reunite the kingdom and duchy under one ruler. While there may have been fewer such lords holding great estates in England and Normandy by 1173, such factors meant that once they had declared for young Henry against his father, men such as Robert of Leicester and Hugh of Chester were irrevocably committed to seeing the Young King obtain direct rule over an undivided Anglo-Norman realm. For his part, young Henry must have realized that his wide-ranging territorial concessions to his allies would seriously weaken Plantagenet power and diminish his own inheritance, at least in the short term. Nevertheless, it was a price worth paying to finally extricate himself from political subordination.

Opening Gambits: Pacy and Gournay

In May, the allies began to probe the defences of the duchy. A force of Flemings pushed down the valley of the Eure towards Pacy, in what was probably an attempt by Robert, earl of Leicester, to regain control of this important fortress and castlery pertaining to his Norman honour of Breteuil.[15] Local Norman forces, however, succeeded in gradually driving them back, and Ralph of Diss recorded the mocking story of how a 'little woman' had broken down the bridge by which they had crossed the Eure, so that in their precipitous retreat many were drowned.[16] The assault on Pacy may have been planned to coincide with an attack in greater force by the Young King himself against Gournay in the Pays de Bray, to which he could rightfully lay claim as part of his wife Margaret's dowry.[17] This key marcher lordship lay well to the north of the near-impregnable fortress of Gisors, yet no major castle stood between it and a direct march on Rouen itself.[18] In a daring ambush, the Young King captured Hugh II de Gournay, his son and eighty knights, burned the town of Gournay and forced its burgesses to ransom themselves.[19] As with other lords of the Vexin caught between competing rulers, the allegiance of the Gournays was as fluid as the political situation demanded: if Hugh was loyal to Henry II, it is unsurprising subsequently to find his son Hugh the younger as an active supporter of the Young King.[20]

For the opening months of the war, and indeed for much of the period of his rebellion, the Young King's own movements remain shadowy: no fiscal records survive pertaining to his own or Louis' expenditure on his behalf, while the chroniclers largely concentrate on the actions of his father. Though William Marshal doubtless had vivid memories of the conflict, the author of the *History* considered it prudent to pass quickly over the events of the great rebellion, save for one incident that served to highlight the honour of the Marshal and his importance to the Young King. According to the *History*, young Henry was just within the frontiers of Anjou at either Vendôme or Trôo when he learned that his father was marching on him from Tours with his army, intending to besiege him and take him prisoner.[21] The Young King took counsel with his followers, including a number of leading French lords. Some argued for withdrawal, but others angrily rejected such advice as cowardly and shameful; the Young King's forces were strong, they argued, and they should make their stand.[22] Once resolved to resist, his men pointed out that the Young King had not yet been knighted: '"We would all be a more effective force if you had a sword girded on; that would make the whole of your company more valorous and more respected, and would increase the joy in their hearts"'.[23] The Young King readily agreed, and, much to the jealousy of many of the French nobles present, he bestowed this great honour on William Marshal as 'the best knight who ever was or who will be', even though 'he had not one strip of land to his name or anything else, just his chivalry (*ne rein fors sa chivalerie*)'.[24] Accordingly, the Marshal girded his young master with a sword 'and kissed him, whereupon he became a knight, and he asked that God keep him most valorous, honoured and exalted, as indeed God did'.[25]

It was not uncommon to knight young men on campaign, usually prior to battle or at a major siege.[26] Yet if young Henry had indeed been girded with the belt of knighthood before his coronation in 1170, then his dubbing in 1173 may have represented a second knighting, this time by his companions in arms, intended to symbolize his new independence from his father.[27] Whatever its veracity, the *History*'s anecdote provides a valuable glimpse of the forces available to young Henry, noting that Louis VII had sent him 400 hand-picked knights, including the French king's youngest brother, Peter de Courtenay, Raoul, count of Clermont-en-Beauvaisis, Bouchard V, lord of Montmorency, and William des Barres.[28] If the *History* does not exaggerate, this was a very powerful field force: 400 knights, for example, had represented the entire strength of Louis VI's army at the battle of Brémule in 1119.[29] As Count Raoul was Louis VII's constable, and William des Barres an experienced knight of the French royal household,[30] Louis was providing the Young King not only with military clout but with the guidance of veteran warriors. If these lords and their military households were assigned to his support from the outset of the war, it would explain the Young King's initial success at Gournay in May. The *History* also states that Geoffrey, count of Brittany, was present among his eldest brother's forces, even though he was then only fifteen and was not to be knighted until 1178.[31] Of all his brothers, young Henry was to be closest to Geoffrey, and his appearance alongside the Young King in 1173 is an early indication of the bond that would subsequently be strengthened first by shared participation in the tournament circuit of northern France from the late 1170s, then again in war itself in 1183.

Diplomatic Moves and the Appeal to Rome

The Young King accompanied these opening military actions by waging war on the diplomatic front. On 3 June, an ecclesiastical council, convened in London under the watchful eyes of Richard de Lucy and Reginald of Cornwall, had elected Richard, prior of Dover, as archbishop of Canterbury.[32] A week later, however, with preparations for the consecration at Canterbury in readiness, Prior Odo produced a letter addressed to himself and the convent of Canterbury from the Young King. Styling himself 'Henry, *Dei gratia*, king of England, duke of Normandy and count of Anjou, son of King Henry', he contested the election as having been held without his consent.[33] This was improper, he explained, because as an anointed king he had been entrusted with the kingdom and its well-being.[34] The Young King notified the prior that he had appealed to Rome both in writing and by messenger to the legates, cardinals Albert and Theodin, as well as to 'our faithful men', the bishops of London, Exeter and Worcester.[35] He also challenged the episcopal elections held in late April, which had seen Richard of Ilchester elected to the see of Winchester, the king's natural son Geoffrey to Lincoln, Geoffrey Ridel to Ely, Robert Foliot to Hereford, Reginald the Lombard to Bath, and Goscelin to Chichester.[36] This was an astute move on the Young King's part, which attempted to block the promotion of some of his father's most loyal servants. He did so, moreover, not simply on the grounds that, as king, his assent was necessary for the legality of the elections, but on the grounds that some of those chosen by Henry II were unsuitable for office. As leading agents of Henry II in his struggle with Archbishop Thomas, Ilchester and Ridel already were of ill repute at the Curia, and the Young King sought to exploit this, accusing Ridel, for example, of 'many things' including immorality and his involvement in Becket's murder.[37] Thomas, moreover, had only very recently been canonized (on Ash Wednesday, 23 February 1173) by Alexander III, who 'commanded that his memorial should be inscribed in the catalogue of the saints, and he further enjoined by his apostolic authority, that the day of his passion should be held and celebrated as a festival'.[38]

As a result, Richard of Canterbury was compelled quickly to send his own messengers with letters to the pope, and soon after hastened to Rome in person.[39] Gilbert Foliot also wrote to the pope supporting the candidacy of the bishops elect of Winchester, Hereford and Ely.[40] He noted that out of respect for the pontiff the consecration would be delayed till Alexander could consider the matter, but informed him that the Young King's letters of objection appeared suspect on a number of grounds.[41] Nevertheless, the Young King succeeded in obtaining postponement of the consecration of all the bishops elect until the following year. Throughout the period of conflict, he and Louis were to keep an influential presence at the Curia: when in late March or early April 1174 Richard and Reginald, elect of Bath, finally travelled to Rome to seek confirmation of their election, they 'found many opponents from France, and a greater number of still more implacable ones from England against them'.[42] One of the Young King's advocates was Master Berter of Orléans, who was said to have jested wryly to Pope Alexander that Geoffrey Ridel had a canonical excuse for not attending the Curia: he had a wife.[43] Though no others are known by name, they may have included men such as Ralph Niger, a former clerk in Thomas' circle and already an implacable opponent of Henry II.[44] Whether for those who had suffered at the Old King's hands on account of their support for Becket, or for university-trained clerics such as Berter ambitious for promotion, championing the cause of the younger Henry held out the prospect of high ecclesiastical preferment: a challenge to the elections to key English bishoprics both prevented Henry II from installing his leading clerks in positions of power and kept these posts open for other aspirants.

The hand of young Henry's clerical advisors can clearly be seen in the long letter sent by the Young King to Pope Alexander, probably in conjunction with his appeals against the episcopal elections, in which he justifies his actions in taking up arms.[45] Again adopting the style *Dei gratia rex*, but deliberately omitting it from references to his father, he began by admitting that many were shocked by the serious and detestable quarrel which had arisen between his father and himself.[46] As many had reminded him, God had especially commanded that one should honour one's parents, and that those persecuting them were disgraced and ill-fortuned. Since he had incurred blame for so inhuman and terrible a crime, to the damage of his renown, the Young King now appealed to the apostolic authority: if he had acted excessively, he would embrace the pope's correction and was ready to accept the counsel of the holy Roman Church.[47] He set out his own grievances against his father, stressing the indignity not only of being an anointed king without any power to implement his duties, but also of being subject to the control of his father's unworthy ministers.[48]

In an astute attempt to win the pope's support the Young King then moved from a rehearsal of his own circumstances to a denunciation of Henry II's flagrant abuses of the Church, and expressed his wish to abrogate a number of offensive clauses of the Constitutions of Clarendon. These included the punishment in royal courts of clerics first convicted in ecclesiastical courts; the prohibition of excommunication without the king's prior consent; the need to seek the king's permission for clerical appeals to Rome; and the king's right both to the revenues of a vacant see and to have elections for abbacies and bishoprics held in the royal chapel.[49] Henry II's record concerning prolonged vacancies and his scarcely concealed manipulation of supposedly 'free' elections to high ecclesiastical offices were notorious, but to press home his point the Young King's letter included the text of a writ purportedly sent earlier that year by Henry II to the chapter of Winchester: 'Henry, king of the English, duke of the Normans and count of the Angevins to his faithful monks of the church of Winchester, greeting. I order you to hold a free election, but nevertheless forbid you to elect anyone but Richard, my clerk, archdeacon of Poitiers.' This writ was undoubtedly an unscrupulous forgery, even if it reflected the reality of Henry II's control over such key appointments.[50] Nevertheless, the Young King's manifesto can only have reinforced papal suspicion of Henry II at a time when Becket's canonization had heightened still further the vivid memories of his martyrdom.

Nevertheless, Alexander III kept a judicious distance from the conflict, neither openly supporting Louis and the allies against Henry II, nor unleashing the thunders of Rome against the Young King in response to the Old King's own appeals for his aid.[51] In his attempt to win hearts and minds, moreover, Henry II also wrote to his allies among European rulers, including William II of Sicily. They expressed their regret, but, other than their sympathies, could send little by way of effective support to him.[52] Still less effectual were the letters composed by Peter of Blois for Archbishop Rotrou of Rouen directly rebuking both Queen Eleanor and the Young King for the folly of their opposition to King Henry and exhorting a swift return to obedience.[53] Nevertheless, Rotrou's censure of young Henry vividly captures the shock and outrage of Henry II's own supporters at his son's inception of what they regarded as an unjust and unnatural conflict, for, Rotrou warned, he was engaged in the worst kind of civil war:

> You fight not against barbarian nations but your own intimate followers and domestics (*familiares et domesticas*). It is not foreign lands you invade, nor hostile strongholds, but your own country. You afflict people who are subject to you; you pursue in a hostile manner not a rebel, not an enemy, but your father – indeed, not your father, but yourself. By fighting, you do not enlarge for yourself that inheritance which was granted to you by paternal concession, by the general wish of the people, and by the oaths of the nobles. Rather, you now usurp it as a tyrant and invader, by spoliation of churches, oppression of the poor, by arsons and homicides, and ultimately, by parricide.[54]

Aumale and Drincourt: The Assault on North-East Normandy

While his agents pursued their diplomatic offensive at the Curia, the Young King prepared for a major campaign. Despite his success at Gournay, any further advance into the duchy would have been dangerous while the strong castles of Aumale and Neufchâtel-en-Bray, also known as Drincourt, remained untaken to the north.[55] Accordingly, around 29 June, Count Philip and young Henry led a large army against Aumale, one of the principal bastions of the duchy's vulnerable north-eastern border.[56] It was held by its count, William 'le Gros', a veteran warrior in his sixties who had distinguished himself at the defeat of the Scots at the Standard back in 1138, and Simon, count of Evreux, an important border lord whose loyalty Henry II had worked hard to maintain.[57] Despite this, Aumale now surrendered to the forces of Philip and the Young King with such indecent haste that its commanders and others in the garrison were strongly suspected of treason.[58] Whether Aumale had fallen through cowardice or complicity, it augured badly for Henry II. The loyalties of frontier magnates in this region were notoriously fragile, and the defection of Henry, count of Eu, quickly followed.[59] Howden directly linked the outbreak of open rebellion in England and elsewhere with the news of Aumale's fall.[60]

The allies moved quickly to exploit these successes. In early July, while King Louis led a great army up through the Chartrain to invest the key town of Verneuil in the south-east, the Young King and his brothers Richard and Geoffrey joined Philip and Count Matthew for an attack on Drincourt.[61] This pushed their advance to the river Béthune: beyond this, only the small castle of Saint-Saëns on the Varenne stood between them and a direct march to Rouen

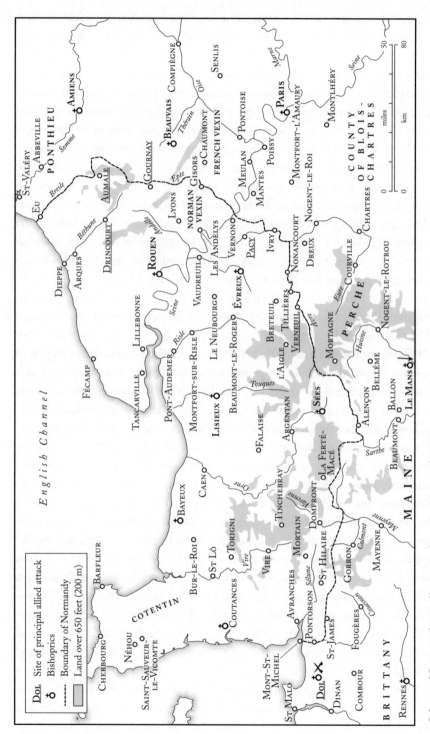

Map 2 Normandy, to illustrate the campaigns of 1173

through Bray and the Roumois. The strategic importance of Drincourt, however, was reflected both in its strength and by its elite garrison of knights commanded by two of Henry's *fideles*, Doun Bardolf and his brother Thomas, who put up a far more spirited resistance than the defenders of Aumale.[62] Nevertheless, after a sustained period of battering by siege engines, the castle's defences began to weaken, and Count Matthew adjudged the time was right for an all-out assault on 25 July. This, however, was the Feast of St James, and the Young King and his nobles, 'showing honour to the blessed apostle', absolutely refused to take up arms that day.[63] Young Henry's reticence reflected the great importance to the Angevin family of the cult of St James, which though soon to be eclipsed by that of Becket remained one of the foremost objects of pilgrimage in England. Henry II invoked the protection of the relic of the hand of St James for Channel crossings and sought the saint's intercession on military campaigns: in 1163, for example, he visited Reading prior to his Welsh campaign.[64] His son had been imbued with a similar reverence, but may also have learned from his father the wisdom of abstaining from fighting on major holy days. During his campaigns of 1166–67 in Brittany, Henry II had prepared his forces for battle on the vigil of the feast of the Apostles Peter and Paul (29 June), but had been dissuaded from giving battle the next day by Hamo of Savigny, a holy man whom he greatly respected. Hamo prophesied that as a result of respecting the apostles' feast day Henry would meet with great success within the year; and so, noted the *Life of Hamo*, it transpired, for King Henry both subdued the Bretons and established a truce with the king of France.[65]

Count Matthew, however, did not share such scruples. On the refusal of the Young King and his supporters to join in the storming, he 'was furious and indignant with them, and demanded that he should be allowed to keep whatever booty and spoils he might take that day'. The Young King consented, despite the great importance of such booty to the morale and finances of his men. Matthew's forces duly attacked the walls of the castle, but during the assault the count of Boulogne was struck just below the knee by a crossbow bolt, 'shot as it were from heaven'.[66] Count Philip had his brother taken back to Flanders, but he died some days later from his wound.[67] Ralph of Diss also saw the workings of divine retribution in Matthew's fatal wounding on the feast of St James, noting that it was five years to the day since the count had sworn fealty to Henry II, touching a number of relics including the hand of St James.[68]

Despite this setback, the allies pressed home their siege. Realizing that they could not resist another such assault, the constables of Drincourt sought and were granted a respite from the besiegers in which to seek King Henry's aid, promising that they would yield the castle on terms if this was not forthcoming.

Notwithstanding Matthew's death, Philip and the Young King were no doubt eager to display chivalric magnanimity to these loyal defenders and thereby encourage the more rapid surrender of other castles to them. Henry II, unable to come to his castellans' assistance, gave them permission to yield the castle to the count of Flanders.[69]

Aumale and Drincourt had fallen to the allies. But the death of Count Matthew had been a bitter blow and immediately confronted Count Philip with a dynastic crisis. Having no children of his own, Philip had made Matthew his heir. He was now forced to break off campaigning to arrange for his other brother, Philip, bishop elect of Cambrai, to demit his ecclesiastical office and take up the arms of knighthood as his new successor.[70] With their offensive on the north-east frontier of the duchy stalled, the Young King moved south to join King Louis at the great siege of Verneuil.[71]

War in the Midlands: The Siege of Leicester[72]

While the allies were pounding at the frontier defences of Normandy, in England it was the turn of Henry II's forces to take the offensive. On 3 July, the justiciar Richard de Lucy and Henry II's uncle Reginald of Cornwall, with 'the army of England', laid siege to the castle and town of Leicester.[73] Though Earl Robert had withdrawn to France, he had left powerful garrisons in Leicester and its two dependent fortifications at Mountsorrel and Groby.[74] Whether the siege was a response to the garrison's depredations or a pre-emptive strike intended to overawe other potential rebels, it indicated the central role the earl of Leicester played in the Young King's rebellion.[75] The Midlands were to prove the epicentre of the insurgency in England: the defection of Leicester along with William, Earl Ferrers, who held the castles of Tutbury and Duffield, created a powerful bloc of rebel castles stretching up to the lands of Earl Hugh of Chester, together with Hamo de Masci's castles of Dunham and Ullerwood, and Geoffrey de Cotentin's castle at Stockport.[76]

Despite their lord's absence, the garrison of Leicester under the constable, Ansketil Mallory, put up a sustained resistance. To co-ordinate their operations with the wider allied strategy, the Young King had sent them one of his trusted household knights, William of Dive, who also had links with the household of Earl Robert, and who was subsequently installed as castellan of the castle of Mountsorrel.[77] In Leicester, the powerful castle, flanked to the west by the river Soar, was situated at the south-west corner of the town, whose walls followed the line of the former Roman defences and probably preserved much of the Roman walls.[78] Pressed home for three weeks, the royalist siege revealed the great resources in men, material and logistics available to Henry II, which the Young King's allies in England, and even Louis VII in northern France, could barely hope to match. The sheriff of Shropshire, for example, sent a force of 410 archers and other infantry, while 156 carpenters and an engineer 'to make machines for the army at Leicester' were paid from the account of the counties of Warwickshire and Nottinghamshire. The sheriff of Gloucester supplied 10,000 crossbow bolts from St Briavels, the royal centre of bolt and arrow production in the Forest of Dean, while other shrievalties furnished more siege materials.[79] These preparations also reveal the crucial role played in the war by the sheriffs, the key agents of royal authority in the shires. The great majority were men of modest rank, career administrators who owed their positions to Henry II: throughout the war, the Young King was unable to detach any of them from his father's cause, and their unshakable loyalty to the Old King was to prove a major factor in his ultimate victory.

Leicester castle continued to remain impregnable against the royalist attacks, but the outbreak of fire within the town finally forced the townsmen to sue for peace. After levying a fine of 300 marks from the leading citizens, de Lucy expelled the burgesses, but permitted them to take their possessions to whichever of the king's towns, castles or vills they wished.[80] He then had the town's gates and part of its walls pulled down. Leicester's fate was both a dire warning to any other towns that might consider insurrection in the name of the Young King, and a deliberate blow to the status and prosperity of the rebel earl of Leicester. Yet before the justiciar and his colleagues could finish their task by reducing Leicester castle itself, news of the invasion of northern England by William the Lion forced them to break off the siege on 28 July and grant the garrison a truce until Michaelmas.[81]

The Invasion of William the Lion

Assembling his army at the traditional mustering site of Caddonlee, Selkirkshire, close to the major royal stronghold of Roxburgh, William had invaded Northumberland, probably in mid July.[82] His army had been stiffened by a force of Flemings, disembarked at Berwick or one of the other Scottish east coast ports.[83] Their first target was the castle of Wark, which had been heavily re-fortified by Henry II after its recovery in 1157.[84] Its castellan, Roger de Stuteville, nevertheless judged his position so grave that he sought a respite of forty days from King William to seek aid from Henry II, and pledged to yield the castle if relief was not forthcoming within this time.[85] The Scots army now moved down the rich coastal plain of Northumberland, harrying and burning. It was not without reason that William of Newburgh called them 'that savage people who would spare neither sex nor age', for the Scots and

Galwegian levies had a black reputation for their ruthless conduct in war.[86] Reginald of Durham describes how the terrified inhabitants fled to take sanctuary in churches, setting up makeshift dwellings and tents in the cemetery enclosures.[87] King William may well have been counting on a shift in loyalties among the northern magnates. Some of the older among them, such as Odinel de Umfraville, lord of Prudhoe, had served his father Earl Henry, while William himself had held the earldom of Northumberland from 1152 to 1157.[88] Even after Henry II's resumption of the northern counties in 1157, William remained lord of extensive holdings in Tynedale, and must have still been a familiar figure in Northumberland.[89] Jordan Fantosme reveals considerable sympathy for William, and has Henry II's castellans, even though opposing him, speak with respect of his claims to the earldom he regarded as his patrimony.[90] Such claims, moreover, had been strengthened by the Young King's grant of the earldom to William in 1173.[91]

Yet if he had hoped to win over the leading northern families such as the Stutevilles, de Vauxs, de Vescis and Umfravilles, King William was to be disappointed. At Alnwick, the Scots were repulsed by the stiff resistance put up by William de Vesci, and though Roger FitzRichard deemed the castle of Warkworth too weak to be defensible, he fell back on Newcastle upon Tyne, a fortress far too powerful for the Scottish army to take by assault.[92] The campaigns of 1173–74 would sharply reveal the absence of an effective siege train to be a critical flaw in King William's ability to wage an effective war of conquest in northern England.[93] Despite this, William now moved his forces into Cumbria and besieged Carlisle, for as Jordan has the king's counsellors tell him, 'of all the lands you lay claim to, Carlisle is the chief'.[94] Henry II had greatly strengthened the castle's outer defences, and it had been put in a state of readiness in 1173.[95] It was thus with some confidence that its castellan, Robert de Vaux, refused the Scots' summons to yield it.

William launched a major assault, probably on the more accessible southern side where the town protected the castle, but the Scots were successfully repulsed.[96] Realizing he must resort to attrition, the king sent out raiding parties to ravage the countryside and collect supplies, while the main army remained investing Carlisle.[97] The king of Scots ordered that churches and religious houses be spared, but the royal mandate was not always obeyed and the Scots and Galwegians were accused of widespread plundering of churches.[98] Yet as William tightened his blockade of Carlisle, he received news that an English army under Richard de Lucy and the constable, Humphrey de Bohun, were hastening to the town's relief. The king, perhaps urged on by some of the younger firebrands, was all for offering battle and winning his inheritance by force of arms, but this time sounder counsel prevailed. For the Scots to hope to vanquish an Anglo-Norman army greatly superior in knights and well-equipped troops in the open field was clear folly, as the rout of David I's mighty host at the battle of the Standard in 1138 had painfully revealed. Bitter at heart, William the Lion bowed to the inevitable, and ordered a precipitous retreat to the safety of Roxburgh.[99] Elements of the Carlisle garrison gave pursuit, and Robert de Vaux employed much of the substantial booty they gained to strengthen his defences and reward his men for their stout resistance.[100] The English field army then advanced into Scotland and de Lucy proceeded to lay waste much of Lothian.[101] No attempt was made to besiege Roxburgh, Edinburgh or other powerful strongholds, for the justiciar's fast-moving force had no siege equipment, and aimed only at a punitive strike to deter the King of Scots from further support for the rebels in England.

Debacle at Verneuil

While war raged in the northern counties of England, Louis had been pressing the siege of Verneuil hard since early July. Defending the line of the river Avre,[102] this fortress town stood as a bastion loyal to Henry II between two principal areas of disaffection on the southern frontier of Normandy. Torigni greatly exaggerates in claiming that the French army contained 7,000 knights and many other troops,[103] but Louis had nonetheless assembled a powerful host, including the forces of counts Theobald of Blois, Henry of Champagne, and Robert of Dreux, as well as troops from Burgundy.[104] Raising and maintaining such a force in the field was a major logistical and financial challenge for the Capetian king, whose resources were proverbially scanty when compared to those of Henry II.[105] To fund it, Louis had levied a special tax throughout his lands: the royal collectors had been ruthless in its collection, while the land had been stripped of supplies and beasts of burden to provision the great army that now encircled Verneuil.[106] The town put up a spirited resistance. Its defences, strengthened by Henry II since Louis' attack in 1152, consisted of a powerful castle and a number of separate boroughs, each defended by its own walls and water-filled moat.[107] It had a strong garrison, commanded by its constables Hugh de Beauchamp and Hugh de Lacy, the latter lately come with other marcher lords from Ireland, while its citizens, who had been granted special privileges by Henry, remained staunchly loyal.[108]

The attackers desperately tried to fill in the ditches with rocks and wood in order to create a level surface over which to wheel great siege towers higher than the walls, while their stone throwers endeavoured to smash the battlements.[109] The castle remained impregnable, so the French chose to concentrate their attacks on the largest of the boroughs, known as the 'great borough' or the

'Queen's borough'. It sheltered a large number of the poor and indigent, and after almost a month of blockade, the inhabitants were beginning to starve. Aware of their growing plight, Louis offered them a respite of three days in which to summon aid from King Henry. Should this not be forthcoming, they would surrender without harm, and the hostages given to guarantee the agreement would be returned in safety. The desperate citizens accepted, and the Young King, counts Theobald, Henry and Robert, and Archbishop William of Sens swore to uphold this agreement.[110] The granting of such respites and terms of conditional surrender was common in warfare of the period, but the space of only three days allowed for Henry to come to the relief of Verneuil was unusually short. Chivalric convention made it hard to refuse the request for a beleaguered garrison to seek its lord's aid before surrender, but after so major an operation, the French were clearly determined to make the chances of the town's relief as slight as possible.[111]

Henry II, however, reacted swiftly to news of Verneuil's plight. From his base at Rouen, he immediately marched to Conches on 7 August at the head of a powerful army. In strategic terms, the withdrawal of Count Philip from north-east Normandy had enabled Henry II to concentrate his forces against Louis and the Young King.[112] He had been busy recruiting large numbers of Brabançon mercenaries, and during the early summer the Plantagenet lands must have seen the passage of many disparate bands or *rutae* of these feared and hated mercenaries flocking north from the Midi to Henry II's service. It is hard to give credence to the figures of upward of 10,000 claimed by the chroniclers, but they undoubtedly constituted a formidable fighting force.[113] Crucially, moreover, their loyalty to the king was assured, though not, observed Howden dryly, 'without the high pay which he gave them'.[114] Accordingly, treasure from Winchester was at the same time being transported via Southampton across the Channel to fund the heavy costs of defence, for as Newburgh noted, 'there was an abundant supply of money from the royal treasures, which were not to be spared in such a crisis'.[115] The provision of armed guards for flotillas, such as that of the chamberlain's ships and the royal esnecca bringing treasure to Normandy in May 1173, indicates Henry's awareness of the possible threat of attack by the naval forces of the Young King's allies.[116]

After further reinforcements had come up to him at Conches, Henry II advanced to Breteuil, just seven miles from Verneuil, where he drew up his army on rising ground.[117] With his forces in readiness, Henry II issued Louis with a formal challenge either to withdraw from the duchy unharmed or to face him in battle.[118] His choice of ground was as much symbolic and psychological as tactical, for Breteuil was the principal Norman lordship of Robert, earl of Leicester. The provocation to Leicester was deliberate; would the rebel earl dare to recover his patrimony by facing Henry in the field? According to William of Newburgh, 'at first the French, by nature both aggressive and arrogant, mocked this ultimatum, especially as they seemed to have superiority in numbers and in military equipment, and they imagined that Henry would certainly not dare to carry through such a plan'.[119] Yet such bluster masked the fact that in reality Henry II's bold gambit had presented the allies with a grave dilemma. If they did not confront Henry, Verneuil might be relieved, and a month's hard and costly fighting would have been wasted. The resulting loss of face would certainly both shame the French and damage the Young King's cause within Normandy and the other Plantagenet domains. It was true that, on more than one occasion in the past, Henry had shown his reluctance to attack the person of his lord, Louis VII.[120] But he was now fighting a desperate war of defence within the borders of his own duchy, and his resolve appeared unshakable.[121] Were the allies prepared to risk the uncertain outcome of a major pitched battle? For the armies of the kings of England and of France to meet in a major set-piece engagement was extremely rare. Indeed, the last occasion had been back in 1119 when, as Louis was uncomfortably aware, his father Louis VI had suffered a crushing defeat at the hands of Henry I.[122] Despite displaying considerable personal bravery on the Second Crusade, Louis VII's own military record did not inspire confidence, while that of his opponent justified his reputation as one of the finest military commanders of the age. The presence, moreover, of so many Brabançons in Henry II's army at Breteuil did not augur well for the allies. Their professionalism, not least as well drilled and steady infantry, would ensure a hard-fought engagement in which the French cavalry might not prevail, while their reputation for ruthlessness only heightened fears of heavy casualties. For the Young King, the dilemma was acute: could he bring himself to fight directly against his own father? Chroniclers describing young Henry's rebellion spoke readily of the sin of parricide, but despite his determination to make war against his father to force political concessions, the Young King almost certainly did not desire the violent death of Henry II. The rebellious Robert Curthose had unhorsed his father at the siege of Gerberoi in 1079, because initially he had not recognized him; once he heard William's voice, however, Robert at once dismounted and gave his father his own horse as a means of escaping further harm.[123] But in the confusion of battle there was no certainty that the Young King would be able to safeguard his own father's life.

For his own part, Henry II doubtless had similar qualms about joining battle with an army that contained the Young King and perhaps his other sons Richard and Geoffrey. Yet he had long since gained the measure of Louis' character, and his actions were carefully calculated. Had he been intent on forcing a decisive engagement, Henry could have launched a direct attack on Louis' army as it lay before Verneuil. Instead, his challenge from Breteuil was a show of strength, but one that allowed the allies room for withdrawal. His instincts were confirmed when Louis, increasingly alarmed by the prospect of an imminent attack, sent Archbishop William of Sens, Count Robert and Count Theobald to parley. Meeting the king riding ahead of his main army with a small retinue, they informed him that the king of France wished to hold talks concerning the establishment of peace between Henry and his sons.[124] Henry II granted them a truce until the following day, and retired with his army back to his camp at Conches, evidently assuming that his preparations for battle and his challenge to Louis had constituted the formal relief of Verneuil. The next morning, 9 August, he again moved up to Breteuil, but waited in vain for the French.[125] For Louis had used the pretence of talks to buy time to occupy the great borough at Verneuil. The French cordon around the town must have prevented the receipt of any further messages bearing news of King Henry's arrival at Breteuil or of the ensuing negotiations, and somehow Louis was able to convince the burghers that no help was forth-coming and demanded their surrender according to the terms of the respite. Thus duped, the townspeople duly capitulated to Louis, but the French imme-diately violated the agreement, sacking and burning the borough and carrying off the townsmen and their goods to France. Louis' forces then beat so hasty a retreat, however, that they were forced to leave much equipment, baggage and supplies behind.[126] 'He fled thus vilely and ignominiously with his army,' noted Roger of Howden, 'to his shame and everlasting opprobrium, not daring to await the attack of the army of the king of England.'[127] Alerted to this perfidy only by the smoke from the blazing town, Henry set off in hot pursuit of the retreating French, but could cut off just part of their rearguard, taking many prisoners.[128] Henry II chose not to pursue Louis or his son further into France, but returned to Verneuil that evening, where his men plundered the aban-doned French camp in which they found 'a great stock of corn, wine, and foodstuffs, together with an assortment of furnishings'.[129] The king formally entered the town amidst celebrations, praised its defenders for their gallant resistance, and ordered the destroyed or damaged walls to be rebuilt.[130]

Ruse, guile and ambush were commonplace in twelfth-century warfare, and were not in themselves deemed unchivalric.[131] But to violate a sworn promise of surrender and safe conduct was a dishonourable act, unbecoming in a knight, still less a king.[132] Louis, moreover, had not only violated his word, failing to keep a pact which young Henry had himself sworn to guarantee, but had profaned the vigil of the feast day of St Laurence, his own patron saint. As Roger of Howden indignantly wrote: 'In order that these events may be kept in memory, be it known that this flight of the king of France took place on the fifth day of the week, upon the vigil of St Laurence, to the praise and glory of our Lord Jesus Christ, who by punishing the crime of perfidy so speedily avenged the indignity done to his martyr'.[133] The reverence displayed by young Henry to St James during the siege at Drincourt suggests he may well have been affronted by his father-in-law's blatant disregard for the feast of St Laurence, some of whose relics were among the treasures of the abbey of Mont Saint-Michel.[134] Whatever part, if any, the Young King had in the treacherous attack on the great borough at Verneuil, he shared in Louis' dishonour and humiliation. In a martial culture where deeds of prowess gained honour and reputation, headlong flight brought ignominy and ridicule.[135] 'So it was', commented Newburgh, 'that those who a little earlier seemed as lions with fierce spirits and the roaring of high sounding words, were suddenly found to be like hares in retreat and flight.'[136] It was for good reason that in his poem, written in the immediate aftermath of the war and urging reconciliation between father and son, Jordan Fantosme told of Count Matthew's death at Drincourt, but studiously avoided any mention whatsoever of the siege of Verneuil. More immediately, the French withdrawal spelt disaster for those Norman lords on the southern frontier, such as Gilbert Crispin, who had come out in support of the Young King. Gilbert had rebelled from the castle of Damville, to the north-east of Verneuil, but with no further hope of reinforcements its garrison surrendered to Henry II's powerful army on 10 August as it marched up the valley of the Iton.[137]

War in the West: Brittany

Despite the failure at Verneuil, the impetus of the allies' attack was far from spent. The Breton frontier was still in turmoil. As the situation had worsened from March 1173, Henry had summoned the Breton magnates and required them to take an oath of loyalty to him. Though many obeyed, Ralph of Fougères ignored the king's summons and had begun to reconstruct his great fortress of Fougères. The Young King sent to his aid a force of picked knights under the command of Hasculf of Saint-Hilaire, one of his leading *familiares*, and William Patrick, who rode across Normandy by circuitous routes to avoid detection by Henry II's men.[138] They were joined by Hugh of Chester, whose influence in the Avranchin was strong, and by Eudo, viscount of Porhoët.[139] It was probably the arrival of some of these reinforcements that allowed Ralph to launch a counter-attack on a force of Brabançons who had been sent by Henry II to devastate the lordship of Fougères.[140] His knights fell on one of their foraging parties between Fougères and Saint James de Beuvron, killing many of them. Following up this success, he took and burned the castles of St James and of Le Teilleul. While Eudo strengthened the castle of Josselin and took that of Ploërmel, Ralph managed to capture the castle of Combour and the city of Dol by suborning the royal castellans,[141] an indication of the fragility of loyalty to the Old King. The situation in Brittany was now deteriorating fast, and Henry II, realizing that he must respond with greater force, sent an advance guard led by William du Hommet, the constable of Normandy, and part of the Norman host, supported by a strong contingent of Brabançons.[142]

On 20 August, the allied forces led by Ralph of Fougères, Hugh of Chester, Hasculf of Saint-Hilaire and William Patrick met in battle with the royal army outside Dol.[143] Why the Young King's supporters chose to give battle, if indeed the choice was theirs, is uncertain; they may not have felt confident about the strength of Dol's defences, as Jordan Fantosme suggests, or they may have risked an attempt to defeat Henry's advanced units before the king himself could come to reinforce his men.[144] The result, however, was swift and decisive. At the first royalist attack Ralph's knights broke and fled, leaving the infantry to be cut down in large numbers.[145] Despite the leavening of knights from the Young King's *familia*,[146] the rebels' hybrid force had stood little chance against the fearsome combination of the elite of Henry II's own household knights and the professional Brabançons. William, Hasculf, fifteen knights and others of rank were taken prisoner, either in the battle or in the rout, and were sent to Pontorson.[147] As William du Hommet had sent part of his force to prevent the escape of the rebels, Ralph, Earl Hugh and some sixty of their knights found their way barred and had no option but to take refuge in the town of Dol. The Brabançons pressed home their attack, overran the town and forced fugitives into the final refuge of the castle's keep.[148] Here they were closely besieged by the *routiers*, the king's knights and the local peasantry raised from the Avranchin, while word was quickly sent to the king at Rouen.[149]

Henry II received the news on the evening of Tuesday 21 August. He moved at once to ensure that the ringleaders neither escaped nor were relieved by Eudo or other Breton insurgents.[150] Henry's speed of movement was proverbial, but in a march that astonished contemporaries he covered the distance of nearly 200 miles between Rouen and Dol in just two days, arriving before the castle on 23 August.[151] In such a dash, the king could only have been accompanied by a comparatively small retinue, but a number of siege engines, possibly already sent for from neighbouring ducal castles, were subsequently set up to begin a bombardment of the keep at Dol. The defenders, realizing their situation was hopeless, surrendered the castle on 26 August after the king had offered lenient terms, agreeing to spare life and limb. The haul of prisoners was enough to show why Henry had regarded the siege of Dol as crucial.[152] It included Earl Hugh, Ralph of Fougères, Ralph de Haye and eighty knights 'of great name', said to be of the Young King's household.[153] In time of war, the small numbers of knights permanently retained in the household of a king or great magnate would be temporarily swelled by stipendiary knights, of whom there was always a ready supply. Those taken at Dol included sons or kinsmen of prominent rebels who had taken the Young King's wages, while others, such perhaps as the warrior known simply by the nickname 'Springald', were free-lances, raised from various regions of France.[154]

To the surprise and approbation of contemporary observers, Henry II dealt mercifully with his defeated opponents at Dol. Some were soon released after giving hostages and pledges, others were kept with him 'in open custody', though Earl Hugh was sent as a prisoner to Falaise castle.[155] His capture removed a major supporter of the Young King not only in south-west Normandy but also in north-west England, and it is notable that, unlike the garrisons of the earl of Leicester, little is heard of the activities of Hugh's castellans in England.[156] The Old King's treatment of rebel lands and castles was more ruthless. He sent his Brabançons on a punitive campaign deep into Brittany, during which they harried and burned Le Porhoët, destroyed the castle of La Guerche, and demolished Fougères and Ralph's other castles.[157] Nonetheless, some of young Henry's adherents on the marches of Anjou and Brittany fought on, waging a guerrilla war from the forests and raiding the lands of the Henry II and his supporters.[158]

Rejecting Overtures of Peace

Such stubborn resistance could not disguise the fact that the Young King and his allies had suffered significant setbacks. Despite the initial successes at Aumale and Drincourt, the offensive in the north had stalled: the French had been shamefully repulsed at Verneuil and at the defeat at Dol had inflicted a major blow to the Young King's support in western Normandy and Brittany. In thanksgiving for his victories, Henry II celebrated the festival of the Birth of the Virgin on 8 September at Le Mans, and remained there till the festival of the exaltation of the Holy Cross, 14 September.[159] Yet he was anxious, from a position of strength, to make peace with his sons. Other forces were also pressing for a reconciliation. Henry II's kinsman King Amalric of Jerusalem, alarmed by Saladin's control of Egypt as vizier of Nur al-Din, had sent a dele-gation to the West headed by the bishop of Lydda, and in one of the letters he sent with the envoys he appealed to Archbishop Henry of Rheims to make peace between the king of England and his sons so that King Henry could come East.[160] Evidently, the extent of Capetian involvement in the inception and sustaining of the rebellion had not been clear to Amalric. The pope, who was doubtless better informed, also urged Archbishop Henry to work for the restoration of peace between the kings of France and England, so that aid could be swiftly sent in this time of crisis to the Holy Land: Christians were fighting each other while Saladin threatened to conquer Christ's patrimony.[161] He also sent a distinguished legation, comprising Peter, archbishop of Tarentaise, Giles, bishop of Evreux, the bishop of Clermont and the abbot of Cîteaux to broker peace talks between Henry II, his sons and King Louis.

It was in such a climate that on 25 September 1173 Henry II met with his sons and the king of France near Gisors. At this great assembly, attended by many of the leading clergy as well as nobles from the Plantagenet and French lands, Henry II first promised to address the grievances that Louis and his men had against him. Though 'against the hope and advice of many', he then made a generous offer which he hoped would reconcile his disaffected sons and detach them from the French. Young Henry was to receive half of the revenues of his demesne lands in England and three 'strong and suitable castles in which he and his household would be able to reside honourably and securely'.[162] Alternatively, he could hold four castles in Normandy instead, with the same revenues suitably adjusted.[163] If he preferred to remain in Normandy, the Young King would receive all the revenues of Normandy with the exception of those from Rouen, Cherbourg and Arques, and three suitable castles, one within the duchy and two on its frontiers.[164] In financial terms, these were very handsome offers.[165] In offering his son a number of castles, moreover, Henry II was granting young Henry a symbolic yet tangible stake in his future inheritance, as well as directly responding to the ostensible *casus belli*, the Young King's anger at the granting of Chinon, Loudun and Mirebeau to John as part of the Maurienne marriage. To Richard, Henry II offered half the revenues of Aquitaine and four castles, and to Geoffrey the lands that would come with Duke Conan's daughter, if the pope granted consent for their marriage. These terms were to be submitted to Peter of Tarentaise, who had played a role in the great peace summit at Limoges earlier that year, and to the papal legates, who could add to these initial terms whatever amounts of revenue they considered just.[166]

The peace negotiations, however, proved fruitless. In his proposals, Henry had sought to share the wealth of his dominions with his sons, and, as his delegation of powers of arbitration reveal, he regarded as the principal issue for negotiation the amount of revenue each of them would receive. Yet just as with his own brother Geoffrey in 1156, the Old King had failed to address the real grievance of his eldest son. There was no offer of rule in Normandy, England or Anjou, and Henry II's terms had explicitly reserved to himself 'justitia et regia potestate'.[167] He doubtless felt he could not be seen to yield to demands for partition or a diminution of his own power made under the threat of force. Young Henry and his brothers accordingly rejected their father's proposals. Roger of Howden believed that King Louis was responsible for persuading them to do so, yet writing to Pope Alexander, Giles, bishop of Evreux, pinned the blame squarely on the Young King.[168] Although Henry II's terms were pleasing to the legates and even to the French king and most of his men, young Henry impudently spurned all his offers 'in contempt of reverence due to a father and divine and human law', while he also offended King Louis by rejecting his counsel. If true, this gives a very different picture from the common assumption that in 1173–74 young Henry was simply the cat's paw of the Capetians.[169] Given how badly the allies had fared in the war up to this point, Louis may well have wanted to cut his losses, but young Henry was not prepared to accept so limited a grant. In all this, warned Giles, the Young King had acquiesced to the counsels of those who, despairing of forgiveness because of the enormity of their iniquity, had set their minds on the killing of the king, the ravaging of the kingdom, and the heavy affliction of the Church. It was now time to demonstrate the apostolic power, given by God, 'to execute vengeance on the nations, and punishments among the peoples'.[170]

Despite this refusal, a second meeting was arranged for the following day between Gisors and Trie, in order to establish some form of peace. Tempers soon flared, however, and an angry exchange took place between Henry II and Earl Robert of Leicester. Whatever his other grievances, the destruction of his comital town had been a bitter blow, and after 'many reproachful and abusive words', Robert even drew his sword on the king before being restrained by those around him.[171] As the conference broke up, skirmishing began between some of the French and English knights, and Ingelram, the castellan of Trie, was captured by William de Mandeville, earl of Essex.[172] Robert of Leicester, however, was already riding hard to Wissant, where he found a powerful force of Flemish mercenary infantry and cavalry, together with transports, ready and waiting.[173] Count Philip had been busy preparing the next stage of the allies' strategy: a field army under the earl of Leicester would land in eastern England, where it could count on the support of Hugh Bigod. It would then march to the relief of the garrison of Leicester castle, for the truce that had been agreed with the justiciar would soon be at an end, reinforce the rebel position in the Midlands and, if possible, join forces with William the Lion as he invaded the northern counties.[174] Accordingly, on the orders of the Young King and Louis, Earl Robert immediately set sail for England, assisted by his cousin Hugh of Châteauneuf, and Normans adhering to the younger Henry's cause.[175] Something of his confidence can be gauged from the fact that, rather than leave her safely in France, Earl Robert brought with him his wife Petronilla, with her household furnishings.[176] King Henry had anticipated some form of landing, but by now he had ordered those ships based at Orford to sail to Sandwich, the traditional base for fleets guarding against invasion.[177]

The Earl of Leicester's Invasion

Leicester's force landed unopposed in the Orwell estuary near Walton, on 29 September, and was quickly joined by Hugh Bigod.[178] Hugh, who held the castles of Framlingham and Bungay, seems to have undertaken little direct military action before Leicester's arrival.[179] The newly completed royal fortress of Orford lay just eighteen miles from Framlingham, and a group of castles, including Eye, Haughley, Thetford, Cambridge, Aldreth and Wisbech, had effectively contained his sphere of operations.[180] The advent of Leicester with a powerful field force, however, greatly enhanced the offensive potential of Bigod's strongholds and boosted the morale of the Young King's supporters in England.[181] The earls' first task was to consolidate their hold on the coast, in order to keep communication with Flanders open and facilitate the landing of reinforcements.[182] They brought up siege engines to attack the clifftop castle at Walton, formerly held by Bigod before being confiscated by Henry II, but despite four days of assault the small royal garrison successfully resisted.[183] An attempt to seize the nearby town of Dunwich was likewise thwarted by a spirited defence by its inhabitants, even though the earl of Leicester had gallows set up to intimidate them into surrendering.[184] Bigod, however, succeeded in taking the greater prize of the port of Ipswich and, aided by the Flemings, he laid siege to Eye, which had been granted to him by the Young King.[185] The earls' forces engaged in widespread plundering, devastating the surrounding area, destroying barns, byres and fishponds and seizing corn and cattle.[186]

These moves helped to consolidate Hugh Bigod's position, but Leicester still needed to break out from the encircling royal garrisons in order to march into the Midlands. His intention may have been to pick up the Icknield Way just to the west of Bury St Edmunds, then head up the old Roman road, the Via Devana, from Babraham to Cambridge and Godmanchester on towards Leicester.[187] On 13 October, the earls stormed and took the large motte and bailey castle of Haughley, held by Becket's old enemy Ranulf de Broc.[188] The attack was not only strategic: it struck a blow for St Thomas, whose aid Earl Robert was invoking for his uprising and the Young King's cause. A polyphonic song, *Novus miles sequitur*, composed for the earl shortly before, envisages the newly canonized St Thomas, and hence a 'new knight' of Christ, supporting young Henry, the new king:

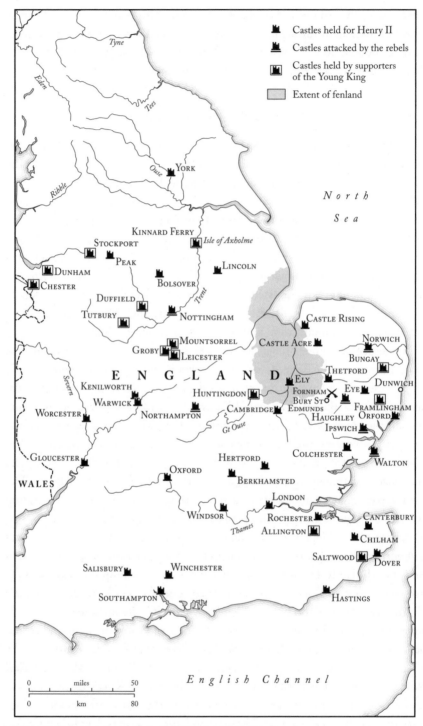

Map 3 East Anglia and the Midlands, 1173–74

A new soldier (*novus miles*) follows
The path of the new king (*novus rex*);
A good shepherd suffers
For the good of his flock . . .
The blood of Thomas the physician
Has healed the wounds
Of a palsied world;
The Lord's flock cries aloud
That the physician of the English
Has renewed the world.

O Thomas, triumphant soldier
Of a young boy,
Be a spiritual shepherd to the clergy and people.
Harken to Leicester!
Direct its clerics
And knights in such a way
That he [the Young King] may reign in the land,
When the wars are done,
With the eternal king.[189]

Just as Thomas' martyrdom has healed the spiritual ills of a corrupt world, so too the reign of the Young King will bring a new beginning, blessed by God and his saint. A rare survival of what must have been a more widespread genre, the song gives a precious glimpse into the efforts of the Young King and his allies to win more widespread support in their struggle against Henry II.

Despite the fall of Haughley, Leicester chose to return to Hugh's principal base at Framlingham rather than continue his push westward, perhaps because, as Howden believed, he shied away from confronting a large force of royalist knights then assembling at Bury St Edmunds.[190] Once back in eastern Suffolk, however, the difficulties of supplying and disciplining so large a force quickly became apparent; Earl Hugh – and, it seems, still more his countess – found the damage inflicted by the Flemish mercenaries on his own lands increasingly intolerable. Whatever his qualms, Earl Robert was soon forced to resume his attempt to reach Leicester.[191]

The Battle of Fornham

The earl's delay in effecting his breakout from East Anglia was to cost him dear. The justiciar Richard de Lucy and Humphrey de Bohun had just burned Berwick as part of their punitive ravaging of Lothian when news reached them of Leicester's landing in East Anglia.[192] Concealing the danger and coolly exploiting the fact that William the Lion himself had not yet been apprised of Earl Robert's invasion, de Lucy negotiated a truce, seemingly from a position of strength, until the feast of St Hilary in January.[193] Free to hasten south, de Bohun joined forces at Bury with the earls of Cornwall, Arundel and Gloucester together with other royalists, including Robert FitzBernard, who led a strong force of veterans drawn from the Anglo-Norman settlers in Ireland.[194] This powerful army, also containing 300 stipendiary knights from the *familia regis*, was further strengthened by a contingent of the abbey's men under Walter FitzRobert, and – perhaps as important for the morale of King Henry's men – with the banner of St Edmund himself.[195] This standard was carried, by hereditary right, by Roger Bigod, Earl Hugh's eldest son, a striking reminder of how the civil war might divide baronial families.[196] A well-informed contemporary believed that the royalists outnumbered Leicester's forces in cavalry by four to one, but that the earl had a significantly larger force of infantry, with the Flemings under his command numbering around 3,000.[197] Leicester was said to have set great store by these mercenaries, for in tight, well-ordered formations the Flemish infantry, armed with long spears, was more than capable of defeating a cavalry charge.[198]

Though he was aware of the royalist build-up at Bury, Earl Robert nonetheless chose a line of march which took him only few miles to the north-west of the town.[199] If he was hoping that the size of his army would deter attack, he was gravely mistaken. Well informed of the earl's movements and apprised of the local terrain by the abbey's knights, Henry II's men launched a bold attack on 17 October, suddenly falling on the Flemings at the little village of Fornham St Genevieve as they were crossing the river Lark, still in their marching order.[200] Leicester was taken completely by surprise, and the engagement was as short as it was sudden.[201] There was some hard fighting, but the Flemings soon broke under the impact of the royalist knights' charge. Scattered and knocked down by the cavalry, some were slain in large numbers by the royalist infantry, while others, driven into the marshy ground by the river, were drowned.[202] Angry peasants finished off stragglers with scythes and pitchforks, but some managed to flee as far at the abbey itself, where they sought sanctuary by the feretory of St Edmund.[203] Those who were not butchered out of hand were imprisoned in wretched conditions, while the bodies of some of the slain rebels were displayed at Bury, Colchester and Ipswich.[204] Earl Robert, Hugh de Châteauneuf and other nobles were taken prisoner, as was the earl's wife Petronilla, a virago said to have been wearing a hauberk and armed with spear and shield.[205] Shipped to the king in Normandy, they soon joinined the earl of Chester at Falaise 'in the strictest custody'.[206]

It had been a notable victory for Henry II and his supporters.[207] For the Young King, however, the defeat and capture of the earl of Leicester and his forces was a terrible blow. Not only had he lost his most powerful supporter in England, but his cause in the kingdom can only have been harmed by the wave of hostility expressed towards the Flemings, whose depredations continued even after the battle, from the castles of Bungay and Framlingham. This rekindled memories of the dark days of Stephen's reign, when Flemish mercenaries had caused widespread devastation.[208] Looking back after the war's end, Jordan Fantosme could mock the Flemings:

My lords, the truth is that most of them were weavers, they do not know how to bear arms like knights, and why they had come was to pick up plunder and the spoils of war, for there is no more prosperous region on earth than Bury St Edmunds ... They made no early start in gathering the wool of England! Crows and buzzards descend on their corpses and bear off their souls to the fire that burns to eternity ... The Flemings would have been worthy enough people had God been their helper, but this they had not deserved because of their vast thievery. It was a disaster that the earl of Leicester ever got mixed up with them ...[209]

Contemporaries, moreover, were quick to attribute the swift and decisive nature of the royalist victory to divine judgement.[210] Leicester may have invoked St Thomas, but at Fornham it was St Edmund, king and martyr, who had punished those who dared to ravage his lands.[211] Howden noted that news of the defeat struck fear into all the king's enemies. The Young King and Louis were greatly saddened, 'and from that time, they feared the king of England more than I am able to express, because God was with him'.[212]

The defeat of Leicester's field army left Hugh Bigod isolated in East Anglia. He nevertheless still retained large numbers of Flemings in his service. Some may have been survivors from the rout of Fornham, but Ralph of Diss' statement that there were 14,000 of them – even if a great exaggeration – strongly suggests that the earl of Norfolk had been reinforced by further contingents from Flanders sent subsequent to the landing of Leicester's force in late September.[213] To contain this threat, Henry II's men mustered contingents against him at Colchester, Ipswich and Bury. Dean Ralph believed that had the earl been closely besieged, the very number of his Flemish troops would have quickly forced Bigod to surrender through lack of supplies. As it was, however, the loyalist magnates were persuaded, for a large sum, to grant a truce to the octaves of Pentecost, whereby the Flemish were allowed safe passage through Essex and Kent to Dover, where ships, doubtless supplied by

Count Philip and the Young King, waited to transport them back to Flanders.[214] Bigod's offensive capabilities had been curbed, but he had not been forced to submit and his castles remained a threat, not least as bases for any fresh invasion that the allies might launch.

With young Henry and his allies defeated or repulsed in Normandy and in England, Henry II was able to campaign beyond the duchy into the Angevin heartlands. Leading his great army of Brabançons into the Touraine, the king compelled the surrender of Geoffrey de La Haye, who yielded up the castle and town of La Haye on 18 November.[215] With the surrender soon after of the castle of Preuilly, held by Peter de Montrabei, and Robert de Blé's stronghold of Champigny, two of the great lordships of northern Poitou were reduced to obedience.[216] The importance of the latter fortress as a focus of resistance is indicated by the substantial list of knights and serjeants taken prisoner there, their names carefully enrolled, to which Roger of Howden had access.[217] Around 30 November, Henry moved against Vendôme, whose count had been expelled by his own son, Brachard de Lavardin, who had sided with the Young King. Henry's Brabançons, however, soon took the place.[218] But this campaign was to bring a far greater prize. Queen Eleanor, attempting to escape the forces of her husband as they marched south into Aquitaine, had attempted to flee north to Paris, to seek refuge with King Louis and join her sons.[219] First she had moved to the castle of her uncle Ralph at Faye-la-Vineuse, but she was captured by Henry's men on the road to Chartres and brought as a prisoner to Chinon.[220] According to Gervase of Canterbury, she had donned the clothes of a man, either for disguise or for ease of fast riding.[221] No contemporary records the impact of Eleanor's capture on young Henry or his brothers, but though she was now Henry's hostage, her captivity did nothing to lessen the vigour with which they prosecuted the war against their father.

A War against Nature

The conflict which had broken out in 1173 had shaken the stability of Henry's lands to the core. It also deeply troubled contemporary writers, who struggled to make sense of a war begun by the king's own sons. For Gerald of Wales, quoting Lucan's famous description of the bitter struggle between Caesar and Pompey, it was *bella plus quam civilia* – 'a worse than civil war'.[222] It appeared not only as illicit and treasonous but as unnatural.[223] The Melrose chronicler saw the conflict in terms of warring members of the body politic: 'A dispute and a war, which may almost be styled inexorable, arose between the belly and the bowels, between the parent and the child.'[224] Such a rebellion of son against father, noted Peter of Blois, ran contrary to the law of Moses, the law of the

Gospels, the censure of the canons, the strictures of the apostles, the imperial laws, the condition of men and natural law itself.[225] Howden agreed, arguing that at Breteuil in 1173 Henry II would have been fully justified in attacking Louis and the French because they had so corrupted Henry's sons that they rebelled against their parent and progenitor, 'forgetful of the dictates of humanity and unrestrained by natural law'.[226] Such an act could only be one of insane folly, bestial because it flew in the face of reason and duty to one's natural lord; the Young King's rebellion was 'the wicked madness of traitors', 'bestial madness', and a *furor* waged with 'diabolical fury'.[227] When Ralph of Diss compiled his lengthy list of examples of earlier filial revolts, he did so less for a historical than for a didactic purpose. For, as he noted, in many of these cases the rebellious son met with divinely ordained punishment, whether by death, demonic possession, exile, imprisonment, deposition as heir or lack of offspring.[228] 'You will be able to frighten whoever you wish away from parricide,' Ralph remarked with vehemence, 'if the Book of Judges, the Book of Kings and the Book of Isaiah are diligently studied concerning the extermination of sons rising up against their parents. Read books, study the scriptures, consult more prudent men, and have before your eyes this little collection.'[229] By contrast, it was little surprise that the Young King's rebellion came to be regarded by some as divine punishment on Henry II for Becket's murder.[230]

Plagued as he was by fears of treachery, Henry II was particularly sensitive to interpretations of the 'Prophecies of Merlin', the supposed utterances of one Merlin Sylvester at the time of King Vortigern. Contained in the seventh book of Geoffrey of Monmouth's *History of the Kings of Britain*, they were a heady mixture of Geoffrey's own invention with an earlier Welsh genre, and they were highly influential.[231] Writing in late 1174, Guernes of Pont-Sainte-Maxence noted of the king how the Prophecies 'really alarmed him, and the fools who interpret them have been no help to him'.[232] Just as the rebellious Eleanor was linked to 'the eagle of the broken covenant' in the Prophecies, so too Roger of Howden saw the Young King's war as being foretold:

> Then indeed was fulfilled the prophecy of Merlin, who spoke thus: 'Then the cubs of the roaring lion shall awaken and coming out of the forests . . . will live again the days of their forefathers'. Merlin made this prophecy about the sons of King Henry, son of the Empress Matilda. When he called them 'the cubs of the roaring lion', he meant they would rise against their father and their lord to make war on him.[233]

Gerald of Wales, who had a deep interest in these prophecies and regarded the rebellion of 1173–74 as preordained retribution for Henry II's supposed crimes and oppression of the Church, similarly recited a prophecy of Merlin which he considered had been fulfilled by young Henry's revolt:

> Because of their father's sin, sons sin against him who begot them, and an earlier crime becomes the cause of subsequent ones. Sons will rise against their parent, and to avenge a crime the bowels will conspire against the belly. His own flesh and blood will rise up against a man of blood, and he will suffer terrible affliction . . .[234]

For the present, however, Henry II had weathered the storm. He and Louis agreed a truce to last from 13 January until 31 March, the close of Easter. He held his Christmas court at Caen, but there can have been little joy in the festivities.[235] His own queen was now his captive, while all of his sons, save John, still remained at the court of the king of France, and had rejected his offer of peace on generous terms. To steady his supporters, Henry II acted with studied sangfroid, being careful to be seen hawking and hunting as if he was unperturbed by the dangers of the situation, and to this end he had hawks and even fallow deer shipped to the duchy from England.[236] Yet fear of betrayal and desertion was ever present. Ralph of Diss claimed that among the defectors were some of his 'household men . . . most intimate in his counsels'. Henry knew well that many nobles secretly favoured the Young King and were merely biding their time for the fortunes of war to turn in the younger Henry's favour.[237]

CHAPTER 9

Invasion

THE ONSLAUGHT RENEWED, 1174

OVER THE WINTER, the Young King and his brothers remained at Louis' court. The campaigns of 1173 had gone badly for the allies, but they still held the strategic initiative. The fires of rebellion in Henry II's dominions were far from extinguished, and the Old King, plagued by fears of disloyalty as yet concealed, was forced to remain on the defensive. Save for some of the younger hotheads, few of the Young King's supporters can have expected that Henry II's position would crumble in the space of only one campaigning season. As in the previous year, the allies sought to keep up military pressure on a number of fronts, to keep Henry guessing and to prevent him concentrating his forces. Philip of Flanders was now fully committed to the war once again, and plans were laid for an invasion of England.

A January Offensive in the Séois

In January, young Henry showed his eagerness to renew hostilities by striking through the county of Perche to attack Sées. He clearly did not regard himself bound by the truce which his father had established with King Louis, that was to last until after Easter 1174, and while the Capetian king himself refrained from taking the field, Count Theobald of Blois, aided by Count Rotrou of Perche and John, count of Sées, provided the bulk of the Young King's forces.[1] As the reverse at Verneuil had starkly shown, the Norman defences on the line of the Avre still remained too strong. But the support of Count Rotrou, who was married to the count of Blois' sister, and of Count John, allowed an allied strike further west on the border of the duchy with Maine.[2] This was a daring move: if Sées fell, the allies could drive up the valley of the Orne to Argentan and from there push deep into central Normandy, threatening Falaise, Caen or Lisieux.[3] Indeed, this strategic potential had long been recognized by Louis VII, who had himself attacked Sées in 1151 in his war against Count Geoffrey le Bel, exploiting the fact that his own brother Robert was then count of Perche.[4] It was also why in 1166 Henry II had constructed defensive earthworks on the borders of Perche, built the castle of Beauvoir in north-east Maine, and taken into his own hands the key castles of this vital yet turbulent frontier, including removing Alençon and La Roche Mabile from the Bellême family.[5] Count John, son of William Talvas, was thus anxious to reassert Bellême influence in the Alençonnais and regain control of his comital seat at Sées. By supporting the Young King, more-over, he hoped to recover the extensive lands in England that had come to him through marriage to a niece of Geoffrey le Bel but had been seized by Henry II in 1166.[6] To the east of Alençon, John held the castles of Essay, Saint-Rémy-du-Val and Mamers, and it may well have been from Essay, due south of Sées, that the allies launched their attack.[7] Sées itself comprised two separate bourgs: on the north bank of the Orne, the Bourg l'Évêque contained the cathedral, while south of the river was the Bourg-le-Comte with its castle.[8] The Young King once again led a powerful force of some 500 knights, indi-cating that the attack was far more than a reconnaissance in force.[9] The garrison and townspeople of Sées, however, put up a spirited resistance, and, lacking a siege train, young Henry and Count John were forced to withdraw in frustration.[10]

For the rest of the winter months, the allies bided their time. Pope Alexander III sent a delegation, headed once more by Peter, the saintly archbishop of Tarentaise, and Alexander, abbot of Cîteaux, to King Louis to establish peace between Henry II and his sons.[11] Their efforts, however, were fruitless, for Louis was already planning a joint offensive, and at Easter, when the truce agreed with Henry II was set to end, the French king summoned his nobles to a great council at Paris.[12] Here, the counts of Flanders, Blois and Clermont, as well as many others, swore on relics that they would sail with the Young King around 24 June, the Feast of St John, to invade England and subjugate it to his rule. Other lords, who were to remain with Louis, pledged that they would enter Normandy with his army, take whatever castles they could and lay waste the land, or that they would lay siege to Rouen.[13] Meanwhile, William the Lion was to invade northern England once more and to join forces there with a group of committed rebels headed by Roger de Mowbray. This campaign would prepare the way for the invasion by the Young King, Philip and their allies, who would sail from Flanders: the young Henry's pres-ence in England would bring over the waverers to his cause and decisively tip the balance against the Old King.

The Second Invasion of William the Lion

Although William the Lion had been forced into a precipitous withdrawal from the north of England in 1173, the earl of Leicester's invasion in East Anglia had prevented the justiciar Richard de Lucy from pressing home his punitive counter-attack. Indeed, King William's position remained strong enough for him to be able to demand the stiff price of 300 marks of silver for granting a truce, brokered by Hugh, bishop of Durham, to the nobles of Northumberland for the same period as Henry II had agreed with Louis – from 13 January, the feast of St Hilary, up to the close of Easter.[14] The very moment the truce expired, William again led his army across the border into Northumberland and, as in the previous year, commenced by attacking Wark.[15] With the Scots controlling Berwick and Roxburgh, Wark alone held out in a salient, which left any Scottish advance to the south-east vulnerable to an attack in its rear. The castle's defences had not been tested in 1173, but Roger de Stuteville was an experienced commander and had made good use of the intervening respite to further strengthen the fortifications. While William made preparations for a major assault, he dispatched a strong force of knights, including some of his Flemish mercenaries, on a surprise dawn raid on the town of Belford.[16] Pillaging the countryside around Bamburgh, they returned to Berwick-upon-Tweed laden with spoils and livestock to help provision the army during the impending siege.[17] Jordan Fantosme gives a vivid impression of what such a raid entailed:

> Some speed into the farms to wreak havoc, some take sheep from their folds, and some set fire to farmsteads ... You could have seen Flemings tying up peasants and leading them off roped together like heathens. Women flee to the church, only to be snatched away naked, leaving behind their garments and their valuables ... They burned the countryside: but God showed his love for these goodly peasants who had no protection, in that their mortal enemies, the Scots, were not there, for *they* would have beaten and killed and ill-treated them. The king of Scotland's men took off an enormous quantity of booty ... they have any number of animals, oxen, horses, fine cows, ewes, lambs, clothes, money, brooches and rings.[18]

William now ordered the attack on Wark with 'his archers, with his catapults and sturdy siege engines, and his slingers and his crossbowmen'.[19] The well-armed Flemings broke through the outer palisades and stormed the ditches, but were repeatedly thrown back from the walls with heavy losses. Attempts to deploy a stone-throwing engine against the gate of the bailey and to set fire to the defences proved equally ineffectual.[20] The following day, acknowledging he

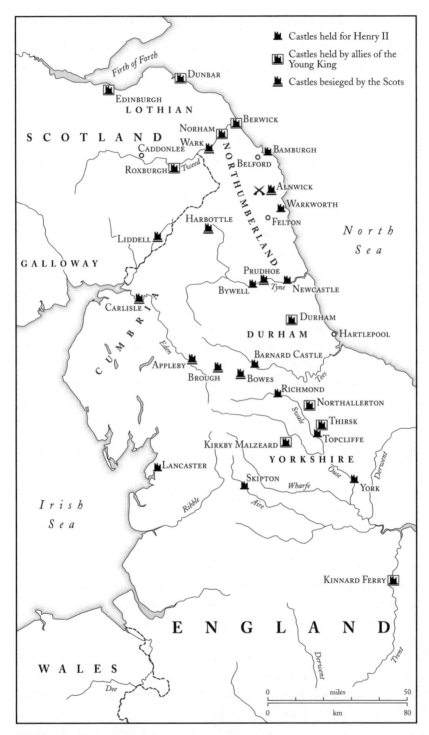

Map 4 Northern England, 1173–74

could not take the castle by force, William ordered the Scottish army to strike camp, burn their temporary huts and retreat across the Tweed to Roxburgh. It is Jordan Fantosme who again captures the noise and commotion of an army on the move:

> Then you would have seen the marshals going hither and thither, taking down the pavilions and folding up the tents and making a tremendous racket throughout the camp of the army of Scotland . . . they set fire to their huts and left them ablaze: the hubbub was enormous . . . that the serving men and the esquires make throughout the camp.[21]

Roger de Stuteville wisely counselled his men not to push their luck by making insulting remarks or jeering at the retreating Scots, but once the enemy were at a safe distance the garrison sounded a fanfare and broke into song to celebrate their victory.[22] It had been a stark demonstration of the great superiority of the art of defence over attack: Roger's garrison of some ten knights and forty serjeants and archers had successfully repulsed William's entire army.[23]

The attack on Wark, however, was only the first stage of William's campaign. As the allies had planned, the powerful Yorkshire magnate Roger de Mowbray now came out openly in revolt. During the time of truce in early 1174, Mowbray had re-fortified the ruined castle of Kinnard Ferry on the Isle of Axholme,[24] and, leaving this and his two other castles of Thirsk and Kirkby Malzeard in the charge of his two eldest sons, he had come north to join William the Lion.[25] He was accompanied by Adam de Port, who had been implicated in a plot to murder Henry II in 1172, with a strong force.[26] The Young King hoped that Mowbray's defection would begin a landslide. According to William of Newburgh, he repeatedly sent secret letters

> either to entice by promises or to assail with threats the English nobles who seemed to be standing by his father so as to bring them over to his faction by any means possible. So it is said that at that time there were in England only a few nobles whose support for the king did not waver, and who would not be ready to abandon him at an opportune moment if their intentions were not countered in good time.[27]

Mowbray's alliance opened up important strategic possibilities for the Young King's coalition. His castle of Kinnard Ferry lay between York and Lincoln, and its position on the river Trent, close to its confluence with the Humber, made it a potential landing base for ships from Flanders, while his other castles threatened York and provided a rebel enclave between the northern counties and the concentration of rebel strongholds in the Midlands. Indeed, the Scots' invasion at Easter had been the signal for these Midlands rebels to mount a sustained series of raids,[28] and William the Lion assisted them by sending his younger brother David to reinforce the garrisons of Leicester castle and Huntingdon.[29]

David's role in the invasion of 1173 is unrecorded, but now, in return for his assistance in the war, King William offered him the earldom of Lennox, as well as confirming the grant made to him by the Young King the previous year of the great honour of Huntingdon for his service.[30] This already included widespread holdings in Northamptonshire, Bedfordshire and Cambridgeshire, but young Henry had added all the county of Cambridgeshire for good measure.[31] The powerful castle of Huntingdon not only controlled the passage of Ermine Street between Stamford and Hertford but also one of the main routes out of Norfolk skirting the Fens.[32] Whatever scruples he may have felt in taking up arms against Henry II, the man who had knighted him in 1170, David now threw his energies into supporting the Young King. The new earl was quickly able to draw on a groundswell of support among the lesser tenants of the honour of Huntingdon, which had close links to Scotland.[33] Earl David 'fortified Huntingdon sufficiently with knights, and with supplies of food' before joining forces with the men of Leicester, then 'molested the whole province with sword and fire, with spoiling and plunderings'.[34] From these two bases, Earl David and Ansketil Mallory launched a successful raid on Northampton, the linchpin of royalist defences in the Midlands.[35] The garrison under Bertram de Verdun, the sheriff of Warwickshire and Leicestershire, sallied out, together with a force of the burgesses, to engage with the rebels but in the ensuing clash many of the townsmen were killed and over 200 captured. The castle and the town were too heavily defended to take, but David and the knights of the earl of Leicester returned in triumph with much booty.[36]

This success may have prompted another leading Midlands rebel, William, Earl Ferrers,[37] to lead the knights of Leicester in a daring dawn attack on Nottingham, which was held by Reginald de Lucy. Achieving complete surprise, the rebels broke into the town with ease, killing and taking prisoner many of the citizens before plundering and putting it to the torch.[38] As at Northampton, Ferrers and his men did not attempt to attack the heavily fortified castle,[39] but the booty and ransoms gained from these attacks, as well no doubt as many smaller raids that went unnoticed by the chroniclers, were vital in sustaining the rebel war effort.[40] As had happened so often in the troubled years of Stephen's reign, churches were plundered of their treasures to provide money for knights' wages. After the end of the war, in late 1175, Abbot William of Peterborough was deposed by the archbishop of Canterbury for having violently entered his own church at the head of a body of knights and wounded the monks who attempted to prevent his seizure of the relics of the saints, including the arm of St Oswald, which, it was alleged, he intended to hand over to the Jews in return for cash.[41] The abbot was also arraigned by the king for having received Ralph de Waterville, his brother, who was an *inimicus regis* and one of the rebel garrison of Huntingdon.[42] The abbot was attempting, or so his accusers must have claimed, to support the rebels with the moveable wealth of his own abbey.[43]

The Siege of Carlisle

While his younger brother harassed the royalist garrisons of the Midlands, King William chose to launch his second attack on Cumberland, probably in early June.[44] Mowbray's presence with the Scots king may well explain the choice of their first target, the powerful earthwork and timber castle of Liddel for this was held by Nicholas, Robert de Stuteville's elder brother.[45] The castle fell to the Scots, who then marched on Carlisle, where King William issued its castellan, Robert de Vaux, with an ultimatum: he could surrender on terms, but if he did not and the castle fell by storm, he would be put to death as a traitor who had withheld William's rightful inheritance from him.[46] De Vaux refused, though he promised he would surrender if King Henry instructed him to do so.[47] The prospect of a direct assault on Carlisle was a daunting one, so leaving part of his army to blockade the town and castle William moved down the Eden valley and attacked Appleby.[48] His aim was to capture the series of more minor royal castles – Appleby, Brough and Bowes – which served as staging posts across the Pennine route to Richmond, in order to isolate Carlisle from the prospects of relief and resupply from other royalist bases, especially Richmond and Barnard Castle, held by Ranulf de Glanville and Bernard de Balliol respectively.[49] Despite its strong stone keep, Appleby was poorly garrisoned and supplied, and its castellan, Gospatric FitzHorm, quickly surrendered, an act for which he was later heavily amerced by Henry II.[50] That Gospatric's sympathies may well have been with William the Lion reflected the competing claims of loyalties in the contested northern counties, and Appleby's capture caused the defection of others previously loyal to Henry II.[51]

With their own constables and a garrison installed in Appleby, the allied army struck east to Brough, where the Flemings and Mowbray's 'marchers' succeeded in taking the bailey by storm. Its small garrison put up a valiant resistance, but when the keep was set on fire they were finally forced to capitulate.[52] Yet Bowes, which served as the western defence for Richmond, successfully held out: Henry II had spent considerable sums on the castle between

1170 and 1172, which probably included the building of the small but strong keep.[53] As the Scots continued to ravage Cumbria, however, victuals began to run low enough within Carlisle for Robert de Vaux to reopen negotiations with King William, who had returned to press the siege. The upgrading of Carlisle's fortifications in the 1160s had made the town an integral element of the castle's defences, but a doubtless unforeseen consequence was that it became harder for its garrison to operate independently of the townsmen, which added to the problems of logistics. It may have been pressure from the burgesses that caused de Vaux to agree to surrender to the Scots if the castle was not relieved by Henry II. Howden, who was particularly well informed about northern affairs in 1174, believed that de Vaux had negotiated a respite until Michaelmas, for which he gave oaths and hostages.[54]

'My Other Sons are the Real Bastards': Geoffrey Plantagenet and the Royalist Revanche

Henry II's commanders in England, however, had already begun a counter-attack. Realizing that it was imperative to prevent William from joining forces with the Midland rebels, they focused their efforts first on Mowbray's castles. Henry II's natural son Geoffrey, the bishop elect of Lincoln, gathered a large force of knights and stipendiaries, as well as summoning the county levy of Lincolnshire.[55] Collecting boats, they crossed to the Isle of Axholme and laid siege to Kinnard castle. Its castellan, Mowbray's son Robert, was captured by a peasant at Clay while trying to make for Leicester to seek aid. The inadequately provisioned garrison quickly surrendered on 5 May through lack of water, and the castle was destroyed.[56] Only a little older than the Young King, Geoffrey was fast emerging as a talented military leader. Loyalty to Henry II in this time of crisis was a marked feature of his illegitimate kinsmen: his natural brother Hamelin de Warenne and his uncle, Reginald of Cornwall, illegitimate son of Henry I, stood by him, but above all it was young Geoffrey who saw in his legitimate brothers' rebellion a major opportunity for his own advancement. According to Gerald of Wales' later encomium on Geoffrey, when in July 1174 the elect of Lincoln came to King Henry at Huntingdon to witness the formal surrender of the rebel castellans, the king greeted him delightedly and publicly proclaimed, 'My other sons are the real bastards. He alone has proved himself legitimate and true!'[57]

From Kinnard, Geoffrey marched to York where he was greeted, or so Gerald claimed, by Archbishop Roger with a great ecclesiastical procession and hailed by the citizens as their saviour from the Scots.[58] Together, Geoffrey and Archbishop Roger raised the levies of Yorkshire to augment the knights of their own military households and those they had been able to raise from their sees' military tenants, and besieged Mowbray's castle at Kirkby Malzeard, just twenty miles from York.[59] The garrison fired some of the outer defences before withdrawing into the main fortifications, but Geoffrey pressed home the attack with siege engines while attempts were made to sap the walls. After only a few days the castle fell, with thirty knights and sixty archers being taken prisoner.[60] Entrusting the castle to the archbishop of York, Geoffrey then moved to contain Mowbray's last stronghold at Thirsk by strengthening the castle at Topcliffe and giving it into the charge of Robert de Stuteville's son William.[61] The royalists also built a siege castle to contain the garrison of Hugh de Puiset's castle at Northallerton.[62] With these immediate threats to York dealt with, Geoffrey's army struck north to secure the crucial stronghold of Richmond, which was being menaced by the Scottish attack on Bowes. News of Geoffrey's approach forced King William to raise the siege and with-draw north-east into Northumberland.[63] The allies' campaign was faltering, and the Midlands rebellion, though still vigorous, remained isolated. All now rested on the Young King and his planned invasion.

Invasion Preparations and Overtures to London

Young Henry and Count Philip had not been idle. An armada was gathering in the Flemish ports in readiness for the planned assault after 24 June, and on 14 May a powerful advance guard sailed from Wissant under the command of Ralph of La Haye, one of the Young King's leading supporters in Anjou.[64] Several thousand strong, it was headed by an elite group of 318 knights hand-picked by Count Philip.[65] They made landfall in the Orwell estuary and joined forces with Earl Hugh Bigod, who had been ordered by the Young King to receive them into his castles.[66] The arrival of this new field army once again allowed Earl Hugh to go on the offensive, and he marched into Norfolk, plun-dering as he went.[67] On 18 June, the allies scored a notable success when they took the city of Norwich by storm, killing some of the burgesses and taking a rich haul of booty and prisoners, from whom they extracted heavy ransoms.[68] These were important developments for the allied cause, for if the coast of East Anglia was largely under rebel control it might serve as a safe landing base for Count Philip and the Young King's invasion force. More immediately, Earl Hugh and his Flemings might attempt to break out of East Anglia and threaten London itself.

The Young King had already attempted to win over the Londoners to his cause. As Jordan Fantosme later reminded Henry II, the citizens had remained loyal to the Old King, despite the fact that they did not lack envoys from Flanders across the sea who promised to give them great honours and rewards. Your own son ... urged them by letter and by envoy to aid him in making war on his father in such terms as you shall hear me state: that he would esteem them all the days of his life, would love them and cherish them, and much he wanted to give them.[69]

London, after all, had claimed a voice in the election of the king of England, and this supposedly 'ancient privilege' had been confirmed by King Stephen in 1135.[70] The city had subsequently played a major role in the political struggles between Stephen and the Empress, and Matilda's catastrophic mishandling of the citizens in 1141 had robbed her of a coronation, of control of the capital's military and financial resources, and ultimately of her own chance of victory over King Stephen. It is unknown if young Henry went so far as to offer the Londoners the grant of a commune, as his younger brother John would do in 1191 to buy the city's support during his own bid for power in Richard's absence on crusade, but he must have promised them liberties exceeding those his father had granted the city soon after his own accession.[71]

The Young King's alliance with Philip of Flanders, moreover, had profound economic implications for the city, as a good deal of its commerce flowed via the Flemish ports, which were also the principal entrepôts for English wool exports: an embargo imposed by the count might prove crippling.[72] Henry II seems to be have been politic in his dealings with the Londoners before the conflict, but the county farm of the city and of Middlesex had risen from £300 under Henry I to a heavy £500 per annum, while in 1173, doubtless as a result of the pressures of war, the king had levied a 'gift' of 1,000 marks on the city.[73] Jordan's statement that the Young King's missives and messengers came from Flanders, rather than from Paris, strongly implies that they were co-ordinated with the invasion plans as the allied fleet and army made ready at Gravelines. These overtures, moreover, seem to have gained some support. Jordan believed that Gilbert de Montfitchet had fortified his castle, which lay within the walls of the city just to the west of St Paul's, and that he proclaimed that he had 'the support of the earls of Clare'.[74] How far Richard de Clare, earl of Hertford, was actually a partisan of the Young King is hard to determine, but his control of the two castles of Clare in Suffolk and Tonbridge in Kent made suspicion as to his loyalty a worrying prospect for Henry II.[75] The fear of crumbling loyalties is reflected in Howden's belief that young Henry and Philip were preparing to invade 'at the summons of the earls and barons of England'.[76]

The gravity of the situation prompted the justiciar and his colleagues to send a number of messengers to Henry II in France, but they had 'received no certain news' that the king intended to return to England.[77] Henry, indeed, was preoccupied with the war in France. Though Louis VII had gathered his forces and was threatening once more to invade Normandy, Henry II had been concentrating his efforts on the Angevin heartlands, where despite his campaign the previous November the Young King's partisans again appear to have been active.[78] In late April Henry II had entered Maine with a powerful army, before rallying his supporters in Anjou. The Angevins, noted Dean Ralph, 'came to meet the king more readily and swiftly than the men of Maine, for they were more devoted to him, and more ready and willing to submit to all his wishes.'[79] He then marched south and celebrated Whitsun in Poitiers.[80] Eleanor's capture in November 1173 had been a major blow to the rebels in Poitou, but as a direct riposte Louis VII had bestowed arms on Richard, an act representing not only his dubbing to knighthood and coming of age, but his investiture of power in the duchy of Aquitaine.[81] Anxious to prove himself, Richard had left the Île-de-France and had rallied opposition in the duchy to his father, whom, admitted the chronicler of the great abbey of St Aubin in Angers, many of the Poitevins hated.[82] In Poitou itself, Henry II's power was strongest in the north-west, where ducal castles, estates and a number of consistently loyal ducal castellans or *prévôts*, such as William Maingot and Fulk de Matha, were concentrated, while the castles of Geoffrey de Rancon and of the count of Angoulême formed a rebel bloc in the Charentais.[83] Though Richard's attempt to take the key port of La Rochelle was repulsed by its citizens, the rival burgesses of Saintes went over to him, and he began to strengthen the town's fortifications, even converting the cathedral into a makeshift castle.[84] When in early June, however, Henry II advanced into the Saintonge against him, Richard dared not face his father and fled to Geoffrey de Rancon's great castle of Taillebourg on the Charente.[85] Despite the fall of Saintes, he would continue his resistance until September, while further east the Limousin remained troubled enough for the citizens of Limoges to build a defensive wall, hurrying in their work before Henry II could forbid such measures.[86]

Henry II had, however, effectively broken the back of the revolt in Aquitaine. Made anxious to return north by news of the Young King and the count of Flanders' preparations, Henry entrusted Maine and Anjou to one of his closest *familiares*, Maurice de Craon.[87] He strengthened the western approaches to Angers against a renewed attack from the Breton rebels by taking the town of Ancenis, on the Loire between Nantes and Angers, from its rebel lord Guivinou de Ancenis, and constructed there a great fortress, 'which displays all the knowledge and skill of the carpenter' – an important reminder of the continuing importance of timber-built fortifications.[88] To make any siege of Ancenis still harder, he devastated the surrounding territory, including the lands of St Florent to the west of Saumur, tearing up the vines and felling fruit trees.[89]

Gathering additional forces of mercenaries as he went, Henry returned to Normandy and held a general assembly of the Norman nobles loyal to him at the ducal castle of Bonneville-sur-Touques on 24 June, at which he urged them to keep their faith to him.[90] He strengthened his castle garrisons on the Norman border with France, removing those castellans whose loyalty he suspected – a telling indication of his fear of defection to his son.[91] But in some quarters, loyalty could still be bought: according to Robert of Torigni, Henry II matched these efforts by a sustained attempt to suborn leading French nobles by great gifts, and as a result was well informed about the Young King and Louis' plans.[92] The *History of William Marshal* similarly alleges that the Young King was deserted by some of the most eminent French barons 'because of their greed for gain from the King who greased their palms. He really knew how to sing the right tunes to them, tunes they found delightful and sweet.'[93] It may have been at Bonneville-sur-Touques that Henry II was met by Richard of Ilchester, now bishop elect of Winchester, sent as a last resort by the justiciar. Implicitly trusted by the king, he was, as Dean Ralph noted, the man best placed 'to point out to the king all the losses, difficulties and risks his people had endured, and to give an accurate picture of the quarrels of the nobles, the unstable situation in the cities, the clamouring of the common people, which would steadily grow worse as they longed for change and would produce movements that would be difficult to suppress.'[94] Richard's presence was a clear sign of the growing panic of Henry's regents in England: the Normans joked that 'since the English have sent so many messengers, and now this man, what else could they send to call the king back to England except the Tower of London itself?'[95] Henry II, however, needed little urging, for he realized that it was imperative to reach England before his son.

Informed of Henry II's planned crossing, the justiciar Richard de Lucy had already begun a major counter-attack in late June, closely investing Huntingdon and building a siege castle in front of the castle gates to deny exit or entry to the defenders, who as a defensive measure had fired the town.[96] On the king's orders, he entrusted this fortification to Simon III de Senlis, who claimed as his own inheritance the great Midlands earldom, which Henry II now granted to him if he could capture Huntingdon.[97] It was probably at this time that the Lord Rhys, prince of Deheubarth, sent a substantial force of Welsh to assist in the siege of the earl of Ferrers' great castle at Tutbury.[98] In marked contrast to Stephen's reign, when Earl Robert of Gloucester had been able to make effective use of Welsh allies in his war against the king, the Young King could attract none of the Welsh princes to his cause. This was in large measure because of Henry II's successful establishment of détente with the Lord Rhys, who had come to exercise effective hegemony over much of south Wales by the early 1170s.[99] The relative peace allowed the marcher lords from south Wales and Ireland to come to the Old King's assistance in Normandy against his son. It also meant that Henry II was able to continue to draw on a supply of Welsh troops for his campaigns in France.[100]

The Race for England

The invasion fleet of the Young King and Count Philip now lay in readiness at Gravelines, but contrary winds detained them in port.[101] With the situation in England now highly volatile, the moment of crisis had come. As so often in such dynastic struggles, the majority of the nobility in England had played a waiting game, biding their time until it became clear which side was gaining the upper hand. If the Young King landed in person in East Anglia or in Kent and marched on London, a tide of desertion might yet sweep the Old King away. Exactly such a landslide was to occur in 1216, when the invasion of Louis of France massively reinvigorated a rebellion against King John that had been close to extinction, and within months the baronial opposition and its French allies had gained control of much of eastern England.[102] Accordingly, as soon as the Old King had sure intelligence that his son had reached the fleet at Gravelines, he ordered the embarkation of his own forces.[103] As William of Newburgh noted, Henry 'preferred to put at risk his territories overseas rather than his kingdom (though he believed that those territories should be carefully fortified), for he foresaw that if he was absent and regarded as non-existent, no-one in England would stand in the way of the person whom they expected to succeed him'.[104] Henry's army was comprised principally of his loyal Brabançons.[105] The cost of retaining so large a number of these mercenaries for so long was financially crippling: Geoffrey of Vigeois noted that after nearly two years of war, Henry II's treasury was so exhausted that he sent his royal coronation sword to his Brabançons as a pledge for his debts to them.[106] Yet they were crucial to his chances of success at a time when Henry II could trust few among the magnates. As professional soldiers, moreover, they were the only force that could match the powerful army of stipendiary knights and serjeants mustered by the Young King and Count Philip. If their armies were to clash, it would be a contest between rival bodies of mercenaries that would decide who would hold the kingdom.[107]

The winds that kept the allied fleet in Gravelines also prevented Henry from sailing from Normandy with his army. But a sudden change in the wind, which Roger of Howden saw as a sure sign of divine favour, allowed Henry to cross with a small retinue from Barfleur on 7 July, while his Brabançons embarked at Ouistreham.[108] With him he brought his youngest children,

Joanna and John, his captive queen Eleanor, and the Young King's wife Margaret, who was also in effect his captive. Also with the king were some of his most important prisoners, including the earl and countess of Leicester, and Hugh of Chester, who were quickly sent to the castle of Devizes for safe-keeping.[109] Why the Young King and the count of Flanders did not avail themselves of the same winds to set sail is unknown, but their delay bought Henry II a precious respite. Landing at Southampton, he made directly for Canterbury, where on 12 July he undertook a dramatic act of penance.[110] Dismounting at Harbledown where the distant cathedral came into view, he walked barefoot to Becket's tomb as a penitent, dressed only in a woollen shirt, having forbidden the monks from their usual practice of meeting him with a procession worthy of his majesty.[111] After publicly confessing that he had been unwittingly responsible for Thomas' death, he submitted himself to a beating by the monks and the bishops present in the chapter house.[112] Then, eschewing all food and drink, he spent the entire night in prayer and vigil at Thomas' shrine. How far Henry felt real contrition is impossible to judge, but it was a powerful act of political theatre, and an attempt to neutralize the widespread outrage felt towards Henry for Becket's murder which the Young King and his partisans had attempted to harness, and to invoke the aid of the new saint for the Old King's cause. As Guernes noted, 'in very pressing need, he went to the baron for help'.[113]

There was, however, also a sound strategic motive for Henry's presence at Canterbury. He had beaten his son and Count Philip in the race to reach England, but the most likely target for their landing was Kent. This was a county in which support for King Stephen had been particularly strong, and, as Henry II knew, it had been promised, together with the castles of Dover and Rochester, to Count Philip by the Young King in 1173. The Medway had long been a favoured point of attack by invading forces, and though Rochester was secure, the castles of Saltwood and Allington were probably in rebel hands.[114] William of Canterbury reports that on the morning on which he completed his vigil at Becket's tomb, 13 July, King Henry ordered the people of Kent to remove their belongings beyond the Medway for fear of the invading forces. Meanwhile, the shire levies of Kent had been called out to guard the coast.[115] Having made his peace with Thomas and seen to the defences of the Kentish coast, Henry hastened to secure London. As he entered the city on 14 July he was greeted by the citizens, clad in their best apparel, in a great ceremony of welcome, the rapturous reception perhaps reflecting their attempts to allay any suspicions the king had concerning their loyalty.[116]

The reaction of young Henry and Count Philip to Henry's arrival in England on 8 July is not recorded: the narratives of the chroniclers and of

St Thomas' hagiographers are alike dominated by the extraordinary events at Canterbury and its aftermath. It seems, however, that the allies still intended to launch their attack, for well after it was known that the Old King had crossed from Normandy, a substantial force of 40 knights and 500 Flemish under the leadership of Hugh of Bar-sur-Seine, the nephew of Bishop Hugh de Puiset, sailed from Flanders and landed at Hartlepool on 13 July, in order to strengthen the garrisons of Bishop Hugh's castles.[117] As with the Flemish forces sent in May to aid Hugh Bigod, such a move can only have been intended to reinforce the northern rebels, to coincide with the Young King's landing in the south. What prompted the Young King to abandon his 'enterprise of England', however, was not his father's presence in the kingdom but news of a devastating and completely unexpected event – the capture of King William the Lion by Henry II's forces.

Aided by the Martyr: The Capture of William the Lion and the Collapse of the Rebellion in England

By early July, the king of Scots had shifted the focus of his attack from Cumbria to Northumberland. Targeting the lands of Odinel de Umfraville, he took his castle of Harbottle, then laid siege to Prudhoe on the Tyne.[118] The garrison put up a fierce resistance, and Odinel himself broke out of the blockade to seek aid from the strong royalist forces that were concentrating in north Yorkshire. On learning that the 'army of Yorkshire' led by Ranulf de Glanville, Bernard de Balliol, Robert de Stuteville, William de Vesci and Odinel were marching against him, William raised the siege of Prudhoe and withdrew north to the village of Felton, whence he dispatched his army to devastate the surrounding region.[119] The Scots divided their raiding forces into three groups, one of which, led by Duncan, earl of Fife, attacked and burned the town of Warkworth. Its inhabitants were said to have been massacred, including those seeking refuge in the church of St Laurence along with its priests.[120] Meanwhile, King William had encamped before de Vesci's castle of Alnwick with a force of around 100 knights, in order to prevent the garrison from attacking the raiding parties.[121] It is unclear why William did not retreat more swiftly, as he had done in 1173, but instead chose to divide and disperse his forces in widespread harrying. He may have wished to punish the nobles of Northumberland for their refusal to support him and perhaps he was over-confident: English chroniclers noted that while his army was engaged in brutal ravaging, he himself was 'engaging in sport with his knights as if safe and fearing nothing' and 'appeared to be on holiday'.[122] But with the proximity of a powerful English field army, it was to prove a very costly mistake.

The royalist army, comprised only of cavalry for speed of movement and numbering some 400 knights, had ridden hard in pursuit, and on arrival at Newcastle on 12 July received good intelligence of William's situation.[123] Discovering that the king was guarded by only a small force of his household knights, they determined on a bold strike. Setting out before dawn the following morning at top speed, they covered twenty-four miles 'before the fifth hour of daylight', with a thick coastal fog making the route difficult but also helping to screen their approach.[124] They halted to re-form in the cover of some trees within sight of Alnwick castle, from where they could assess the Scottish positions. William was at breakfast, and took the advancing horsemen to be part of his army returning from foraging. Only as they grew closer did he realize from their banners that they were Henry II's men.[125] The king of Scots, who had a reputation as a fine knight, flew to arms and led his household knights into combat, but despite their fierce resistance, they were soon over-whelmed. The English knights took care to spare their Scottish counterparts as prisoners for ransom, for many were well known to them, but they ruthlessly cut down the Flemish infantry. Most of William's retinue were taken captive, and the king himself was captured when his horse was run through and he became trapped beneath it.[126] Glanville's force then immediately withdrew at great speed with their prize to Newcastle before the remainder of the Scots army realized what had befallen their king.[127]

It had been a brilliant military operation, exploiting good intelligence by audacity, speed and surprise. Its impact was equally dramatic. Deprived of the unifying force of the king, William's hybrid army rapidly disintegrated, with rival elements even turning on each other as they withdrew north. Uctred and Gilbert, the lords of Galloway, immediately seized the opportunity to return to their province and launched a widespread attack on the castles of the French and English colonists settled there by the king of Scots.[128] The Scots' contribution to the Young King's war was over at a stroke. Roger de Mowbray had narrowly escaped capture at Alnwick, but it was now clear that the revolt in the north was also doomed. As soon as he heard news of the defeat, Bishop Hugh of Durham immediately dismissed the Flemish mercenaries who had disembarked on the very day of King William's capture, and ships returning directly to Flanders must soon have apprised young Henry and Count Philip of the catastrophe.[129] The rebel garrisons of the Midlands were now not only cut off from external aid but deprived of their most effective leader as Earl David, on hearing of his brother's fate, immediately left Leicester and headed back to Scotland with his men.[130]

Henry II himself learned the astonishing news on 18 July, when a messenger from Ranulf de Glanville arrived post-haste from the north.[131] Church bells were rung in celebration and thanksgiving throughout the country.[132] To contemporaries, the fact that King William had been captured on the very morning that King Henry had completed his vigil at Becket's tomb at Canterbury could not be a coincidence: it was a miraculous sign that St Thomas had accepted the repentance of his old friend, and come to his aid in a time of dire need.[133] William himself certainly saw the hand of St Thomas at work, for in 1178 he would dedicate his new abbey of Arbroath to the martyr.[134] For young Henry, it was a bitter blow. He had espoused the cause of St Thomas to rally support against his father, yet now it seemed that the saint had dramatically manifested his displeasure at the Young King's enterprise and shown forgiveness to Henry II. If he landed in England now, would anyone rise in his name? Would he in turn feel the wrath of the martyr? At Gravelines, there must have been a heated counsel of war as to whether to proceed with the invasion.

Henry II, however, was taking no chances despite this upsurge in his fortunes, and moved rapidly to crush the remaining rebel areas in eastern England before his son could invade. The same day that news reached him of William the Lion's capture, the king marched from London at the head of a large army, and laid siege to Huntingdon.[135] Three days later, the garrison bowed to the inevitable and surrendered, placing themselves at the king's mercy but with a guarantee that they would be spared in life and limb.[136] Hugh Bigod still commanded a large force of Flemings based at Framlingham, but Bungay had already been besieged, and the royalist forces had succeeded in digging a mine under the south-west corner of the keep.[137] When Henry II moved into Suffolk, pitched his tents at the vill of Seleham near Framlingham and prepared to lay siege, Bigod swiftly capitulated.[138] On 25 July he came to the king, made his peace and yielded up his castles. Henry II was in no mood for bargaining, but Earl Hugh 'with great difficulty' obtained the king's permission for his Flemish allies to leave the kingdom under safe conduct.[139] By the time Bigod finally surrendered, the Young King and Count Philip had abandoned their invasion plans. Deprived of Earl Hugh's bases in East Anglia, any landing of forces on the Suffolk coast would be fraught with danger, while even if they attempted a landing in Kent, the capture of King William meant that the allied forces would alone have to confront a powerful royal army led by Henry II in person.[140] Whatever the reasons why young Henry and the count of Flanders had not launched their fleet around 11–12 July, delay had been fatal to their chances of success. The Young King had lost the initiative, and with it the last chance to gain sole rule of his kingdom by force of arms. Yet he and Count Philip still had a powerful army at their command. Even if England had eluded his grasp, an assault on Rouen might yet break his father's hold on the duchy and destabilize his position in his continental lands. The campaigns of 1173 had weakened the eastern defences of Normandy, making a direct attack on the city possible.[141] If the allies moved fast, they might with luck take Rouen while Henry II was still occupied in suppressing the uprising in England. Accordingly, young Henry and Count Philip turned their army of invasion against Normandy and, joining forces with King Louis, they laid siege to Rouen on 22 July 1174.[142]

The departure of the allied army from Gravelines, however, rang the death knell for the rebellion in England. On 31 July at Northampton, the centre of royal power in the Midlands, the leading rebels came to submit to Henry II in a carefully choreographed ritual of surrender. Bishop Hugh of Durham yielded up the castles of Durham, Norham and Nothallerton, and also gained the king's reluctant permission to allow the French forces commanded by his nephew, Hugh de Bar, to leave for France.[143] Roger de Mowbray yielded his remaining fortress of Thirsk, while the earl of Ferrers surrendered Tutbury and Duffield. The diehard garrisons of Leicester, Mountsorrel and Groby also finally surrendered, but only after Henry II had threatened that their captured lord, the earl of Leicester, would not taste food or drink until they did so.[144] For William the Lion, there was to be studied humiliation: he was paraded before the assembled royal host and the gathering of his erstwhile allies, with his feet bound beneath his horse.[145] Within less than a month and to the wonder of contemporaries, Henry II's position in England had been transformed from acute crisis to firm control.[146] Now all depended on whether the Young King and his allies could finally wrest the duchy's capital from him.

The Siege of Rouen

Rouen was a great prize. In wealth and population it far outstripped Paris, and within the Angevin empire it was surpassed in political and fiscal importance only by London.[147] Henry II had been careful to retain the loyalty of the Rouennais, granting the citizens extensive judicial and trading privileges, including a virtual monopoly on trade from Normandy to Ireland, especially that in wine.[148] The financiers of Rouen had helped to bankroll Henry II's campaigns in the 1150s, which secured the kingdom of England for him, although their interests may have suffered from Henry's increasing reliance on both Flemish and Jewish moneylenders.[149] Rouen itself was home to a large and flourishing Jewish community, and it seems likely that during the troubles of 1173–74 the Old King drew on their financial support, whether proffered or compelled. Certainly in its aftermath he reaffirmed their privileges, including freeing them from taxes on either side of the Channel. Henry II's control of

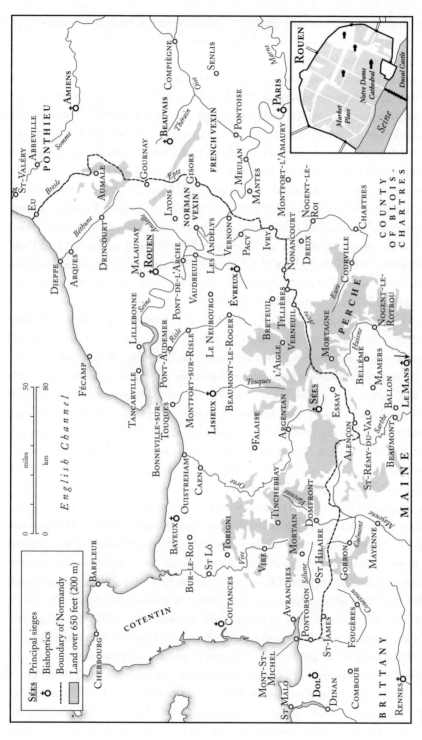

Map 5 Normandy, to illustrate the campaigns of 1174

Jewish finance within the empire deprived the Young King of this major source of credit, though he evidently borrowed heavily elsewhere.[150]

The combined allied army which now pitched its tents before the walls of Rouen was a mighty one, containing not only the counts of Flanders, Burgundy, Champagne, Blois and many other of Louis' leading nobles, but a great number of infantry, many of which had been levied from royal towns.[151] Yet the city's defences were equally formidable. In the south-east corner close to the river was the great donjon, built in the later tenth century and enclosed by an enceinte with mural towers added by Henry I.[152] Although in January 1144 Henry's father Geoffrey le Bel had accepted the bloodless surrender of the city, the keep itself continued to hold out until late April, defying Geoffrey's siege engines, and capitulated at last only when its defenders faced starvation.[153] The fortifications, dating in part back to the walls of the Roman *civitas*, had been strengthened by Henry II in the 1160s.[154] Moreover, the city, which had its own marshal, had been reinforced by a powerful garrison drawn from the knights and nobles of the duchy.[155]

The key to the city's defence, however, was its situation. 'It lies on the Seine, broadest of rivers,' noted Newburgh, 'by which merchandise from many regions is transported into the city. It is so effectively protected by this river and also by overhanging hills that scarcely a third of it can be put under siege by an army.'[156] A fine stone bridge, which had been built by the Empress Matilda, crossed from regions to south and east of the Seine.[157] In times of peace this had greatly facilitated the city's trade and commerce, but in time of war it formed a vital lifeline, allowing Rouen to be resupplied from the left bank of the Seine. Downstream, there was no other bridge, while upstream the powerful fortress of Pont de l'Arche guarded the nearest crossing point, at the confluence of the Seine and the Epte. The topography of Rouen was well known to King Louis, for as a younger man he had brought his forces to assist Count Geoffrey in his siege of 1144.[158] Yet despite the fact that the allies' combined army 'was greater than any seen in Europe for many years previously', they could only bring their forces to bear against part of the city. Crucially, they were unable to command the south bank of the river and hence could not interdict access to the city via the bridge.[159] Even if they had been able to reach the southern end of the bridge, to divide their army was to invite being attacked and defeated in detail.

This inability to prevent the city from being resupplied made blockade impossible, leaving no option but to try and take it by direct assault. Siege artillery began to bombard the walls while the attackers, who had divided their forces into three units, sought to maximize their advantage in numbers by establishing three eight-hour shifts, with each section attacking in turn, then being replaced by fresh troops while the others rested.[160] 'In this way,' noted

Newburgh, 'they attacked continuously, so as not to allow the defenders of the walls any respite for even a short period of the day or night.'[161] The citizens matched these arrangements by organizing the defenders into three similar watches, and, by carefully deploying their men, were able to repulse all the assaults.[162] According to a Norman thirteenth-century vernacular prose history, 'Even the ladies of the town carried stones and boiled water and pitch to throw down upon their enemies.'[163] The siege wore on, but on 10 August King Louis granted the citizens a day's respite in honour of St Laurence, his patron saint. This they readily used to demonstrate their high morale: 'Youths and maidens, old and young sang lustily with tuneful voices within the city, both rejoicing in the day and also to provoke the enemy: and a force of knights even engaged in jousting on the river bank in sight of the enemy'.[164] This galling spectacle caused Count Philip, or so ran the report which William of Newburgh had heard, to approach Louis and urge a surprise assault while the unsuspecting citizens were distracted by their merrymaking. It was a pragmatic but dishonourable ruse, and Louis at first indignantly refused to blemish his reputation by so treacherous an act. But the weight of his council was behind the count's plan: too much was at stake to forgo this chance because of honourable scruples.[165] Louis was finally persuaded, and orders were given for the army to quietly prepare their ladders for the assault.[166] Whether or not the Young King approved of this course of action is unknown, but like his allies, he was acutely aware that Henry II would soon come to the city's relief, and that it was imperative to strike before he did so.

The allied army stealthily made ready for an assault, with orders given in whispers. By chance, however, their preparations were spotted by a cleric high up in the city's belfry, who rang 'Ruvell', the alarm bell which had been sounded each time an assault had been attempted on the city. Forewarned, the citizens rushed to arms. Some of the attackers had already climbed ladders and gained the top of the wall, but the defenders counter-attacked fiercely, and after much hard fighting, in which the besiegers suffered heavy losses, they were compelled to abandon the assault. Louis, noted Newburgh, 'pinned the blame on the count of Flanders, but the stain of so foul a transgression clung more to the king's person'.[167] The use of such a breach of truce to seize a key town did not stand in isolation. In 1175, for example, Emperor Frederick Barbarossa, frustrated by his long but unsuccessful siege of the north Italian town of Alessandria, attacked it during a truce he himself had granted, not just in Lent but on Good Friday itself.[168] The fact that Louis had now violated his patron saint's day twice, at the two greatest sieges of the war, reflected the desperation of besiegers confronted by near-impregnable civic fortifications. Louis himself must have been acutely reminded of the dismal failure of the siege of

Damascus during the Second Crusade, when the crusaders not only turned on a former ally but fatally mismanaged the siege itself.

But time was running out for the Young King and Louis. The very next day, 11 August, Henry II arrived at Rouen, relieving the city from the left bank.[169] He had landed at Barfleur on 8 August and had marched directly on the duchy's capital at the head of his army of Brabançons, some 1,000 Welsh troops and a force of knights from the royal military household led by Earl William de Mandeville.[170] The day after his arrival, echoing his successful tactics at Chaumont-sur-Epte in 1167, Henry immediately sent his Welsh across the river, into the forest areas that lay to the south-east of the city, to wreak havoc with the French supply lines. Experts in guerrilla warfare, the Welsh soon ambushed a major supply train of forty wagons coming to re-victual the besiegers. Falling upon the terrified carters, capturing some and killing others, they made off with the draught horses and broke open the tuns containing wine.[171] Rumours that the woods were alive with Welsh soon circulated, creating panic in the French camp, and supplies began to dwindle.[172]

The following day, Henry II had the city gates, which had been blocked up by the citizens, reopened, and in preparation for an attack on the allied camp he had the great ditch outside the walls filled up with stones, timber and earth, then made level so that 200 knights could cross it in formation.[173] As at Verneuil the year previously, Henry was making his aggressive intentions clear, once more confronting Louis with the stark choice of withdrawing or engaging in what was certain to be a major pitched battle. If Louis and the Young King had shied away from such an engagement in 1173, by August 1174 their run of defeats and the collapse of the rebellion in England made the prospects of a bloody confrontation seem still more unpalatable. There was little choice but to retreat. Louis gave orders for his stone-throwers and other siege machines to be burned, a symbolic act to signify the end of the siege as well as a pragmatic move to stop these costly weapons from falling into Henry II's hands.[174] Henry II, however, was determined to harry the allied forces, and advanced towards King Louis' tents. The French knights and serjeants who had been stood to arms sallied out to meet the oncoming Angevin knights, and fierce fighting ensued in which some were wounded and others captured.[175]

Had Henry pressed home his attack, the allies might well have found themselves in a grave situation, but the king was wise enough to let his son and King Louis escape comparatively unscathed. On 13 August, the archbishop of Sens and Count Theobald obtained his permission for the allied army to withdraw unmolested to Malaunay, some nine miles north of Rouen, pledging that, the day after, they would hold talks for peace there. The Young King and Louis had the army pitch their tents there, but, as Henry II probably suspected, they hurriedly slipped away under cover of darkness back into France.[176] For young Henry, the retreat from Rouen must have seemed an all too inglorious end to what was to be his final action in the war.[177]

The citizens of Rouen, by contrast, gave thanks to the Virgin for their liberation, for the great besieging army had departed on the eve of the feast of the Assumption.[178] The significance of Marian feasts in the peace process was again indicated when, the day after the allies' departure, French envoys met with Henry II and arranged for peace talks to be held at Gisors on 8 September, the Nativity of the Virgin.[179] The *History of William Marshal* recounts how the archbishop of Sens and his party found Henry between Conches and Verneuil, and that on hearing their message he remarked wryly, '"Who will repair the damage I have sustained, the great losses sustained by my lands, destroyed through all this war-mongering of theirs?"'[180] The intended summit at Gisors failed to take place, and a new meeting was arranged at Montlouis, on the river Loire just to the east of Tours, for 29 September.[181] Henry made it clear, however, that in the intervening period he would again march against Richard, who was still putting up resistance in Poitou. The Young King and Louis VII pledged that neither they nor any of their supporters would give Richard assistance.[182] Left isolated both militarily and diplomatically, Richard's position quickly became untenable. When his father moved with a large army into Poitou, the young count fled, not daring to face his father in the field and abandoning those fortifications he had taken earlier.[183] Incensed to discover that his elder brother and Louis had made a truce with Henry II from which he was specifically excluded, and now with no hope of external aid, Richard bowed to the inevitable. On 23 September he came to submit, throwing himself at his father's feet and begging pardon. Henry treated his son affectionately, giving him the kiss of peace, and at once sent him to inform Louis and the Young King that he had made peace with his father.[184] It cannot have been a happy encounter; though in truth after the debacle at Rouen the younger Henry and King Louis had had little option but to withdraw support from Richard in order to secure peace, Richard felt himself betrayed and no doubt looked askance at the military failings of his elder brother and his allies in Normandy. Whatever the feelings between the brothers had been before then, the events of September 1174 may well have sown the seeds of a lasting enmity.

The Young King's gambit had failed, despite an ambitious strategy that had exploited the widespread opposition to Henry II and kept up a war on several fronts. Insurrection throughout the empire had been crushed, many of young Henry's supporters, including the king of Scots, had been captured and his mother, Queen Eleanor, was now a prisoner of her husband. The repulse of the combined forces of Count Philip of Flanders and King Louis laid bare as never before the dominant power and resources of Henry II. The Young King's ability to prosecute the war had remained completely dependent on the fiscal and military aid of Louis, Count Philip of Flanders and the great barons of France, as well as on loans. But Louis himself was feeling the fiscal burden of funding so sustained a series of campaigns: the siege of Rouen alone had represented a huge investment, and the impact of the war on Capetian finances may go far in explaining Louis' quiescence in the later 1170s.[185] The allies had poured their resources into the struggle, but now had little to show for two years of war save ruinous debt. As the *History of William Marshal* recalled, young Henry's supporters 'were in such a sorry state that the great majority of them had nothing to put in the hand of the smallest creditor. Nor could they find credit, despite securities offered and pledges made . . . and their debts were on such a scale that they had not the wherewithal to pay them off.' Some were reduced to such penury that they were forced to sell their arms, horses and pack animals.[186]

Henry II's command of greater financial resources had been a crucial element in his ability to overcome his son's rebellion.[187] The continuing operation of the sophisticated administrative machinery of government, made possible by the resolute loyalty of sheriffs, baillis and other regional officers, had allowed him to supply and pay garrisons in a network of royal castles in his English and continental lands, field a powerful force of mercenaries and even to undermine the allied coalition by suborning leading French nobles.[188] While the allies had achieved some successes in taking castles on the Norman frontier and in northern England, the chain of royal fortresses that formed 'the bones of the kingdom', in William of Newburgh's famous phrase, had succeeded in their primary wartime function of keeping groups of active rebels from uniting, containing the incursions of invading forces, and acting as bases for the effective operations of royalist field forces. Though much less can be recovered of the warfare within Henry's continental domains, the pattern appears similar. Both here and in England, the royalists succeeded in maintaining their lines of communication, while Henry II's continued control of the Channel and ability to ship over forces and treasure had been instrumental in moving his armies swiftly to the points of greatest danger.[189]

The Young King's failure to win the support of London, Rouen or other towns, save for Leicester and Huntingdon which were dominated by their rebel earls, proved critical. Fearful of a reversion to the miseries of the reign of King Stephen and mindful of the liberties granted to them by Henry II, their citizens' loyalties to the Old King remained steadfast.[190] Allied attempts to take key towns by force, as at Verneuil, Sées and Rouen, had been costly failures. By contrast, Henry II's forces were compelled to undertake only a limited number of sustained sieges. The efforts required by the justiciar to reduce the town of Leicester in 1173 and the continuing resistance of its castle revealed how fortunate the Old King was that William the Lion's capture led to a landslide of surrender of rebel garrisons in England, and that he was not forced to engage in a prolonged campaign of reduction of a series of powerful baronial castles in 1174. Yet if castles and fortified towns had dominated the strategy of the war and much of the fighting, the outcome of the campaigns of 1173–74 had been largely decided by the engagements in the field at Dol, Fornham and Alnwick.[191] Henry II's lieutenants had shown a marked willingness to engage in battle to exploit tactical advantages as well as their superiority in professionalism and sometimes in numbers. With the exception of the ambush of William the Lion at Alnwick, however, the principals of the conflict had not been directly involved in such engagements, and the Young King and Louis VII had baulked at engaging in a major pitched battle with Henry II both at Verneuil in 1173 and at Rouen in 1174. Yet Henry II's aggressive proffer of battle on both occasions had been a bluff, a cool and calculated act of brinksmanship. For in reality, the very real fear that he would be betrayed by some of his own nobles in the heat of combat made resort to pitched battle all the more hazardous for the Old King, as it did for other rulers facing a major baronial rebellion. Even if he had not been captured or killed, a victory by the Young King might well have caused Henry II's position to collapse. Yet young Henry, whether through scruple or the unwillingness of Louis to commit his forces to so dangerous an undertaking, had been unable to join in an ultimate confrontation with his father and so exploit such a weakness. As battle was seen as an ordeal – a judicial combat writ large, with God awarding victory to the side whose cause was more just – to be seen to refuse such arbitration not once but twice could only undermine the Young King's position and strengthen that of Henry II.[192] Not only that, but St Thomas had declared for his father through the miraculous defeat of William the Lion. Not only had Young Henry lost the war, but the justice of his cause had been thrown into deep doubt.

CHAPTER 10

A Fragile Peace, 1175–1177

The son honoureth the father, and the servant his master: if then I be a
father, where is my honour? and if I be a master, where is my fear?
– Malachi 1:6

L ATE SEPTEMBER 1174 was a time of fear and deep misgiving for the
Young King. On the advice of King Louis, young Henry and his brothers
had placed themselves at their father's mercy (*in misericordia*), thereby acknowledging a state of unconditional surrender.[1] Henry II had received Richard,
defeated and humbled, into his grace. But as the focus of the great rebellion,
could young Henry and his leading supporters expect similar clemency? In
view of the great threat the war had posed to the Old King's position, the scale
and cost of the hostilities, and his undoubted feeling that he had been betrayed
by his own wife and children, Henry II might be expected to be vengeful.
Contemporaries were fully aware that righteous anger was a prerogative of
kings, firmly grounded in biblical precedent. According to Peter of Blois, in the
aftermath of the rebellion Henry II told the abbot of Bonneville that 'I read in
the Old Testament of leaders, kings and even prophets frequently pursuing
very harsh vengeance against their enemies ... Have I no right to become
enraged when anger is a virtue of the spirit and a natural power? By nature I
am a son of anger, why then should I not grow angry? God himself becomes
angry ...'[2] As Becket had been reminded in 1169, the king had not been
beyond having the rebel Manceaux lord Robert de Sillé captured and imprisoned even after granting him the kiss of peace.[3] Displays of royal anger – the
ira regis – were an integral element in the exercise of kingship, and Henry II
knew as much as any ruler about the conscious manipulation of anger as political theatre. Yet Henry's notorious outbursts of fury could also be genuine and
uncontrolled: his fateful reaction to Becket's excommunication of the bishops

in December 1170 was spontaneous and exasperated rage, with disastrous and wholly unplanned consequences.[4]

Rebellious sons might hope for clemency from their wronged fathers, but it was by no means a foregone conclusion. It was only with great difficulty and after powerful intercession from leading nobles and ecclesiastics that William the Conqueror had been persuaded to make peace with Robert Curthose after his first rebellion.[5] Their reconciliation, moreover, was of brief duration, and Robert soon left Normandy for an exile that lasted until his father's death. In the aftermath of the rebellion of his illegitimate son Jordan, c.1083–84, Count Roger of Sicily had ordered twelve of the 'depraved young men' who had led his son astray to be blinded. Then summoning Jordan to court, Roger pretended he would do the same to him, having arranged beforehand for his vassals physically to restrain him from harming the terrified young man.[6] In 1234, Frederick II would treat his rebellious son still more harshly: despite Henry's complete and humiliating abasement, he was imprisoned for many years. When finally released, he feared even worse punishment and chose instead to take his own life by riding over a cliff, aged only thirty.[7]

Such reactions reflected the dilemma which filial rebellion, even when defeated, posed to ruling fathers: how to punish a dangerous act of disobedience severely enough to deter its recurrence, yet without inflicting lasting harm on the person or the authority of the heir.[8] In such circumstances, the trope of a young prince flawed only through immaturity, and led astray by 'evil counsellors' from his inherent good nature and filial duty, was an invaluable fiction.[9] Thus in the *History of William Marshal* the French ambassadors seeking peace in September 1174 urge Henry II: '"Dear lord, you should not show your anger to your son or those in his company, but to those who advised him to act as he did. The ones to suffer for it should be those who advised him to turn traitor, and they should be considered the more base for what they did." "Upon my soul!" Henry replies. "That is how it will be: never will there be a single day that [my anger] will not be shown to them and their heirs, either in the morning or the evening."'[10] Writing much closer to events, Guernes of Pont-Sainte-Maxence stressed how the Angevins' enemies had played upon the Young King's immaturity:

[T]he whole of England was heading for disaster ... they did not want to have a powerful king over them but preferred to have a mere suckling amongst them whom they could twist around their little finger like a glove. By their loyalty to him they had a malevolent influence, and they used the child as a cover for their own treachery. The child was incapable of governing the kingdom. No one could be a more reliable guardian of it than his father.

For any right-minded person, father and son are one. Those who sought to separate son from father wanted to deprive each one of his hereditary rights.[11]

Such sentiments were intended to help exonerate young Henry, but by stressing his youth in such terms they must have further undermined his authority and the view that he was ready for independent rule.

The Establishment of Peace: The Treaty of Montlouis, 1174

In the event, Henry II treated his sons and their supporters with a clemency that elicited both surprise and admiration from contemporaries, as well as later historians.[12] Wace, writing in the immediate aftermath of the rebellion, noted of the rebels that 'the king had their vineyards and their woods destroyed, their houses burnt and their castles laid waste. The only thing they had to show for their efforts was their shame; nevertheless, they were lucky to escape as lightly as they did.'[13] He believed that those who had been taken prisoner were particularly fortunate to avoid heavier punishment: 'he put them in chains and fetters, but, being such a noble man, he did not want to hang them or tear them limb from limb ... They were indeed treated much more mercifully by him than they deserved.'[14]

The tone was set by the settlement drawn up at Montlouis on 30 September.[15] A summary of its principal terms was circulated to the king's men, in which Henry declared peace to have been made with his sons and with the king of France 'to God's honour and my own'.[16] King Louis and Count Philip had agreed to give up the fortresses they had taken in Normandy, but the treaty now drawn up was concerned exclusively with Henry's own domains.[17] It was a statesmanlike settlement, designed to heal the wounds of two years of civil war and to return Henry's realms, in so far as was possible, to the *status quo ante bellum*. King Henry and his men, and those who had fought against him, were to hold the lands and castles they had held fifteen days before the outbreak of the war.[18] All prisoners on both sides were to be freed, but Henry reserved the right to take any hostages he should choose from those released, or to accept security by fealty or oath from them and their friends.[19] Those, however, of Henry's prisoners, such as William the Lion, Ralph of Fougères and the earls of Leicester and Chester, who had already made terms with Henry II were to remain at the king's will, and were specifically exempted from this agreement, as were those who had already pledged to stand surety for them.[20] As a mark of affection to his sons, Henry conceded that all those whose lands or goods had been forfeited on their departure to join the Young

King were to be restored to the king's peace; they were not to answer for any chattels they had removed on their departure, but would have to stand to right according to the law of the land for any acts of murder, mutilation or treason. Similarly, any who before the war had fled, for whatever reason, and had subsequently entered the service of his sons, were, for the love he bore his eldest son, to be restored to the king's peace, provided they gave pledges to stand to right for the offences for which they had been outlawed.[21]

The dissolution of ties of the sworn alliance and the annulment of all the Young Henry's grants to his erstwhile supporters was an essential prerequisite for a lasting peace. The treaty had opened by proclaiming that the three young men had 'returned to their father and to his service, as to their lord, free from all oaths and undertakings they had made among themselves or with others, against him or his men'.[22] Henry II, moreover, pledged to remit any rancour against those of his men who had supported his sons, and to cause them no harm, as long as they accepted him as their liege lord and served him faithfully. Such terms gave a degree of assurance to the Young King's followers, who not unnaturally had feared Henry II's imminent *ira et malevolentia*. Yet the treaty also addressed the dilemma in which the young King's rebellion had placed Henry II's own loyal men. The homage they had sworn to the young Henry in 1162 and again in 1170 had been explicitly saving the fidelity owed to his father, and, as was their duty as loyal vassals, they had supported the Old King to whom they owed liege homage. Nevertheless, in so doing, they had taken up arms against the Young King, who was both an anointed sovereign and the man who would before too long inherit the rule of England, Normandy and Anjou. Accordingly, Henry II's *fideles* looked with trepidation to the future: once their lord and protector was dead, might not the Young King or his partisans attempt to settle old scores? The Treaty of Montlouis thus declared explicitly that, in turn, the Young King had put aside all malice against all men, both clerics and laymen, who had supported his father. He pledged, with his hands in his father's, that he would, for all his life, neither do nor seek to do any ill or harm to those who had served Henry II. So important was this promise that Henry II's grant to the Young King of revenues specified in the treaty was made specifically 'on this condition'. King Henry also demanded a pledge from his eldest son that he would firmly observe all the grants that Henry II had made or would make in the future both to his men in reward for their service and to churches in free alms.[23] The evident concerns reflected in these clauses – that young Henry would revoke grants made by his father after the Old King's death – goes far to explain why many felt it so important to obtain charters of confirmation from the Young King while the elder king was still alive.

The Old King abided in large measure by the terms promised to the rebels. Ralph de Faye, however, was banished for his leading part in plotting the rising, his treasure confiscated and his offices redistributed, while his English honour of Bamley, Surrey, was forfeit and later granted to Baldwin de Béthune.[24] After a period of temporary custody, Hugh of Chester, Robert of Leicester and Ralph de Fougères were released, though their lands were taken into the king's hands. Hugh Bigod emerged from the failed rebellion with his power curbed but not broken. He was amerced £466, but initially was allowed to keep Bungay castle.[25] As he had surrendered on terms, he fared better than some of the leading lords who were captured during the rebellion itself and thus excluded from the provisions of the settlement of Montlouis. Unsurprisingly, the earl of Leicester's men were among those feeling the king's greatest indignation: some, including the constable Ansketil Mallory, suffered lasting disseisin, while tenants of the honour of Leicester paid a punitive aid.[26] Leicester's own lands were gradually restored in instalments: in 1179–80, his steward was still accounting to the Exchequer for one-third of the earl's lands in Leicestershire and Warwickshire.[27] Seizure of lands occurred on a scale large enough to make a significant increase in the sums returned to the Exchequer by sheriffs from the county farms.[28] Nevertheless, according to Ralph of Diss, Henry II freed no fewer than 969 prisoners of seigneurial or knightly rank without ransom, though he took hostages or pledges of surety from them.[29] The Young King, by contrast, extracted ransom from the hundred or so prisoners he or his allies had captured 'according to the laws of war (*jure belli*)', an action against the spirit of the peace but reflecting his dire financial circumstances.[30] Henry II, however, subsequently paid off the Young King's creditors, as well as honouring the extensive purveyances for provisions made by his own officials in Normandy, Maine and Anjou during the hostilities.[31]

Writing in the years after the war, the royal treasurer Richard FitzNigel not only praised Henry II's great clemency, but held it up as an example for his sons to emulate:

> When his enemies had been captured, his unprecedented mercy pardoned the perpetrators for terrible crimes, so that few of them suffered the loss of their possessions, and none lost their rank or life. If you were to read of the revenge which David took on the corrupters of his son Absalom, you would say that King Henry far surpassed him in gentleness ... So although the renowned King Henry had many examples and could have justly inflicted the most severe punishment upon the rebels, he preferred to spare them, rather than to punish them, so that, though unwillingly, they would see his kingdom grow. Therefore, long live that glorious and happy king, and for the grace that

he has shown may he receive grace from on high. And long live his noble offspring, subject to their father and not unlike him, and, because they were born to rule over nations, may they learn from both their father's example and their own how glorious it is to spare the conquered and beat back the rebels.[32]

There was, however, one glaring omission from the general amnesty. Queen Eleanor received no mention in the Treaty of Montlouis, and the silence of the chronicles concerning her fate is deafening. In Aquitaine, Richard the Poitevin lamented his duchess' captivity, but in the north, only the Frenchman Guernes of Pont-Sainte-Maxence dared to put in a plea for her, alluding to the association of Eleanor with 'the eagle of the broken covenant' in the 'Prophecies of Merlin':

> But there is no need for the king to fear this eagle any more. She will never make her nest somewhere else, since she has lost her feathers and will never hatch anything again. Let him keep his eye on the country, however. It is badly in need of it![33]

The queen appears not to have been subjected to any form of trial, but her lands were confiscated by Henry II and she was kept a prisoner at the king's pleasure.[34] By October 1175, Henry II seems to have seriously contemplated divorcing her, as he is said to have sought a papal annulment from the visiting legate Cardinal Pierleone. There can be little doubt that young Henry and his brothers were implacably opposed to such a plan, but its failure may have been due more to ecclesiastical opposition.[35] Determined to keep Aquitaine in his control, Henry II chose instead simply to keep Eleanor a captive. Her custody amounted to comfortable house arrest at major royal residences such as Salisbury and Winchester, and she was later permitted to attend some major court festivals and even to visit Aquitaine in 1184.[36] Nevertheless, she did not completely regain her liberty until her husband's death in 1189. Of all the leading rebels, Eleanor was thus the most severely punished, a reflection of her key role in the conspiracy and the continuing danger Henry II judged her as posing to him if she was again set free. How much contact young Henry had with his mother during her captivity is unknown, but for him and his brothers her prolonged confinement must have been a continuing source of grievance against their father.

Revenues and Castles: Henry II's Provision for his Sons

The second crucial issue addressed by the settlement at Montlouis was the provision for Henry II's sons. The Old King's terms were not punitive, for he sought a genuine rapprochement with his sons. Nevertheless, the terms did reflect the overwhelming strength of his position and pointedly granted considerably less than he had first offered young Henry and his brothers in the talks in September 1173 but they had rejected. The Young King was to have two castles in Normandy, to be chosen by Henry II, and an annual revenue of 15,000 *livres angevins* (£3,750).[37] This was at a time when the average audited income from England as recorded on the Pipe Rolls between 1165/6 and 1189 was £20,400 and the estimated revenue for Normandy in 1180 was 27,000 *livres angevins*.[38] The revenue from the duchy in the 1170s is unknown, but it is evident that the Young King was being offered a very substantial percentage of the duchy's fixed income. Richard gained half the revenues of Poitou and two dwellings (*receptacula*) 'from whence no harm could come to the King', a telling recognition by Henry II of the potential danger posed by the young count of Poitou. Geoffrey was to have half the income of the marriage portion of his future wife, Constance, and all of it following the marriage itself.[39] Henry II, however, held back the county of Nantes from this agreement, possibly as a mark of his displeasure at Geoffrey's involvement in the rebellion.[40]

The Young King himself received a clear rebuke in Henry II's provision for his youngest son John, who alone had remained in Henry's charge during the war.[41] John was to hold three castles, one in each of the counties of Anjou, Maine and Touraine: the treaty does not name them, but they were clearly intended to echo the original provision of Chinon, Loudun and Mirebeau in the Maurienne dower. In addition, he was to have 1,000 *livres angevins* (£250) from the lands of the count of Anjou, 1,000 *livres angevins* from Normandy and two castles in the duchy to be chosen by his father.[42] In England, he received the county of Nottinghamshire and Nottingham castle, the castle of Marlborough with its appurtenances, £1,000 from royal lands and any escheats the king should choose subsequently to give him. In other words, John was now given significant revenues in all of the Young King's lands, and though his income was considerably less than that of his elder brother, he held more castles. It was a handsome provision, and an early manifestation of what would become evident favouritism by Henry II for John, doubtless intensified by the king's disillusionment with the conduct of his elder sons in 1173–74.[43] It was little wonder that Henry II had made young Henry swear to observe his grants inviolably. Only months later, on the death of Henry II's uncle Reginald, earl of Cornwall, John was granted his extensive lands in England, Normandy and Wales, even though this effectively disinherited Reginald's three daughters and would force the hitherto loyal Count Aimar of Limoges into open rebellion.[44]

Aware that the question of income and territorial settlement had been a driving factor behind the rebellion, Henry extracted a promise from young Henry and his brothers 'that they would never demand anything more of the Lord King their father, beyond the prescribed and determined settlement, against the will and pleasure of the Lord King their father, and that they would withdraw neither themselves nor their service from their father'. Young Henry, Richard and Geoffrey put their seals to the treaty.[45] To make the settlement more binding, Richard and Geoffrey performed homage to Henry for their grants, but although the Young King wished to do likewise, Henry II 'would not receive it, because he was a king, but he took securities from him'.[46] Although his son had submitted, Henry was concerned that this should be an agreement between two kings, without any damage to his son's regal status. The Young King accordingly swore an oath to observe the terms of the treaty 'in the hand of the lord king his father', perhaps a handshake as in the reconciliation between Henry II and Louis VII at Montmirail rather than an act of homage involving the ritual of a vassal placing his hands within those of his lord – the *immixio manuum*.[47] Henry II, however, had no such qualms concerning William, the captive king of Scots, who performed homage to both Henry II and his eldest son at Valognes on 8 December, when the treaty he had been forced to accept as the price of his release was ratified.[48]

The Young King and his brothers could have counted themselves fortunate in their father's leniency and generosity. Nevertheless, the crucial issue that had lain at the heart of the rebellion by Henry II's sons – their desire to exercise direct authority over the territories assigned to them by their father – remained unresolved. Ironically, indeed, the rebellion itself made the granting of direct rule to young Henry still more difficult for Henry II. From the early months of 1175, the Old King would use the process of restoring order to the Angevin lands as a means of granting Richard and Geoffrey a more active role in the governance of his empire, turning their energies towards the suppression of their erstwhile allies. Yet Henry II felt unable to do likewise with his eldest son: not only would a grant of direct rule appear to have been extracted by coercion, but, still worse, Henry now distrusted young Henry, fearing that any designated rule in England, Normandy or Anjou would only be turned against him. In turn, as events were soon to show, the Young King mistrusted his father, suspecting that his forgiveness was not genuine.

Lord and Father: Submission and the Security of Homage

Henry II held his Christmas court at Argentan before moving through Anjou to Poitou, where he strengthened his castles' garrisons.[49] The Young King joined his father at Le Mans for the feast of the Purification of the Virgin, 2 February 1175, and here both Richard and Geoffrey performed homage to Henry II.[50] Travelling to Normandy together, the two kings held a conference with Louis at Gisors on 24 February, before returning to Rouen.[51] It may be doubted that the citizens of Rouen gave the younger Henry a joyous welcome; the city still bore the scars of the recent siege, and the allied army had wreaked havoc on the surrounding countryside during the weeks of futile investment. Nevertheless, Henry II left his eldest son in Rouen while he again toured the major fortifications in Anjou, restocking them with victuals and garrisons, and ordering that some of the castles held against him during the war were to be destroyed and others reduced to their state fifteen days before the war began.[52] Meanwhile, he had given Richard command of the army of Poitou to do likewise to the castles of the Poitevin lords who had taken part in the rising.[53]

The all too visible contrast between the authority Henry II bestowed on Richard and the close scrutiny under which young Henry was now kept gave King Louis the chance to play once more upon the Young King's fears. While his father was absent, the French king repeatedly sent messengers to Rouen warning his son-in-law not to cross over to England; were he to do so, his father would seize and imprison him, and across the Channel, Louis would be powerless to help him.[54] Had Henry II not imprisoned Queen Eleanor? For the Young King, Louis' scaremongering must have brought back all the uncertainties of early 1173, when it had been rumoured that his father might make him a prisoner: perhaps this was really why the Old King had refused his homage, so that he could take sterner measures against him, unrestrained by a lord's obligations to his vassal. Accordingly, when Henry II returned to Normandy in late March 1175 and summoned the Young King to join him at Caen to prepare to journey to England, his son flatly refused. 'He was "soft as wax for moulding to evil"', noted Howden, sourly quoting Horace on the follies of youth, 'nor did he dare to return to his lord father'.[55] Henry was compelled to send messenger after messenger, until their reassurances finally won young Henry over and he came to his father at the palace at Bur on 1 April.[56] There, in the presence of Archbishop Rotrou, Bishop Henry of Bayeux, Earl William de Mandeville, Richard de Humez the constable 'and many others of the households of both kings', the Young King 'fell flat on the earth at the feet of the Lord King his father, begging him with tears to receive homage and allegiance from him, as he had done from his brothers'. He wished to do so 'in order that he might remove all mistrust from his father's mind', and the Young King added 'that if the king refused to accept his homage he would not believe that he loved him'.[57]

Henry II was deeply moved by his son's abject abasement. While the Young King had to all intents and purposes surrendered to his father at Montlouis the previous September and had sworn to observe the terms of the settlement, there had as yet been no truly cathartic act of submission and reconciliation. The French, as well as many magnates from the Angevin territories, had been present at Montlouis, and Henry II had been extremely concerned not to damage young Henry's regal dignity, attained at such cost in 1170.[58] Now, with the pleas of his own men added to those of his son, Henry took liege homage from the Young King.[59] William of Newburgh later reflected on the significance of this act:

> As scripture says, 'A three-ply rope is not easily broken.' If he warred against nature in breach of observance of the natural law towards a father, he would at any rate have to continue to bear in mind his homage and the twofold guarantee of his oath and the surety provided by others. He would have to ensure that the words spoken of old by the Lord of Lords through the prophet to the sinning people could not justly be addressed to him by his father, who was now not merely his father, but also his lord: 'If I am your father, where is the honour owed to me? And if I am your lord, where is your fear of me?'[60]

As a gesture of his good intentions, Henry II even gave young Henry permission to visit King Louis.[61] On his return from the Île-de-France, he met his father at Cherbourg on 12 April, and here they celebrated Easter together. The king now extended his act of reconciliation to Geoffrey, whom he ordered to destroy the castles in Brittany that had been held against his father.[62]

The work of dissolving the former *conjuratio* continued when on 22 April Philip of Flanders came to the kings at Caen. At Henry II's prompting, he and the Young King absolved each other of any obligations they had made during the war. In return for surrendering the Young King's charter granting him the earldom of Kent, with the castles of Dover and Rochester, and for quitclaiming the Young King of all promises made to him, Henry II renewed the annual money fief of 1,000 marks, and young Henry confirmed this grant with his own charter.[63] The renewal of the *conventio* of 1163 was a visible sign of the realignment of Flanders with the Angevins and away from Louis, and Henry bestowed great honour upon the count before he again left 'with the licence of both kings'.[64] Shortly before his visit to Caen, Count Philip, his brother Peter, and many of his men had taken the cross, intending to leave for the Holy Land the following summer.[65] The hostile Ralph of Diss believed that they had done so to expiate the outrages the Flemings had committed in the recent war against the English and Normans, and added that the souls of all those Flemish slain at Fornham would proclaim the iniquities of Count Philip before the

Great Judge.[66] Though he subsequently took pains to delay Philip's crusade, Henry II pledged him a sum of money 'for the soul of Matthew, count of Boulogne', to help retain knights in defence of the land of Jerusalem.[67] The war of 1173–74 had been not only a conflict between father and son; it had been a war between kinsmen.

Reassured of his father's good intentions and forgiveness, the Young King and Margaret crossed with Henry II from Barfleur to Portsmouth, arriving on 9 May 1175.[68] As a public and potent symbol of the love and reconciliation between father and son, 'every day at the stated hour for meals they ate at the same table, and rested their limbs in the same bedroom'.[69] After the power struggles between father and son in 1173–74 over high clerical appointments, the return of order and harmony was symbolized by the two kings jointly presiding over an ecclesiastical council, convened 'by the consent and wish of both of them' by Richard, the new archbishop of Canterbury, at Westminster on Rogation Sunday, 18 May.[70] In the great hall of the royal palace, a series of canons were promulgated, largely restating existing decrees, although the presence of the Young King led to a subtle amendment to the canon strictly forbidding the marriage of children. Everyone present was all too aware that young Henry had been married to Margaret as a mere infant, so a saving clause was added stating that an exception could be made in urgent necessity for the establishment of a firm treaty of peace.[71]

Business pertaining more directly to the settlement of the realm was discussed at a great council held two days later, on 20 May.[72] The Westminster council was of particular importance, as it represented the first major convocation of Henry's magnates since the establishment of peace. The question of the Young King's status remained a pressing issue. For although he had made a dramatic and complete submission to his father at Bur-le-Roi, this ritual had occurred in Normandy, and before a comparatively small number of nobles. Accordingly, in order to make more widely known the nature of his son's submission and to explain his new feudal subordination, Henry II commanded a letter, whose text was subsequently circulated as a newsletter, to be read out at the opening of the council:

> King Henry, the father of the King, to his faithful subjects, greeting. I give thanks to almighty God and to the saints, whose grace, although not because of my merits, has visited and gladdened me beyond belief. My son, King Henry, came to me at Bur, and on the Tuesday next before Palm Sunday ... with great shedding of tears and many sobs, he prostrated himself before my feet, humbly begging for mercy; and that I would, with fatherly love, grant forgiveness for what he did to me before the war and

during the war and after the war. He also begged with all humility and as much devotion as he could that I, as his lord and father, would accept his homage and allegiance, asserting that he would never believe that I had given up my indignation against him unless I would do to him what I had done to his brothers, at their petition and humble insistence. I, therefore, moved by pity and believing that he spoke from his heart and that he was remorseful and humbled before me, put away my anger and indignation (*ira et indignatio*) against him, and wholly took him into my fatherly favour (*in gratiam paternam*), having received homage from him and an oath upon the holy relics placed before him that he would bear me faith against all men and abide by my counsel henceforth in all his doings, and that as long as he lived he would seek no harm to either my men or his who had served me in this war, but that he would honour and advance them as my faithful subjects and his, and that he would order all his household and all his state by my advice and henceforth do likewise in all things.[73]

This rehearsal of the Young King's earlier submission has been seen as Henry II's deliberate humiliation of his son.[74] No doubt it made for uncomfortable listening, but it scarcely compared with Henry II's act of contrition at Avranches in 1172 or his penance at Becket's tomb, and still less with the public humiliation of William the Lion at Northampton in July 1174. Rather, it may have been intended to limit further damage to the Young King's royal dignity, for by merely reading a narrative of events at Bur-le-Roi Henry II informed the political community of young Henry's suitable contrition, of the reconciliation between father and son, and of the reason for the Young King's new status as his homager, all without the need to actively carry out any further ceremony of abasement before the assembled magnates.[75] The letter, moreover, stressed reconciliation and, closely echoing the Treaty of Montlouis, assured the Old King's *fideles* that an integral aspect of Henry II's acceptance of young Henry's submission was its guarantee of their future safety from reprisals, and from the *ira* of the future king of England.

Such concerns are prominently reflected in Jordan Fantosme's remarkable poem on the events of 1173–74. Written soon after the war for a court still traumatized by the recent conflict, it was perhaps performed at just such a great assembly as that at Westminster in May 1175, where men who had but recently fought against each other now rubbed shoulders in a highly charged atmosphere. The Young King's war is presented as unlawful, unnatural and unjust, but equally Jordan boldly points out that by crowning his son, then denying him any real authority, Henry II himself must take the ultimate blame for his son's frustrations.[76] Skilfully weaving praise of loyalty with rebuke for the folly of rebellion, Fantosme provides a roll call both of those lords who remained faithful to the Old King and of those who were the Young King's key supporters. The rebels are censured, but neither denounced nor vilified; though they have erred through folly, they are nonetheless still part of the community of nobles, and by coming back to their senses and due loyalty to Henry II they too should be restored to their rightful place within this society. Vividly capturing the hopes and fears of his contemporaries in the immediate post-rebellion period, Jordan's overriding theme is one of reconciliation. As he urges Henry II:

> Noble king of England, do what I desire: love those whose wish it is to serve you faithfully. It is not right that any evil should befall the Young King, since his better nature made him regret bringing in foreigners to bring shame on his countrymen who after his father's lifetime are to support him. Before this world approaches its end many strange things can come to pass. You never had to sustain a war so bad that your son may not have a worse one on his hands! Now let him think of improving the lot of his own people![77]

The message to young Henry was clear: just as he and his supporters should be forgiven and taken back into Henry II's grace, so in turn the Young King should show his favour to those who had served his father so loyally. For, in due course, they would become *his* liegemen, and as king he would need their support just as much in any future conflicts. One tangible demonstration of just such a rapprochement was the confirmation by the Young King of his father's grants to loyal *curiales*. It may, for example, have been during the Westminster council that the Young King confirmed Henry II's grant of the chapelry at Blythe to Walter of Coutances, his former chaplain, who had been one of those members of his household who had refused to swear uncondi-tional loyalty to young Henry after his flight to France in 1173, and who had accordingly been sent back to Henry II.[78]

It was with a similar plea for reconciliation, not only between father and sons but between all members of the Angevin family, including both Queen Margaret and Queen Eleanor, that Guernes chose to conclude his *Vie de Saint Thomas le Martyr*:

> The king should know it well – and I am telling him the absolute truth – that his sons will be honourable, strong and brave. The more they stand by each other, the more powerful they will be. English, Poitevins and Normans will be in great fear of them. Some who are laughing now will end up

weeping. As long as father and son continue to love each other, as long as both love their mother and the king's daughter-in-law, as long as the children stay close as brothers should, as long as the king reigns over them, as emperor and as king, then anyone who meddles with the sauce will find it tastes very bitter. I pray to God and to the martyr whom I have long served, that he bring peace to the kingdom, sustain the affection between father, son, daughter-in-law and wife, and grant them happiness and long life without any change in sovereignty. And may God encourage them to look favourably on me![79]

Henry II himself never adopted an imperial title, and readily recognized the more exalted rank of the German emperor. Nevertheless, Guernes here encapsulates perfectly Henry II's own vision of his 'empire' as a family enterprise over which he presided, as well as the political reality that, if united, the Angevins would be the dominant power in France. The question in 1175 was how far such family unity could be rebuilt, and for how long it could be maintained.

As a further gesture of their reconciliation, the two kings then made their way to Canterbury, where the great new choir of the cathedral of Christ Church, ravaged by a devastating fire only the year before, was beginning to rise from the ashes under the direction of the French architect William of Sens.[80] Here, on 28 May 1175, in an atmosphere very different to that of the Old King's urgent visit to the shrine in July of 1174, Henry II gave thanks to God and St Thomas 'for the peace so gloriously restored to him'. Father and son spent the night in vigil and prayer, united in veneration of the martyr.[81] After holding court and 'a feast of the kings' at Reading for Pentecost on 1 June, the kings progressed to Gloucester for a second major council on 29 June.[82] There was an urgent need to reassert royal authority in the marches, where rising tensions between the Welsh and the Anglo-Norman marcher lords had been compounded by the recent slaying of Henry, lord of Brecknock and Upper Gwent, by Seisyll ap Dyfnwall.[83] Henry II also had pressing business with his cousin William, earl of Gloucester and lord of Glamorgan. Although he had been one of the magnates leading the royalist forces in the victory at Fornham in 1173, William was married to Hawise, the sister of Robert, earl of Leicester, and it is clear that Henry held him in mounting suspicion. Even before the outbreak of the war, the king had taken the great castle at Bristol into royal hands. This was a major affront to Earl William, for Bristol was the seat of his treasury and comital government, and he had retaliated by driving out the royal garrison during the war and holding the castle for its duration. For this act of defiance he was now impleaded by King

Henry, and, bowing to the inevitable, Earl William returned the keep to the king.[84] Henry may already have been planning to divert the inheritance of the earl's rich lands to John, thereby further providing for his youngest son while at the same time removing any future threat from the great lordship of Gloucester.

The council at Gloucester also gave the Young King the opportunity to see at first hand the workings of the successful policy of détente and devolved authority his father had adopted towards the Lord Rhys, prince of Deheubarth. Recognized as Henry II's 'justice' over much of south Wales, Rhys had remained Henry's 'right loving friend' during the great rebellion and now stood as patron and mediator for other princes – of Gwent, Gwynllwg, Gwerthrynion, Morgannwg, Elfael and Maelienydd – as they made their peace with King Henry and were confirmed in their lands.[85] But the king tempered conciliation with insistence that the marchers show a determined face against any future Welsh aggression. By early July, the kings were back at Woodstock, where they presided over a great gathering of bishops and abbots assembled in council to elect and install abbots to twelve vacant houses in the archdiocese of Canterbury and to appoint a new bishop of Norwich.[86] Geoffrey Plantagenet was confirmed as elect of Lincoln, having received papal dispensation 'in respect of his age and his birth', but it may not have been coincidental that, later that summer, Henry II sent Geoffrey to the school in Tours 'until he should be worthy of the dignity of such an honour'.[87] The stated reason was that Geoffrey was still under the canonical age of thirty required to hold priestly office, but as he had been so active in the defeat of the rebels in 1174, his absence may also have been a diplomatic move by Henry II to place some distance between the Young King and his more loyal natural son.[88]

The Impact of the War

Speaking of the rebellion, Richard FitzNigel noted that Henry II had 'so prevailed against almost all the rebels that he was established in the kingdom far more strongly than before, by the very circumstance that should have weakened him'.[89] Historians have largely followed the Treasurer's assessment. The post-war period has been seen as ushering in an age of stability, paving the way for impressive legal and governmental reforms; 'unbroken tranquillity and steady prosperous growth, social, intellectual, political, constitutional'.[90] Henry had overcome baronial opposition, and his judicial and fiscal measures to restore his authority between 1175 and 1176 left him stronger than ever before. The Becket crisis was now in the past: the king and the martyr were reconciled, and relations had been restored with the Church and the papacy.

Though it was an unintended consequence of the war, he had established an unprecedented and unambiguous overlordship over Scotland, and was unchallenged overlord of Britain and Ireland. The dazzling match between his daughter Joanna and William II of Sicily, celebrated in 1177, and his arbitration in the same year of a settlement between the kings of Castile and Navarre, were but highlights in a period of successful international diplomacy that saw Henry II at the zenith of his prestige and influence in Europe.[91]

Yet this resurgence was neither inevitable nor untroubled. The Young King's relations with his father between 1175 and 1177 reveal a period of continuing tension, deteriorating at least once into a serious political crisis that again threatened war. When Norgate wrote of a period of 'unbroken tranquillity' after 1174, she was only considering England, but even the kingdom was far from immune from the impact of Henry II's fears of fresh insurrection in 1176. His stated plans for a crusade, halted by the reaction to Becket's murder but brought back to the fore by the penance accorded at Avranches, had now been rendered all but impossible by fear of his sons' further disloyalty. The Young King's actions in 1173–74 were a stark warning to Henry that if he left for the East, he might find his ability to resume power on his return seriously challenged. Though he continued to support the Holy Land with very considerable sums of money, it was a risk he could no longer take.[92] The rebellion continued to cast a long shadow and left 'a legacy of bitterness and mistrust which darkened all the rest of his reign'.[93]

Indeed, in its immediate aftermath, despite the public reconciliation of the Young King and his father, Henry II feared for his own safety. Twelfth-century kings normally eschewed overt measures of personal security as unbecoming: fear of one's own subjects appeared an admission of misrule.[94] Walter Map told how King Louis, reproved by Count Theobald for falling asleep in a wood when only accompanied by two knights, had answered, 'I may sleep alone quite safely, for no-one bears me any ill-will.' 'What other king,' asked Map, 'can claim so much for himself?'[95] Henry I, by contrast, 'dreading night's terrors' after an attempt on his life by his own chamberlain, had increased his guards, often changed beds and slept with a sword and shield within reach.[96] Henry II did not resort to such measures, but at the great council at Woodstock in July 1175, it was publicly proclaimed that none of his opponents in the recent war were to come to court without his expressed consent, on pain of being arrested as an enemy of the king. No one was to linger at court after sunset, nor come to it before sunrise, while no one dwelling east of the river Severn was to bear bows and arrows, or carry daggers, for these were the weapons of an attack by stealth.[97] Only the marchers to the west could not be so disarmed, for fear of the Welsh. As Howden noted, these new measures – in any case far too impracticable – were not adhered to for long, but they sharply reveal that a climate of fear and suspicion still pervaded the court.[98]

The task of recovery was a formidable one, for the Young King's rebellion had brought devastation to many areas of the Angevin lands. As the annals of St Aubin bewailed, 'the kingdoms of the earth were overthrown, churches laid waste, religion dragged through the mire and peace lost throughout the land'.[99] Though in England the Exchequer had continued to function at a fairly high level of efficiency, some counties had not rendered account, and the war had caused a sharp drop in revenue.[100] The northern counties had been ravaged by the Scots, while areas of the Midlands and East Anglia had suffered from the depredations of the rebel garrisons there. To make matters worse, a plague broke out in England in 1175, followed by a severe famine.[101] In Normandy, the earliest surviving Exchequer roll, that of 1179–80, still revealed the impact of the war, both in repairs needed to castles and in fall in revenue from those areas worst affected by the conflict.[102] The estates of Archbishop Rotrou of Rouen, for example, including those centred on Les Andelys which were among his key sources of income, had suffered badly at the hands of the French. In vain had he begged Archbishop William of Sens to urge Louis to refrain from destroying church lands, had complained bitterly to Pope Alexander, and in a letter of admonition to the Young King during the war, had tried to entrust his lands to his protection.[103]

From Woodstock, the two kings, accompanied by a number of justices, including William FitzRalph, Bertran de Verdun and William Basset, undertook a progress north intended to reassert order and royal prerogatives and to replenish the exhausted treasury.[104] Henry II not only was keeping young Henry close for reasons of security but regarded his presence as important in the process of pacification. At Lichfield, Henry II had four knights and their associates hanged for the murder of Gilbert, a royal forester, and his men: the killing of royal officers could not be tolerated. Such an example was also part of a forceful general reassertion of the king's rights over the forest.[105] Moving to Nottingham on 1 August, in the heart of the great royal forest of Sherwood but also near one of the major epicentres of the rebellion, the king impleaded 'all the barons and knights of the country concerning his forests, and placed them all in mercy for the taking of game'.[106] In vain did the justiciar Richard de Lucy show the king his own writ by which he had authorized de Lucy to make it known that woodland could be exploited and game and fish taken from the royal reserves during the course of the war without offence. Henry II had evidently made such a concession to win political support in the crisis; also, no doubt to provide royalist garrisons with a ready supply of victuals. But now the king rejected this plea out of hand, insisting that royal forests and hunting rights had been abused to his great detriment.[107]

The Young King continued to witness at first hand the oppressive power of the forest law as an arbitrary royal tool of fiscal extortion and political repression.[108] With Henry II presiding, the justices proceeded heavily to amerce those who had violated its rigid strictures. When the court moved to York in early August, 'the lord king sued the earls and barons and also the clergy of Yorkshire, concerning the forests and the taking of venison', especially in connection with the great royal forests of Galtres and Pickering.[109] Much of the driving force behind these measures was Henry II's urgent need for money to recoup the massive expenditure he had incurred during the war, but there can be little doubt that the forest law was also used to punish the king's erstwhile opponents.[110] William Ferrers, earl of Derby, for example, was fined 200 marks, Robert de Mowbray's brother Nigel 100 marks and Adam de Port, the king's particular enemy, a still heavier £200.[111] The proceedings of 1175, moreover, were only the beginning; a circuit of itinerant justices continued through the following year and the net was cast wide: fines for forest offences were recorded from twenty-nine counties and the record of the Pipe Rolls fully bears out Howden's statement that many nobles, knights, peasants and clergy were amerced to the limits of their means by what contemporaries rightly regarded as naked extortion.[112]

The principal reason for the arrival of the Young King and Henry II in York on 1 August, however, was to receive the formal submission of William the Lion and to confirm the Treaty of Falaise.[113] Remarkably, William had not been forced to pay a ransom, but nevertheless the political price of his freedom was high. In the great cathedral church of St Peter, the king of Scots, followed by his brother David and all their leading magnates and ecclesiastics, performed homage first to Henry II, then to the Young King, 'saving his faith to the Lord King his father'.[114] William was also forced to recognize the subjection of the Scottish Church and its clergy to both Henry II and his son, and he may have placed his lance, saddle and equipment on the high altar of St Peter's as a further symbol of his submission.[115] William's disastrous intervention in the war had resulted in the most explicit act of feudal submission undertaken by a Scots king since the Conquest. William doubtless hoped that when Henry II died, the Young King would honour the grant of Northumberland and Cumberland he had made to him in 1173, but for the present he had to submit to the humiliation not only of having the key castles of lowland Scotland held by English garrisons, but also of having to pay for their upkeep.[116] Gerald of Wales regarded Henry II's assertion of overlordship over the Scots as a crowning triumph and the high-water mark of Plantagenet power:

Contrary to anything which had occurred before, adding so noble an increase to the English crown, he gloriously extended the boundaries and limits of the kingdom from the southern ocean to the northern islands of the Orkneys, by his powerful hand including in one monarchy the whole island of Britain as it is bounded by the ocean. We have no authentic account that anyone had ever done this before, from the time when the Picts and the Scots first occupied the northern parts of the island since the days of Claudius Caesar . . .[117]

Nevertheless, Henry II's control of these lowland fortresses was intended less as an act of aggressive Angevin imperialism than as a safeguard against future Scottish support for any future insurrection by the Young King: only after the death of the young Henry in 1183 did Henry II feel able to relax the terms of the Treaty of Falaise.[118] William's explicit subjection to the Young King as well as to Henry II stood in marked contrast to the terms agreed later that year at Windsor on 6 October by Ruaidhrí Ua Conchobhair, king of Connacht, who claimed the high kingship of Ireland. In return for recognition of his lordship over that part of Ireland not held by Henry II or the Anglo-Norman settlers, Ruaidhrí agreed to pay tribute and became Henry's man, but though he did so in the presence of the Young King and a great council of magnates, there was no mention of any similar pledge to young Henry. Unlike Geoffrey's duchy of Brittany, John's lordship of Ireland was not to be under the superior lordship of the Young King, at least not while Henry II still lived.[119]

The two kings seem to have spent the closing months of 1175 in the south of England, and in late October they honourably received the new papal legate, Hugo Pierleone, at Winchester. If, as Gervase of Canterbury reported, Henry II unsuccessfully attempted to use this legatine mission to gain an annulment of his marriage to Eleanor, his plans must have caused renewed tensions between young Henry and his father and their joint Christmas court at Windsor is likely to have been a fraught one.[120] Despite this, it was ostensibly 'by the counsel of King Henry his son' that Henry II issued a new assize at a great council held at Northampton on 26 January 1176.[121] The process had already begun of demolishing the castles of leading rebels, including those of the earls of Leicester, Ferrers and Norfolk, and of others such as Roger de Mowbray and Gervase Paganel.[122] But in the new assize, in essence a revised and enlarged version of the Assize of Clarendon of 1166, Henry II pressed ahead with measures to reassert justice and strengthen royal authority in the wake of the rebellion, and it was not coincidental that it was promulgated at the very location that had witnessed the great ceremony of surrender of the rebel castellans to Henry II in July of 1174.[123] Teams of three justices, assigned to six circuits to cover the kingdom, were instructed to receive oaths of fealty to Henry II from all men from the rank of earl down even to the unfree villeins (*rustici*), and any refusing were liable to arrest as the king's enemies.[124] Henry II was determined upon a universal reaffirmation of loyalty to him, and anyone who had not yet performed liege homage to the king was to do so at an appointed time.[125] The names of those outlawed for refusing to stand to trial were to be reported to the Exchequer and a list sent to the king himself, which indicates that Henry II had in mind not only petty malefactors but political opponents of standing.[126] The justices were to review custody of royal castles and to assess available resources for castle guard, while there was to be a careful audit of the progress of demolition of the castles of erstwhile rebels.[127] Fearing lest the influence of local magnates would interfere with the effective destruction of these strongholds, the king decreed that the justices fulfil this work of security without fear or favour, on pain of being arraigned themselves.[128]

Beyond such immediate measures, the assize sought to address the baleful impact of the war on law and order. Harsh penalties for theft, robbery, forgery and arson were decreed for those found guilty after accusation by a jury of presentment, though in recognition that the widespread plundering of livestock was an inevitable accompaniment to the recent hostilities, these were not to apply 'in cases of petty thefts and robberies which have been committed in time of war (*tempore guerrae*), as of horses and oxen and lesser things'.[129] The war had provided ample opportunity for appropriation at the expense either of enemies or of weaker neighbours, but some had continued to take advantage of the confusion; the justices were commanded to investigate dispossessions made contrary to the assize 'since the lord king's coming to England immediately following upon the peace made between him and the king, his son'. They were also to undertake a thorough review of the king's rights, including those 'escheats, churches, lands and women' (the latter referring to heiresses and wards) who were in the royal gift.[130] Anticipating resistance in areas where the authority of erstwhile rebel lords was still strong, the assize noted that the justices should nevertheless 'hold the assize for wicked robbers and evildoers throughout the counties they are about to traverse, for this assize is enacted in accordance with the advice of the king his son, and his vassals'.[131] This was a vital clause: no one was to be let off by exploiting their loyalty to the son, and it was to be made clear to all that these measures were the agreed policy of both kings.

The Old King had regarded the Young King's participation in the major councils and itinerant government of 1175–76 as an important aspect of the re-establishment of his own authority in the kingdom, while in turn this was a public demonstration of young Henry's restoration as his father's principal heir. Nevertheless, by Easter 1176 young Henry had been under his father's close supervision for nearly a year and was beginning to chafe against such restraint. In March, he pressed his father for permission to leave England. Roger of Howden believed his stated reason was that he wanted to undertake a pilgrimage to the shrine of St James at Compostella.[132] As his conduct at the siege of Drincourt in 1173 had indicated, the Young King had a particular devotion to St James, and the earlier pilgrimages of his erstwhile allies King Louis VII and Count Philip afforded ample precedent.[133] Henry II, however, suspected his son's motives, and that his request came less from genuine piety than from the bad advice of the young Henry's counsellors who were attempting to extract him from his father's control.[134] A pilgrimage to Compostella, moreover, would take young Henry not only through Aquitaine, but further into Gascony, and run the risk of further destabilizing an area under only the loosest of Angevin hegemony, where lords such as the count of Bigorre and the viscounts of Dax and Bayonne needed little excuse to attempt to throw off ducal control.[135] Henry II tried to persuade his son to abandon the idea, but when the young man could not be convinced, Henry eventually agreed, and gave the Young King permission to cross to Normandy with his household.[136]

The *History of William Marshal*, by contrast, saw young Henry's request to leave England, made 'upon the counsel and advice of his companions', as stemming from boredom and a desire for chivalrous adventure through errantry.[137] Young noblemen had long sought martial glory and advancement beyond their fathers' lands, but the idea of knight-errantry was being greatly popularized in the 1170s by Chrétien de Troyes, whose Arthurian romances had at their centre the questing adventures of knightly heroes who won renown and riches through feats of arms. Chrétien's romances, aimed precisely at the aristocratic youth of the courts of northern France, reflected, but also helped to formulate and disseminate, a burgeoning chivalric ideology. Thus in *Cligès*, Chretien's second great romance written *c*.1176, Alexander, son of the emperor of Greece, seeks his father's leave (and a suitable supply of treasure), in order to travel to Britain to prove himself through arms and to be knighted by Arthur himself. When his reluctant father offers to knight Alexander himself, to crown him, give him Greece and the homage of all his barons, the young man still refuses:

> Many high-born men through indolence have forfeited the great fame they might have had, had they set off through the world. Idleness and glory do not go well together, it seems to me; a noble man who sits and waits gains

nothing ... Dear father, as long as I am free to seek glory, if I am worthy enough I wish to strive and work for it.[138]

The analogy here with the Young King cannot have been lost on Chrétien's audiences, just as the coronation of Erec which concludes his first romance, *Erec and Enide*, called to mind young Henry's own coronation in 1170. Such sentiments are closely echoed in the *History of William Marshal*, who has young Henry ask for permission to leave England in 1176 because it 'could be a source of much harm to me to stay idle for so long, and I am extremely vexed by it. I am no bird to be mewed up; a young man who does not travel around could never aspire to anything worthwhile and he should be regarded of no account'.[139] In a thought world where fame and honour required constant refreshing and reinforcement by new feats of arms, lethargy ran the risk of reproach and dishonour. 'I can tell you in a word', noted the *History*, 'that a long period of rest is a disgrace to a young man.'[140] As Philippe de Novare, also writing in the 1220s, counselled in his *Les Quatre Ages de l'homme*:

> In his youth a man should use without laziness or delay, his prowess, his valour and the vigour of his body for the honour and profit of himself and his dependants; for he who passes his youth without exploit may have cause for great shame and grief. The young nobleman, knight or man-at-arms should work to acquire honour, to be renowned for valour, and to have temporal possessions, riches and heritages on which he can live honourably.[141]

It was for just this reason that soon after his knighting *c.*1178, Arnold of Ardres and his knightly companions had 'preferred to go into exile in other places for the love of tournaments and for glory than to spend time in his homeland without warlike entertainments ... so that he could live gloriously and attain secular honour'.[142] By the mid 1170s, such things were most readily to be gained in the flourishing tourneying circuit of northern France, where there was ample opportunity for deeds of arms, glory, excitement and profit. In England, by contrast, Henry II had re-established his grandfather's prohibition on tournaments, and thus it was that the Young King begged his father's leave 'to go over the Channel for my sport'.[143] As the chamberlain of Tancarville had earlier warned his young protégé William Marshal, England was no place for a young man seeking renown through feats of arms, and anyone 'wishing to devote his time and effort to travelling the world and tourneying was usually sent to Brittany and to Normandy to frequent the company of knights, or indeed, anywhere where tournaments were held'.[144]

Whether his stated reason was pilgrimage or martial sport, the Young King clearly regarded a return to the continent as restoring a considerable degree of his personal freedom. On receiving his father's leave to cross to Normandy, he and Margaret hurried to Portsmouth, but were delayed by unfavourable winds.[145] By now, Easter was approaching, so Henry II summoned the Young King back to hold court with him at Winchester, where Henry was expecting the imminent arrival of Richard and Geoffrey. He returned, but left Margaret at Porchester to mark his intention of leaving England as soon as he might. Delighting, noted Roger of Howden, in the presence of three of his sons, Henry II held a magnificent court. Even Queen Eleanor was probably allowed to attend this family reunion.[146] But there was also pressing business to discuss, for once again serious discontent had arisen in Aquitaine, fomented by Vulgrin Taillefer III, count of Angoulême, and his brothers, their half-brother, Aimar of Limoges, Raymond II, viscount of Turenne, and other lords such as Echiward of Chabanais and William Mastac.[147] Fuel had been added to the fires of rebellion by Henry II's own policies, for which Richard was now paying the price. While the sons of Count William of Angoulême had been hostile in 1173–74, Henry II's decision to keep the lion's share of the inheritance of Reginald of Cornwall in his own hands, to give to his son John, had deprived Aimar of Limoges of a rich inheritance and forced him into the rebel camp.[148]

Henry II persuaded the Young King to defer his pilgrimage and to help Richard to restore peace in Aquitaine; the campaign would give his eldest son valuable military experience as well as some of the freedom he clearly craved, and direct his energies against the family's enemies. The Young King and Margaret sailed on 20 April from Porchester, and on landing at Barfleur they at once hurried to see King Louis, though evidently with Henry II's permission.[149] It was probably soon thereafter that the Young King and his household journeyed from the Île-de-France to Arras to visit Count Philip.[150] The count gave young Henry a warm welcome, as 'they were cousins and good friends', and 'took him round his castles and cities, had him stay with him, and had him honoured as the king he was'.[151] Hearing that there was to be a major tournament near Ressons-sur-Matz, a town within Count Philip's county of Montdidier and a favoured tourneying venue on the border with the Capetian lands, Philip provided the Young King and his *mesnie* with horses, arms and fine equipment so that they could participate.[152] The author of the *History* noted that the Young King's troops did well, maintaining their discipline and fighting 'with great ferocity'.[153] Although this is the first specific tournament in which the Young King is known to have participated, there is no indication here that he was a novice; it was, however, his first opportunity to engage in a major feat of arms since the conclusion of the war, and it was doubtless for this reason that, as the *History* notes, Henry and his companions 'were keen to do well'.[154]

War in Aquitaine

Choosing not to wait for the Young King's arrival, Richard had marched with a powerful army against the insurgents in Poitou. During his absence, Theobald Chabot, Richard's *magister militum*, and John, bishop of Poitiers, had defeated a force of Vulgrin of Angoulême's mercenaries near Barbezieux. Exploiting this success, Richard himself won a victory in open battle against a force of Brabançons between St Maigrin and Bouteville in late May.[155] Moving against Aimar of Limoges, he took the castle of Aixe, which guarded an important crossing of the Vienne, then laid siege to Limoges itself, which fell to him within a few days.[156] It was only after 24 June that the Young King finally joined forces with Richard, who had returned victorious from the Limousin to meet him at the ducal capital of Poitiers.[157]

After holding a council of war with their magnates, the brothers marched into the lands of Vulgrin of Angoulême, who had refused to keep the duke's peace. They besieged Châteauneuf, which fell to them after fifteen days, but not before at least one knight in young Henry's contingent, Geoffrey of Saumur, had been mortally wounded.[158] With the castle taken, however, the Young King refused to stay longer with Richard. Howden noted that his decision to leave had been made 'according to ill-counsel', though he declined to specify who gave such advice or why.[159] It is likely, however, to have been the result of Poitevin barons hostile to Richard attempting to drive a wedge between the two brothers by playing on their rivalry. If so, it was the beginning of the Young King's fateful involvement in the troubled politics of the south. Though brief, these operations could not but have fuelled Young Henry's sense of frustration and his jealousy of his brother, for though Richard's authority remained delegated, he now effectively commanded the resources of the duchy.[160] How little the Young King's military aid meant to Richard, moreover, was painfully underlined when, despite the departure of his elder brother, Richard pressed on with his campaign with dramatic success. After a siege of only six days, he took Angoulême itself, capturing within it many of his leading opponents, including Count William, Aimar of Limoges, and the viscounts of Ventadour and Chabanais. Richard sent them back to his father in England, where at Winchester on 21 September they submitted and implored his mercy.[161] It had been a masterful campaign, and young Henry had missed out on any share of the glory.

A Crisis of Loyalty: Adam of Churchdown

The summer of 1176, moreover, witnessed a serious deterioration in relations between young Henry and his father. Between 1170 and 1173 the only witnesses appearing on the Young King's *acta* had been those *tutores* appointed by his father, which reflects their effective control of his actions. From 1175 onwards, by contrast, the Young King's own household knights and other members of his *familia*, such as the chaplains Nicholas and William, are found attesting his writs and charters, marking a significant step towards his greater autonomy.[162] Henry II nevertheless still exercised control of key members of his son's clerical staff. Indeed, Roger of Pont L'Évêque, archbishop of York, had purchased from Henry II the post of chancellor to the Young King for his nephew, Geoffrey, archdeacon of York and provost of Beverley, for the huge sum of 1,100 marks of silver.[163] In turn, Geoffrey had appointed another of Archbishop Roger's clerks, Adam of Churchdown, as his vice-chancellor.[164] Archbishop Roger had been a staunch ally against Thomas Becket and conspicuously loyal during the rebellion of 1173–74, so that in making these appointments the Old King was clearly seeking to install men drawn from the archbishop's circle to keep close watch on his son's activities.

It was inevitable, however, that young Henry, ever more sensitive concerning his own independence, should view officials selected by his father as at best a burdensome imposition, and at worst a fifth column. The invidious position in which this placed the new vice-chancellor was dramatically revealed while the Young King was at Poitiers on his return journey from the siege of Châteauneuf. According to Roger of Howden, young Henry had met with several nobles from Normandy and France, and despite the fact that these men were known enemies of his father he retained them in his household.[165] Alarmed by these developments, Adam of Churchdown attempted to warn Henry II. His letters, however, were intercepted – a telling insight into the tension and suspicion that existed between the Young King's friends and those appointed to his household by Henry II. Though Adam was acting out of a strong sense of duty to Henry II, the Young King regarded his actions as treason, and, wanting to stress the absolute loyalty he demanded from his men, he sought to make an example of the unfortunate vice-chancellor. Asked for their verdict on the matter, the Young King's counsellors judged that Adam be put to death for such betrayal, either by hanging or flaying alive. The bishop of Poitiers, however, intervened, claiming that as a clerk Adam was immune from secular jurisdiction. Yet though this saved him from a worse fate, the Young King nevertheless ordered Adam to be scourged through all the town squares along the court's journey to Argentan, where he was to be imprisoned. Incensed by his son's actions, Henry II sent four of his household knights to order Adam's immediate release and return to him.[166]

Yet if Henry II had been angered by the manner in which the Young King treated one of his own clerks, he was still more troubled by the news that Adam had attempted to convey. Was the Young King seeking to rekindle rebellion? How gravely Henry II took the situation is shown by his actions at Michaelmas when, following a great council at Windsor, he ordered that all castles in England were to be taken into royal hands; those in the hands of earls or barons were now to receive royal garrisons.[167] Even his loyal justiciar, Richard de Lucy, described by Howden as the king's *familiarissimus*, was forced to surrender his castle of Chipping Ongar, which was the centre or *caput* of his estates.[168] It was a remarkable display of force, but also of deep insecurity. Measures to ensure the demolition of castles were speeded up, and it was now, in the autumn of 1176 rather than in the immediate aftermath of the war, that Henry ordered the destruction of some of the castles of leading rebels of 1173–74. The castle at Leicester was demolished by the king's engineers, together with what remained of the town walls, while the earl's castle at Groby was razed. Roger de Mowbray's castles of Thirsk and Malzeard, and those of Hugh Bigod at Framlingham and Bungay, suffered a similar fate.[169] Similar measures were taken in Normandy, where Richard of Ilchester, bishop of Winchester, was made effectively the justiciar of Normandy, and took into Henry II's control the castles of all the Norman counts and barons, installing ducal garrisons in them.[170] Nor does it seem coincidental that in 1176 a number of erstwhile rebels, including Hugh Bigod and Hasculf of St Hilaire – the same man whom Henry II had expelled as a troublemaker from his son's household in 1173 – left on pilgrimage to the Holy Land.[171] Their decision to journey east is unlikely to have been a voluntary one, and the elderly Hugh was to die en route to Jerusalem.

Henry also now pressured Earl William of Gloucester into making John his principal heir. John was to marry the earl's daughter Isabella and to inherit the great honour of Gloucester. If Earl William should have a son by his wife, the honour was to be divided between this heir and John. The earl's other daughters were simply to receive an annuity from the revenues of England.[172] Like the settlement on John in the Treaty of Montlouis in 1174, Henry's lavish endowment of John appears in part to have been a further reaction to his eldest son's disloyalty, and Henry II may have been intending increasingly to establish his youngest son John as a check on the Young King's position in England.

By the late summer, however, relations between Heny II and the Young King had been patched up sufficiently for young Henry to obey his father's command to meet his sister Joanna as she crossed from England to Normandy in the company of Richard, archbishop of Canterbury, Geoffrey, bishop of Ely, and the Sicilian ambassadors who had negotiated her marriage to King William II.[173] Their ultimate destination was Saint-Gilles, where the Sicilian galleys were waiting. The dictates of security as well as state required a powerful escort, for the party bore rich gifts including horses, clothes, and gold and silver plate from Henry II. Young Henry received his sister and the ambassadors with the utmost honour and escorted them as far as Poitou, where he entrusted them to Richard for their onward journey to the lands of Toulouse.[174]

Châteauroux, Berry and the Reckoning with Louis

While Henry II celebrated Christmas at Nottingham, the Young King and Margaret held their own court at Argentan.[175] Early in the new year of 1177, however, young Henry received an urgent mandate from his father. Ralph de Déols, the most important baron in Berry, had died, leaving a three-year-old daughter, Denise, as the heiress to a wealthy and strategically crucial lordship centred on the castle of Châteauroux.[176] Controlling a major crossing of the river Indre, Châteauroux lay on the borders of both the Touraine and Poitou, within striking distance of Poitiers and of the heartlands of Anjou alike. As overlord, Henry II claimed the right of wardship over the girl and thus the opportunity to marry her to one of his own leading supporters. Resisting this imposition that went against local custom and family interest, Ralph's kinsmen refused to hand over Denise, carried her off and fortified their castles in expectation of the Angevin retaliation they knew must come.[177] In their defiance, they may have received the support of Louis VII, who directly controlled the viscounty of Bourges in eastern Berry and had long been seeking to expand Capetian power westward.[178] Angevin claims to control stemmed from the fact that Berry had long been regarded as part of the duchy of Aquitaine, but in January 1177, Richard was preoccupied by a major campaign against Dax and Bigorre which had taken him as far south as St Pierre-de-Cize and to the foothills of the Pyrenees.[179] The crisis in Berry demand a swift response, so Henry II ordered the Young King immediately to raise an army and take control of the lands of Ralph de Déols.[180] The Old King's mandate added a revealing comment that when he alone had been in control of the kingdom he had never lost anything pertaining to his right, and so in the same way it would be dishonourable, now that several were involved in the rule of the land, to lose anything from it: the prestige and honour of the Angevins as a family were at stake.[181] Glad of the commission and eager to make his own military showing, the Young King summoned the host of Normandy and Anjou and marched

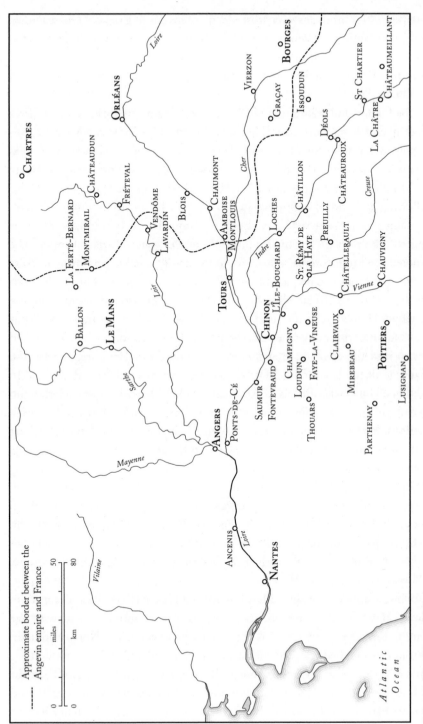

Map 6 The Loire Valley

into Berry. No chronicler records any details of his ensuing siege of Châteauroux, but its defenders evidently regarded his forces as overwhelming, for the castle was surrendered to him. Capture of the heiress Denise, however, eluded him, for she remained securely in the custody of her kinsman, the lord of La Châtre.[182]

Such a forceful reassertion of Plantagenet suzerainty in Berry was a direct challenge to King Louis, and Henry II doubtless intended the Young King's agency as an indicator of his son's political realignment. Moreover, whereas Henry II had been reconciled with his sons and their supporters by the Treaty of Montlouis, no formal peace had been drawn up with the French king following the end of hostilities in 1174. With his position within his own domains now reasserted, Henry II was determined on a showdown with Louis and to take revenge for his leading role in the war.[183] In late February, he ordered his English tenants-in-chief to muster at London on 8 May to cross to Normandy and be prepared to serve in the defence of his continental lands for a whole year.[184] Meanwhile, Henry II prepared his ground carefully, aiming to detach Louis from his most powerful allies, and to neutralize as far as possible support for any renewed rebellion by his eldest son. In January, he had pressurized the count of Flanders into turning down Louis' request for the marriage of the late Count Matthew's daughters to Louis' son Philip and to the son of Theobald of Blois.[185] Although in 1175 Henry had persuaded Philip to defer his planned pilgrimage to the Holy Land, he now provided him with funds for his journey, and in a gesture symbolizing their reconciliation, the king and count jointly undertook a pilgrimage to Becket's tomb in April.[186] Philip, accompanied by a number of French and Anglo-Norman barons, including William de Mandeville, left for the Holy Land in early May.[187] The Young King was still on the continent, and it seems likely that he met Count Philip before his friend and erstwhile ally departed. Whether he expressed any desire to accompany him on his eastern expedition is not known, but his father needed him in France. By early 1177, moreover, it was clear that his queen, Margaret, was pregnant.[188]

Philip's absence considerably strengthened Henry II's position in regard to King Louis, but the king also took care to seek a rapprochement with the leading former rebels within his realm. At a great council at Northampton in mid January he had restored their lands in England and in Normandy to the earls of Leicester and Chester, though he retained Mountsorrel and Pacy, the only castles of Earl Robert left standing, and the castle of Chester.[189] Earl Robert had shown himself to be obedient and humbled, and Henry had no wish to foment further enmity by dispossessing him. In a masterly move, Henry subsequently dispatched Earl Hugh to Ireland, suitably shadowed by

1. The Young King, labelled as Henricus junior, appears in a small arch between his father, Henry II, and his brother Richard in the line of kings of England, as depicted in Matthew Paris' *Historia Anglorum*, c.1250–59. By the mid-thirteenth century, the title of Henry III, given to the Young King by his contemporaries, had been transferred to his nephew Henry, shown here in the bottom right-hand panel.

2. The coronation of the Young King by Roger, archbishop of York, at Westminster in 1170, from an illustrated Anglo-Norman verse, Life of Thomas Becket, c.1220–40. At the coronation banquet, depicted to the right, Henry II serves young Henry at table, offering him a cup, to emphasize his new regal status. As the rubric above proclaims, some found this gesture shocking and injurious to Henry II's own majesty.

3. Though the Young King did not enjoy Henry II's reputation for learning, his father had ensured that he received a good education. From an early age, he was schooled in the workings of law and government, as well as in courtly accomplishments. Here, from the early fourteenth-century Codex Manesse, a king instructs his son.

4. A charter of the Young King granting rents to Christ Church cathedral priory, Canterbury, probably dating from late 1175 or early 1176, with his great seal appended. Among the witnesses are Adam d'Yquebeuf, William Marshal's great rival in the Young King's household, and his vice-chancellor, Adam of Gloucester, who was soon to be tried for treason for betraying young Henry's letters to his father.

5. The seal of King Louis VII of France, on which the Young King's own seal was modelled. The adoption of a single-sided seal served as an easy means of distinguishing the Young King's charters from those of his father, which bore a double-sided seal, but it also reflected the strong Capetian influence on the Angevins' perception of kingship.

6. The murder of Thomas Becket in Canterbury cathedral on 29 December 1170, here depicted in a psalter dating to *c.*1220, shocked Christendom. In refusing to see Thomas in person after his return to England, young Henry had unwittingly played a part in this tragic event, and his grief at the death of his old tutor was matched by a mounting sense of guilt and remorse.

7. The Young King's pilgrimage in 1172 to Canterbury, made before the canonization of Becket the following year, was the first of many royal pilgrimages to the martyr's shrine. The miraculous correlation of Henry II's own dramatic penance at Becket's tomb in Canterbury with the capture of William the Lion at Alnwick in 1174 convinced many that St Thomas was now reconciled with King Henry, depicted here in prayer at the shrine in a thirteenth-century stained-glass window, Canterbury cathedral.

8. Heads of a young king and queen, perhaps representing young Henry and Queen Margaret, from the early thirteenth-century portal of the church of Candes-Saint-Martin, Anjou, close to the abbey of Fontevraud.

9. The great castle of Chinon, on the river Vienne in the Touraine, combined the roles of palace, treasury, and fortress. It was here that, in March 1173, young Henry and his companions escaped from his father's control and made their daring ride to the safety of Louis VII's lands.

10. The image of two hands pulling the crown in opposite directions represents the struggles between Henry II and his sons in this list of marginal signs, intended to direct readers to key topics, from the chronicle of Ralph of Diss. Above the hands are items of regalia representing the counts of Anjou, the dukes of Normandy, and the kings of England.

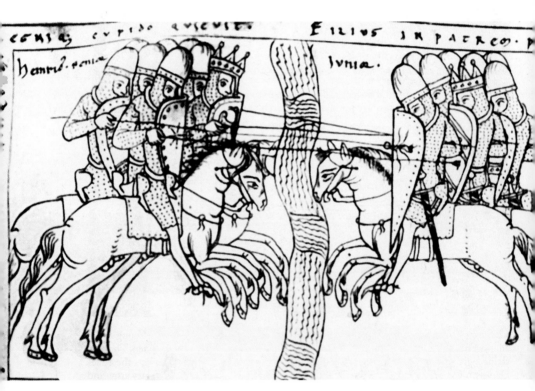

11. The rebellion of sons against fathers was commonplace in dynastic politics of the eleventh and twelfth centuries. In this mid-twelfth-century illustration from Otto of Freising's *Chronicle*, Henry IV of Germany, to the left, confronts his son Henry (labelled, respectively, as Henricus senior and junior) at the river Regen in 1105, while the rubric bemoans such internecine strife. In the war of 1173–74, the Young King and Louis VII shrank from engaging in pitched battle with Henry II.

12. Sieges dominated twelfth-century warfare, but, in the war of 1173–74, the Young King and his allies were unable to overcome the defences of towns such as Verneuil and Rouen. Though this stained-glass window, from the north quire aisle of Canterbury cathedral, depicts the attack of the Danes on Canterbury in 1011, it dates from the 1170s and features contemporary arms and armour.

13. In this illumination from the Morgan Bible, *c.*1250, a captive king is led away together with other prisoners and livestock. In contrast with the bloody combat depicted here, no knights were killed in the engagement at Alnwick in 1174, in which King William the Lion was surprised and captured, although his Flemish and Scots foot soldiers were treated more ruthlessly.

14. A cast of the tomb of William Marshal (d. 1219), from the Temple Church, London, made before the original was badly damaged by fire during bombing in 1941. Regarded as one of the greatest knights of his day, William Marshal served as young Henry's tutor in arms from 1170, and he became one of his closest companions.

15. The violence of the mêlée is vividly captured in this depiction of the tournament from the Codex Manesse. Deliberate killing or serious wounding, however, was forbidden, and the aim was to capture opponents, often by tearing off their helms or wrestling them from their saddles.

16. The Young King was famed for his generosity and open-handed giving, which attracted knights from many regions to his service in the tournament and in war. Here, from the Codex Manesse, a king distributes largesse to his knights, clerks, and minstrels.

17. The Young King's participation in the coronation of Philip Augustus at Rheims in November 1179 was later seized on by French royal propagandists to demonstrate the subjection of the kings of England to those of France. In this illumination by Jean Fouquet, from the *Grandes Chroniques de France, c.*1455–60, the Young King, holding the crown and standing next to Count Philip of Flanders, who bears the sword of Charlemagne, is depicted anachronistically wearing the royal arms of England, adopted by his brother Richard in the 1190s.

18. The seal of Philip Augustus, 1198. Young Henry played a prominent role in supporting King Philip, his brother-in-law, in the first troubled years of his reign. Though their own relations were cordial, the Young King's death ushered in a period of unrelenting hostility from the king of France towards the Angevins.

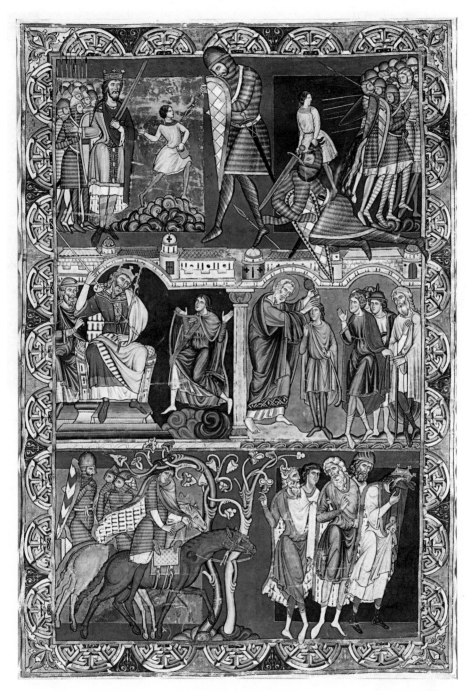

19. The Old Testament afforded many exemplars of good and bad kingship, as well as of divine punishment of filial disobedience. In the bottom register of these scenes by the Master of the Morgan Leaf, Winchester, *c*.1160–80, illustrating the life of David from the Book of Samuel, King David's rebellious son Absalom, to whom the Young King was compared by contemporaries, is run through as his hair is caught in a tree while attempting to flee. Like King David, depicted hiding his face in his cloak, Henry II felt bitter grief at the death of his son.

20. The Young King as imagined by the late nineteenth-century restorers of his tomb, now in the north aisle of the quire of Rouen cathedral. The tomb effigy itself probably dates from the early fourteenth century, but it was badly damaged in the Wars of Religion and the French Revolution. The head, shown here, and other details, as well as the tomb base and inscription, are later restorations.

William FitzAdelin, with orders to subdue it on behalf of John, whom Henry was planning to make king of Ireland.[190] A further indication of the rebels' political rehabilitation was the fact that the earls of Leicester, Chester and Ferrers, as well as Roger de Mowbray, were among the witnesses to the agreement between the kings of Navarre and Castile brokered by Henry II and ratified at Windsor on 9 March.[191] Nevertheless, when news reached him of the death of Hugh Bigod on pilgrimage in Palestine, Henry II moved to weaken Bigod power; his agents seized all of the earl's treasure and, despite the fact that his eldest son Roger had been a loyal supporter in the war of 1173–74, the king exploited a challenge by Hugh Bigod's second wife Gundreda in favour of her own son Hugh to take a significant number of Bigod lands into royal control and to withhold from Roger the grant of the earldom itself.[192]

The extent to which Henry II still feared a potential uprising in England during his projected campaign against Louis is starkly indicated by the fact that at a council at Windsor in May, convened to deliberate 'the peace and stability of the realm', the king – ostensibly on the advice of the assembled magnates – 'removed the custodians of the castles of England' and replaced them with knights from his own household.[193] Similarly, in a bid to prevent the Scots from attempting to regain the key strongholds of Lothian, Henry II entrusted them to the very men who had proved so steadfast in the defence of the north against William the Lion in 1173–74: William de Stuteville was installed at Roxburgh, hitherto in the custody of Archbishop Roger, who was instead granted control of the great Yorkshire stronghold of Scarborough, while Roger de Stuteville held Edinburgh and Geoffrey de Neville Berwick.[194] The defection of Hugh of Durham, who had served the king 'badly and deceitfully' in the recent war, had pointed up the Achilles heel of the defences of the north-east. The bishop had proffered the huge fine of 2,000 marks to have the king's goodwill, to save his castles from demolition, and to secure the manor of Wicton for his son Henry de Puiset. Nevertheless, King Henry now had his castle of Northallerton demolished, and the keep of Durham castle placed in the custody of Robert de Conyers, while the episcopal castle of Norham was committed to William de Neville.[195] Henry looked equally to the security of his western borders. At Oxford, he met with a great assembly of Welsh princes, who, after suitable grants, swore homage and fealty to him and pledged to keep peace with him.[196]

With the chances of renewed Scottish aggression or insurrection in England thus diminished, Henry II embarked on an aggressive game of brinkmanship with Louis. The muster of the English host was pushed back to early June but it was to take place at Winchester, while a great fleet of ships from the ports of England and Normandy were assembled at Portsmouth and Southampton to carry the army across to Normandy.[197] Then, with his intentions of deploying massive force made clear, Henry II announced the postponement of the expedition until 1 July, while he sent a high-powered delegation, led by Geoffrey Ridel, bishop of Ely, Richard of Ilchester, bishop of Winchester, and Archbishop Rotrou of Rouen to King Louis, to whom they presented an astonishing ultimatum. In order to ratify the terms of the marriage agreements made with his sons, the French king was to cede to the Young King 'the whole of that territory which is called the Vexin, that is to say all the land which is between Gisors and Pontoise', which had been promised when young Henry married Margaret. Louis was also to cede the city of Bourges and its appurtenances, which he had purportedly granted as her dower when Richard should marry Alice.[198] These were extraordinary claims, to which Henry II cannot seriously have expected Louis to accede. Margaret's dowry had only been the contested Norman Vexin, not the French half of it, while the agreement of Montmirail had explicitly stated that the marriage of Richard and Alice was not to entail a territorial dowry. Henry II's actions have been seen as a flagrant pretext for premeditated aggression, or as a means by which he sought to achieve his primary goal of securing fuller recognition of his rights in Berry and the Auvergne and to obtain a promise that the French would not intervene while he pursued these aims.[199] Yet while his authority in these regions and the issue of the honour of Châteauroux were a cause of contention,[200] there was a more immediate and alarming reason for the heightened tension between the kings of France and England. For Margaret, the Young King's wife, who was heavily pregnant, had left the Angevin lands without consulting Henry II and without his permission, and gone to her father, King Louis.[201] When Henry's ambassadors demanded the French Vexin and Bourges from Louis, they also demanded that he send back his daughter to Normandy immediately.[202] If the child of Margaret and young Henry was born in the Île-de-France, the Capetians would have control over the future heir of the heartlands of the Angevin empire. This was an acute danger that Henry II was not prepared to tolerate.

Roger of Howden, the only chronicler to mention Margaret's flight to Louis' court, gives no explanation of the circumstances which lay behind it, nor of the Young King's role in this drama. Yet it is hard to believe that Queen Margaret could have withdrawn to Paris without young Henry's knowledge or consent. He must have viewed his father's aggressive stance towards King Louis, his father-in-law and erstwhile ally, with deep ambivalence, and perhaps saw the refuge of his wife and future child in the Île-de-France as safeguarding his own position. Henry II had sent Geoffrey of Ely and Walter of Coutances, the archdeacon of Oxford, as messengers to the Young King, but when they brought his response to his father's mandates back to the Old King at Woodstock, 'it did not please him in any respect'.[203] This suggests more than merely a report that the French had refused Henry II's ultimatum. Had young Henry opposed his father's demands on Louis, or refused to assist him in any campaign against the French king? Henry II's response was to summon the bishops of the realm to be ready to cross to Normandy with him on 1 July, but once again he postponed transferring his assembled army to the duchy while he waited for news of his envoys to France.[204]

The immediate diplomatic crisis provoked by Margaret's flight, however, was ended by a personal tragedy. In Paris, around 19 June, Margaret gave birth to a boy who was baptized William, but the infant, who may have been prema-ture, survived only three days.[205] Little William's death helps to explain why Henry II did not press home his military plans against Louis but instead allowed himself 'to be talked rather easily into drawing up a non-aggression pact with Louis'.[206] Louis, moreover, had neatly turned the tables on Henry II's demands concerning his daughters' dowries by appealing to the papal legate in France, Peter, cardinal bishop of Saint Chrysogonus and formerly bishop of Meaux, over the fact that the marriage of Alice and Richard had, in contraven-tion of their agreement, been repeatedly delayed, even though the girl had long been in Angevin custody. Unless the marriage was now ratified, the legate threatened to place all Henry's lands on both sides of the Channel under inter-dict. Henry responded by an appeal to the pope, but though he did indeed transport his great army to Normandy he did not turn it against Louis, but sent part of it with his son Geoffrey to quell insurgents in Brittany.[207] The Young King joined his father at Rouen on 11 September, where they received the legate Peter, still bent on carrying out his threatened interdict, but he was persuaded to desist until talks could be held with Louis.[208] Accordingly on 21 September, the three kings held a summit between Nonancourt and the great Norman border fortress of Ivry. Here, Henry II concluded a general peace with King Louis, and agreed that Richard would marry Alice, while he and Louis also pledged to take the cross.[209]

Soon after these negotiations, however, tragedy struck the Angevin court when a ship carrying Geoffrey of Beverley, the Young King's chancellor, sank in severe storms off St Valéry on 27 September as it crossed from England to Normandy.[210] Roger of Howden also noted the loss of Robert, master of the York schools, but though the names of no others on board are known, it is likely that young Henry also lost further members of his household and those close to him among the 300 souls who perished in the wreck. Nevertheless, the Young King was soon engaged in leading an army into Berry at his father's command to put down their enemies, while Richard was sent into Poitou to suppress further rebellion there.[211] Little is recorded about young Henry's campaign, though it seems to have been unsuccessful; hearing of his lack of progress, or so Howden believed, Henry II invaded Berry himself with a large force, took Châteauroux and moved to besiege La Châtre where the Déols heiress was being held. Faced with such overwhelming force, the castellan made peace with Henry II and surrendered Denise, who was sent to Chinon to be guarded.[212] Henry II then turned against those nobles in the Limousin who had supported his sons against him in the war of 1173–74, and imposed heavy fines on them.[213] His success was completed in December when at Grandmont he managed to purchase La Marche from its count, Adalbert, for 15,000 *livres angevins*, a coup that markedly strengthened Angevin power in Aquitaine.[214] The Young King, Richard and Geoffrey all attended Henry II's magnificent Christmas court of 1177 at Angers, where the Old King celebrated a triumphal year. Robert of Torigni could not remember another occasion, even at Henry II's coronation or that of the Young King, when the king had so many knights with him.[215] It was the conclusion of a period of pacification and restoration of power, at times halting and uncertain, that had begun in September 1174; only now was Henry II secure, even if relations with his eldest son were still unsettled. For young Henry, however, the year equally marked an important turning point. Whether through a genuine rapprochement or merely resignation to his inability to alter his position vis-à-vis his father, the Young King entered into a period of more stable and peaceful relations with Henry II that would last until 1182.

CHAPTER II

Apogee

KING OF THE TOURNAMENT, 1177–1182

> The Young King, a worthy, fine and courtly man later in his life performed
> such high exploits that he revived the notion of chivalry which, at that time,
> was close to extinction. He was the gate, the way and the door through
> which chivalry returned, and he was her standard bearer . . .
>
> – *History of William Marshal*[1]

DESPITE THE RENEWED tensions of 1176–77, the next five years would witness a period of comparative stability in relations between the Young King and his father. This peace was in no small measure due to the close involvement of the Young King in the tournament circuit of northern France. It was in these years that he gained a glittering reputation as a *roi chevalier*, admired not only for feats of arms, but for the size of his retinues, his open-handed generosity, and his embodiment of the chivalric virtues, which the tournament itself helped to disseminate.[2] His participation in the tournaments of the later 1170s and early 1180s, moreover, is among the best-recorded aspects of his life, thanks largely to the invaluable record of the *History* itself. Almost a third of this long poem is devoted to descriptions of William Marshal's tourneying exploits before 1183, many of which were undertaken while in the service of, and often in company with, the Young King.

By the 1170s the tournament was already well developed, with northern France as its epicentre.[3] Tournaments frequently took place in border areas, notably those between Normandy and the Île-de-France, or further to the north-east where the Capetian lands marched with those of the counts of Flanders. A number of favoured sites had emerged, such as between Anet and Sorel-Moussel on the river Eure, or between Gournay-sur-Aronde and Ressons-sur-Matz, while a tournament season had been established, running between Lent and Whitsuntide. Indeed, so frequent had tournaments become that in the season there might be as many as one every two weeks.[4] With its opportunities for training in cavalry warfare, for the winning of a martial reputation through feats of arms and profit through ransoms, and for conspicuous display and noble conviviality, the tournament had rapidly become an integral aspect of aristocratic culture. Its allurements were neatly summed up in the late twelfth-century German romance *Lanzelet*, in which a herald proclaims:

> At these jousts are to be won fame and honour: there one can thrust and slash at will; all the celebrities will participate; and there one can meet distinguished knights and ladies. To stay away were a disgrace. All that can delight the knightly soul is there to be had: fighting, horse racing, jumping, running, fencing, wrestling, play at tables and at bowls, the music of the rote, the fiddle and the harp; and besides these, the opportunity of buying things from all over the world.[5]

It was into this world that the Young King threw himself, armed with youthful enthusiasm and a seemingly limitless supply of his father's money.

Although its origins are obscure, the tournament's growth was inextricably linked to increasing stability within the territorial principalities of northern France and the concomitant curbing of small-scale but endemic warfare among the nobility. Galbert of Bruges had directly equated the frequent participation of Count Charles the Good of Flanders (d. 1127) in tournaments to the firm peace he had established in his own lands, and to absence of war on his frontiers. With no other fighting to be done, he 'undertook chivalric exploits for the honour of his land and the training of his knights in the lands of the princes of Normandy or France, sometimes even beyond the kingdom of France; and there with two hundred knights on horseback he engaged in tourneys, in this way enhancing his own fame and the power and glory of his country'.[6] Similarly, John of Marmoutier noted how Count Geoffrey le Bel of Anjou, 'stoking up his own reputation and keen for further contests, began to engage in tournaments within the borders of Flanders and even further afield'.[7] If Charles appears to have been precocious as a count in participating in a sport initially regarded more as the preserve of mere knights, by the 1160s and 1170s many greater magnates and the territorial princes of northern France were doing likewise, and for very much the same reasons.[8] Count Baldwin V of Hainault, for example, is recorded as having participated in at least thirteen tournaments between 1168 and 1184, while there was nothing exceptional in finding Duke Hugh of Burgundy and the counts of Clermont, Beaumont and Blois attending a great tournament at Pleurs, *c.*1178.[9] Count Philip of Flanders and Count Henry 'the Liberal' of Champagne had become especially renowned as great patrons of the tournament. The close correlation between the holding of tournaments and major fairs, such as those of Champagne, stimulated regional economies and yielded revenue through tolls and entry charges.[10] Yet still more important for these princes, such patronage – both through sponsorship and through personal participation in combat – brought martial prestige and served as a means of extending political and cultural influence. The honour and reputation gained by feats of arms in the tournament was a crucial factor in explaining its lasting importance. 'The fact is', noted the messengers bringing William Marshal the prize at a tournament at Pleurs in 1178, 'that high deeds are witnessed by many men when one is in such a situation.'[11] Such was the allure of tournaments that King William the Lion of Scotland and some of his leading nobles, such as Peter de Valognes, had crossed from Scotland to France in 1166 to engage in them.[12]

Before the Young King, kings of England had not patronized or personally participated in the tournament. Henry II permitted tournaments to be held on the borders of Normandy, but had strictly prohibited them in England, fearing they would be a source of potential disorder and rebellion. In doing so, he was re-establishing a similar ban imposed by Henry I, which had lapsed during the troubles of Stephen's reign.[13] Henry II, like his grandfather, was a brave and seasoned warrior, but considerations of status and regal dignity, as much as concerns for personal safety, kept him aloof from tourneying himself.[14] Henry II's reticence was shared by the kings of France. Louis VII was not a martial king, but neither Philip Augustus nor his son Louis VIII would participate in tournaments despite much campaigning in actual warfare. A century later the French herald Sarrazin commented with evident disapproval that 'No king of France has ever participated in a tournament from the time when Noah entered the ark, and no-one knows if a king ever did more than come to one'.[15] Young Henry's leading role in the tournament stood in marked contrast. In a revealing passage, Ralph of Diss noted under the year 1179 that:

> Young King Henry, the king's son, left England and passed three years in tournaments, spending a lot of money. While he was rushing all over France he put aside the royal majesty and was transformed from a king into a knight, carrying off victory in various meetings. His popularity made him famous; the old king was happier counting up and admiring his victories, and although the Young King was still under age his father restored in full his possessions which he had taken away.[16]

Far from disapproving of his son's involvement, Henry II took paternal pride in his high-profile sporting achievements and was more than willing to bankroll the Young King's tourneying activities. For he realized that the tournament provided young Henry and his companions with a vital safety valve through which to exercise their martial aggression, as well as a means for his son to enhance his status and reputation. Thus preoccupied, the Young King might be less minded to press his father for direct rule of any part of the Angevin dominions. Equally, just as he had readily appreciated the political value of Becket's extravagant display of his king's wealth, so Henry II fully recognized that the Young King's lavish patronage of an international body of knights reflected the wealth of the Angevin empire and augmented its prestige. The Young King's leadership in the tournament projected a strong and vigorous image of Plantagenet rulership. Indeed, young Henry began a new trend by which English kingship took on a self-consciously chivalric dimension, and employed royal participation in the tournament as a crucial means of forging bonds between the king and his aristocracy: after a hiatus under John and Henry III, this would be developed by Edward I and reach its apogee with the enthusiastic tourneying of Edward III and the Black Prince.[17]

A winning combination of young Henry's personal charisma and great wealth, moreover, served to draw to him otherwise disparate sections of the nobility of the Angevin empire. In the tournament, two main teams fought each other, each team often comprising contingents with distinctive regional identities. At a tournament in 1166 near Le Mans, for example, knights from Anjou, Maine, Poitou and Brittany opposed those from England, France and Normandy.[18] More usually, however, teams reflected political alignments: thus at one tournament in the late 1170s a French team fought one led by the Young King comprising Norman and English knights, who, noted the *History of William Marshal*, vied with each other to be the best.[19] Such rivalry doubtless arose between other constituent regions of the Angevin empire, yet the leadership of the Young King brought knights together from these diverse areas in a common purpose and shared identity. If one of the great weaknesses of Henry II's rule was the all too evident monopoly by Anglo-Normans of patronage and influence at court and the exclusion of members of other regional aristocracies, the composition of the Young King's tourneying teams was far more inclusive. At the tournament held between Anet and Sorel, probably in the spring of 1178, Normans, Bretons, English, 'men from Le Mans and Anjou, along with the men from Poitou, with their lord, the Young King' fought as a team against one drawn from France, Flanders, Brie and Champagne.[20] Similarly at the great tournament at Lagny in November 1179, the Young King's team included English, Norman and Angevin knights, but also some from France and Flanders.[21] The composition of this team at Lagny, which is recorded in unusual detail by the *History*, indicates how participation in the tournament also served as an invaluable mechanism for reintegrating a divided aristocracy in the wake of the civil war of 1173–74, bringing together men who had fought on opposing sides, such as Robert de Stuteville, who had played such a key role in holding northern England for Henry II, and Earl David of Huntingdon, one of the leading rebels in the Midlands.[22] Ralph of Diss clearly regarded the Young King's great success in the tournament between 1176 and 1179 as a means of his political rehabilitation in the eyes of his father.[23]

The Young King's leadership and patronage, however, extended well beyond the nobility of the Angevin lands to embrace knights from all over France and the Low Countries. At Lagny, for example, he retained Robert count of Dreux and famous French knights, including William des Barres and his son of the same name, as well as leading Flemish knights such as Baldwin de Béthune, William de Cayeux and Baldwin le Caron.[24] As the *History* noted, he

> gathered so many worthy men around him that no emperor, king or count ever had such an experienced company, nor would such have been found at any time, for there is no doubt that he had the pick of the bravest young knights (*les buens bacheliers*) of France, Flanders and Champagne. He did not haggle with them, but he acted in such a way that all the worthy men (*tuit li buen*) came and joined him.[25]

One such knight was the Fleming Roger de Jouy, for 'there was no man between Dieppe and Baugé more successful at winning booty or more valorous', and William Marshal was himself to exploit Roger's talents for gain by entering into a very profitable business partnership with him for taking ransoms in the tournament.[26] At a tournament at Eu, in either 1178 or 1179, the Young King had a force of over 100 knights, 'the best that could be found', but at the exceptionally grand tournament at Lagny in 1179, held to celebrate the coronation of Philip Augustus, young Henry fielded a great retinue of over 200 knights, including nineteen counts and fifteen knights banneret.[27] An emerging rank within the aristocracy, bannerets were lords of greater wealth and status, who were capable of retaining a number of other knights in their service. By the 1170s they were coming to distinguish themselves by bearing distinctive square or rectangular banners, in contrast to the smaller pennon, usually with a forked tail, borne by lesser knights, who now formed the lowest tier of the nobility.[28] Beyond the wages paid to his own knights, each of the fifteen bannerets retained by the Young King at Lagny received 20 shillings a day for every knight in his unit, 'whether they were on the move or in lodgings, from the moment they left their own lands'.[29] The daily expense of well over

£200 that this represented was a staggering sum.[30] 'It was a source of wonder where this wealth was to be found,' mused the *History*, 'and one can only say that God had shared out to him the wealth placed at his disposal.'[31] Not infrequently, however, the Young King's spending outstripped his access to ready money and he was forced to rely on credit:

> It is true that the Young King, in castle and town, led such a lavish life that, when it came to the end of his stay, he would have no idea how to take his leave. When it came to the last day, creditors would appear, men who had supplied him with horses, garments and victuals. 'This man is owed three hundred pounds; this one a hundred and that one two hundred,' the household clerks would say ... 'My lord has no ready money with him, but you shall have it within a month.'[32]

His creditors could at least comfort themselves that the ultimate source of young Henry's money, and if need be their own redress, was the royal coffers of Henry II himself.

Entry into the Young King's retinue was not automatic. Though the *History* does not record the reason for young Henry's repeated refusal to take on Sir Reginald de Nevers, a younger son of Count William III of Nevers, such a rebuff clearly rankled and made Reginald an implacable opponent when fighting against the Young King's team.[33] For even temporary service in the tourneying retinues of the great magnates enhanced a man's standing and provided a valuable source of employment for the 'bachelors' – young or landless knights. They thereby gained not only wages but opportunities for advancement and the patronage of influential lords. Those knights who served with the Young King, moreover, gained kudos that might aid their subsequent careers. Though he does not name him, Lambert of Ardres relates how one Flemish knight, 'a man vigorous in arms, who had previously been a fellow knight and associate of Henry the Young King of England', was made 'teacher and instructor in arms' to the young Arnold, lord of Ardres, in a role closely analogous to that of William Marshal. Unlike the Marshal, however, he was swiftly rewarded by Arnold with a fief: that of Verlinghem near Licques.[34]

In a world where prestige and status were measured not only by conspicuous consumption in dress, equipment and at table but also by the size and excellence of one's retinue, the great lords competed to hire the best knights for their teams. In such a bidding war, the Young King's wealth put him at a great advantage, and his extravagant generosity meant that knights flocked to his banner. As the *History* noted: 'No amount of expense would stop the King enticing to his side any good, valiant and experienced knight who could be found, for in his generosity, high exploits (*par largesse e par bien feire*) and all other fine qualities he surpassed all princes'.[35] It was this patronage of knights that, in the eyes of the author of the *History*, made the Young King the very model of chivalry, 'for at that time men of high rank were doing nothing for any young nobleman (*bachiler*). But he was the flower and cream of men as regards keeping worthy followers in his service; for he wanted all of these to be with him.'[36] As a result, claimed the *History*, the other great lords, and especially Count Philip of Flanders, followed his example, 'for they saw very well that neither king nor count could raise his standing except through the worthy men he had with him'. In reality, the Young King was merely following the well-established practice of other great lords. Gilbert of Mons notes, for example, how, as a new knight, Count Baldwin of Hainault had 'sought tournaments everywhere and attached to himself whatever virtuous knights and companions and household knights of great name that he could'.[37] Nevertheless, the advent of the Young King certainly increased competition between the great princes, and may well have served to push up wages demanded by the best knights.[38]

Among those eager to serve with the Young King was his younger brother Geoffrey of Brittany. Roger of Howden records how, immediately after he had been knighted by Henry II at Woodstock in July 1178, and evidently with his father's approbation, Geoffrey

> crossed over to Normandy, and on the borders of Normandy and France, but also on the frontiers of other countries, he exercised his strength, and took pleasure in making himself a match for knights of reputation in arms. And he sought to acquire glory by his prowess all the more because he knew that his brothers, that is to say King Henry and Richard, count of Poitou, had increased in renown through knightly arms. They were all of one mind, namely to excel others in feats of arms, because 'the arts of war, if not practised beforehand, are not to be had in time of necessity'.[39]

This period of Geoffrey's military apprenticeship in the tournament circuit under the Young King's tutelage doubtless helped to strengthen the close bond between them that emerged clearly in the political crisis of 1183.

A School of Arms: The Nature of the Tournament

The *History* presents the Young King's fortunes in the tournament as rising gradually from a run of defeats suffered in 1176 and 1177 to increasing success, achieved by greater tactical sagacity and skill. This development was naturally attributable to the sound instruction and tutoring of the Marshal, who 'was for many a day lord and master of his lord', though the *History* does not trouble to explain why it took the Marshal so long to impart such wisdom.[40] Nevertheless, once lessons were learned, the Young King excelled in arms. At a tournament held between Gournay-sur-Arnode and Ressons-sur-Matz in late 1182, 'the King performed with such vigour that his boldness and valour, his skill and his speed, gave pleasure to many, and his men performed so well that all the others, on all sides, fell silent as a result of their exploits'.[41] Indeed, the combination of the young Henry's prowess with his ability to field a side of the best knights made his teams formidable. 'He made the whole world tremble in the battles in which he took part,' claimed the *History*:

> Many a time it happened that, when he spurred on, so the companies with him spurred on too, so vigorously as they advanced that those riding towards them from the other side could not withstand their charge. And it often happened that the other side had far more men than they, and yet they were soon thrown into disarray by the mighty power of the King's companies.[42]

In actual warfare, knights rarely had the opportunity to charge in large groups, as the limited number of such actions in the recent war of 1173–74 had shown. The tournament, by contrast, provided an effective means by which to regularly practise the group drill and disciplined manoeuvre that were essential to the effective operation of units of knights.[43] During the twelfth century, its essential element remained the mêlée, in which two teams of knights charged each other, then engaged in close-quarter combat, with the aim of routing the opposing team, seizing horses and capturing prisoners for ransom. A series of individual jousts known as *commençailles* or *jostes de pladïeces* might take place the day before the main tournament in a preliminary event known as the 'vespers'.[44] As these could be more easily observed and appreciated than in the press and confusion of the mêlée, such jousts were particularly favoured by younger knights seeking to make their reputation, yet combat in the mêlée was deemed worthy of greater honour.[45] Though it was fast becoming a highly popular spectator sport, the mêlée itself might range over a wide area of several miles. A palisaded area known as the lists (*lices*) was usually erected, to protect a routed team from further attack, and these might even be guarded by infantry. Similarly, certain areas, often fenced off, were designated as 'refuges' (*recez*) in which knights could arm in safety before the combat and form up, or into which they could retire to rest.[46]

On the main day of the tournament, teams of knights would be drawn up and at a given signal charge each other. Cohesion was the key to success.[47] In some combats, when both sides managed to retain sufficient cohesion, there was no clear victor; at the tournament in late November 1182 held between Gournay-sur-Aronde and Ressons-sur-Matz, for example, the fighting was ended by mutual consent, although here the Young King and his team were nevertheless awarded the prize.[48] More often, one side would gain a decisive advantage through greater discipline in attack. At Ressons-sur-Matz in 1176, the Young King and his *conroi* or troop performed well, for they 'kept themselves serried and in close ranks', whereas the opposing forces, through over-confidence and ill-discipline, came on 'in too great a disarray', never kept tight formation, and were consequently routed by the Young King's squadron.[49] 'A man who breaks ranks too early is a fool,' noted the *History*.[50] Similarly, at the tournament held probably in early 1178 between Anet and Sorel, the French charged so impetuously that their *conrois* collided together, disrupting the effect of their impetus. The Young King allowed them to come on sufficiently for their ranks to become still more disordered, then launched a powerful charge which drove right through the French and put them to flight.[51] In the pursuit, however, the Young King's men in turn 'lost all self-control and gave chase, so intent on booty that they left the king all alone, except for the Marshal'.[52] The rout of the French had been so complete that on this occasion there were no ill consequences, but in a real battle such *'desmesure'* or ill-discipline – which left their lord without a reserve company and thus vulnerable to counter-attack, or which left his own person exposed to danger – could have spelt disaster.[53] At Lagny in 1179, the Young King's retinue drove their opponents from the field, but they had advanced so precipitously that the king himself was left almost unattended. Promptly targeted by other groups of knights joining the field, he was subjected to sustained attack and was rescued from capture by the Marshal only with great difficulty.[54]

As well as tight formation, the timing of a charge was critical to success. The *History* recounts how Count Philip, who had revealed himself as a ruthless pragmatist in the war of 1173–74, held back when the Young King's powerful troop was initially engaged, and 'only joined in the tournament when all were weary, disarrayed and disorganized'. When he was certain of the advantage, he would launch an attack on the flank of the opposing force.[55] At Lagny, he 'held back cleverly, until he saw that the time was exactly right', and his counter-attack completely routed part of the Young King's team led by his brother Geoffrey.[56] The author of the *History*, however, saw no cause for censure; Count Philip's conduct was that of a 'man both brave and wise (*proz e sages*)', and was just the kind of hard-headed approach to the art of war counselled by the Marshal himself.[57] Indeed, according to the *History*, the Young King soon learned from Philip's tactics, and imitated them to good effect. On one occasion, he went so far as pretending he and his men were not going to engage in a tourney, before suddenly falling upon his opponents. Such was his success that 'after that, the King never came to the site of a tourney without availing himself of this sort of trick and deception (*de ceste bole e de tel guile*)'.[58] This was not seen as in any way unchivalrous, for, as the *History* notes, 'high valour needs to be allied to good sense'.[59] Less justifiable was an incident in 1178 when, having routed their French opponents, the Young King and William Marshal broke the rules by riding into the town of Anet, which was the base for the French team and thus technically off limits. They rushed a group of infantry gathered to protect the lists and seized their commander Simon de Neuphle.[60]

As in real war, further cohesion within each team was afforded by the use of distinctive war cries, blazon and banners. The Young King and his knights used the rallying cry of the dukes of Normandy, 'Dex aïe!' ('God aid us!'), as well as 'Alez lor reals!' ('At them, king's men!').[61] More effective in the din of the mêlée was the visual identity provided by heraldry. By at least the 1170s, great lords carried heraldic devices on their shields, banners and horse trappers, while members of their retinues might also wear livery with their lord's colours, device or arms. The arms of neither Henry II nor the Young King are known for certain, but the lion emblem was closely linked to Henry II and some of his courtiers, while young Henry's uncle William FitzEmpress certainly bore a single lion rampant as his arms.[62] It is probable that the Young King bore a single golden lion rampant on a red field (gules, a lion rampant or), the same arms that Richard I subsequently carried as king until he adopted the new royal arms of three lions (gules, three lions passant guardant or) in the later 1190s.[63] If so, William Marshal was consciously echoing the arms of his lord, but subtly 'differenced', when he adopted a red lion rampant on a half-yellow, half-green background (party per pale or and vert, a lion rampant gules), which he seems to have first displayed when he appeared as a knight banneret at the great tournament of Lagny in 1179.[64]

In the initial charge, known as the *estor*, knights aimed to strike their opponents with their lances and, if possible, unhorse them.[65] At Lagny, the Young King boldly attacked a larger group of knights, 'and the clash was so ferocious that his lance was shattered as easily as if had been made of glass'.[66] Once lances were broken or discarded, close combat was joined with swords and maces.[67] Such combat demanded skill in handling weapons, accomplished horsemanship and a good deal of physical strength and stamina. It was also very dangerous, the greatest risk being that an unhorsed knight might be trampled or suffocated in the press. When at a tournament between Maintenon and Nogent, probably in the summer of 1179, the count of Clermont was knocked from his horse, a fierce combat ensued between those trying to capture him and those trying to defend him. The Young King ordered his knights to withdraw a little 'for he feared that they would constrict him so much that they would crush him with their weight'.[68] Though the count was rescued, he had taken such a battering in this particularly fierce mêlée that he and his men were forced to withdraw behind the safety of a ditch to bandage their wounds.[69] High mettled warhorses might throw their riders or bolt; reins could snap, saddle girths could slip or break, and even the most skilled rider might be dragged with a foot caught in the stirrup. The risks were all too clearly demonstrated when the Young King's brother Geoffrey died of wounds received at a tournament in Paris in August 1186. Howden recorded that 'knights coming at him from different directions had knocked to the ground with their lances both him and the horse upon which he was mounted. When he by no means wished to yield to them, he was trampled by the hooves of their horses and so violently shaken up by the hard blows of these aforesaid knights that he soon died.'[70]

Though the killing or serious wounding of opponents was forbidden, there was a risk that even a rebated lance might cause a fatal injury, or that blows from maces or swords might cause broken bones or concussion. Nevertheless, the mêlée accustomed knights not only to bearing the weight of their armour in sustained action but to receiving as well as giving blows. The royal clerk Roger of Howden made the point well when, in describing the tourneying activities of the Young King and his younger brother Geoffrey in 1178 without any hint of disapproval, he enthusiastically adapted a passage from Seneca:

Nor indeed can the athlete bring high spirit to the contest, who has never been trained to practise it. It is the man who has seen his own blood, whose teeth have rattled beneath another's fist, who when tripped up has striven against his adversary with his entire body, and though thrown, has not lost his mettle, and who, as often as he fell has risen more determined, more bold – it is he who goes forth with ardent hopes to the combat. For valour when aroused adds greatly to itself; transitory is the glory of the mind that is subjected to terror. Without any fault of his, he who bears a burden to which he is unequal is overcome by the immensity of the weight, no matter how zealous he may be. Well is the reward paid for toil, in the temples of victory.[71]

The ability to withstand repeated blows in such fighting necessitated good armour, and it is probable that it was the desire for better protection in the tournament as much as in actual warfare that stimulated the development of additional body defences worn over the mail hauberk, and often made of lighter materials such as hardened leather or baleen, and of the full-faced helm.[72] The *History* records how in one tournament *c.*1179, the Marshal's helm had been so dented by the blows he had received that he was unable to remove it without the aid of a blacksmith. Indeed, the helm's protection was so important that one prominent method of attempting to capture an opponent in the tournament was to try and tear off his helmet; to do so was effectively the equivalent of disarming him.[73] At Lagny, the Young King came close to being overwhelmed by a group of knights who succeeded in pulling off his helmet.[74] Though he was extricated, another group of Flemish knights, seeing he was without a helmet, rushed to make what they thought would now be an easy capture, but were driven off by a fierce countercharge by the Marshal, which allowed the Young King to escape.[75]

Such techniques highlighted the fact that the essential purpose of combat in the tournament was to take opposing knights prisoner, not to wound and still less to kill them. Once he admitted defeat, a knight would pledge his word to become his captor's prisoner, whereupon he was released and the captor was free to rejoin the mêlée.[76] Before that, however, he could be rescued by members of his own team or he might attempt escape before he could be brought to the *recez*. The *History* recounts the humorous incident of how, at Anet in 1178, the Marshal had taken the French knight Simon de Neuphle by seizing his bridle, then had ridden through the town, leading Simon on his horse as a prisoner, with the Young King following behind. Simon, however, caught a low-hanging gutter and held on as the Marshal, not looking behind, rode on, oblivious to his escape. The Young King deliberately said nothing until the Marshal commanded a squire to take his prisoner into custody, only to find a horse with an empty saddle. Only then did young Henry explain to William the means of Simon's escape, and all burst out laughing.[77]

An opponent could be captured by being either knocked from his mount or wrestled from the saddle.[78] Although undertaken at a remove from the confusion of real battle, such manoeuvres gave knights essential training in the practical business of taking an opponent prisoner in combat without killing or seriously wounding him, thus helping to reinforce the custom of ransom and the chivalric expectation that a knight should spare a vanquished opponent. The capture of William the Lion and his household knights at Alnwick in 1174, despite fierce fighting, or of the earl of Leicester's noble followers at Fornham in 1173, were vivid examples of this in practice. Particularly skilful tourneyers such as William Marshal could capture an opponent by riding at him at high speed, then seizing his bridle to lead him to the *recez*, whereby he was technically made a prisoner.[79] The *History* vividly recounts how the Young King narrowly escaped capture at the tournament at Lagny when a group of

Flemish knights surrounded him and firmly seized his bridle. Cutting his way through to his lord, the Marshal could only free him by pulling the bridle and harness completely off the Young King's warhorse, so that his opponents had nothing by which to restrain him. Another of his retinue, William de Préaux, then put his arm around the neck of the Young King's horse and led him away, while Henry used his shield to defend William from a rain of blows.[80]

That the Young King was never captured in the many tournaments in which he fought was in large part due to the efficacy of William as his body-guard, or so the *History of William Marshal* insisted. 'He was always close to him,' the *History* noted, 'to offer help, to defend and rescue him. No man dared stretch out his hand towards him to seize him or to take his bridle, and this because of the mighty blows dealt by the Marshal, blows exceedingly mighty and dangerous.'[81] The Marshal's own success undoubtedly had much to do with his outstanding physical prowess: at a tournament at Pleurs, he was said to have 'struck and hammered like a woodcutter on oak trees'.[82] Yet he had not always fulfilled his role as bodyguard with such care. At Ressons-sur-Matz, the first of the Young King's tournaments to be described by the *History*, young Henry had been angered because the Marshal, instead of fighting alongside his lord as a team player, had left the king's troop to engage in individual feats of arms to boost his own reputation and purse.[83] Young Henry upbraided his tutor in arms for thus abandoning him in the mêlée:

> 'I really think it's about time you came back, Marshal,' he said. 'Any man who leaves his lord in such a situation behaves very badly. You saw fit to do that just now, and I am not the one to teach you in such matters, but this much I do wish to tax you with, that you did not behave in a rightful manner when you left me at such a time. It was not right, indeed, it was wrong.'[84]

Ever the accomplished courtier as well as warrior, the Marshal sought to defuse this rebuke by flattery, replying 'in a gentle joking manner': 'Sire', he said, 'so God help me, it is true that I left you here. But I can tell you this, that when I left, I still had no idea that your wish was to surpass your ancestors in feats of arms. Since your wish is to excel in this field, and that is where your aspirations lie, I shall henceforth devote myself to the matter.'[85] Henry secured a pledge that in future William would direct all his efforts to assisting the king in gaining victory in the tournament.[86] 'Never since the day the King rebuked the Marshal,' noted the *History*, 'was the latter to be found in any place, in any camp, without standing close by the King, whatever the outcome might be for him.'[87] Yet the *History* protests too much: its repeated insistence that William was constantly rescuing the Young King at subsequent tournaments strongly suggests that the

incident at Ressons did not stand in isolation and that the Marshal had attracted
much criticism for his self-interested pursuit of individual glory and ransoms.[88]
The incident reveals serious tension between the king and his tutor, and highlights the strains that the highly competitive nature of the tournament and the
quest for honour and gain might create between team and individual, and
between a lord and a highly talented household knight.

With the handsome revenues he was granted by his father, the Young King
had no pressing need for the spoils of the tournament. Nevertheless, for his landless household knights such booty was an important source of revenue. It was for
this reason that even if he himself was unable to participate because of other
business, young Henry was quite willing to allow members of his *mesnie* such as
William Marshal to go off tourneying when he did not immediately require their
services.[89] The operation of ransom in the later twelfth-century tournament is
obscure, but it would seem that, unlike in real warfare, in tourneys ransoms took
the more limited form of the captor taking only the horses and equipment of a
vanquished knight: the payment of heavy and often arbitrarily set sums of money
to regain personal liberty would have made the tournament prohibitively costly
and too great a risk.[90] The *History of William Marshal* mentions warhorses from
Spain, Sicily and Lombardy,[91] regions held to produce the best chargers, and
such destriers could be extremely valuable.[92] It was for good reason that the rules
of the tournament strictly forbade the killing of an opponent's mount, and that
these costly warhorses were increasingly protected by barding of mail as well as
of leather.[93] Horses could be seized as prizes during the mêlée itself, while a
knight taking part in a capture might claim half the value of the vanquished
knight's horse.[94] So integral an aspect had the seizure of horses become that
Henry de Laon would later complain that 'tournaments were not originally held
as way of capturing horses, but so as to learn who was manly in his conduct'.[95]

The *History of William Marshal* focuses almost exclusively on the winnings
of the Marshal, but these are revealing. At the tournament at Eu, for example,
William took ten knights prisoner, and seized twelve horses and their equipment. At another between Sainte-Jamme and Valennes in 1166, the Marshal's
two prisoners brought him four warhorses and a half-share in a third, but also
'hacks and palfreys, fine pack horses and harnessess'.[96] He subsequently teamed
up with another member of the Young King's tourneying *mesnie*, Roger de
Jouy, and in one tournament season they reputedly took 103 knights prisoner,
'not to mention the horses and equipment which were never taken into
account'.[97] These winnings were recorded by Wigain, the Young King's clerk
of the kitchen, and by other clerks, and it is possible that, as the Marshal's lord,
Young Henry was entitled to a share of the booty taken by his household
knights, as he would have been in real warfare.[98]

Profits, however, depended on the fortunes of combat, and for young or poorer knights – the *bacheliers* – the loss of their horse or equipment could be a crippling financial blow. It seems not to have been uncommon to ask for the return of a warhorse as an act of largesse on the captor's part. The *History* tells a revealing story of how at a tournament at Eu in 1178 or 1179, the Marshal had unhorsed the Hainaulter knight Matthew de Walincourt in the *commençailles* or preliminary jousts and taken his horse. Matthew went directly to the Young King, whom he found arming for the main tournament, and asked him for the return of his horse. Young Henry in turn requested the Marshal to restore the horse to Matthew, which he did. In the ensuing mêlée, however, William once again defeated Matthew, and took back his horse. But when Matthew returned to the Young King at the tournament's close and asked again for the restoration of his mount, the Marshal refused. Instead, he reminded Matthew of how, at a tournament earlier in the Marshal's career, the leading men had requested Matthew to return a horse he had taken from the Marshal, but he had absolutely refused.[99] The ability of the Young King to resupply his knights with horses and arms lost as ransoms was an important factor in making service with him particularly attractive.[100] At one tournament held between Maintenon and Nogent, the Young King told his knights to try and capture Sir Reginald de Nevers, who on the previous day had captured two of the king's knights, so that he could redeem their ransoms in exchange.[101]

The *History of William Marshal* vividly captures the hubbub of the throng of people more 'than at a fairground' in the immediate aftermath of a tournament at Pleurs in 1178, when the serious business of counting profit and loss, and negotiating ransoms and sureties took place:

> Some were looking for their friends, captured during the combat, whilst others were searching for their equipment. Others were making persistent enquiries of many who had taken part in the tournament as to whether they had heard any news of their kinsmen, of their friends, and as to whether they knew who had taken them. And, for their part, those who were in pledge (*cil qui erent fiancié*) wanted a ransom or surety to be forthcoming, through the offices of a friend or acquaintance. The reason why the throng was so enormous was that everyone asks in this way after a tournament for some indication of the losses he has sustained.[102]

Beyond the Tournament: Court and Culture

The opportunity to display prowess in arms and to gain prisoners and booty was but one aspect of the tournament. For there was an important social dimension to these great gatherings, which brought together magnates and knights from all parts of France and beyond. After the exertions of the mêlée came the post-match analysis of the performance of teams and of individuals' prowess. After the combat at Eu in 1178 or 1179, for example, 'all the high-ranking men there that day gathered around the King, and they spoke of many a matter as people are bound to do on such occasions'.[103] As significantly, there was feasting and entertainment on the nights preceding and following the main tournament. The *History of William Marshal*, focused as it was on feats of arms and the business of fighting, says regrettably little about the Young King or the Marshal's participation in such gatherings, though it speaks of warm hospitality offered to the Marshal by great magnates on his visits to claim ransom or seek redress. Yet it is likely that the Young King's celebrity led him frequently to be an honoured guest at the table of his fellow princes, and that in turn his own largesse extended to hosting splendid festivities. These served as an important forum for the discussion and dissemination of chivalric and courtly values, while a significant dimension was added by the increasing presence of noblewomen, both as spectators of the tournament itself and as participants in the post-tournament celebrations.

At gatherings such as the great seasonal courts held by the Young King and Henry II a variety of entertainments were provided by minstrels, jesters, mummers and other performers, which might range from the edifying to the earthy.[104] The former probably included recitations and discussion of the new genre of Arthurian romances that were to have such an extraordinarily profound influence on chivalric culture. The extent to which Henry II, Eleanor and the Plantagenet court actively patronized Chrétien de Troyes and other exponents of Arthurian literature or adopted it for their own propaganda purposes has been much debated, and direct evidence of young Henry's own sponsorship of such writing remains elusive.[105] When Marie de France noted in the prologue to her *Lais* – intriguingly complex short stories set in an Arthurian milieu – that she wrote 'in your honour, noble king, so worthy and courtly (*pruz et curteis*), before whom all joy bows its head, and whose heart is the root of all virtue', she could have been referring to the Young King as much as to Henry II, but as with his links to Chrétien de Troyes, there is no certainty.[106] Nevertheless, Chrétien was writing many of his Arthurian romances at the very time the Young King was playing so central a role in the tournament circuits of northern France, and he certainly had close contact with those known to be among Chrétien's chief patrons. Chrétien wrote *Lancelot* or *Le Chevalier de la Charrette* for the wife of Count Henry the Liberal, Marie de Champagne, who was the Young King's half-sister, and it was one of Count Henry's clerks, Godfrey de Lagny, who completed this romance.[107]

Chrétien's last work, *Perceval* or *Le Conte du Graal*, was dedicated to Count Philip of Flanders.[108] Both Henry of Champagne and Philip were also great patrons of the tournament, and it is no coincidence that in Chrétien's stories the tourney itself finds an increasingly important place in the tales of romance that surround his heroes. Written as they were as much for the ladies of the great courts of France as for the magnates and their knights, his romances achieved their enormous popularity through the winning fusion of erotically charged tales of love, both licit and illicit, with the magical world of 'the matter of Brittany' and the questing exploits of Arthur's paladins.

While there is no evidence that real tournaments of the 1170s and 1180s were influenced by the kind of Arthurian role play and imagery which would become so prominent a feature of 'Round Tables' and other forms of hastiludes from the early thirteenth century, Chrétien's tales undoubtedly served to augment their glamour and prestige, and to give greater emphasis to the role of ladies.[109] A noblewoman awarded the prize at the tournament at Pleurs, for example, while at Joigny, William Marshal and his men danced with the countess and her ladies while waiting for the challengers' team to arrive.[110] Writing in the 1220s, the author of the *History* was doubtless influenced by the romance tropes of Chrétien in which heroes such as Lancelot battle against the odds in tournaments to prove their love. At the tournament at Joigny, the knights 'were convinced that they had become better men as a result of the ladies' arrival, and so they had, for all those there felt a doubling of strength in mind and body, and of their boldness and courage ... because of the ladies present the least bold among them was emboldened to be the victor at the tournament that day'.[111] As early as the 1130s, however, Geoffrey of Monmouth could note that knights might carry their ladies' tokens into the tournament and be inspired to greater feats of arms by their love.[112] Such would have been a familiar concept to young Henry and his knights. Yet though it paints a vivid picture of other aspects of the tournament, the *History of William Marshal* maintains a discreet silence on the amorous liaisons of the Young King's *mesnie* and the sexual pleasures that are likely to have been a common part of the entertainments of the 'après-tournoi'. Whether courtesans frequented Young Henry's court is unknown, but the fact that Henry II had a marshal of whores (*marscallus custodiendi meretrices de curia domini regis*) at his own is suggestive.[113]

Though the Arthurian romances of Chrétien were highly fashionable from the 1170s, the diversity of literary entertainment available at courts such as that of the Young King should not be underestimated. The older genre of the *chansons de geste* remained highly popular, as frequent allusions to their characters in other contemporary texts indicate, but beyond the songs of the jongleurs, talented and ambitious clerks could turn their hand to a number of different literary forms. Devotional literature included edifying stories of saints' lives, which authors such as Denis Pyramus rendered into French either from Latin or other vernaculars, 'for both the great and the least can understand it in French'.[114] In addition to his great works of the *Roman de Rou* and the *Roman de Brut*, Wace composed *sirventes* and religious works, of which three saints' lives are known, while Gervase of Tilbury also composed works on the life of the Virgin.[115] Much of the literature composed for the court, however, was of a decidedly secular bent. For among the highly educated clerical elite, many of whom were of noble birth, distinctions between clerical and secular, the sacred and the profane, were often blurred. Several of Thomas Becket's *eruditi* could share his love of worldly magnificence, and Henry II himself had joked about the proud and haughty bearing of Herbert of Bosham.[116] Jordan Fantosme may have been educated in schools of Chartres and Poitiers, but his verse account of the war of 1173–74 reveals his familiarity, and that of his courtly audience, with many *chansons de geste*, while his own *estoire* itself has an epic flavour.[117]

Interest in the heroic deeds of antiquity was reflected in the rendering of classical works into the vernacular, such as Benoît of Sainte-Maure's *Roman de Troie* (composed *c*.1155–60), or the series of romances telling the story of Alexander, such those by Thomas of Kent (*c*.1175–85) and Alexandre de Paris (*c*.1180–85).[118] 'Our books have taught us', wrote Chrétien in his *Cligès*, in which Alexander also plays a role, 'that chivalry and learning first flourished in Greece; then to Rome came chivalry and the sum of knowledge, which now has come to France.'[119] The Young King undoubtedly had heard such romances, and he in turn was to be likened to Hector in the Latin *Iliad* of Joseph of Exeter, composed in the mid 1180s. After mourning the death of Hector, Joseph added:

> Even so great and so valiant a man was our king, Henry III, who had grown to a lordly rage like Hector's. He who was our king and Normandy's duke, had spent his youth in France. The warlike French, vanquished by him in battle, did not so much begrudge him his superiority in fighting as they begrudged us our superiority in wisdom.[120]

If Joseph's sophisticated Latin verse was accessible only to the highly educated and primarily clerical elite, the range of courtly genres composed by just such clerks in the service of secular lords is suggested by Chrétien de Troyes' reminder, in the preface to his *Cligès*, that it was he 'who translated Ovid's *Commandments* and the *Art of Love* into French, who wrote the *Shoulder Bite*, and about King Mark and Isolde the Blonde, and of the metamorphosis of the hoopoe, swallow and nightingale'.[121] The composition of love lyrics was by no means the preserve of the troubadours: Peter of Blois admitted that 'at one time I devoted myself to frivolities and songs of love (*nugis et cantibus veneris*)', some of a most lascivious nature, while Denis Pyramus related how at court in 'the merry days of my youth (*mes jurs jolifs de ma joefnesce*)' and before he became a monk at the abbey of St Edmunds, he had likewise composed love songs and poems on current matters.[122] Such poetry, often written by and for the young, would have been of particular appeal to young Henry and his equally youthful companions. Nor were such amorous interests of his clerical courtiers confined to verse. Gervase of Tilbury, who was in the Young King's service, was said to have made advances to a pretty girl walking in a vineyard, though she rebuffed him with tragic consequences.[123]

More edifyingly, Gervase wrote a *Liber facetiarum*, or 'Book of Entertainments', at the command of the Young King.[124] Though now lost, it appears to have contained a wide-ranging compendium of subjects – probably akin to his subsequent *Otia imperialia*, which he had also intended for the Young King.[125] This second book was composed 'in recognition of his kindness', and, as Gervase explained,

> was to be divided into three sections, and was to contain a description, at least in brief, of the whole world, and its division into provinces, naming the greater and lesser sees. Then I intended to add the various marvels of each province. Their very existence is remarkable, and to hear of them should afford pleasure to a listener who is not already informed of them and is able to appreciate such things. No longer need great men learn of God's power, as happens all too often, from the lying tongues of players or actors: now they will have a reliable account which we have either culled from books of ancient authors or established from eye witness testimonies . . .[126]

Gervase's work, which also includes a digest of Geoffrey of Monmouth's *History of the Kings of Britain* as well as histories of the kings of France and of England, allows a precious glimpse of the wider cultural tastes and intellectual life of the Young King and his courtiers. He and his knights may have excelled in the tournament, but they were no mere boorish prizefighters, addicted solely to fighting and feasting.

The knights themselves, moreover, might entertain and edify. Wace noted that it was the duty of clerks to read stories at feasts so that they were not forgotten, but it was not only the clerical elite who were the repository of such material.[127] The Young King's contemporary, Arnold of Ardres, loved hearing stories told by one of his household knights 'on the subject of the Roman emperors and on Charlemagne, Roland and Oliver, and King Arthur of Britain'. Another spoke 'to his ears' delight of the land of Jerusalem and the siege of Antioch and of the Arabs and Babylonians and deeds done overseas', while Walter of le Clud 'diligently informed him of the deeds and fables of the English, of Gormond and Isembard, of Tristan and Isolde, of Merlin and Morolf' and the deeds of his ancestors the lords of Ardres.[128] In such a world, the prince's intimates were as much entertainers and instructors of past history, whether of family or of great kings, as companions-in-arms. It may be that some of young Henry's household knights had won their place in his *mesnie* less by their skill in arms than by just such talents.

CHAPTER 12

Keeping the Balance of Power
FRANCE, 1178–1182

Gracious heaven! If such brothers would have regarded the fraternal compact between each other, if they would have looked towards their father with filial affection ... how great, how inestimable, how renowned, how incomparable to all future time would have been the glory of their father and the victory of his offspring! ... For what valour could resist these powers, what kings could stand against these kings, or what kingdoms could successfully oppose such leaders in war?[1]
– Gerald of Wales, *De principis instructione*, II: 11

FROM THE *HISTORY of William Marshal* alone, it would be easy to gain the impression that the Young King did little else but frequent the tournament circuit of northern France between 1178 and 1182.[2] In reality, young Henry continued to play a significant role in the military and political affairs of the Angevin territories during these years. In the aftermath of the major confrontation with Louis VII in 1177, the ageing Capetian monarch had accepted an entente based on the acceptance of Plantagenet supremacy. The accession of his heir Philip in 1180, however, resulted in a period of political destabilization in northern France, as rival factions vied for control of the young ruler, pitting Philip of Flanders against the queen mother Adela and the house of Blois. Such divisions only served to strengthen the Plantagenets' hegemony, but in marked contrast to the years of bitter conflict with Louis, the early 1180s witnessed Henry II acting as peacemaker and the young Henry as a protector of the youthful Philip, his brother-in-law and overlord.

Little can be traced of the Young King's movements during 1178, not least because Roger of Howden's narrative for this year is notably scanty, even in regard to Henry II.[3] Nevertheless, he is found on 19 March 1178 with his father and his youngest brother John at a great ceremony to consecrate the magnificent new abbey church of Bec, which Robert of Torigni, who had been a monk there, claimed 'had no equal for its beauty in the whole of Normandy'.[4] The ties between the ducal house and Bec, one of greatest monasteries in Normandy, were as close as they were long-standing, and young Henry's grandmother, a particularly generous patron, was buried there.[5] During the service, performed by Archbishop Rotrou and the bishops of Bayeux, Avranches and Evreux,[6] King Henry II granted the house 100 *livres* 'in the money of Normandy' annually, by placing his hat on the main altar, while the Young King confirmed his father's gift by likewise placing a ring on it.[7] Young Henry himself may have had no landed endowment from which to make his own territorial grants to religious foundations, but he regularly confirmed those of his father.[8] Following the re-foundation of Waltham abbey as a college of secular canons by Henry II in 1177, for example, the Young King issued his own charter at Argentan, which follows the list of the abbey's possessions in Henry II's initial grant almost verbatim but adds a lengthy preamble in which he propounds the merits of confirming and supporting religious establishments as greatly befitting the royal majesty.[9] Such confirmations also reflected his authority to grant exemptions from tolls, such as the freedom from prisage of wine and other levies throughout his dominions which he granted to the monks of the abbey of Le Valasse in the Pays de Caux.[10] Likewise, in a charter to the great abbey of Fontevraud by which he confirmed a number of Henry II's earlier grants as well as those of other donors, the Young King conceded to the abbess and the community a range of tolls, revenues and jurisdictional rights linked to lands at Ponts-de-Cé, near Angers, which formerly had pertained to the count of Anjou and his local agents or baillis. These included the right to levy *minagium* or a tax on wheat and salt, and the profits of justice from an extensive range of pleas. He reserved to himself the power to punish 'in life and limb', only because, as he explained, it was not appropriate for clergy and the religious to be involved in judgments resulting in the shedding of blood.[11] The Young King not only confirmed the charters of other donors but can be glimpsed urging others to make charitable bequests, as in his notification of the grant of the church of Nointot made 'at my beseeching' by John de Mara to the leper house of Sainte Catherine de Monte in Rouen.[12]

After holding his Christmas court in Normandy, the Young King sailed from Wissant to Dover on 26 February 1179, after a three-year absence from the kingdom. Riding high on the reputation he had gained on the tournament circuit, he was received with honour by his father.[13] Ralph of Diss noted that 'although the Young King was still under age his father restored in full his possessions which he had taken away'.[14] That Dean Ralph could regard young Henry, who was now twenty-five, as still being in some form of minority is striking, and though no details of exactly what was restored to him are known, it seems that his return was marked by some kind of formal political rehabilitation. The two kings made a progress to Gloucestershire, hunting at Bicknore on the Wye, and the Young King probably also visited Worcestershire before father and son returned to Winchester to celebrate the feast of Easter on 1 April.[15] Among the reasons for the Young King's return was the need to consult with his father over important reforms to the system of the general eyre by itinerant royal justices, and jointly to preside over a great council at Windsor on 10 April in which the new arrangements were set out.[16] These changes had been prompted by the retirement from public life of Richard de Lucy, the king's eminent and long-serving chief justiciar, but also by the results of an inquiry into the conduct of the royal justices which Henry II had held on his own return from the continent in July 1178.[17] Revising the provision of justices set out in the assize of Northampton, Henry and his counsellors devised a new system by which the kingdom was divided into four circuits, with a group of six itinerant justices assigned to each.[18] In addition, a panel of five justices, comprising three laymen and two clerks and based in the *curia regis*, were to hear all the *clamores* or legal appeals of the kingdom. If they encountered a question they could not resolve among themselves, they could refer the cases to the king and other councillors.[19] It is likely that the council's deliberations also involved the introduction of the 'grand assize', a crucial reform which for the first time offered men engaged in a dispute over seisin of land the chance to avoid a judicial duel and instead have the case decided by a jury of twelve law-worthy knights of the neighbourhood.[20] How far young Henry was an active participant in these legal reforms is unknown, though Henry II clearly regarded his consent and presence at Windsor as important. We should be wary of assuming that his passion for the tournament necessarily excluded a concern for the development of judicial procedures, and from the time of his early training in the operation of justice under the tutelage of William FitzJohn he had been made fully aware of the great significance of these processes for the exercise of royal power.

After holding a joint court with his father at Pentecost, 20 April, the Young King immediately sailed back to Flanders with his father's blessing.[21] His speedy return may well have been prompted by a desire not to miss a great tournament between Maintenon and Nogent-le-Roi on the river Eure on the south-east border of Normandy held in late May, but also by the preparations being made by King Louis for the coronation of his son Philip, who was now approaching fifteen.[22] The great lords and ecclesiastics had been summoned to Rheims, the great coronation church of the kings of France, for the feast of the Assumption, 15 August, and as seneschal of France young Henry would have a leading part to play in the ceremony.[23] But then events took a sudden and

dramatic turn. When out hunting near Compiègne, Philip had become separated from his companions; disorientated and increasingly terrified, he had
spent the night in the forest, and was later discovered in a state of shock by a
charcoal burner. As a result of this trauma, he fell dangerously ill.[24] Were he to
die, the succession to the throne of France would again be thrown into question and the Young King, as the husband of Louis' daughter Margaret, would
have a strong claim. Not only that, but the Angevins, reunited and dominant
within France, had the power to make such a claim good. In desperation, Louis
sought the intercession of St Thomas by making a pilgrimage to Canterbury,
where a flood of miracles had already proclaimed him as one of the most potent
of saints.[25] So spontaneous was his visit that Henry II was caught unawares
and had to ride through the night to greet Louis, the first king of France ever
to set foot in England.[26] After being warmly welcomed at Dover by King
Henry 'as his most dearly loved liege lord and friend', Louis journeyed in the
company of Count Philip of Flanders to the martyr's shrine, where he prayed
and then offered lavish gifts, including a great cup of gold, 100 tuns of wine
yearly in perpetuity to the monks, and freedom from tolls and customs for
whatever was purchased in his domains for the use of the convent.[27] On his
return to France, Louis found his son restored to health, and amidst general
rejoicings, he ordered that Philip's coronation should proceed. Yet the strain
had been too much for Louis. At St Denis, where he had gone to give thanks,
he suffered a severe stroke that left his right side paralysed and prevented him
from attending the coronation.[28]

Philip was duly anointed and consecrated by his uncle William, archbishop
of Rheims, on 1 November 1179. In the procession from the palace to the
cathedral, Count Philip of Flanders bore the coronation sword, said to be that
of Charlemagne,[29] while the Young King also walked before the future
monarch, carrying the crown of gold. During the ceremony itself he helped
support its great weight when it was placed on the boy Philip's head.[30] Henry
evidently regarded his role in the coronation as a high honour, and it is possible
that he performed it in his office as seneschal of France, as a prerogative
claimed by the counts of Anjou.[31] Yet his participation raised a crucial question
concerning the status of Angevin kingship. When, in 1169, young Henry had
as seneschal of France served Louis at table in Paris he had not yet been
crowned, but in 1179, by contrast, he was an anointed monarch in his own
right. Did not his performance of duties at Philip's coronation imply the subordination of the kings of England to the kings of France? Was it not directly
analogous to the position of the kings of Scots or Welsh princes at the crown-
wearings of English monarchs? Such was the inference readily seized upon by
Capetian chroniclers from the 1190s. Thus Rigord, who had completed the

first recension of his *Gesta Philippi* by 1196, noted of the coronation that: 'Henry king of England was present and in due dependence (*ex debita subjectione*) humbly supported the crown on the head of the king of France, while all the princes of the realm and the whole of the clergy and people shouted "Long live the king! Long live the king!"'[32] For the Minstrel of Rheims, writing in the 1260s, it was the Young King's role as seneschal at the coronation banquet which demonstrated his subordinate status to Philip, for he noted how 'at the dinner, King Henry of England, on his knees, served him, and cut his food for him'.[33] The Angevin chroniclers were equally aware of the possible implications of the Young King's participation. When in the mid 1190s Roger of Howden came to revise his *Gesta Henrici*, he was careful to add the statement that the Young King had borne the crown as the prerogative of the duke of Normandy.[34] Ralph of Diss was more explicit in his rejection of any implication of subordination of the crown of England:

> Henry, son of Henry II, king of England, the husband of the French king's sister, attended the coronation because he was a close relation and because he was invited to observe. Although Britain almost deserves to be called another world and you will often hear that Britons are divided among themselves, it remains clear that no king of Britain or England ever acknowledged the king of France as a superior, rather they were more accustomed to be friends. In the letters passing between them, they decided that they would call each other brothers, a custom which even Charlemagne had observed after he had been made emperor by the Romans. The young King Henry, realizing that he had an interest in the solemnities, exercised his prerogative and talked with all the nobles in his presence, and thus from the mouths of the French people, he learned of future events. King Henry of England held the crown on the new king's head, lest, since he was still young, it injure him, the claims of those more suited to this duty being rejected. This implied that if ever the French needed help they could safely ask it from one who had helped the king at his coronation.[35]

Dean Ralph's studied refutation of any claims to Capetian suzerainty over the kingship of England, however, reflected the attitude of the Angevin court after the Young King's death and a dramatic deterioration in Plantagenet–Capetian relations. The atmosphere in the first years of Philip's reign was very different, as the Plantagenets' support for young Philip between 1179 and 1182 was to show. Had Henry II feared for the prestige and independence of the kingship of England in 1179, he would have forbidden the Young King's participation rather than lavishly funding it.

Indeed, rather than an act which damaged their royal prestige, both father and son regarded the Young King's presence at the coronation as a great opportunity to display Angevin power and wealth. The Old King sent Philip great gifts in gold and silver, but also game from England.[36] On learning that Philip had ordered the construction of a wall to enclose his hunting park at Vincennes, Henry II had a large number of roe deer, small fallow deer and forest goats collected from all parts of England and Normandy to help him stock it. The beasts were carefully shipped down the Seine to Paris and presented as a magnificent gift.[37] On his father's orders Young Henry himself brought such a bountiful supply of provisions with him that he had no need to receive hospitality either on the journey to Rheims or during the festivities.[38] At the magnificent tournament held in celebration of the coronation at Lagny, some ten miles from Paris, his dazzling retinue of over 200 knights, and the presence in it of nineteen counts, was intended as a clear statement of Angevin power and influence. In its size and composition and in the generous wages he paid, the Young King was directly vying with Count Philip, who had in turn a powerful retinue drawn from Flanders, Hainault and lands of the empire, for, as the *History* noted, 'there was no doughty knight anywhere between here and the mountains of Great Saint Bernard whom he did not seek out for his company'.[39]

On 1 April 1180, the Young King crossed from Normandy 'and was received with great honour' by his father.[40] The two kings had come together to consult over a rapidly developing political crisis in France. King Louis' paralysis and removal from active government had been increasingly exploited by Count Philip of Flanders to assert influence over the boy king Philip, undermining the previously dominant influence at court of Louis' queen, Adela of Blois, and her brothers, Counts Henry of Champagne, Theobald of Blois, Stephen of Sancerre and William, archbishop of Rheims.[41] Count Philip may have been recognized as young Philip's guardian, and King Louis had agreed that his son should marry Philip of Flanders' niece, Isabella of Hainault.[42] The match promised to significantly enhance Capetian power, since Count Philip provided as her dowry the wealthy lands of Artois, including the towns of Arras, St Omer, Bapaume and Aire, on condition that he continued to hold them during his lifetime.[43] It would also place Count Philip in a position of great influence, and for this reason the marriage had been opposed by Adela and her brothers. But in April 1180, the count of Flanders had quickly moved to have the marriage solemnized at Bapaume.[44] Then, in order to circumvent any opposition by Archbishop William, he had Isabella crowned queen and had Philip re-crowned by a rival metropolitan, the archbishop of Sens, at a dawn ceremony at St Denis on 29 May.[45] King Philip, who had seized the opportunity to break free from his mother's dominance, had removed Louis' seal from the ailing king to prevent its use by the Champagne faction, and when Adela began fortifying her dower lands, Philip confiscated them, forcing her to flee for refuge to her brother Count Theobald.[46]

In this crisis, the queen mother, Count Theobald and former councillors of Louis appealed to Henry II for assistance.[47] While it might have been in Angevin interest to see the Capetians weakened by infighting, King Henry was justly concerned by the potential destabilization the looming civil war might bring. Equally, he saw the threat posed by an overmighty Flanders should Count Philip succeed in dominating King Philip. Accordingly, Henry II and the Young King prepared to cross to Normandy. Before they did so, however, the two kings visited Reading, where King Henry required his son to swear in the presence of relics – no doubt including the hand of St James – that he would faithfully observe his father's disposition in all matters, and would inviolably observe his grants, whether in respect of castles, manors or benefices, as set out in the king's charters.[48] The reasons for this striking and public reassertion of the Young King's compliance with his father's wishes are nowhere recorded. Though it suggests a continuing anxiety on the part of the Old King regarding his eldest son, no chronicler mentions renewed requests by young Henry for lands to rule directly or any open tension between the two. It may be that Henry II was attempting to ensure his son's absolute loyalty during the forthcoming negotiations in France, which would involve a number of the Young King's former allies. The kings proceeded to cross to Normandy, where they were met by Adela, Theobald and other French nobles; as Roger of Howden noted pointedly, those who formerly hated Henry II were now imploring him for aid.[49]

To lend his diplomacy the backing of military force, Henry II had ordered a muster of his armies in England and his continental territories.[50] His aim, however, was to establish peace, not only between the rival factions around King Philip but between the Angevins and the new French monarch, for already King Philip had threatened to lead an expedition to assert his rights in the Auvergne, long contested with Henry II, and had gone so far as to raise forces.[51] On 28 June, at the great elm tree which marked the traditional conference site between Gisors and Trie, Henry II, 'partly by smooth words and partly by threats', persuaded King Philip to restore Adela, her brothers and their supporters and to remit his ill will against them; Adela was promised an allowance as long as her husband King Louis lived, and possession of her dower lands on his death, saving only the castles.[52] By way of security, Henry II took Philip of Flanders' homage, but as a salve to the count he again renewed the Anglo-Flemish convention by which Philip was to receive an annual sum of £1,000, in return for providing 500 knights to serve if required.[53] To complete the peace settlement, Henry II renewed the treaty of Ivry, which he had made with Louis in 1177.[54]

The political situation in northern France, however, remained volatile, and during 1181 King Philip's relations with the count of Flanders rapidly deteriorated.[55] The threat of escalating hostilities arising from a quarrel between Count Philip and Raoul de Coucy, who enjoyed the French king's backing, caused King Henry to delay his planned embarkation for England in late April and to respond to King Philip's request for aid.[56] Arriving with a small retinue, but one which included King William the Lion, he and the Young King met King Philip and the count of Flanders at Gisors, where Henry II successfully brokered a further peace settlement.[57] 'We have read', noted Ralph of Diss wryly, 'of four kings having fallen at the same time in one battle, but have very seldom heard of four kings having come to one conference in peace, and in peace having returned.'[58] Yet Henry II was sincere in his attempts to establish a peaceful balance of power in northern France, and is even said to have counselled the young King Philip on the ways of government in imitation of his own successful policies.[59] The Young King, moreover, was envisaged as playing a key element in maintaining this status quo, and before returning to England, Henry II devolved effective power in Normandy to him. As Dean Ralph noted:

> The elder king placed all of Normandy under the control of his son, the younger king, charging all the ministers of that land with obedience to him, and left him to watch over and protect Philip, king of France, should the need arise. Now that all the provinces were ordered according to his wishes and, respectful of his laws, were enjoying the benefits of peace brought by his rule, he returned to England on 28 July, making a visit to St Thomas in order to pray.[60]

The Young King's commission was an important indication of the renewed trust his father was willing to place in him. He was soon called upon to fulfil his role as protector, for, despite the settlement at Gisors, the breach between the king of France and the count of Flanders continued to deepen. The Angevin chroniclers saw Count Philip's growing hostility to the French king as the result of his jealousy of the latter's new alliance with Henry II. Flanders' influence was certainly waning fast, but the count himself seems to have regarded Raoul, count of Clermont and constable of France, 'who was very powerful in the counsels of the king', as a principal fomentor of discord between them.[61] When King Philip supported Raoul's refusal to comply with Count Philip's demand to return the castle of Breteuil, which he held from him, war broke

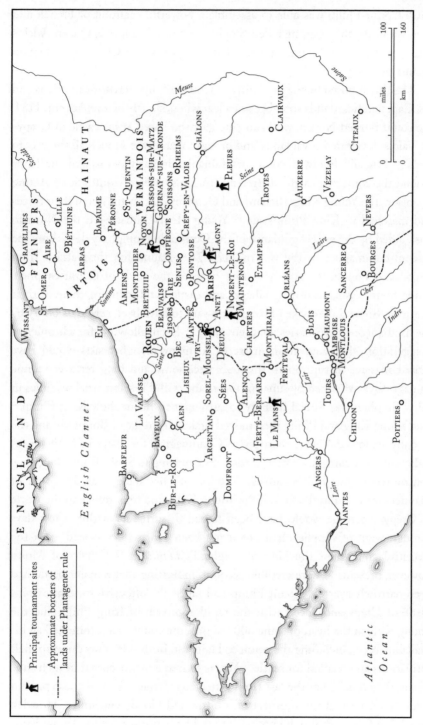

Map 7 Northern France in the late twelfth century

out.[62] Count Philip was able to assemble a powerful coalition of French and Flemish lords; this even included Stephen, count of Sancerre, Queen Adela's youngest brother, reflecting the wider discontent of the Champagne faction against the king.[63]

The threat posed by the proximity of Count Philip's territories to Paris and the Capetian heartlands soon became clear when, shortly before Advent, 1181, the count burned Noyon, while an elite garrison based at his castle of Crépy-en-Valois devastated royal lands 'and brought fear to the French all the way to Paris'.[64] His ally, Baldwin, count of Hainault, similarly devastated the lands around the contested castle of Breteuil from his base at Montdidier.[65] Acting in unison, the Young King, Richard and Geoffrey quickly mustered their forces and marched to King Philip's aid.[66] Young Henry himself led the Norman host, aided by the expert guidance of the Constable Humphrey de Bohun, the veteran commander of the war of 1173–74.[67] Launching their attack from Anjou and Poitou, the Angevins first targeted the lands of Count Stephen, laying them waste, destroying villages and castles, and stripping them of their livestock. Some 5,000 yoke of oxen were said to have been seized as booty by the Brabançon mercenaries in their army.[68] Even allowing for chroniclers' exaggeration, the removal en masse of so many plough beasts would have caused massive disruption to the arable economy and long-term economic damage. Overwhelmed by superior forces and with his seigneurial revenues in ruins, Stephen was forced humbly to surrender to his nephew King Philip.[69] The Young King and Philip then moved against the duke of Burgundy and the recently widowed Marie, countess of Champagne, 'the sister of both kings', inflicting great damage on their lands before moving to Senlis from where they confronted Count Philip himself.[70] Ralph of Diss states that the count of Flanders retreated in the face of the Young King, and took refuge in the castle of Crépy, where he would have been forced to surrender within a few days through want of supplies, had not it not been – or so it was said – for the 'deceitful counsel of the king of England's *familiares*'.[71] Gilbert of Mons, however, presents a more credible account, indicating that a major battle had been narrowly averted. Count Philip had taken the offensive to reinforce his castle of Crépy and, faced with the rapid approach of King Philip and the Young King at the head of some 600 knights, the count had summoned all his available forces, including the count of Hainault. Both sides now drew up their formations and readied for battle.[72] Yet, as so frequently occurred in such situations, they flinched at the last from actual engagement. Few of those present could have relished the prospect of a bitter and bloody encounter; Howden noted that Count Philip did not wish to fight a battle against the Young King, and Henry in turn must have been very reluctant to attack in earnest his old

ally and mentor in chivalry.[73] Though Gilbert is silent on the matter, interme-
diaries must have persuaded both sides to parley, and a truce was arranged to
last over Christmas.[74]

The situation was further aggravated shortly before Easter 1182, by the
death of the Count of Flanders' wife Elizabeth. Count Philip had held the
Valois and the Vermandois only by right of his wife, and King Philip moved
swiftly to seize these lands, ostensibly in the interests of Elizabeth's sister
Eleanor of Beaumont, to whom they should have legally reverted.[75] When the
count of Flanders refused to relinquish them and a renewed war loomed, it was
the Angevins who again brokered a peace. After crossing from England to join
the Young King, Henry II and his son held initial talks in early April with
Count Philip and Baldwin of Hainault at Gerberoy before helping to negotiate a settlement between King Philip and the count at La Grange-Saint-
Arnoul, between Senlis and Crépy, around 11 April.[76] Here it was agreed that
Count Philip would retain the Vermandois during his lifetime, but Eleanor
was granted the Valois, while the count ceded Amiens to the king, and promised reparation for war damages.[77]

While waiting at Bishop's Waltham to cross to Normandy for these negotiations, Henry II had drawn up his testament.[78] As was customary, his bequests
did not relate to the succession to his lands, but were restricted to gifts of land
and money to religious houses and other institutions for the benefit of his soul.
These totalled the massive sum of 41,000 marks of silver (£27,333 6s. 8d.) and
500 marks of gold (£3,000).[79] Had the Old King died soon thereafter, the
Young King would have found himself in a serious dilemma, having to decide
how far he was prepared to honour his father's lavish legacies, which would
have enormously depleted the Angevin treasury.[80] Despite such intimations of
mortality, however, Henry II was only forty-nine and still in good health.
Almost a decade had now passed since the inception of the great war, yet
despite his recent role as his father's deputy in Normandy, the Young King was
still no nearer to achieving his longed-for goal of direct rule over a part of his
father's great empire. Though the revenues granted to him were generous, they
remained but an allowance. By contrast, his younger brothers Richard and
Geoffrey had become increasingly established in their respective territories.
After Richard's triumph over a rebel coalition in 1179, Henry II had officially
restored his title as count of Poitou, recognizing the de facto authority he had
long since wielded.[81] In October 1181, Geoffrey had strengthened his hold on
Brittany by finally marrying Constance; he assumed the title 'dux Britanniae et
comes Richemundie', and was allowed by his father to exercise direct lordship
over the greater part of the duchy, though not the county of Nantes.[82] Unlike
the Young King, he was now no longer entirely dependent on his father's

beneficence but could command his own resources in lands, men and money.[83] The war of 1173–74 had painfully reinforced the fact that, even with a great coalition of allies, the Young King could not wrest England, Normandy or Anjou from his father by force. Petition and plea had equally failed, and his father remained in robust good health. In such circumstances, the Young King increasingly looked with envious eyes on the duchy of Aquitaine. Henry II had received Normandy as his maternal inheritance in 1151 while his father Count Geoffrey still ruled Anjou. If the Old King would not part with rule of any portion of the Anglo-Norman and Angevin heartlands in his lifetime, why by this analogy could not the Young King, as the eldest son, assume direct rule of Aquitaine as *his* maternal inheritance?[84] Had not Charlemagne made his eldest son Louis king of Aquitaine?[85] Once his father died and young Henry gained control of the heartlands of the empire, perhaps Aquitaine or other territories might revert to Richard. The Young King knew that his younger brother would not willingly accept such a move, and that their father might only do so if presented with a fait accompli. One powerful factor, however, drove forward the Young King's designs – the seething discontent of many of the Aquitanian nobility with Richard.

Henry II had singularly failed to incorporate leading nobles from Poitou and Aquitaine into the wider governance of his great conglomeration of territories.[86] Feelings of political marginalization and exclusion from the court, with its opportunities for royal favour and personal advancement, only served to fuel the resentment still felt in Aquitaine at being under the sway of the 'king of the North', whose designs for ever-increasing dominance of the region had seemingly been confirmed by his purchase of the county of La Marche from its count, Adalbert, in 1177.[87] Nevertheless, Angevin control of La Marche had been fiercely contested by the powerful Lusignan family, and by the autumn of 1182 Geoffrey de Lusignan had succeeded in taking possession of it, claiming that it belonged to him by right of inheritance.[88] Yet if Henry II's overlordship was resented, the nobility of Aquitaine chafed still more at the direct and increasingly masterful rule of young Duke Richard. He 'oppressed the Poitevins', noted Ralph of Diss, 'with unaccustomed burdens and violent domination'.[89] Any hopes, raised by his proactive role in the rebellion in Aquitaine in 1174, that Richard would be a protector of the duchy's independence and customs had been dashed. He had showed himself to be fully the heir of his father's policies of enforcing rights of overlordship, notably wardship and marriage of heirs, contrary to local custom.[90] Indeed, the period from 1175 onwards had witnessed a marked intensification of such intervention by both Henry and Richard, and a corresponding incidence of rebellion within Aquitaine.[91] On each occasion Richard's daring generalship, military skill and superior resources had crushed the opposition. Rebels' castles were slighted, city walls torn down, and leading opponents had quit the duchy on what may well have been involuntary or penitential pilgrimages.[92] In 1181, the fragile peace which had prevailed in the duchy since late 1179 had again been ruptured when, on the death of Count Vulgrin of Angoulême, Richard had seized his young daughter into his wardship, thereby claiming control of the comital lands, a high-handed act which set the duke at war with the girl's uncles, Aimar and William.[93] Richard's opponents, moreover, claimed that he had 'carried off his subjects' wives, daughters and kinswomen by force and made them his concubines; when he had sated his own lust on them he handed them down for his soldiers to enjoy. He afflicted his people with these and many other wrongs.'[94] Such charges were the stock-in-trade of political defamation and were used to justify a vassal's renunciation of homage: similar accusations had been levelled against Henry II by his Breton opponents, as they would be against King John by his baronial enemies. Yet though brief and sometimes formulaic, the reports of the English chroniclers leave little doubt that Richard was regarded by many of his Aquitanian subjects as a tyrant. Tellingly, in an early version of his *De principis instructione* written after Richard had become king, Gerald of Wales felt obliged to excuse at some length an evident reputation for harshness, acknowledging that he had been 'generally hated for his cruelty'.[95]

Conversely, the Young King held out the promise of change: Poitevins had been welcomed into his *mesnie* for the great tourneys in which he was winning a glowing reputation for his his *franchise*, or greatness of chivalric spirit. Young Henry's reckless generosity struck a deep chord with the nobility of southern France. Acts of conspicuously extravagant spending at a great court festival held at Beaucaire in 1174, supposedly in celebration of Henry II's establishment of peace between Raymond of Toulouse and Alfonso of Aragon, had already become the stuff of legend and epic exaggeration by the time Geoffrey of Vigeois denounced them:

The count of Toulouse gave 100,000 sous to Raimon d'Agout, a liberal knight, who at once divided the thousands by a hundred and distributed single thousands to a hundred individual knights. Bertran Raimbaut had the castle grounds ploughed by twelve pairs of oxen, and then had coins to the value of 30,000 sous sown into it. Guilhem the Fat of Martello, who had 300 knights with him [the court in fact comprised about 10,000 knights], is reported to have cooked all the food from the kitchen with wax and pitchpine torches . . . Raimon of Vernoul burned thirty horses in a fire with everyone watching, because of a boast.

The contrast between the characters of the two brothers had never been more evident. As Gervase of Canterbury explained:

> The nobles of Aquitaine hated their lord, Count Richard, on account of his great cruelty. They planned to drive him by force from the duchy of Aquitaine and the county of Poitou, and greatly desired to transfer the principality to the good and benign Young King ... For he was amiable to everyone, of handsome countenance, and especially famous for his military glory, to such an extent that he appeared second to none. He was self-effacing, responsive and affable, so that he was loved with very great affection by those both near and far. By contrast, Count Richard was most hateful to almost everyone, and they desired to eradicate him from the land.[96]

If the less heavy-handed rule of the Young King offered the Aquitanian nobility the prospect of greater autonomy, a conflict between the brothers also afforded a chance to settle local scores. Thus the minor Limousin lord and troubadour Bertran de Born, whose poems provide a precious glimpse into the thought-world of the aristocracy, saw in the developing struggle an opportunity to take control of the family castle of Hautefort, disputed with his younger brother Constantine, who in turn sought the support of Duke Richard.[97] War, moreover, opened the purse strings of the great lords. 'Don't take me for a troublemaker,' remarked Bertran, 'if I want one great man to hate another; then vavasors and castellans will be able to get more sport out of them. I swear it by the faith I owe you, a great man is more free, generous and friendly in war than in peace.'[98] For members of the lesser aristocracy such as the castellan of Hautefort, such times of open hostilities held out the prospect not only of wages, but also of plunder, booty and brigandage, as Bertran frankly admitted:

> Trumpets, drums, standards, and pennons and ensigns and horses white and black we shall soon see and the world will be good. We'll take the usurers' money, and never a mule driver will travel the roads in safety, nor a burgher without fear, nor a merchant coming from France. He who gladly takes will be rich.[99]

Seen in such a light, it is little wonder that the nobility of Aquitaine jealously guarded its right to wage 'private' war. Yet Bertran also gave voice to a fierce sense of local independence, and anger against Richard's harsh rule. 'Let us challenge him for the territory he took out of our hands,' he would later proclaim to his fellow nobles in Aquitaine in 1183, 'until he gives us justice.'[100]

By 1182, a major rebellion was being fomented, led by William and Aimar of Angoulême, and their half-brother Aimar, viscount of Limoges. An oath of mutual support was pledged on a missal in the church of St Martial in Limoges, and the league soon grew to include the three other viscounts of the Limousin, Eble IV of Ventadorn, Archambaut V of Comborn and Raymond II of Turenne, together with Elias, count of Périgord, William of Gourdon, and the lord of Montfort.[101] Bertran de Born called on leading Poitevin lords to join the rising, including Geoffrey de Rancon, Geoffrey de Lusignan, Aimery IV, viscount of Thouars, and the lords of Mauléon and Tonnay, and also looked further south to Gascony for support from Gaston IV of Béarn, the viscounts of Dax and Bigorre, and the count of Lomagne.[102] Catching wind of the allies' plans, however, Richard launched a surprise attack on Puy Saint-Front, the thriving settlement beyond the city of Périgueux, then, striking north up the valley of the L'Isle to Excideuil, one of Count Elias' principal castles, he devastated his lands from there to Cornac.[103] By mid May, the counts of Périgord and Angoulême, and Aimar of Limoges had opened peace negotiations, not with Richard, but with his father, meeting Henry II at the king's favoured monastery of Grandmont after 16 May.[104] The talks, however, came to nothing as it became clear that, instead of curbing his son, Henry had brought his forces to Richard's assistance. Aiming to drive a wedge between the areas under the control of Aimar of Limoges and Count Elias, the king took first Saint-Yrieix, then Pierre-Buffière after a siege of twelve days, while Richard attacked Excideuil, taking the town but not the powerful castle. The duke then invested Périgueux itself with a large army, and was soon joined by his father.[105] The gravity of the rebellion led Henry II also to summon the Young King to bring further aid, hoping that the brothers might work as well together against the Aquitanian rebels as they had against Stephen of Sancerre.

The Old King, however, must have been not a little alarmed when, en route to Périgueux, the Young King was not only admitted to Limoges but 'joyfully received' by the monks of St Martial's abbey and the citizens.[106] The shrine of St Martial was a major pilgrimage site, yet to undertake such a visit when Viscount Aimar was still engaged in hostilities with Richard was ominous. It was, moreover, one of the two traditional sites for the double investiture of the dukes of Aquitaine. As counts of Poitou, they first received the sacred lance and banner from the bishop of Poitiers and the archbishop of Bordeaux at the church of St Hilaire in Poitiers; then, as duke of Aquitaine, they were invested with the ring of Sainte Valérie at the abbey of St Martial in Limoges.[107] It was at this very time, however, that the monks of St Martial's were attempting to assert their pre-eminence over St Hilaire as the principal site of investiture, and developing more elaborate rituals, similar to those involved in the creation of dukes of

Normandy.[108] It was, therefore, a highly charged gesture when the Young King proceeded to gift to the abbey a rich robe 'of silk woven with gold thread' with the embroidered inscription 'Henricus Rex'.[109] It was a barely concealed challenge to Richard for the legitimate rulership of Aquitaine. If they had not already done so, it was probably at this time that the members of the league against Richard made overtures to young Henry, offering him their allegiance.[110] Geoffrey of Brittany, who was in the Limousin at just this time, appears to have already been involved in the Young King's plans to take Aquitaine; indeed, he may even have been their principal architect.[111] It was only after celebrating the feast day of St Martial on 30 June, when amidst a great gathering in the abbey Abbot Theobald of Cluny celebrated Mass, that the Young King left Limoges to join his father and Richard at the siege of Périgueux.[112]

In the rebel camp, Bertran de Born was full of fighting talk: 'At Périgueux, near the wall, I'll ride out on my Bayard as far as I can throw a club. And if I find there a potbellied Poitevin, he'll know how my blade cuts − on top of his head I'll make him a slop of brains mixed with mail.'[113] But with the Angevins united − or so it still seemed − the rebels had little choice but to seek peace. Elias yielded the city, and Richard at once had the towers of its walls destroyed.[114] At an assembly at St Augustine's abbey, Limoges, Aimar surrendered his two sons as hostages into Richard's keeping, and pledged to give no further aid to his Taillefer half-brothers.[115] When Henry II returned to Normandy to welcome his daughter Matilda and her husband Henry the Lion, duke of Saxony and Bavaria, who had been exiled by Emperor Frederick Barbarossa, he may have brought potential dissidents north with him.[116] Henry seems to have established Henry the Lion and Matilda at Argentan, which after Rouen and Caen was one of the most important administrative centres of the Norman duchy. It was while the court was residing there that Bertran de Born flattered Matilda with his amorous verse, wryly commenting that he wished he had the love not only of duchess of Saxony but also of her brother, Duke Richard.[117] He satirized the Norman court as a dull and joyless one compared to the *joie de vivre* of the south:

> A court is never complete without joking and laughter; a court without gifts is a mere mockery of barons! And the boredom and vulgarity (*l'enois e e la vilania*) of Argentan nearly killed me, but the noble, lovable body and sweet, mild face and good companionship and conversation of the Saxon lady protected me.[118]

Despite pockets of resistance from the Taillefers, which required further actions by Richard in November, the insurrection in Aquitaine appeared to have been quelled.[119] Yet all was not well. For now the Young King once more began to press his father to grant him Normandy 'or another territory where he and his wife could dwell, and from which he would be able to reward his knights for their service'.[120] The recent sojourn in Aquitaine, on a campaign that had only served to strengthen his brother's hold on the duchy, had fuelled the younger Henry's sense of frustration at his continued lack of a realm of his own and the demeaning nature of his dependent status. It is possible that a catalyst for young Henry's discontent was Henry II's allocation of Argentan to Matilda and Henry the Lion, as this had probably been one of the castles assigned to the Young King in the wake of the peace of 1174. Howden, however, believed that his demands were made 'by the counsel of evil men', chief among whom was King Philip.[121] If so, the king of France was following in his father's footsteps, seeking to weaken Angevin power by setting son against father. Henry II, acutely aware that such demands had been the prelude to the great rebellion in 1173, was said to be 'tormented with inner anxieties': indeed, so worried was he about his son's possible actions that he felt unable to leave Normandy to aid the justiciar Ranulf de Glanville in suppressing a major Welsh attack.[122] Henry nevertheless refused the Young King's petition. Recent events in Brittany had only served to compound his innate reluctance to alienate any part of the empire's core lands: Geoffrey, who had assumed effective authority in the duchy in 1181 on his marriage to Constance, had almost immediately begun to assert his independence from his father by armed resistance, perhaps intending to press his claims to the honour of Richmond and the county of Nantes, which Henry II still held in his own hands.[123] The king was forced to send an army into Brittany; it took and garrisoned the castle of Rennes, but Geoffrey had responded by burning much of the town and attacking Bécherel, one of Roland de Dinan's castles.[124] Father and son were reconciled by June of 1182, but the incident must have confirmed Henry II's fears about what might happen should he grant young Henry direct rule over Normandy, or Anjou or England.

In high dudgeon at his father's response, young Henry left for the court of King Philip, saying that he intended to undertake a pilgrimage to Jerusalem: if he was to be denied a realm in his father's lands, then he would depart for Outremer, where he might serve some worthy purpose and gain high honour fighting the enemies of Christ.[125] Only the year before, Henry II and King Philip had held a summit in April near Nonancourt, at which a delegation of Templars and Hospitallers had produced a bull of Alexander III, *Cor nostrum*, warning of the parlous state of the Holy Land under the ailing leper king, Baldwin IV, and offering remission of sin for those taking up arms for its aid.[126] The two kings had pledged their support, and Henry II had attempted to divert to the Holy Land a planned crusading expedition to Spain led by Hugh, count of Bar, one of the Young King's former allies in the war of 1173–74.[127] As yet, however, there had been no serious response from the Angevin or Capetian monarchs themselves. To send young Henry east at the head of an expedition would have fulfilled the Plantagenet commitment to aid the Holy Land while at the same time offering an outlet for the Young King's frustrations. All knew that Baldwin had not long to live, and that his death might easily turn bitter factional tensions in the kingdom of Jerusalem into a dangerous civil war unless a new leader could be found behind whom all could unite against the onslaught of Saladin. Many would doubtless have welcomed the charismatic young Plantagenet; had the Young King headed East in 1182, he would have been one of the most powerful contenders for the throne of Jerusalem, and might well, like his great-grandfather Fulk V, have become its king. Yet Henry II was unwilling to endorse such a plan: it may have been that he feared that the challenges of crusade and the fierce political infighting of the Latin kingdom were beyond the capacities of his eldest son. Yet his subsequent refusal in 1185 to send any of his other sons east when begged to do so by the Patriarch Heraclius suggests instead that he was not willing to upset his plans for succession and division of his empire by risking any of his heirs on such an expedition.[128]

Anxious to prevent the Young King from taking the cross without his consent, Henry II quickly sent messengers offering to give young Henry a stipend of 100 *livres angevins* (£25) each day, and 10 *livres angevins* daily for his wife, Queen Margaret.[129] This total sum of 40,150 *livres angevins* (£10,037) was an enormous increase on the yearly sum of 15,000 *livres angevins* which young Henry had been assigned by the peace settlement of 1174. Henry II also promised that within the year he would provide 100 knights for service in the Young King's household. As this was a very high number of knights to retain permanently within the *familia*, it may be that Henry II was pledging to fund this number of knights on a more ad hoc basis, as and when they were required to form the mainstay of the Young King's tourneying retinue.[130] Even if this was so, the rates of pay given by young Henry to his knights at the tournament at Lagny in 1179 indicate that it represented a very heavy additional outlay for Henry II. The Young King accepted his father's terms, and swore that he would not withdraw in any way from his father's wishes or council, and that he would make no further demands.[131] Henry II had, or so it seemed, succeeded in purchasing the quiescence of his eldest son. Yet though it made the Young King wealthy, the settlement – in essence a money-fief writ large – still failed to address the fundamental problem which lay at the heart of conflict between father and son, and which also embittered relations between the brothers: he remained a king without a kingdom. For a man in twelfth-century noble society to move from the condition of the unmarried and landless 'youth' (*juvenis*) to the attainment of full adult status required the acquisition of land, whether by inheritance, marriage, gift or war.[132] The manner in which contemporaries continued to refer to the Young King clearly indicates his dependent status. Ralph of Diss, writing of the Young King's return to England in 1179, regarded him as 'still under age (*adhuc minoris aetatis*)', even though he was by then twenty-four, while in 1182 Geoffrey of Vigeois could still refer to him as 'rex adolescens'.[133] Without a realm to govern in his own right, it was young Henry as much as his youngest brother John who merited the epithet 'Lackland'.

A Crisis of Faith: The Quarrel with the Marshal

The question of the Young King's ability adequately to reward his household knights, which had in part prompted the demands he had made on his father, equally lay at the heart of a crisis which that same year had shattered the frail unity of young Henry's own *mesnie*. For his lack of lands with which to endow his men impacted directly on their own status and prospects. By now, William Marshal had served his lord for twelve years but had not gained a foot of land; nor had any of his fellow knights in the Young King's household, even though many of them had risked much by following him into war in 1173 against Henry II. It is telling that the Young King's charters regarding former members of his uncle William Longsword's household who entered his own are only confirmations, not grants from the younger Henry himself. It was Henry II's own men and established nobles who had first claim on wealthy heiresses or lands that had escheated to the crown, and the financial resources to purchase them from the king. Henry II's policy in the later 1150s and 1160s had been to recover, not disburse, royal lands and prerogatives, and his subsequent grants of royal demesne were very limited. Nor were there ready opportunities for young Henry and his companions to gain land by the sword. In Wales, the recognition by Henry II of the position of the Lord Rhys, prince of Deheubarth, as his 'justice of all south Wales' was a tacit acceptance that marcher expansion had been successfully halted. In Ireland, the English colonists had made impressive gains since 1169, but here again the tide of conquest appeared to have been slowed, and, as importantly, Henry II was increasingly coming to regard Ireland as the land for his youngest son John.

It was little wonder, then, that members of the household of the Young King, trapped as he was in a position of equivocal and secondary status, were in fierce and divisive competition among themselves for any chances of advancement.[134] William Marshal may not have received a fief, yet by dint of his skill in the tournament and his relentless pursuit of ransoms and other profits he had done very well for himself. At the great tournament at Lagny in late 1179 he appeared as a banneret, an elevated rank which proclaimed him as a man of sufficient wealth and status to lead a company of knights in his own right, and to carry his own device on a banner.[135] Yet this very prominence had earned him enemies among his fellows in the Young King's household. The *mesnie*, no less than the wider royal court, was a place rife with envy and plots, and defamation by *losengiers* or 'tale-bearers' was an ever-present risk.[136] A jealous clique headed by Adam d'Yquebeuf, Thomas de Coulonces and someone who with deliberate vagueness the *History of William Marshal* refers to as the 'seneschal and master of the king's household' sought to discredit him in the eyes of their lord.[137] They complained that on the tournament field he had put his own interests far ahead of those of the Young King, disloyally leaving his royal master in danger in order to accrue both glory and ransoms for himself. Much of his success, it was alleged, came from the practice of one of the Marshal's supporters, Henry the Northerner, who in the heat of the mêlée drew knights to the Marshal by crying out, 'This way, God is with the Marshal! (*Ça, Dex aïe li Mareschal!*)'. This quickly attracted such a great throng about William that no attention was paid to the Young King. Still worse, by adopting this cry the Marshal had even usurped the war cry of the Norman dukes – 'Dex aïe!' – as his own.[138]

In addition to these charges, the *History* claims that his detractors accused the Marshal of being the lover of the Young King's wife Margaret. To sleep with the wife of one's lord was not only an act of personal betrayal but an act of treason, because it threatened the purity of the seigneurial or royal bloodline. Allegations of sexual impropriety were thus powerful political weapons at court, both in romance literature and in reality.[139] A major political crisis had disrupted the rule of Fulk V as king of Jerusalem, when the handsome young lord of Jaffa, Hugh II de Puiset, was accused by his rivals of being overly intimate with Fulk's queen, Melisende.[140] The Young King's own mother, Queen Eleanor, had aroused much suspicion in 1148 by her conduct with her uncle Raymond, prince of Antioch, when she and King Louis sojourned there following the Second Crusade. While some among the troubadours claimed that true love only existed outside marriage, the reality for those caught engaging in extramarital affairs could be brutal.[141] When in 1175 Count Philip discovered the infidelity of his wife, Elizabeth of Vermandois, she was spared, but her lover Walter was beaten with clubs and hung over a privy to suffocate.[142] Events such as these must have lent a real frisson to the exploration of adulterous love in romances such as *Tristan*, where an older king is cuckolded by a supposedly loyal younger man, and it was at the behest of his patron, Marie, countess of Champagne and the Young King's half-sister, that in the later 1170s Chrétien de Troyes wove one of the most famous tales of adulterous love, that between Arthur's queen Guinevere and his best knight, Lancelot, in his *Chevalier de la Charette*.[143]

It has been argued, however, that the allegations of adultery levelled at the Marshal were more likely to have been an invention of the author of the *History of William Marshal*, influenced by just such romances. For although the *History* stridently denounced them as false, these charges of illicit love with the queen afforded a more glamorous explanation for the estrangement of William from the Young King, drawing attention away from the accusations of disloyal self-serving and *lèse-majesté* which in reality had probably soured relations between the two men.[144] No other chronicler mentions an affair, real or alleged, nor is any disgrace known to have fallen upon Margaret.[145] The affair of Adam of Churchdown in 1179 had shown how vehemently the Young King reacted to what he saw as betrayal, yet William was not threatened with any of the condign punishments for such treason.

According to the *History*, when the Young King heard the charges brought against the Marshal by Ralph Farci, a young nobleman whom the conspirators had chosen because of his intimacy with young Henry, he initially refused to believe them. When five other knights came forward as witnesses, however, the Young King was convinced and, greatly angered, refused to speak to William.[146] He nevertheless recalled the Marshal for an important tournament between Gournay and Ressons in November 1182, which suggests that he still felt the need for his skill in the mêlée.[147] Yet although William performed well in the fighting, the subsequent attempt by Count Philip to effect a reconciliation between the Young King and his most acomplished household knight met with failure, and the two men parted 'in shame and anger' without a word.[148]

The Young King returned to Normandy from the Île-de-France in time to join his father for the Christmas festivities of 1182 at Caen. Intent on making this a particularly magnificent court, Henry II had forbidden his barons from holding their own Christmas courts. As a result, in addition to a throng of leading prelates and nobles, over 1,000 knights were said to have attended.[149] The presence of Henry the Lion and the Duchess Matilda, as well as Richard and Geoffrey, made this a great Plantagenet family gathering. Not everything, however, went smoothly: William Marshal appeared to demand justice from the Young King and the chance to prove his innocence by wager of battle against his accusers, who were present at court. When he was denied this request, he indignantly protested to Henry II that the judgement of his court was 'weighted against right and the law of the land', and sought safe conduct

from the Old King to leave the realm.[150] He soon received several offers of
retainer and accepted that of Count Philip of Flanders, who granted him a
lucrative money fief from the rents of St Omer.[151] Philip's reception of the
Marshal – a man who, whatever the validity of the charges, had been publicly
branded a traitor – was an indication of the extent to which relations had deteriorated between the count and the Young King in the wake of young Henry's
support of King Philip against him in 1181–82.[152]

Despite all the distortions inherent in the *History of William Marshal*'s
version of events and the probability that tensions between the Marshal and
his lord may have been simmering for some time, it seems likely enough that
the Young King keenly felt William's supposed betrayal and fall from grace.
His overwhelming desire during the 1170s to escape from the tutelage of his
father's ministers had made him place a high premium on absolute loyalty, and
his own insecurities, already reflected in his uncharacteristically harsh treatment of Adam of Churchdown, may have made him all too susceptible to the
charges of disloyalty and *lèse-majesté* brought against the Marshal by his
enemies in young Henry's household.

In an incident that may have been related to the Marshal's demand for
trial by combat, the Christmas festivities at Caen were again disrupted when
the Marshal's former lord, William de Tancarville, came to assert his own rights
as chamberlain of Normandy.[153] Striding into the hall, he seized the basin used
for washing the king's hands from an attendant and personally washed Henry
II's hands: he may have fallen from favour at court, but the office of chamberlain was still his by hereditary right, and the king should not forget it.[154] As
seneschal of France, the Young King could appreciate as much as any the significance of his former ally's gesture, and as some present may well have reflected,
it was now a decade since the Young King's first and fateful independent court,
likewise held at Caen, at which plans for the great rebellion against Henry II
had begun to form. The protests of both William Marshal and the chamberlain
of Tancarville were dramatic reminders of how highly politically charged the
great seasonal courts which brought together the king and many of the nobility
of the Angevin lands might be. Yet in contrast to 1172, the nobility of Normandy
now appeared quiescent. The power of many of the former rebels in the duchy
had been broken or contained, and Henry II's grant of what was effectively the
regency of Normandy to the Young King in 1181 had demonstrated that he no
longer feared a renewed rebellion there headed by his eldest son. The Old King
had good reason to celebrate in such magnificent style at Christmas 1182.
From being at bay against a powerful coalition of enemies, Henry II had
become unchallenged, and since 1180 he had been peacemaker and the arbiter
of the political status quo in northern France.

For the Young King, the years between 1178 and 1182 had been a period of successful political rehabilitation and reintegration. Restored unequivocally as Henry II's principal heir, his relations with his father appeared far more cordial than in the strained, volatile years immediately following the war. The ultimate cause of his discontent was unresolved, but his acceptance of Henry II's generous financial settlement suggests that young Henry had resigned himself to the fact that neither by threat, force or entreaty would his father grant him direct rule of any part of the Angevin heartlands while the Old King yet remained in robust good health. If, however, his regal status still suffered from his lack of a kingdom, his lavish funding had allowed young Henry to forge a new image as a pre-eminent figure of the tournament and a king among knights, whose free-handed generosity astonished and delighted, winning him kudos and much support. By 1182, his chivalric reputation had reached its apogee. Yet dark clouds were gathering that would soon shatter the apparent unity of the Angevin family and plunge them into a bitter civil war.

CHAPTER 13

The Brothers' War, 1183

A king who fights for his rights has a better right to his heritage;
Because Charles conquered Spain, men have been talking about him
ever since.
For with effort and generosity, a king both conquers merit and wins it . . .
The Young King has acquired merit from Burgos to Germany.
                    – Bertran de Born, 'Ieu chan que.l reys m'en a preguat'[1]

The Castle of Clairvaux and the Breach with Richard

The spark that would ignite war had already been kindled in Aquitaine. It
was most probably during the Young King's visit to Limoges in June of
1182, but certainly before Christmas, that young Henry had secretly accepted
pledges from the dissident barons of Poitou that they would follow him as
their liege lord and not withdraw from his service.[2] The question of his support
was becoming ever more pressing, for by late 1182 the Taillefers and Aimar
of Limoges had once more come out in open rebellion against Richard,
summoning mercenaries to their aid.[3] The Young King's propensity to aid
his brother's enemies had been increased by his own quarrel with Richard
over the latter's construction of a castle, Clairvaux, on the border of Anjou
and Poitou.[4] Geoffrey Greygown, count of Anjou, had forcibly annexed the
castle from Poitou, though he had acknowledged Count William III's ultimate
title by performing homage for it. Over time, however, this homage had lapsed,
and Clairvaux had been assimilated into Anjou.[5] Richard may well have
been reasserting an ancient claim, but in 1182 it was Henry II, not the Young
King, who had actual control of Anjou, and Richard can scarcely have felt
threatened by his father after the latter's evident support for him against
the Aquitanian rebels. Richard may have been strengthening his position in

relation to the viscount of Châtellerault, one of his leading Poitevin vassals whose own fortress at Châtellerault controlled a key crossing of the river Vienne.[6] But his motives may have been as much economic as strategic. A mid-thirteenth-century inquest reveals that in 1184 Richard had established a castle, but also a new town dependent on it, at Saint-Rémy-de-la-Haye on the river Creuse, which formed the border between Poitou and the Touraine. Burgesses were attracted to the 'free town' by the rent or sale of plots to be held by burgage tenure, and the count's officials collected tolls and dues.[7] Richard's founding of the castle at Clairvaux in 1182 appears closely analogous. In his *sirventes* which speaks of Clairvaux, Bertran de Born gives the Young King the mocking *senhal* or coded name 'Sir Carter' (*en Charretier*), and the poem's thirteenth-century *razo*, or introduction, explained this by noting that Henry II had given young Henry an income of tolls from carts, but that these had been taken away by Richard.[8] Little reliance can be placed on these quasi-historical *razos*, but the presence of a new bourg at Clairvaux may well have led to conflict over local rights, not least with comital officials in Anjou. The Young King's unusually complete dependence on assigned revenues doubtless made him particularly sensitive to such issues. Yet what rankled most was that, as in 1173, he felt his patrimony was being encroached upon by a younger brother before he himself had even obtained it. Bertran de Born was quick to point up the insult and, by extension, the Young King's lack of power:

> Between Poitou and L'Île Bouchard and Mirebeau and Loudun and Chinon, at Clairvaux they have built a beautiful castle without a by-your-leave and put it in a flat field. I don't want the Young King to know it or see it, because he would not like it, but I'm afraid he will see it from Mateflon, since it shines so bright.[9]

Bertran's naming of the three Angevin castles of Chinon, Loudun and Mirebeau was a deliberate and provocative reminder of the quarrel over them that had wrecked the Maurienne marriage plan in 1173 and precipitated young Henry's rebellion.

A superficial peace had been maintained during the Christmas celebrations at Caen, but tensions between the brothers were soon brought to a head when the court reached Le Mans. In an attempt to establish the relationship between his sons and their respective lands after his own death, Henry II ordered Richard and Geoffrey to perform homage to their elder brother.[10] The Old King was clearly anxious that the younger Henry should step into his shoes not only as king of England, duke of Normandy and count of Anjou, but as the head of the family, a position already suggested by the Young King's acceptance of the homage of Raymond V of Toulouse in 1173.[11] This unambiguous establishment of young Henry's overlordship can be seen in part as an extension of Henry II's recent settlement with him, and as an attempt to reassure the Young King of the pre-eminence of his position.[12] By securing Richard's homage to the Young King, moreover, Henry II was seeking to bypass Capetian claims to direct overlordship of Aquitaine.

Geoffrey readily obeyed his father's command and performed liege homage to the Young King: such an act merely reaffirmed the homage he had performed to young Henry as duke of Normandy in 1169.[13] But obtaining Richard's homage was a very different matter. The count of Poitou indignantly refused, protesting that, having the same illustrious birth as his brother, he was young Henry's equal.[14] 'He exploded in anger,' noted Ralph of Diss,

> declaring (so it was reported) that since he came from the same father and the same mother as his brother, it was not right for him to acknowledge his elder brother as superior by some sort of subjection. Rather, by the law of firstborn sons (*lege primogenitorum*), the paternal goods were due to his brother, and he claimed equal right to legitimate succession to the maternal goods.[15]

Such a stance reflected a very different view of the future of the Angevin 'empire' from that of his father: on Henry II's death, Aquitaine would go its own separate way under Richard and his heirs, its duke bound only as the vassal of the king of France.[16] Richard was eventually persuaded by his father, though with great reluctance, to perform homage to his older brother, but only on condition that Henry II ensured that the Young King should grant the duchy of Aquitaine to Richard, 'to be held by Richard and his heirs by an undisputable right'.[17] Richard evidently feared for the security of his hold on Aquitaine once Henry II was dead. Young Henry's own insistence on performing homage to his father in 1175 had underlined its great significance as a form of security. In turn, Richard's performance of homage to his elder brother, though unpalatable, would obligate the Young King to recognize his rightful inheritance and to support and protect Richard as his lord.

To Henry II's complete exasperation, however, the Young King now refused to accept Richard's homage. It was a lord's duty to aid his man against his enemies, and the ties of homage meant that the Young King would be unable, either in good conscience or in feudal law, to give any support to those rebelling against Richard. Yet equally, if kept hidden, his earlier intrigues with the disaffected barons of Aquitaine might so anger his father that the generous settlement recently agreed might be jeopardized. There was no option but to make a clean breast of it. Accordingly, on 1 January 1183, in the presence of a large gathering of clerics and laymen, young Henry swore an oath on the Gospels 'of his own accord, with no-one compelling him, that from that day forward, and for all the days of his life, he would keep complete faith with King Henry, as his father and his lord, and always show the honour and service he owed to him'.[18] Yet this, an affirmation of his earlier oath of 1182, was the prologue to a shocking revelation. As Roger of Howden, who was evidently an eyewitness to the events at Le Mans, recorded:

> And because – as he asserted – he desired to retain in his mind no malice or rancour whereby his father might afterwards be offended, the Young King made it known to him that he was bound by an agreement with the barons of Aquitaine against his brother Richard. He had been moved to do so because his brother had fortified the castle of Clairvaux against his wishes, in the patrimony which would come to him after their father's death. He therefore besought his father to take that castle from Richard, and retain it in his own keeping.[19]

Not unnaturally, given his brother's league with the Aquitanian rebels, Richard refused Henry II's initial command to hand Clairvaux over to him. He was, however, eventually prevailed upon by his father and 'freely made it over to him to dispose of it according to his good pleasure'.[20] Doubtless he judged it expedient to prevent his elder brother from any subsequent meddling with the dissident lords of Aquitaine.

To further quell the discord between the brothers, Henry II summoned them to Angers, where he made young Henry, Richard and Geoffrey swear a compact of perpetual peace. Each then swore an oath of fealty to their father against all men, pledging they would maintain his honour and service, and would observe the peace between them according to their father's dispositions.[21] To tackle the divisive issue of the rebels in Aquitaine, it was agreed that a new peace summit would be held at Mirebeau, to which the dissidents would be invited. Geoffrey was accordingly sent to the Limousin soon after 2 February 1183, to arrange a truce and to summon the rebel lords to the conference.[22] In what appears to have been a move prearranged with the Young King, however, Geoffrey immediately sided with the rebels and began to plunder with units of *routiers*.[23] The Young King at once offered to act as an intermediary, and convinced his father that if the dissident barons were dissatisfied with terms of the agreement made in the summer of 1182, they should be allowed to appeal for justice to Henry II's court. This move seems to have been the last straw for Richard, and there can be little doubt that the Young King was deliberately attempting to provoke his brother. The surrender of Clairvaux was galling, and to have agreed to his father's request that he perform homage to his elder brother was a bitter pill to swallow. Yet now Richard's acquiescence appeared to be for nothing. Young Henry had leagued with his enemies, and by supporting their claims against him before Henry II, he now sought to undermine the terms Richard had succeeded in imposing on the rebel nobles after so long and hard-fought a campaign. On top of this, his brother had the temerity to demand he swear fealty to him, a man who had formed a secret alliance with his enemies. Without taking leave, Richard stormed from the court, 'leaving nothing but insults and threats behind him'.[24]

Provoked beyond patience, Henry II fell into a rage and 'threatened difficulties for Richard, saying that the Young King should rise up and tame Richard's pride. He told Geoffrey count of Brittany to stand faithfully by his brother as his liege lord.'[25] The History of William Marshal has the Young King tell Henry II, '"For a long time they [the barons] were my men, and it would not be right of me to fail them or allow them to be ill-treated; it is only right that I should come to their aid." "Go on then, go to their aid," said the father, "I'll permit that."'[26] It was not to be the last time that Henry, in a moment of deep anger and frustration, would sanction war between his sons. Yet it proved a fatal miscalculation and, as Prior Geoffrey of Vigeois lamented, the quarrel between the king's three sons was soon to be the cause 'of a lamentable calamity for Aquitaine'.[27]

Mindful of the events of 1173, when he had escaped to France but Margaret had been left behind to become his father's hostage, the Young King sent his wife to the safety of the court of her brother King Philip, then set out for Limoges in early February.[28] As he journeyed through Poitou, the insurgents placed their castles under the Young King's control.[29] Arriving at Limoges, he joined forces with Viscount Aimar and Geoffrey, who had brought a large force of knights and other troops from Brittany and had assembled a great host of Brabançons.[30] As Gerald of Wales reflected, young Henry had gathered together an army 'greater than was ever before assembled at any time by a man having neither territory or treasure'.[31] By now, the extent of the alliance headed by the Young King against Richard was becoming apparent. As the History of William Marshal noted,

> the high ranking barons of the region, whom the count, whom they hated
> bitterly, had treated badly, rode there in great numbers, everyone of them with

a mind to fight, for they would dearly have loved to humble the pride of Count Richard, if only they had the opportunity and could get the upper hand.[32]

They included Aimar of Limoges, the Taillefer brothers of Angoulême and one of their leading vassals, Fulcaud of Archiac in the Saintonge, the viscounts of Ventadour, Comborn, Turenne and Castillon, Oliver de Chalais, and Bernard of Montfort.[33] These lords, who together with the count of Périgord, had formed the core of opposition to Richard in 1182, were concentrated in the Angoumois, Limousin and Périgord, but now the Lusignans, who had remained quiescent in 1182, joined the coalition, with other Poitevin lords.[34] It was a sign of the upheaval that had taken place within the Young King's household that at Limoges he welcomed Geoffrey de Lusignan, the sworn enemy of the now disgraced and exiled William Marshal.[35] All the chroniclers stress the size and power of the forces assembled by the coalition. At Limoges, the Young King and Geoffrey retained in their service 'knights and sergeants, and *routiers* and crossbowmen, fine footsoldiers and good archers'.[36] The *History* noted that the Young King had summoned stipendiary knights from all over northern France, some of whom had evidently seen previous service with him, whether in war or in his tournament retinues; 'in France and Normandy, in Anjou and the Lowlands, and throughout Flanders he called up his young knights (*ses bachilers*)', who came 'out of the great affection they had for their lord'.[37] Whether they had existing ties to young Henry or not, all these knights were attracted by his reputation as a generous paymaster.

'The Legions of Hell': Brabançons and *Routiers*

The elements of the Young King's forces which most attracted the wholly negative attention of the chroniclers were the bands of mercenary *routiers* or *rutae* who in ever increasing numbers had become the scourge of southern France by the 1170s.[38] 'They are now multiplied above numbering,' noted Walter Map, 'and so strong have these armies of Leviathan grown that they settle in safety or rove through whole provinces or kingdoms, hated of God and man.'[39] The multiplicity of local lordships in southern France, often in fierce competition, the comparative weakness or absence of direct rule by princes and the distance from the power bases of the kings of France and England, made this an ideal arena for mercenary bands to flourish. The counts, viscounts and other local magnates lacked extensive military resources of their own, yet commanded sufficient wealth drawn from a prosperous region to employ mercenaries for short periods of war against either their local rivals or nominal overlords such as the duke of Aquitaine. The later 1170s and early

1180s, moreover, witnessed a particularly intense period of war and turmoil in the Auvergne and much of Aquitaine.[40] Disbanded mercenaries employed in Frederick Barbarossa's wars in northern Italy had moved into southern France after the Treaty of Venice in 1177, while by 1179 the archbishop of Narbonne could single out Count Raymond V of Toulouse, and his enemies Roger Trencavel of Béziers and Bernard Ato of Nîmes, as notorious employers of the *routier* bands.[41] To this bitter regional struggle was added the conflict between the king of Aragon and the count of Toulouse over their competing claims to Provence, which had erupted into war in 1181 after Alfonso II's brother Raymon Berenguer IV, the count of Provence, was murdered, a deed in which Raymond was deeply implicated.[42] Rigord, carefully omitting Philip Augustus' role in the troubles of 1183, says that the war between the count of Toulouse and the king of Aragon caused terrible devastation, while the prominence of Basques among the chroniclers' lists of various *routier* bands seems closely connected to the presence of Aragonese forces in Aquitaine.[43]

Though often referred to in the narrative sources by names indicating their broad regional origins, such as Brabançons from the Low Countries, or Basques, Navarrese and Catalans from south of the Pyrenees, these *routiers* were in reality hybrid groups attracting a volatile mix of criminals, renegades and outcasts, all 'armed cap-à-pied with leather, iron, clubs and swords'.[44] Once out of the pay and direct control of a ruler or lord, these bands rapidly became a serious threat to local order, but equally their ruthless conduct on campaign was rarely restrained by their employers, who appreciated the political and military value of the terror which they inspired.[45] These 'legions from Hell', as Geoffrey of Vigeois termed them, had a particularly evil reputation for cruelty and sacrilege.[46] Walter Map, who had seen their handiwork in the Limousin in 1183, noted how they 'lay monasteries, villages and towns in ashes, and practise indiscriminate adulteries with force, saying in their hearts, "There is no God"'.[47] Likewise, to Ralph of Diss, they were 'those wicked overthrowers of castles, slaughterers of peasants, burners of churches, and oppressors of monks'.[48]

Local populations had attempted to organize resistance to these predators when they could, but the support of the powerful was crucial. In 1177, Abbot Isembard of St Martial's had led a local peace guild against them, while the bishop of Poitiers had assisted Duke Richard's forces to destroy a concentration of *routiers*.[49] So grave had the depredations of these mercenary bands become that in 1179 the Third Lateran Council took drastic steps against them. Anyone who, under the guidance of bishops or priests, took up arms against these mercenaries was to be placed under the protection of the Church as if they were journeying to Jerusalem, and would gain remission from two years of penance.

It was both licit and meritorious to kill such men, who were branded as heretics, while if captured they could be enslaved.[50] Those who killed women, children, clergy and the old without pity deserved none themselves. It was not only the *routiers*, however, who faced the thunders of the Church. Those who took such mercenaries into their service, associated with them or supplied them were to be excommunicated, with the extinguishing of candles and ringing of bells, and any who owed obligations of service to such renegade lords were freed from their oaths of homage and fealty. Their lands were placed under interdict; save for baptism and penitence, they were to be denied the sacraments, including the viaticum.[51] The primary target of these papal strictures had been those lords in southern France suspected of harbouring or supporting the dualist heretics increasingly known as Albigensians or Cathars, whose spread was perceived by the Church as an ever-increasing threat. Yet by taking the *routier* bands into his pay, the Young King himself was in violation of the canons of the Lateran Council and thereby was putting his mortal soul in grave peril.

The War against Richard and the Siege of Limoges

From their base at Limoges, the Young King and Geoffrey began to plunder and lay waste Richard's lands.[52] With his very survival at stake, the young duke's response was typically bold. In the art of war, he had already learned much from his father, one of the greatest generals of the age, and knew the value of good intelligence and of the use of surprise to offset superior numbers ranged against him. A large body of *routiers* under Raymond 'Brennus' had moved north from Gascony and with Viscount Aimar were laying siege to the church at Gorre, a little to the south-west of Limoges. Apprised of this, Richard and a small force, probably comprising only his household knights, dashed south from near Poitiers and after almost two days' hard riding they fell upon the unsuspecting enemy on 12 February. The mercenaries were routed, many were slain, and Richard himself laid low William Arnald, Raymond's nephew. Had Richard been able to capture Aimar and other leaders he might have dealt the insurgents a fatal blow, but the horses of the Poitevins were exhausted from their forced marches, and the viscount and his allies were able to escape.[53] Richard, however, also knew the value of terror: determined to make an example of the Basques who had fallen into his hands, he dragged his prisoners a few miles north-east to Aixe on the south bank of the river Vienne, virtually within sight of Limoges, where he had some drowned, others executed, and around eighty blinded.[54] Richard's actions were a direct challenge not only to Aimar but to the Young King and Geoffrey within the city. The slaying of these 'sacrilegious people, detested by the Roman church', as Roger of Howden called them, was not a cause for censure. It was a very different matter, however, when he ordered that if anyone belonging to the households of the Young King or Geoffrey was captured, they were to be beheaded at once, whatever their rank.[55] To execute knights once taken prisoner was a major breach of chivalric convention, and took the war to a new level of ruthlessness. It was a revealing indication of how desperate Richard felt his position to be and the extent of hatred that now existed between the brothers.

The victory at Gorre only bought Richard a breathing space. Realizing that alone he had little chance of withstanding so powerful a coalition of enemies, he appealed to his father for aid.[56] Henry II, admitted Roger of Howden, had allowed his sons to fight against each other for some time, but he too now saw that Richard might be forcibly deposed. Indeed, so bitter had the conflict become that he was said even to have feared for Richard's life should he fall into the hands of his brother's forces.[57] Nevertheless, the Old King still believed the Young King's protestations that he was acting as a peacemaker on behalf of the rebel lords and, on his eldest son's advice, he travelled to Limoges with only a small retinue.[58] By the later twelfth century, the city of Limoges had developed into two distinct areas, situated adjacent to each other on the north bank of the river Vienne. The oldest district, known as the Cité, was established on the site of the Roman town of Lemovincensium and had grown up around the cathedral church of St Etienne. Defended by its own circuit of walls and gates, it contained the episcopal palace and the residences of the canons. An intense rivalry existed between the inhabitants of the Cité and those of the thriving and more populous urban centre surrounding the great abbey of St Martial, a little to the north-west, which was known as the Château of St Martial (or the Château of Limoges). The Château's separate defensive perimeter also enclosed the castle of the viscount of Limoges, held as fief of the abbot of St Martial's, but with whom the viscounts were often in dispute.[59] The Young King and his allies had established themselves in the Château, and Viscount Aimar had intimidated the burgesses into joining them against Richard.[60]

On his arrival at Limoges, Henry II expected to be welcomed into the Château by his sons. Instead, he was suddenly met by a hail of arrows, one of which pierced his surcoat. A sally in force by the defenders of the Château drove the king's retinue back, preventing them from entering either the Château or the Cité, and in the resulting skirmish one of Henry II's household knights was wounded.[61] According to Geoffrey of Vigeois, the defenders of the Château had mistakenly believed – or so they claimed – that they were being assaulted by the burgesses of the Cité, while in the confusion the cry was raised that Duke Geoffrey was outside the walls and in great danger. It was only when an English knight recognized the king's standards and his arms that a full-scale attack by the

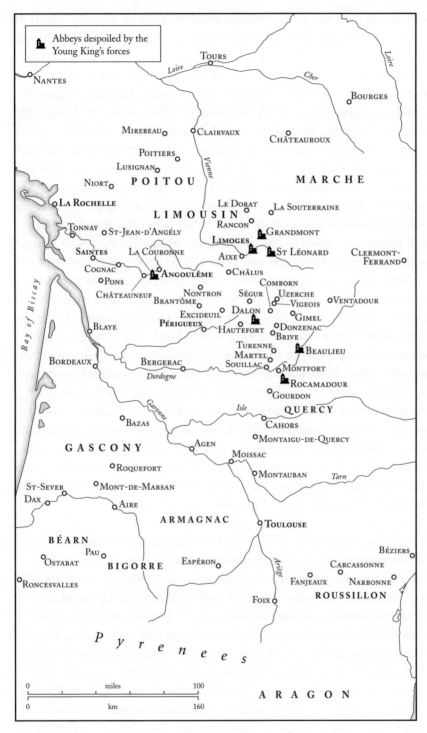

Map 8 Aquitaine, to illustrate the war of 1183

forces within the Château was prevented and the fighting stopped.[62] Henry II now took up residence in the Cité, but when he rode out to talk peacefully with the Young King and Geoffrey, he was again shot at, and would have received a potentially fatal wound had not his horse suddenly raised his head and been struck by the arrow or bolt intended for Henry.[63] Enraged and badly shaken, the Old King withdrew across the Vienne to Aixe.[64] That evening, the Young King visited his father, but he came wearing his hauberk and declined his father's invitation to dinner – clear signs of renewed tension between father and son.[65] In turn, Henry II refused to listen to the Young King's excuses and entreaties on behalf of the burgesses of the Château, for in attacking the person of their overlord they had committed a grave offence.[66] The Young King may have been genuinely distressed by the attack on his father, but as Roger of Howden was quick to point out, while he condemned those responsible, he neither avenged his father nor handed the guilty over to the Old King for punishment.[67]

Henry II's refusal to excuse those in the Château seems to have been a crucial turning point, marking the shift from war against Richard to overt rebellion against Henry II himself. At the command of Viscount Aimar, 'the people swore fealty to the Young King in the church of St Peter du Queiroix', then immediately began to strengthen the defences of the Château and the viscount's castle. Walls were constructed, ditches of exceptional depth were dug and the ramparts reinforced with hoarding and brattices of wood.[68] Though swiftly erected and only of timber, such defences could be formidable. Everything outside them was ruthlessly levelled to deny cover to attackers and to obtain materials for the defences, creating a bleak wasteland between the Château and the Cité. Not even churches were spared, for these could be used as extemporized fortifications. Prior Geoffrey recorded a graphic picture of an urban landscape devastated by the demands of war:

> They entirely uprooted the garden of St Martial's, full of trees of many different varieties, together with those trees which surrounded the Château. But why should these trees be the cause of wonder? Putting aside reverence for the divine, they pulled down the church of Mary the Mother of God [Sainte-Marie-des-Arènes], the basilica of the Hospital of St Gerold, the house of St Valéry, the church of Saint Maurice and certain others. They burned up in flames – for shame! – the wooden spire and *signa* of Saint Martin's, and almost completely destroyed the stone belfry, enclosure walls and outbuildings, the monastery itself and its adjacent bourg. The vill and church of Saint Symphorien of the Bridge were demolished in a similar fashion, together with certain other churches, both by the men of the Château as well as by those of the Cité.[69]

Now dug in, the rebels in Limoges were soon reinforced by further bands of *routiers* summoned by Viscount Aimar and Raymond, viscount of Turenne.[70] Prominent among their leaders were Sancho de Savannac, and Curbaran, who with grim irony had adopted the name of the Muslim emir Kerbogha who had given battle to the men of the First Crusade at Antioch.[71] The strategy of the Young King and his allies at this time and in subsequent months is far from clear: the chroniclers record only sporadic and isolated incidents, resulting in the (probably mistaken) impression of uncoordinated and apparently purpose-less campaigns of devastation. One immediate goal, however, appears to have been to reverse some of the gains made by Henry II and Richard at the expense of the viscounts of Limoges and Périgord the year previously, for Ademar immediately led the forces of Sancho and Curbaran to lay siege to Pierre-Buffière, which commanded the approach to Limoges from the south-east.[72] They succeeded in capturing the town, upon which Peter of Pierre-Buffière negotiated terms and surrendered the castle and its keep. There followed one of those striking rituals which, though rarely glimpsed in the sources, were a common feature of such warfare. First, the banners of Ademar, the Young King and Curbaran were flown from the battlements, thereby proclaiming their legal ownership of the castle and all spoils taken within. Then, after the viscount had celebrated his triumphal capture for a day and a night with the sounding of trumpets, the castle was promptly returned to Peter.[73] The whole affair represented a public assertion by Ademar of his direct lordship of Pierre-Buffière; this was contested with the abbey of St Martial, which claimed the viscount held it only as its vassal. Like Bertran de Born's feud with his brother Constantine over possession of Hautefort, local turf wars were inexo-rably bound up with the wider struggle of young Henry and his Aquitanian allies against Richard. Similarly, it was on behalf on the viscount of Turenne that the *routiers* next attempted, but failed, to take Brive, before establishing a base at Yssandon.[74]

Still more mercenaries flocked towards Limoges from the north-east, sent by Philip Augustus to aid young Henry, his brother-in-law. Philip had begun his attempts to undermine Plantagenet lordship in Aquitaine the year previ-ously by accepting the homage of the count of Angoulême, which was claimed by Richard as duke.[75] Yet though this was a serious challenge to both Richard and Henry II, Philip did not dare to openly declare war or to send French troops. But Capetian silver paid – initially at least – for a large but heterogeneous force of *routiers*, known collectively as 'Palearii' or 'strawmen', an allusion either to their lowly status or perhaps to their rapacity, as they stripped victims of their goods down to the very straw.[76] They marked their arrival in the Limousin by sacking the town of Noblat, putting over 150 of the towns-

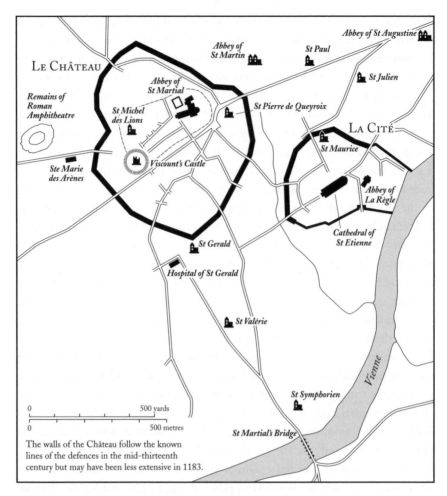

Map 9 Limoges in the late twelfth century

people to the sword, and plundering the famous pilgrimage church dedicated to St Leonard, the patron saint of prisoners.[77] Soon after, they moved into the Périgord, plundering the town and monastery of Brantôme, while other *routier* bands extended their ravages to the Périgord, Angoumois and Saintonge.[78]

It was now evident to Henry II that the situation in Aquitaine was spiralling dangerously out of control. Until the reinforcements he had summoned arrived, he was forced to wait at Aixe, but by the end of February he had summoned Alfonso of Aragon to his aid, and his own forces, raised from the feudal hosts of Normandy and Anjou, as well as from other bands of *routiers*, were assembling in strength.[79] As the *History of William Marshal* noted, Henry II quickly assembled a big army on horse and a great body of knights. They were Normans and men from Anjou, men from Flanders and from Picardy and men from Poitou, and mercenaries of many sorts (*e rotiers de maintes manieres*) and many a pennant and banner you would have seen gleaming as it fluttered in the wind. The king rode on in a great fury to meet his sons in Limoges. There were so many tents, pavilions and marquees, that no man could give an account of them, for the King did things there on a very grand scale.[80]

The king began his siege of the rebel forces in the Château of Limoges on Shrove Tuesday, 1 March. He had the fine stone bridge over the Vienne cleared of any buildings that would obstruct the constant flow of supplies necessary to maintain this great host. Henry took up residence in the Cité, while Richard encamped with his troops in the suburb of St Valéry, between the Château and the river.[81]

Meanwhile, the Young King continued to act as an intermediary between the rebel lords and Henry II. He told his father that if he could not persuade them to seek peace at Henry II's feet, he would abandon the Aquitanian lords. Won over by his son's assurances, the Old King accordingly renewed the terms he had previously offered them. Yet when young Henry carried this news back to Geoffrey and the nobles in the rebel camp, he appeared to meet with no success in persuading them to submit. Denouncing the allies as disobedient rebels, the Young King returned to his father, promising to serve him faithfully.[82] Soon afterwards, however, Geoffrey led a force of Brabançons out of Limoges in a campaign of devastation, burning lands, laying waste towns and villages, plundering churches, and slaying indiscriminately.[83] The hostile Roger of Howden believed the Young King to be complicit in these actions, but it was Geoffrey who increasingly appears as the driving force of the rebels' military actions in the spring of 1183. Indeed, Gerald of Wales regarded him as 'the moving spirit of the whole evil venture', using his smooth tongue to corrupt and deceive, while the *senhal* 'Rassa' given to him by Bertran de Born may derive from the Occitan noun *rassa*, meaning to plot or intrigue.[84] Given the markedly hesitant and indecisive nature of young Henry's own actions during these critical months – at least as they can be glimpsed from Howden's partisan account – Geoffrey may well have been the prime mover in the Young King's attempt to wrest Aquitaine from Richard. It is likely that the Young King had promised to grant him the county of Nantes and the honour of Richmond to gain his support in 1182–83.[85] Yet Geoffrey seems to have had grander ambitions, and sought to exploit the war between his two elder brothers to realize them. Bertran de Born, disillusioned by the Young King's lack of decisive action, regarded the count as the best of Henry's sons, declaring, 'I wish Count

Geoffrey ... were the firstborn, for he is courtly (*es cortes*), and I wish the kingdom and duchy were in his command'.[86] Geoffrey doubtless welcomed such sentiments, but for the present he saw in Richard's disinheritance the opportunity for a partition of the Angevin lands along new lines.[87] If young Henry was established as duke of Aquitaine as well as future king of England and duke of Normandy, might he not cede Poitou or perhaps even Anjou to Geoffrey, to be held of him after their father's death?[88]

On hearing of Geoffrey's raiding, the Young King disavowed these actions, claiming that whatever his part had been in the undertakings, it had been at Geoffrey's counsel. He voluntarily surrendered his horse and arms as a symbol of his submission, and stayed with his father for a number of days.[89] Howden regarded such actions as wholly disingenuous, claiming that the Young King had been intent on treachery from the start.[90] This is not, however, how things appeared to Bertran de Born, who, incensed by young Henry's apparent abandonment of the league, composed a biting *sirventes*:

> I have heard a great story about the Young King, who has dropped his claim
> on his brother Richard, because his father told him to. He says he was
> driven to it! Since Sir Henry neither holds nor governs lands, let him be
> King of the Fools (*reis del malvatz*)![91]

He goes on to pour scorn on the Young King's dependent status as shameful and contemptible, for in such a condition he can never achieve great deeds. The Young King

> acts like a fool, living this way entirely on an allowance, by count and by
> measure. A crowned king who takes victuals from another scarcely resem-
> bles Arnaut, the marquis of Bellande, or brave William who stormed the
> tower at Mirmanda. How high he was praised! Since in Poitou Sir Henry
> lies to his men and cheats them, he will never be loved there as much. Never
> by dozing will he be king of the Cumberland English, or conquer Ireland,
> or hold Angers or Montsoreau or Candes, or the watchtower of Poitiers, or
> be duke of Normandy or count palatine (*coms palatz*) either of Bordeaux or
> of the Gascons beyond the Landes, or lord of Bazas.[92]

Here Bertran compares young Henry unfavourably not only with the deeds of two legendary heroes of the *chansons*, William of Orange and his grandfather Arnaut de Beaulande, but also with those of his own father, King Henry, whose vigour has forged a great empire. While his brother Richard was busy laying siege to his wayward vassals and destroying their land and castles, jibed Bertran, the Young King 'will be up there tourneying' in northern France. Such passivity, warns the troubadour, has so weakened young Henry's position that Richard no longer has any need to 'flatter his men for fear they might turn to his brother'.[93]

Whether or not he was moved by such taunts, the Young King now renewed his oath to his allies. Telling his father that he could not bear to see the harm Henry II was inflicting on his men in Limoges, he left for Le Dorat before returning to the Château at Limoges.[94] Entering the abbey of St Martial, he made a highly dramatic gesture: on the relics of the saint, he vowed that he would take the cross. On hearing this news, Henry II was deeply troubled, uncertain whether young Henry had done so out of devotion or more out of rancour towards him because of his landless state. Father and son met, and in a highly emotional scene, young Henry insisted that he had taken the cross to absolve himself of the sins which he had committed against Henry II, and that unless his father desisted from his attempts to prevent him, he would take his own life. He revealed that he had taken the cross some time earlier, but had not wished to make this known until he stood better in his father's grace and might gain his permission for his pilgrimage.[95] Writing with the benefit of hindsight of the ensuing denouement, those in the Old King's entourage such as Roger of Howden and Walter Map regarded such drama as part of a cynical sham, intended to dupe his father. Walter Map, with Henry II at Limoges, recorded how 'again and again, as I witnessed myself, he was perjured to his father: repeatedly he set snares in his way, and when foiled returned to him, ever the more prone to crime the more clearly he saw that it was impossible not to forgive him'.[96]

Rather than studied duplicity, however, it is more likely that young Henry's conduct reflected his own troubled state of mind.[97] He was increasingly aware that control of events, never secure, was slipping further from his grasp. His quarrel had been with Richard alone and, despite the allegations of attempted parricide flung at him by his father's courtiers, young Henry seems to have genuinely wished no harm to his father. Yet now Henry II had sided with Richard, and appeared implacable against the rebellious nobles of Aquitaine, who had looked to young Henry as their liberator. Having pledged his aid, he could not in all conscience abandon them, yet in supporting their cause he was being drawn inexorably into conflict with his father, something he wished to avoid. He may well have seen taking the cross as the only way out of an increasingly impossible conflict of loyalties that had plunged him into emotional turmoil. Henry II's reaction bears out such an interpretation. Unlike in 1182, when he had suspected the Young King's wish to take the cross as being merely a means of political leverage, King Henry was now convinced of his son's sincerity. He may reluctantly have realized, moreover, that young Henry's absence in the Holy Land might help defuse the serious political dissensions within his lands that had been brought to a head by the animosity between his sons. The Old King not only consented to the Young King's request but promised to equip him with a retinue and supplies that would make his expedition to Jerusalem the grandest yet seen.[98]

Effusive in his thanks to his father, young Henry asked that he treat the men in the Château and the nobles of Aquitaine mercifully. Henry II agreed to his son's petition, whereupon the Young King led a number of the burgesses to his father, and joined them on his knees to implore forgiveness for them. This was granted, on condition that a small number of hostages would be given. This settlement promised to mark an end to the fraught stand-off at Limoges. Yet Roger of Howden claimed that when Henry II's envoys went to collect these hostages they were set upon, barely escaping with their lives, while shortly afterwards, members of another delegation bringing a truce at the request of the Young King were killed in young Henry's very presence.[99] A few days later, so Howden alleged, it was Geoffrey's turn to preside over another outrage when two members of Henry II's household, bearing another truce at the count of Brittany's request, were attacked; Ger de Musterol was wounded by a sword blow, while Oliver FitzErnis was thrown from the bridge into the Vienne.[100] But Roger was not with King Henry II at Limoges during these events, and his reportage is impressionistic and imprecise.[101] He evidently received information from members of the Old King's household, but his account reads like a series of hearsay allegations of treachery stemming from the court but lacking accurate chronology and any sense of their wider political context or knowledge of the situation among the defenders of the Château. If such attacks did occur in the manner Howden alleges, how far was young Henry responsible? He may have found himself unable to control the forces within the Château: it is quite possible that Count Geoffrey, or those Aquitanian lords implacably opposed to Henry II, were attempting to wreck any peace settlement by such actions and drive a wedge between the Young King and his father in order to fan the flames of the rebellion anew. The deficiencies of the sources make it impossible to know. It seems, however, that these events marked a critical turning point in the relations between Henry II and his son. Young Henry now unequivocally threw in his lot with the defenders of Limoges, while Henry II recommenced the siege in earnest. Father and son would never meet again.

Within the Château, the besieged inhabitants sought to augment their defences by invoking divine protection. In the Young King's presence, the clergy led a procession around the inside of the walls, bearing the relics of the saints, including those of St Martial and St Austriclinianus, praying to God to deliver them. The womenfolk tied a thread of tow round the whole circumference of the walls, then cut this up to make wicks for many candles,

which they offered up at the abbey of St Martial and other churches.[102]
Incessant rain and bitter cold, however, began to sap morale: many lords who
had come to the Young King's aid departed for home, and in vain he reminded
them of the fealty they had sworn to him.[103] As the siege intensified, moreover,
tensions began to surface within the Young King's own household. Such at
least was the belief of the *History of William Marshal*, which tells how the Young
King's anonymous 'seneschal', one of the ringleaders in the earlier attempt to
discredit the Marshal, now protested that, as he was Henry II's liege man, he
dare not remain and asked for leave to join King Henry. The younger Henry
was, claims the *History*, so angry at this betrayal that he snatched up the sword
by his bedside and would have attacked him, had not Geoffrey of Brittany
physically held him back. Instead, on Geoffrey's advice, the seneschal was ignominiously banished, while the Young King's chamberlain, Ralph FitzGodfrey,
was sent to recall the Marshal to his service.[104] The author of the *History*,
however, was less concerned with the facts than with presenting a morality tale:
those who had falsely denounced the Marshal as as a traitor showed the reality
of their base and cowardly nature by deserting their lord the Young King in his
hour of great need, while young Henry, realizing he had been deceived, turned
in this crisis to the one man he now knew he could rely on, the Marshal.

Young Henry's *routiers*, by contrast, stayed loyal as long as he had the money
to pay them. But his funds were now close to exhaustion. To keep his own
forces in the field, Henry II had his war chests regularly replenished from
England; treasure had been shipped from Southampton to Normandy at
Easter and Whitsun.[105] By contrast, the Young King had no such resources on
which to draw. As Geoffrey of Vigeois remarked, the Young King had been not
so much generous as prodigal with his daily allowance of 1,500 shillings, but
once he had leagued against Richard, his father had cut off this subsidy.[106] Now
he asked the burgesses of the Château for a loan of 2,000 shillings, but this was
soon consumed in supplies and wages for the Palearii, Count Ademar's
Brabançons, Basques and other groups.[107] Fearful lest these bands desert to his
father for the promise of greater pay, young Henry had been ruinously generous
to them. In a desperate search for money, he turned to the greatest source of
wealth in Limoges – the abbey of St Martial itself. By the 1180s, this was
among the richest and most powerful abbeys in Aquitaine, with many
dependent priories in southern France. The wealth brought by the stream of
pilgrims to the tombs of St Martial and of St Valérie had allowed the monks
to build on a grand scale; the infirmary buildings constructed under Abbot
Isembard (1174–98) alone were likened to a royal palace.[108] But as a strong
supporter of Duke Richard and Henry II, Isembard had been forced to flee
Limoges, and the monks were leaderless. They watched helplessly as the Young

King's men entered the cloisters and expelled the younger monks, who might be most capable of any resistance. The pleas of the remaining brothers were of no avail and on the following day they bowed to the inevitable, handing over many of the church's most precious religious artefacts as a 'loan'. These included richly worked golden altar tables and their frontals, adorned with figures, a golden chalice, an exquisitely worked silver vase, two great crosses, one of which alone was made of fifty marks of gold, as well as 103 marks of silver, and even the reliquary casket of St Austriclinianus.[109] All of this was assessed at a value of 22,000 shillings, and the Young King solemnly gave the monks a charter in the form of a chirograph, validated with his seal, promising to repay this sum. But, noted Geoffrey of Vigeois bitterly, these treasures were worth far more, and no account was taken of the value of the goldsmithing or the gold used to gild the silverware.[110] Worse still, he lamented, these sacred objects, reflecting the pious donations of many, were to be given to the sacrilegious *routiers*, the very men whom the Lateran Council had condemned as godless heretics.[111]

Young Henry realized that he needed to make better strategic use of such ruinously expensive troops than merely garrisoning the Château of Limoges. His Taillefer allies had urgent need of his support against a vigorous counterattack by Richard, for while Henry II had pressed the siege of Limoges, the count of Poitou had taken the offensive and in a lightning campaign had recovered control of the Angoumois and the Saintonge, even raiding into Brittany in reprisal against Geoffrey.[112] Accordingly, the Young King led his *routiers* out of Limoges south-west to reinforce Angoulême, and celebrated Easter there on 17 April. In Aquitaine, the allies were on the back foot, but the shock waves of the war were now threatening to destabilize other parts of Henry II's domains. The Old King himself had celebrated Easter at Limoges, but shortly before this he had given orders to his officials in England and his continental lands to seize and imprison all those who had been his enemies in the war of 1173–74.[113] He clearly feared that the Young King or his supporters would attempt to revive the fires of rebellion. Among those to suffer arbitrary arrest were Robert, earl of Leicester, and his countess, Petronilla. His lands were taken into royal control, chattels were sold and the sheriff took the earl's third penny for the Exchequer.[114] King Henry's suspicions may not have been groundless: the king's justices heavily fined a number of burgesses of Northampton for sending to Leicester for hauberks and for communicating with the king's enemies, which perhaps suggests a plan to seize this vital royal base in the Midlands.[115] Howden notes that many of the most powerful and wealthy lords in England were also seized, including William, earl of Gloucester.[116] Repairs were made both to key fortresses such as Northampton, reflecting Henry II's fear of fresh insurrection in the former rebel heartlands in the Midlands, but also to coastal strongholds such as Dover, Colchester and 'New Hastings', to guard against possible invasion from Flanders.[117] Henry II's anxiety that the war would spread from Aquitaine to his northern lands receives support from Bertran de Born, who eagerly anticipated hostilities in the Vexin and Normandy, and the direct involvement of the count of Flanders and the king of France in the developing struggle: 'It started in the Limousin, but it will end somewhere else. Between the Île-de-France and Normandy, towards Gisors and Neufmarché, I hope they'll hear shouts of "Arras!" and "Montjoie!" and "Dieu Aie!"'[118] A further troubling echo of the events of 1173 came when the Young King again challenged the episcopal election of one of Henry II's trusted clerical servants, this time that of Walter of Coutances to the see of Lincoln. Despite the unanimous consent of the chapter to Walter's elevation, young Henry protested that Walter had not been elected with his consent, and so forbade his consecration and appealed to the pope.[119]

Despite Richard's military successes, moreover, Henry II's position in the Limousin was weakening. His army had now been besieging Limoges for over a month and a half, but with little effect. As the war of 1173–74 had so graphically shown, major towns presented attackers with a formidable challenge. Though the urban fortifications of the Château at Limoges were makeshift, it was defended in strength, and the Young King's ability to lead his army out to reinforce Angoulême indicates that Henry II's forces had been unable to establish an effective cordon around it. Yet in the circumstances of rebellion, sustaining a major siege presented a king with more than simply tactical, logistical and financial problems: the drawn-out nature of such an investment allowed ample opportunities for fifth-column elements within his own forces secretly to assist the besieged, either by allowing in reinforcements and supplies, or by keeping the enemy informed of his dispositions and intentions. With so many nobles brought together in the siege camp from all parts of his realm, there was a very real danger that disaffection, even treason, might spread rapidly among his erstwhile supporters. Indeed, it was now Henry II's turn to suffer widespread desertion. Walter Map, an eyewitness to the siege, complained bitterly how young Henry had

> stirred up all Aquitaine and Burgundy, and many of the French, against our lord his father, and all them of Maine, Anjou and the Bretons; and of those who were fighting on our side the more part fell away to him. They of Maine and Anjou indeed, when we were besieging Limoges, set at naught our tears and entreaties and openly deserted us and set off for home, forcing us to disband our army because so few were left.[120]

Bertran de Born more gleefully recorded the desertion of the Angevin levies: 'This game I consider won for our side and begun again. We've cleared the board of the pawns of La Vallée; without taking leave – none of them did – all of them ran away scared.'[121] Infantry were a vital component of Anglo-Norman and Angevin armies, especially for siege warfare. Yet among those serving out of customary obligation rather than as stipendiaries, desertion was common, and it was notoriously diffficult to keep such troops in the field beyond their stipulated period of service.[122] Map, however, suggests a collapse of loyalty beyond such considerations: the fidelity of the Manceaux to Henry II in 1173–74 had at best been equivocal, and, as events would soon show, they regarded the Young King with far greater affection. It is probably to this time that we can date Peter of Blois' reproach to Ralph, bishop of Angers, regarding the treachery of the Angevin people and the army of Anjou which had deserted the king.[123] The combination of dwindling numbers, the threat of an attack on Normandy by Philip Augustus or Count Philip of Flanders, and the need to show his presence in the Angevin heartlands forced Henry II to lift the siege of Limoges and return north.[124]

His father's retreat gave the Young King the opportunity to return to Limoges, where he attempted to take the Cité. The citizens, however, refused to submit and drove him off.[125] He had greater success at Aixe, which he took on 23 May: a ruse had reduced the garrison of the keep to only two knights and twelve serjeants, who now surrendered the castle. Having thus gained control of the left bank of the Vienne, young Henry swung his forces north-east of Limoges to the nearby abbey of Grandmont. Only the year before, Count Geoffrey, together with his father, had been entertained by the monks in their refectory, a singular honour.[126] Nonetheless, its treasures now met the same fate as those of the abbey of St Martial. Geoffrey of Vigeois was particularly appalled that a golden dove to hold the Eucharist, which had been given by Henry II himself to this, his most favoured foundation, was not spared.[127] During his earlier stay in Angoulême, the Young King had also seized the moveable wealth of the rich Benedictine abbey of La Couronne, which lay a short distance to the south-west, and in the Limousin had similarly extorted valuables from the monasteries of Dalon and Beaulieu.[128] The commandeering of church wealth in times of war was far from unprecedented, and these religious houses in all probability received pledges of repayment from the Young King similar to those given to the monks of St Martial.[129] Yet to expropriate ecclesiastical treasures on such a scale was rare, and to do so to fund troops that were seen as the particular enemies of the Church shocked ecclesiastics. Clerical writers regarded such a violation as a grievous sin, and the outrage which coloured their description of the Young King's last campaign contributed much to the negative image of him which they bequeathed to posterity.

Seen with hindsight, following his untimely death and the subsequent collapse of the rebellion in Aquitaine, the stripping of these great abbeys of the Angoumois and Limousin has often been regarded as the last desperate move by the Young King in a rapidly failing campaign. In reality, however, it seems likely that he was raising funds for a major new phase of operations. For from Grandmont he led his army south, reaching Uzerche on 26 May, where a rendezvous had been scheduled with reinforcements brought by Count Raymond of Toulouse, Raymond II, viscount of Turenne, and Odo, eldest son of Duke Hugh of Burgundy.[130] While Raymond of Turenne seems to have been a member of the original coalition against Richard, the involvement of the counts of Toulouse and Burgundy represented a very significant escalation in the scope of the war. Count Raymond V, who had become young Henry's vassal in 1173, was the duke of Aquitaine's greatest rival in the region, and the alliance of his opponent Alfonso II of Aragon with Henry II and Richard gave him still greater reason to side with the Young King. Burgundy was a staunch supporter of the Capetians, and Bertran de Born had eagerly expected his aid: 'The duke of Burgundy has sent word that he'll help us in summer, with the aid of Champagne. Some five hundred armed men will come, so when we are all joined, Poitiers [i.e. Richard] will be sure to complain.'[131] Born also implies that in Gascony those sympathetic to or actually in league with the Young King included Gaston VI, viscount of Béarn, and Vezian II, viscount of Lomagnac, as well as Bernard IV, viscount of Armagnac, and the viscounts of Dax and Marsan.[132] It seemed, as Walter Map put it, that 'all the power of the world was flocking to Absalom'.[133] It was also at this time that William Marshal rejoined the Young King's service. The *History* claimed that he had obtained letters of protection from King Philip, the archbishop of Rheims and the counts Robert of Dreux and Theobald of Blois, and that on the strength of these, Henry II allowed him safe conduct to join his son in the Château of Limoges.[134] As he was accompanied by Hugh de Hamelincourt and the notable Flemish lord Baldwin de Béthune, and as William, castellan of St Omer, is known to have been with the Young King at this time, it seems more likely that the Marshal had come as part of a force of Flemish knights to young Henry's summons for stipendiary knights.[135]

On the very day the reinforcements joined the Young King at Uzerche, a very different kind of assembly took place in Normandy at the great abbey of St Etienne in Caen. So serious and protracted had the hostilities in Aquitaine become that, on Henry II's orders, Richard, archbishop of Canterbury, together with the bishops of Bayeux, Evreux, Lisieux, Sées and Rochester, with many of the abbots of Normandy, solemnly and publicly pronounced excommunication against anyone who attempted to stand in the way of peace or who sowed discord between King Henry and his sons, though the sons themselves were excepted from such anathema.[136] Archbishop Richard himself wrote to the Young King, urging him to make peace with his father, reminding him of a range of biblical and classical examples of both loyal and rebellious sons but adding that 'concerning Absalom I shall remain silent, for his story is known to all'. Richard rebuked young Henry for becoming a leader of Brabançons, 'people excommunicate and utterly lost', and for despoiling churches, warning that if he did not cease hostilities against his father, then he would with reluctance be forced to excommunicate him.[137] The action of the clergy at Caen was a dramatic gesture, informed by the strictures of the 1179 Lateran Council, but one that reflected a sense of desperation on Henry II's part. More tangibly, he summoned aid from his ally, Alfonso of Aragon.[138]

It was at Uzerche, however, that young Henry began to feel the first signs of a sickness that rapidly became increasingly severe. He moved via Donzenac on 27 May to the small fortified town of Martel on the 28th, where Viscount Raymond put on a horse race 'to delight the common people'.[139] Here, young Henry recovered sufficiently to ride due south to the great pilgrimage church of Rocamadour, the famous the shrine to the Virgin. Henry II had travelled there in 1170 when recovering from his near-fatal illness, and it seems most likely that young Henry similarly came as a pilgrim, seeking healing from his growing sickness.[140] Yet the chroniclers naturally saw a more impious purpose when his men stripped the gold, silver and gems off the feretory of St Amator and took away the treasures in the church.[141]

The allies' intention appears to have been to march north against Henry II, who had now returned to the Limousin. Roger of Howden believed that, misled by evil counsel, the Young King was bent on joining battle with his father around 6 June. On learning of his intentions, the Old King had been greatly disturbed, for he had few forces with him, and was uncertain of the loyalty of some of his nobles. He was faced with the choice of trying to escape capture by his son by flight, to his everlasting shame and opprobrium, or risking the doubtful outcome of battle.[142] Roger's account, occurring as it does in a speech given by him to Henry II immediately on hearing of the Young King's death, must be treated with caution, and it seems highly improbable that young Henry was actively seeking a pitched battle with his father. But if the newly reinforced allied army was indeed significantly stronger than the forces assembled by Henry II at Limoges, a bold strike to force the Old King to again withdraw from the Limousin made good strategic sense. Yet as he returned north from Rocamadour, the Young King was struck once more by his illness.

Howden believed this was 'in consequence of indignation and rancour of mind' because he 'could not do any material injury to the king, his father'.[143] He had, in fact, contracted dysentery and was 'attacked first by a fever, then by a flux of the bowels, which reduced him to the point of death'.[144] He was forced to remain at Martel, where he lay ill in the house of Stephen, 'surnamed the Smith'.[145] The Young King's life, and the success of the allies' war in Aquitaine, alike hung in the balance.

CHAPTER 14

Vir Sanctus

DEATH, COMMEMORATION AND LEGACY

In mercy's name I pray to my companion, if ever I wronged him may he forgive it; and may he pray to the Lord Jesus on His throne, both in Romance and in what Latin he knows.

I have lived my life in prowess and joy, but now we both part company, and away I shall go to Him in Whom all sinners find their end ...

All have I quit that I used to love, chivalry and noble pride; and since it pleases God, all this I accept, and pray to him to keep me by His side.

All my friends I pray, at my death, to come and do me great honour, for I have known joy and delight both far and near, and within my own bounds.

Thus I quit joy and delight, rich clothes and precious sable.
              – William IX, duke of Aquitaine, *Pos de chanter m'es pres talentz*[1]

AS HIS SYMPTOMS grew worse, it was evident that Henry would not recover.[2] He sent to his father, begging him to come to him, but after the events of the past months, Henry II could no longer bring himself to trust his son. Fearing a trap, he refused.[3] He did, however, send Bishop Bernard of Agen and Rotrou, count of Perche, to the Young King bearing a letter and a precious sapphire ring as a token of his pardon.[4] Young Henry in turn sent his father letters in which he begged his forgiveness, and implored him to take pity on both his mother, Queen Eleanor, and on his wife, Queen Margaret.[5] Conscious of his duty as a good lord, he also looked to the well-being of his own men: he besought the Old King to provide for his knights and servants, to whom he had promised much but now, because of his imminent death, was unable to reward.[6] Fearing that they, as well as the dissident nobles who had recently been his allies, would be exposed to Henry II's vengeance, he implored the king his father to set aside his *ira et malevolentia* towards his knights and other retainers and to treat the barons of Poitou mercifully.[7]

In these last letters, young Henry also asked his father to make reparation on his behalf for whatever he had despoiled from the Church. Ecclesiastical writers were naturally swift to see in his illness and untimely death God's punishment for his rebellion and recent acts of sacrilege.[8] As Walter Map grimly punned, 'he took an oath against his father at Martel, and on that same day smitten with the hammer (*martellus*) of death by the all-righteous avenging hand, he was not, and riot was turned to quiet'.[9] Young Henry is likely to have seen the tympanum above the west door of the church in Martel itself, which depicts Christ as judge, stern and unbending, with hands outstretched to reveal the wounds of the cross. He is flanked by two angels holding instruments of the passion, while with their trumpets two other angels summon the dead from their tombs to face the Last Judgment.[10] Fears of such a judgment and the fate of the damned must have deeply troubled the Young King, for his conscience was heavy. In violation of repeated oaths of fidelity, he had rebelled against his father and lord; he had stirred up mortal war against his brother; and he had stripped the shrines of some of the holiest places in Aquitaine. Accordingly, Henry now subjected himself to a harsh penance. In what the *History of William Marshal* called 'his seemly act of repentance (*sa bone repentance*)', he confessed his sins to the clergy who were in attendance, including Bishop Bernard, first in private, then publicly, as was required of penitents.[11] The leading bishops then granted him absolution and remission of his sins.[12] Even the hostile Geoffrey of Vigeois was moved by young Henry's fulsome contrition.[13] Roger of Howden, who clearly had access to an eyewitness account of the Young King's last days, records how young Henry then put off his princely finery and assumed the garb of a penitent:

> After this, laying aside his fine garments, he put on a hairshirt, and fastening a noose around his neck, said to the bishops and other religious men who stood around him, 'By this halter I deliver myself, an unworthy, guilty and culpable sinner, to you, the ministers of God, beseeching that our Lord Jesus Christ, who remitted his sins to the thief when confessing upon the cross, will, through your prayers and his ineffable mercy, have compassion upon my most wretched soul.' To which all made answer, 'Amen.'[14]

Henry then ordered his men to drag him from his bed by the rope around his neck, symbolizing his status as a traitor and felon to God, to another bed strewn with ashes, and to place under his head and feet 'two large square stones' instead of pillows.[15] Such 'exaggerated, almost extravagant humility' did not stand in isolation.[16] In 1039, on the last of his four pilgrimages to Jerusalem, his great Angevin forebear, Fulk Nerra, was said to have ordered his men to drag him round the Holy City with a halter around his neck while a servant scourged his naked back and the count cried to heaven for mercy.[17] Similarly, Abbot Suger of St Denis reported how, when in 1138 Louis VI knew himself to be dying, he made his confession, then 'ordered that a carpet be spread on the ground and ashes be shaped on the carpet in the form of a cross', on which he was then laid.[18] Though young Henry was urged by one of the clergy to give away the ring sent by his father, lest possession of any earthly goods impede his salvation, he vehemently refused, insisting on keeping this token of his father's forgiveness and benediction which he could show at the Last Judgment.[19]

The Young King then commanded his testament, 'a will well and wisely made', to be read.[20] Though this has not survived, he must have relied on his father to disburse the sums he allocated, as he himself was now without either money or land to fulfil any bequests. His unfulfilled crusading vow weighed heavily on his mind. He entrusted the cloth cross which he had received on becoming a *crucesignatus* to his old friend and tutor in arms, William Marshal, begging him to fulfil this pilgrimage to Jerusalem in his stead.[21] 'Marshal, Marshal,' the *History* has the Young King declare, 'you have ever been loyal to me, a staunch supporter in good faith. I leave you my cross, so that on my behalf you can take it to the Holy Sepulchre and with it pay my debts to God.' The Marshal thanked Henry for giving him the honour of performing this task, and assured his lord that 'I shall certainly do it gladly, for that man is no loyal friend who is found wanting in help in a moment of great need.'[22] His presence at young Henry's deathbed and his acceptance of the proxy pilgrimage made a fitting gesture of reconciliation between the two men who had forged such a close bond in life. It was for good reason that Geoffrey of Vigeois could refer to the Marshal as one very dear to the Young King – his *carissimus*.[23]

The king commanded that his eyes, brain and intestines were to be buried before the shrine of St Martial at Limoges, as a token of reverence and contrition.[24] His body, however, was to be buried at Rouen, in the cathedral of St Mary, next to the tomb of his uncle, William FitzEmpress.[25] Such a division of the body was a common practice among royalty and the nobility: its practical function was to remove the organs which would decay the quickest if the corpse itself needed to be transported any distance, but it also allowed the continued presence in death of the individual at more than one site within his lands.[26] Bishop Bernard and many others, mindful of how long and difficult the journey from Martel to Rouen would be, urged him to be buried instead at Grandmont, which was considerably closer, and was already a foundation greatly favoured by Henry II. Henry, however, remained adamant in his choice of Rouen.[27]

Racked with fever, the Young King now became delirious: according to the subsequent testimony of his chaplain Thomas of Earley, he saw a vision of the saints Eustace and Thomas Becket standing before him, and took comfort that Thomas, his old *nutricius*, had come to safeguard his soul as he passed from this life.[28] 'His face grew pale,' noted the *History of William Marshal*, 'and that fresh and youthful complexion, so fair and pleasant to behold, became sallow, wan and livid.'[29] Finally, the end came, and 'being fortified with the viaticum of the holy body and blood of our Lord, in the fear of the Lord, he breathed forth his spirit'.[30] The messenger sent by his father to tell the Young King that Henry II would, as requested, pay whatever his son had promised, arrived too late.[31] 'King Henry the Third, son of King Henry, son of the Empress Matilda, daughter of King Henry I', as Howden calls him, died on 11 June, on the feast of St Barnabas the Apostle.[32] He was 'in the flower of his youth, having lived twenty eight years, fourteen weeks and six days', noted Ralph of Diss, adding regretfully that he had died 'among very barbarous peoples'.[33]

The day after his death, the Young King's body began its long journey north to Normandy, the bier being borne on the shoulders of his 'fellow knights (*commilitones*)'. As they passed by the villages, castles and towns on the route, the people hurried to watch.[34] They proceeded via Brive to the monastery of Vigeois, where Prior Geoffrey and a group of monks and laymen observed the procession's passing, then on to Uzerche, where Abbot Bernard provided candles for the obsequies. Geoffrey, keen to draw a contrast with the riches the young Henry had impiously taken from St Martial's and other monasteries just days before, stressed the poverty of the Young King's household: a collection for Masses raised only twelve pence, which were promptly seized by one of the Young King's chaplains, while his retainers were reduced to selling the king's fine horse to buy supplies. Such was their need that the monks gave food to the famished retinue.[35] Yet given that Viscount Aimar, Geoffey de Lusignan and other knights soon arrived to grieve for the Young King, it is unlikely that they left his *mesnie* in so abject a state as Prior Geoffrey wished to convey. The presence of clergy and loyal men, moreover, including William Marshal, meant that at least the younger Henry was spared the indignity that would befall Henry II in 1189, when his corpse was plundered of jewellery and clothes by his servants, and deserted with indecent haste by those seeking to ingratiate themselves with the new political order.[36]

From Uzerche, the cortège skirted the east of Limoges, still closely besieged by the forces of Henry II and Richard, and came to the monastery of Grandmont. Here, three days after his death, more elaborate obsequies were carried out by the monks and higher clergy, including John, bishop of Nevers, Theobald, abbot of Cluny, Sailbrand, priest of Limoges, and Bertrand, bishop of Agen. The solemnities, however, were threatened by the bishop of Limoges, who denounced the deceased king as an excommunicate. He was finally pacified by William, the prior of Grandmont, who offered sureties that Henry II would restore any treasure taken from St Martial's and other churches by the Young King.[37] It was here that his body was prepared for its journey further north and its eventual burial. Perhaps because of the dangers of the ongoing siege of Limoges, his viscera, brain and eyes were interred at Grandmont, rather than at St Martial's as he had requested, while the young Henry's corpse was embalmed with aromatic spices, or more functionally, according to Howden, with large quantities of salt.[38] It was then wrapped in a white linen cloth, consecrated with the holy oil used at his coronation, covered with a bull's hide, and sealed in lead, while a rich cloth of green sendal was placed over it.[39]

Henry II did not attend these rites at Grandmont, even though it was but a few miles away from Limoges, where he continued his siege. The dire news of his son's death had been brought to him by a monk of Grandmont, Bernard de Reynat, who had found the king taking shelter from the summer heat in a peasant's hut as the army lay encamped around the city.[40] According to Howden, Henry had been incredulous on hearing the first tidings of his son's death, until it was confirmed by the arrival of other messengers. Ordering his men to leave him, the Old King was overwhelmed by paroxysms of grief.[41] Despite the periods of tension between them, the sources leave little doubt that Henry II loved his son deeply, and that his death was, as the *History* noted, 'a bitter shock'.[42] His grief was such that Peter of Blois felt compelled to compose a letter of consolation to the king, replete with biblical citations, urging him to moderate his sorrow and assuring him that young Henry's deep contrition and pious death would spare him from divine punishment.[43] Nevertheless, in this time of crisis, Henry II realized it was imperative not to show weakness: withholding his emotions from his forces, he immediately sent word to Richard, who was besieging Aixe, and ordered the siege of Limoges to be pressed home with greater vigour.[44] Repeated attacks finally wore down the defenders, weakened by hunger and demoralized by the realization that the chance of the rising's success had died with the Young King. Finally, on 24 June, Viscount Aimar and the men of the Château surrendered the castle and all the defences to Henry II. The king thereupon completely demolished the fortifications, not leaving one stone upon another, and likewise ordered the destruction of other rebel castles.[45]

Resistance was crushed elsewhere in the Limousin. Aided by Alfonso of Aragon, Richard laid siege to Hautefort on 30 June, and on 6 July he took it by storm, having routed the forces of Raymond of Toulouse in a memorable engagement.[46] Bertran de Born, who complained bitterly that his erstwhile allies had made peace without including him, was forgiven by Richard, who gave him the kiss of peace, but Hautefort was taken from him and restored to his brother Constantine.[47] The roving bands of *routiers* who had been at the centre of the hostilities now found themselves under attack not by the royal or ducal forces but by members of a sworn peace league, known as the Capuchins after the distinctive white hood bearing an image of the Virgin worn by its members. Founded by Durand, a carpenter of Le Puy in the Auvergne who had been inspired by a vision of the Virgin, this armed confraternity quickly gained ecclesiastical backing in its attempts to rid the region of the scourge of the hated mercenaries. Not long after the Young King's death they achieved the first of a number of military successes against bands of *routiers*, but, alarmed by the growing power of the peace league, the local nobility finally rounded on the Capuchins and in turn slaughtered them without mercy.[48]

Count Geoffrey submitted to his father at Angers, probably in July, swore fidelity to him, and was compelled to surrender all his castles in Brittany.[49] But Henry II's desire to reassert direct control in all his domains was also indicated by the fact that, despite his successes, Richard too was commanded by his father to yield into his keeping all the castles with which he had been entrusted as duke prior to the outbreak of the war.[50] With the Young King's death, the turmoil in Aquitaine finally died down: referring to the mythical serpent of Delphi slain by Apollo, Walter Map noted that 'riot was turned to quiet, and so the world was at rest when Python perished'.[51] Likewise Ralph of Diss noted that the Young King's life 'was cut short, as if by a weaver, and with it the hopes of many fighting for him and hoping to rule with him after his father's death'.[52] Among those who, deprived of the Young King's protection, were forced to seek Henry II's peace was Bertran de Born. According to the fictionalized *razos* explaining the context of Bertran's poems, the king ironically demanded of him, 'You were wont to boast of possessing more wits than you ever needed to use – what has become of them now?' To which Bertran replied, 'Sire, on the day that the valiant Young King your son died, I lost my knowledge, my wits and my skill.' Dissolving into tears, Henry II forgave Bertran and restored Hautefort to him.[53] Imaginary though such a story may be, it echoes that related in the *History of William Marshal*, which recounts how, on the Young King's demise, William had immediately been seized by the *routier* captain Sancho de Savennac as a pledge for 100 marks owed to him by the late king. Unable to pay such a sum out of his own purse, the Marshal deftly convinced Sancho that Henry II would settle his debt. When confronted with this pledge, Henry was at first indignant, but finally agreed to pay the 100 marks to Sancho: '"My son has cost me much more than that",' the *History* has him say, '"and would that he were still costing me!" His eyes filled with tears of sorrow and, for a brief moment, he looked like giving way to it.'[54]

He subsequently gave the Marshal 100 *livres angevins* towards the costs of his pilgrimage to fulfil young Henry's vow, though considering the expense involved in so long a journey, this was a modest sum. It is clear that the Marshal's involvement in the Young King's final rebellion had earned him Henry II's displeasure and that his two-year sojourn in the East was a timely period of political cooling off. Nevertheless, mindful of his earlier service, the Old King promised him a place in his household on his return, a pledge he subsequently honoured.[55]

Even in death, the Young King was to be a continuing source of contention. From Poitou, his funeral cortège had passed through Anjou, crossing the Loire and continuing as far as Le Mans. There, the bier was placed overnight in the choir of the great cathedral of St Julian, next to the magnificent tomb of his grandfather, Count Geoffrey V, and a vigil was kept with hymns and psalms around the body of the king.[56] The following morning, as the bearers prepared to leave for Rouen, a group of the leading citizens entered the cathedral and, to great acclamation from the populace, promptly dug a grave in the cathedral choir and interred the body with great honour, with the bishop of Le Mans presiding.[57] It was a forceful demonstration of young Henry's great popularity, of the strength of feeling between the citizens of le Mans and the Angevin comital dynasty, and of the benefits in prestige and patronage expected from the possession of the tomb of a king.[58] The actions of the Manceaux, however, caused outrage among the Rouennais, who regarded this as an intolerable insult. They demanded that the Young King's body be given up to them, even threatening to destroy the city of Le Mans, but they met with obstinate refusal. Young Henry lay for thirty-four days in St Julian's, while Henry II sought to arbitrate between the representatives of the two cities whom he had summoned before him.[59] Letters confirming that Rouen had been the place of burial expressly wished for by the Young King were sent to Pope Lucius III by a number of leading men who had been present to hear the Young King's dying wishes, including Count Raymond V of Toulouse, the duke of Burgundy, William, castellan of St Omer, and Bishop Bernard of Agen.[60] On ascertaining that it had been his son's wish to be buried in the cathedral church of St Mary in Rouen, Henry commanded that the body be exhumed and taken to the place chosen by the Young King. Archbishop Rotrou sent his nephew Robert of Neubourg, dean of Rouen cathedral, aided by the archbishop of Canterbury, to Le Mans to secure the safe release and transit of the Young King's body.[61]

Once in Rouen, he was buried 'with the honour due to a prince' in the cathedral on 22 July, in the north ambulatory of the choir, close to the high altar dedicated to the Virgin.[62] Henry was an anointed king of England, yet his choice to be buried neither at the existing royal mausolea of Reading or

Westminster, nor in Anjou, but in the capital of the duchy was a powerful reflection of the significance Normandy had come to hold for him. Beginning in earnest with his regency in 1171–72, his association with the Normans had intensified in the later 1170s and early 1180s, by which time Henry II had effectively delegated authority in the duchy to him. At St Mary's cathedral, as the Norman Robert of Torigni explained with evident pride, were laid his fore-bears, the earliest dukes of Normandy, including Rollo, founder of the duchy itself, and his son, William Longsword, as well as the Young King's beloved uncle, William FitzEmpress.[63] The contemporary tombs of Louis VII and Henry, count of Champagne, are known to have been surmounted by a life-sized effigy, but it is far from certain that the effigy of the Young King now visible in the cathedral, and heavily restored following damage in the Wars of Religion and the Revolution, is part of his original monument.[64] Around 1300, the canons of St Mary's commissioned a new series of effigies of the early dukes of Normandy buried there as part of an ambitious programme to celebrate their foundation's illustrious ducal and royal heritage, and it seems likely that the Young King's tomb was remodelled at this time with a new effigy.[65]

Thomas of Earley and the Cult of the Young King

Among those attending the Young King during his last days had been Thomas of Earley (also known as 'Agnellus' or 'de Agnellis'), who had been one of his clerks and his confessor. A canon of Wells cathedral and a kinsman of the influential Reginald, bishop of Bath, he was author of a considerable number of sermons.[66] Thomas had been appointed archdeacon of Bath and Wells by Henry II by 1168, and had been associated with young Henry as early as 1170 when he had carried a letter from Henry II to Rotrou of Rouen accepting terms of peace for Becket prior to the Young King's coronation.[67] In 1183, he was dispatched to bear the sad tidings of her son's death to Eleanor at Salisbury, her principal residence during her captivity, and it was doubtless with the queen's encouragement that not long thereafter he preached a sermon in which he proclaimed the Young King's sanctity.[68] A nascent cult had already sprung up around the Young King and healing miracles were reported at his tomb. As William of Newburgh later noted, 'even when he was dead many extraordinary things were related of him'.[69]

Nevertheless, Thomas' task was no easy one. Of all young Henry's qualities in life, piety had not been the most prominent. He had not washed the feet of paupers, as his sainted ancestor St Edward had reputedly done, and though he had confirmed grants to religious houses, he had not been in a position to endow his own monastic foundation. If he had been generous in almsgiving, it went unrecorded, unlike his expenditure on the tournament. In his later years, indeed, he had spent much of his time engaged in a sport loudly and repeatedly condemned by the Church. On his own deathbed, William Marshal was reminded of the clerical stricture that salvation would be difficult unless he gave back his winnings from the tournament – a suggestion the Marshal rejected with anger and exasperation.[70] Aware too of the charge that young Henry had despoiled several of the great churches of the Limousin and Angoumois, Thomas claimed that he had taken these treasures in a just cause to fund a war to free Aquitaine – and its churches – from tyranny. He was, however, careful never to name Richard, and treated the conflict in the most general and guarded of terms, as Eleanor's patronage doubtless demanded. Undeterred by such difficulties, Thomas chose to focus on Henry's last days as a sign that the Young King was a 'vir sanctus'.[71] He speaks of his illness as a form of martyrdom, and uses martial language to describe the Young King's battle against sickness; he 'fought on (*militavit*) for many days under such penitential discipline and wonderful devotion of contrition' that he set an example even to the men of religion who attended him.[72] 'The glory of a martyr should thus not be denied to he who ended his life by the violence of such persecution, instead of by the sword'.[73]

Thomas relates how Queen Eleanor had told him of a dream in which she had foreseen her son's death and beatitude. She saw young Henry lying, hands in prayer, with a serene visage, wearing two crowns, one with the brightness of an earthly crown, but the other far more brilliant:

> What meaning could one give to that crown, other than eternal bliss, which knows neither beginning nor end? What meaning can one see in the splendour of such intensely brilliant light, other than the glory of felicity on high? That superior crown surpassed anything that can be seen on earth by the eyes of men. Truly, 'eye hath not seen, nor the ear heard, neither have entered into the heart of man, the things which God hath prepared for them that love him'.[74]

Earley claimed, moreover, that almost immediately after the Young King's death miracles had begun, attesting to his sanctity and God's favour towards him. Drawing on Christ's healing miracles as recorded in Matthew's Gospel, an analogy that would have been readily recognized by contemporaries, he reported how the sick were healed by touching his corpse.[75] A woman suffering from a haemorrhage was cured by touching the hem of his robes, and Thomas himself claimed to have seen a man completely cured of debilitating ulcers within two days, who had showed the scars of his healed wounds to witnesses.[76]

A further potent sign of the deceased king's sanctity occurred when a leper was healed at the Young King's bier as it was being carried out of the gates of Martel. To commemorate this miracle, a church was constructed on the site in honour of the Young King, where, noted Thomas, the memory of the martyr continued to be venerated.[77] Further along the route, as those who were carrying the bier were hastening to reach the monastery of St Savin before nightfall, a long shaft of very bright light appeared from the heavens, and for more than a hour illuminated the church until the entourage had arrived there safely.[78] Similarly, four miles from Le Mans, a shaft of light shone down on the bier, and above it a cross of light appeared in the sky, which continued to shine until the cortège was safely in the cathedral of St Julian. This divine sign encouraged the people of Le Mans to bury the Young King on the spot, and further healing miracles took place there before his body was finally removed to Rouen.[79]

William of Newburgh, looking back from the later 1190s, may have had Thomas in mind when he noted how after the Young King's death 'some persons, induced by the love of falsehood and most unblushing vanity, widely disseminated a report that cures of diseased people took place at his tomb, insomuch as he was believed either to have had good grounds for offence against his father, or to have highly pleased the Almighty by his last repentance'. 'As it is written,' he added dismissively, '"The number of fools is infinite".'[80] It is clear from Thomas' own sermon that there were already sceptics: he obliquely refers to 'Pharisees' among those who had the temerity not to believe in the miracles, and alleges that attempts were made by 'iniquitous persecutors' to remove offerings left at the Young King's tomb by the faithful and to suppress his veneration.[81] Had Queen Eleanor been at liberty to foster the cult directly, it might perhaps have had a longer vitality. Yet grief-stricken as he was at his son's death, Henry II had little wish to see another figure of sanctity, who, like Thomas Becket, might afford a focus of opposition to the king, while Richard must have been actively hostile to any such veneration of a man he had come to hate cordially.[82] The cult itself and attributions of miracles reflected a spontaneous outpouring of grief as much for dashed hopes of a better future as for the untimely death of a highly popular prince.[83] Yet without the concerted and sustained clerical support that had helped propel Thomas' cult, that of young Henry, more improbable from the first, could only be short-lived. There is little or no trace of claims to the Young King's sanctity in any of the vernacular sources, though Bertran de Born no doubt spoke for many of the nobility and knighthood when he expressed the fervent hope that God would forgive young Henry's sins and 'that He might set him among the honoured companions, there where there never was grief, nor will be sorrow'.[84]

Commemoration

Less dramatic but more lasting than the efforts of Thomas of Earley was the commemoration of the Young King in a series of bequests to religious houses by members of his family and by his men. In 1184, Geoffrey of Brittany, the brother who was closest to him, founded a chaplaincy at the cathedral of Rouen for the benefit 'of the soul of my venerable brother Henry the Young King', providing an annual rent of 20 *livres* from the ducal mills at Guingamp.[85] The following year, in a charter which affords a rare glimpse of a strong bond of affection between the couple, his widow Margaret, 'ever preserving the memory of her lord and husband, King Henry the Younger, and anxious to maintain the same union of minds when dead as when alive', pledged revenues from the income she was to receive from her future husband, King Béla of Hungary, for other chaplains in Rouen cathedral to say Masses for the Young King, and arranged that they be supported by a fund supervised by the abbot of Clairvaux.[86] The charter was witnessed by at least two other great ladies, Marie, countess of Champagne, the Young King's half-sister, and Hawise, countess of Gloucester and sister to Earl Robert of Leicester, suggesting their own attachment to the young Henry.[87] Further benefactions to the cathedral of Rouen for the Young King were to follow. In November 1189, his youngest brother John, now count of Mortain, granted it the chapelry of St Nicholas in the castle of Blyth, Nottinghamshire, for the health of his soul and those 'of Henry the King his father, of happy memory, and of his brother Henry the Young King, buried in the church of Rouen, and all my other ancestors'. The revenues were to supply two priests, while other funds were set aside for an annual commemoration of young Henry's death.[88] The establishment of these chaplaincies and altars for the Young King has been seen as an early and important stage in the development of the institution of the endowed chantry, as well as being influential in the growth of chantries in secular cathedrals.[89]

John's charter granting of the chapelry of Blyth noted that his gift had been made at the prayers of 'most dear Richard, illustrious king of England and my most beloved mother Eleanor, queen of England'.[90] How far Eleanor was the driving force behind this benefaction cannot be known, but it has been argued that the considerable size of the queen's own clerical establishment was a reflection of her desire to maintain elaborate liturgical commemoration for her family and affinity.[91] Her concern with her son's spiritual well-being in death, already visible in the promotion of his cult of sanctity, was again evident when shortly after Richard's own death in April 1199 Eleanor made a grant of 100 *livres angevins* to the abbey of Fontevraud 'for the health of our soul and the pious commemoration of our revered husband King Henry, and King Henry our son of good memory, and the powerful man King Richard and our other sons and daughters'.[92] Richard's own orders as he lay mortally ill following his wounding by a crossbow bolt at the siege of Châlus in 1199 were that his body was to be buried at Fontevraud at the feet of his father, an act not only of filial piety but also of contrition for having brought about his downfall. His heart, however, was to be taken to Rouen cathedral, a gesture which an anonymous contemporary author believed was intended to reward the city of Rouen for its exceptional loyalty and to safeguard Normandy by striking terror into the French.[93] Yet in his stipulation that his heart was to be buried opposite the tomb of his brother Henry we may perhaps see another act of posthumous reconciliation.[94]

If the Angevin family took a lead in the spiritual commemoration of young Henry, several of his former men were also concerned to remember a lord dear to them. When at last William Marshal found himself in possession of sufficient lands to found the Augustinian priory of Cartmel, Lancashire, he did so for the salvation of his soul and that of his family, yet also for the soul of Henry II and young Henry 'our lord'.[95] Similarly, in 1200 Peter de Préaux made a grant of rents from the market and fairs of Rouen to the canons of Notre Dame de Beaulieu, on condition that they should pay 20 shillings annually to the Hospital of St Mary Magdalene for the soul of Henry the Young King, 'my lord'.[96] William and Peter were among those knights formerly in the Young King's *mesnie* who subsequently took service with Henry II and Richard, and were men of rising prominence. Yet lesser figures, who presumably had also served young Henry, remembered him with affection in their benefactions. Thus Osbert, son of William, who founded the chapel of North Cove, Suffolk, endowed it for the soul of King Henry the Younger, of himself, his parents, his wife and his children, while John Lestrange granted lands at Edgefield to the monks of Binham priory, Norfolk, in perpetual alms for his soul and those of his family, but also for the soul 'of the lord king Henry junior and Queen Eleanor and of her sons'.[97]

The Young King's own cult was to be of limited impact and short duration, but his widow Margaret and his sisters Matilda, Eleanor and Joanna played a role in disseminating that of Thomas Becket more widely through Europe. When in 1186 Margaret married Béla III, king of Hungary, she took with her a devotion to St Thomas, which must have been a constant reminder of her late husband, and Béla established a religious chapter dedicated to St Thomas close to his castle and royal centre at Esztergom.[98]

Legacy

If the Young King's death had allowed Henry II and Richard finally to triumph over the rebellious nobles of Aquitaine, it almost immediately provoked another dangerous crisis. Philip Augustus' relationship with young Henry had been cordial, but with his brother-in-law dead, he at once demanded that Henry II return Gisors and the Norman Vexin, which had been assigned as Margaret's dower. He also insisted that she receive those lands in England and Normandy which had been assigned to her as her marriage portion, but which Henry II had withheld.[99] His hand had been strengthened by the fact that Margaret herself was now out of Henry II's reach, having been sent to the safety of the Capetian lands by young Henry before the outbreak of war in Aquitaine. Henry II, however, refused to grant Margaret these lands and revenues, claiming with evident sleight of hand that they had been ceded to Queen Eleanor. To confirm this transfer and deny any French claim, the king ordered Eleanor's release from custody, commanding that she make a progress around her dower lands.[100] Henry was equally determined to maintain possession of the Vexin. He replied to Philip that Gisors was his by right, for it belonged to the duchy of Normandy, while if King Louis had had any rights in it at any time, he had quitclaimed these on behalf of himself and his heirs when he gave Margaret in marriage to young Henry. Philip refused to accept this and a series of further conferences between the two kings failed to reach any agreement.[101] Finally, on 6 December 1183, at a large assembly held between Gisors and Trie, Henry met with Philip. It was agreed that Margaret and Philip would quitclaim Margaret's dower lands, as well as Gisors, in return for an annual payment of 1,700 *livres angevins* for her lifetime.[102] Henry was to give Gisors and the Vexin to whichever of his sons he chose, but on condition that the recipient should marry Alice, who still remained in Henry II's custody at Winchester and who had been betrothed to Richard since 1169.[103] Margaret, unlike her unfortunate sister, was now finally free of the Angevins.[104]

Philip's price for such concessions, however, went far beyond an annual pension for Margaret: he demanded that Henry II perform homage to him. If the Norman Vexin belonged by right, as Henry claimed, to the duchy of Normandy, then Henry must also perform homage for it as the duke of Normandy.[105] Henry II had been caught by his own logic. Despite the fact that, as Howden noted tersely, 'he had never wished to perform homage', he now had little choice but to do so.[106] On 6 December 1183, Henry 'swore homage and allegiance for all his lands across the sea to Philip, King of France'.[107] It was no little irony that, for all Henry II's attempts to enhance and preserve the status of Angevin kingship, the Young King's death had brought about circumstances in which, for the first time, Henry himself as king of England was compelled to perform homage to a king of France. Philip's demand, moreover, was the harbinger of a sustained, aggressive and ultimately successful attack on Henry II's position, starkly symbolized when in 1188 Philip hewed down the great elm tree near Gisors which had been a traditional site for talks between the kings of France and the king-dukes of England and Normandy.[108] The political landscape had changed profoundly since young Henry had held the crown over Philip's head at Rheims in November 1179.

Much of Philip's success would stem from the continuing disputes between Henry II and his surviving sons over the question of succession and the division of the Angevin empire, and here the Young King's legacy cast a long and baleful shadow. Richard absolutely refused to countenance Henry II's plan that Richard would step into the Young Henry's shoes as his principal heir to England, Normandy and Anjou, while John would replace Richard in Aquitaine and Geoffrey continue to hold Brittany: he had not engaged in ceaseless campaigns since 1175 to impose his rule on the duchy, then surmounted the massive rebellion of 1183, only to yield it to his youngest and untried sibling.[109] But still more, he saw that, if he did so, his father would be no more willing to grant him direct rule in England, Normandy or Anjou than he had been to grant it to the Young King. He successfully resisted Henry II's efforts to bestow the duchy on John, and easily repelled the attempts of the latter, aided by Geoffrey, to take Aquitaine by force.[110] As the eldest surviving son, however, Richard had good cause to expect that as of right he would succeed on his father's death to the heartlands of Henry's empire as his principal heir, and contemporaries shared this view. Indeed, in the immediate aftermath of young Henry's death, Bertran de Born even assumed that Richard in turn would be crowned as associate king of England:

> One thing the Bretons and Normans and Angevins, Poitevins and people from Maine should know; from Ostabat to Montferrand, and from Rosiers to Mirebeau, everyone will see Richard's armour, and since a count wants a free hand, and it's his right, let him ask at once for the land of Saint Edmund [England], until they put the sacred oil on his forehead.[111]

There is no evidence that Richard himself ever sought such associative coronation, but he was naturally anxious to secure Henry II's recognition as his successor. Henry, however, dreaded a repetition of the Young King's rebellion.[112] He not only procrastinated but engaged in a dangerous policy of attempting to control Richard by deliberately keeping him in uncertainty. Even after the issue of the succession had been sharply foregrounded by Richard's taking of the cross in late 1187 on hearing of the fall of Jerusalem to Saladin, Henry II's continuing equivocation, then his outright refusal publicly to acknowledge Richard allowed Philip Augustus to play on Richard's growing, though probably unfounded, fear that Henry would disinherit him in favour of

John. Henry II had already driven Geoffrey of Brittany into the arms of King Philip by refusing Geoffrey's demands that he grant him Anjou, and Philip had fuelled this division by granting Geoffrey the seneschalship of France, in circumstances very different from those of young Henry's tenure of the office.[113] By 1188, Richard himself had drawn closer to Philip and the following year, pushed beyond endurance by Henry's intransigence, Richard repeated young Henry's actions in 1173 by allying with the king of France and waging war against his father. Henry II's inability to trust Richard, fuelled by the traumatic experiences of the wars of 1173–74 and 1183, had ultimately provoked the very revolt of which Henry had been so fearful. This time, the rebellion was successful: whatever Richard's intentions, it brought about the downfall and death of his defeated father at Chinon on 6 July 1189.[114]

In his *Collection of the History of England* of 1618, dedicated to James VI and I's queen, Anne of Denmark, the historian Samuel Daniel reflected on the fate of the Young King.[115] The subject was an all too poignant one, for only six years earlier James' eldest son, another Prince Henry (1594–1612), also highly praised for his charm, courtliness and excellence in martial sports and as a leading figure in a chivalric revival, had met an untimely death through illness, shattering the hopes of many and causing an outpouring of grief.[116] There were striking parallels between the two young men, but what set them apart were the Young King's royal title and the ensuing conflict with his father. Daniel found Henry II's decision to crown his son bewildering, not least as at that time 'the King of England stood safe enough and was like to have his businesses runne in a strong and entire course'. Yet 'by casting to make things safer than fast, hee lays open a way both to disjoynt his own power and embroil his people open to division'. Henry's motive was, it seemed, 'the love he bore his sone' and his belief that it was insufficient security even to have had the nobles of the realm swear young Henry homage on two occasions. In a revealing reflection on the perceived power of the great councils convoked by Henry II, Daniel also remarked that it was 'strange that a Parliament, an assembly of State, convoked for the same businesse, would in so wise times, consent to communicate the Crowne, and make the commonwealth a Monster of two heads'. 'Howsoever,' he noted, 'this young King shewed shortly thereafter that a Crowne was no state to be made over in trust, and layd much griefe, and repentence, upon his father's forwardnesse'. Little wonder that his associative crowning had been 'an act without example in this Kingdome'.[117]

For thirteen years England had had two kings, yet the Plantagenet experiment in co-rulership failed catastrophically. The strife, tension and mutual suspicion that had marred the years between 1173 and 1183 ensured that the practice of associative kingship in England and the coronation of the heir in the lifetime of the ruler died with young Henry. Nor may it have been mere coincidence that Philip Augustus, fully alive to the opportunities such division had brought, was the first Capetian to forgo the long-standing practice of anticipatory succession.[118] Yet sufficient examples of associate rule in territories as divergent as the empire, the Norman kingdom of Sicily, and the county of Flanders showed that the failure of such condominium was far from inevitable. The plan to crown young Henry had been motivated by far weightier considerations than Henry's undoubted love for his eldest son. By it, Henry II sought to stabilize the succession to his great empire and thereby avoid a repeat of the kind of disastrous civil war that had engulfed the Anglo-Norman realm under King Stephen. At the same time, it was an integral part of his measures to restore and enhance the dignity of Angevin monarchy and bestow on his dynasty the regal lustre befitting the vast territories it now controlled. The counts of Anjou had come far very fast, but if Henry's status as king could be impugned by his enemies, that of his son, born in the purple, could not. The title of *rex filius regis* applied to young Henry was far more than a convenient designator; it held a deep significance. There was nothing inherently unworkable in Henry II's plan that, from 1162, England should be ruled by his young son through his trusted friend Thomas Becket, wielding the joint office of chancellor and archbishop of Canterbury. Had this arrangement been implemented, the course of Henry II's reign, including perhaps relations with his eldest son, would have been very different. Responsibility for its collapse must be laid principally at the door of Becket for his resignation of the chancellorship, for it is impossible to believe he had not decided on this before he accepted the archbishopric.

As a result, young Henry's coronation was delayed for a further eight years during Henry II's acrimonious quarrel with Becket, then carried out by the archbishop of York in highly contentious circumstances. Inauspicious as these may have been, however, contemporaries – including Thomas himself – were anxious to stress that the usurpation of Canterbury's prerogative in no way detracted from the legitimacy and sacrality of the Young King's regal status. It was only after Becket's murder and canonization that young Henry's coronation came to be seen as the baleful harbinger of Thomas' martyrdom and an affront which would bring divine retribution on young Henry as well as his father. In reality, the wisdom of young Henry's coronation had been thrown into sharp relief by Henry II's near-fatal illness in the late summer of 1170.

Why then did all go awry? In part, the problem was the nature of the relationship between the two royal authorities. As Samuel Daniel noted of young Henry's crowning: 'But now with what reservations this was done we are not particularly informed: whether there was an equal participation of rule, or only but of Title; and that the Father, notwithstanding this act, was to have the especial manage of the Government, and the Sonne, though a King, yet a sonne with limited power'.[119] Young Henry's contemporaries shared, and his opponents exploited, such uncertainty, which had been compounded by Henry II's insistence on his son's equality of royal status, so that even after two years of bitter war the elder king was still highly reluctant to accept the homage of his royal son. Unlike Frederick Barbarossa, moreover, who had created his son Henry king, Henry II did not have an imperial title which clearly marked a higher sovereignty.[120] Such ambiguities, however, were not in themselves the cause of friction, and little suggests that young Henry did not similarly expect to rule under his father's overarching authority. Far more significant was Henry II's refusal to grant any such devolved and direct rule to young Henry in England, Normandy or Anjou, and his inability to see that by withholding the governance that such regal status required he was undermining the very regalian authority he had created and was placing his son in an impossible situation.

This, moreover, was at a time when Henry II held more territories than any previous ruler of England. Just as William the Conqueror's acquisition of England had raised Robert Curthose's expectation for the rule of Normandy, so the very size of Henry's empire, and his continuing expansionist policies, added further weight to young Henry's natural expectation that his father would delegate rule of one major component of it. Further, Henry II's unrelenting grasp on power stood in all too marked a contrast with contemporary examples of condominium and with the powerful precedent of his own receipt of direct rule of Normandy in the lifetime of his father, Geoffrey of Anjou. It was a perfect storm. Nevertheless, young Henry was far from blameless in resorting to arms against his father: as Jordan Fantosme has Henry II's loyal barons tell him, 'Your son is in the wrong to make war on you'.[121] More than rash impatience and disloyalty, the Young King's readiness to confront his father reflected too great a propensity to be swayed by those seeking their own interests in attacking Henry II. In 1173, Henry II had refused his son's demands for direct rule in part because he believed the impetus for them had come from Louis VII and those who sought to weaken his empire through division. Paradoxically, however, had he not alienated the Young King, the enmity of Louis and the plots of Eleanor and his baronial opponents would have been far less effective. As it was, young Henry became an 'anti-king', all the more dangerous because of his status as an anointed sovereign, and the focal point for the many who resented what they regarded as the overbearing and oppressive rule of Henry II. Yet young Henry was no mere cat's paw of the Capetian king or of his mother; he was an Angevin, well schooled in realities of power politics and well aware of the conflicts in his family's own past, including a tradition of disaffected cadets resorting to the kings of France for aid. His rejection of his father's terms for peace in September 1173 reveals him as resolute in his opposition at a time when Louis VII's commitment to the war was faltering.

The gravity of the threat posed to Henry II by the great war of 1173–74 trapped both father and son in its legacy of fear and mistrust and made it all the harder for Henry II subsequently to grant young Henry the very power necessary to place their relations on a more secure footing. Henry II's attempt to use the wealth of the Angevin lands as a way of pacifying his son met with some success between 1176 and 1182, when the acclaim and kudos the Young King gained in the tournament circuit, combined with his leadership of a number of military expeditions, helped to allay his frustrations and project an imposing image of Angevin authority. Yet no matter how generous, an allowance in revenues could only be a temporary solution and it failed to address the fundamental problem that young Henry remained 'a king without a kingdom'. Young Henry's support of the dissident nobles of Aquitaine from 1182 in an attempt to replace Richard was jealously opportunistic, showed scant regard for his younger brother's rights of inheritance and created renewed and dangerous division within the Angevin lands. Yet equally it was a mark of his desperation. Unlike the war of 1173–74, the Young King's campaigns in 1183 had not been intended as an attack on Henry II himself, and his father's subsequent support for Richard placed young Henry in an agonizing dilemma. Though hostile writers in Henry II's court such as Roger of Howden and Walter Map saw only calculated duplicity by a would-be parricide, young Henry's actions, including repeated attempts at negotiation and even the taking of the cross in a moment of evident crisis, were not the conduct of a ruthless heir bent on the destruction of his father. Rather, his unwillingness to launch an all-out attack on Henry II may well have resulted in his losing control of the war to those, including his brother Geoffrey, with far fewer scruples.

It is little surprise that the rebellion of 1173–74 and the circumstances of young Henry's death during renewed conflict with his father dominated assessments of the Young King by writers in the orbit of the court of Henry II and then of Richard I. Yet their overwhelmingly critical voices have exerted too great an influence on more recent historians. In the early sixteenth century, Samuel Daniel offered a less hostile view and an acute summary. The Young King, he noted, was 'a Prince of excellent parts, who was first cast away by his father's indulgence, then after by his rigor; not suffering him to be what he himselfe had made him; neither got he so much by his Coronation, as to have a name in the Catalogue of the Kings of England'.[122] Claims that he was feckless, unintelligent and uninterested in government have little foundation. He had been well trained in the practical skills of governing, both by Henry II's ministers and by his father, and had jointly presided over many important secular and ecclesiastical councils. If as a child his role in their deliberation and policy making was more of a formality, the same cannot be assumed from his adolescence, and his father's evident concern from 1175 that he should be party to major initiatives in justice implies a more active involvement. Henry II's readiness to leave him as effective regent of Normandy in the early 1180s reflects a confidence in his abilities which appears not to have been misplaced. Nothing suggests that he was unready for or incapable of the direct rule he so ardently sought.

Had he outlived his father, moreover, young Henry would have inherited a highly efficient governmental structure, at least in England and Normandy, as well as the cadre of talented officials who ran it and who were already familiar to him. In the cultural sphere, his retention in his household of highly educated clerks such as Ralph Niger and Gervase of Tilbury points to his varied intellectual interests, and though, just as for Henry II and Eleanor's courts, firm evidence of his literary patronage is all too slight, it is very likely that the Young King's wealth and position made his court an attractive one for other writers and poets. Indeed, in this respect there may even have been a more positive rivalry between the courts of father and son.[123] On the death of the Old King, men such as Walter Map and Roger of Howden would, it might be thought, have been able to make the transition to the service of the Young King with little difficulty.

Between 1170 and 1183 all in the Angevin empire lived with the assumption that young Henry would one day succeed to sole rule of England, Normandy and greater Anjou. Henry's charm and winning personality, combined with his open-handed giving, would have made him a very different ruler from his father. He was, noted Bertran de Born, 'generous and well spoken, a good horseman, handsome and humble in conferring great honours'.[124] In leading teams of knights from across the lands under Plantagenet rule, the Young King provided a strong unifying influence, and from the evidence of those he recruited into his great tourneying retinues, his patronage would have reached well beyond those Anglo-Normans on whom his father's favour seems to have been primarily focused. There was a truth beyond the mere topos of a troubadour *planh* in Bertran's reflection that on news of young Henry's death: 'Bretons and Irishmen, Englishmen and Normans, Aquitainians and Gascons, should be sad and still for your sake ... And Poitou suffers, and Maine, and Tours'.[125]

A king among counts and knights in the dynamic military, social and cultural milieu of the tournament circuit of northern France, young Henry had forged a new image of chivalric kingship in a manner that was not to find an equivalent among monarchs of England until Edward III. His prominent participation in tourneying, combined with a largesse that amazed observers, created strong bonds between him and the aristocracy both in and beyond the Angevin lands as well as projecting Plantagenet power and wealth. It is hard to form an accurate assessment of young Henry's skill as a warrior and commander beyond the tournament field, but contemporaries were united in their praise for his martial skill and reputation. If the all too laconic record of his campaigns implies that he lacked the outstanding generalship of Henry II and Richard, the military and fiscal resources of the lion's share of the Angevin empire and his ability to field large groups of elite knights closely bound to him by ties of loyalty nevertheless made the armies he led formidable.[126]

What the fortunes of the Angevin empire might have been under his sole rule is impossible to know. His enmity with Richard suggests that Aquitaine would have become detached from it, as had been envisioned by Louis at the settlement of Montmirail, but dissident elements of its nobility could still have looked to the Young King either for support for insurrection within the duchy or patronage beyond it. Given his marriage to Margaret, there was less reason for the issue of the Vexin to become a source of friction with her brother King Philip than was the case under Henry II and Richard. Yet even if Philip had pursued a more hostile policy towards his brother-in-law, young Henry's support and popularity with the Norman aristocracy would have made the loss of Normandy, as well as the Angevin heartlands, which occurred in the debacle of 1202–4 under King John, most improbable. What is more certain is that on the death of the Young King in 1183 many believed they had lost a great king. 'Let each one model himself on the young English king,' ran one lament, 'who, in the whole world, was the most valiant of the worthy. Now is his noble, lovely person gone, whence there is grief, and dismay and sorrow.'[127] Bertran de Born gave powerful and poignant voice to the sentiments of the Young King's knightly companions in war and the tournament:

> Lord, in you there was nothing to change: the whole world had chosen you for the best king who bore a shield, the bravest one and the best knight in a tourney. Since the time of Roland, and even before, no one ever saw so excellent a king or one so skilled in war, or one whose fame so spread through the world and gave it new life, or one who sought fame from the Nile to the setting sun, looking for it everywhere.[128]

The overwhelming sense of loss and dashed expectation is captured just as powerfully by Gervase of Tilbury. Remembering his former lord with admiration and affection, he remarked of young Henry: 'As he was a solace to the world while he lived, so it was a blow to all chivalry (*universe milicie*) when he died in the very glow of youth . . . When Henry died, heaven was hungry, so all the world went begging.'[129]

Notes

Preface

1. *Jordan Fantosme's Chronicle*, ed. and trans. R. C. Johnston (Oxford, 1981), ll. 21–2.
2. *The Chronicle of Richard of Devizes of the Time of Richard the First*, ed. J. T. Appleby (1963), 2–3.

A Note on Terms and Currency

1. D. Broun, 'Britain and the Beginnings of Scotland', *Journal of the British Academy*, 3 (2015), 107–37, at 117, n. 66, noting Ralph's attestation in a number of charters as *de Disci* or *de Disei*. In references to the Rolls Series edition, *Opera Historica: The Historical Works of Master Ralph de Diceto, Dean of London*, ed. W. Stubbs, 2 vols (London, 1876), the Latin form Diceto has been retained.
2. For further details, see B. J. Cook, '*En Monnaie Aiant Cours*: The Monetary System of the Angevin Empire', *Coins and History in the North Sea World, c.500–c.1250: Essays in Honour of Marion Archibald*, ed. B. J. Cook and G. Williams (Leiden, 2006), 617–86; and for England, M. Allen, 'Henry II and the English Coinage', *Henry II. New Interpretations*, ed. C. Harper-Bill and N. Vincent (Woodbridge, 2007), 257–77.

Chapter 1: A Forgotten King?

1. *The Poems of the Troubadour Bertran de Born* (Padern), ed. W. D. Padern, T. Sankovitch and P. Stablein (Berkeley, 1986), no. 15; *L'Amour et la guerre. L'oeuvre de Bertran de Born* (Gouiran), ed. G. Gouiran, 2 vols (Aix-en-Provence, 1985), no. 12, ll. 15–28.
2. For contemporary use of the title 'Rex Henricus tertius' see, for example, *Gesta regis Henrici secundi Benedicti abbatis: The Chronicle of the Reigns of Henry II and Richard I, AD 1169–1192* (*GH*), ed. W. Stubbs, 2 vols (London, Rolls Series, 1867), I, 301; Peter of Blois, *Epistolae*, nos 33, 47 (*Patrologia Latina* (*PL*), CCVII, cols 109–10, 137); *Expugnatio Hibernica: The Conquest of Ireland, by Giraldus Cambrensis* (*Expugnatio*), ed. and trans. A. B. Scott and F. X. Martin (Dublin, 1978), 224; *Radulphi de Coggeshall Chronicon Anglicanum* (Coggeshall), ed. J. Stevenson (London, Rolls Series, 1875), 15; *De principis instructione liber* (*De principis*), ed. G. Warner, in *Giraldi Cambrensis Opera* (Gerald, *Opera*), ed. J. S. Brewer, F. Dimock and G. Warner, 8 vols (London, Rolls Series, 1861–1891), VIII, 173, 219; *De vita Gaufridi*, ed. J. S. Brewer, Gerald, *Opera* IV, 363; William of Newburgh, *Historia rerum Anglicarum* (*WN*), in *Chronicles of the Reigns of Stephen, Henry II and Richard I*, ed. R. Howlett, 4 vols (Rolls Series, London, 1884–1889), I, 233.
3. Geoffrey of Vigeois, *Chronica* (Vigeois), ed. P. Labbe, *Novae Bibliothecae manuscriptorum et librorum rerum Aquitanicarum*, 2 vols (Paris, 1657), II, 336, calls him 'rex puer'. In Roger of Howden's *Gesta Henrici*, he is often styled *rex filius regis* as well as *rex junior*, styles also adopted in official records such as the Pipe Rolls (see, for example, *Pipe Roll (PR) 18 Henry II*, 94, 144).
4. For Fontevraud and the Angevin tomb effigies, T. S. R. Boase, 'Fontevrault and the Plantagenets', *Journal of the British Archaeological Society*, 3rd series, 34 (1971), 1–10; E. Hallam, 'Royal Burial and the Cult of Kingship in France and England, 1060–1330', *JMH*, 8 (1982), 339–80; K. Nolan, 'The Queen's Choice: Eleanor of Aquitaine and the Tombs at Fontevraud', *Eleanor of Aquitaine. Lord and Lady*, ed. B. Wheeler and J. C. Parsons (New York, 2003), 377–405; and C. T. Wood,

'Fontevraud, Dynasticism and Eleanor of Aquitaine', *Eleanor of Aquitaine. Lord and Lady*, ed. J. C. Parsons and B. Wheeler (Basingstoke, 2002), 407–22.

5. For the Young King's effigy, see M. Schlicht, *La Cathédrale de Rouen vers 1300* (Caen, 2005), 347–55, and below, 313 and n. 65.

6. Of these, the most significant remains the depiction of young Henry at his coronation in 1170 and the ensuing banquet from an illustrated early thirteenth-century Anglo-Norman verse, Life of Thomas Becket (London, British Library, Loan MS 88, f. 3r, reproduced in J. Backhouse and C. De Hamel, *The Becket Leaves* (London, 1988), f. 3r). For the Candes sculptures, S. Lutan, 'L'Iconographie royale de Saint-Martin de Candes', *Aliénor d'Aquitaine* ed. M. Aurell (303: Arts, recherché et créations, Nantes, 2004), 108–17. If the well-known but enigmatic wall painting at the chapel of Sainte-Radegonde at Chinon does indeed portray Eleanor of Aquitaine and elements of her family, young Henry may perhaps be one of the two young noblemen, the other being Richard, depicted riding behind the queen, one of whom reaches out to either give or receive a bird of prey in a scene held to refer to her captivity (as, for example, by N. Keenan-Kedar, 'Alienor d'Aquitaine conduite en captivité. Les peintures murales commémoratives de Sainte Radegonde de Chinon', *Cahiers de civilisation médiévale* (*CCM*) 41 (1998), 317–30; and J. Flori, *Aliénor d'Aquitaine. La reine insoumise* (Paris, 2004), translated by O. Classe as *Eleanor of Aquitaine: Queen and Rebel* (Edinburgh, 2007), 115–17. The scene's interpretation, however, remains much debated; see C. Voyer, 'Les Plantagenêts et la chapelle de Sainte-Radegonde de Chinon: en débat', *Alienor d'Aquitaine*, ed. Aurell, 187–93; and the discussion of the wall painting and its historical context by N. Keenan-Kedar, D. Kleinmann, Y. Cloulas and U. Nilgen in *Cinquante années d'études médiévales: à la confluence de nos disciplines. Actes du Colloque organisé à l'occasion du cinquantenaire du CESCM, Poitiers, 1–14 septembre 2003*, ed. C. Arrignon, M.-H. Debiès and E. Palazzo (Turnhout, 2005), at 43–9, 51–8, 59–60, and 61–7 respectively.

7. On the nature of the Angevin empire, see J. Le Patourel, 'The Plantagenet Dominions', and idem, 'Angevin Successions and the Angevin Empire', in J. Le Patourel, *Feudal Empires: Norman and Plantagenet* (London, 1984), 289–308, 1–17; R.-H. Bautier, '"Empire Plantagenêt" ou "Espace Plantagenêt". Y eut-il une civilisation du monde Plantagenêt?', *CCM*, 29 (1986), 139–47; J. Gillingham, *The Angevin Empire* (2nd edn, London, 2001); idem, 'Problems of Integration within the Lands Ruled by the Norman and Angevin Kings of England', *Fragen der Politischen Integration im Mittelalterlichen Europa*, ed. W. Maleczek (Ostfildern, 2005), 85–135; and M. Aurell, *L'Empire des Plantagenêt, 1154–1254* (Paris, 2003), translated by D. Crouch as *The Plantagenet Empire* (Harlow, 2007).

8. Gervase of Tilbury, *Otia imperialia*, ed. and trans. S. E. Banks and J. W. Binns (Oxford, 2002), 486–7.

9. 'Mon chan fenis ab dol et ab maltraire' (Padern, no. 15, Gouiran, no. 12), ll. 18, 45–56.

10. 'Si tuit li doil e-il plor e-il marrimen' (Gouiran, no. 14), ll. 6, 30, 14; *Anthology of Troubadour Lyric Poetry*, ed. and trans. A. R. Press (Edinburgh, 1971), 168–71.

11. *History of William Marshal* (*HWM*), ed. A. J. Holden, with English translation by S. Gregory and historical notes by D. Crouch, 3 vols (Anglo-Norman Text Society, London, 2002–2006), ll. 6874–8. Paul Meyer's earlier edition, with a modern French précis of the text, remains valuable for its extensive notes: *L'Histoire de Guillaume le Maréchal, comte de Striguil et de Pembroke, régent d'Angleterre de 1216 à 1219: poème français* (*HGM*), ed. P. Meyer, 3 vols (Société de l'Histoire de France, Paris, 1891–1901). On its composition see D. Crouch, 'Writing a Biography in the Thirteenth Century: The Construction and Composition of the History of William Marshal', *Writing Medieval Biography, 750–1250: Essays in Honour of Professor Frank Barlow*, ed. D. Bates, J. Crick and S. Hamilton (Woodbridge, 2006), 221–35; and idem, 'Biography as Propaganda in the History of William Marshal', *Convaincre et persuader: communication et propagande aux XII et XIIIe siècles*, ed. M. Aurell (Poitiers, 2007), 503–12.

12. For Latin verses probably composed on the death of the Young King, see *Planctus in mortem cuiusdam nobilissimi Regis Henrici*, printed in C. L. Kingsford, 'Some Political Poems of the Twelfth Century', *EHR*, 5 (1890), 311–26, at 315–16.

13. *The Chronicle of Robert of Torigni* (Torigni), in *Chronicles of the Reigns of Stephen, Henry II and Richard*, ed. R. Howlett, 4 vols (London, Rolls Series, 1884–1889), IV, 305. It may not be coincidental that Robert presented the first recension of his chronicle to Henry II soon afterwards, in 1184.

14. *Annales de Saint-Aubin*, in *Recueil d'Annales Angevins et Vendômoises*, ed. L. Halphen (Paris, 1903), 21, 'Obiit Henricus rex Junior, mortem cujus fere universus orbis lamentatur'; *Annales de Waverleia*, in *Annales monastici*, ed. H. R. Luard, 4 vols (London, Rolls Series, 1864–1869), II, 243, 'Obiit vir illustris et mirae indolis Henricus tertius rex, filius Henrici secundi regis Anglorum'.

15. British Library, Royal MS 14 C VII, f. 9r; S. Lewis, *The Art of Matthew Paris in the Chronica Majora* (Berkeley, 1987), plate VII. In the same text, however, Matthew refers to the coronation of

'Henricus III Junioris' in 1170 (*Matthaei Parisiensis, monachi Sancti Albani, historia Anglorum* (Paris, *Historia Anglorum*), ed. F. Maddern, 3 vols (London, Rolls Series, 1866–1869), I, 352).

16. *Annales de Bermundeseia*, in *Annales monastici* (*AM*), ed. H. R. Luard, 5 vols (Rolls Series, London, 1864–1869), III, 445, though it nevertheless noted the thirteen-year reign of 'Henricus rex tertius'. Hostility to the 'most hateful' coronation as prejudicial to St Thomas, however, was already well developed in Paris' *Historia Anglorum* (I, 352–3).

17. The majority of contemporaries who refer to the Young King as 'Henricus tertius', including in his obits, were writing before the birth of John's son Henry on 1 October 1207 (or in the case of the later recension of Gerald of Wales' *De principis instructione*, reworking texts begun before then), but exactly when and why this transference occurred remains unclear. The Annals of Margam note the coronation in 1216 of 'Henricus tertius' (*AM*, I, 33), while on Henry III's new coinage introduced from 1247 he appears first as 'Henricus tercius', then 'Henricus III'. I am most grateful to David Carpenter for these points. It is notable that the rubric attached to Matthew Paris' depiction of Henry III reads simply 'Henricus rex octavus' [i.e. post-Conquest] and that the Roman numeral III has been squeezed in above, as if as an afterthought, whereas by contrast that for Henry II reads 'Henricus Secundus rex quintus'. That the Young King could still be counted as Henry III and his later namesake as Henry IV into the early fourteenth century is reflected in testimony given during the canonization process of Thomas Cantilupe, bishop of Hereford, where a witness referred to Thomas' father as 'William de Cantilupe knight and baron who was a powerful man and of great authority and seneschal to the lord King Henry the fourth of the English (dominus Henricus quartus rex Anglorum)' (MS Vatican City, Bibliotheca Apostolica Vaticana, Vat. Lat. 4015, fol. 92v). My thanks to Rob Bartlett for kindly supplying this reference.

18. Bern, Burgerbibliothek MS 113, f. 143v, noting that Henry II 'avoit. iii. fix. Li ainsnés avoit a non li jovenes rois Henris ke on nouma lion qui giest a Martiaus qui fuu li plus larges cuers de prince né de roi qui onques fust puis le tans Judas Macabeu s'il eust vescu, mais il fu mors ains que ses peres. Li autres oy a non Richars et estoit quens de Poitiers. Li tiers avoit a non Jehans sans Terre'. While other versions of the *Chronique d'Ernoul*, composed in its final form in the 1230s, speak only of Richard and John as the sons of Henry II, the interpolator of the Bern ms has deliberately sought to rectify this by the addition of the sentence on young Henry. I am most grateful to Peter Edbury, who is currently preparing a new edition of the *Chronique d'Ernoul*, for this reference. For the growth of Richard's legendary reputation see: B. B. Broughton, *The Legends of King Richard I Coeur de Lion* (The Hague and Paris, 1966); J. Gillingham, 'Some Legends of Richard the Lionheart: Their Development and Influence', *Riccardo Cuor di Leone nella storia e nella leggenda, Accademia Nazionale dei Lincei, problemi attuali di scienza e di cultura*, 253 (1981), 35–50, and reprinted in J. Gillingham, *Richard Coeur de Lion: Kingship, Chivalry and War in the Twelfth Century* (London, 1994), 181–92; idem, '*Stupor mundi*: 1204 et un obituaire de Richard Coeur de Lion depuis longtemps tombé dans l'oubli', *Plantagenêts et Capétiens: confrontations et héritages*, ed. M. Aurell and N.-Y. Tonnerre (Turnhout, 2006), 397–412.

19. *Récits d'un ménestrel de Reims au treizième siècle*, ed. N. de Wailly (Société de l'histoire de France, Paris, 1876), 7 (ch. 12), 9–10 (chs 17–19), 'Henriz au Court Mantel'. For his treatment by the Minstrel, see O. H. Moore, *The Young King Henry Plantagenet 1155–1183 in History, Literature and Tradition* (Columbus, Ohio, 1925), 29–34. In this extraordinary romance (which has Queen Eleanor attempt to elope with Saladin during the Second Crusade), Young Henry's wife Margaret is conflated with her sister Alice, and the prince dies of grief on learning that his father has seduced her. The Minstrel also has Henry II, not his son, being buried in Rouen. Henry II's nickname 'Shortcloak' is recorded by both Gerald of Wales, *De principis*, 304, and the *Histoire des ducs de Normandie*, which speaks of 'li rois Henris au Court-Mantiel, li peres le jouene roi Henri' (*Histoire des ducs de Normandie et des rois d'Angleterre*, ed. F. Michel, Paris, 1840, 82). Ironically, in the town of Martel itself, the plaque marking the house in which the Young King supposedly died repeats this same error of calling him 'Curtmantle'.

20. *Il Novellino*, ed. A. Conte (Rome, 2001), nos XIX and XX; Moore, *The Young King*, 53–55.

21. Moore, *The Young King*, 54; M. Dauzier, *Le Mythe de Bertran de Born du Moyen Âge à nos jours* (Paris, 1986), 17–32.

22. Dante, *The Divine Comedy, I: Inferno*, ed. and trans. J. D. Sinclair (Oxford, 1939), Canto XXVIII, ll. 118–42: '. . . know that I am Bertran de Born, he that gave evil backing to the Young King. I made rebellion between the father and the son; Achitophel did no worse for David and Absalom with his wicked goading.'

23. For Geoffrey, M. Aubrun, 'Le Prieur Geoffroy du Vigeois et sa chronique', *Revue Mabillon*, 58 (1974), 313–25.

24. For the imagery of David and Absalom in views of father–son rebellion, see K. H. Krüger, 'Herrschaftsnachfolge als Vater–Sohn-Konflikt', *Frühmittelalterliche Studien*, 36 (2002), 225–40; and X. Storelli, 'La Figure d'Absalon dans la famille royale anglo-normande (XIe–XIIe siècles)', *La Parenté déchirée: les luttes intrafamiliales au Moyen Âge*, ed. M. Aurell (Turnhout, 2010), 321–41.

25. Walter Map, *De nugis curialium* (Map), ed. and trans. M. R. James, revised by C. N. L. Brooke and R. A. B. Mynors (Oxford, 1983), 280–3.
26. Map, 282–3.
27. *Opera Historica: The Historical Works of Master Ralph de Diceto, Dean of London* (Diceto), ed. W. Stubbs, 2 vols (London, Rolls Series, 1876), II, 19.
28. Map, 282–3, 'he left his brother Richard (with hate of whom his heart was withered) heir'.
29. *De principis*, 173–4, where Gerald states he has taken this encomium from the *Topographia*. Only elements of it, however, appear in the version of it printed in the Rolls Series (Gerald, *Opera*, V, 193–5), though Gerald must have been drawing on a version of the first or second recension written before July 1189. For the recensions and their dating, see R. Bartlett, *Gerald of Wales. A Voice of the Middle Ages* (new edn, Stroud, 2006), Appendix I, 174–5. Gerald repeats his verses in praise of young Henry in his *Symbolum Electorum*, a collection of his poems and letters, composed *c.*1204–1205 (Gerald, *Opera*, I, 355).
30. *Expugnatio*, 22–3.
31. *Expugnatio*, 22–3.
32. For Howden, see D. Corner, 'The Earliest Surviving Manuscripts of Roger of Howden's *Chronicle*', *EHR*, 98 (1983), 297–310; idem, 'The *Gesta regis Henrici secundi* and *Chronica* of Roger, parson of Howden', *Bulletin of the Institute of Historical Research*, 56 (1983), 26–44; J. Gillingham, 'The Travels of Roger of Howden and his View of the Irish, Scots and Welsh', *Anglo-Norman Studies*, 20 (1997), 151–70, reprinted in J. Gillingham, *The English in the Twelfth Century: Imperialism, National Identity and Political Values* (Woodbridge, 2000), 69–91; J. Gillingham, 'Writing the Biography of Roger of Howden, King's Clerk and Chronicler', *Writing Medieval Biography*, 207–20.
33. *GH*, I, 122–3; Gillingham, 'The Travels of Roger of Howden', 74–6; and below, 230–1.
34. *Chronica magistri Rogeri de Hoveden* (Howden), ed. W. Stubbs, 2 vols (Rolls Series, London, 1868–1871), II, 46; J. Flori, *Aliénor d'Aquitaine. La reine insoumise* (Paris, 2004), trans. O. Classe as *Eleanor Aquitaine* (Edinburgh, 2007), 104. This passage was inserted into a later copy of the *Gesta* (British Library, Cotton Vitellius E. xvii) labelled MS B by Stubbs, who suggested that it might have been copied from the *Chronica* (*GH*, I, 43; Howden, II, 46, n. 2).
35. *GH*, I, 292; Howden, II, 274; J. Gillingham, *Richard I* (New Haven, Conn., and London, 1999), 66 and n. 44.
36. *GH*, I, 300–2.
37. The accounts were seemingly so different in their tone and content that Stubbs regarded this as evidence that the author of the *Gesta* (long assumed to be Benedict, abbot of Peterborough) could not have been Roger of Howden (*GH*, I, 304, n. 1). As David Corner has demonstrated beyond doubt, however, Roger was indeed the author of both works (Corner, 'The *Gesta Regis Henrici Secundi*', 126–44).
38. Howden, II, 279–80.
39. J. Gillingham, 'Royal Newsletters, Forgeries and English Historians: Some Links between Court and History in the Reign of Richard I', *La Cour Plantagenêt (1154–1204)*, ed. M. Aurell (Poitiers, 2000), 171–86; idem, *Richard I*, 6–7.
40. J. Gillingham, 'Events and Opinions: Norman and English Views of Aquitaine, *c.*1152–*c.*1204', *The World of Eleanor of Aquitaine: Literature and Society in Southern France between the Eleventh and Thirteenth Centuries*, ed. M. Bull and C. Léglu (Woodbridge, 2005), 57–81, at 77–8.
41. Howden, II, 272–3. This passage in the *Chronica*, though inserted *s.a.* 1182, was probably penned *c.*1200–1201 (Gillingham, 'Events and Opinions', 77, n. 110).
42. *Vita Sancti Thomae archiepiscopi et martyris, auctore Heberto de Boseham* (Bosham), in *Materials for the History of Thomas Becket, Archbishop of Canterbury* (*MTB*), ed. J. C. Robertson and J. Brigstock Sheppard, 7 vols (Rolls Series, London, 1875–1885), III, 460–1. The date of the completion of the *Vita* is usually regarded as between 1184 and 1186, but this passage also suggests Herbert was aware of the death of Henry II in July 1189, as well as that of Count Geoffrey, whose death in 1186 was also predicted in Thomas' vision.
43. *De principis*, 302; B. S. Bachrach, 'Henry II and the Angevin Tradition of Family Hostility', *Albion*, 16 (1984), 111–30, at 112. Gerald had already begun to develop this theme in his *Expugnatio Hibernica*, where he noted that 'it befell that there was never true affection felt by the father towards his sons, nor by the sons towards their father, nor harmony among the brothers themselves' (*Expugnatio*, 387–8).
44. *De principis*, 176; trans. J. Stevenson, *The Church Historians of England*, 8 vols (London, 1853–1858), V, part I, 150.
45. For the *De principis* as 'a drama of kingly hubris', Bartlett, *Gerald of Wales*, 64.
46. *De principis*, 172, and 155, where Gerald notes that although the rebellions of Henry II's sons were pleasing to God as instruments of his vengeance, yet 'their private intentions were displeasing to him in every way', and that they were themselves punished accordingly.

47. A not untypical comment is that of Walter de Gray Birch that 'modern historians are remarkable for their omission of this young king's name in the fasti of England's rulers'. But, he added, 'fortunately, perhaps, the untimely death of Henry Junior, during the lifetime of his father, Henry II, relieved the country of many misfortunes, as it is most probable that his failure to show respect to his father indicated a want of mental character which those whose lot it is to govern others ought to make manifest' (W. de Gray Birch, *Seals*, London, 1907, 35).

48. Howden, I, lxviii.

49. K. Norgate, *England under the Angevin Kings*, 2 vols (London, 1887), II, 220–1.

50. K. Norgate, *Richard the Lionheart* (London, 1924), 36, 45, a verdict drawn very largely from an uncritical reading of Gerald's comparison of the two brothers.

51. Norgate, *Angevin Kings*, II, 221.

52. Moore, *The Young King*, 26–7, appears to be borrowing directly from Norgate, but without citation, in his statement that his 'entire life was a record of the meanest ingratitude and the basest perfidy', and that 'his merits, so far as they existed, were of the superficial kind'.

53. W. L. Warren, *Henry II* (London, 1973, new edn) New Haven, Conn., and London, 2000), 580, and 118, 'a charming, vain, idle spendthrift'.

54. W. L. Warren, *King John* (London, 2nd edn, 1978), 31. A more restrained tone is that of Ralph Turner, *Eleanor of Aquitaine* (New Haven, Conn., and London, 2009), 206, 'this thoughtless, whimsical yet winning boy'. Likewise, John Gillingham, *Richard I* (New Haven, Conn., and London, 1999), 63, recognizes young Henry's chivalrous qualities and skill in the tournament, but 'in politics and real war he was a child, incapable of concentrating for long. Unable to see beyond the short term gain he went from whim to whim, reacting without thought to whatever gossip he happened to have heard last'.

55. D. Crouch, *Tournament* (London, 2005), 21–7; idem, *William Marshal: Knighthood, War and Chivalry, 1147–1219* (2nd edn, London, 2002), 45.

56. The career of Geoffrey has been well covered by J. Everard, *Brittany and the Angevins: Province and Empire, 1158–1203* (Cambridge, 2000); *The Charters of Duchess Constance of Brittany and her Family, 1171–1221*, ed. J. Everard and M. Jones (Woodbridge, 1999); and see also M. Jones, 'Geoffrey, duke of Brittany (1158–1186), prince', *ODNB*.

57. C. E. Hodgson, *Jung Heinrich, König von England, Sohn König Heinrichs II* (Jena, 1906); and see the review by H. W. C. Davis in *EHR*, 22 (1907), 826–7. Moore's brief treatment of the Young King's historical career, which takes up barely a quarter of a short book of some hundred pages, is drawn primarily from the narratives of Norgate.

58. A. Duggan, 'The Coronation of the Young King in 1170', *Studies in Church History*, 2, ed. G. J. Cumming (London, 1968), 165–78; T. M. Jones, 'The Generation Gap of 1173–1174: The War of the Two Henries', *Albion*, 5 (1973), 24–40; idem, *The War of the Generations. The Revolt of 1173–4* (Medieval Text Association, University Microfilms International, Ann Arbor, 1980); R. V. Turner, 'The Households of the Sons of Henry II', *La Cour Plantagenêt (1154–1204). Actes du Colloque tenu à Thouars du 30 avril au 2 mai 1999*, ed. M. Aurell (Poitiers, 2000), 49–62; and see also M. J. Strickland, 'On the Instruction of a Prince: The Upbringing of Henry, the Young King', *Henry II. New Interpretations*, 184–214.

59. R. J. Smith, 'Henry II's Heir: The *Acta* and Seal of Henry the Young King, 1170–1183' (Smith, '*Acta*'), *EHR*, 116 (2001), 297–326. Much valuable analysis of the Young King is also contained in Roger Smith's unpublished thesis 'The Royal Family in the Reign of Henry II' (Master of Arts Thesis, University of Nottingham, 1961), especially 50–119, and 120–63.

60. V. L. Puccetti, *Un fantasma letterario. Il «Re Giovane» del Novellino* (Bologna, 2008). I am indebted to Martin Aurell for drawing this book to my attention.

61. It is thus remarkable that in his classic study J. E. A. Joliffe, *Angevin Kingship* (London, 1955) makes only fleeting reference to the Young King ('Henry FitzRoy', at 20, n. 2, 176, n. 3, and 260) and does not discuss his associative status.

62. R. V. Turner, 'The Problem of Survival for the Angevin Empire: Henry II's and his Sons' Vision compared to late Twelfth-Century Realities', *American Historical Review*, 100 (1995), 78–95.

63. For approaches to the genre, see W. L. Warren, 'Biography and the Medieval Historian', *Medieval Historical Writing in the Christian and Islamic Worlds*, ed. D. O. Morgan (London, 1982), 5–18, and the studies collected in *Writing Medieval Biography*.

64. N. Vincent, 'The Strange Case of the Missing Biographies: The Lives of the Plantagenet Kings of England, 1154–1272', *Writing Medieval Biography*, 237–58.

65. *The Chronicle of Richard of Devizes of the Time of Richard the First*, ed. J. T. Appleby (1963), 2–3.

66. A. Grandsen, *Historical Writing in England, c. 550–c. 1307* (London, 1982), 220–1.

67. J. C. Holt and R. Mortimer, *Acta of Henry II and Richard I* (List and Index Society, Special Series, 21, Gateshead, 1986); N. Vincent, *Acta of Henry II and Richard I. Part Two* (List and Index Society, Special Series, 27, Kew, 1996); J. C. Holt, 'The Acta of Henry II and Richard I of England,

1154–1189: The Archive and its Historical Implications', *Fotographische Sammlungen Mittelältischer Urkunden in Europa*, ed. P. Rück (Sigmaringen, 1989), 137–40; *The Letters and Charters of Henry II King of England (1154–1189)*, ed. N. Vincent *et al.*, 5 vols (Oxford, forthcoming). This paucity for young Henry is despite the explosion in the number of charters issued under Henry II, which may be compared to the 180 known *acta* of his father Count Geoffrey for Anjou and Normandy (K. Dutton, 'Geoffrey, Count of Anjou and Duke of Normandy, 1129–51' (unpublished Ph.D thesis, University of Glasgow, 2011), Appendices I–VI).

68. Smith, '*Acta*', 297.
69. *GH*, I, 77, 83, and 286. An exception is probably his confirmation of the grant by the count of Eu of privileges to the burgesses of Eu, likely to have been issued in 1173 during or shortly after the siege of Drincourt (Smith, '*Acta*', no. 18).
70. Smith, '*Acta*', 297–314.
71. For these authors, M. Staunton, *Thomas Becket and his Biographers* (Woodbridge, 2006), and idem, *The Lives of Thomas Becket* (Manchester, 2001).
72. *Jordan Fantosme's Chronicle (JF)*, ed. and trans. R. C. Johnston (Oxford, 1981); and for the author, I. Macdonald, 'The Chronicle of Jordan Fantosme: Manuscripts, Author and Versification', *Studies in Medieval French presented to Alfred Ewart* (1961), 242–58.
73. Jordan himself does not give his work a title. That ascribed to it by P. A. Becker, 'Jordan Fantosme, la guerre d'Ecosse, 1173–14', *Zeitschrift für romanische Philologie*, 64 (1944), 449–556, reflects its principal focus, but the poem is more wide ranging. For interpretations of the poem and its purpose, R. C. Johnston, 'The Historicity of Jordan Fantosme's *Chronicle*', *JMH*, 2 (1976), 159–68; M. J. Strickland, 'Arms and the Men: War, Loyalty and Lordship in Jordan Fantosme's *Chronicle*', *Medieval Knighthood, IV: Papers from the Fifth Strawberry Hill Conference 1990*, ed. C. Harper-Bill and R. Harvey (1992), 187–220; A. Lodge, 'Literature and History in the *Chronicle* of Jordan Fantosme', *French Studies*, 44 (1992), 257–70; J. Blacker, 'Oez veraie estoire; History as Mediation in Jordan Fantosme's Chronicle', *The Formation of Culture in Medieval Britain*, ed. F. H. M. Le Saux (Lampeter, 1995), 27–35; P. Damian-Grint, 'Truth, Trust and Evidence in the Anglo-Norman *Estoire*', *ANS*, 18 (1995), 63–78; P. Bennett, 'La Chronique de Jordan Fantosme', *CCM*, 40 (1997), 35–56; L. Ashe, *Fiction and History in England, 1066–1200* (Cambridge, 2007), 81–120; and G. Rector, '"Faites le mien desir": Studious Persuasion and Baronial Desire in Jordan Fantosme's Chronicle', *JMH* (2008), 311–46.
74. G. Gouiran, 'Bertran de Born, troubadour de la violence?', *La Violence dans le monde médiéval* (Aix-en-Provence, 1994), 237–51.
75. *Poésies complètes de Bertran de Born*, ed. A. Thomas (Toulouse, 1888), *vida* no. 1; Norgate, *Richard*, 40–1.
76. On the poet and his work, *HGM*, III, iv–xiv; *HWM*, III, 3–9; Crouch, 'Construction and Composition of the History of William Marshal', 221–35; idem, 'The Hidden History of the Twelfth Century', *Haskins Society Journal*, 5 (1993), 111–30.
77. Crouch, 'Hidden History', 122, who points to the influence not only of Chrétien's romances, but of gestes such as *Feurres de Gadres* or possibly *Guy of Warwick*. See also L. D. Benson, 'The Tournament in the Romances of Chrétien de Troyes and *L'Histoire de Guillaume le Maréchal*', *Chivalric Literature. Essays on Relations between Literature and Life in the later Middle Ages*, ed. L. D. Benson and J. Leyerle (Toronto, 1980), 1–24, 147–51; and the important studies of R. W. Kaeuper, 'William Marshal, Lancelot and the Issue of Chivalric Identity', *Essays in Medieval Studies. Proceedings of the Illinois Medieval Association*, 22 (2005), 1–19; and L. Ashe, 'William Marshal, Lancelot and Arthur: Chivalry and Kingship', *Anglo-Norman Studies*, 30 (2008), 19–40.

Chapter 2: Born in the Purple

1. *The Anglo-Saxon Chronicle. A Collaborative Edition*, ed. D. Dumville and S. Keynes (Cambridge, 1983), vol. 7. *MS E*, ed. S. Irvine (Cambridge, 2004), 1154; Henry of Huntingdon, *Historia Anglorum* (HH), ed. D. Greenway (Oxford, 1996), 774–5; WN, I, 95–6; *The Historical Works of Gervase of Canterbury* (Gervase), ed. W. Stubbs, 2 vols (Rolls Series, London, 1879–1880), I, 159–60.
2. For the opening of Henry II's reign see M. Chibnall, 'L'Avènement au pouvoir d'Henri II', *CCM*, 37 (1994), 41–8; E. Amt, *The Accession of Henry II in England. Royal Government Restored, 1149–1159* (Woodbridge, 1993); G. J. White, *Restoration and Reform, 1153–1165. Recovery from Civil War in England* (Cambridge, 2000); and E. King, 'The Accession of Henry II', *Henry II. New Interpretations*, ed. C. Harper-Bill and N. Vincent (Woodbridge, 2007), 24–46.
3. *Anglo-Saxon Chronicle*, 'E', 1137. In the weeks between Stephen's death and Henry's arrival in England on 7 December, Henry of Huntingdon was moved to write a poem of relief and joy, though he failed to realize his intention that 'a new book must be devoted to a new king' (HH, 776–7).

4. Sir Roger Twysden, *Historiae Anglicanae decem scriptores* (London, 1652), col. 347; *Aelred of Rievaulx: The Historical Works*, ed. M. L. Dutton and trans. J. P. Freeland (Kalamazoo, 2005), 42.

5. HH, 772–3; WN, I, 101; William of Newburgh, *The History of English Affairs, Book II*, ed. and trans. P. G. Walsh and M. J. Kennedy (Oxford, 2007), 15. For his military reputation, *Policraticus*, ed. C. C. J. Webb, 2 vols (Oxford, 1909), Bk VI: 18; *The Statesman's Book of John of Salisbury*, trans. J. Dickinson (New York, 1963), 236–7.

6. WN, I, 93.

7. *The Historia Pontificalis of John of Salisbury*, ed. and trans. M. Chibnall (London, 1956), 52–3; P. McCracken, 'Scandalizing Desire: Eleanor of Aquitaine and the Chroniclers', *Eleanor of Aquitaine. Lord and Lady*, ed. B. Wheeler and J. C. Parsons (New York, 2003), 247–64; M. Aurell, 'Aux origines de la légende noire d'Aliénor d' Aquitaine', *Royautés imaginaires (XIIe–XIVe siècles)*, ed. A.-H. Allirot, G. Lecuppre and L. Scordia (Turnhout, 2005), 89–102; Flori, *Eleanor*, 209; R. V. Turner, 'Eleanor of Aquitaine, Twelfth-Century English Chroniclers and her "Black Legend"', *Nottingham Medieval Studies*, 52 (2008), 17–42; R. V. Turner, *Eleanor of Aquitaine* (Yale, 2009), 87–92.

8. Torigni, 214. See J. A. Brundage, 'The Canon Law of Divorce in the Mid-Twelfth Century: Louis VII c. Eleanor of Aquitaine', *Eleanor of Aquitaine. Lord and Lady*, 213–22; and C. B. Bouchard, 'Eleanor's Divorce from Louis VII: The Uses of Consanguinity', *Eleanor of Aquitaine. Lord and Lady*, 223–36.

9. Diceto, I, 296; Torigni, 176, who gives the date as 17 August. For other possible infant deaths during the marriage, C. N. L. Brooke, 'The Marriage of Henry II and Eleanor of Aquitaine', *The Historian*, 20 (1988), 3–8.

10. Torigni, 183; Diceto, I, 30; *Annales sancti Albini Andegavensis (Annales de St Aubin)*, in *Recueil d'annales angevines et vendômoises*, ed. L. Halphen (Paris, 1903), 14; *Radulphi Nigri chronica* (Ralph Niger, *Chronicle*), ed. R. Anstruther (London, 1851), 189.

11. Torigni, 176, specifically notes that he was named William 'quod nomen quasi proprium est comitibus Pictavorum et ducibus Aquitanorum'. Nevertheless, it equally evoked Henry II's Norman forebears from the second Norman duke, William Longsword, to Henry I's son William Aetheling. For Torigni, see E. M. C. van Houts, 'Le Roi et son historien: Henri II Plantagenêt et Robert de Torigni, abbé du Mont-Saint-Michel', *CCM*, 37 (1994), 115–18.

12. 'Roger of Pontigny', in *Materials for the History of Thomas Becket, Archbishop of Canterbury (MTB)*, ed. J. C. Robertson and J. Brigstock Sheppard, 7 vols (Rolls Series, London, 1875–1885), IV, 19, calls him 'magnificus et potentissimus rex'; *Policraticus*, Bk VI: 18, trans. Dickinson, 233; Map, 440–1. Indeed, early in his reign Henry II could himself be referred to as 'Henry the Younger' (HH, 776–7; *Chronicle of Battle Abbey*, ed. and trans. E. Searle (Oxford, 1980), 174–5, which refers to events 'in the third year of the reign of King Henry the Younger, daughter's son to the great Henry'.

13. Howden, I, 215; Warren, *Henry II*, 219. Earlier, in 1154, Henry II's coronation charter had granted the Church and his vassals all customs and liberties 'as freely and peaceably and fully in everything as King Henry, my grandfather, granted and conceded to them and confirmed by his charter' – W. Stubbs, *Select Charters and other Illustrations of English Constitutional History* (Oxford, edn 1913), 158; *English Historical Documents, II, 1042–1189 (EHD)*, ed. D. C. Douglas (2nd edn, Oxford, 1961), 440, no. 23).

14. Henry I's widow Adeliza of Louvain had commissioned a verse history by a poet named David, and in the mid 1130s, Constance, the wife of a Lincolnshire lord, Ralph FitzGilbert, could possess a copy, 'which she often read in her chamber' (Geffrei Gaimar, *Estoire des Engleis*, ed. and trans. I. Short (Oxford, 2009), ll. 6483–96). The Empress Matilda commissioned a *vita*, also now lost, of her father from Robert of Torigni (E. van Houts, *Memory and Gender in Medieval Europe, 900–1200*, Houndmills, 1999), 71, 74). It is likely that that similar works were available at the court of Henry II. For Brémule, *Policraticus*, VI: 18, trans. Dickinson, 233.

15. J. Green, 'Henry I and the Origins of the Court Culture of the Plantagenets', *Plantagenêts et Capétiens*, 485–96; Turner, *Eleanor*, 156.

16. *Regesta regum Anglo-Normannorum (RRAN)*, III, ed. H. A. Cronne and R. H. C. Davies (Oxford, 1968), no. 635; M. Chibnall, *The Empress Matilda. Queen Consort, Queen Mother and Lady of the English* (Oxford, 1991), 145 and n. 1; *Policraticus*, VI: 18; trans. Dickinson, 233.

17. In his epilogue to the *Roman de Rou*, composed c.1174, the poet Wace made this link explicit: 'I have known three King Henrys and seen them all in Normandy: all three had lordship over Normandy and England. The second Henry, about whom I am talking, was the grandson of the first Henry and born of Matilda the empress, and the third was the son of the second' (*Wace's Roman de Rou*, trans. G. S. Burgess, with the text of A. J. Holden and notes by G. S. Burgess and E. M. C. van Houts, St Helier, Jersey, 2002, ll. 11431–8, and cf. ibid., III, l. 177–80).

18. Diceto, I, 301. Gervase, I, 161, believed he was baptized by Theobald of Canterbury, and in this is followed by Turner, *Eleanor*, 132. Diceto, however, is likely to have been more accurate on matters

pertaining to the bishops of London, and in 1152 had been made archdeacon of Middlesex in Robert's stead when the latter was raised to the episcopacy (Diceto, I, xxv–xxvi).

19. William FitzStephen, *Vita sancti Thomae Cantuarensis archiepiscopi et martyris* (FitzStephen), *MTB*, III, 7–8, 12–13, 'Henricus rex tertius'; trans. *EHD*, II, 1027, 1030.

20. Torigni, 184; Gervase, I, 162, 'conventus generalis'; Eyton, 9–10. Fears of William's health are perhaps reflected in a general confirmation by Henry II to the Hospitallers of all their possessions in England, issued at Winchester 'in concilio' in September, given for the souls of his grandfather and his father, and 'for my health, and that of my mother the Empress, and of my queen Eleanor and my children' (*Recueil*, I, no. 6).

21. C. F. Slade, 'Wallingford Castle in the Reign of Stephen', *Berkshire Archaeological Journal*, 58 (1960), 33–43; C. N. L. Brooke, with G. Kier, *London 800–1216: The Shaping of the City* (London, 1975), fig. 3 and fig. 5, for aerial view and plan of Wallingford; and see also N. Christie, O. Creighton, M. Edgeworth and H. Hamerow, *Transforming Townscapes. From Burgh to Borough: The Archaeology of Wallingford, 800–1400* (Society for Medieval Archaeology, 2013).

22. *Gesta Stephani*, ed. and trans. K. R. Potter, with notes by R. H. C. Davis (Oxford 1976, reprinted 2004), 236–9; J. C. Holt, '1153: The Treaty of Winchester', *The Anarchy of Stephen's Reign*, ed. E. King (Oxford, 1994), 291–316.

23. As the Walden chronicler noted, he had been crowned 'absque ullius reclamatione' (*The Book of the Foundation of Walden Monastery*, ed. D. Greenway and L. Watkiss (Oxford, 1999), 24–5).

24. *RRAN*, III, no. 272; J. H. Round, *Studies in Peerage and Family History* (London, 1907), 147–80; and T. K. Keefe, 'William [William of Blois], earl of Surrey [Earl Warenne] (c.1135–1159)', *ODNB*.

25. Torigni, 161, 'heritatem suam ex parte matris', 162–4; Gervase, I, 147; Ralph Niger, *Chronicle*, 188, who refers to Geoffrey as 'Guafridus Plantagenest comes Andegaviae'.

26. Torigni, 123, records Geoffrey's birth as 3 June 1134; and WN, I, 112–14, for the story of Geoffrey's deathbed testament, by which supposedly the count willed that should Henry succeed in gaining England, he was to relinquish Anjou to his brother. Some historians have accepted the story, notably T. K. Keefe, 'Geoffrey Plantagenet's Will', *Albion*, 6 (1975), 226–74; C. W. Hollister and T. K. Keefe, 'The Making of the Angevin Empire', *Journal of British Studies*, 12 (1973); and Gillingham, *The Angevin Empire*, 12, 17. As early as 1145, however, a charter of Duke Geoffrey suggests Henry was earmarked as heir to Anjou as well as Normandy (Chibnall, *Empress Matilda*, 145), and it seems improbable that a father would compel an eldest son to forgo the patrimony, especially when in 1150 King Stephen's defeat was far from certain. As Warren, *Henry II*, 46–7, 64, suggests, the whole story may well have been fabricated by Geoffrey or his partisans to justify his renewed rebellion in 1156.

27. Torigni, 165–6, 169–70.

28. *Chronicon Turonense magnum*, in *Recueil des chroniques de Touraine*, ed. A. Salmon (Tours, 1854), 135; Turner, *Eleanor*, 107.

29. *Chronica de gestis consulum Andegavorum*, in *Chroniques des comtes d'Anjou*, 71. Helias was imprisoned at Tours from 1145 to his death in 1151 (*Recueil d'annales angevines*, 11, n. 2, and 71).

30. *Chroniques des comtes d'Anjou*, 232; Orderic, II, 104–5; L. Halphen, *Le Comté d'Anjou au XIe siècle* (Paris, 1906), 146; O. Guillot, *Le Comte d'Anjou et son entourage au XIe siècle*, 2 vols (Paris, 1972), I, 105–15.

31. Nevertheless, B. S. Bachrach, 'Henry II and the Angevin Tradition of Family Hostility', *Albion*, 16 (1984), 111–30, has argued that co-operation rather than conflict was the norm among members of the early Angevin dynasty, and that if Henry II and his sons had looked to a tradition of familial hostility, it was more readily to be found in the disputes of their Norman forebears. For the problems of younger brothers, K. Thompson, 'L'Héritier et le remplaçant: le rôle du frère puîné dans la politique anglo-normande (1066–1204)', *Tinchebray, 1106–2006. Actes du colloque de Tinchebray (28–30 septembre 2006)*, ed. V. Gazeau and J. Green (Caen, 2009), 93–100.

32. W. M. Aird, *Robert Curthose, Duke of Normandy (c. 1050–1134)* (Woodbridge, 2008), 245–81.

33. Y. Sassier, *Louis VII* (Paris, 1991), 196–8; L. Grant, *Abbot Suger of St Denis* (Harlow, 1998), 172–4.

34. He probably adopted the sobriquet from the second duke of Normandy, William Longsword (d. 942). In turn, Henry II's illegitimate son William, who became earl of Salisbury, took the name Longsword, as did William, the third son of Henry the Lion, duke of Saxony, and Matilda, Henry II's daughter (Gervase, *Otia imperialia*, 488–9).

35. Torigni, 186.

36. E. Amt, 'William FitzEmpress (1136–1164)', *ODNB*, who notes that by 1162 he was receiving geld exemption of over £500 on lands in fifteen counties; Amt, *The Accession of Henry II*, 75–6, 127, 153.

37. Torigni, 186–7; WN, I, 113–14; *Recueil*, I, nos 13, 14 and 16. Torigni, 163, noted that Count Geoffrey had granted Geoffrey four castles, three of which are named by Newburgh (WN, I, 113), as Chinon, Loudun and Mirebeau.

38. Torigni, 186, n. 4; *Recueil d'annales angevines*, 14, 102.
39. Torigni, 187, who estimated the county of Nantes to be worth 60,000 shillings *angevin*; WN, I, 114; *Chronicon Britannicum, RHF*, XII, 560; J. Dunbabin, *France in the Making, 843–1180* (Oxford, 2000), 330–3; J. Everard, *Brittany and the Angevins. Province and Empire, 1158–1203* (Cambridge, 2000), 38–40.
40. Torigni, 189; and for the moving simile, Gervase, *Otia imperialia*, 486–7. It is possible that Henry II and Eleanor later had a second son who died in infancy, perhaps between the birth of Geoffrey (1158) and Eleanor (1161), or between 1161 and the birth of Joanna (1165); Diceto, II, 16–17, 269–70; A. W. Lewis, 'The Birth and Childhood of King John: Some Revisions', *Eleanor of Aquitaine. Lord and Lady*, 159–75, at 161.
41. Torigni, 189; J. M. Luxford, 'The Tomb of King Henry I in Reading Abbey: New Evidence Concerning its Appearance and the Date of its Effigy', *Reading Medieval Studies*, 30 (2004), 15–31. Matthew Paris provides the date of his burial, and speaks of him as 'infirmatus Willelmus' (*Matthaei Parisiensis monachi sancti Albani, Historia Anglorum*, ed. F. Madden, 3 vols, Rolls Series, London, 1865–1869, I, 307).
42. F. T. Wethered, *St Mary's Hurley in the Middle Ages* (London, 1898), no. 15; *Letters and Charters of Henry II*, no. 231; C. R. Cheney, 'A Monastic Letter of Fraternity to Eleanor of Aquitaine', *EHR*, 51 (1936), 488–93; Turner, *Eleanor*, 130; N. Vincent, 'Patronage, Politics and Piety in the Charters of Eleanor of Aquitaine', *Plantagenêts et Capétiens*, 17–60, at 22, n. 30.
43. WN, I, 106.
44. R. V. Turner, 'Eleanor of Aquitaine and her Children: an Inquiry into Medieval Family Attachment', *JMH*, xiv (1988), 325–6; H. Vollrath, 'Aliénor d'Aquitaine et ses enfants: une relation affective?', *Plantagenêts et Capétiens*, 113–24; and C. M. Bowie, *The Daughters of Henry II and Eleanor of Aquitaine* (Turnhout, 2014), 55–63.
45. Eyton, 16; Turner, 'Eleanor of Aquitaine and her Children: an Inquiry into Medieval Family Attachment', 325–6; idem, *Eleanor*, 150–74. For a valuable comparative study, R. V. Turner, 'The Children of Anglo-Norman Royalty and their Upbringing', *Medieval Prosopography*, 11 (1990), 17–52; M. Goodrich, 'Bartholemeus Anglicus on Child-rearing', *History of Childhood Quarterly/Journal of Psychohistory*, 3 (1975), 75–84.
46. Turner, 'Eleanor of Aquitaine and her Children', 326; N. Orme, *From Childhood to Chivalry: The Education of English Kings and the Aristocracy, 1066–1530* (London, 1984), 11–12.
47. Turner, 'Eleanor of Aquitaine and her Children', 325–6. To cover his expenses, Mainard received £6 per annum from the vill of Tarentford, Kent (*The Great Rolls of the Pipe for the Second, Third and Fourth Years of the Reign of Henry II, 1155–1158* (*PR 2, 3, 4 Henry II*), ed. J. Hunter (Record Commission, 1844), 66, 101, 180; *PR 5 Henry II*, 58).
48. Turner, 'Eleanor of Aquitaine and her Children', 325–6.
49. *PR 2, 3, 4 Henry II*, 66, 101, 180; *PR 5 Henry II*, 58; K. Dutton, '*Ad erudiendum tradidit*: The Upbringing of Angevin Comital Children', *ANS*, 32 (2010), 24–39. Some of Fulk V's charters are witnessed by one Richard, styled *pedagogus* or *nutritor* to the count's brother Philip (*Grand Cartulaire de Fontevraud*, ed. J.-M. Bienvenue, R. Favreau and G. Pon, 2 vols (Poitiers, 2000, 2005), I, nos 139, 153, 204, II, no. 850).
50. Turner, *Eleanor*, 161–7; J. Dor, 'Langues françaises et anglaises, et multilinguisme à l'époque d'Henri II Plantagenet', *CCM*, 29, 61–72; Turner, *Eleanor*, 127.
51. Chibnall, *Empress Matilda*, 151.
52. Chibnall, 'The Empress Matilda and her Sons', *Medieval Mothering*, ed. J. C. Parsons and B. Wheeler (New York and London, 1996), 279–94, at 285–9; Turner, *Eleanor*, 132.
53. Diceto, I, 302; *PR 2, 3, 4 Henry*, 4; Eyton, 18, for corrodies for the queen and subsequent payments for prince Henry, his new sister and his aunt.
54. *PR 2 Henry II*, 5; Eyton, 18.
55. *RHF*, XII, 121; *Recueil*, IV, 66; Eyton, 19–20; *PR 2 Henry II*, 5; *PR 3 Henry II*, 71, 107; R. Smith, 'The Royal Family in the Reign of Henry II', 50, n. 2. Payments to the queen and her children from the Pipe Rolls included 44 shillings 'for rushes' for young Henry's use, presumably for a mattress or floor covering.
56. J. H. Le Patourel, 'Le Gouvernement de Henri II Plantagenêt et la mer de la Manche', *Recueil d'études offerts au Doyen M. de Bouärd* (Annales de Normandie extra, Caen, 1982), II, 323–33, noting that between 1154 and 1189 Henry II crossed the Channel at least twenty-six times. For the esnecca, FitzStephen, 26; C. H, Haskins, *Norman Institutions* (Cambridge, Mass., 1918), 121–2; R. H. F. Lindemann, 'The English Esnecca in Northern European Sources', *Mariner's Mirror*, 74 (1988), 75–82; D. Gilmour, 'Bekesbourne and the King's Esnecca, 1110–1445', *Archaeologia Cantiana*, 132 (2012), 315–27.
57. J. H. Round, *The King's Serjeants and Officers of State* (London, 1911), 18.
58. William of Malmesbury, *Gesta regum Anglorum*, ed. R. A. B. Mynors, R. M. Thompson and M. Winterbottom, 2 vols (Oxford, 1998–1999), I, 760–1.

59. *The Chronicle of John of Worcester*, ed. R. R. Darlington and P. McGurk, 3 vols (Oxford, 1995–), III, 202–3.

60. K. Leyser, 'Frederick Barbarossa, Henry II and the Hand of St James', *EHR*, 90 (1975), 481–506; N. Vincent, 'King Henry III and the Blessed Virgin Mary', *The Church and Mary*, ed. R. Swanson (Boydell, 2004), 126–46, at 129. In 1154, for example, he crossed to England on the eve of the Conception of the Virgin (7 December), and in 1158 he crossed to Normandy on the vigil of the feast of the Assumption (14 August) (ibid.; Torigni, 186, 196; Eyton, 15–16, 40–1). It may well have been anxieties about the Channel crossing after a period of rough weather that led Henry II to make his will just before sailing to Normandy in March, 1182 (J. Gillingham, 'At the Deathbeds of the Kings of England', *Herrscher- und Fürstentestamente im westeuropäischen Mittelalter*, ed. B. Kasten (Vienna, 2008), 509–30, at 517–18; and below, 269).

61. William of Canterbury, *Vita, Passio et Miracula Sancti Thomae*, ed. J. C. Robertson, *MTB*, I, no. 90; and for wider context L. Musset, 'Un Empire à cheval sur la mer: les périls de la mer dans l'État anglo-normand d'après les chartes, les chroniques et les miracles', *Les Hommes et la mer dans l'Europe du Nord-Ouest de l'Antiquité à nos jours*, ed. A. Lottin, J.-C. Hoquet and S. Lebecq (Villeneuve d'Ascq, 1986), 413–24. William of Canterbury seems to have compiled the *Miracula* after May 1172, but probably before completing his *Vita* of Becket. The monks of Christ Church presented Henry II with a copy, apparently at his request (*MTB*, I, xxx, 137).

62. *GH*, I, 4, 30.

63. *GH*, I, 195; Diceto, I, 422.

64. *PR 2, 3, 4 Henry*, 171; *PR 5 Henry II*, 45.

65. Torigni, 195.

66. Eyton, 21–5; Warren, *Henry II*, 66–8.

67. For the ambush and the campaign, D. J. Cathcart-King, 'The Fight at Coleshill', *Welsh Historical Review*, 2 (1965), 367–73; J. G. Edwards, 'Henry II and the Fight at Coleshill: Some Further Reflections', *Welsh Historical Review*, 3 (1967), 253–61; J. Hosler, 'Henry II's Military Campaigns in Wales, 1157–1165', *Journal of Medieval Military History*, 2 (2004), 53–71.

68. *The Letters of John of Salisbury (LJS)* ed. W. J. Millor, H. E. Butler and C. N. L. Brooke, 2 vols (Oxford, 1979, 1986), I, 32.

69. Eyton, 32.

70. *Chronique de Robert de Torigni* (Torigni, ed. Delisle), ed. L. Delisle, 2 vols (Rouen, 1872–1873), I, 298, and cf. II, 166. Earlier, Henry had named his favoured natural son Geoffrey, born probably in 1151 and before Henry's marriage to Eleanor, after his own father (Gerald of Wales, *De vita Galfridi Eboracensis archiepiscopi*, in Gerald, *Opera*, IV, 363). Yet it is striking that, thereafter, it was only Henry's fourth legitimate son who received the name of Geoffrey, and equally that Henry II was to call none of his children Fulk. This was despite the prominence of the name among his Angevin comital ancestors, and the fact that his paternal grandfather Fulk V had raised the dynasty to new heights of prestige by becoming the third Latin king of Jerusalem in 1131 (Diceto, II, 15; William of Tyre, *Chronique* (William of Tyre), ed. R. B. C. Huygens, 2 vols (Corpus Christianorum, Continuatio medievalis 63–63a, Turnhout, 1986), XIV: 1). This reticence may well have reflected Henry's sensitivity to the fact that the Angevins had long been a traditional enemy of the Normans, and that, despite Count Geoffrey's marriage to Henry I's daughter Matilda, he had only wrested Normandy from King Stephen by force of arms and a prolonged war of attrition, still etched in recent memory.

71. Eyton, 40.

72. *PR 26 Henry II*, xxviii; M. Biddle and B. Clayre, *Winchester Castle and the Great Hall* (Winchester, 1983), 7. Stephen's crown had been kept at Winchester, from whence Matilda took it in 1141 (*Gesta Stephani*, 118–19), while at Michaelmas 1157, 2 shillings was paid to transport the new king's crown from Winchester to Bury St Edmunds (*PR 3 Henry II*, 107).

73. *The History of the King's Works*, ed. H. M. Colvin, 8 vols (London, HMSO, 1963–1982), II, 855–7.

74. *JW*, III, 294–5, 298–9; William of Malmesbury, *Historia Novella*, ed. K. Potter and E. King (Oxford, 1998), 102–3 and n. 245; *JW*, III, 298–301, and 300, n. 10.

75. Turner, *Eleanor*, 125–6.

76. *PR 2, 3, 4 Henry II*, 115.

77. J. Boorman, 'Hugh de Gundeville', *ODNB*; N. Vincent, 'Hugh de Gundeville (fl.1147–81)', *Records, Administration and Aristocratic Society in the Anglo-Norman Realm. Papers Commemorating the 800th Anniversary of King John's Loss of Normandy*, ed. N. Vincent (Woodbridge, 2009), 125–52.

78. Vincent, 'Hugh de Gundeville', 131–2. He later became sheriff of Hampshire and keeper of the city of Winchester from 1170 to 1179 (ibid., 132).

79. The Astronomer, *Vita Hludowici imperatoris*, ed. E. Tremp, *MGH SRG*, 44 (Hanover, 1995), 294. For such military training, J. Le Jan, 'Apprentissages militaires, rites de passage, et remises d'armes au haut Moyen Âge', *Éducation, apprentissages, inititiation au Moyen Âge. Actes du premier colloque international de Montpellier, Cahiers du CRISIMANO*, 1 (1993), 214–22.

80. *PR 6 Henry II*, 13; M. T. Flanagan, 'William fiz Aldelin [William Fitzaldhelm], (d. before 1198), administrator', *ODNB*.

81. *PR 6 Henry II*, 49.

82. *PR 2, 3, 4 Henry II*, 115, 175.

83. *PR 5 Henry II*, 45.

84. *Recueil*, I, no. 62; *Letters and Charters of Henry II*, no. 2381.

85. Eyton, 49.

86. J. Dunbabin, 'Henry II and Louis VII', *Henry II. New Interpretations*, 47–62.

87. For the extent of the Vexin ceded by Geoffrey, see J.-F. Lemarignier, *Recherches sur l'hommage en marche et les frontieres féodales* (Lille, 1945), 45 and n. 53.

88. FitzStephen, 29–31.

89. L. Diggelmann, 'Marriage as a Tactical Response: Henry II and the Royal Wedding of 1160', *EHR*, 119 (2004), 954–64, at 956, n. 13.

90. Dunbabin, 'Henry II and Louis VII', 50.

91. Torigni, 196; *Continuatio Beccensis*, in *Chronicles of the Reigns of Stephen, Henry II and Richard I*, ed. R. H. Howlett, 4 vols (Rolls Series, London, 1884–1889), IV, 318.

92. *Continuatio Beccensis*, 319.

93. Gillingham, *The Angevin Empire*, 10–12.

94. WN, I, 123–4; T. M. Bisson, *The Medieval Crown of Aragon* (Oxford, 1986), 27–35.

95. Diceto, I, 303. For the political symbolism of such conduct, and of Henry's lavish hospitality to Louis during the king's return visit to Normandy that November, J. Gillingham, 'The Meeting of the Kings of France and England, 1066–1204', *Normandy and its Neighbours, 900–1250. Essays for David Bates*, ed. D. Crouch and K. Thompson (Turnhout, 2011), 17–42, at 34–6. For the relations between Henry II and Louis, I. Wolff, *Heinrich II von England als Vasall Ludwigs VII* (Breslau, 1936); and Y. Sassier, '*Reverentia Regis*; Henri II face à Louis VII', *1204. La Normandie entre Plantagenêts et Capétiens*, ed. A.-M. Flambard-Héricher and V. Gazeau (Caen, 2007), 23–35.

96. Torigni, 196–7.

97. *LJS*, II, no. 288, p. 639; J. Gillingham, 'Doing Homage to the King of France', *Henry II. New Interpretations*, 63–84, at 74.

98. For the near-contemporary case of Agnes, the daughter of Henry of Essex, betrothed aged only three to Aubrey de Vere, earl of Oxford, in the mid 1150s and placed in the charge of Aubrey's brother, Geoffrey de Vere, see R. C. DeAragon, 'The Child-Bride, the Earl and the Pope: The Marital Fortunes of Agnes of Essex', *Haskins Society Journal*, 17 (2007), 200–16. Adam of Eynsham noted that in the early 1190s, Adam de Neville, brother of the chief forester, Hugh de Neville, married Grace, the supposed heiress of the Lincolnshire knight Thomas of Saleby, when she was only four (Adam of Eynsham, *The Life of St Hugh of Lincoln*, ed. D. L. Douie and H. Farmer, 2 vols (Oxford, 1961–1962), II, 20–7.

99. Torigni, 197 and 203; *Continuatio Beccensis*, 324, noting that Robert, 'vir magnae prudentiae et bonitatis', fell ill, took the habit at Bec and died soon after on 30 August 1159; *The Correspondence of Thomas Becket, Archbishop of Canterbury, 1162– 1170 (CTB)*, ed. A. J. Duggan, 2 vols (Oxford, 2000), I, no. 24.

100. *Continuatio Beccensis*, 320; Torigni, 198; Gervase, I, 166.

101. R. Benjamin, 'A Forty Years War: Toulouse and the Plantagenets, 1156–1196', *Historical Research*, 61 (1988), 270–85; J. Martindale, '"An Unfinished Business": Angevin Politics and the Siege of Toulouse, 1159', *ANS*, 23 (2000), 115–54.

102. Torigni, 200.

103. Torigni, 203.

104. FitzStephen, 33; WN, I, 125; Stephen of Rouen, *Draco Normannicus*, in *Chronicles of the Reigns of Stephen, Henry II and Richard I*, II, 608–9; Vigeois, 310; and Diceto, I, 303.

105. In 1151, Henry had withdrawn from the siege of Torigni on Louis' approach, and when later that year Louis had aided Stephen's son Eustace in besieging Arques, Henry had moved to attack him but was prevented by his senior Norman, Breton and Angevin magnates (Torigni, 161; Sassier, 'Reverentia regis', 26–8, 31.

106. FitzStephen, 34; Grim, *MTB*, II, 365; Bosham, 176; *Continuatio Beccensis*, 323; Torigni, 205.

107. Diceto, I, 303. For this reverse as a turning point in the reign, Warren, *Henry II*, 9.

108. Torigni, 205–6; Warren, *Henry II*, 87–8.

109. Torigni, 206. They reached England on 31 December 1159 (Eyton, 51).

110. Torigni, 207; *Recueil*, I, no. 141; *Letters and Charters of Henry II*, no. 1666; Eyton, 50.
111. Torigni, 207–8; Howden, I, 218; *RHF*, XVI, 21–2; *Recueil*, I, no. 141; and *Letters and Charters of Henry II*, no. 1666. For discussion of whether the pact should be dated to May or October, Diggelmann, 'Marriage as a Tactical Response', 957, n. 15.
112. Torigni, 207.
113. *RHF*, XVI, 700–1, for the text, issued at Beauvais in July 1160. For Henry's recognition of Alexander, M. Cheney, 'The Recognition of Pope Alexander III: Some Neglected Evidence', *EHR*, 84 (1969), 474–97, which takes issue on the date with F. Barlow, 'The English, Norman and French Councils called to deal with the Papal Schism of 1159', *EHR*, 51 (1936), 264–8. Cf. *Councils and Synods*, I, vol. 2, 835–41; and for Henry II's control over ecclesiastical recognition of the pope within his lands, A. Duggan, 'Henry II, the English Church and the Papacy, 1154–76', *Henry II. New Interpretations*, 154–83, at 168–70.
114. Diggelmann, 'Marriage as a Tactical Response', 958.
115. Torigni, 208, 'de ducatu Normanniae, qui est de regno Franciae'.
116. Gillingham, 'Doing Homage', 63–84, at 77; William of Malmesbury, *Gesta regum*, I, 758–9; HH, 708; Torigni, 132; *The Ecclesiastical History of Orderic Vitalis* (Orderic), ed. M. Chibnall, 6 vols (Oxford, 1969–1980), VI, 482. Gillingham, 'Doing Homage', 66–7, shows that Gervase, I, 112, was mistaken in noting that Eustace performed homage to Louis VII in 1140.
117. Torigni, 162 Gillingham, 'Doing Homage', 63–77; K. van Eickels, *Vom inszenierten Konsens zum systematisierten Konflikt: Die englische–französischen Beziehungen und ihre Wahrnehmung und der Wende vom Hoch-zum Spätmittelalter* (Stuttgart, 2002), 318; and idem, 'L'Hommage des rois anglais et de leurs héritiers aux rois français au XIIe siècle: subordination imposée ou reconnaissance souhaitée?', *Plantagenêts et Capétiens*, 377–85. It is probable that Geoffrey le Bel never performed homage for Normandy (Gillingham, 'Doing Homage', 69).
118. Torigni, 207; Gervase, 167; *Historia gloriosi regis Ludovici*, ed. A. Molinier (Paris, 1887), 129.
119. Diceto, I, 303. Louis thus became the brother-in-law of his two sons-in-law.
120. *RHF*, XIII, 517–18; Diggelmann, 'Marriage as a Tactical Response', 957.
121. Howden, I, 218, 'pueruli in cunis vagientes'; Torigni, 208; Diceto, I, 304; Diggelmann, 'Marriage as a Tactical Response', 960.
122. Torigni, 208; Diceto, I, 303–4.
123. For Gisors, see J. Mesqui and P. Toussaint, 'Le Château de Gisors aux XIIe et XIIIe siècles', *Archéologie médiévale*, 20 (1990), 253–317; and A. Baume, 'Le Document et le terrain: la trace du système défensif normand au XIIe siècle', in *1204: la Normandie entre Plantagenêts et Capétiens*, ed. A.-M. Flambard-Héricher and V. Gazeau (Caen, 2007), 93–112.
124. Diceto, I, 304.
125. Diceto, I, 303; Diggelmann, 'Marriage as a Tactical Response', 960–1.
126. Howden, I, 218, who notes that the Templars were welcomed by Henry II; Diceto, I, 304.
127. Torigni, 208–9; Diceto, I, 303–4; *Recueil*, I, no. 201. Henry entrusted it to Hugh of Amboise, a mortal enemy of Count Theobald, because his father Sulpitius had perished in his prison (Torigni, 208–9).
128. Torigni, 209–11; Diceto, I, 305.
129. In 1165, for example, not only was Henry II's daughter Matilda, then aged eight, betrothed to the thirty-six-year-old Henry the Lion, duke of Saxony, but her three-year-old sister Eleanor was betrothed to Frederick Barbarossa's son Henry, who was not yet a year old (Torigni, 224).
130. John's birth may have been in late 1166 or early 1167 (Lewis, 'The Birth and Childhood of King John', 159–65).
131. G. Duby, 'Youth in Aristocratic Society', in G. Duby, *The Chivalrous Society*, trans. C. Postan (London, 1977), 112–22; and idem, *Medieval Marriage* (Baltimore, 1979), 10–13; D. Bates, 'The Conqueror's Adolescence', *ANS*, 25 (2002), 1–18.
132. Below, 316.
133. *GH*, I, 177. Margaret appears to have had no children with her second husband, King Béla III of Hungary. For this marriage, below, 317 and n. 98. For wider context, J. Gillingham, 'Love, Marriage and Politics in the Twelfth Century', *Forum for Modern Language Studies*, 25 (1989), 292–303, reprinted in idem, *Richard Coeur de Lion. Kingship, Chivalry and War in the Twelfth Century* (London, 1994), 243–55.
134. *CTB*, I, no. 24.
135. Rigord, *Histoire de Philippe Auguste* (Rigord), ed. É. Charpentier, G. Pon and Y. Chauvin (Paris, 2006), 120; *De principis*, 292.
136. Gillingham, 'The Meeting of the Kings of France and England', 17–42, and especially 23, noting that the marriage of the young Henry to Margaret and the betrothal of Alice to Richard in 1169 'ensured that these meetings of kings retained the character of family conferences to a degree not seen since the many meetings of Carolingian kings in the ninth century'.

137. Gillingham, 'Doing Homage', 78. For the status of the Vexin and its place in Anglo-French diplomacy, L. Landon, *The Itinerary of Richard I* (Pipe Roll Society, new series, xiii, London, 1935), 219–34, Appendix H, 'The Vexin'.

Chapter 3: *Rex Puer*

1. *Raoul de Hodenc: Le Roman des Eles*, ed. and trans. K. Busby (Amsterdam and Philadelphia, Pa., 1983), 163.
2. Matthew Paris, *Historia Anglorum*, I, 315.
3. F. Barlow, *Thomas Becket* (London, 1986), 69.
4. W. H. Hutton, *Thomas Becket* (Cambridge, 1926), 51.
5. FitzStephen, 104, 'prima elementa morum et litterarum'; M. G. Cheney, *Roger Bishop of Worcester, 1164–1179* (Oxford, 1980), 7; A. L. Poole, 'Henry Plantagenet's Early Visits to England', *EHR*, 47 (1932), 447–51; Chibnall, *Empress Matilda*, 144. He also spent some time with his mother the Empress at Devizes (M. Chibnall, 'The Empress Matilda and her Sons', *Medieval Mothering*, 279–94, at 284).
6. M. Innes, '"A Place of Discipline": Carolingian Courts and Aristocratic Youth', *Court Culture in the Early Middle Ages. Proceedings of the First Alcuin Conference*, ed. C. Cubitt (Turnhout, 2003), 59–76; and C. Dette, 'Kinder und Jungendliche in der Adelsgesellschaft des frühen Mittelalters', *Archiv für Kulturgeschichte*, 76 (1994), 1–34.
7. Henry I's natural son Richard, for example, was brought up in the household of Robert Bloet, bishop of Lincoln, which was famed for its magnificence; another of that king's illegitimate sons, Robert of Gloucester, had also received schooling there at some stage in his youth (HH, 594–5).
8. *HWM*, ll. 743–804, 'pris e . . . onor'; Map, 488–9; Crouch, *William Marshal*, 22–8. William, however, joined the Tancarville household at the rather later age of about twelve (*HWM*, III, 61, note to line 773).
9. One of Henry II's closest companions, William de Mandeville, had as a second son been brought up from his youth in the court of Philip of Alsace, count of Flanders, and had been knighted by him (*Foundation of Walden*, 44–5, 80–1). His father Earl Geoffrey had Flemish knights in his service, and William may have been sent to Flanders for safety around 1143, when Geoffrey's political position in England was under attack (ibid., xxiv).
10. J. R. Lyon, 'Fathers and Sons: Preparing Noble Youths to be Lords in Twelfth-Century Germany', *JMH*, 34 (2008), 291–310.
11. Henry I's only legitimate son, William Aetheling, had grown up at the royal court, together with the king's nephew Stephen of Blois and sons of the greatest nobles such as Waleran and Robert, heirs to Robert, count of Meulan. King Stephen's son Eustace was probably also raised in his father's court after 1135. Henry FitzEmpress' fosterage with his uncle Robert of Gloucester had in this respect been unusual, motivated as much by political expediency as by the desire for education at a court renowned for its cultural patronage, for it was hoped the presence of the Matilda's son and heir in England would bolster the beleaguered Angevin cause there.
12. *CTB*, II, no. 243, 'ut ei alendum et instiuendum'. By contrast, the future Louis VI was said to have come with a group of followers to the court of Henry I early in the latter's reign 'to attend him as a distinguished young knight' (Orderic, VI, 50–1).
13. These included the sons of several earls: N. Vincent, 'Did Henry II have a Policy towards the Earls?', *War, Government and Aristocracy in the British Isles, c. 1150–1500. Essays in Honour of Michael Prestwich*, ed. C. Given-Wilson, A. Kettle and L. Scales (Woodbridge, 2008), 1–26, at 11. Geoffrey of Monmouth, writing *c.*1139, reflected the practice at the court of Henry I when he described King Arthur's reception of young nobles: 'during that time the youthful sons of noble families come to him from the remotest parts; gladly the king honours them and makes them his young warriors (*neoptolomos*), ennobling them with horses and armour and enriching them with gifts': *The Historia Regum Brittaniae of Geoffrey of Monmouth, V. Gesta Regum Britanniae*, ed. and trans. N. Wright (Cambridge, 1991), 190–1 (VII: 154).
14. *The Letters of Arnulf of Lisieux*, ed. F. Barlow (Camden Society, 3rd series, lxi, 1939), 18–20.
15. M. Keen, *Chivalry* (New York and London, 1984), 66–9; Le Jan, 'Apprentissages militaires', 211–32.
16. FitzStephen, 35; William of Malmesbury, *Gesta regum*, I, 542–3, noting that Lanfranc 'reared him and made him knight (*eum nutrierat et militem fecerat*)'; F. Barlow, *William Rufus* (London, 1983), 22. I am grateful to John Gillingham for this point. Lanfranc also knighted the future Henry I, though he may have been educated in the household of Bishop Osmund of Salisbury rather than that of the archbishop (*Anglo-Saxon Chronicle*, E, 1086; William of Malmesbury, *Gesta regum*, I, 710; Green, *Henry I*, 22–3).
17. FitzStephen, 18. The most extensive discussion of Becket's role as chancellor remains L. B. Radford, *Thomas of London before his Consecration* (Cambridge, 1984), especially 57–152.

18. Gervase of Canterbury, I, 169, could later claim that by 1161 Thomas was said to be '*in* Anglia potentissimus', and that he 'was also the king's guide, and, as it were, his master (*sed et regis rector et quasi magister*)'.
19. N. Vincent, 'The Court of Henry II', *Henry II. New Interpretations*, 278–34, at 288–92.
20. L. Grant, *Abbot Suger of St Denis* (Harlow, 1998), 124–5; E. Bournazel, *Le Gouvernement capétien, 1108–1180* (Paris, 1975), 104; F. Funck-Bretano, *The Middle Ages* (London, 1922), 130. His role equally echoed that of Roger, bishop of Salisbury, in the government of Henry I (E. J. Kealey, *Roger of Salisbury, Viceroy of England*, Berkeley and London, 1972).
21. FitzStephen, 25; and cf. Howden, I, 216. As John of Salisbury informed Becket himself in 1160, 'common report and rumour seems to indicate that you are so strongly of heart and mind, that in view of such intimate friendship your desires and dislikes must coincide' (*LJS*, I, no. 128, 221).
22. FitzStephen, 22; Staunton, *Lives*, 50–1.
23. Ibid.
24. Matthew Paris, *Historia Anglorum*, I, 315, 'unde postea idem Thomas ipsum Henricum jocose filium suum adoptivum appellavit'; *Thómas Saga Erkibyskups*, ed. and trans. E. Magnusson, 2 vols (Rolls Series, London, 1875–1883), I, 120–1, similarly says he regarded young Henry as his foster son.
25. In a like manner, the Englishman Ralph, bishop of Bethlehem and chancellor of the Latin kingdom of Jerusalem, had been prominent in the regency of Queen Melisende, widow of Henry II's grandfather Fulk V, who from 1143 acted as co-ruler with her son Baldwin III (B. Hamilton, 'Ralph (d. 1174), administrator and bishop of Bethlehem', *ODNB*).
26. In addition to his archdeaconry of Canterbury, the provostship of Beverley and several other livings, Becket held the castles and honour of Eye, with its service of 140 knights, Berkhamsted and the Tower of London 'with knight service provided' (FitzStephen, 20).
27. FitzStephen, 22; Staunton, *Lives*, 50.
28. Bosham, 176. He even had his own fleet of six or more ships, and once presented the king with three fully equipped vessels (FitzStephen, 22, 26). Becket's near-contemporary, the Englishman Roger of Selby, had, as chancellor to King Roger II of Sicily, a similar reputation for splendour and extravagance (D. H. S. Abulafia, 'Robert of Selby [Salesby], Robert of (*fl.* 1137–1151), administrator', *ODNB*).
29. *La Vie de Saint Thomas le Martyr par Guernes de Pont-Sainte-Maxence* (Guernes) ed. E. Wahlberg (Lund, 1922), ll. 341–3; *Garnier's Becket*, trans. J. Shirley (Chichester, 1975), 10.
30. FitzStephen, 20–1; Staunton, *Lives*, 50. For the rebuke of an anonymous French scholar, writing *c.* 1156 x 1164 but probably before Becket's elevation to the archbishopric, B. Ross, 'Audi Thoma … Henriciani Nota: a French Scholar Appeals to Thomas Becket?', *EHR*, 89 (1974), 333–8, especially 336, 'Listen, Thomas! With that which you spend to buy beasts, ransom prisoners; whence you feed wild beasts, nourish the poor; whence you arm men, bury the innocent dead!'
31. For Thomas' sense of the magnificent, Barlow, *Becket*, 219.
32. FitzStephen, 20–1; Staunton, *Lives*, 50.
33. FitzStephen, 36. As a youth, Becket himself had been captivated by the knightly lifestyle of one of his father's friends, Richer de Laigle, who had taught him horsemanship and hunting, the essential prerequisites of the aristocratic life for which Becket yearned (Grim, *MTB*, II, 359–61; Guernes, ll. 206–13; *Thómas Saga Erikibiskups*, I, 30–5; and for Richer himself, Barlow, *Becket*, 19–20).
34. These included Baldwin, son of Count Arnold of Guines, who as count himself later obtained relics of St Thomas to place in his chapel of St Catherine at La Montoire, and showed the saint particular devotion, 'because Thomas had administered the oath of knighthood to him and granted and bestowed on him the name and duty of a knight' (*Lamberti Ardensis historia comitum Ghisnensium*, ed. J. Heller, *MGH SS*, 24: 550–642, cc. 75, 87; Lambert of Ardres, *The History of the Counts of Guines and Lords of Ardres*, trans. L. Shopkow, University of Pennsylvania, 2001, 110, 121).
35. FitzStephen, 33, 34–5. Guernes noted of Becket in Normandy that 'I myself saw him riding several times against the French; his trumpets did much to further the king's cause' (ll. 358–60). On Thomas as a commander, J. D. Hosler, 'The Brief Military Career of Thomas Becket', *Haskins Society Journal*, 15 (2006), 88–100, and on the size and nature of the forces under Becket's command, Strickland, 'On the Instruction of a Prince: The Upbringing of Henry, the Young King', 192.
36. FitzStephen, 35.
37. Equally, the power and glamour with which Becket had imbued the chancellorship goes far to explain why, when confronted in 1181 by a papal demand that he should finally be consecrated bishop of Lincoln or surrender the office after a scandalously long tenure merely as bishop elect, young Henry's half-brother Geoffrey unhesitatingly chose to abandon the bishopric in favour of becoming chancellor to Henry II, a role far better suited to his skills as a soldier and all too evident ambitions (*GH*, I, 271–2).
38. HH, 586–7.
39. HH, 586–7.

40. Warren, *Henry II*, 207 and n. 1.
41. Torigni, 215.
42. Map, 116–17; Vincent, 'The Court of Henry II', 308–9; and S. Schröder, *Macht und Gabe: Materielle Kultur am Hof Heinrichs II von England* (Husum, 2004).
43. Diceto, II, 3; D. Crouch, 'The Court of Henry II of England in the 1180s, and the Office of King of Arms', *The Coat of Arms: The Journal of the Heraldry Society*, 3rd series, 5 (2010), pt 2, 47–55; and on the court's protocol, Vincent, 'The Court of Henry II', 323–8.
44. *GH*, I, 291; and below, 276.
45. Soon after Theobald's death, the king had granted Becket custody of all the temporalities of the see (Bosham, 180); Knowles, *Becket*, 50; Barlow, *Becket*, 53 and n. 24).
46. John of Salisbury, *MTB*, II, 306; Lambeth Anonymous, *MTB*, IV, 86; William of Canterbury, 7–8; Grim, *MTB*, II, 365–7; Barlow, *Becket*, 65.
47. Bosham, 180–1: Lambeth Anonymous, *MTB*, IV, 85–6; William of Canterbury, 7–8; 'Roger of Pontigny', *MTB*, IV, 18.
48. Warren, *Henry II*, 91–2.
49. *MTB*, VII, no. 310; Duggan, 'Coronation', 168–74 for the crucial re-dating of the mandate from 1170 to 1161, and 177–8 for the text of the letter; *CTB*, I, 262 n. 13. A second mandate, *Quanto personam*, dated 13 July 1162, confirmed York's privileges, including authority to crown the king; *MTB*, V, letter 13, 'regem quoque coronare'; Duggan, 'Coronation', 168, suggesting this ambiguous phrase probably was intended to apply only to crown-wearings.
50. *The Red Book of the Exchequer*, ed. H. Hall, 3 vols (Rolls Series, London, 1896), II, 695, 'et Willielmo Cade, xxxviii l. vi s. pro auro ad coronam filii Regis et Regalia paranda'; *PR 8 Henry II*, 43. Barlow, *Becket*, 68, noted that the sum of £38 6s. would, with gold prices at around 15 shillings the ounce, provide some 50 ounces of gold. For royal goldsmiths, including Solomon who may well have been one of those employed in 1162, see E. M. C. van Houts, 'Nuns and Goldsmiths: The Foundation and Early Benefactors of Saint Radegund's Priory, Cambridge', *Church and City, 1000–1500. Essays in Honour of Christopher Brooke*, ed. D. Abulafia, M. Franklin and M. Rubin (Cambridge, 1992), 59–79, at 65–9. Among other goldsmiths was Geoffrey of Caen (*aurifaber nostrum*) who received a grant from Henry II, *c.*1177–80 (*Recueil*, II, no. 562; *Letters and Charters of Henry II*, no. 396).
51. When, following the coup which put an end to the Merovingian dynasty, Pope Stephen II anointed Pippin at Saint-Denis in 754, he also consecrated his two sons, Charles and Carloman as kings, and in turn Charles had his own sons, Pippin and Louis, anointed as kings by Pope Hadrian at Rome in 781 (*Annales regni Francorum*, 741–829, ed. F. Kurze, *MGH SRG* (Hanover, 1895), *s.a.* 754, 781). Pippin had famously been first anointed by Boniface in 750 after Pope Zacharias had been persuaded that 'it was better to call him king who had the royal power than the one who did not' (ibid., *s.a.* 749, 750).
52. 1 Samuel 16:1: 'And the Lord said unto Samuel, "How long wilt thou mourn for Saul, seeing that I have rejected him from reigning over Israel? Fill thy horn with oil, and go, I will send thee to Jesse the Bethlehemite, for I have provided me with a king among his sons"'; W. Levison, *England and the Continent in the Eighth Century* (Oxford, 1946), 115–17.
53. W. Ohnesorge, 'Die Idee der Mitregenschaft bei den Sachsenherrschern', *Mitteilungen des österreichischen Staatsarchivs*, 25 (1972), 539–48, and reprinted in idem, *Ost-Rom und der Western* (Darmstadt, 1983), 117–27. Otto I associated his son Otto II with his rule first as king in 961, then as emperor in 967, and he in turn associated his son Otto III with his kingship in 983. For Staufen practice, see B. Weiler, 'Suitability and Right: Imperial Succession and the Norms of Politics in Early Staufen Germany', *Making and Breaking the Rules of Succession in Medieval Europe, c.1000– c.1600*, ed. F. Lachaud and M. Penman (Turnhout, 2008), 71–86.
54. J. Dhondt, 'Élection et hérédité sous les Carolingiens et les premiers Capétiens', *Revue belge de philologie et d'histoire*, 18 (1939), 913–53; R. Fawtier, *The Capetian Kings of France. Monarchy and Nation, 987–1328* (London, 1960), 48–50; A. W. Lewis, 'Anticipatory Association of the Heir in Early Capetian France', *American Historical Review*, 83 (1978), 906–27; idem, *Royal Succession in Capetian France: Studies on Familial Order and the State* (Cambridge, Mass., and London, 1981), especially 44–77. The Capetians, however, could look to late Carolingian practice, for in 979 Lothar had his son Louis V, who would be the last Carolingian monarch, anointed 'rex acclamatus' (Richer of Saint-Rémi, *Histories*, ed. and trans. J. Lake, 2 vols (Cambridge, Mass., and London, 2011), II, 156–7; *Recueil des actes de Lothaire et de Louis V*, ed. L. Halphen and F. Lot (Paris, 1908), nos 9 and 56).
55. Claiming that he intended to aid the count of Barcelona against a Muslim invasion, Hugh convinced the Frankish nobles that the kingdom's safety required Robert's establishment as king lest he himself die on the expedition. Robert was duly consecrated, but Hugh's campaign never materialized (Richer, *Histories*, II, 222–5).
56. Fawtier, *Capetian Kings*, 49.
57. Thus, for example, following the premature death of his eldest son Hugh in 1025, Robert II had attempted to secure the throne for his second son Henry, crowned in 1027, in the face of a serious

challenge mounted by his youngest son Robert, who was supported by King Robert's queen, Constance (C. Pfister, *Études sur le règne de Robert le Pieux, (996–1031)* (Paris, 1885), 77.

58. *Recueil des actes de Louis VI roi de France (1108–1137),* ed. R.-H. Bautier and J. Dufour, 3 vols (Paris, 1992–1993), I, nos 3–6, 'Dei gratia Francorum rex designatus'. This coronation had been in part to counter the threat posed to him by his half-brothers Philip and Florus (A. Fliche, *Le Règne de Philippe Ier, roi de France (1060–1108)* (Paris, 1912), 78–83; A. Luchaire, *Louis VI le Gros. Annales de sa vie et de son règne (1081–1137),* Paris, 1890, nos 8, 11, 16, 31).

59. Though Louis himself had been crowned again, together with Eleanor, following their marriage at Bordeaux in 1137. For the ceremony and its probable *ordo,* E. A. R. Brown, ' "Franks, Burgundians and Aquitanians" and the Royal Coronation Ceremony in France', *Transactions of the American Philosophical Society,* 82 (1992), 1–189, at 36–8.

60. *Recueil des actes de Louis VI,* I, nos 182, 229; L. delisle, 'Sur la date de l'association de Philippe, fils de Louis le Gros, au gouvernement du royaume', *Journal des savants* (1898), 736–40; Luchaire, *Louis VI le Gros,* xlix–liii, and nos 399, 420, 433. Thereafter, Louis makes a number of grants 'concedente Philippo filio nostro, iam in regem coronato' (*Recueil des actes de Louis VI,* nos 283–6, 289, 292–304), and one jointly as 'Ludovicus et Philippus, filius ejus, divina ordinante providencia reges Francorum' (ibid., no. 281).

61. Torigni, 120.

62. Henry I of France had his eldest son Philip consecrated as king when aged only seven (*RHF,* XI, 32–3); J. Dhondt, 'Les Relations entre la France et la Normandie sous Henri Ier', *Normannia,* 12 (1939), 465–86; *Recueil des actes de Philippe Ier, roi de France (1059–1108),* ed. M. Prou (Paris, 1908), xxviii–xxxii. Louis VII, however, declined the suggestion of Archbishop Henry of Champagne to crown his son Philip in 1172, when he was seven, perhaps regarding his son as unready (Sassier, *Louis VII,* 467; J. Bradbury, *Philip Augustus, King of France, 1180–1223* (London, 1998), 38).

63. *Recueil des actes de Louis VI,* no. 305.

64. For Byzantine co-rulership, W. Ohnesorge, 'Das Mitkaisertum in der abendländischen Geschichte des früheren Mittlealters', in idem, *Abendland und Byzanz* (Darmstadt, 1963), 261–87; G. Ostrogorsky, 'Das Mitkaisertum im mittelalterlichen Byzanz', *Doppelprinzipat und Reichsteilung im Imperium Romanum,* ed. E. Kornemann (Leipzig and Berlin, 1930), 166–78.

65. William of Tyre. She was styled *filia regis et regni Jerosolimitani haeres* (B. Hamilton, 'Women in the Crusader States: The Queens of Jerusalem, 1100–1190', *Medieval Women,* ed. D. Baker (Ecclesiastical History Society, 1978), 143–74).

66. William of Tyre. Though in different circumstances, Queen Urraca of Leon-Castlile (r. 1109–1126) had similarly had her son Alphonso crowned and anointed as king of Galicia and her co-ruler in 1111.

67. William of Tyre, XXII: 30; B. Hamilton, *The Leper King and his Heirs. Baldwin IV and the Crusader Kingdom of Jerusalem* (Cambridge, 2000), 194–5. Baldwin V was the son of Baldwin IV's sister Sybilla and her first husband, William of Montferrat.

68. *Historia Pontificalis,* 69; Torigni, 178, 'Willelmus, filius suus, quem pater ante mortem suam sublimatum in regem consortem regni fecerat'. D. Matthew, *The Norman Kingdom of Sicily* (Cambridge, 1992), 170, regards Roger's actions as 'plainly adopted from the custom long observed in France', and in playing down the Byzantine influence on Roger's kingship follows L. R. Ménager, 'L'Institution monarchique dans les états normands d'Italie', *CCM,* 2 (1959), 303–31 and 445–68.

69. Duggan, 'Coronation', 166–7.

70. *Anglo-Saxon Chronicle, s.a.* 785 (C. Plummer, *Two of the Saxon Chronicles Parallel,* 2 vols (Oxford, 1892), I, 53–5, 'to cyninge gehalgod').

71. In this context, it is significant that the ceremony of 787 also appears to be the first recorded consecration of an English king (F. M. Stenton, *Anglo-Saxon England,* 3rd edn, Oxford, 1989, 218–19). Levison, *England and the Continent,* 118–19, believed that by having Ecgfrith consecrated, Offa 'first introduced a Christian element into the initiation of English kings', but E. John in *Orbis Britanniae* (Leicester, 1966, 28–35) has argued for an insular origin for anointing of kings. J. M. Wallace-Hadrill, in *Early Germanic Kingship in England and on the Continent* (Oxford, 1971, 114–15), suggests that Ecgfrith's coronation was performed either by the legates or the newly elevated archbishop of Lichfield, given the hostility of Archbishop Jaenberht of Kent. By contrast, the archbishop of Canterbury performed the consecration of Ceolwulf I of Mercia (821–3) (Levison, *England and the Continent,* 119).

72. S. E. Kelly, 'Offa (d. 797), king of the Mercians', *ODNB.* Ecgfrith's premature death in the same year was seen by Alcuin as punishment for his father's ruthlessness, 'for you know very well how much blood his father shed to secure his kingdom on his son' (*Alcuini Epistolae,* ed. E. Dümmler, *MGH, Epist. Karol. Aevi,* II (Berlin, 1895), no. 27; *English Historical Documents, I, c.500–1042,* ed. D. Whitelock (2nd edn, London, 1979), 854–6).

73. G. Garnett, *Conquered England: Kingship, Succession and Tenure, 1066–1166* (Oxford, 2007), 185–6, however, argues that the claims made by William the Conqueror to justify his succession to the

throne of England only served to strengthen 'the existing Norman assumption that rulership was neither sharable nor divisible'.

74. The magnates of Normandy swore homage to William Aetheling at Rouen in 1115, and the 'leading men and barons of all England' did so at the assembly at Salisbury in 1116 (William of Malmesbury, *Gesta regum*, I, 758–9: *Anglo-Saxon Chronicle*, E, 1115; *JW*, III, 138–9; *RRAN*, II, no. 1074; C. W. Hollister, *Henry I* (New Haven, Conn., and London, 2001), 238 and n. 20.

75. *RRAN*, II, nos 1189, 1191, 1192, 1201 and 1202; Hollister, *Henry I*, 365–6.

76. *RRAN*, II, no. 1204 and printed in full in *The Cartulary of St John's, Colchester*, ed. S. Miller (Roxburghe Club, 1897), 4–10, though doubts as to the charter's authenticity were raised by J. H. Round, 'The Early Charters of St John's Abbey, Colchester', *EHR*, 16 (1901), 721–30; Hugh the Chanter, *The History of the Church of York, 1066–1127*, ed. and trans. C. Johnson (London, 1961), 99; J. Green, *Henry I. King of England and Duke of Normandy* (Cambridge, 2006), 149; Garnett, *Conquered England*, 207, n. 593.

77. *The Warenne (Hyde) Chronicle*, ed. and trans. E. M. C. van Houts and R. C. Love (Oxford, 2013), 80–1 and n. 154.

78. Hollister, *Henry I*, 274–5; Green, *Henry I*, 163–8.

79. *The Charters of King David I: The Written Acts of David I King of Scots, 1124–53, and of his Son Henry Earl of Northumberland, 1139–52*, ed. G. W. S. Barrow (Woodbridge, 1999), nos 126 and 129.

80. Barrow, *RRS*, I. *The Acts of Malcolm IV*, 4, n. 3.

81. *Charters of King David I*, 34: 'David's was a dual reign . . . with joint or at least coadjutorial royal government'; K. J. Stringer, 'State-building in Twelfth-Century Britain: David I, King of Scots, and Northern England', *Government, Religion and Society in Northern England, 1000–1700*, ed. J. C. Appleby and P. Dalton (Stroud, 1997), 40–62; G. W. S. Barrow, 'The Scots and the North of England', *The Anarchy of King Stephen's Reign*, ed. E. King (Oxford, 1994), 231–53; idem, 'King David I, Earl Henry and Cumbria', *Transactions of the Cumberland and Westmorland Antiquarian and Archaeological Society*, new series, 99 (1999), 117–27.

82. *Liber S. Marie de Calchou. Registrum Cartarum abbacie Tironensis de Kelso*, ed. C. Innes, 2 vols (Edinburgh, 1846), I, plate.

83. *CTB*, I, no. 153; Warren, *Henry II*, 32–4; E. King, *King Stephen* (London, 2010), 237, 262–4, for a full discussion; and cf. Garnett, *Conquered England*, 264–5.

84. E. King, 'Eustace (*c.* 1129–1153), count of Boulogne', *ODNB*, 18, 649–50. He married Constance, Louis VII's daughter, in or shortly after 1140.

85. *Gesta Stephani*, 208–9. King, *King Stephen*, 237–8, notes that while this is normally taken to refer to his investiture with the county of Boulogne, the *Gesta* notes only his elevation to unspecified comital rank ('ad consulatus').

86. *Historia pontificalis*, 85–6, 'inhibens ne qua fieret innovatio in regno Anglie circa coronam, quia res erat litigiosa cuius translatio iure reprobate est'; King, *King Stephen*, 263.

87. John of Hexham, *Historia*, in *Symeonis monachi opera omnia*, ed. T. Howlett, 2 vols (Rolls Series, London, 1882–1885), 325–6; *Historia pontificalis*, 83, 86. Stephen's position was not helped by the fact that he had alienated both Pope Eugenius III and Archbishop Theobald of Canterbury by his unsuccessful attempts to prevent the latter from attending the Council of Rheims, while Angevin influence at the Curia was strong. Thomas Becket was said to have played an important role in obtaining the papal prohibition (Gervase, I, 150; *MTB*, VI, no. 250; Radford, *Thomas of London*, 45; D. Knowles, *Thomas Becket* (London, 1970), 26, 127; A. Saltman, *Theobald. Archbishop of Canterbury* (London, 1956), 36–8).

88. King, 'Eustace'. He died *c.*17 August 1153.

89. S. D. Church, 'Succession and Interregnum in the Kingdom of England and the Kingdom of Ireland in the Twelfth and Thirteenth Centuries', forthcoming. I am grateful to Stephen Church for sending me this paper before publication.

90. Chibnall, *Empress Matilda*, 102. Though in the wake of Stephen's capture at the battle of Lincoln in 1141 she had entered London, she alienated her erstwhile supporters by her arrogance, and her disastrous mishandling of the citizens caused them to expel her before she had the opportunity to be consecrated at Westminster (ibid., 102–5).

91. *Recueil*, I, no. 61. Ralph Niger is barely less dismissive in referring to her, in regard to the start of the civil war, as 'quondam imperatrice' (Ralph Niger, *Chronicle*, 92).

92. *Historia pontificalis*, 83–5; *Letters of Gilbert Foliot*, no. 26; King, *King Stephen*, 102–4.

93. FitzStephen, 98–101; Barlow, *Becket*, 141; F. Barlow, 'Herbert of Bosham (d. *c.*1194)', *ODNB*; Vincent, 'The Court of Henry II', 333–4.

94. Matthew Paris, *Historia Anglorum*, I, 353.

95. Warren, *Henry II*, 78.

96. Vincent, 'The Court of Henry II', 334.

97. William was made to yield the castles of Norwich and Pevensey, and Earl Hugh all his castles.

98. *Chronicle of Battle Abbey*, 174–7; *PR 3 Henry II*, p. 107, recording the sum of 22s. 'for carrying the crowns to St Edmunds'. The plural *coronis* implies Eleanor's presence (Norgate, *Angevin Kings*, I, 430, n. 3).

99. Norgate, *Angevin Kings*, I, 430. For a study of the more traditional locations for crown-wearings, M. Biddle, 'Seasonal Festivals and Residence: Winchester, Westminster and Gloucester in the Tenth to Twelfth Centuries', *ANS*, 8 (1985), 51–72, with appendices tabulating known sites of crown-wearings by the first three Norman kings.

100. To wipe away the shame of this humiliation, Stephen himself had held a crown-wearing at Lincoln at Christmas 1146, in defiance of a superstition that held it was unlucky for kings to wear a crown within the city (HH, 748–9; King, *King Stephen*, 228–9). Henry, by a surely deliberate contrast, held his crown-wearing just outside the city, in the church of St Mary in the suburb of Wigford, on the south side of the river, where he nevertheless had a palace erected for the purpose, and celebrated the festival in great style (WN, I, 117–18 (wrongly dated to 1158); Howden, I, 216; *PR 4 Henry II*, 136; D. Stocker, *St Mary's Guildhall, Lincoln* (London, 1991), 38–9).

101. The choice of site may be connected to the fact that in 1153 Henry had moved against Waleran of Meulan, earl of Worcester, whom he had long held in suspicion, stripping him of lands in both Normandy and England, including his honour of Worcester (D. Crouch, *The Beaumont Twins. The Roots and Branches of Power in the Twelfth Century*, Cambridge, 1985, 71, 74–6).

102. Howden, I, 216. Ralph of Diss similarly noted that Henry 'coronam super alter posuit, nec ulterius coronatus est' (Diceto, I, 302).

103. This was an imperial crown, used by Emperor Henry V, and brought back from Germany by Matilda (Chibnall, *Empress Matilda*, 189). For votive crowns, P. Schramm, *Herrschaftszeichen und Staatssymbolik*, 4 vols (Stuttgart, 1954–1978), III, 910–12. William the Conqueror had granted the English royal regalia to his foundation of St-Etienne, Caen, though they seem to have been brought back by William Rufus (*The Gesta Normannorum Ducum of William of Jumièges, Orderic Vitalis and Robert of Torigni*, ed. E. M.C. van Houts, 2 vols (Oxford, 1992–1995), I, lxiii–lxiv; F. Barlow, *William Rufus* (London, 1983), 50, 58).

104. Some days before his formal crown-wearing at Gloucester at Pentecost 1138, King Stephen had offered his royal ring on the altar of the cathedral, 'which the royal chaplains brought back to him the same day, it having been redeemed for 500 shillings' (*JW*, III, 242–3).

105. Norgate, *Angevin Kings*, I, 439. Vincent, 'The Court of Henry II', 326, by contrast, suggests that the decision to cease formal crown-wearings may have 'been motivated by a desire to replace the expensive and dispute-ridden ceremony of coronation at the hands of the archbishop of Canterbury with a no less lavish display of alms-giving to the poor'.

106. Howden, I, 216; Diceto, I, 302, n. 1. By the 1240s Matthew Paris believed Henry's gesture to have been informed by the example of King Cnut, who, as a lesson to his courtiers on the vanity of earthly power, had famously had his throne placed on the seashore, and in vain ordered the waves not to encroach further on his domains. Then, noted Paris, as a continuing gesture of humility, he had removed his crown, carried it to the nearest church and placed it on the head of a statue of Christ (Matthew Paris, *Historia Anglorum*, I, 308–9).

107. Haskins, *Norman Institutions*, 131; Warren, *Henry II*, 32–3.

108. M. Chibnall, 'Charters of the Empress', *Law and Government in Medieval England and Normandy*, ed. J. Hudson and G. Garnett (Cambridge, 1994), 276–98, at 288–9.

109. Barlow, *Becket*, 68.

110. This was already clear from the division of time the king had spent between England and his lands in France. From December 1154 to early January 1156 Henry had been in England, then stayed in France between January 1156 to March 1157. He was in the kingdom again between April 1157 and mid August 1158, but from mid August 1158 to January 1163, he remained on the continent.

111. Barlow, *Becket*, 68.

112. Diceto, I, 308.

113. B. Smalley, *The Becket Conflict and the Schools* (Totowa, NJ, 1973), 118, noting that 'we are still in the early summer of the reform movement', so that by holding both posts 'Becket would have caused more scandal in 1162 than Hubert Walter did thirty years later'.

114. Guernes, ll. 745–7.

115. Smalley, *The Becket Conflict and the Schools*, 118, 145–6; Barlow, *Becket*, 67.

116. Grim, *MTB*, II, 366, trans. Staunton, *Lives*, 62.

117. 'Roger of Pontigny', *MTB*, IV, 16.

118. Eyton, 56.

119. Gervase, I, 169; 'Roger of Pontigny', *MTB*, IV, 14–16. For Becket's election and its context, Knowles, *Becket*, 50–76; Barlow, *Becket*, 64–73; A. Duggan, *Thomas Becket* (London, 2004), 22–32, and Barlow, *Becket*, 72, on Henry II's absence.

120. Bosham, 82; Anonymous II, *MTB*, IV, 85.
121. 'Roger of Pontigny', *MTB*, IV, 16; Diceto, I, 307, gives the date.
122. Diceto, I, 306. Matthew Paris, *Historia Anglorum*, I, 315 adds, most improbably, that when Becket swore fealty, the prince, 'so it was said', refused to accept the saving clause guaranteeing ultimate loyalty to Henry II ('quam adjectionem dicitur filius non acceptasse'). Becket had probably performed the customary homage required of a bishop elect before consecration to Henry II before leaving Normandy (Barlow, *Becket*, 71).
123. Diceto, I, 306.
124. *Thómas Saga Erkibyskups*, I, 66–7: cf. 'Roger of Pontigny', *MTB*, IV, 16.
125. 'Roger of Pontigny', *MTB*, IV, 17; Diceto, I, 306–7.
126. 'Roger of Pontigny', *MTB*, IV, 17–18; Grim, *MTB*, II, p. 367, Bosham, p. 185. In describing this election, 'Roger' anachronistically refers to young Henry as 'rex junior' and 'rex puer' (*MTB*, IV, 16, 17).
127. Gervase, I, 150; Radford, *Thomas of London*, 45; *MTB*, VI (250), 58; Knowles, *Becket*, 26, 127.
128. Bosham, 188–19, 187–8; *LJS*, no. 261; FitzStephen, *MTB*, III, 36; 'Roger of Pontigny', *MTB*, IV, 18–19; Lansdowne Anonymous, *MTB*, IV, 154–6; Gervase, I, 170–1.
129. Bosham, 188–9; Staunton, *Lives*, 66.
130. Barlow, *Becket*, 72. On the unpopularity of the choice of Becket, Duggan, *Thomas Becket*, 23–5.
131. Barlow, *Becket*, 70.
132. Ibid.
133. William of Canterbury, 9; FitzStephen, 36; Guernes, ll. 514–30; 'Roger of Pontigny', *MTB*, IV, 17–18; Anonymous II, *MTB*, IV, 104–5; Bosham, 185; *Thómas Saga Erkibyskups*, I, 79–81; Barlow, *Becket*, 71–2.
134. Thus, for example, the Lansdowne Anonymous believed that just prior to Thomas' consecration by the bishop of Winchester, prince Henry confirmed his quittance from secular liabilities, and that the exemption was ratified by several of Henry's officials, including Robert, earl of Leicester, the justiciar (*MTB*, IV, 154–5).
135. Diceto, I, 307; Gervase, I, 172; Barlow, *Becket*, 82–3; Duggan, *Thomas Becket*, 25–7.
136. Diceto, I, 307–8, and 268, where Ralph places his *signum* for 'de controversiis inter regnum et sacerdotium' beside the *capitulum* 'Thomas archbishop of Canterbury sent the royal seal back to Normandy'.
137. M. Staunton, 'Thomas Becket's Conversion', *ANS*, 21 (1998), 193–211.
138. Bosham, 202, 226–31; Barlow, *Becket*, 74–7.
139. Bosham, 227–8, who notes that just as the king had the right to service at his table from the eldest sons of the nobility, so the archbishop claimed the same right from their second-born sons until the age for them to be knighted. Herbert calls Henry 'egregrius ille . . . puer . . . alumnus pontificis' (ibid., 228).
140. Torigni, 216.
141. Torigni, 216.
142. Diceto, I, 308.
143. Bosham, 251–2; Staunton, *Lives*, 72; and Torigni, 216, who also notes that young Henry was at the forefront of the party that welcomed the royal arrival.
144. Diceto, I, 308, 'receptus est in osculum, sed non in plenitudem gratiae'.
145. Diceto, I, 308.
146. In May 1163, Pope Alexander III summoned a great ecclesiastical council at Tours, and when the archbishop left to attend with the king's permission, he entrusted young Henry back temporarily into the keeping of his father (Bosham, 253).
147. Grim, *MTB*, V, 27–8.
148. In 1159, on the death of William of Blois, William FitzEmpress had been granted part of his estates, and holding the vicomté of Dieppe and lands in eleven English counties, he enjoyed an estimated annual income of between £1,000 and £1,700 (T. K. Keefe, 'Place Date Distribution of Royal Charters and the Historical Geography of Patronage Strategies at the Court of Henry II Plantagenet', *Haskins Society Journal*, 1 (1990), 179–88, at 185–7).
149. *Draco Normannicus*, 676; Barlow, *Becket*, 103. According to FitzStephen, 142, one of Becket's murderers, Richard le Bret, struck him with the words, 'Take that, for the love of my lord William, the king's brother.'
150. Torigni, 306, who notes that William was 'vir per omnia plangendus'. Count Raymond of Toulouse's disposition to Pope Lucius III concerning the final wishes of the Young King also made clear his desire to be buried beside William (*CDF*, I, no. 38; Rouen, Archives départementales de la Seine-Maritime, G 3569 (3)). See below, 312–13. I am most grateful to David Crouch for drawing this to my attention, and for providing me with a transcript of Raymond's original letter.

151. See, for example, Warren, *Henry II*, 453–9; Barlow, *Becket*, 88–116; while for a robust defence of Becket's actions, Duggan, *Thomas Becket*, especially 33–60.
152. For the council of Westminster, *Councils and Synods*, I, 848–52; Warren, *Henry II*, 464–70; Barlow, *Becket*, 94–5; Duggan, *Thomas Becket*, 39–40.
153. For the issue of criminous clerks, see F. W. Maitland, 'Henry II and the Criminous Clerks', *EHR*, 7 (1892), 224–34; C. Duggan, 'The Becket Dispute and Criminous Clerks', *Bulletin of the Institute for Historical Research*, 35 (1962), 1–28; Knowles, *Thomas Becket*, 77–87; Warren, *Henry II*, 459–70; Barlow, *Becket*, 90–4; Duggan, *Thomas Becket*, 39–58.
154. *MTB*, IV, 201–5; Bosham, 274; William of Canterbury, 12–15; 'Roger of Pontigny', *MTB*, IV, 25–9.
155. Bosham, 275; Eyton, 65; Barlow, *Becket*, 95.
156. For detailed discussion of the Council and the Constitutions of Clarendon, on which what follows is based, see *Councils and Synods*, I, 852–93; Warren, *Henry II*, 97–8, 473–84; Barlow, *Becket*, 98–106; Duggan, *Thomas Becket*, 44–60.
157. Warren, *Henry II*, 98, noting that Henry's 'high-handed treatment of the bishops at Clarendon had converted a serious but resolvable problem in the relations of Church and State into a major dispute between Crown and Papacy'.
158. Gervase, I, 178–80; *MTB*, V, pp. 71–9. It went on to urge that the 'many other great customs and privileges' not here recorded should be kept safe 'for holy Church and for our lord the king and his heirs and the barons of the realm'.
159. For detailed discussion of the events at Clarendon and the Constitutions, Warren, *Henry II*, 473–84; Barlow, *Becket*, 98–106; Duggan, *Thomas Becket*, 39–60.
160. Torigni, 221; Bosham, 260–1; Staunton, *Lives*, 74.
161. Barlow, *Becket*, 108–11.
162. Barlow, *Becket*, 111–16; and Duggan, *Thomas Becket*, 61–83, for a close analysis of the proceedings. In a letter to King Louis requesting that he give Becket no refuge, Henry II calls him 'an outlaw and perjured traitor' (*MTB*, V, no. 71).
163. For such royal 'anger and ill-will', see Joliffe, *Angevin Kingship*, 87–109.
164. FitzStephen, 75–6.

Chapter 4: Training for Kingship, 1163–1169

1. *GH*, I, 302.
2. Diceto, I, 309.
3. Eyton, 60. The Pipe Rolls record expenditure on 'pigs and sheep and other small items for the feast of the king's son' (*PR 9 Henry II*, 72).
4. For Thierry, who had become count of Flanders on William Clito's death in 1128 and married Sybila, Fulk V's daughter, in 1134, see T. De Hemptinne and A. Verhulst, *De oorkunden van de graven van Vlanderen (Juli 1128–17 Januari 1168)* (Brussels, 1988); R. Nip, 'The Political Relations between England and Flanders, 1066–1128', *ANS*, 21 (1998), 145–67, at 164–6; and E. Oksanen, *Flanders and the Anglo-Norman World, 1066–1216* (Cambridge, 2012), 29–35. His presence at Dover may well have been connected to Henry's plans for an imminent Welsh campaign, as William Cade was paid £100 for the transport of Flemish troops (*PR 9 Henry II*, 71).
5. Torigni, 193, 205; *Continuatio Beccensis*, 317. He returned in 1159. Although King Henry had ordered the expulsion of all Flemish stipendiary troops from England soon after his accession, he permitted Flemings engaged in commerce to remain, and gradually built up an affinity among the Flemish nobility by a series of money fiefs (E. Varenbergh, *Histoire des relations diplomatiques entre le comté de Flandre et l'Angleterre au Moyen Âge* (Brussels, 1874), 73–9; D. Nichols, *Medieval Flanders* (London, 1992), 70; Amt, *The Accession of Henry II*, ch. 5, 'The Anglo-Flemish Community', and Oksanen, *Flanders and the Anglo-Norman World*, 82ff).
6. *Diplomatic Documents Preserved in the Public Record Office, 1 (1101–1272)*, ed. P. Chaplais, (London, 1964), 1–4, and 5–8; Hemptinne and Verhulst, *De oorkonden der graven van Vlananderen*, I, no. 208. The 1101 treaty is translated by E. van Houts, 'The Anglo-Flemish Treaty of 1101', *ANS*, 21 (1998), 169–74, while the Anglo-Flemish treaties are discussed by Oksanen, *Flanders and the Anglo-Norman World*, 54–72, and 68–72 for the particular significance of the 1163 treaty.
7. In 1164, Thierry left for his third journey to the East, leaving Philip as count. His marriage to the daughter of Ralph of Vermandois brought him the county of Vermandois and Mondidier (Torigni, 220).
8. *Diplomatic Documents*, nos 3, 8–12; ibid., nos 4, 12–14, which details the money fees to be received by the Flemish barons and castellans from Henry II.

9. Torigni, 218: Diceto, I, 311. Malcolm was then convalescing from a severe illness (Torigni, 218). For Henry II's expedition against Rhys which had preceded the submissions at Woodstock, J. E. Lloyd, *A History of Wales, from the Earliest Times to the Edwardian Conquest*, 2 vols (London, 1911), II, 511–13.

10. *Brut y Tywysogion, Peniarth MS 20*, ed. and trans. T. Jones (Cardiff, 1941), 62–4; *Brut y Tywysogion, Red Book of Hergest Version*, ed. T. Jones (Cardiff, 1955), 147; WN, I, 145; Torigni, 218, 'de pace tenenda et pro castellis suis'. Howden, I, 219, noted Malcolm's recovery at Doncaster, presumably on his way to Woodstock, and that 'a firm peace was made' between him and Henry. It is possible, however, that as suggested by A. A. M. Duncan, *Scotland. The Making of the Kingdom* (Edinburgh, 1975), 226–7, Malcolm only performed homage to the younger Henry, and only for the earldom of Huntingdon, as he had already performed homage to Henry II in 1157. David was released on Malcolm's death, and was back in Scotland by 1165 (*Regesta regum Scottorum, II. The Acts of William I, King of Scots, 1165–1214 (RRS, II)*, ed. G. W. S. Barrow with W. W. L. Scott (Edinburgh, 1971), 30, 79; K. J. Stringer, *Earl David of Huntingdon, 1152–1219: a Study in Anglo-Scottish History* (Edinburgh, 1985) 12.

11. Stringer, *Earl David*, 11, noting that, if so, this demand predated by over a decade the surrender of the major fortresses of Lothian required by the Treaty of Falaise in 1174. This would also explain why, in listing key rebels and their strongholds in the rising of 1173, Roger of Howden lists Stirling, Edinburgh, Jedburgh and Berwick, as well as Annan and Lochmaben in the west (*GH*, I, 48).

12. Warren, *Henry II*, 96, 162–3, argues that rather than treating them as client rulers acknowledging only his personal overlordship, he may have demanded fuller and more explicit subordination as his feudal vassals, together with the obligations inherent in this status. For a more cautious assessment, P. Latimer, 'Henry II's Campaigns against the Welsh, 1165', *Welsh History Review*, 14 (1989), 523–35. For the reaction, Lloyd, *A History of Wales*, II, 514–15; Warren, *Henry II*, 96. Malcolm was wise enough not to attack Henry II directly, but he was in communication with Louis VII at a time when Henry faced serious rebellions in Poitou and Brittany, whose count, Conan, had married Malcolm's sister Margaret in 1160 (*The Acts of Malcolm IV, King of Scots, 1153–1165 (RRS, I)*, ed. G. W. S. Barrow (Edinburgh, 1960), 13).

13. *English Episcopal Acta, II: Canterbury, 1162–1190*, ed. C. R. Cheney and B. E. A. Jones (Oxford, 1986), no. 2.

14. Thus, for instance, in 1138 a charter of Geoffrey Plantagenet in favour of the abbey of St Florent, Saumur, was attested by his sons Henry, Geoffrey and William, then aged five, four and two respectively (*Recueil*, I, no. 1, while the young Henry FitzEmpress witnessed Matilda's charter for St Nicholas, Angers (*RRAN*, III, no. 20). By contrast, Henry I's son William Aetheling seems to have first attested royal charters at the age of ten, in 1113, the year of his betrothal to Matilda, daughter of Fulk V (J. F. A. Mason, 'William [William Aetheling, William Adelinus, William Adelingus] (1103–1120)', *ODNB*).

15. As Adam, *nutricius* of Fulk V when still a small child, is recorded as having done in a grant to Ronceray (*Cartularium monasterii beatae Mariae Caritatis Andegavensis*, Archives d'Anjou III, ed. P. Marchegay, Angers, 1854, no. 313). He did likewise for Fulk V's son Geoffrey; Dutton, 'The Upbringing of Angevin Comital Children', 27–30.

16. Chibnall, *Empress Matilda*, 144–5.

17. Bosham, 261; *Councils and Synods, with other Documents Relating to the English Church, I, AD 871–1204*, ed. D. Whitelock, M. Brett and C. N. L. Brooke, 2 vols (Oxford, 1981), I, 849–50; *Ricardi de Cirencestria speculum historiale de gestis regum angliae*, ed. J. A. B. Mayor, 2 vols (London, 1869), II, 325–7; *The Life of Aelred of Rievaulx by Walter Daniel*, ed. F. M. Powicke (London, 1950), xlix; E. Bozoky, 'Le Culte des saints et des reliques dans la politique des premiers rois Plantagenêt', *La Cour Plantagenêt (1154–1204)*, ed. M. Aurell (Poitiers, 2000), 277–91, at 278–9.

18. B. W. Scholz, 'The Canonization of Edward the Confessor', *Speculum*, 36 (1961), 38–49; E. Bózoky, 'The Sanctity and Canonization of Edward the Confessor', *Edward the Confessor. The Man and the Legend*, ed. R. Mortimer (Woodbridge, 2009), 173–86; E. Mason, '"The Site of King-Making and Consecration": Westminster Abbey and the Crown in the Eleventh and Twelfth Centuries', *The Church and Sovereignty*, ed. D. Wood (Oxford, 1991), 57–76, at 73. Stephen, whose natural son Gervase was abbot of Westminster 1138–c.1157), had been supported by Henry of Blois in his petition to Innocent II for canonization, but hostile papal reaction to Stephen's outrageous treatment of the bishops in June 1139 probably lay behind its rejection by the Curia in December 1139.

19. Schramm, *Herrschaftszeichen und Staatssymbolik*, III, 757–8; N. Cantor, *Church, Kingship and Lay Investiture in England, 1089–1135* (New York, 1969), 173–4.

20. *The Life of Edward who Rests at Westminster*, ed. F. Barlow (revised edn, Oxford, 1992), 155–6.

21. WN, I, 116–17; Torigni, 220; P. Muntz, *Frederick Barbarossa* (Ithaca, NY, 1969), 238–9; K. Görich, *Friedrich Barbarossa. Eine Biographie* (Munich, 2011), 271; B. Hamilton, 'Prester John and the Three Kings of Cologne', *Studies in Medieval History presented to R. H. C. Davis*, ed. H. Mayr-Harting and

R. I. Moore (London, 1985), 177–91; P. Geary, *Living with the Dead in the Middle Ages* (London, 1994), 243–56, 'The Magi and Milan'; R. C. Trexler, *The Journey of the Magi: Meanings in History of A Christian Story* (Princeton, NJ, 1997), 75, 78; and for a valuable contextual study, J. P. Huffman, *The Social Politics of Medieval Diplomacy. Anglo-German Relations, 1066–1307* (Ann Arbor, Mich., 2000).

22. R. Folz, *La Souvenir et la légende de Charlemagne dans l'empire germanique médiéval* (Paris, 1950), 197, 203–4; W. Kleinast, *Deutschland und Frankreich in der Kaiserzeit*, 3 vols, Stuttgart, 1974–1975, 516–20.

23. *Decem scriptores*, cols 347–50, 368–70; WN, I, 76–8, 147–8; W. W. Scott, 'Malcolm IV', *ODNB*.

24. M. L. Dutton, 'Aelred Historian: Two Portraits in Plantagenet Myth', *Cistercian Studies Quarterly*, 20 (1993), 113–44; L. Jones, 'From Anglorum Basileus to Norman Saint: The Transformation of Edward the Confessor', *Haskins Society Journal*, 12 (2002), 99–120; J. E. Lawyer, 'Ailred of Rievaulx's Life of Edward the Confessor: a Medieval Idea of Kingship', *Fides et Historia*, 31 (1999), 45–65.

25. *Decem scriptores*, col. 370; *The Life of Edward*, ed. Barlow, 161–2 and 130.

26. *Decem scriptores*, cols 350–70; *PL*, CXCV, cols 711–38; King, 'The Accession of Henry II', 41–2. This genealogy was incorporated by Ralph of Diss into his chronicle, *s.a.* 1154 (Diceto, I, 299).

27. E. King, 'Henry of Blois (*c.*1093–1171), bishop of Winchester', *ODNB*; and idem, 'Henry of Winchester: The Bishop, the City and the Wider World', *ANS*, 37 (2014), forthcoming. This reburial, which occurred soon after Bishop Henry's return from his self-imposed exile at Cluny, was an act of political reintegration intended to win Henry II's favour, though it also proclaimed the bishop's own exalted ancestry and the significance of his see.

28. The Capetians could only claim descent from Charlemagne after the marriage of Louis VII to Adela of Blois in 1160, and of Philip II to Isabella of Hainault, both of whom could trace their line to the Carolingians (E. A. Brown, 'La Notion de la légitimité et la prophétie à la cour de Philippe Auguste', *La France de Philippe Auguste*, ed. R. H. Bautier, Paris, 1982, 77–111, at 81–2).

29. *The Historia Regum Brittaniae of Geoffrey of Monmouth, V. Gesta Regum Britanniae*, ed. and trans. N. Wright (Cambridge, 1991); J. Gillingham, 'The Context and Purposes of Geoffrey of Monmouth's *History of the Kings of Britain*', *ANS*, 13 (1991), 99–118, and reprinted in J. Gillingham, *The English in the Twelfth Century* (Woodbridge, 2000), 19–40.

30. *Wace's Roman de Brut. A History of the British. Text and Translation*, ed. and trans. J. Weiss (Exeter, revised edn, 2002). The dedication is noted by Layamon, *Brut*, ed. G. L. Brook and R. F. Leslie, 2 vols (Early English Text Society, 1963, 1978), I, ll. 20–3.

31. For the question of patronage, see J. Gillingham, 'The Cultivation of History, Legend and Courtesy at the Court of Henry II', *Writers of the Reign of Henry II: Twelve Essays*, ed. R. Kennedy and S. Meecham-Jones (New York, 2006), 25–52.

32. A. Chauou, *L'Idéologie Plantagenêt. Royauté arthurienne et monarchie politique dans l'espace Plantagenêt (XIIe–XIIIe siècles)* (Rennes, 2001), especially 88–125; and M. Aurell, *La Légende du roi Arthur 550–1250* (Mesnil-sur-l'Estrée, 2007), especially 210–52, 'Henri II, ses fils et la légende authurienne'. For a valuable review of the extensive secondary literature, see also M. Aurell, 'Henry II and Arthurian Legend', *Henry II: New Interpretations*, 362–94.

33. For the use of Arthur in anti-French propaganda, D. Crouch, 'The *Roman des Franceis* of Andrew de Coutances: Significance, Text and Translation', *Normandy and its Neighbours, 900–1250. Essays for David Bates*, ed. D. Crouch and K. Thompson (Turnhout, 2011), 175–98.

34. *La Vie d'Édouard le Confesseur*, ed. O. Södergard (Uppsala, 1948), ll. 4969–5006, ll. 105–30; D. M. Legge, *Anglo-Norman Literature and its Background* (Oxford, 1963), 60–3, points out the close connection between the abbesses of Barking and the crown, as does Aurell, *Plantagenet Empire*, 136–7. The abbess at the time of writing was probably Adeliza, sister of Eustace and Payn FitzJohn.

35. Torigni, 212–13; Torigni, ed Delisle, I, 336 and n. 5; and Aurell, *Plantagenet Empire*, 137–9, also noting the significance of the relic of the Holy Blood kept there. For the ducal complex at Fécamp, A. Renoux, *Fécamp. Du palais ducal aux palais de Dieu* (Paris, 1991), and for its significance J. A. Green, 'Fécamp et les rois anglo-normands', *Tabularia. Sources écrites de la Normandie médiévale*, 2 (2002), 9–18.

36. F. H. M. Le Saux, *A Companion to Wace* (Cambridge, 2005), 160–208; A. Scaglioni, *Knights at Court. Courtliness, Chivalry and Courtesy from Ottonian Germany to the Italian Renaissance* (Berkeley, Los Angeles and Oxford, 1991), 74–5; P. Damien-Grint, 'Benoît de Sainte-Maure et l'idéologie Plantagenêt', *Plantagenêts et Capétiens*, 413–28.

37. J. Martindale, '"*Cavalaria et Orgueill*". Duke William IX and the Historian', *Ideals and Practice of Medieval Knighthood, II. Papers from the Third Strawberry Hill Conference*, ed. C. Harper-Bill and R. Harvey (Woodbridge, 1988), 87–116; idem, 'Secular Propaganda and Aristocratic Values: The Autobiographies of Count Fulk le Réchin of Anjou and William of Poitou, duke of Aquitaine', *Writing Medieval Biography*, 143–59.

38. *Chroniques des comtes d'Anjou et des seigneurs d'Ambroise*, ed. L. Halphen and R. Poupardin (Paris, 1913); J. Bradbury, 'Geoffrey V of Anjou, Count and Knight', *The Ideals and Practice of Medieval*

Knighthood, III, ed. C. Harper-Bill and R. Harvey (Boydell, 1990), 21–38. John dedicated his text to William Passavant, bishop of Le Mans, rather than to Henry II himself.

39. J. Chartrou, *L'Anjou de 1109 à 1151: Foulques de Jérusalem et Geoffreoi Plantagenêt* (Paris, 1928), 86–8. Its inscription runs 'Ense tuo, princeps, praedonum turba fugature; Ecclesiisque quies, pace vigente, datur'. See D. Christophe, 'La Plaque de Geoffroy Plantagenêt dans la cathédrale du Mans', *Hortus Artium Medievalium*, 10 (2004), 74–80.

40. *Actus pontificum Cenomannis in urbe legentium*, ed. G. Busson and A. Lédru (Le Mans, 1901), 416–17; and on the importance of the cult of St Julian to the projection of Angevin power, K. Dutton, 'The Assertion of Identity, Authority and Legitimacy: Angevin Religious Patronage in the County of Maine, 1110–1151', *Monasteries on the Borders of Medieval Europe: Conflict and Cultural Interaction*, ed. E. Jamroziak and K. Stöber (Turnhout, 2014), 211–36.

41. *Actus pontificum Cenomannis*, 432. Geoffrey's burial in the cathedral in 1151 was an honour not even accorded to the bishops (Torigni, 163; Chartrou, *L'Anjou*, 86).

42. *De principis*, 283. A charter of Henry II (1154 x 1158), provided 40 *livres angevins* for two priests to say Masses daily at the altar before his father's tomb (*Recueil*, no. 70; *Letters and Charters of Henry II*, no. 1514, and cf. no. 1695; *Nécrologie-Obituaire de la cathédrale du Mans*, ed. G. Busson and A. Ledru (1906), 155–6).

43. Below, 312.

44. Eyton, 77–8. There is no indication that young Henry had joined Eleanor, Matilda and Richard in Normandy when they met the king during negotiations for Matilda's marriage to Henry of Saxony, and that of her sister Eleanor to a younger son of Frederick Barbarossa (ibid.). Henry II was back in England by mid May 1165, to launch an expedition against the Welsh. William FitzJohn appears in charge of both young Henry and Geoffrey, and he escorted Henry II's natural sister Emma to Wales to marry David ap Owen (*PR 11 Henry II*, 73; *12 Henry II*, 71, 96, 100–1; *PR 13 Henry II*, 169; *PR 20 Henry II*, 16).

45. Between 1158 and 1160, he tried land pleas in Yorkshire, Devon, Gloucestershire and Somerset; Warren, *Henry II*, 285, and n. 3, 325; White, *Restoration and Reform*, 153, and n. 105, 184, 187.

46. *Historia Ecclesia Abbendonensis*, ed. J. G. Hudson, 2 vols (Oxford, 2002, 2007), II, 242–3, in describing the abbot's case against Turstin FitzSimon. William's role was probably analogous to that of Ranulf de Glanville, who served as John's *magister* from 1182 and doubtless was tasked with instilling in him a knowledge of the law and the functioning of the courts (*GH*, I, 7, 304–5, 307–8). Henry II himself had been associated with his father's rule in Anjou and Normandy from 1145, when he likewise had been introduced 'to the practical work of government in England and Normandy' (Chibnall, *Empress Matilda*, 144–5).

47. Warren, *Henry II*, 93, 97.

48. J. Hudson, *The Formation of the English Common Law* (Harlow, 1996), 146–56.

49. *Dialogus de Scaccario and the Constitutio Domus Regis*, ed. E. Amt and S. Church (Oxford, 2007), 114–15.

50. *Dialogus*, 4–5.

51. *Dialogus*, 40–1, and for Thomas Brown, ibid., 52–5; R. C. Van Caenegem, *English Lawsuits from William I to Richard I*, 2 vols (London, 1990–1991), II. no. 446. On Ilchester see C. Duggan, 'Richard of Ilchester, Royal Servant and Bishop', *TRHS*, 5th series, 16 (1966), 1–21; and J. G. Hudson, 'Ilchester, Richard of', *ODNB*, 29, 195–8.

52. He is found commanding units of the king's knights in the 1165 Welsh campaign (Eyton, 80).

53. Smith, 'Royal Family', 52; *Red Book of the Exchequer*, I, 408, where he is described as 'pincerna domini Henrici filii domini regis'; Eyton, 86; and see also *Letters and Charters of Henry II*, no. 5272. By 1170, payments were made to Ailward as *camerarius* for the expenses of young Henry, *rex filius Regis* (e.g. *PR 16 Henry II*, 61, 111, 112, 118, 128, 162).

54. *LJS*, II, no. 136.

55. *CTB*, I, 262–3.

56. For Hugh, see *CTB*, II, 1376.

57. *MTB*, V, no. 169.

58. *Red Book of the Exchequer*, I, 412–13; *EHD*, II, 971. On the inquest of 1166, see T. K. Keefe, *Feudal Assessments and the Political Community under Henry II and his Sons* (Berkeley, Los Angeles and London, 1983), 6–19. The fiscal intentions behind the survey are demonstrated by the fact that whereas before 1166, annual audited revenue from England was £13,300, it rose thereafter to £20,000 (N. Barratt, 'Finance and the Economy in the Reign of Henry II', *Henry II. New Interpretations*, 242–56, at 249–50, 253). The aid was levied in 1168 for the marriage of Matilda, and raised £4,300 in 1167/8 alone (ibid., 253).

59. *Red Book of the Exchequer*, I, 442; Smith, 'Royal Family', 54.

60. *Red Book of the Exchequer*, I, 400; E. King, *Medieval England, 1066–1485* (Oxford, 1988), 74.

61. On the performance of homage and the ritual gesture of the *immixtio manuum*, J. Le Goff, 'The Symbolic Ritual of Vassalage', in idem, *Time, Work and Culture* (Chicago, 1980), 237–87.

62. Eyton, 103. Queen Eleanor, however, returned to England where, at Oxford, she gave birth to John, Henry and Eleanor's last child.

63. Eyton, 137; Smith, 'Royal Family', 52–3.

64. Torigni, 235–6; William of Malmesbury, *Historia Novella*, ed. E. King and trans. K. Potter (2nd edn, Oxford, 1998), 126–31; Warren, *Henry II*, 29.

65. Torigni, 235–6; *HWM*, ll. 1565–1651.

66. Peter of Blois, *Epistolae*, no. 67 (*PL*, CCVII, col. 211); J. Appleby, *Henry II, the Vanquished King* (London, 1962), 70.

67. *Epistolae*, no. 67 (*PL*, CCVII, cols 210–13).

68. *Chroniques des comtes d'Anjou*, 140–1. The tag was already familiar: William of Malmesbury tells the (implausible) story of how the Conqueror's son Henry made play of the proverb 'a king unlettered is a donkey crowned' even in the hearing of his father (*Gesta regum*, II, 710–11).

69. J. Bradbury, 'Fulk le Réchin and the Origin of the Plantagenets', *Studies in Medieval History Presented to R. Allen Brown*, ed. C. Harper-Bill, C. Holdsworth and J. Nelson (Woodbridge, 1989), 27–42.

70. William of Conches, *Opera omnia*, I. *Dragmaticon philosophiae*, ed. I. Ronca (Corpus Christianorum Continuatio mediaevalis, 152, Turnhout, 1997); idem, *A Dialogue on Natural Philosophy*, trans. I. Ronca and M. Curr (Notre Dame, Indi., 1997); Warren, *Henry II*, 38–9.

71. Map, 476–7; Gerald, *Opera*, V, 302–3; W. Stubbs, *Seventeen Lectures on the Study of Medieval and Modern History* (3rd edn, Oxford, 1900), nos 6 and 7.

72. *Epistolae*, no. 66 (*PL*, CCVII, col. 198).

73. Gerald of Wales only joined Henry II's court in 1184, the year after the Young King's death.

74. Map, 278–9, with the translation slightly adapted. The quote is from the *Aeneid*, v. 79. Henry I could be considered 'literatus' by Orderic Vitalis (Orderic, II, 214, III, 120, and cf. *Gesta regum*, I, 710; Green, *Henry I*, 22–3).

75. Bk XIV: 21; M. Aurell, *Le Chevalier lettré: savoir et conduite de l'aristocratie au XII et XIIIe siècles* (Paris, 2011), 96–8.

76. Walter Map famously noted that Henry II 'had a knowledge of all the tongues used from the French sea to the Jordan, but spoke only Latin and French' (Map, 476–7). For the extent of literacy among the nobility, see M. Clanchy, *From Memory to Written Record. England, 1066–1307* (2nd edn, Oxford, 1993), and Aurell, *Le Chevalier lettré*, especially 47–114.

77. Gerald of Wales, *Liber de invectionibus*, I: 5 (*Opera*, III, 30), where Gerald's concern was more to belittle Hubert Walter's education than praise Richard's, although his disparaging view was shared by the scholarly Ralph Niger, a member of the Young King's court, who noted that Hubert 'parum . . . literatus fuit' (Ralph Niger, *Chronicle*, 101); S. Church, *King John, Magna Carta and the Making of a Tyrant* (London, 2015), 15, and 5–6 for John's 'privileged education, the best his world could give'.

78. For books owned by John, Church, *King John*, 14–15, and for Gervase, below, 257.

79. Map, 280–1.

80. *Expugnatio*, 196–7, where Gerald also notes of Henry II that 'he was a prince of great eloquence'; John of Marmoutier, *Historia Gaufridi ducis Normannorum et comitis Andegavorum*, in *Chroniques des comtes d'Anjou*, 218.

81. *Policraticus*, IV: 8, trans. Dickinson, 38.

82. Map, 102–3; and see Gillingham, 'The Cultivation of History, Legend and Courtesy', 39–40; and idem, 'From Civilitas to Civility: Codes of Manners in Medieval and Early Modern England', *TRHS*, (2002) 267–89.

83. Etienne de Fougères, *Le Livre des manières*, ed. J. T. E. Thomas (Paris and Louvain, 2013). The work was written some time during Stephen's episcopacy, between 1168 and 1178 (ibid., 10).

84. C. S. Jaeger, *The Origins of Courtliness. Civilizing Trends and the Formation of Courtly Ideals, 939–1210* (Philadelphia, Pa., 1985), 127–75. For the inculcation of manners in dress, hygiene and at table, see Aurell, *Le Chevalier lettré*, 312–64.

85. *Expugnatio*, 172–3, though Gerald, who harboured a particular animus against him, alleged that in reality he 'was full of guile, a flatterer and a coward, addicted to wine and lust'.

86. Gervase, *Otia imperialia*, 486–7.

87. Cited in Keen, *Chivalry*, 42; L. Paterson, 'Knights and the Concept of Knighthood in Twelfth-Century Occitan Epic', *Forum of Modern Language Studies*, 17 (1981), 117–30; and see W. M. Hackett, 'Knights and Knighthood in *Girart de Roussillon*', *Ideals and Practice of Medieval Knighthood*, II, ed. C. Harper-Bill and R. Harvey (Woodbridge, 1988), 40–5.

88. A. Luchaire, *Social France at the Time of Philip Augustus* (New York, 1912), 315–21. John of Salisbury informed Becket in 1164 that when he came to Count Philip of Flanders at the castle of Lécluse, 'in the manner of the wealthy, who love this way of wasting time, he was hawking; and with this in view he was scouring rivers and pools and marshes and springs' (*LJS*, II, no. 136, at 2–5).

89. *PR 8 Henry II*, 39: Eyton, 139.

90. *PR 16 Henry II*, 15. Though the exact circumstances are unknown, in 1164 Henry II was so enraged with Robert Belet, one of the king's hereditary butlers, 'on account of a sparrow-hawk', that he fined him £100 and confiscated most of his lands (*Curia Regis Rolls*, ix, 332).

91. *Dialogus*, 30–1; and the *Constitutio Domus Regis*, 212–14, which clearly indicates the number, diversity and significance of the various royal huntsmen. See G. H. White, 'The Constitutio Domus Regis and the King's Sport', *Antiquaries Journal*, 30 (1950), 52–63, and more generally J. Cummins, *The Hound and the Hawk. The Art of Medieval Hunting* (London, 1988).

92. Map, 476–7; Gerald, *Opera*, V, 302; WN, I, 280; Warren, *Henry II*, 393. For Thomas' love of hunting 'with dogs and birds, his hawks and falcons', FitzStephen, 20.

93. Duggan, *Thomas Becket*, 163–4 and 162–72 for these two men and their legation. The meetings took place at Argentan (15–16 August), Domfront (23–24 August), Bayeux (31 August) and Bur-le-Roi (1–2 September).

94. *CTB*, II, 980–1 and n. 6, *c*.3 September 1169.

95. J. Jarnut, 'Die Frühmittelalterliche Jagd unter Rechts- und sozialgeschichtlichen Aspekten', *L'uomo di fronte al mondo animale nell'alto medioevo* (XXXI Settimana, Spoleto, 1985), 765–98; J. L. Nelson, 'Carolingian Royal Ritual', in *Rituals of Royalty. Power and Ceremonial in Traditional Societies*, ed. D. Cannadine and S. Price (Cambridge, 1987), 137–80.

96. Orme, *From Childhood to Chivalry*, 196–8.

97. R. Almond, *Medieval Hunting* (Stroud, 2003), 17.

98. Thus Orderic, III, 114–15, noted the death of William the Conqueror's second son Richard, 'who had not yet received the belt of knighthood', struck by a branch while hunting in the New Forest. Fulk V was fatally injured by a fall from his horse while hunting a hare outside Acre in 1142 (William of Tyre, Bk 15: 27).

99. Sassier, *Louis VII*, 468, and below, 264.

100. FitzStephen, 11; trans. *EHD*, II, 1029.

101. Gottfried von Strasbourg, *Tristan*, trans. A. Hatto (Harmondsworth, 1974), 69, where Tristan is said to have 'often sought recreation in fencing, wrestling, running, jumping and throwing the javelin'.

102. Gerald, *De rebus a se gestis*, *Opera*, I, 50; *The Autobiography of Gerald of Wales*, trans. H. E. Butler (new edn, Woodbridge, 2005), 70. The chanson *Girart de Roussillon* similarly describes how newly dubbed knights ran courses at the quintain, which in this instance was a manikin 'equipped with a new shield and a strong and glittering hauberk' (Luchaire, *Social France*, 321).

103. FitzStephen, 11–12; trans. *EHD*, II, 1028–9.

104. Ibid.

105. Everard, *Brittany and the Angevins*, 41–7. Conan was, however, allowed to retain the lordship of Guingamp and the honour of Richmond during his lifetime.

106. Lloyd, *A History of Wales*, II, 518–22.

107. For discussion of the threats posed to Henry in 1166–1168, Warren, *Henry II*, 102–8, on which this summary is based.

108. *LJS*, II, no. 288, stating that they discussed the 'secret undertakings' that Henry was giving Louis; Warren, *Henry II*, 108–10. For the broader context, L. Halphen, 'Les Entrevues des rois Louis VII et Henri II durant l'exil de Thomas Becket en France', in idem, *A travers l'histoire du Moyen Âge* (Paris, 1950), 266–74.

109. *LJS*, II, no. 288. John adds, however, that 'he had previously offered him secret undertakings, too, by messengers, but all these secrets will (as we believe) be general knowledge'.

110. *LJS*, II, no. 288: William of Canterbury, 73–4.

111. Gillingham, 'Doing Homage', 73. As Dunbabin, 'Henry II and Louis VII', 47, remarks, as count of Anjou 'Henry belonged to a line that had for a long time demonstrated rather ostentatiously its loyalty to the Capetian kings'.

112. Gillingham, 'Doing Homage', 63–77.

113. *Draco Normannicus*, 680.

114. *LJS*, II, no. 288; Torigni, 240.

115. *Draco Normannicus*, 664, 675, 'indomitusque leo respuit omne jugum'. On this work, see I. Harris, 'Stephen of Rouen's *Draco Normannicus*: a Norman Epic', *The Epic in History*, ed. L. S. Davidson, S. N. Mukherjee and Z. Zlatar (Sydney, 1994), 112–24; and E. Kuhl, 'Time and Identity in Stephen of Rouen's *Draco Normannicus*', *JMH*, 40 (2014), 421–34.

116. *Draco Normannicus* 664–74, 'tertia pars regni Karoli sibi sola relicta a se vix regitur, vix sibi tota favet'.

117. Gillingham, 'Doing Homage', 72–6. Henry and Louis 'shook hands and gave each other the kiss of peace (*sibi dextras et oscula dederunt*)', and Henry promised that he would 'keep faith with him as his lord, to whom he did homage and fealty before he himself became a king, against all men, and give him the aid and service due from a duke of the Normans to the king of the French' (*LJS*, II, no. 288).

118. Gillingham, 'Doing Homage', 67–8, noting that once a lord had accepted homage, 'he had lost some freedom of manoeuvre: a useful card in the game of diplomacy'; Van Eickels, 'Vom inszenierten Konsens', 312–24, 333–4.

119. J. C. Holt, 'Politics and Property in Early Medieval England', *Past and Present*, 57 (1972), 3–52, and reprinted in idem, *Colonial England, 1066–1215* (London, 1997), 113–60; J. C. Holt, 'Feudal Society and the Family in Early Medieval England, II: Notions of Patrimony', *TRHS*, 5th series, 33 (1983), 193–220, and reprinted in idem, *Colonial England*, 197–222.

120. Le Patourel, 'Angevin Successions', 16.

121. Warren, *Henry II*, 108.

122. *LJS*, II, no. 272. These terms had been formulated at Soissons in March 1168, following the intervention of Count Philip and Count Henry of Champagne on Henry II's behalf.

123. *LJS*, II, no. 272, 564–5.

124. Turner, *Eleanor*, 210.

125. Torigni, 208, 'fecit homagium regi Francorum de ducatu Normanniae, qui est de regno Franciae'.

126. *LJS*, II, no. 288, 'for the king himself remains in Count Theobald's homage for Touraine'. On this, *Chronique des comtes d'Anjou*, 125; J. Boussard, *Le Comté d'Anjou sous Henri Plantagenêt et ses fils (1151–1204)* (Paris, 1938), 70–1, 74–6.

127. Gervase, I, 208, 'suscepit a rege Franciae dominium Brittaniae'. For Norman claims to overlordship, Everard, *Brittany and the Angevins*, 126–7.

128. Ibid., 127.

129. Torigni, 241. Later in 1169, Geoffrey was ceremonially welcomed by the clergy, including Abbot Robert of Mont St Michel, at the church of St Peter in Rennes, where he received the homage of all the barons of Brittany (*Annals of Mont St Michel*, s.a. 1169, in Torigni, ed. Delisle, II, 228).

130. For Eleanor's consent, Turner, *Eleanor*, 208–11.

131. *LJS*, II, no. 288; Gervase, I, 208.

132. *LJS*, II, no. 288.

133. Ibid.; *MTB*, VI, 488–9; Becket's letter to Henry from Sens, *MTB*, VI, 509.

134. *LJS*, II, 644–5.

135. Torigni, 240.

136. Torigni, 240, noting that the office 'pertains to the county of Anjou'. Torigni was here drawing on the *De majoratu et senescalcia franciae* (see below, note 138).

137. Gervase, I, 166, who notes that Thomas 'optinuit ut quasi senescallus Regis Francorum intraret Britanniam, et quosdam ibidem inter se inquietos et funebre bellum exercentes coram se convocaret et pacificaret, et quem invenieret rebellem violenter coherceret'; Norgate, *Angevin Kings*, I, 450, n. 5; A. Luchaire, 'Hugh de Clers et le "De senescalcia Franciae"', *Mélanges d'histoire du Moyen Âge*, ed. A. Luchaire, I (Paris, 1897), 1–38. For context, J. Le Patourel, 'Henri II Plantagenêt et la Bretagne', *Mémoires de la Société d'Histoire et d'Archéologie de la Bretagne*, 58 (1981), 99–116; reprinted in idem, *Feudal Empires: Norman and Plantagenet* (London, 1984), 1–17.

138. The text is edited in *Chroniques des comtes d'Anjou*, 239–46. Considerable debate has surrounded both the authenticity of this tract and the claims it puts forward. Dismissed by Mabille, the authenticity of Hugh de Clers' assertions was defended by C. Bémont, 'Hugues de Clers et le de senescalcia Franciae', *Études d'histoire au Moyen Âge dédiées à Gabriel Monod* (Paris, 1896), 253–60, but again challenged by Luchaire, 'Hugues de Clers et le "De senescalcia Franciae"', 1–38. Yet as John Gillingham, 'Problems of Integration within the Lands Ruled by the Norman and Angevin Kings of England', 132 and n. 233, has pointed out, Hugh attests a charter of Henry II dated 1158 in which the king claimed that the custody of the abbey of St Julian at Tours 'ad me pertinent ex dignitate dapiferatus mei, unde debeo servire regi Francie sicut comes Andegavorum' (*Recueil*, I, no. 87: *Letters and Charters of Henry II*, no. 2663), and that the *De senescalia* may be the only 'historical' work in Latin Henry is known to have commissioned.

139. For the Clers family, Chartrou, *L'Anjou*, 101, and 99–106; Dutton, 'Assertion of Identity', 352, n. 139; and for a useful biographical note on Hugh, *CTB*, II, 1376. I am grateful to Katy Dutton for discussion of this subject.

140. Torigni, 240.

141. Torigni, 222, who noted that Theobald had been granted the 'dapiferatum Franciae quem comes Andegavensis antiquitus habebat' on his marriage to Louis' daughter Alice; J. W. Baldwin, *The Government of Philip Augustus* (Berkeley, 1986), 15, and 32–3 for the offices of the French royal household.

142. Torigni, 241.

143. C. W. Hollister, 'Normandy, France and the Anglo-Norman Regnum', *Speculum*, 51 (1976), 202–42, and reprinted in idem, *Monarchy, Magnates and Institutions in the Anglo-Norman World* (London, 1986), 17–57, at 56; J. Le Patourel, 'The Norman Conquest, 1066, 1106, 1154', *Proceedings of the Battle Conference*, 1978, 103–20, 216–20, at 118; D. Carpenter, *The Struggle for*

Mastery in Britain, 1066–1284 (London, 2003), 193–4; and for a contrary view, Gillingham, *The Angevin Empire*, 122–5; and idem, 'Doing Homage', 63–84.

144. J. Dunbabin, 'Henry II and Louis VII', 61; Gillingham, 'Doing Homage', 83–4.

145. As Dunbabin, 'Henry II and Louis VII', 47, notes in relation to the counts of Anjou, Henry II 'belonged to a line that had for a long time demonstrated rather ostentatiously its loyalty to Capetian kings'.

146. *LJS*, II, no. 288, 'honorum distributione'.

147. Gillingham, 'The Meeting of the Kings of France and England', 37–9.

148. First at Saint-Léger-en-Yvelines, then at Saint-Germain-en-Laye (Guernes, 128; Torigni, 241).

149. Gillingham, 'The Meetings of the Kings of France and England', 38–9, 'for Louis to lose one daughter may have been a misfortune, but to lose two was carelessness . . .'

150. At the time of young Henry's death in 1183, Alice still remained unmarried, detained virtually as a high-ranking hostage by the Angevins. Philip's attempts to transfer the Vexin from Margaret to Alice as her dowry only made Henry II and Richard yet more unwilling to ratify the marriage, and when finally in 1190 Richard rejected Alice in order to marry Berengaria of Navarre, he told her brother King Philip that his reasons for so doing were that, while she was in his custody, Henry II had fathered a child by her (*GH*, II, 160; Gillingham, *Richard I*, 77–8, 81–2, 142–3, 294–5). Alice was subsequently married to the count of Ponthieu.

151. U. Schmidt, *Königswahl und Thronfolge im 12 Jahrhundert* (Cologne, Weimar and Vienna, 1987), 180–5; Görich, *Friedrich Barbarossa*, 421–4.

152. R. C. Smail, 'Latin Syria and the West, 1149–1187', *TRHS*, 5th series, 19 (1969), 1–20, at 14–16; C. Tyerman, *England and the Crusades, 1095–1588* (Chicago, 1988), 39–40, and n. 13.

153. Diceto, II, 15.

154. Torigni, 176, for example, recorded Baldwin III's capture of the vital coastal city of Ascalon in 1153, 'gratia Dei praecurrente', and later recorded how, after Amalric's successful expedition to Egypt in 1164 against Shirkuh, the grand vizier had doubled the annual tribute, previously set at 30,000 gold pieces, rendered by Cairo to the king of Jerusalem (ibid., 223–4).

155. Smail, 'Latin Syria', 8–9; *RHF*, XVI, 66; *Gilbert Foliot and his Letters*, ed. A. Morey and C.N.L. Brooke (Cambridge, 1967), 241 n. 3, suggesting a date of 1163.

156. *PL*, CC, cols 384–6; Smail, 'Latin Syria', 11–12.

157. Gervase, I, 198–9; S. K. Mitchell, *Taxation in Medieval England* (New Haven, Conn., 1951), 115; Smail, 'Latin Syria', 12, 14. It is possible, but not certain, that the payment recorded in *PR 13 Henry II*, 194, for the esnecca 'ad elemosinas ecclesiae orientalis deferendas', refers to the monies collected. In 1167, Henry met with Louis 'about collecting the money for the defence of Jerusalem, which had been collected at Tours', but this led to a major dispute, ostensibly about its transport (Torigni, 230).

158. *Gilbert Foliot and his Letters*, no. 170, and for scepticism, ibid., at 241, n. 3; *The Life and Letters of Thomas à Becket*, trans. J. A. Giles, 2 vols (London, 1846), I, 395; *Gilbert Foliot and his Letters*, n. 173. The same year the archbishop was also informed of rumours that Richard de Lucy had taken the cross (*MTB*, V, *Epistolae*, 254).

159. Ralph Niger, *Chronicle*, 94.

160. Gerald, *Opera*, I, 60–1; *De principis*, 209, 251, 255.

161. Tyerman, *England and the Crusades*, 41.

162. R. Röhricht, *Regesta regni Hierosolymitani* (Innsbruck, 1893), no. 497, 498; *RHF*, XVI, 198–9. In his *Topographia Hibernica*, dedicated to Henry II in 1188, Gerald of Wales himself had told the king that it was his sons' rebellion 'most damaging to the whole Christian world', which had 'postponed your eastern victories in Asia and Spain, which you had had already decided in your noble mind to add to those of the West and so extend in a signal way the Faith of Christ' (Gerald, *Opera*; Gerald of Wales, *The History and Topography of Ireland*, trans. J. O'Meara (London, 1982), 124).

163. Tyerman, *England and the Crusades*, 41.

164. *LJS*, II, no. 272. William, who was translated to the archbishopric of Sens later in 1168, was the brother of Henry of Champagne and Theobald of Blois (ibid., at 567, n. 28).

165. *LJS*, II, no. 272.

166. *LJS*, II, nos 568–9, where John reports that Louis 'would not on any ground believe in the sincerity of King Henry's statement until he saw his shoulders marked with the sign of the cross'.

167. The great Muslim chronicler Ibn al-Athir has King Amalric note that Nur al-Din's capture of Cairo would mean '"death to the Franks and their expulsion from the land of Syria"' (*The Chronicle of Ibn al-Athir for the Crusading Period from al-Kamil fi'l-ta'rikh. Part 2. The Years 541–589/1146–1193: The Age of Nur al-Din and Saladin*, trans. D. S. Richards (Aldershot, 2007), 172).

168. Alexander III, *Epistolae, PL*, CC, cols 599–601; Smail, 'Latin Syria', 13; J. G. Rowe, 'Alexander III and the Jerusalem Crusade. An Overview of Problems and Failures', *Crusaders and Muslims in Twelfth-Century Syria*, ed. M. Shatzmiller (Leiden, 1992), 118–23. The pope also urged Louis' brother Henry of Rheims to press the king of France to summon a council to discuss an expedition to the East (*PL*, CC, cols 601–2).

169. *LJS*, II, nos 297–8; *MTB*, V, no. 537 (wrongly dated 1169); 646, 637–8; Barlow, *Becket*, 198–9.

170. *MTB*, VII, no. 538.

171. Torigni, 193, 220; A. E. Verhulst, 'Note sur une charte de Thierry d'Alsace, comte de Flandre, pour l'abbaye de Fontevrault (21 avril 1157)', *Études de civilisation médiévale (IXe–XIIe siècles): Mélanges offerts à Edmond-René Labande* (Poitiers, 1974), 711–19; Lewis, 'Anticipatory Association of the Heir', 917–18.

172. Chartrou, *L'Anjou*, 21–4; Hollister and Keefe, 'The Making of the Angevin Empire', 15.

Chapter 5: *Novus Rex*

1. *LJS*, II, nos 297–8; *MTB*, VII, no. 537 (wrongly dated 1169); 646, 637–8; Torigni, 249: Barlow, *Becket*, 198–9. The departure for the East of Stephen, count of Sancerre, and his nephew Odo, duke of Burgundy, bearing the money King Louis had raised to aid the Church in the Latin states, may have added further pressure on Henry to take action.

2. *MTB*, nos 623–5, 635; Barlow, *Becket*, 202. For the significance of this gesture, H. Vollrath, 'The Kiss of Peace', *Peace Treaties and International Law in European History*, ed. R. Lesaffer (Cambridge, 2004), 162–83.

3. Barlow, *Becket*, 205.

4. In this case, the pope appears to have meant the decrees of 1169, Duggan, *Thomas Becket*, 180.

5. *MTB*, VII, no. 647; *CTB*, II, no. 266.

6. Barlow, *Becket*, 204.

7. *CTB*, II, 296.

8. *CTB*, II, 296.

9. Duggan, 'Coronation', 167.

10. *GH*, I, 5.

11. Diceto, I, 388; Bosham, 458; William of Canterbury, 82. Ralph Niger was later careful to point out that at Henry II's own coronation in 1154, Roger of York was present but 'manus non apponente', with Theobald conducting the ceremony (Ralph Niger, *Chronicle*, 189).

12. *CTB*, II, nos 286 and 277.

13. *Councils and Synods*, I. ii, 926–39; 'Roger of Pontigny', *MTB*, IV, 65–6.

14. *GH*, I, 4.

15. *GH*, I, 5.

16. *GH*, I, 4.

17. *GH*, I, 5; Gervase, I, 217; *PR 19 Henry II*, 182; *Select Charters*, ed. Stubbs, 174–8; Warren, *Henry II*, 287–91.

18. Gervase, I, 219.

19. For a list of those sheriffs who were dismissed, appointed or stayed in office, see *GH*, II, lxvii–lxviii; *EHD*, II, no. 47. As Warren, *Henry II*, 290–1 notes, Howden (*GH*, I, 4–5) misplaces the dismissal of the sheriffs, which occurred not before the inquest, but after its findings.

20. On the inquest and its remit, J. H. Round, 'The Inquest of the Sheriffs (1170)', in idem, *The Commune of London* (London, 1899), 125–36; J. Tait, 'A New Fragment of the Inquest of Sheriffs (1170)', *EHR*, 39 (1924), 80–3; H. Suggett, 'An Anglo-Norman Return to the Inquest of Sheriffs', *Bulletin of the John Rylands Library*, 27 (1942–1943), 179–81; Warren, *Henry II*, 287–8, and 290–1; J. Boorman, 'The Sheriffs of Henry II and the Significance of 1170', *Law and Government in Medieval England and Normandy. Essays in Honour of Sir James Holt*, ed. G. Garnet and J. Hudson (Cambridge, 1994), 255–75. As Warren, *Henry II*, 290, remarks, 'it is perhaps no small wonder that England was soon to be engulfed in a baronial revolt'.

21. *CTB*, II, no. 289, and no. 296, which stresses the effectiveness of the royal embargo; Duggan, 'Coronation', 174–6.

22. FitzStephen, 103; *Councils and Synods*, I, ii, 941–2. Yet as Duggan, 'Coronation', 176, points out, even if this was the case, he had very probably received an earlier letter of papal prohibition, *Illius dignitatis*, in 1166 (*MTB*, V, letter 169).

23. FitzStephen, 103.

24. Flori, *Eleanor*, 94–5.

25. *CTB*, II, no. 296.

26. *CTB*, II, no. 296; Eyton, 139. Torigni, 245, believed that Margaret had been brought to England, but too late for the coronation.

27. *CTB*, II, no. 296. An anonymous correspondent told Becket that, shortly after his son's coronation, Henry II had ordered that Margaret and her household be supplied with fine clothing and horses in readiness to cross to England, 'so that the French king might hear of it and quieten to some extent the indignation he felt at the insult to his daughter' (*CTB*, II, no. 297). The purchase of clothing for 'the daughter of the King of France and her household', costing no less than £26 17s. 5d. is confirmed in the Pipe Rolls while Queen Eleanor received cloth worth £6 19s. 9d (*PR 16 Henry II*, 15).

28. For the date, Duggan, 'Coronation', 165, n. 1; Eyton, 138; *MTB*, VII, 673, 679. As well as the feast of St Basil, it was 'the vigil of the holy martyrs Vitus and Modestus and the holy virgin Crescentia' (*GH*, I, 5).

29. *CTB*, II, no. 297, 'transacta Dominica, rex apud Londonias filium suum cingulo militiae donavit, eundemque statim Eboracensis in regem inunxit'; Gervase, I, 219, 'ipsa die Henricum filium suum ... militem fecit, statimque eum ... in regem ungui praecepit et coronari'. This testimony is accepted by the editors of the *History* (*HWM*, III, 69, note to l. 2072), and Crouch, *William Marshal*, 46, n. 13.

30. Thus, for example, the future Henry I was nineteen when knighted by William the Conqueror at Westminster in 1086 (William of Malmesbury, *Gesta regum*, I, 71: *ASC*, E, 1086), while the Young King's brother Geoffrey was twenty when knighted at Woodstock by Henry II in 1178 (*GH*, I, 207). Nevertheless, fifteen had been a common age for German royal princes to be knighted in the later eleventh and twelfth centuries (J. Flori, *L'Essor de la chevalerie, XIe-XIIe siècles* (Geneva, 1986), 57–8), and Henry V, husband of the Empress Matilda, had been knighted at fifteen (Chibnall, *Empress Matilda*, 21 and n. 5). William Clito was knighted by Baldwin VII of Flanders when aged only fourteen in 1116 (C. W. Hollister, 'William [called William Clito]', *ODNB*) and similarly, Geoffrey le Bel was only fourteen when knighted by his prospective father-in-law King Henry I, immediately prior to his marriage to Matilda.

31. Chrétien de Troyes, *Arthurian Romances*, trans. W. W. Kibler (London, 1991), 402; Keen, *Chivalry*, 64–82; Flori, *L'Essor de la chevalerie*, 304–20; D. Barthélemy, *La Chevalerie. De la Germanie antique à la France du XIIe siècle* (Paris, 2007*)*, 168–78, 238–43. For an important new study, M. Lieberman, 'A New Approach to the Knighting Ritual', *Speculum*, 90 (2015), 391–423.

32. Flori, *L'Essor de la chevalerie*, 58; idem, *Eleanor*, 105–6; J. D'Arcy Boulton, 'Classic Knighthood as a Nobiliary Dignity: The Knighting of Counts and Kings' Sons in England, 1066–1272', *Medieval Knighthood. Papers from the Sixth Strawberry Hill Conference, 1994*, ed. S. D. Church and R. E. Harvey (Woodbridge, 1995), 41–100.

33. *Gesta Stephani*, 208–9; *GH*, I, 336, 'honoravit Johannem filium suum armis militaribus. Et statim misit eum in Hiberniam, et eum inde regem constituit'.

34. K. Norgate, *The Minority of Henry III* (London, 1912), 5 and n. 1. Faced with an analogous succession of a minor in 1249, the nobles of Scotland debated whether the inauguration of young Alexander III, then nearly eight, should be postponed by a day to allow his knighting beforehand (M. D. Legge, 'The Inauguration of Alexander III', *Proceedings of the Society of Antiquaries of Scotland*, 80 (1945–1946), 77–80; and A. A. M. Duncan, *The Kingship of the Scots, 842–1292* (Edinburgh, 2002), 132–3, and 132, n. 21 for a discussion of the place of knighting in contemporary French and Iberian coronations). In the event, the inauguration went ahead and Alexander was knighted by Henry III on Christmas Day at York, 1250 when he was eight. On this ceremony, see B. Weiler, 'Knighting, Homage, and the Meaning of Ritual: The Kings of England and their Neighbors in the Thirteenth Century', *Viator*, 37 (2006), 275–300.

35. *Policraticus*, VI: 10; Etienne de Fougères, *Le Livre des manières*, ed. J. T. E. Thomas (Paris and Louvain, 2013), ll. 617–32; J. Flori, 'Chevalerie et liturgie', *Le Moyen Âge*, 4e série, 23 (1978), 247–78, 409–42.

36. *Chroniques des comtes d'Anjou*, 179, trans. Bradbury, 'Geoffrey V of Anjou, Count and Knight', 32; Flori, *L'Essor de la chevalerie*, 305–6.

37. *HWM*, ll. 15306–24, 's'avra dues reis faitz chivaliers'. The *History* has one noble say, ' "Who can do that except one man? ... he who already knighted one young king ... Let him gird the sword on this child so he shall have worthily knighted two kings" ' (ibid., ll. 15309–20).

38. For the central importance of dubbing to knighthood within chivalric culture, see Keen, *Chivalry*, 64–82.

39. When, for example, Frederick Barbarossa knighted his two sons at Mainz in 1184, he held a court of exceptional magnificence and festivities, which involved tournaments (J. Fleckenstein, 'Friedrich Barbarossa und das Rittertum. Zu Bedeutung der grosser Mainzer Hoftage von 1184 und 1188', *Festschrift für Heinrich Heimpel zum 70 Geburtstag 1971*, 3 vols (Göttingen, 1972), II, 1023–41; H. Wolter, 'Der Mainzer Hoftage von 1184 als politische Fest', *Feste und Feiern im Mittelalter*, ed. D. Alterburg, J. Jarnut and H.-H. Steinhof (Sigmaringen, 1991), 193–99; and W. H. Jackson, 'Knighthood and the Hohenstaufen Imperial Court under Frederick Barbarossa 1152–1190', *Ideals*

and Practice of Medieval Knighthood, III. Papers from the Fourth Strawberry Hill Conference, 1988, ed. C. Harper-Bill and R. H. Harvey (Woodbridge, 1990), 101–20.

40. GH, I, 63 (Richard); 207 (Geoffrey); 336 (John); and for David, GH, I, 4.

41. Keen, Chivalry, 69–70. Prior to the coronation of Erec in Chrétien de Troyes' first known romance, Erec et Enide, probably written in the early 1170s and very possibly alluding to the Young King's own coronation, King Arthur knights and richly equips no fewer than 400 young men, 'all sons of counts and kings' (Chrétien de Troyes, Arthurian Romances, tr. Kibler, 119).

42. Gesta Stephani, 214–17; Continuatio Beccensis, 323; A. C. Lawrie, Annals of the Reigns of Malcolm IV and William, Kings of Scotland, AD 1153–1214 (Glasgow, 1910), 43–4. Similarly, in 1212, William the Lion's son Alexander knighted twelve Scots nobles immediately after his own knighting by King John at Clerkenwell (Memorials of St Edmund's Abbey, ed. T. Arnold, 2 vols (Rols Series, London, 1890), II, 20).

43. Warren, Henry II, 278–81, who notes that debts owed for the aid 'ad maritandum filiam regis' were pursued by the Exchequer until as late as 1187.

44. PR 16 Henry II, 15, 'roba de viridi essaia et caligis et ocreis et tribus pannis sericis ad opus Regis filius Regis'. Other robes worth over £9 for the Young King and his familia had also been purchased (PR 16 Henry II, 61). It is impossible to know if the expense of 18s. 'for work on four helmets for the use of the King', recorded on the Berkhamsted account, was connected in any way with the bestowal of arms (ibid.).

45. As suggested by the editors of the History of William Marshal, III, note to l. 2091. Crouch, William Marshal, 44, accepts the Marshal's knighting of young Henry in 1173.

46. For an important assessment of the context and limitations of English sacral kingship in the twelfth century see G. Koziol, 'England, France and the Problem of Sacrality in Twelfth-Century Ritual', Cultures of Power. Lordship, Status and Process in Twelfth-Century Europe, ed. T. Bisson (Philadelhia, Pa., 1995), 124–48.

47. GH, I, 6. On Westminster, R. D. H. Gem, 'The Romanesque Rebuilding of Westminster Abbey', Proceedings of the Battle Conference on Anglo-Norman Studies, 3 (1980), 33–60; E. Mason, '"The Site of King-Making and Consecration": Westminster Abbey and the Crown in the Eleventh and Twelfth Centuries', The Church and Sovereignty, c. 950–1918. Essays in Honour of Michael Wilks, ed. D. Wood (Studies in Church History, Subsidia, 9, Oxford, 1991), 57–76.

48. Torigni, 245, who notes that the sees of Carlisle, Hereford, Bath, Lincoln, Chichester and Ely were at that time still vacant. Roger of Worcester had been detained in Normandy, while Henry of Winchester and William of Norwich excused themselves on grounds of sickness.

49. Howden, II, 4–5; and Torigni, 245, 'cum magna cleri et populi laetitia'.

50. Anglo-Saxon Chronicle E, 1154; Torigni, 245; WN, I, 101. Even the chronicler closest to Henry II, Robert of Torigni, 245, concentrates on listing the clergy present, and of the ceremony in Westminster simply notes that Henry was 'ab omnibus electus et in regem unctus est'.

51. Ralph of Diss, usually coolly distanced in his treatment of the Becket controversy, was careful to follow his very brief notice of the Young King's coronation by giving the text of Alexander's letter of prohibition, and noted that the coronation took place 'inconsulte' (Diceto, I, 228); and A. Duggan, 'Ralph de Diceto, Henry II and Becket', Authority and Power. Studies in Medieval History Presented to Walter Ullman, ed. B. Tierney and P. Linehan (Cambridge, 1980), 59–81. Newburgh calls it 'that most ill-starred coronation (illi infautissimae coronatio)' (WM, I, 160). Torigni, 245, alone sought to defend the coronation by Roger of York, citing the precedent of the Conqueror's coronation by Ealdred of York.

52. GH, II, 79–83. Howden, III, 247–8, similarly provides a detailed account of Richard's crown-wearing in 1194, as does Gervase, I, 524–5, citing parts of the ordo used. For twelfth-century English coronations, P. E. Schramm, A History of the English Coronation (Oxford, 1937), 27–73; H. Richardson, 'The Coronation in Medieval England: The Evolution of the Office and the Oath', Traditio, 16 (1960), 111–202; and R. Strong, Coronation. A History of Kingship and the British Monarchy (London, 2005), 35–69, which provides a valuable survey and discussion of the corona-tion service from the Conquest to 1189. For wider context of the study of such rituals, see the introduction by J. M. Bak in Coronations: Medieval and Early Modern Monarchic Ritual, ed. J. M. Bak (Berkeley, 1990), 1–151.

53. The text of the Third Recension ordo is printed and translated in English Coronation Records, ed. L. G. Wickham Legg (London, 1901), 30–45. On this recension, see J. Bruckmann, 'The Ordines of the Third Recension of the Medieval English Coronation Ordo', Essays in Medieval English History Presented to Bertie Wilkinson, ed. T. A. Sandquist and M. R. Powicke (Toronto, 1969), 99–115; and G. Garnett, 'The Third Recension of the English Coronation Ordo: The Manuscripts', Haskins Society Journal, 11 (1998), 43–71. For a valuable study of coronation in the eleventh century see J. Nelson, 'The Rites of the Conquereor', The Proceedings of the Battle Conference on Anglo-Norman Studies, 4 (1982 for 1981), 117–32, 210–21, and reprinted in J. Nelson, Politics and Ritual in Early Medieval Europe (1986), 375–401.

54. Aurell, *Plantagenet Empire*, 110–12; King, *King Stephen*, 47–8, 176–7.

55. *GH*, II, 80.

56. *Coronation Records*, ed. Wickham Legg, 30.

57. *GH*, II, 81.

58. In 1189, Howden notes these were 'tres gladios cum vaginis aureis sumpos de thesauro regis' (*GH*, II, 81). That these played a similar role in young Henry's coronation in 1170 is confirmed by the payments in the Pipe Rolls for the refurbishment of the swords (*PR 16 Henry II*, 16). For the office, Round, *The King's Serjeants*, 337–47.

59. *Heinrich der Löwe und seine Zeit. Herrschaft und Repräsentation der Welfen*, 1125–1235, ed. J. Luckhardt and F. Niehoff, 3 vols (Munich, 1995), II, 374–5 and 365 for a detailed illustration of the scabbard; *A Brief Guide to the Kunsthistorisches Museum, II: Masterpieces of the Secular Treasury*, ed. W. Seipel (Vienna, 2008), 8–9.

60. As in April 1194, when King William performed this role at Richard's great crown-wearing at Winchester on the latter's return from crusade and captivity (Howden, III, 248). At the coronation of 1189, his brother Earl David had done so as his representative, though in this instance the central position was taken by John, count of Mortain, as the king's brother (*GH*, II, 81). For Curtana, see M. R. Ditmas, 'The Curtana or Sword of Mercy', *Journal of the British Archaeological Association*, 3rd series, 29 (1966), 122–33.

61. Godred's presence at the coronation is noticed by the Chronicle of Northampton, Cambridge, Corpus Christi College MS 281, f. 100v. I am most grateful to Dauvit Broun for this reference. Godred, who had been in receipt of small grants from the Exchequer since 1156, may have been anxious to gain Henry II's protection against the Anglo-Norman invaders of Ireland, not least because he had briefly held control in Dublin before Strongbow and his allies took it in 1170 (S. Duffy, 'Godred Crovan [Guðrøðr, Gofraid Méránach] (*d.* 1095), king of Man and the Isles', *ODNB).*

62. See Duncan, *The Kingship of the Scots*, 127–50.

63. *GH*, II, 81. The chequered board used for accounting, whence the Exchequer received its name, thus symbolized the wealth of the kingdom. In 1189, the great crown was borne by William de Mandeville, earl of Essex, and it is possible that given William's eminence and closeness to Henry II he may also have borne it in 1170.

64. For the text, *Coronation Records*, ed. Wickham Legg, 30–1. On the oath and its significance, H. G. Richardson, 'The English Coronation Oath', *TRHS*, 4th series, 23 (1941), 129–58; idem, 'The English Coronation Oath', *Speculum*, 24 (1949), 44–75.

65. In 1166, Becket told Henry: 'Remember also the profession concerning the preservation of the liberty of God's Church which you made when you were consecrated and anointed by our predecessor, and placed in writing upon the altar at Westminster' (*CTB*, I, 288–9). See R. Foreville, 'Le Sacre des rois anglo-normands et angevins et le serment du sacre (XIe–XIIe siècles)', *Proceedings of the Battle Conference on Anglo-Norman Studies*, 1 (1978), 49–62.

66. *GH*, II, 81–2; *Coronation Records*, ed. Wickham Legg, 30–1.

67. *MTB*, VII, 426–7, 'in coronatione sua manifeste juravit se observaturum omnia ecclesia jura, sicut in antique et communi consecrationis canonae continentur, neque de novae consuetudinibus mentione aliqua fact est'. Roger likewise assured the pope 'quod ipse in coronatione filii regis debitum iuramentum integre recepit, nec aliquid omisit quod in coronatione regis Anglie prestari solet' (ibid., 942).

68. *Coronation Records*, ed. Wickham Legg, 31.

69. William of Newburgh could describe Henry II as having been consecrated as king 'mystica unctione' in 1154 (WN, I, 101).

70. *Coronation Records*, ed. Wickham Legg, 31.

71. *CTB*, I, 295; and Howden, who, speaking of Richard I's coronation, noted that this 'signifies glory, courage and knowledge' (*GH*, II, 82).

72. Howden refers to this as the *pileus regalis* (*GH*, II, 81). For such caps of state, D. Crouch, *The Image of Aristocracy in Britain, 1000–1300* (London, 1992), 208–10.

73. Diceto, II, 20. Similarly, in 1199 Richard was buried in the regalia in which he had been crowned, and which 'he had been adorned with' (*infulatus*) at his crown-wearing in 1194 at Winchester (*Annales de Wintonia, AM*, II, 71).

74. W. Ullmann, *Growth of Papal Government* (London, 1955), 225ff.; Morey and Brooke, *Gilbert Foliot and his Letters*, 176.

75. N. F. Cantor, *Church, Kingship and Lay Investiture in England, 1089–1135* (New York, 1969), 137.

76. *MTB*, V, 532; *Letters and Charters of Gilbert Foliot* (no. 170), 236; Morey and Brooke, *Gilbert Foliot and his Letters*, 176–7.

77. Cantor, *Church, Kingship and Lay Investiture*, 180.

78. *Libelli de lite imperatorum et pontificum*, ed. E. Bernheim et al., 3 vols, *MGH* (Berlin, 1892–1897), iii, 667, 679; Cantor, *Church, Kingship and Lay Investiture*, 191.

79. *Letters and Charters of Gilbert Foliot*, no. 170; *MTB*, V, 532–3. Gilbert's stance here is discussed by R. Foreville, *L'Eglise et la royauté en Angleterre sous Henri II Plantagenêt* (Paris, 1943), 244–5; D. Knowles, *The Episcopal Colleagues of Thomas Becket* (Cambridge, 1951), 171ff.; and Morey and Brooke, *Gilbert Foliot and his Letters*, 174–80.
80. *Letters and Charters of Gilbert Foliot* (no. 170), 236.
81. *Epistolae*, no. 150 (*PL*, CVII, col. 440); F. Barlow, 'The King's Evil', *EHR*, 95 (1980), 3–27, at 19.
82. Barlow, 'The King's Evil', 19.
83. M. Bloch, *Les Rois thaumaturges* (Strasbourg, 1924), trans. J. E. Anderson as *The Royal Touch: Sacred Monarchy and Scrofula in England and France* (London, 1973); Cantor, *Church, Kingship and Lay Investiture*, 173; P. Buc, 'David's Adultery with Bathsheba and the Healing Power of Capetian Kings', *Viator*, 24 (1993), 101–20; and cf. Koziol, 'The Problem of Sacrality', 128, 139–40.
84. *GH*, II, 82; *CTB*, I, 294–5. Becket's quotation is from Claudian, *De quarto consulate Honorii Augusti*, I, 299.
85. That the attachment of such spurs was not a novelty in the coronation of 1189 is suggested by Howden's statement that those used were 'calcaria aurea sumpta de thesauro regis' (*GH*, II, 82), implying they were already items of regalia. A pair of finely worked gold spurs, of twelfth-century date, used in the coronation of the French kings, was kept with the royal treasure at St Denis, and survive in the Musée du Louvre (D. Gaborit-Chopin, 'Le Trésor au temps de Suger', in *Le Trésor de St Denis, les dossiers d'archéologie*, 158 (1991), 19, at 10). For this 'encroachment of knighthood upon kingship', Koziol, 'The Problem of Sacrality', 135–6.
86. *Coronation Records*, ed. Wickham Legg, 34–6; Strong, *Coronation*, 48, and cf. *GH*, II, 82.
87. At Richard's coronation, this was described as 'a great and heavy crown of gold, adorned on all sides with precious stones', but it is not known if this was the same one that was used in 1170 (Howden, III, 10). The crown may have been made especially for the Young King's coronation, for the great imperial crown, brought back from Germany by the Empress Matilda and used for the crowning of Henry II in 1154, had been gifted by the Empress to the abbey of Bec (Chibnall, *Empress Matilda*, 189).
88. E. H. Kantorowicz, *Laudes Regiae: a Study in Liturgical Acclamations and Medieval Ruler Worship* (Berkeley and Los Angeles, 1946), 171–9.
89. Howden, III, 11, noting that 'talis enim oblatio decet regem in singulis coronationibus suis'.
90. In Geoffrey of Monmouth's *History of the Kings of Britain*, this is the age at which Arthur is crowned king (Bk IX: 1).
91. Howden, II, 4, n. 3, for the text of an anonymous Latin verse in praise of young Henry, penned in the margin of the earliest extant manuscript of the *Chronica* (BL, MS Reg. 14 C. 2), and possibly in Howden's own hand (Howden, I, lxxiv–lxxv).
92. *HWM*, ll. 1956–8.
93. *Histoire des ducs*, 65. For Westminster hall, *The History of the King's Works*, I, 45–7.
94. Eyton, 139–40. Edward Blund received expenses of £30 'ad coronationem Regis filius Regis' (*PR 17 Henry II*, 80).
95. William of Canterbury, 83, 'post coronationem celebrato convivio, rex regi, pater filio dignatus est ministrare, et se regem non esse protestari'.
96. FitzStephen, 107. It is difficult to accept that Henry II regarded his son's coronation merely as a ruse to prevent Thomas Becket from excommunicating Henry, as suggested by U. Vones-Liebenstein, 'Alienor d'Aquitaine, Henri le Jeune et la révolte de 1173: un prélude à la confrontation entre Plantagenêts et Capetiéns?', *Plantagenêts et Capétiens: confrontations et heritages*, ed. M. Aurell and N. Y. Tonnerre (Brepols, 2006), 75–93.
97. *La Chronique de Giselbert de Mons*, ed. L. Vanderkindere (Brussels, 1904), c. 70; trans. Napran, 63, 'King Henry … embraced his sons with great esteem and raised them to their own properties with all honour and placed them in charge by themselves. For he put aside the royal crown and caused his son Henry to be crowned.' Nevertheless, Gilbert understood that 'of the entire land, King Henry II retained for himself the fruits and profits belonging to that kingdom, and kept for himself the administration of his son the new king.'
98. Matthew Paris, *Historia Anglorum*, I, 352–3; above, 45.
99. J. Backhouse and C. De Hamel, *The Becket Leaves* (London, 1988). The rubric above the scene reads: 'Celebratur convivium coronationis, ministrat pater filio et se regem esse diffitetur.'
100. Howden, II, 4, n. 3. These verses, probably by Howden himself, are followed by another stanza praising the young Henry's good looks in fulsome terms. Roger would similarly use the juxtaposition of a series of favourable and critical verses in lieu of an obit for Richard I (Howden, IV, 84–5).
101. *Historia pontificalis*, 69.
102. *GH*, I, 6, 'et omnes comites, et barones et francos tenentes regni sui, devenire homines novi regis filii sui, et fecit eos super sanctorum reliquias iurare illi ligantias et fidelitates contra omnes homines salva fidelitate sua'.

103. JF, ll. 5–12.
104. Torigni, 245.
105. Torigni, 245.
106. *FitzStephen*, 104 trans. Appleby, *Henry II*, 162.
107. Guernes, ll. 2756–60; trans. Short, 92.
108. *GH*, I, 6; *CTB*, II, no. 296.
109. Torigni, 246; *GH*, I, 6, noted that he landed at Barfleur *c.* 24 June.
110. *MTB*, VII, 331 (no. 685); Barlow, *Becket*, 208
111. FitzStephen, 109; Staunton, *Lives*, 175.
112. FitzStephen, 109–10; Staunton, *Lives*, 175.
113. FitzStephen, 110; Staunton, *Lives*, 175. This account tallies closely with the report of the meeting at Fréteval sent by Becket himself to Pope Alexander (*CTB*, II, no. 300; Duggan, *Thomas Becket*, 184–5).
114. *MTB*, VII, 331 (no. 685); Guernes, ll. 4371–90.
115. WN, I, 172.
116. As the author of the *History of William Marshal* sententiously noted from the vantage point of the 1220s, 'I would add my opinion that the King did not act wisely when he forced all his barons to pay homage to his son. Once the deed had been done, many was the day afterwards that he readily would have undone it. But here I make a parenthesis for you: men often do many things readily, only to regret them; but no man can predict the future' (*HWM*, ll. 1925–34).
117. *GH*, I, 6.
118. Torigni, 247.
119. *GH*, I, 6–7, where Howden states that both Aquitaine and Brittany were 'tenendum de rege Franciae'.
120. *GH*, I, 7, 'ad provenendum et manutenendum'. In his later *Chronica*, Howden (II, 6) says that Henry II also granted John the county of Mortain at this time, but in reality this appears to have been a statement of wish and future intent. John was only to receive the county on Henry's death in 1189, when Richard granted him 'omnes terras quas dominus rex pater suus ei dederat', including Mortain (*GH*, II, 73; K. Norgate, *John Lackland* (London, 1902), 3–4, 24–5). I am grateful to Stephen Church for this point.
121. *GH*, I, 7. For Henry's devotion to Grandmont, E. Hallam, 'Henry II, Richard I and the Order of Grandmont', *JMH*, 1 (1975), 165–86; C. A. Hutchison, *The Hermit Monks of Grandmont* (Kalamazoo, Mich., 1989), 57–64.
122. *GH*, I, 7: Torigni, 262. N. Vincent, 'Henry III and the Blessed Virgin Mary', *The Church and Mary*, ed. R. Swanson (Boydell, 2004), 126–46, at 130, suggests that Henry's choice of this Marian pilgrimage site may be linked to the fact that the onset of his sickness had occurred close to the feast of the Assumption (15 August).
123. E. Mason, 'Rocamadour in Quercy above all other Churches: The Healing of Henry II', *The Church and Healing*, ed. W. J. Sheils (Studies in Church History, 19, 1982), 39–54. For the cult of the Virgin see J. Roacher, *Rocamadour et son pèlerinage: Étude historique et archéologique*, 2 vols (Toulouse, 1979); and M. Bull, *The Miracles of Our Lady at Rocamadour* (Woodbridge, 1999), which analyses a miracle collection composed in 1172–73.
124. Torigni, 262; Mason, 'Rocamadour in Quercy', 39.

Chapter 6: The Regent and the Martyr, 1170–1172

1. 'Vox vatis velata diu', in P. A. Thompson, 'An Anonymous Verse Life of Thomas Becket', *Mittellateinisches Jahrbuch*, 20 (1985), 147–54, ll. 3–5; A. G. Rigg, *A History of Anglo-Latin Literature, 1066–1422* (Oxford, 1992), 82.
2. *GH*, I, 6. The Pipe Roll for 1171 records considerable expenditure for the Young King on robes and clothing of scarlet, green and coloured serge, as well as furs of ermine, while more than £27 was also spent on robes for Margaret and her household (*PR 17 Henry II*, 147).
3. *GH*, I, 6; Smith, '*Acta*', 305. His privy seal has not survived, but Jordan Fantosme noted that in 1173 the Young King sent King William the Lion a letter, written in French (*en romanz*), sealed with his ring (*d'un anel*) (JF, ll. 245; M. T. Clanchy, *From Memory to Written Record*, 2nd edn, Oxford, 1993, 219). That of his brother Richard, incorporating a classical Roman cameo depicting Mercury, is illustrated in Gillingham, *Richard I*, pl. 3.
4. For Henry II's seals, W. de Gray Birch, 'On the Seals of King Henry the Second, and of his Son the so-called Henry the Third', *Transactions of the Royal Society of Literature of the United Kingdom*, 2nd series, no. xi (1878), 301–37; and N. Vincent, 'The Seals of Henry II and his Court', *Seals and their Context in the Middle Ages*, ed. P. Schofield (Oxford, 2015), 7–34.

5. For a discussion of the Young King's seal, Smith, '*Acta*', 304–7. Only two near-complete seals survive, though both are worn, leaving much of the detail indistinct. One is attached to a charter to Christ Church cathedral priory, Canterbury, granting rents in Barksore (Canterbury Cathedral Archive, Chartae Antiquae, B336; Smith, '*Acta*', no. 10), and the second to a charter in favour of Montjoux hospital (Oxford, New College MS Archive no. 10679; reproduced in H. E. Salter, *Facsimiles of Early Charters in Oxford Muniment Rooms* (Oxford, 1929), no. 37; Smith, '*Acta*', no. 24). A cast of another seal is preserved in the British Library (W. de Gray Birch, *Catalogue of Seals in the Department of Manuscripts in the British Museum*, 6 vols (London, 1887–1900), I, no. 79 (ii.4). For the reproduction of another seal of the Young King, A. B. Wyton, *The Great Seals of England from the Earliest Period to the Present Time* (London, 1887), no. 34. A drawing of the Young King's seal was made by F. Sandford, *A Genealogical History of the Kings of England and Monarchs of Great Britain* (London, 1677), 54, where he is shown bearded, while the French antiquary Roger de Gaignières recorded the seal once attached to the charter of the Young King in favour of Fontevraud abbey (Paris, Bibliothèque nationale, MS Latin 5480, Gaignières transcripts; Smith, '*Acta*', no. 20).
6. Smith, '*Acta*', 304–7.
7. M. Dalas, *Les Sceaux des rois et de la régence* (*Corpus de sceaux français du Moyen Âge*, ii, Paris, 1991), 150 and n. 1, and nos 70, 70 bis. For Louis' seal, B. Bedos-Rezak, 'Suger and the Symbolism of Royal Power: The Seal of Louis VII', *Abbot Suger and St Denis. A Symposium*, ed. P. L. Gerson (New York, 1986), 95–103. On both Young Henry and Louis' seal, the throne with finials as lions' heads is near identical, and on both the sceptre terminates in a fleur-de-lys.
8. Only for the period 1137–1152, when he was duke of Aquitaine by virtue of his marriage to Eleanor, did Louis VII use a double-sided seal, with the reverse depicting him as duke as a mounted warrior. With his divorce from Eleanor, he resumed a single-sided seal.
9. Suger, *Vie de Louis VI le Gros*, ed. H. Waquet (Paris, 1964), 86; trans. R. Cusimano and J. H. Moorhead, *The Deeds of Louis the Fat* (Washington, DC, 1992), 63.
10. Smith, '*Acta*', 305.
11. It is possible, however, that the absence of a counter-seal depicting Young Henry as duke of Normandy may reflect limitations on his authority in the duchy, even though the legend on the single face bore the title Dux Normannorum (Smith, '*Acta*', 307–9). Certainly there is no record of young Henry having been invested as duke in 1170, or on any subsequent occasion.
12. *HWM*, ll. 1936–8.
13. They witness three of the Young King's administrative writs between his coronation and November 1172 when he left for Normandy (Smith, '*Acta*', 298, and nos 7, 15, 28).
14. On Ridel, see *English Episcopal Acta, XXXI: Ely, 1109–1197*, ed. N. Karn (Oxford, 2005), lxxix–lxxxii; A. J. Duggan, 'Geoffrey Ridel (d. 1189), administrator and bishop of Ely', *ODNB*; and for Richard of Ilchester, see above, 60, n. 51.
15. William of Canterbury, 108–9; Smith, '*Acta*', 299, n. 1. The first three also appear in the witness list to the Mandeville charter.
16. For William, *Recueil, Introduction*, 500–1; *CTB*, II, no. 311, n. 7. He was, for example, sole witness to writs of the Young King in favour of Bury St Edmunds and Biddlesden Abbey, as well as that commanding Peter of Studely to keep an agreement with Godwin of Warwick concerning land at Enborne, Berkshire (14 June 1170 x November 1172); Smith, '*Acta*', nos 8, 2, 33.
17. Vincent, 'Hugh de Gundeville', 131–3.
18. J. Boorman, 'Ralph FitzStephen (d. 1202)', *ODNB*. He received payments from Henry II's chamber from 1156/7, and attests as a chamberlain in 1178. He was sheriff of Gloucestershire 1171–75, and later was one of those responsible for the upkeep of Eleanor during her captivity.
19. Smith, '*Acta*', nos 2 (Windsor), 3, 8 (Winchester), 7 (Newbury), 33 (Oxford). For Eleanor's regency, Turner, *Eleanor*, 150–61.
20. J. H. Round, 'A Glimpse of the Young King's Court (1170)', in J. H. Round, *Feudal England* (London, 1909), 503–8, at 504.
21. This was probably in 1171. G. H. Fowler, 'Henry FitzHenry at Woodstock', *EHR*, 39 (1924), 240–1.
22. *History of the King's Works*, II, 1009–10.
23. *PR 17 Henry II*, 23.
24. Smith, '*Acta*', nos 8, 7.
25. *Cartulary of the Monastery of St Frideswide*, ed. S. R. Wigram, 2 vols (Oxford Historical Society, xxviii, xxxi, 1895–1896), i. 260, no. 338; Smith, '*Acta*', no. 26; ibid., no. 15; *Cartularium Monasterii de Ramesia*, ed. W. H. Hart and P. A. Lyons, 3 vols (Rolls Series, 1884–1893), I, 254, no. 190; *Recueil, Introduction*, 253; Smith, '*Acta*', no. 28.
26. Smith, '*Acta*', nos 4, 5 and 6.
27. For Barre's career, R. V. Turner, 'Richard Barre and Michael Belet: Two Angevin Civil Servants', *Medieval Prosopography*, 6 (1985), 25–49, on which what follows is largely based. From a family

hailing from La Barre to the east of Lisieux, he served in the household of Robert de Chesney, bishop of Lincoln, and by 1165 had secured a position at the royal court.

28. *CTB*, II, nos 227, n. 18, 229, n. 3, 244, n. 1; *MTB*, VII, nos 536–7, 554, 564–7.

29. *MTB*, VII, 227, 440–43, 443–5, 471–5, 475–87; *GH*, I, 19; Howden, II, 25–8.

30. *GH*, I, 43, indicating that Walter was his father's appointment. Subsequently, William 'my chaplain' appears as a witness to a number of the Young King's charters, which also mention John *capellanus* (Smith, '*Acta*', nos 30, 31, 32). For Walter, R. V. Turner, 'Walter de Coutances (d. 1207), administrator and archbishop of Rouen', *ODNB*. Geoffrey, the king's chaplain, who was in the service of both the Young King and Henry II, appears as a canon of Lincoln cathedral (*English Episcopal Acta, I: Lincoln, 1067–1185*, ed. D. M. Smith (Oxford, 1980), nos 205 and 280).

31. Warren, *King John*, 153; *Foundation of Walden*, 82, n. 62; *PR 16 Henry II*, 15.

32. *Foundation of Walden*, 80–83; and below, 111, for Queen Margaret's chapel.

33. *MTB*, III, 30–1; Staunton, *Lives*, 56.

34. *HWM*, ll. 3417–24.

35. For a valuable discussion of the nature of the royal household in the earlier twelfth century, *Dialogus de Scaccario and the Constitutio Domus Regis*, ed. and trans. E. Amt and S. Church (Oxford, 2007), lv–lviii; Hollister, *Henry I*, 361–4; and G. H. White, 'The Household of the Norman Kings', *TRHS*, 4th series, 30 (1948), 127–55. For the household of Henry II, Warren, *Henry II*, 254–5.

36. *GH*, I, 43, and 46, for Solomon *hostiarius*, listed among those fleeing with young Henry to France in 1173.

37. D. Crouch, 'The Court of Henry II of England in the 1180s, and the Office of King of Arms', *The Coat of Arms: The Journal of the Heraldry Society*, 3rd series, 5 (2010), pt 2, 47–55.

38. R. V. Turner, 'The Households of the Sons of Henry II', *La Cour Plantagenêt (1154–1204). Actes du Colloque tenu à Thouars du 30 avril au 2 mai 1999*, ed. M. Aurell (Poitiers, 2000), 49–62, at 53; *Facsimiles of Early Charters from Northamptonshire (Northamptonshire Charters)*, ed. F. M. Stenton (Northampton Record Society, 4, Northampton, 1930), nos VI and VII; *Feudal Documents from the Abbey of Bury St Edmunds* (London, 1932), nos 96, 98, 99; Smith, '*Acta*', no. 30. Subsequently, John Malherbe, one of Earl William's household, appears among the Young King's retinue at Lagny in 1179 (*HWM*, I, 4690; *HWM*, III, note to line 4690; *HGM*, III, 60, note).

39. *HWM*, ll. 1936–48.

40. *HWM*, ll. 184–282; Crouch, *William Marshal*, 12–23. John Marshal had played a notable role in saving the Empress from capture in 1141 following the rout of Winchester.

41. *HWM*, ll. 1565–758.

42. *HWM*, ll. 1864–82. The relations between the queen and the Marshal are briefly examined in E. Mullally, 'The Reciprocal Loyalty of Eleanor of Aquitaine and William Marshal', in *Eleanor of Aquitaine. Lord and Lady*, ed. B. Wheeler and J. C. Parsons (New York, 2003), 237–46.

43. *Recueil*, I, nos 257, 258, 260, 261, 268, 269; Smith, '*Acta*', nos 13, 14, 27, 29, 30, 31, 32; S. Painter, *William Marshal. Knight-Errant, Baron and Regent of England* (Baltimore, Md., 1933), 32; Crouch, *William Marshal*, 38–44.

44. *HWM*, ll. 1939–34; Turner, 'The Households of the Sons of Henry II', 52.

45. *GH*, I, 45–6.

46. Adam's importance in the household is indicated by the fact that he attests eight of the Young King's known charters, one more than William Marshal (Smith, '*Acta*', 300; *HWM*, III, note to l. 4685).

47. *Recueil, Introduction*, 258–9, 260, 262–3, 268; *HGM*, III, 60 note. The family was from Troisgots, Manche, cant. Tessy-sur-Vire (*HWM*, III, note to l. 4693). For Coulances (Calvados, cant. Vire), *HWM*, III, note to line 4697; Talbot, probably from the Pays de Caux, *HWM*, III, note to l. 4677; and Tinténiac, *HWM*, III, note to line 4743.

48. *HWM*, III, note to line 4623; and for possible identifications for Robert, perhaps from an Anglo-Norman marcher family in south Wales, *HWM*, III, note to line 4621.

49. Vincent, 'The Court of Henry II', 295–6.

50. Smith, '*Acta*', 298–9, 301.

51. The Young King, for example, received a writ from his father commanding him to issue two of his own charters to confirm those Henry II had issued on behalf of Master David, who was acting on behalf of the king and the bishop of London at the papal Curia, concerning the provision of an annuity for £20 (Z. N. Brooke, 'The Register of Master David of London and the Part he Played in the Becket Crisis', *Essays in History Presented to R. L. Poole*, ed. H. W. C. Davis (Oxford, 1927), 227–45, at 240; Clanchy, *From Memory to Written Record*, 44–5).

52. J. C. Holt, 'The Writs of Henry II', *Proceedings of the British Academy*, 89 (1996), 47–64.

53. William of Canterbury, 84–5; FitzStephen, 112; trans. G. Greenaway, *The Life and Death of Thomas Becket* (London, 1961), 138; *MTB*, VII, no. 690; Diceto, I, 339.

54. Barlow, *Becket*, 211–12.

55. Barlow, *Becket*, 221; Duggan, *Thomas Becket*, 187–90.

56. *LJS*, II, no. 302; FitzStephen, 112–13; and for the dating of these orders, Barlow, *Becket*, 213 and n. 32.

57. Barlow, *Becket*, 213. Ranulf, the king's hereditary doorkeeper, had vociferously denounced the archbishop as he fled from the tumultuous council of Northampton in 1164 (ibid., 114, 225).

58. Barlow, *Becket*, 213. The fact that Ranulf de Broc accounted for £1,560 5s. 5d. at the Michaelmas Exchequer, 1170, indicates the extent of the sums involved (ibid., 221).

59. Barlow, *Becket*, 214–15; Duggan, *Thomas Becket*, 189–92.

60. Barlow, *Becket*, 215.

61. *CTB*, II, no. 311.

62. Ibid., dated before 15 October 1170.

63. *CTB*, II, no. 311, where Duggan notes that William FitzAldelin had accounted for the scutage of the knights of Canterbury in 1161, while it is possible that Ralph may have been related to Becket's clerk and biographer William FitzStephen.

64. For Reginald, see D. Crouch, 'Reginald, earl of Cornwall (d. 1175)', *ODNB*.

65. For Walter, *CTB*, II, no. 311, n. 8. He had been one of the commissioners involved in the Inquest of Sheriffs early that year (*PR 19 Henry II*, 182).

66. Herbert goes on to note that he had heard that the Young King and his advisors had immediately sent letters back to Henry II in Normandy, but that he was ignorant of their purport (*CTB*, no. 311).

67. *CTB*, II, no. 311.

68. *LJS*, II, no. 304.

69. Barlow, *Becket*, 221.

70. William of Canterbury, 87–8; FitzStephen, 116–18; Bosham, 471–2; Guernes, ll. 4681–700. These letters had been issued by Alexander III before news had reached him of the peace settlement of Fréteval, and on receiving them, probably in late October, Becket had initially refrained from deploying them, realizing not only that they were out of date in regard to the current political situation, but also that their tone and reference to the highly contentious 'evil customs' were highly inflammatory. Moreover, in late November, Thomas had received a second batch of papal letters expressing joy at the news of the peace established at Fréteval, confirming Thomas' powers as legate and strengthening the authority of his other legates to impose an interdict on Henry II's continental lands should he not fulfil its terms. Yet Alexander, as well as several cardinals who wrote separate letters to Becket, urged him to be conciliatory and not to seek revenge, lest the hard-won peace be ruined. Becket, however, could not bring himself to heed this wise advice. For detailed analysis of these developments, Barlow, *Becket*, 216–24.

71. *CTB*, II, no. 311; Anon. II, *MTB*, IV, 123, 125–6.

72. Barlow, *Becket*, 223.

73. As the bishops' representatives who met with Thomas at Canterbury on 2 December had told him, the sentences were contrary to the peace at Fréteval; Barlow, *Becket*, 226.

74. William of Canterbury, 99–102; FitzStephen, 118–19; Bosham, 477–8; *CTB*, II, no. 326.

75. Barlow, *Becket*, 226.

76. William of Canterbury, 102–5; FitzStephen, 120; Bosham, 480; Barlow, *Becket*, 227.

77. FitzStephen, 121–2; Howden, II, 13. Diceto, I, 342, incorrectly has the Young King at Woodstock. Earlier, in a letter to the pope reporting his meeting with Henry II at Fréteval, Becket reports how the king had told Thomas that young Henry 'loves you with such great affection that he refuses to see any of your enemies in a true light' (*CTB*, II, no. 300).

78. Barlow, *Becket*, 230.

79. William of Canterbury, 105–8; FitzStephen, 122.

80. FitzStephen, 122; trans. Staunton, *Lives*, 185. These may well have been procured by the archbishop's agents from the horse fair held every Saturday at Smithfield, then just beyond the walls of London (FitzStephen, 6). As FitzStephen notes, Becket 'loved him very much as his lord king, whom as a boy he had reared in his house and court when he was chancellor to his father the king' (FitzStephen, 122; trans. Staunton, *Lives*, 185).

81. William of Canterbury, 109–10.

82. William of Canterbury, 110–11.

83. William of Canterbury, 111.

84. He had been made archdeacon of Canterbury at Henry II's insistence in 1163, and continued to hold the archiepiscopal church at Otford in Kent (William of Canterbury, 111; Duggan, 'Geoffrey Ridel', *ODNB*).

85. *MTB*, VII, 412; Gervase, I, 223. According to William of Canterbury, the archdeacon's message informed young Henry that: 'I know your father's wishes; and never will I be a party to admitting into your presence a man who purposes to disinherit you' (William of Canterbury, 111; Duggan, 'Geoffrey Ridel', *ODNB*).

86. William of Canterbury, 111–12; FitzStephen, 123; Diceto, I, 342. Jocelin was the brother of Queen Adeliza, widow of Henry I.
87. William of Canterbury, 111–12.
88. FitzStephen, 123.
89. FitzStephen, 123; Staunton, *Lives*, 186.
90. William of Canterbury, 113, 'Ergo diffiduciat me?'
91. William of Canterbury, 114–19; FitzStephen, 124–6; Barlow, *Becket*, 230, n. 8.
92. William of Canterbury, 118–19.
93. William of Canterbury, 114–15.
94. Howden, II, 14.
95. FitzStephen, 124.
96. Grim, *MTB*, II, 429; Barlow, *Becket*, 235.
97. FitzStephen, 128.
98. For these men, N. Vincent, 'The Murderers of Thomas Becket', *Bischofsmord im Mittelalter*, ed. N. Fryde and D. Reitz (Göttingen, 2003), 211–72.
99. William of Canterbury, 127; FitzStephen, 129–30, 139, Bosham, 488.
100. FitzStephen, 129.
101. The fullest reconstruction of the course of events and Thomas' murder is provided by Barlow, *Becket*, 237–50, on which what follows is based, and W. Urry, *Thomas Becket. His Last Days* (Stroud, 1999).
102. Grim, *MTB*, II, 431–2.
103. Barlow, *Becket*, 241–9.
104. Henry II received the news at Argentan. Overwhelmed by a mixture of grief and fear that he would be blamed for the crime, he shut himself away for three days, refusing to eat or to see anyone; *GH*, I, 14; *MTB*, VII, no. 738.
105. FitzStephen, 149.
106. There is no contemporary support for the statement by Turner, *Eleanor*, 214, that Becket's death 'had already inflamed the Young King's hostility to his father', or that Henry II's 'less than whole-hearted repentance at Avranches further undermined his son's respect for him'.
107. A. Duggan, 'Diplomacy, Status and Conscience: Henry II's Penance for Becket's Murder', *Forschungen zur Reichs-, Papst- und Landesgeschichte. Peter Herde zum 65. Geburtstag von Freunden, Schülern und Kollegen durchgebracht*, ed. K. Borchardt and E. Bünz, 2 vols (Stuttgart, 1998), 265–90, reprinted in A. J. Duggan, *Thomas Becket: Friends, Networks, Texts and Cult* (Aldershot, 2007), with original pagination.
108. *MTB*, VII, no. 739.
109. *MTB*, VII, no. 440; Duggan, 'Diplomacy, Status and Conscience', 267.
110. Torigni, 249.
111. *GH*, I, 14–19; *MTB*, VII, no. 735.
112. For the embassy and its dealings, Duggan, 'Diplomacy, Status and Conscience', 268–72.
113. *GH*, I, 19–22.
114. *MTB*, VII, 443, 476–8.
115. Torigni, 252; *PR 17 Henry II*, 19, 34, 40, 42, 47, 148; Eyton, 162. She crossed in the royal esnecca, while a separate ship transported the horses of the princess and her retinue.
116. Warren, *Henry II*, 529–30, who regards as erroneous Howden's statement that a legation had arrived in Normandy before Henry left the duchy but that he departed without seeing them, having made an appeal to Rome (*GH*, I, 24). Howden may be correct, however, in stating that Henry forbade the legates to enter England in his absence, and required that anyone crossing to England had first to swear an oath not to harm the king or his kingdom (*GH*, I, 24; Gervase, I, 234).
117. M. T. Flanagan, 'Strongbow, Henry II and Anglo-Norman Intervention in Ireland', *War and Government in the Middle Ages. Essays in Honour of J. O. Prestwich*, ed. J. Gillingham and J. C. Holt (Woodbridge, 1984), 62–77; idem, *Irish Society, Anglo-Norman Settlers, Angevin Kingship: Interactions in Ireland in the Late Twelfth Century* (Oxford, 1989); and J. Gillingham, 'The English Invasion of Ireland', *Representing Ireland: Literature and the Origins of Conflict, 1534–1660*, ed. B. Bradshaw, A. Hadfield and W. Maley (Cambridge, 1993), 24–42, and reprinted in Gillingham, *The English in the Twelfth Century*, 145–60.
118. *GH*, I, 24.
119. *Expugnatio*, 92–3.
120. M. T. Flanagan, 'Household Favourites: Angevin Royal Agents in Ireland under Henry II and John', *Seanchas. Studies in Early and Medieval Irish History and Literature in Honour of Francis J. Byrne*, ed. A. R. Smith (Dublin, 2005), 357–80. Together with Hugh de Lacy, FitzAldelin nego-tiated with Ruaidri, king of Connacht, while King Henry was at Dublin receiving the submission of other Irish chiefs (*Expugnatio*, 94–5 and notes 156, 157). On Henry's departure from Ireland, he was given custody of Wexford (*Expugnatio*, 105, 169, 336, n. 329; Howden, II, 134).

121. *GH*, I, 24, n. 2, an event noticed only by the B text of the *Gesta*; Eyton, 158–9.
122. *Expugnatio*, 90–7.
123. Torigni, 252.
124. M. T. Flanagan, 'Henry II, the Council of Cashel and the Irish Bishops', *Peritia*, 10 (1996), 184–211.
125. *GH*, I, 28.
126. Diceto, I, 350.
127. Provisions, as well as silks and rich furs – perhaps intended for diplomatic gifts to Irish chiefs – were sent to Henry II in Ireland by the writ of the Young King (*PR 18 Henry II*, 21, 79, 84, 86, 87; Eyton, 163).
128. In his charters, he is typically styled 'Henricus rex Anglorum, dux Normannorum, et comes Andegaviae Regis Henrici filius' (see, for example, Smith, '*Acta*', no. 23).
129. Smith, '*Acta*', 322–3, no. 23, and printed in *Recueil, Introduction*, 254. As Eyton, 159, n. 2, noted, however, Reginald and Hugh also accompany Henry II to Ireland, which may suggest a date in late July or August 1171, or after Henry II's own return to Normandy in May 1172.
130. *Recueil*, I, no. 305.
131. *HWM*, ll. 1950–74.
132. A hint that this may have been so is expenditure on a number of helmets for the Young King's use, perhaps intended to equip him and his *mesnie* (*PR 18 Henry II*, 46).
133. *Lamberti Ardensis historia comitum Ghisnensium* (*History of the Counts of Guines*), ed. J. Heller, *MGH, Scriptores*, XXIV (1879), c. 90; trans. L. Shopkow, *Lambert of Ardres, The History of the Counts of Guisnes and Lords of Ardres* (Philadelphia, Pa., 2007), 123.
134. Eyton, 166; *PR 18 Henry II*, 84. Considerable work was being undertaken in these years on the castle, both on its walls and on the royal accommodation within (*History of the King's Works*, II, 855–7).
135. Eyton, 166–7; *PR 18 Henry II*, 84, 33.
136. *Expugnatio*, 96–7; Howden, II, 32, 253. For the wider context of such festivals, and their prominence in the 1170s and 1180s, see L. Patterson, 'Great Court Festivals in Southern France and Catalonia in the Twelfth and Thirteenth Centuries', *Medium Aevum*, 51 (1982), 213–21, who at 217, compares this and Henry II's great court feast of 1182 with the contemporary lavish festivals visible in both southern France and Germany.
137. *History of the Counts of Guines*, c. 87; trans. Shopkow, 120, recounting that a feast was given in honour of William, archbishop of Rheims, who was en route to visit Becket's shrine at Canterbury.
138. Torigni, 253; Appleby, *Henry II*, 188. For William de St John, Torigni, ed. Delisle, II, 31, n. 2.
139. *HGM*, note to l. 1960; M. Jones, 'Geoffrey, duke of Brittany (1158–1186)', *ODNB*.
140. Torigni, 249–50.
141. Diceto, I, 350; *Chronicon Turonense magnum*, 138; and for the lordship of St Maure, Boussard, *Le Comté d'Anjou*, 50, n. 5, 78, 80.
142. *Expugnatio*, 220–1.
143. Torigni, 251.
144. Diceto, I, 350.
145. Diceto, I, 351; *GH*, I, 30. Howden's chronology of events, however, is very confused; he has Henry II arrive in Normandy on 25 May, by which time he had in fact met with the legates several times and been absolved; and he wrongly places Henry's settlement with the legates at Avranches on 27 September, on the eve of a great ecclesiastical council (A. Duggan, '*Ne in dubium*: The Official Record of Henry II's Reconciliation at Avranches, 21 May 1172', *EHR*, 115 (2000), 643–58, at 649).
146. *MTB*, VII, 518; Appleby, *Henry II*, 192.
147. *Expugnatio*, 104–5.
148. Though Gerald was very well informed about the expedition and its immediate aftermath, he was also writing with full hindsight of the rebellion of 1173–74 and, indeed, of Henry's future problems with his sons until his death, reflected in a number of self-fulfilling prophecies (for example *Expugnatio*, 108–13).
149. The king's agents, however, met considerable resistance from the lay magnates, while the ecclesiastics refused to pay anything on new enfeoffments made after 1135 (J. H. Ramsay, *The Angevin Empire, or the Three Reigns of Henry II, Richard I and John (1154–1216)*, 2 vols, London, 1903, I, 111–13).
150. R. A. Brown, 'Royal Castle-Building in England, 1154–1216', *EHR*, 70 (1955), 353–98, reprinted in R. A., Brown, *Castles, Conquest and Charters* (Woodbridge, 1989), at 46; J. Beeler, *Warfare in England, 1066–1189* (Ithaca, NY, 1966), 167.
151. *GH*, I, 35 and n. 2. Howden records these events as his last entry for 1172, but when in the year these charges were made is unknown. In 1166, Adam's barony comprised some 23 knights' fees in

England; E. Cownie, 'Adam de Port (*fl.* 1161–1174)', *ODNB*; J. H. Round, 'The Families of St John and of Port', *The Genealogist*, new series, 16 (1899–1900), 1–13.

152. JF, ll. 1334, 1354, 1840–47; *RRS*, II, 22, n. 19a. After refusing to appear at court, Adam had fled to Scotland. In 1180, he proffered 1,000 marks to gain his lands and the inheritance of his second wife, Matilda d'Orval, to remit the king's anger and for Henry II to accept his homage (*PR 26 Henry II*, 135; *GH*, I, 35, n. 2).

153. *MTB*, VII, no. 771. For the so-called 'Compromise of Avranches', Foreville, *L'Eglise et la royauté*, 330–67; Warren, *Henry II*, 532–4.

154. *MTB*, VII, nos 774, 771. As Henry was a major benefactor to Savigny, the venue seems to have been mutually agreed upon as a fitting place for the king's public reconciliation; F. R. Swietek, 'King Henry II and Savigny', *Citeaux*, 38 (1987), 14–23.

155. *Recueil, Introduction*, 256–7; Torigni, ed. Deslisle, II, 303–6.

156. *MTB*, VII, no. 771; *Councils and Synods*, I, ii, 942–4; Foreville, *L'Eglise et la royauté*, 335ff.

157. *MTB*, VII, no. 771.

158. Ibid., nos 771, 774. The version of Henry's purgation in the Lambeth Anonymous has Henry swear that 'he had been no less alarmed by his [Becket's] unexpected death than if it had been his own son' (*MTB*, IV, 173–4; Staunton, *Lives*, 216).

159. Duggan, 'Diplomacy, Status and Conscience', 265–90.

160. A. Forey, 'Henry II's Crusading Penances for Becket's Murder', *Crusades*, 7 (2008), 153–64.

161. *MTB*, VII, no. 771; Diceto, I, 352.

162. *MTB*, VII, no. 771: *EHD*, II, no. 156.

163. *MTB*, VII, no. 771. For the formal agreement, *Ne in dubium*, recording the terms of Henry's oath, penance and absolution, sealed by the king and the legates on 21 May, *MTB*, VII, no. 772; Duggan, '*Ne in dubium*', 643–58. The full oath is also given by Gervase, I, 238–9.

164. *MTB*, VII, no. 772; *GH*, I, 33; Duggan, '*Ne in dubium*', 650, noting the corrected reading supplied from the letters of Herbert of Bosham (Cambridge, Corpus Christi College, MS 123, f. 59r–v); 'juravit et filius vester, excepto eo quod personam vestram contingebat'. A version of the oath at Caen was included in the Life of Alexander III by Boso (*Liber pontificalis*, ed. L. Duchesne, 3 vols (2nd edn, Paris, 1955–1957), II, 425; Duggan, '*Ne in dubium*', 566–67).

165. *MTB*, VII, no. 771: *EHD*, II, no. 156; Diceto, I, 352; *MTB*, II, no. 772, 518; Duggan, '*Ne in dubium*', 651, and 653 for the subsequent papal bull ratifying the Avranches agreement, which reminded Henry II that 'your eldest son who was crowned as king also swore to remove the new customs'.

166. *MTB*, VII, no. 772; Duggan, '*Ne in dubium*', 658. A later interpolation into the *Vita Alexandrini*, probably written after King John's quarrel with Innocent III, makes Henry II and the Young King receive back and hold their kingdom from the pope (Foreville, *L'Église et la royauté*, 342–56; *Councils and Synods*, I, ii, 950 and n. 2).

167. Torigni, 254; *GH*, I, 31; Diceto, I, 352; Lansdowne Anonymous, *MTB*, IV, 178; *PR 19 Henry II*, 51.

168. 'Upon entering into this pact of peace,' wrote Gerald of Wales, 'the malicious plotting of his sons and their accomplices, plotting so monstrous in its conception and so furtive, fell into abeyance until the following year' (*Expugnatio*, 108–9).

169. *GH*, I, 31, noted of Margaret that Rotrou 'unxit in reginam et consecravit et coronavit'; the Lansdowne Anonymous, *MTB*, IV, 174, records that Margaret was anointed 'juxta morem patriae'; Diceto, I, 35 misdating the coronation to 21 August. For the coronation of the queen, *Coronation Records*, ed. Wickham Legg, 41–2; J. L. Nelson, 'Early Medieval Rites of Queen-making and the Shaping of Medieval Queenship', in *Queens and Queenship in Medieval Europe*, ed. A. J. Duggan (Woodbridge, 1997), 301–15; and L. Gathagan, 'The Trappings of Power: The Coronation of Matilda of Flanders', *Haskins Society Journal,* 13 (2000), 21–39.

170. *PR 19 Henry II*, 152, 184, the latter recording the sum of £42 12s. 6d. 'for the purchase of robes for the king, the son of the king, for the queen his mother, and for the queen his wife'; and *PR 18 Henry II*, 144, for the swords.

171. In 1174, an Exchequer clerk could refer to her as 'Regina Juniora' (*PR 20 Henry II*, 21). In the only extant charter issued by Margaret, her agreement with Henry II in 1186 concerning her dower, she styles herself 'Dei gratia regina Anglorum, soror Philippi regis Francie' (*Recueil*, I, no. 660; *Letters and Charters of Henry II*, no. 1755). Howden refers in 1183 to Margaret 'quae regina Angliae existerat' (*GH*, I, 306). Her seal is recorded as having depicted a queen with a sceptre in one hand and a bird on the other (*Letters and Charters of Henry II*, no. 1755). For the wider context, B. Bedos-Rezak, 'Women, Seals and Power in Medieval France, 1150–1350', *Women and Power in the Middle Ages*, ed. M. Erhler and M. Kowalaski (Athens, Ga, 1988), 61–82.

172. 'Henricus III coronam portavit apud Wintoniam' (Ralph Niger, *Chronicle*, 174). As K. Leyser, 'Ritual, Ceremony and Gesture: Ottonian Germany', in K. Leyser, *In Communications and Power*

in Medieval Europe. The Carolingian and Ottonian Centuries, ed. T. Reuter (London, 1994), 189–213, at 190, notes, 'a crown-wearing was only a ceremony which solemnly presented this charismatic persona to his followers and *fideles'*.

173. For Richard's crown-wearing in 1194, likewise held at Winchester, and similar confirmatory or 'strengthening coronations' *(Befestigungskrönung)* as a response to damaged honour and status see K. Görich, 'Verletzte Ehre. König Richard der Löwenhertz als gefangener Kaiser Heinrichs VI', *Historisches Jahrbuch,* 123 (2003), 65–91, at 89–91; and J. Gillingham, 'Coeur de Lion in Captivity', *Quaestiones medii aevi novae,* 18 (2013), 59–83, at 73–5. John's magnificent crown-wearing at Christmas 1204, following Philip's invasion of Normandy and the loss of the Angevin heartlands, may well have a served a similar function (Church, *King John,* 129–31).

174. Predictably, however, the Canterbury monks, jealous of all their prerogatives, regarded the second coronation as another affront to Canterbury's rights, as it was performed by an archbishop from another kingdom (Gervase, I, 237–8).

175. Diceto, I, 352–3; Lansdowne Anonymous, *MTB,* IV, 175.

176. *GH,* I, 31.

177. Lansdowne Anonymous, *MTB,* IV, 176.

178. On his return to Canterbury, Becket had intended to depose Odo. His popularity with the chapter, however, is shown by the fact that in 1184 the monks again put him forward as their candidate for the archbishopric (Barlow, *Becket,* 248, 271).

179. Lansdowne Anonymous, *MTB,* IV, 178. The more sceptical Gervase of Canterbury stressed the hostile agency of Henry's *tutores* in controlling the 'election', referring to them as 'more his masters than his ministers (*magistros magis quam ministros)'* (Gervase, I, 239–40).

180. Lansdowne Anonymous, *MTB,* IV, 179–80.

181. Ibid., 178; *RHF,* XVI, 644; *Councils and Synods,* I, 958, n. 2.

182. For the remarkable growth of the cult, Barlow, *Becket,* 264–70; and G. Oppitz-Trotman, 'Penance, Mercy and Saintly Authority in the Miracles of St Thomas Becket', *Studies in Church History,* 47 (2011), 136–47.

183. Barlow, *Becket,* 249–50. This was the form of the shrine between 1171 and 1220, and is depicted in a thirteenth-century stained-glass roundel from the south aisle of the Trinity chapel in Canterbury cathedral (Barlow, *Becket,* pl. 36).

184. Lansdowne Anonymous, *MTB,* IV, 178–9.

185. Ibid., 179. It may have been at this time that young Henry also confirmed some grants made by Thomas, including that of the chapel of Penshurst to William, a poor curate of Chiddingstone, who was reported to have given Becket a number of relics shortly before the archbishop's martyrdom, on the insistence of none other than St Laurence (FitzStephen, 124–5, 131).

186. Lansdowne Anonymous, *MTB,* IV, 179.

Chapter 7: 'A King Without a Kingdom'

1. JF, ll. 17–20, 'Après icest curunement, e après caste baillie,/Surportastes a vostre fiz auques de seignurie,/Tolistes lui ses voluntés, n'en pot aver baillie./La crut guerre senz amur: Damnesdeus la maladie!'

2. *GH,* I, 34, 'multum tamen invitus'; Gervase, I, 242. Some time between August and October 1172, the Young King commanded the monks of Ely to send six representatives to his father the king in Normandy in order to elect the new bishop of Ely, a position intended for Geoffrey Ridel (Smith, '*Acta'*, no. 16; *EEA, Ely,* 32 (E), 132–3 (F), and nos 97 and 130–3; and for the text of the writ, *The Memoranda Roll for the Michaelmas Term of the First Year of the Reign of King John (1199–1200),* ed. H. G. Richardson (Pipe Roll Society, 59, new series xxi, 1943), lxx).

3. Smith, '*Acta'*, 298.

4. *GH,* I, 34.

5. Ibid.

6. Walter Map noted that while he was 'a man of such kindliness and simple mindedness (*tam simplicis mansuetudinis*), showing himself affable to any poor man, to his own or to strangers, that he might have been thought imbecile, he was the strictest of judges ... stiff to the proud and to the meek not unfair' (Map, 442–3).

7. To Ralph Niger, for example, he was 'by nature most mild, the father of clerics and a lover of peace, a zealot for justice, the model of liberality, the protector of the church, a consoler of the poor, a raiser up of the oppressed – and a drinker of wine' (Ralph Niger, *Chronicle,* 166).

8. *GH,* I, 34.

9. Torigni, 250; *GH,* I, 35.

10. *GH,* I, 35.

11. Diceto, I, 353.

12. F. L. Cheyette, *Ermengard of Narbonne and the World of the Troubadours* (Ithaca, NY, 2001), 269.

13. Torigni, 250, 255; C. W. Previté Orton, *The Early History of the House of Savoy (1000–1233)* (Cambridge, 1912), 337–8, 339–41 for the proposals, and for the rule of Humbert III, 316–52. Alice's mother was Clementia of Zähringen.

14. *GH*, I, 36–41; *Recueil*, II, no. 455; *Letters and Charters of Henry II*, no. 1779; K. Norgate, *John Lackland* (London, 1902), 2.

15. The lands, including Humbert's claims in Grenoble and the Val d'Aosta, are detailed in *GH*, I, 37–8; Norgate, *John Lackland*, 4–5; and for Savoy see E. L. Cox, *The Eagles of Savoy. The House of Savoy in Thirteenth Century Europe* (Princeton, NJ, 1974).

16. Diceto, I, 353. Following his daughter Alice's death, Humbert did in fact bear a son by his fourth wife, Beatrice de Mâcon; see U. Vones-Liebenstein, '*Vir uxorious*? Barbarossas Verhältnis zur Comitissa Burgundiae in Umkrieg des Friedens von Venedig', *Stauferreich im Wandel. Ordungsvorstellungen und Politik in Zeit Friedriech Barbarossas*, ed. S. Weinfurter, Mittelalter Forschungen, 9 (Stuttgart, 2002), 189–219, at 195.

17. *De principis*, 157; *Anonimi laudenensis chronicon universale, MGH SS*, xxvi, 447; Peter of Blois, *Epistolae*, no. 113 (*PL*, CXIII, col. 340); Warren, *Henry II*, 220–1.

18. Diceto, I, 353; Previté Orton, *House of Savoy*, 341 and n. 1; and J. O. Prestwich, *The Place of War in English History, 1066–1214* (Woodbridge, 2004), 22, who sees the marriage proposal as 'linked with Henry's cautious probing in northern Italy at a time when German power and influence there had been temporarily weakened'. As Torigni, 250, noted, 'it was not possible for anyone to go into Italy except through his [Humbert's] lands'.

19. Warren, *Henry II*, 221 argues that Raymond's submission was the major reason why the scheme was not revived after 1173–74, despite Henry having made a down payment of 2,000 marks, and provision having been made in the treating for a second daughter to replace Alice, who had died. On Raymond's relations with the Angevins, see Benjamin, 'A Forty Years' War', 270–85.

20. Alfonso's brother Raymond-Berengar had inherited the county of Provence, which posed an added threat to the count of Toulouse (Previté Orton, *House of Savoy*, 337; Bisson, *The Medieval Crown of Aragon*, 37). For the growth of Raymond's influence and the strength of his position by 1172, see Cheyette, *Ermengard*, 253–67.

21. *GH*, I, 36: Torigni, 255. Peter, archbishop of Tarentaise, had a role in bringing about this regional peace summit, which he also used to gain support for a drive against the Cathar heretics in southern France (Previté Orton, *House of Savoy*, 338 and n. 4; *Letters and Charters of Henry II*, no. 1779 n). Walter Map, with King Henry at Limoges, was entrusted to see to Peter's upkeep, and witnessed him performing a healing miracle in the city (Map, 134–7).

22. See Benjamin, 'A Forty Years' War', 270–85; and L. Macé, *Les Comtes de Toulouse et leur entourage, XIIe–XIIIe siècles. Rivalités, alliances et jeux de pouvoir* (Toulouse, 2000), 28– 30.

23. *GH*, I, 36; Torigni, 255; Vigeois, 319. Diceto, I, 353, however, noted that Richard was absent from the initial meeting, so the count of Toulouse deferred his homage to the 'octaves of Pentecost'.

24. *GH*, I, 36; Torigni, 255; Vigeois, 319. As Cheyette, *Ermengard*, 268, notes, 'by accepting Raymond's oath of homage, the king implicitly renounced Eleanor's claims and recognized him as legitimate successor to the county'.

25. *GH*, I, 36.

26. Similarly, despite the importance of his treaty with Humbert, Henry II evidently did not exert pressure on Raymond to yield to Humbert's claims to the Dauphiné, held by Raymond's brother Alfonso (Previté Orton, *House of Savoy*, 337, 339–40).

27. Diceto, I, 353.

28. *GH*, I, 41. Geoffrey le Bel, for example, had granted them to his second son, Geoffrey (*Recueil des chroniques de Touraine*, ed. A. Salmon (Tours, 1854), 136; Torigni, 163, noting that Geoffrey received four castles.

29. Diceto, I, 353; and for John's education at Fontevraud, Church, *King John*, 4–5. John was born in late 1166 or early 1167, or perhaps in December 1167 as recorded by Torigni, 233 (Lewis, 'The Birth and Childhood of King John', 161–3; Church, *King John*, 1).

30. *GH*, I, 41.

31. Ibid.

32. For the text of the treaty, *GH*, I, 36–9.

33. See K. H. Krüger, 'Herrschaftsnachfolge als Vater–Sohn-Konflikt', *Frühmittelalterliche Studien*, 36 (2002), 225–40; and B. Weiler, 'Kings and Sons: Princely Rebellions and the Structures of Revolt in Western Europe, *c*.1170–*c*.1280', *Historical Research*, 82 (2009), 17–40, especially valuable for a comparison of the Young King's rebellion with those of Henry (VII) of Germany against Frederick II in 1234, and of the Infante Sancho against his father Alphonso X of Castile in 1282.

34. The *Obituaire de Saint-Serge* spoke of this conflict as 'bellum illud execrabile quod contra patrem sum per annos fere VII subsequentes impie gessit' (*Recueil d'annales angevines et vendômoises*, ed.

L. Halphen, Paris, 1903, 107). Nevertheless, Bachrach, 'Henry II and the Angevin Tradition of Family Hostility', 118–25, in providing a detailed analysis of the conflicting accounts of the sources, suggests that this was probably a heated but non-violent *dissensio* which in later chronicles became exaggerated into open war. By contrast, Fulk le Réchin could write in his own chronicle that Geoffrey 'contra suum etiam patrem guerram habuit in qua mala multa facta fuerunt, unde postea valde penituit' (*Fragmentum historiae andegavensis*, in *Chroniques des comtes d'Anjou*, 235).

35. Guillot, *Le Comte d'Anjou*, I, 117–18.
36. C. W. David, *Robert Curthose, Duke of Normandy* (Cambridge, Mass., 1920), 17–41; W. M. Aird, *Robert Curthose, Duke of Normandy (c. 1050–1134)* (Woodbridge, 2008), 60–98.
37. Diceto, I, 355–66.
38. Suger, *Vie de Louis*, 82; idem, *Deeds of Louis*, 62. Robert the Pious' son Hugh, for example, had gone into exile following a quarrel with his father (Fulbert of Chartres, *Letters and Poems*, ed. F. Behrends, Oxford, 1976, 101).
39. Wace, *Roman de Rou*, ll. 10141–2, 10149–6: 'William, Henry's son, gave and spent generously and dwelt with his father, who loved him very much. He did what his father asked and avoided what his father forbade. The flower of chivalry from England and Normandy set about serving him and had great hopes of him.'
40. W. M. Aird, 'Frustrated Masculinity: The Relationship between William the Conqueror and his Eldest Son', *Masculinity in Medieval Europe*, ed. D. M. Hadley (Harlow, 1999), 39–70; idem, *Robert Curthose*, 62–83; and V. L. Bullough, 'On Being a Male in the Middle Ages', *Medieval Masculinities: Regarding Men in the Middle Ages*, ed. C. A. Lees (Minneapolis, 1994), 31–43. As Orderic, III, 98–9, has Robert ask William, 'What am I to do, and how am I to provide for my dependants (*clientes*)?' For a discussion of Robert's expectations of succession, E. Z. Tabuteau, 'The Role of Law in the Succession to Normandy and England', *Haskins Society Journal*, 3 (1991), 141–69, and G. Garnett, *Conquered England: Kingship, Succession and Tenure, 1066–1166* (Oxford, 2007), 163–9; idem, 'Robert Curthose – the Duke who Lost his Trousers', *ANS*, 35 (2012), 213–44.
41. *GH*, I, 41.
42. WN, I, 170; trans. *EHD*, II, 370.
43. *Memorials of the Church of SS Peter and Wilfrid*, ed. J. T. Fowler, 3 vols (Surtees Society, 1882–1888), I, no. cxlii; *Early Yorkshire Charters*, ed. W. Farrer and C. T. Clay, 12 vols (Edinburgh, 1914–1965), I, no. 123; Eyton, 170; *English Episcopal Acta, XX. York, 1154–1181*, ed. M. Lovatt (Oxford, 2000), Appendix II, no. 1.
44. JF, ll. 21–2, 'Reis de terre senz honur ne set bien que faire: nu sout li juefnes curunez, li gentilz de bon aire'.
45. JF, ll. 17–20.
46. Wace, *Roman de Rou*, ll. 67–69.
47. Luchaire, *Louis VI le Gros*, no. 4; Orderic, VI, 54–5 and n. 3; ibid., IV, 264, n. 1.
48. Guillot, *Le Comte d'Anjou*, I, 117 and n. 528; Orderic, VI, 68, n. 1.
49. As Torigni, 243, noted, on Thierry's death in 1168 he was succeeded by Philip, 'who had now long ruled that county, as his father frequently made the journey to Jerusalem'. Flanders had had a long tradition of such associative rulership. Robert, son of Robert I le Frison, for example, had been associated with the governance of Flanders from 1086 to his father's death in 1093 (C. Verlinden, *Robert I le Frison* (Antwerp and Paris, 1935), 136–7).
50. For Barbarossa's successful policy of delegating power to his sons, U. Schmidt, *Königswahl und Thronfolge im 12. Jahrhundert* (Cologne, Weimar and Vienna, 1987), 195–224; F. Opll, *Friedrich Barbarossa* (Darmstadt, 1990), 166–70; P. Csendes, *Heinrich VI* (Darmstadt, 1993), 35–73; and see now the important study by A. Plassmann, 'The King and his Sons: Henry II and Frederick Barbarossa's Succession Strategies Compared', *ANS*, 36 (2013), 149–66. I am grateful to Alheydis Plassman for sending me a copy of this paper before publication.
51. *Gesta Stephani*, 208–9.
52. *The Charters of David I*, ed. Barrow, 5, who notes that from *c*.1135 David exercised 'genuinely joint kingship' with his son Henry. From 1107 to 1124, during the reign of his brother Alexander I, David himself had been granted a great appanage in southern Scotland, encompassing much of Lothian and Cumbria north of the Solway, by his brother King Edgar (R. Oram, *David I. The King Who Made Scotland* (Stroud, 2004), 59–72).
53. D. Matthew, *The Norman Kingdom of Sicily* (Cambridge, 1992), 49, 52–3, 165. When in 1182 the Young King's sister Joanna had given birth to a son, Bohemond, his father King William II invested him with a golden sceptre as duke of Apulia as soon as he had been baptized, but the child seems to have died in infancy (Torigni, 303). William's successor, Tancred, likewise invested his son Roger with the duchy of Apulia and subsequently had him crowned as co-ruler in his lifetime (Matthew, *Norman Kingdom of Sicily*, 165–6, 288).
54. Norgate, *Angevin Kings*, II, 190.

55. Guernes, l. 6149; *Garnier's Becket*, 163; below, 219.
56. Norgate, *Angevin Kings*, II, 191, 'to place his mother's duchy and his father's counties in other hands – to reduce them to the rank of under-fiefs, keeping for himself no closer connection with them than a mere general overlordship – would have been, in principle, to renounce his birthright; while in practice it would probably have been equivalent to complete abdication, as far as his continental empire was concerned'.
57. As Orderic has William tell Robert, 'My son, you ask the impossible. By Norman strength I conquered England: I hold Normandy by hereditary right, and as long as I live I will not relax my grip on it' (Orderic, III, 98–9).
58. JF, ll. 81–2.
59. Gillingham, *The Angevin Empire*, 12.
60. Orderic, VI, 444–5; HH, 254–5; Torigni, 128; Chibnall, *Empress Matilda*, 60–2.
61. William of Tyre, Bk 7: 13–14.
62. William I of Sicily's son Roger had been used as a figurehead by a powerful baronial coalition in 1160–61, when they seized the king and paraded Roger, aged only nine, as his successor (*Falconis Beneventi Chronicon*, in *Cronistie scrittori sincroni napoletani*, ed. G. Del Re, 2 vols (Naples, 1845, reprinted Aalen, 1975), I, 323–5; *Romualdi Salernitani chronicon*, ed. C. A. Garufi (Rerum Italicarum Scriptores, Città dei Castello, 1935); *The History of the Tyrants of Sicily by 'Hugo Falcandus', 1154–69*, trans. G. Loud and T. Wiedemann (Manchester, 1998), 110–14, 230–1).
63. *Ottonis episcopi Frisingensis chronica sive historia de duabus civitatibus*, ed. A. Hofmeister, *MGH, SS rer. Germ.* 45 (1912), VIII: 9.
64. For his rebellion, see I. S. Robinson, *Henry IV of Germany, 1056–1106* (Cambridge, 1999), 323–43, and 286–8 for the rebellion of Henry IV's eldest son Conrad a decade earlier; G. Althoff, *Heinrich IV* (Darmstadt, 2006), 228–53. The comparable rebellion of Frederick II's son, Henry (VII), in 1234–35 is discussed in detail in B. Weiler, *Kingship, Rebellion and Political Culture. England and Germany, c. 1215- c. 1250* (Basingstoke, 2007), 3–11 and 53–75.
65. Diceto, I, 236, and 363, where Ralph added that his lack of offspring was a mark of divine vengeance for his impious rebellion against his father.
66. Orderic, III, 96–101; and for Robert's supporters, S. L. Mooers, '"Backers and Stabbers": Problems of Loyalty in Robert Curthose's Entourage', *Journal of British Studies*, 21 (1981), 1–17. Similarly, the rebellion against Geoffrey Le Bel by his younger brother Helias took place when he was still deemed a *iuvenis*, and was said to have been at the instigation of 'impious men' (*Chronica de gestis consulum andegavorum*, in *Chroniques des comtes d'Anjou*, ed. L. Halphen and R. Poupardin (Paris, 1913), 25–73, at 71; Bachrach, 'Henry II and the Angevin Tradition of Family Hostility', 113, n. 11).
67. *History of the Counts of Guines*, ch. 92; trans. Shopkow, 125. Father and son were reconciled, with the aid of Count Philip of Flanders, with the compromise that Arnold received Ardres and some of the other property he was demanding, but accepted the nomination of Arnold of Cayeux, 'a man learned in arms, and discreet in advice', as his advisor 'in tournaments and when he disposed of his possessions and as his guardian and, as it were, his teacher' (ibid.).
68. Torigni, 255–6, notes that the expulsions took place during Lent, which began on Wednesday 21 February. Hasculf was a lord of some standing in the county of Mortain (Torigni, ed. Delisle, II, 35, n. 7; *RHF*, XXIII, 697; D. Power, *The Norman Frontier in the Twelfth and Thirteenth Centuries* (Cambridge, 2004), 401, 422).
69. Torigni, 255–6, believed this was the direct cause of the younger Henry's flight from his father.
70. JF, ll. 378–82.
71. *Letters and Charters of Henry II*, no. 1771; N. Vincent, 'William Marshal, King Henry II and the Honour of Châteauroux', *Archives*, 35 (2000), 1–15; Crouch, *William Marshal*, 61.
72. *HWM*, ll. 1975–96.
73. *HWM*, ll. 1997–2002.
74. WN, I, 170; trans. *EHD*, II, 370.
75. *History of the Counts of Guisnes*, ch. 96; trans. Shopkow, 129.
76. Similarly, William of Tyre notes how the counsellors of the young Baldwin III encouraged him to reject the authority of his mother Melisende, for 'it was unseemly, they said, that a king who ought to rule others should constantly be tied to the apron strings of his mother like the son of a private person' (William of Tyre, Bk 16: 3, trans. Babcock and Krey, II, 140).
77. *Brut y Tywysogion or the Chronicle of the Princes (Peniarth MS. 20 Version)*, ed. T. Jones (Cardiff, 1952), 69. This text appears to have been translated into Welsh from an original Latin chronicle, possibly compiled in the later thirteenth century at the Cistercian house of Strata Florida (ibid., xxxiv).
78. Printed in *RHF*, XVI, 643–8, from Paris, BN Ms. Lat. 14876, a group of letters attached to a fifteenth-century collection of works by St Bernard from Saint-Victor; calendared in Smith, '*Acta*', no. 1; and discussed in *Councils and Synods*, I, 958, n. 2.

79. *RHF*, XVI, 644.
80. Ibid. On the importance of regal honour in this context, see Weiler, 'Kings and Sons', 20–1, and further references there cited.
81. *RHF*, XVI, 644.
82. Orderic, III, 98–9, with Book V: 10 probably written in late 1127.
83. Gervase, II, 80.
84. As Gerald of Wales noted, at Easter young Henry revealed 'the evil plot, which he had long since hatched against his father under the influence of wicked men' (*Expugnatio*, 120–1).
85. *GH*, I, 42. N. Vincent, 'King Henry II and the Poitevins', *La Cour Plantagenêt*, ed. M. Aurell (Poitiers, 2000), 103–35, at 122. Ralph was the brother of Eleanor's mother Aéonor de Châtellerault.
86. Vincent, 'King Henry II and the Poitevins', 122–3, who notes that Ralph was the only Poitevin known to be have been granted land in England. According to a moralizing tale of Gerald of Wales, Ralph had lost his right eye in a hunting accident at Woodstock when his horse had bolted into thick briars, after he had gone hunting on Good Friday against the advice of Henry II (Gerald, *Opera*, II, *Gemma Ecclesiastica*, I. dist. 54).
87. *CTB*, I, 216–17, and n. 9. Whether or not John's words hint at Eleanor's infidelity, at the time of writing in early August 1165 she was already heavily pregnant with her daughter Joanna, who was born at Angers in October.
88. *RHF*, XII, 477; *Chronicon Turonense magnum*, 128.
89. *GH*, I, 39; *Foedera*, I, 28; Eyton, 170.
90. Matthew Paris, *Chronica majora*, II, 285; trans. Flori, *Eleanor*, 101.
91. WN, I, 170; trans. *EHD*, II, 370.
92. Vigeois, 319; *GH*, I, 41.
93. *The Chronicle of Melrose*, ed. A. O. Anderson and M. O. Anderson (London, 1936), 40.
94. The contradictory and confused chronology of the Young King's flight given by Roger of Howden and Ralph of Diss is discussed by Norgate, *Angevin Kings*, II, 134, n. 7, who suggests that his escape from Chinon occurred during the night of 20 March. His route, however, and the timing of the stages of his journey is impossible to establish with any certainty. Diceto, I, 355, has no mention of Chinon and believed it was at Argentan than the Young King gave his father's ministers the slip.
95. *Brut y Tywysogion (Peniarth)*, 69.
96. Howden believed that having fled in the night, the young Henry's party arrived at Alençon the next day, which by Norgate's reckoning would be Wednesday, 21 March (*GH*, I. 41; Norgate, *Angevin Kings*, II, 134, n. 7). Even with spare mounts, however, this would have been an extraordinary, though not perhaps an impossible feat, and Howden's chronology may well be unreliable here. That the party only travelled some 25 miles between Alençon and Argentan on their next stage, however, does suggest that they were exhausted. I am grateful to John Gillingham for this point.
97. A journey directly north would have brought the party to Caen. It may be more than coincidence that Port-en-Bessin, held till recently by Adam de Port, lay only a few miles further to the north-west, on the coast just beyond Bayeux.
98. R. Barber, *Henry Plantagenet. A Biography* (London, 1964), 168.
99. *GH*, I, 42; Diceto, I, 355, who dates young Henry's flight from Argentan to 23 March.
100. K. Thompson, *Power and Border Lordship in Medieval France: The County of Perche, c. 1000–1226* (Woodbridge, 2002), 96; Power, *The Norman Frontier*, 361.
101. *GH*, I, 42; Torigni, 256; Diceto, II, xxxvi, n. 6.
102. *GH*, I, 51.
103. *PR 21 Henry II*, 47, 77, 106, 137.
104. Torigni, 256.
105. Torigni, 256.
106. Torigni, 256.
107. Whether she had remained in Normandy during the Maurienne negotiations, or whether she had accompanied the royal court in its itineraries and was left behind at Chinon is unknown. She next appears in Henry II's keeping in 1174, when, with Eleanor, she was taken to England (Torigni, 263).
108. *GH*, I, 43. As Smith, '*Acta*', 304, suggests, this makes it likely that the seal used by the Young King after the end of the war in 1174 was this original seal, restored to him by his father.
109. *GH*, I, 43.
110. Some, such as John of Salisbury and Herbert of Bosham, refused to do so (FitzStephen, *MTB* III, 99–101); A. Duggan, 'The Price of Loyalty: The Fate of Thomas Becket's Learned Household', in idem, *Thomas Becket: Friends, Networks, Texts*, 1–18, at 8–9.
111. *GH*, I, 43: Howden, II, 46.

112. Turner, 'Richard Barre', 25–48. Walter's appointment occurred in either 1173 or 1174 (R. V. Turner, 'Walter of Coutances (d. 1207), administrator and archbishop of Rouen', *ODNB*).

113. *Northamptonshire Charters*, no. 6; *GH*, I 46. After the war, the Young King confirmed the grant of North Luffenham given by Earl William to Solomon (*Northamptonshire Charters*, no. 7; Smith, '*Acta*', no. 30).

114. *GH*, I, 42; Diceto, I, 355.

115. *The Deeds of the Normans in Ireland*, ed. E. Mullally (Dublin, 2002), ll. 2864–945; Warren, *Henry II*, 123.

116. Warren, *Henry II*, 123 and n. 4; R. A. Brown, 'Royal Castle Building in England, 1154–1216', *EHR*, 70 (1955), 353–98, reprinted in idem, *Castles, Conquest and Charters*, 19–64, at 26, and 46–7.

117. Gillingham, *Richard I*, 42–3; Flori, *Eleanor*, 100–1.

118. WN, I, 170–1: trans. *EHD*, II, 371.

119. *GH*, I, 42.

120. Diceto, II, 67, and for discussion of Eleanor's association with the eagle of the prophecies, Flori, *Eleanor*, 112–17. Ralph Niger, writing in the later 1190s, twice refers to her explicitly as 'Alienor, dicta aquila rupti foederis' (Ralph Niger, *Chronicle*, 95, 98).

121. Turner, *Eleanor*, 207; and for Eleanor's role in the rebellion, Flori, *Eleanor*, 97–110.

122. Though it is often claimed that Richard was Eleanor's favourite son (for example, Turner, *Eleanor*, 240, 'obviously Eleanor's favourite'), much of the evidence for the closeness of their relationship comes from after Richard's accession in 1189, and the almost complete dearth of information regarding her feelings for the Young King until his death in 1183 urges caution about such claims.

123. *RHF*, XII, 420: Flori, *Eleanor*, 111–12.

124. Peter of Blois, *Epistolae*, no. 154 (*PL*, CCVII, cols 448–9).

125. Peter of Blois, *Epistolae*, no. 154; trans. Flori, *Eleanor*, 108.

126. Vigeois, 318–19.

127. Everard, *Brittany and the Angevins*, 127.

128. William the Conqueror's queen Matilda had incurred her husband's wrath for sending money to her eldest son Robert Curthose during his estrangement from his father, an act that William not without reason saw as an act of betrayal, as his son was openly in arms against him. He ordered her messenger, Sampson, to be blinded, though he escaped to become a monk at St Evroult (Orderic, III, 102–5). William of Malmesbury believed that Robert raised troops from the revenues sent by his mother from her estates (*Gesta regum*, I, 500–1). For Matilda's actions, Aird, *Robert Curthose*, 83–6.

129. Diceto, I, 350.

130. Gillingham, *Richard I*, 43; and Flori, *Eleanor*, 101–5 for a detailed analysis of the chronicles' treatment of Eleanor's involvement. Howden, for example, noted that she was among the main authors of the conspiracy, 'ut a quibusdam dicebatur' (*GH*, I, 42).

131. Melrose, 40.

132. Flori, *Eleanor*, 122–3.

133. For Rosamund, T. A. Archer, revised E. Hallam, 'Rosamund Clifford [*called* Fair Rosamund] (*b.* before 1140?, *d.* 1175/6)', *ODNB*; Flori, *Eleanor*, 97, suggests that the relationship had begun in about 1166–67. Henry's relations with Rosamund may have been of long standing by 1173, but among the king's earlier mistresses was Ida de Tosny, the mother of Henry II's natural son William Longespée, born in or before 1167 (P. C. Reed, 'Countess Ida, mother of William Longespée, illegitimate son of Henry II', *American Genealogist*, 77 (2002), 137–49; and R. W. Phair, 'William Longespée, Ralph Bigod and Countess Ida', *American Genealogist*, 77 (2002), 279–81). Another natural son, Geoffrey, was born *c.*1151, for whose possible maternity, and a discussion of Henry II's extramarital liaisons, see M. Lovatt, 'Geoffrey (1151?–1212)' *ODNB*; and idem, 'Archbishop Geoffrey of York: a Problem in Anglo-French Maternity', *Records, Administration and Aristocratic Society in the Anglo-Norman Realm*, ed. N. Vincent (Woodbridge, 2009), 91–124.

134. Aurell, 'Aux origines de la légende noire', 89–102. For the notorious record of Henry II's grandfather in this regard see K. Thompson, 'Affairs of State: The Illegitimate Children of Henry I', *JMH*, 2 (2003), 129–51.

135. Warren, *Henry II*, 120–1.

136. *RHF*, XII, 419.

137. Gillingham, *Richard I*, 47; Flori, *Eleanor*, 98–9.

138. *RHF*, XVI, 158–9; Sassier, *Louis VII*, 449; Flori, *Eleanor*, 98, and for another translation of the complete letter, Cheyette, *Ermengard of Narbonne*, 268–9. On Ermengard, see also J. Caille, 'Ermengarde, vicomtesse de Narbonne (1127/29–1196/97), une grande figure féminine du Midi

aristocratique', *La Femme dans l'histoire et la société mediévale, 66th Congress of the Federation Historique du Languedoc-Roussillon* (Narbonne, 1994), 9–50.

139. *RHF*, XVI, 628, no. XX1, 'in coronae suae dispendium comitem Sancti Egidii in ligium hominem recepistis'. For Henry's undermining of Louis' position more generally, Sassier, 'Reverentia regis', 28–31.

140. Vones-Liebenstein, 'Aliénor d'Aquitaine, Henri le Jeune et la révolte de 1173', 85, who also notes that at Montmartre in November 1169, Louis had promised 'to summon the count of St Gilles to Tours to answer to Richard for the county of Toulouse'. This, however, was to happen once Richard was handed over to him for his upbringing at the Capetian court, something which, unsurprisingly, Henry did not allow to happen (*CTB*, II, no. 243).

141. Sassier, *Louis VII*, 448–51.

142. Flori, *Eleanor*, 98–9; Sassier, *Louis VII*, 44–50.

143. Wace, *Roman de Rou*, ll. 94–6.

144. Gervase, I, 243; JF, ll. 30–32, who puts the council at St Denis.

145. *GH*, I, 44; Gervase, I, 243.

146. *GH*, I, 44.

147. JF, ll. 31–58.

148. Peter of Blois, *Epistolae*, no. 153 (*PL*, CCVII, cols 446–8).

149. WN, I, 170; trans. *EHD*, II, 370–1.

150. Peter of Blois, *Epistolae*, no. 153 (*PL*, CCVII, cols 446–8); Sassier, *Louis VII*, 448–51.

151. *GH*, I, 43–4; Sassier, *Louis VII*, 451.

152. As William of Newburgh sourly observed: 'Their pretext was zealous support for the son against the father – and certainly nothing could have been more stupid (*nil stultius*) than such support – but in reality they were seeking the opportunity for the business of private hatred, as in the case of the king of France, or that of gain, as in the case of the count of Flanders' (WN, I, 172–3; trans. Kennedy and Walsh, 120–1).

153. No seals from this matrix are known to have survived, for Henry II had it and documents sealed during the war by the Young King subsequently destroyed.

154. *GH*, I, 44–5.

155. Fresh hostility had flared up as recently as 1169, when Henry II had obtained control of the castles of Montmirail and St Aignan, claimed by Theobald (Torigni, 243–4).

156. The *Feoda* listed in all some 1,900 lords and knights, all of whom acknowledged their obligation to serve the count in time of war (T. Evergates, *Feudal Society in the Baillage of Troyes under the Counts of Champagne, 1152–1284* (London, 1975), 9–10, 60–2, 91–5; J. Dunbabin, *France in the Making, 843–1180* (Oxford, 1985), 250–3, 312–14).

157. JF, l. 28, 'le Puignaire'. He and the Young King were thus first cousins once removed, as his father Thierry had married Geoffrey of Anjou's sister Sybil, while Philip's wife Elizabeth of Vermandois was Queen Eleanor's niece (*HWM*, ll. 2459–60, and ibid., III, 73, note to line 2460). For Philip, see H. van Wereke, *Een Vlaamse graff van Europees formaat. Filips van de Elzas* (Haarlem, 1976).

158. For an overview of Philip's position between 1168 and 1173, Oksanen, *Flanders and the Anglo-Norman World*, 35–9. Philip had succeeded Thierry as count, though by virtue of his father's frequent absences in Jerusalem, he had been effective ruler of Flanders for some time (Torigni, 234).

159. *GH*, I, 44; Gervase, I, 243; Oksanen, *Flanders and the Anglo-Norman World*, 39–40. As Gilbert of Mons put it, 'to help his lord the young king of England', Count Philip 'rose up in great strength against his first cousin the elder king of England' (Gilbert of Mons, c. 73; trans. Napran, 65). William of Ypres had been entrusted with control of Kent (Gervase, I, 121, II, 73; Warren, *Henry II*, 122; R. Eales, 'Local Loyalties in Norman England: Kent in Stephen's Reign', *ANS*, 8 (1985), 88–108; idem, 'William of Ypres, styled Count of Flanders (*d.* 1164/5)', *ODNB*).

160. WN, I, 171; trans. Kennedy and Walsh, 119, and on the county's resources. P. Trio, 'Vlaanderen in de twaalfe eew: een hoogtepunt in de geschiedenis van het graafschap', *Thomas Becket in Vlaanderen. Waarheid of Legende?* (Kortrjk, 2000), 17–36, with English summary at 234–5.

161. Before Philip Augustus' acquisition of Artois in 1191, the only coastal possession of the king of France was the castle of Montreuil-sur-Mer.

162. Torigni, 238; Diceto, I, 303. For the county of Boulogne and its English holdings, J. H. Round, 'The Counts of Boulogne as English Lords', *Studies in Peerage and Family History* (London, 1901), 147–81; and H. A. Tanner, *Families, Friends and Allies: Boulogne and Politics in Northern France and England, c. 879–1160* (Leiden, 2004). King Stephen's ability to draw on the naval resources of the county of Boulogne had been an important factor both in his successful acquisition of the throne in 1135, and in his subsequent struggle against the Empress and her adherents.

163. Gervase, I, 203, and II, 78. In 1168, Henry II had promised Matthew a large annual cash revenue in return for relaxing his claim on the county of Mortain, and Matthew had accordingly brought both a naval force and many knights to aid Henry in his campaign in Brittany (Torigni, 238).

164. *GH*, I, 44; Gervase, I, 243. For the extent of the honour of Mortain, F. M. Powicke, 'The Honour of Mortain in the Norman *Infeudationes Militium* of 1172', *EHR*, 26 (1911), 89–93.

165. WN, I, 105; *RRS,* I, 9–10. For the wider context, J. Green, 'Anglo-Scottish Relations, 1066–1174', *England and Her Neighbours, 1066–1453*, ed. M. Jones and M. Vale (London: Hambledon, 1989), 53–72.

166. *RRS*, I, 10 and n. 1, also noting that in the Cartae Baronum of 1166 King William did not make any return for either Huntingdon or Tynedale, suggesting a privileged form of tenure (ibid., 10, n. 1; *Calendar of Documents Relating to Scotland Preserved in Her Majesty's Public Record Office*, ed. J. Bain, 5 vols (Edinburgh, 1881–1886), I, no. 205).

167. G. W. S. Barrow, 'The Reign of William the Lion, King of Scotland', *Historical Studies*, 7 (1969), 21–44, reprinted in G. W. S. Barrow, *Scotland and its Neighbours in the Middle Ages* (London. Hambledon, 1992), 67–90; *RRS II*, 1–21; and D. D. R. Owen, *William the Lion, 1143–1214: Kingship and Culture* (East Linton, 1997). Within a year of his accession in 1164, William was at odds with Henry over the latter's refusal to restore the county to him, while he can only have been further alienated by Henry II's effective deposition in 1166 of Duke Conan of Brittany, who was married to William's sister Margaret (*CTB*, I, no. 112; *MTB*, VI, 72; A. O. Anderson, *Early Sources for Scottish History, AD 500 to 1286*, 2 vols (Edinburgh, 1922, reprinted Stamford, 1990), II, 264).

168. *LJS*, II, no. 279, at 606–7.

169. Melrose, 40, 'hoping he would find a remedy for old injuries in this new strife, [William] waged a fierce war against his kinsmen and lord, Henry, king of England'.

170. JF, ll. 271–337, who has William's messenger, the Hospitaller William de Olepen, propose that the claim to Northumberland be settled by a judicial duel between two knights.

171. JF, ll. 338–79.

172. JF, l. 378. Howden lists Robert and Adam de Brus, and Everard de Ros among the loyalists to Henry II (*GH*, I, 51, n. 4).

173. JF, ll. 245–70, and ll. 410–36, noting that the two envoys, William of Saint-Michael and Robert of Huseville, sailed from Berwick to Flanders before travelling south to the court of King Louis.

174. *GH*, I, 62 and 47. For a valuable discussion of the role of the Poitevin nobility in the revolt of 1173–74 and other risings against Henry and Richard, see A. Debord, *La Société laïque dans les pays de La Charente. X–XIIe siècles* (Paris, 1984), 382–96. For Preuilly-sur-Claire (Indre et Loire, arr. Loches), Boussard, *Le Comté d'Anjou*, 11–12; idem, *Le Gouvernement d'Henri II Plantagenêt* (Paris, 1956), 21, 102, 483, 226–7.

175. *GH*, I, 46–7; Norgate, *Richard*, 15; Gillingham, *Richard I*, 53.

176. Flori, *Eleanor*, 108; M. Brand'honneur, 'Seigneurs et réseaux de chevaliers du nord-est du Rennais sous Henri Plantagenêt', *Noblesses de l'espace Plantagenêt*, ed. M. Aurell (Poitiers, 2001), 165–84; Gillingham, *Richard I*, 43.

177. Torigni, 259. Ralph had led an earlier rebellion against Norman domination in 1164, and his continued resistance with other discontented lords in Brittany and Maine had led to a punitive campaign by Henry, which included the razing to the ground of Ralph's castle at Fougères in 1166 (Torigni, 214; *LJS*, II, no. 173; Everard, *Brittany and the Angevins*, 41–2, and n. 32). Styling himself '*Dei gratia dux Britannorum*' in a charter of 1153, Eudo had been a leading figure in the revolt of 1167–68, and may have been in arms again in 1170 (Torigni, ed. Delisle, II, 42, n. 4; Everard, *Brittany and the Angevins*, 45–8; *GH*, II, 3). Among the leading Breton rebels in 1173 were William de Tinténiac, Guethenoc d'Ancenis and 'Gwenis' de Palvel (*GH*, I, 46–7).

178. Everard, *Brittany and the Angevins*, 35–6.

179. Power, *The Norman Frontier*, 397–8.

180. Boussard, *Le Gouvernement*, 102, 'un bastion féodal avec lequel, après ses ancêtres, Henri II devra compter'.

181. Warren, *Henry II*, 132.

182. Dunbabin, *France in the Making*, 339.

183. K. Dutton, 'The Personnel of Comital Administration in Greater Anjou, 1129–1151', *Haskins Society Journal*, 23 (2011), 125–54.

184. Ibid., 125, 136; John of Marmoutier, *Historia Gaufridi ducis*, 185.

185. M. Billoré, *De gré ou de force. L'aristocratie normande et ses ducs (1150–1259)* (Rennes, 2014), 175–217. For the wider context of Henry's rule in the duchy, D. J. Power, 'Angevin Normandy', *A Companion to the Anglo-Norman World*, ed. C. Harper-Bill and E. M. C. van Houts (Woodbridge, 2003), 63–85; and idem, 'Henry, Duke of the Normans (1149/50–1189)', *Henry II. New Interpretations*, ed. C. Harper-Bill and N. Vincent (Woodbridge, 2007), 85–128.

186. F. Neveux, *La Normandie des ducs aux rois, Xe–XIIe siècle* (Rennes, 1998), 538, 'de territoires traditionnellement frondeurs'; D. Power, 'Henry, Duke of the Normans', 91–4; Billoré, *De gré ou de force*, 176–8.

187. J. A. Green, 'Lords of the Norman Vexin', *War and Government in the Middle Ages*, ed. J. Gillingham and J. C. Holt (Woodbridge, 1984), 47–63.

188. D. Crouch, 'Normans and Anglo-Normans: a Divided Aristocracy?', *England and Normandy in the Middle Ages*, ed. D. Bates and A. Curry (London, 1994), 51–67, at 60.

189. Crouch, 'A Divided Aristocracy?', 59; idem, *Beaumont Twins*, 64–79. Waleran of Meulan had joined forces with King Louis in 1161.

190. He was the son of Waleran de Beaumont; *Magni Rotuli Scaccarii Normanniae sub regibus Angliae*, ed. T. Stapleton, 2 vols (London, 1840–1844), I, cxviii; E. Houth, *Les Comtes de Meulan, ix–xiii siècles* (Mémoires de la société historique et archéologique de Pontoise, du Val d'Oise et du Vexin, vol. 70 (Pontoise, 1981); Crouch, *Beaumont Twins*, 60. An edition of Robert's charters is currently being prepared by David Crouch, who kindly made this available to me. Robert was joined in revolt by his kinsman Robert de Montfort-sur-Risle (Torigni, 257; Torigni, ed. Delisle, II, 38–9 and notes).

191. Crouch, 'A Divided Aristocracy?', 59; D. J. Power, 'King John and the Norman Aristocracy', in *King John. New Interpretations*, ed. S. D. Church (Woodbridge, 1999), 117–36, at 127; idem, *The Norman Frontier*, 186–7.

192. Power, *The Norman Frontier*, 398–400.

193. J. Everard, 'Wace: The Historical Backround: Jersey in the Twelfth Century', *Maistre Wace: A Celebration. Proceedings of the International Colloquium held in Jersey, 10–12 September 2004*, ed. G. S. Burgess and J. Weiss (Société Jersaise, 2006), 1–16, at 2.

194. Neveux, *La Normandie*, 538; and Billoré, *De gré ou de force*, 177–9, with a map showing principal areas of rebellion.

195. Boussard, *Gouvernement*, 477–8, had dismissed earlier views that Normandy was the epicentre of the rebellion, and that many lords were involved. Yet as Nicholas Vincent, 'Les Normands de l'entourage d'Henri II Plantagenêt', *La Normandie et l'Angleterre au Moyen Âge*, ed. P. Bouet and V. Gazeau (Caen, 2003), 75–88, at 86–7, argues, an analysis of the major rebels shows this view to be untenable, and that Boussard's own list of rebels 'semble démontrer précisément le contraire de ce qu'il avance'.

196. Vincent, 'Les Normands', at 85–7, and Table 5, listing the principal Norman rebels, together with their fiefs as recorded in the Inquest of 1172.

197. D. Crouch, 'Robert de Breteuil, [Robert ès Blanchmains, Robert the Whitehanded, Robert de Beaumont], third earl of Leicester (c.1130–1190)', *ODNB*; idem, 'Robert de Breteuil, fourth earl of Leicester', *ODNB*.

198. T. F. Tout, 'Hugh, fifth earl of Chester', revised T. K. Keefe, *ODNB*; A. T. Thacker, 'The Earls and their Earldom', *The Earldom of Chester and its Charters*, ed. A. T. Thacker (Chester Archaeological Society, vol. 71, Chester, 1991), 7–22, at 22, 'Appendix: The Earl's Norman Estates'. He held fifty-one fiefs in the duchy, and his position as a great baron of Lower Normandy led Wace to include his ancestor in the list of key companions of the Conqueror at Hastings, which may well have displeased Henry II (M. Bennett, 'Poetry as History? The *Roman de Rou* of Wace as a Source for the Norman Conquest', *ANS*, 5 (1985), 21–39, at 32–4).

199. In addition to William, holding Meols in the Wirral, these included Richard de Lovetot and Richard de Combray (*Charters of the Anglo-Norman Earls of Chester, c. 1071–1237*, ed. G. Barraclough (Lancashire and Cheshire Record Society, cxxvi, 1988), nos 171, 126, 132); Thacker, 'The Earls and their Earldom', 10, n. 11.

200. *GH*, I, 46; JF, ll. 105–8, 'The chamberlain of Tankarville is his sworn enemy, he brings a hundred knights in armour in his train, and they all threaten to bring him [Henry II] so low that they will not leave him as much land as would suffice to buy a lady's saddle-horse'.

201. Vincent, 'Les Normands', 87. In regard to the 1172 inquest, however, one should equally note the caveat of Power, 'Henry, Duke of the Normans', 87, that 'the relationship between a baron's assessed number of knights ... and his power in reality, is almost impossible to gauge'. More minor figures, such as William de Falaise and Landric de Orbec, appear in Howden's list of those who first defected with young Henry (*GH*, I, 46).

202. *GH*, I, 48.

203. After initial support for King Stephen, Bigod, who enjoyed virtually autonomous rule of eastern Suffolk during the civil war, remained 'an inveterate enemy of the king's cause' and was rewarded by Henry II with a confirmation of the earldom of Norfolk in 1154 (*Gesta Stephani*, 223; A. Wareham, 'The Motives and Politics of the Bigod Family, c.1066–1177', *ANS*, 17, 1994, 223–42).

204. Wareham, 'Motives and Politics', 223 and n. 3. Hugh also held considerable lands in Normandy (Power, *The Norman Frontier*, 91 and n. 4). Coggeshall, 19, calls him 'vir magnificus'.

205. W. L. Warren, *The Governance of Norman and Angevin England* (London, 1987), 120.

206. *GH*, I, 51–2. The later B manuscript of the *Gesta* also contains a fuller list of Henry II's supporters, including a number of northern English lords such as the Stutevilles, Robert and Adam de Brus,

Thomas M Jones

'The Generation Gap of
1173 - 1174: The War
of The Two Henries'
Albion, 5, (1973): 24-40.

Matthew Paris
Vol I, II, III

Roger of Wendover
Vol I, II

Romance of The
  Three kingdoms,

Geoffrey Trussebut, Odinel de Umfraville, William de Vesci, Everard de Ros and Philip and Simon de Kyme (ibid., 51, n. 4).

207. For the Norman lands of these lords, Power, *The Norman Frontier*, 91 and notes 3 and 4.

208. *GH*, I, 51, n. 4, 106, 166; JF, ll. 1597–600. Howden's mention (*GH*, I, 47) of 'Willemus archiepiscopus' has been taken to refer to the Englishman William, archbishop of Bordeaux (for example Norgate, *Richard*, 15–16; and Gillingham, *Richard I*, 47), but it is far more probable that he was referring to William l'Archevêque, lord of Parthenay. Similarly, it is more likely that the Roger 'abbas de Turnai' listed among a group of Norman dissidents (*GH*, I, 46) was not an ecclesiastic, but from a Norman knightly family named Abbas or Abbé, perhaps from Tournai-sur-Dives near Argentan. Likewise, the Geoffrey and Hamelin 'abbas' listed among those rebels captured at Dol in 1173 were not abbots but knights (*GH*, I, 58). I owe these points to the kindness of Dan Power.

209. *GH*, I, 51, n. 4, where Howden claims he had harboured kinsmen who were rebels; J. Peltzer, 'Henry II and the Norman Bishops', *EHR*, 119 (2004), 1202–29, at 1217–18; Vincent, 'Les Normands', 82. For Arnulf, C. P. Schriber, *The Letter Collections of Arnulf of Lisieux* (Lampeter, 1997), letter no. 2.17, which may hint at his involvement; and G. Teske, 'Ein unerkanntes Zeugnis zum Sturz des Bischofs Arnulf von Lisieux?', *Francia*, 16 (1989), 185–206. In his *Liber Melorum* (*MTB*, III, 548–50), Herbert of Bosham gives a lengthy account of a prophetic dream Thomas had recounted to him, in which Henry II was attacked by a multitude of birds of prey aided by one of the king's most trusted and intimate courtiers (*unus de aulicis regis familiarissimus*) before Thomas miraculously came to Henry's aid. Though Henry II had pressed Herbert to reveal the name of this person, he declined, as the person was now dead and he feared that such a revelation might undeservedly throw the suspicion of treason upon the man's kinsmen. It seems very likely, however, that he had Arnulf in mind.

210. *RHF*, XVI, 643–8.

211. Diceto, I, 371; Warren, *Henry II*, 124; Barber, *Henry Plantagenet*, 169.

212. The Normans were, indeed, in Maïté Billoré's words, 'une noblesse étroitement surveillée et assujettie' (*De gré ou de force*, 175); and cf. M. Billoré, 'Y a-t-il une oppression des Plantagenêts sur l'aristocratie à la veille de 1204?', *Plantagenêts et Capétiens*, 145–61.

213. Torigni, 179.

214. Boussard, *Le Gouvernement d'Henri II*, 421–3; Warren, *Henry II*, 93 and n. 1. When the seneschal of Normandy, Robert of Neubourg, retired to take the habit at Bec in August 1159, Henry did not replace him, instead taking direct control himself. A new seneschal was only appointed on Henry's departure for England in early 1163.

215. Torigni, 209.

216. Torigni, 211–12; Warren, *Henry II*, 95, 235–6; Torigni, 227.

217. Brown, 'A List of Castles, 1154–1216', *EHR*, 74 (1959), 249–80, and reprinted in Brown, *Castles, Conquest and Charters*, at 91–2, indentifying over thirty such castles.

218. K. Thompson, 'Lords, Castellans, Constables and Dowagers: The Rape of Pevensey from the Eleventh to the Thirteenth Century', *Sussex Archaeological Collections*, 135 (1997), at 213–14; idem, 'The Lords of Laigle: Ambition and Insecurity on the Borders of Normandy', *ANS*, 18 (1996), at 191–2.

219. Torigni, 217; Warren, *Henry II*, 95.

220. Stubbs, *Select Charters*, 175–8.

221. Ibid., 177; *EHD*, II, no. 48, clause 8.

222. D. Crook, 'The Earliest Exchequer Estreat and the Forest Eyres of Henry II and Thomas FitzBernard, 1175–80', *Records, Administration and Aristocratic Society*, ed. Vincent, 29–44, at 34–5.

223. Warren, *Henry II*, 95–6, 121; Power, 'Henry, duke of the Normans', 100–2, 117–19.

224. Wace, *Roman de Rou*, ll. 37–42.

225. Guernes, ll. 6081–7; trans. Short, 173.

226. *De principis*, 183–6; J. C. Holt, *Magna Carta* (Cambridge, 3rd edn, 2015), 85–6.

227. Ralph Niger, *Chronicle*, 167–70. For Ralph, see G. B. Flahiff, 'Ralph Niger: an Introduction to his Life and Works', *Mediaeval Studies*, 2 (1940), 104–26.

228. R. V. Turner, 'Changing Perceptions of the New Administrative Class in Anglo-Norman and Angevin England: The Curiales and their Conservative Critics', *Journal of British Studies*, 29 (1990), 93–117, at 93–5.

229. Map, 484–5; Warren, *Henry II*, 214; Aurell, *Plantagenet Empire*, 34.

230. Crouch, *Beaumont Twins*, 79–95; idem, 'Robert [Robert de Beaumont], second earl of Leicester (1104–1168)', *ODNB*.

231. Gillingham, 'Problems of Integration', 105, n. 99.

232. Vincent, 'Les Normands', 88.

233. Vincent, 'Did Henry II Have a Policy towards the Earls?', 1–13, noting that of twenty-three earldoms existing in 1154, there remained only twelve by 1189.

234. D. Bates, 'The Prosopographical Study of Anglo-Norman Royal Charters', *Family Trees and the Roots of Politics: The Prosopography of Britain and France from the Tenth to the Twelfth Century*, ed. K. S. B. Keats-Rohan (Woodbridge, 1997), 89–102; Vincent, 'Les Normands', 85–7 and Table 3; and Gillingham, 'Problems of Integration within the Lands Ruled by the Norman and Angevin Kings of England', 117–18. The exception was Arnulf of Lisieux, who attests more than fifty royal charters, but the extent of his complicity in the rebellion is uncertain.

235. Vincent, 'Les Normands', 86, 'une sombre séparation d'avec la cour'; idem, 'Did Henry II Have a Policy towards the Earls?', 13.

236. E. King, 'William Peverel (*b. c.*1090, *d.* after 1155), baron', *ODNB; GH*, I, 45; A. F. Wareham, 'Hugh (I) Bigod, first earl of Norfolk (*d.* 1176/7), magnate', *ODNB*.

237. *Annales Cestrienses (Chester Annals)*, ed. R. C. Christie (Lancashire and Cheshire Record Society, vol. 14, 1886), 24–5; T. F. Tout and T. K. Keefe, 'Hugh, fifth earl of Chester (1147–1181)', *ODNB*; B. E. Harris, 'The Earldom of Chester, 1070–1301', *A History of the County of Chester*, II, ed. B. E. Harris (Oxford, 1979), 1–6; J. W. Alexander, 'New Evidence on the Palatinate of Chester', *EHR*, 85 (1970), 717–27; and idem, 'The Alleged Palatinates of Norman England', *Speculum*, 56 (1981), 17–27.

238. *RRAN*, III, no. 180.

239. Thacker, 'The Earls and their Earldom', 11; P. Dalton, 'Aiming at the Impossible: Ranulf II Earl of Chester and Lincolnshire in the Reign of King Stephen', *The Earldom of Chester and its Charters*, ed. A. T. Thacker (*Journal of the Chester Archaeological Society*, 71, 1991), 109–34.

240. A. T. Thacker, 'The Cult of King Harold at Chester', *The Middle Ages in the North West*, ed. T. Scott and P. Starkey (Oxford, 1995), 155–76; *V. C. H. Cheshire*, V, part 1, 26. For the rumour that both Harold and his brother Gyrth had survived Hastings and were living as hermits at Chester until Henry II's reign, Ralph Niger, *Chronicle*, 161.

241. For the influence of the Stutevilles, see H. Docherty, 'Robert de Vaux and Roger de Stuteville, Sheriffs of Cumberland and Northumberland, 1170–1185', *ANS*, 28 (2005), 65–102.

242. Diceto, I, 374.

243. Thus, for example, Saher de Quincy 'the younger', Geoffrey de Lavardin, son of the count of Vendôme, and Baudry, son of Goel de Baudemont supported the Young King while their fathers took the side of Henry II (Power, *The Norman Frontier*, 400–1).

244. *GH*, I, 56–7, 48.

Chapter 8: 'The Cubs of the Roaring Lion Shall Awaken'

1. JF, ll. 70–76.

2. Diceto, I, 355; Hallam, *Plantagenet Chronicles*, 124.

3. *GH*, I, 47; Howden, II, 47. Easter fell on 15 April that year. Fantosme, l. 63, says that the French host was summoned in April, but it is more likely that this is when the summons went out for a muster in late June or early July, in readiness for Louis' investment of Verneuil.

4. For a useful contextual overview of strategy, see J. F. Verbruggen, *The Art of Warfare in Western Europe during the Middle Ages* (2nd edn, Woodbridge, 1997), 276–350.

5. Neveux, *La Normandie*, 528–30.

6. B. Gauthiez, 'Paris, un Rouen capétien? Développements comparés de Rouen et Paris sous les règnes de Henri II et Philippe Auguste', *ANS*, 16 (1993), 117–36, at 123; Aurell, *Plantagenet Empire*, 27; Vincent, 'Les Normands', 78–9, including a valuable table of the location of charter issues, which also highlights the significance of Argentan and Caen. Henry's two-year stay in England from January 1163 to February 1165 was his longest absence from the duchy (ibid., 79–81).

7. Carpenter, *The Struggle for Mastery*, 193. It was little wonder that by far the longest of all Henry's stays in the duchy was the period between April 1173 and April 1175 (Vincent, 'Les Normands', 78, 87).

8. Warren, *Henry II*, 124–36, remains the best overview of the war, and has a number of valuable maps. Other accounts include F. Michel, 'Deux années du règne de Henri II (1173–1174)', *Revue Anglo-Française*, 2nd series, 2 (Paris, 1841), 5–44; Norgate, *Angevin Kings*, II, 135–67; Boussard, *Le Gouvernement d'Henri II*, 471–88; Beeler, *Warfare in England*, 166–86, which concentrates only on the warfare within the kingdom; Jones, 'The Generation Gap of 1173–1174', 24–40; idem, *War of the Generations*; Carpenter, *The Struggle for Mastery*, 223–7; J. Hosler, *Henry II. A Medieval Soldier at War, 1147–1189* (Leiden, 2007), 195–220.

9. A. Baume, 'Le Document et le terrain: la trace du système défensif normand au XIIième siècle', *1204. La Normandie entre Plantagenêts et Capétiens*, 93–112, at 104.

10. Power, *The Norman Frontier*, 4; and A. Lemoine-Descourtieux, *La Frontière normande de l'Avre. De la fondation de la Normandie à sa réunion au domaine royal (911–1204)* (Mont-Saint-Aignan, 2011).

11. Torigni, 175. In 1167, Louis had attacked the Vexin while the counts of Flanders, Boulogne and Ponthieu invaded at Eu, though they were repulsed at Drincourt; Torigni, 227; *HWM*, ll. 805–1106, and for the date, ibid., III, 61–2, note to l. 805.

12. Wace, *Roman de Rou*, ll. 59–61.

13. *GH*, I, 44.

14. JF, ll. 51–4.

15. Diceto, I, 367; Torigni, 175, noting that it had been granted to Robert II de Beaumont by Henry II in 1153. His son Robert III probably held this and other of the Norman lands of Leicester from this date; Crouch, *Beaumont Twins*, 89, 175–6, 193. For the castlery of Pacy, Power, *The Norman Frontier*, 28–9, 209 and 259.

16. Diceto, I, 367. This reverse supposedly prompted King Louis' lugubrious remark, 'The elements themselves are fighting for the Normans. When I invaded Normandy last time, a large part of my army died from thirst, and now we can complain of too much water!' (ibid; Hallam, *Plantagenet Chronicles*, 124).

17. Diceto, I, 355.

18. For Gournay, which owed distinctive services 'ad marchiam' to the Norman dukes, see Power, *The Norman Frontier*, 27.

19. Diceto, I, 369, says they were taken by guile.

20. For the lords of Gournay and their allegiances, Power, *The Norman Frontier*, 355–7. Henry II had punished Hugh II for his support for Stephen and had deprived him of the manor of Wendover in Buckinghamshire in 1156–57 (*Recueil*, I, no. 325; *PR 2, 3, 4 Henry II*, 21, 24; *Calendar of Charter Rolls*, 6 vols (Public Record Office, 1903–27), II, 34; Diceto, I, 369; Vincent, 'Les Normands', 86, n. 37. In England, some of Hugh's men plundered royal estates in Suffolk, presumably as part of the rebel forces of the earls of Leicester and Norfolk, leading to Henry II's confiscation of Hugh II's manor of Houghton Regis (Diceto, I, 369; *PR 20 Henry II*, 39, 86; *PR 21 Henry II*, 108, 110; Power, *The Norman Frontier*, 356).

21. *HGM*, III, 30, n. 2, for the identification with Trôo (Loir-et-Cher, cant. Montoire-sur-le Loir); *HWM*, ll. 2023–40.

22. *HWM*, ll. 2023–70.

23. *HWM*, ll. 2071–7.

24. *HWM*, ll. 2097–103.

25. *HWM*, ll. 2079–95.

26. Keen, *Chivalry*, 79–80.

27. Above, 82–4. The event as related by the *History* is difficult to locate within the known chronology of either the Young King or Henry II's movements (Eyton, 177; *HWM*, III, 69, note to line 2025). Henry II is known to have been at Vendôme in late November 1173, but the Young King had seen action well before then at Gournay in May, then again at the siege of Drincourt in June. If he had indeed been knighted in the field, it is more likely to have occurred during these earlier campaigns, not as late as November.

28. *HWM*, ll. 2123–43; *HGM*, III, 31, n. 3.

29. Orderic, VI, 236–7. It is probable, moreover, that many of these knights would have brought squires, serjeants or other retainers with them, thereby considerably increasing the overall fighting force under the Young King's command.

30. A. Luchaire, *Études sur les actes de Louis VII* (Paris, 1885), 51; *HWM*, III, 70, note to line 2130. See, however, *HWM*, III, 70, note to line 2135, suggesting that as there is no known reference to William des Barres (the Elder) in the royal household before the 1180s, the *History* may be anachronistic here.

31. *HWM*, III, 71, note to l. 2153 and l. 2159.

32. Gervase, I, 245.

33. Smith, '*Acta*', no. 11; Gervase, I, 245, who inserts the full text of the Young King's letter; *Councils and Synods*, I, 961–3.

34. Gervase, I, 245, 'qui ratione regiae unctionis regnum et totius regni curam sucipimus'.

35. Gervase, I, 245; *Letters of Gilbert Foliot*, no. 221 (soon after 10 June).

36. Diceto, I, 368. For discussion of these elections and the councils of late April and June, *Councils and Synods*, I, no. 167, 956–60; Foreville, *L'Église*, 373ff.; H. Mayr-Harting, 'Henry II and the Papacy, 1170–1189', *Journal of Ecclesiastical History*, 16 (1965), 39–53, at 50–3.

37. Gervase, I, 245.

38. Melrose, 40.

39. Gervase, I, 245.

40. *Letters of Gilbert Foliot*, nos 223, 224, 225.

41. *Letters of Gilbert Foliot*, no. 221. For the lengthy discussions of the appeal at the Curia, Diceto, I, 388.

42. *GH*, I, 69. Howden seemingly takes the phrase from the letter of Reginald to Henry II reporting on their mission, 'nos in curia domini papae duros de regno Francorum, et de terra vestra duriores adversarios invenisse' (ibid., I, 70).

43. Howden, II, 58–9. Whether Berter was attached to the Young King's household is uncertain, but he is best known for the lament he composed, among other verses for the loss of the Holy Land to Saladin in 1187, which Howden included in his *Gesta Henrici (GH*, II, 27–8).

44. For Ralph's hostility to 'iste Henricus', Ralph Niger, *Chronicle*, 92–3, and 95

45. Printed in *RHF*, XVI, 643–8, from Paris, BN MS. Lat. 14876, a group of letters attached to a fifteenth-century collection of works by St Bernard from St Victor; and calendared in Smith, '*Acta*', no. 1. For comment, *Councils and Synods*, I, ii., 958, n. 2, where it is noted that while 'not perhaps above suspicion . . . it seems probable that it is a contemporary broadside' created within the Young King's court.

46. H. Prentout, *De l'origine de la formule 'Dei gratia' dans les chartes d'Henri II* (Caen, 1926), 26–7; Smith, '*Acta*', 303.

47. *RHF*, XVI, 644.

48. See above.

49. Namely clauses 3, 7, 8 and 12; *Councils and Synods*, I, ii, 946–9.

50. *Councils and Synods*, I, ii, 958, n. 2. As Arnulf of Lisieux informed the pope, however, the election of Richard of Dover had taken place without any interference by Henry II, and he told Alexander that he should be wary of the Young King's attempts to exercise such control (*Letter Collections of Arnulf*, ed. Scriber, no. 2.28).

51. *Recueil*, II, no. 460; Warren, *Henry II*, 536.

52. Howden, II, 47–8: *GH*, I, 54, n. 6.

53. Peter of Blois, *Epistolae*, nos 33, 154 (*PL*, CCVII, cols 109–10, 448–9).

54. Peter of Blois, *Epistolae*, no. 33 (*PL*, CCVII, cols 109–10); Schluntz, 'Archbishop Rotrou', 125. Peter was a canon of the cathedral of Notre-Dame, Rouen, between 1173 and 1181, and as a number of letters in Rotrou's name exist among his letter collection, he may have acted as secretary to the archbishop. For his reflections on the rebellions of sons, see R. R. Bezzola, *La Cour d'Angleterre comme centre littéraire sous les rois Angevins (1154–1199)* (Paris, 1963), 134.

55. Torigni, 258.

56. *GH*, I, 47; Diceto, I, 372.

57. Torigni, 257. One of the greatest barons of Yorkshire, William had during Stephen's reign been 'more truly the king, beyond the Humber', but soon after 1154 Henry II had compelled him to yield much of his autonomy. Despite this, however, the two men appeared to have remained, super-ficially at least, on reasonable terms (P. Dalton, 'William le Gros, count of Aumale and earl of York (*c.* 1110–1179)', *ODNB*). For Henry II's granting of the daughter of Robert, earl of Gloucester, to Simon's son Amaury in 1170, Torigni, 247.

58. *GH*, I, 47 'sine aliqua difficultate'; WN, I, 173; Diceto, I, 373, 'which I am unable to report without much shame'. Howden lists Ralph and Gilbert de Aumale among those who sided with the Young King at the outbreak of the revolt (*GH*, I, 46).

59. Torigni, 257. Howden, however, lists Count Henry as among the initial rebels declaring for the Young King after his flight to France (*GH*, I, 45).

60. *GH*, I, 47. The great importance of Aumale to the defence of Normandy was reinforced when in 1180 Henry II gave William de Mandeville, earl of Essex and one of the king's closest friends, the hand of Hawise, countess of Aumale, precisely to prevent a recurrence of the events of 1173 (Diceto, II, 3; and cf. *Foundation of Walden*, 60–1).

61. *GH*, I, 49; Diceto, I, 373; Torigni, 258.

62. *GH*, I, 49; Diceto, I, 373; Torigni, 258.

63. B. Kemp, 'The Miracles of the Hand of St James', *Berkshire Archaeological Journal*, 65 (1970), 1–19, at 17 (Miracle no. 25); and for context, D. Bethell, 'The Making of a Twelfth-Century Relic Collection', *Popular Belief and Practice*, ed. G. J. Cumming and D. Baker (Studies in Church History, 8, Cambridge, 1972), 61–71. One of the very few among the miracle collection not to involve healing, this story presumably reached Reading through the narration of one of the Young King's followers or even young Henry himself, perhaps during his vist to Reading at Pentecost, 1 June 1175 (*GH*, I, 91).

64. Above, 64. Eyton, 61–2; N. Vincent, 'The Pilgrimages of the Angevin Kings of England', *Pilgrimage. The English Experience from Becket to Bunyon*, ed. C. Morris and P. Roberts (Cambridge, 2010), 20–28, at 24.

65. *Vitae B. Petri Abricensis et B. Hamonis monachorum coenobii Saviniacensis*, ed. E. P. Sauvage, *Analecta Bollandiana*, II (1883), 523–4; Swietek, 'Henry II and Savigny', 20–21.

66. Kemp, 'The Miracles of the Hand of St James', 17.

67. Ibid., 17; Diceto, I, 373; *GH*, I, 49; JF, ll. 87–90, 91–8.

68. Diceto, I, 373, who confirms the date of 25 July, but mistakenly places the siege of Drincourt before the surrender of Aumale.

69. Torigni, 258. It was probably at this time that the Young King, in a charter issued at Drincourt, confirmed the commune of Eu at the request of Count Henry of Eu (*Livre rouge d'Eu*, ed. A. Legris (Société de l'Histoire de Normandie, Rouen et Paris, 1911), 17–18; *Recueil, Introduction*, 255–6; Smith, '*Acta*', no. 18; Power, *The Norman Frontier*, 400, n. 68). It was witnessed, among others, by William of Tancarville and, significantly, William of Saint Maure, whose kinsman Hugh was regarded as one of the principal fomentors of the rebellion (*Chronicon Turonense magnum*, 128).

70. *GH*, I, 49; Gilbert of Mons, ch. 73, 76; Count Philip bestowed on him the lordships of Lillers and Saint-Venant, and in 1174 or 1175 he married Matilde, widow of Count Guy of Nevers. The union produced no sons, but a daughter, Sibylle, who married Robert I of Wavrin, steward of Flanders (Gilbert of Mons, ch. 47; trans. Napran, 47, notes 204 and 205).

71. Howden, II, 49.

72. The *Red Book of the Exchequer*, I, ccxiv, calls this campaign 'the Leicester War' (*Guerra Leicestriae*).

73. *GH*, I, 58; Diceto, I, 376; and for de Lucy, see E. Amt, 'Richard de Lucy, Henry II's Justiciar', *Medieval Prosopography*, 9 (1988), 61–87. It is possible that in late June Henry II had made a lightning visit to England, during which he inspected the strategically crucial fortress of Northampton, and perhaps conferred with de Lucy about plans to attack Leicester, before returning to Normandy via Winchester (Norgate, *Angevin Kings*, II, 143 and n. 4, where the Pipe Roll evidence is set out, and for the suggestion of a date of June, earlier than that proposed by Eyton, 173). The visit is accepted by Warren, *Henry II*, 127 and n. 2, but the failure to note this visit by both Torigni and Howden, otherwise scrupulous in recording the king's Channel crossings, has led John Gillingham to doubt if the visit did in fact take place ('Writing the Biography of Roger of Howden', 212 and n. 32).

74. *GH*, I, 48; King, *Castellarum anglicanum* (2 vols, London, 1983), I, 252–5, and 253 for the suggestion that the large ringwork castle of Hinckley may have been one of Earl Robert's castles, destroyed after 1174. For a plan of Groby, *The Victoria History of the County of Leicester*, I, ed. W. Page (1907), 259.

75. WN, I, 177. William of Newburgh believed that Earl Robert had been first to take up arms against Henry II.

76. *GH*, I, 48.

77. *GH*, I. 73; *Recueil, Introduction*, 258–9, 259–60; *HWM*, III, note to line 4701.

78. D. Cathcart King, *Castellarium Anglicanum*, 2 vols (London, 1983), I, 256–7. For a map of the medieval town and its surroundings, M. Bateson *et al.*, *Records of the Borough of Leicester*, vol. 1 (London, 1899), lxviii–1; L. Fox, *Leicester Castle* (Leicester, 1944); A. E. Brown, 'Roman Leicester', and L. Fox, 'Leicester Castle', in *The Growth of Leicester*, ed. A. E. Brown (Leicester, 1970), and especially 21 and 30 for maps of the castle and town.

79. *PR 19 Henry II*, 107–8, 156, 163, 173, 178; Beeler, *Warfare in England*, 175. For a valuable analysis of the Pipe Roll evidence for the garrisoning of royal castles and Henry II's war effort in England, see P. Latimer, 'How to Supress a Rebellion: England, 1173–74', *Rulership and Rebellion in the Anglo-Norman World, c. 1066–c. 1216. Essays in Honour of Professor Edmund King*, ed. P. Dalton and D. Luscombe (Farnham, 2015), 163–77, which appeared as this book was going to press.

80. Matthew Paris believed that some were given refuge in the towns of St Albans and Bury St Edmunds, 'as if to a protecting bosom, because these martyrs were at that time held in such great reverence that the inhabitants of those places afforded an asylum and safe protection from their enemies to all refugees'. He also adds a marginal illustration of the town's defences (Lewis, *The Art of Matthew Paris*), 67–8 and fig. 30).

81. Diceto, I, 376.

82. For the date, *Annals of the Reigns of Malcolm IV and William, Kings of Scotland, AD 1153–1214*, ed. A. C. Lawrie (Glasgow, 1910), 132–3; *RRS*, II, 96.

83. JF, ll. 417–20, A. Stevenson, 'The Flemish Dimension of the Auld Alliance', *Scotland and the Low Countries, 1124–1994*, ed. G. Simpson (East Linton, 1996), 28–42.

84. Some £380 was spent on Wark between 1158 and 1161, probably including the construction of a polygonal stone keep on the motte: *History of the King's Works*, II, 852–3; Brown, 'Royal Castle-Building in England', 45, 58; R. A. Brown, *Castles from the Air* (Cambridge, 1989), 221–2.

85. JF, ll. 491–519. He also pledged not to strengthen his defences during the time of truce.

86. WN, I, 177; and for the alleged atrocities of the Scots and Galwegians, M. J. Strickland, *War and Chivalry. The Conduct and Perception of War in England and Normandy, 1066–1217* (Cambridge, 1996), 291–329.

87. *Reginaldi monachi Dunelmensis Libellus de Admirandis Beati Cuthberti*, ed. J. Raine (Surtees Society, 1835), 275.

88. JF, ll. 591-6. For the wider context, J. Green, 'Aristocratic Loyalties on the Northern Frontier of England, circa 1100-1174', *England in the Twelfth Century: Proceedings of the 1988 Harlaxton Symposium*, ed. D. Williams (Woodbridge, 1990), 83-100, at 99.
89. *PR 4 Henry II*, 177, 179. Odinel d'Umfraville, for example, witnesses a charter of William the Lion granting part of the vill at Haughton to Reginald Prat of Tyndale, possibly dating to 1173 before the outbreak of war (*RRS*, II, no. 143).
90. JF, ll. 275, 304, 330-3, and 1386-92.
91. JF, ll. 743-5, and cf. ll. 254-70. As Jordan has King William say, 'I too shall hold it from my liege lord the king, the son of that father who granted me the right to it'.
92. JF, ll. 545-68.
93. JF, ll. 581-2.
94. JF, ll. 609-10. The great keep at Carlisle may have been begun by Henry I and completed by David I, who made the city one of his principal centres where he kept an archive and treasury (M. R. McCarthy, H. R. T. Summerson and R. G. Annis, *Carlisle Castle. A Survey and Documentary History* (Historic Buildings and Monuments Commission, London, 1990), 121-2).
95. Ibid., 211-12.
96. Ibid., 211-12, 123.
97. WN, I, 177.
98. JF, ll. 681-2, ll. 683-8; and *RRS*, II, no. 144 for the charter of protection to Furness abbey, issued at Carlisle, probably in 1173.
99. JF, ll. 705-58.
100. JF, ll. 759-62.
101. *GH*, I, 61; Diceto, I, 376.
102. *GH*, I, 49, has the siege begin around 6 July; Torigni, 257, after June 24; and Diceto, I, 374, on 15 July.
103. Torigni, 257.
104. *GH*, I, 50; *Chronicle of Saint-Aubin*.
105. Map, 450-1. Some indication of the disparity is suggested by the fact that Philip's conquest of Normandy in 1204 increased French royal revenues by around 70 per cent: J. Baldwin, 'Qu'est-ce les Capétiens ont appris des Plantegenêts?', *CCM*, 29 (1986), 3-8.
106. Diceto, I, 372, refers to the levy as a 'descriptio generalis'. It was perhaps similar to the levy of serjeants and baggage wagons raised from all towns and abbeys in the royal demesne by Philip Augustus in 1194, or a tax paid in commutation of this obligation (Baldwin, *Government of Philip Augustus*, 171-4).
107. Torigni, 170; *GH*, I, 50, who notes the town had three boroughs, but Diceto, I, 372, speaks of seven. For Verneuil, F. Salet, 'Verneuil-sur-Avre', *Congrès d'Archéologie de France*, 1953, 407-58; A. Lemoine-Descourtieux, 'Les Pouvoirs sur la frontière de l'Avre (XIe-XIIIe siècle), Eure, du pouvoir seigneurial au pouvoir ducal, puis à l'autonomie urbaine', *Les Lieux de pouvoir au Moyen Âge en Normandie et sur ses marges*, ed. M.-M. Flambard-Héricher (Tables Rondes du CRAHM, 2. Caen, 2006), 101-18; and idem, *La Frontière normande de l'Avre*. Significant sections of the town's outer water-filled ditches are still visible, though the great cylindrical donjon, known as the Tour Gris, is most probably the work of Philip Augustus following his conquest of Normandy.
108. Torigni, 257-8; *Ordinances des roys de France de la troisième race*, 21 vols (Paris, 1723, reprinted Farnborough, 1967-1968), IV, 638, 643.
109. Diceto, I, 374.
110. *GH*, I, 50; Diceto, I, 374. Howden, II, 49, explicitly adds the Young King's name to the list of those pledging the return of the hostages and the freedom of the burghers if they surrendered on these terms if not relieved.
111. Diceto, I, 374, notes explicitly that Louis believed such relief to be impossible. On such conventions, Strickland, *War and Chivalry*, 204-29.
112. Diceto, I, 374.
113. WN, I, 172, '*Bribantionum copias quas Rutas vocant*'; JF, l. 66; *GH*, I, 51; and Howden, II, 47, where the number has risen to 20,000. For these *routiers*, see H. Grundmann, 'Rotten und Brabazonen. Söldner-heere in 12. Jahrhundert', *Deutsches Archiv für die Erforschung des Mittelalters*, 5 (1942), 419-92; H. Géraud, 'Les *Routiers* au XIIe siècle', *Bibliothèque de l'École des Chartes*, 3 (1841-42), 125-47; idem., 'Mercadier: Les *Routiers* au XIIIe siècle', *Bibliothèque de l'Ecole des Chartes*, 3 (1841-1842), 417-43; and J. Boussard, 'Les Mercenaires aux XIIe siècle. Henri II Plantagenêt et les origines de l'armée de métier', *Bibliothèque de l'Ecole des Chartes*, 106 (1945-1946), 189-224; J. Schlight, *Monarchs and Mercenaries* (New York, 1968); and below, 287-9.
114. Howden, II, 47.
115. *PR 19 Henry II*, 54-5, detailing four crossings of the esnecca with treasure before September 1173; WN, I, 172; trans. Kennedy and Walsh, 120-1.

116. *PR 20 Henry II*, 134–5; Eyton, 175.
117. *GH*, I, 51; Torigni, 259, 'magno exercitu tam equitum quam peditum'.
118. Diceto, I, 375.
119. WN, I, 174; trans. Kennedy and Walsh, II, 123.
120. Above, 28. Similarly, Henry II had not attacked Louis in 1161 when both their armies had faced each other, and a truce was arranged (Torigni, 210–11).
121. Diceto, I, 374, believed that Henry intended to give battle (*praelium inire*) 'if he found the king of the Franks within the boundaries of Normandy'.
122. M. J. Strickland, 'Henry I and the Battle of the Two Kings: Brémule, 1119', in *Normandy and its Neighbours, 900–1250: Essays for David Bates*, ed. D. Crouch and K. Thompson (Brepols, 2011), 77–116.
123. JW, III, 30–3; Aird, *Robert Curthose*, 87–8.
124. *GH*, I, 53; WN, I, 174.
125. *GH*, I, 53–4.
126. *GH*, I, 54; Diceto, I, 375. Torigni, 259; WN, I, 175.
127. *GH*, I, 54.
128. *GH*, I, 55.
129. Torigni, 259; WN, I, 175.
130. *GH*, I, 55; WN, I, 175.
131. For a valuable analysis, focusing primarily on the period post 1300, see D. Whetham, *Just Wars and Moral Victories: Surprise, Deception and the Normative Framework of European War in the Later Middle Ages* (Leiden, 2009).
132. Sassier, *Louis VII*, 453, 'une vilaine manoeuvre qui jette une ombre trouble sur la personalité du roi'.
133. *GH*, I, 55; Warren, *Henry II*, 128.
134. Torigni, 226. Robert of Torigny recorded how, in 1165, he had commissioned a new arm reliquary of gold and silver for an arm bone and other smaller bones of St Laurence.
135. Compare, for example, Jordan's mockery of William the Lion's precipitous flight 'in arrant cowardice' from de Lucy's army, which incurs 'vilanie' (JF, ll. 699–758).
136. WN, I, 175; trans. Kennedy and Walsh, II, 125. He notes, however, that they 'remained armed and in formation, so as not to give the appearance of flight'.
137. *GH*, I, 56; Diceto, I, 371; F. M. Powicke, *The Loss of Normandy, 1189–1204* (2nd edn, Manchester, 1961), 71; Power, *The Norman Frontier*, 353. The removal of Tillières from his family and the installation of a royal constable appears to have been Gilbert's principal grievance against Henry II.
138. Torigni, 259; Diceto, I, 273.
139. The *History of William Marshal* demonstrated his sympathies when in describing 1173 he referred to Eudo of Porhoët as the count of Nantes and duke of Brittany, 'who performed many a fine exploit' (*HWM*, ll. 2151–92).
140. *GH*, I, 56, notes that immediately on his return to Rouen from the relief of Verneuil, Henry II had dispatched some units of his Brabançons against the Breton rebels.
141. Torigni, 259–60.
142. JF, ll.145–8, and ll. 164–70; Torigni, 260. Torigni noted that rumours of Henry's advance had forced Ralph to flee, and to order his men to bring their arms, possessions and cattle into the safety of the forest, but many of them were cut off and seized by Henry's forces. This may well refer to the arrival of du Hommet's advanced contingent, but Torigni's narrative of the war in Brittany is incoherent and the chronology uncertain.
143. Torigni, 260; *GH*, I, 56.
144. As suggested by JF, ll. 186–7.
145. Torigni, 260, 'quasi in momento dispersi'; JF, ll. 188–94.
146. Diceto, I, 378, 'electam Regis filii regis militiam'.
147. Torigni, 260; *GH*, I, 56–7.
148. WN, I, 176.
149. Torigni, 260; JF, ll. 188–203.
150. Torigni, 260, says he left Rouen at first light the next day.
151. Diceto, I, 351; WN, I, 176; Peter of Blois, *Epistolae*, no. 66 (*PL*, CCVII, col. 197). Wace's *Roman de Rou*, ll. 70–1, vividly remembered Henry's exploit: 'Then you would have seen Henry racing through the border country, dashing from one area to another and doing three days' journey or more in a single day; his men thought he must be flying.' Little is known about the provision of staging posts in the Angevin empire, but Henry must have had access to considerable numbers of fresh horses to have covered such a distance at this speed.
152. *GH*, I, 57–8, lists the knights and serjeants taken at Dol. For the connections of some of these men to Juhel de Mayenne and the lordships of Fougères and Dol, Power, *The Norman Frontier*, 399, n. 65.

153. *GH*, I, 57–8, and 57, n. 19; Diceto, I, 273, 378; WN, I, 176.
154. *GH*, I, 57–8. Thus, for example, as well as Robert and Engeram Patrick, the sons of William Patrick, the list provided by Howden includes two brothers of Hasculf de Saint-Hilaire, Henry and Philip, Juel, son of Ralph de Fougères, and William de Fougères, whom Torigni also lists as his son.
155. Torigni, 261; JF, ll. 228–31. According to Torigni, however, Ralph of Fougères fled to the forest, while similarly he names Ralph de Haye, who must have been released after his capture at Dol, among those who continued to fight on in a guerrilla war against Henry II. Ralph was probably the younger brother of the important Anglo-Norman lord Richard de la Haye, but also held lands in both England and Normandy. My thanks to Dan Power for this identification.
156. John, the constable of Chester, moreover, is listed by Howden as among the leading magnates to remain loyal to Henry II (*GH*, I, 51, n. 4).
157. Torigni, 261; *Chronicle of Saint-Aubin*, I, 279–80, which notes that, after Dol, Henry 'completely destroyed the castles of those who were fomenting the war'; Boussard, 'Les Mercenaires', 207.
158. Torigni, 261. These included the Angevin knight nicknamed the Bon Abbé de Rougé, Geoffrey de Poencé, and others 'disinherited' from the district of La Meé, in the diocese of Nantes (Torigni, ed. Delisle, II, 45–6, and 46, n. 1). The Bon Abbé de Rougé is mentioned by the *History of William Marshal* as attending a tournament in Maine in 1166 in the company of John de Subligny, who may later have been one of the Young King's household knights, and who held lands in the Avranchin and Bessin. Rougé (Maine-et-Loire, cant. Seiches, comms. Jarzé, Echeminé and Char) was a forest in Anjou (*HWM*, III, 65, note to line 1465).
159. *GH*, I, 59.
160. Röhricht, *Regesta regni Hierosolymitani*, nos 497, 498; *RHF*, XVI, 198–9; Smail, 'Latin Syria', 16.
161. 'Non sine gravi dolore', *PL*, CC, cols 927–8, no. 1047. Smail, 'Latin Syria', 17, also suggests a date of 1173–74 for 'Ingemiscimus et dolemus' (*Papsturkunden für Kirchen im Heiligen Lande*, ed. R. Hiestand (Göttingen, 1985), no. 109; *Guilielmi Neubrigensis historia . . . libris quinque*, ed. T. Hearne, III, Oxford, 1719, 664).
162. In addition to Howden's summary (*GH*, I, 59), details of the king's offers were set out in a letter of Giles, bishop of Evreux, to Pope Alexander reporting on the unsuccessful peace negations (London, Lambeth Palace Library, MS 96, f. 1r). I am most grateful to Nicholas Vincent for generously providing the text of this and the shorter summary of the proceedings (ibid., f. 1v), in advance of their publication by him in a forthcoming article in *EHR*. This notes that the moiety of demesne revenues were to be 'in burgis et maneriis atque nemoribus', but excluding any sums already granted in alms or by existing charters (ibid., f. 1r).
163. London, Lambeth Palace Library, MS 96, f. 1r.
164. Ibid. Howden records different terms, namely half the revenues of Normandy, all the revenue of the lands that Count Geoffrey had held, and three castles in Normandy (*GH*, I, 59) and in his *Chronica*, II, 53, adds the offer of one castle in Anjou, Maine and Touraine respectively. It is possible that this latter clause, clearly echoing the grant to John, was an additional demand made by the Young King in the negotiations.
165. Bishop Giles regarded it as 'paterne mansuetudinis largitas' (London, Lambeth Palace Library, MS 96, f. 1r).
166. *GH*, I, 59.
167. *GH*, I, 59.
168. *GH*, I, 58; London, Lambeth Palace Library, MS 96, f. 1r.
169. For example Norgate, *Richard the Lionheart*, 16, could state that 'throughout the rebellion of 1173–4 the young king was a mere tool – and a very inefficient one at that – in the hands of Louis', in contrast to Richard's independent actions in Aquitaine.
170. London, Lambeth Palace Library, MS 96, f. 1r. Giles here quotes Psalm 149: 7–9.
171. Howden, II, 54.
172. *GH*, I, 60.
173. *GH*, I, 60; Diceto, I, 377.
174. Diceto, I, 377, notes that the earl's return to England was also motivated by the fact that the funds he had taken to France were now almost exhausted.
175. *GH*, I, 60; Diceto, I, 377, 'tam Normannorum quam Flandrensium, tam equitum quam peditum, plurima comitante caterva'. Hugh III was the son of Hugh II and Albereda de Meulan, the aunt of Earl Robert III of Leicester. Torigni calls him Leicester's *consobrinus*, or maternal cousin (Torigni, ed. Delisle, II, 45, n. 2; Crouch, *Beaumont Twins*, 16–17; Power, *The Norman Frontier*, 260–1).
176. Diceto, I, 377.
177. VCH, Suffolk, ii, 166.
178. *GH*, I, 60; Diceto, I, 377.

179. For Bungay, guarding a strategic crossing of the river Waveney, see H. Braun, 'Some Notes on Bungay Castle', *Proceedings of the Suffolk Institute of Archaeology*, xxii (1947) 109–19. Ironically, Bungay may have originally been conceived, together with Walton and the royal castle of Orford, as a defence against threatened invasion from France or Boulogne, and was begun by Hugh in 1165 with royal consent. The large fine of £1,000 paid by Bigod may have been for licence to do so, but once he had paid the initial instalments the Exchequer noted he was not to be summoned to pay more of the remaining 500 marks debt unless the king ordered it (Wareham, 'Motives and Politics', 239–40, idem, 'Hugh (I) Bigod', *ODNB*).

180. Beeler, *Warfare in England*, 174. If Bungay was indeed begun with royal licence, the view that the royal castle of Orford, constructed between 1165 and 1168, was part of an arms race against Earl Hugh's own castle-building must be substantially qualified (R. A. Brown, 'Framlingham Castle and Bigod 1154–1216', *Proceedings of the Suffolk Institute of Natural History and Archaeology*, 25 (1950), 127–48, and reprinted in *Castles, Conquest and Charters*, 187–208. Nevertheless, it is surely indicative of Orford's strength that there is no record of the rebels making any attempt to attack it. This crisis, or the earlier invasion scares in the 1160s, may well be the context for the massively reinforced earthwork defences at Castle Rising in Norfolk, then held by the royalist earl of Arundel, William d'Albini.

181. *GH*, I, 60.

182. Diceto, I, 377, notes that Robert quickly sent his fleet back to Flanders, probably to facilitate the sending of further troops as much as to discourage any premature departure by the Flemish troops.

183. Diceto, I, 377. The garrison comprised four knights, all from local Suffolk families, two mounted serjeants and twenty infantry (*The Victoria History of the County of Suffolk*, II, ed. W. Page (London, 1907), 166). The significance of Walton to the king is indicated by the fact that the sum of £96 12s. 8d. spent in the fiscal year 1158–59 on maintaining a garrison there was the highest sum recorded for such wages since the beginning of the Pipe Rolls for the reign (*PR 5 Henry II*, 9; *PR 6 Henry II*, 2; Beeler, *Warfare in England*, 165). Walton, however, was destroyed by Henry after the war.

184. JF, ll. 839–80.

185. Hugh had earlier enjoyed substantial customs from Dunwich, while the honour of Eye included the commendation of many of its burgesses (Wareham, 'Motives and Politics', 241). Bigod had been forced to surrender Ipswich castle to Stephen in 1153.

186. *Memorials of St Edmund's Abbey*, I, 364; *PR 21 Henry II*, 126, which also records works strengthening the castle of Eye; *VCH*, Suffolk, ii, 166.

187. Beeler, *Warfare in England*, 176.

188. The garrison of thirty knights was ransomed, and the castle fired (Diceto, I, 377; *GH*, I, 61; WN, 178–9; *Florentii Wigorniensis monachi chronicon ex chronicis*, ed. B. Thorpe, 2 vols, London, 1848–1849, II, 153). For the castle, E. Martin, 'Haughley Castle', *Proceedings of the Suffolk Institute of Archaeology ad History*, 42 (2012), 543–9. I am indebted to David Sherlock for this reference.

189. For this three-part *conductus*, which must have been composed between Thomas' canonization in February 1173 and Leicester's capture at Fornham on 17 October, see S. D. Stevens, *Music in Honour of St Thomas* (Sevenoaks, 1975), 10–11; A. Duggan, 'The Cult of St Thomas Becket in the Thirteenth Century', *St Thomas Cantilupe, Bishop of Hereford. Essays in His Honour*, ed. M. Jancey (Hereford, 1982), 32 and n. 73. It is recorded by Gothic Voices, *Music for the Lionhearted King* (Hyperion, 1989), directed by Christopher Page, from whose programme notes, 6–7 (no. 2), the translation is taken.

190. *GH*, I, 61; R. J. Eaglen, *The Abbey and Mint of Bury St Edmunds to 1279* (British Numismatic Society Special Publication, no. 5; London, Spink, 2006), 110–11. Bury had no castle, but the town was well fortified with a wall and gates, built, probably in response to the unrest of Stephen's reign, by Henry the Sacrist during the rule of Abbot Anselm (1121–48) (*Gesta Sacristarum*, in *Memorials of St Edmund's Abbey*, II, 290); and for a map of the medieval town, M. D. Lobel, *The Borough of Bury St Edmunds* (Oxford, 1935).

191. Diceto, I, 377. He may well have been forced to move west, as suggested by Barber, *Henry Plantagenet*, 177, before he could be reinforced by contingents from other dissident lords, but these forces would have had to run the gauntlet of the royalist castles, and they ran the risk of being defeated in detail.

192. *GH*, I, 61.

193. *GH*, I, 61; Howden, II, 54; Diceto, I, 376; JF, ll. 766–829.

194. *GH*, I, 61; JF, ll. 1012–15, who also mentions the presence of Hugh de Cressy; *The Song of Dermot and the Earl*, ed. G. H. Orpen (Oxford, 1892), ll. 2946–79. For Robert FitzBernard, who had been given charge of Wexford and Waterford by Henry II in 1172 see *Expugnatio*, 94–5 and n. 155, 318 and n. 193; G. H. Orpen, *Ireland under the Normans, 1169–1333*, 4 vols (Oxford, 1911–1920), I,

256, 263, 281, 327; and JF, ll. 1051–2, and ll. 1554–6, where he and his brother Thomas are mentioned as loyal supporters of Henry II.

195. *GH*, I, 61; JF, ll. 1008–13.
196. JF, ll. 1029–31.
197. Diceto, I, 377.
198. Diceto, I, 377.
199. The *Vita et passio cum miraculis Sancti Edmundi* believed the earl intended to seize Bury, but this is unlikely, given its defences and the strong royalist presence there (*Memorials of St Edmund's Abbey*, I, 364–5).
200. Diceto, I, 378; *GH*, I, 61–2, which has the date as 16 October and notes that the earl was hoping to cross 'a certain marsh, not far from the church of St Genevieve' without impediment; Beeler, *Warfare in England*, 177–8.
201. *GH*, I, 62, notes that the royalists triumphed 'in momento, in ictu oculi', while the *Vita et Passio cum Miraculis Sancti Edmundi* believed that 'in barely an hour' a thousand Flemings had been slain close to the gates of the town (*Memorials of St Edmunds Abbey*, I, 364–5). Diceto, I, 377–8, suggests a more hard-fought engagement. The royalist attack was spearheaded by Walter FitzRobert and the knights of Bury: JF, ll. 1008–11.
202. The chroniclers were, however, eager to exaggerate the extent of the carnage, with Howden giving the impossibly inflated figure of 10,000 slain (*GH*, I, 62). For a tantalizing description of the discovery of what is taken to be a mass grave of the fallen Flemings, J. G. Rokewood, *Chronica Jocelini de Brakelonda* (Camden Society, London, 1840), 105–6.
203. JF, ll. 1032–9; Diceto, I, 378; *Memorials of St Edmund's Abbey*, I, 365.
204. Norgate, *Angevin Kings*, II, 150.
205. Diceto, I, 378, who names Walter de Wahelle among the captives. For Petronilla's Amazonian context, J. A. Truax, 'Anglo-Norman Woman at War: Valiant Soldiers, Prudent Strategists or Charismatic Leaders?', *The Circle of War in the Middle Ages*, ed. D. J. Kagay and L. J. Villalon (Woodbridge, 1999), 111–26.
206. *GH*, I, 62; Melrose, 40.
207. *Annales Cestrienses*, 24–5. The chronicler Jocelin of Brakelond noted that his chronicle begins 'from the year in which the Flemings were taken prisoner outside the town, that being the year in which I assumed the religious habit' (*Chronicle of Jocelin of Brakelond*, ed. H. E. Butler, London, 1949, 1).
208. See, for example, Gervase, I, 110–11. To the chronicler of Bury St Edmunds, they were 'viros bellatores, praedatores, rapaces et maleficos' (*Memorials of St Edmund's Abbey*, I, 364). For praise of Henry II's expulsion of the Flemings in 1155, Torigni, 183; Gervase, I, 161; FitzStephen, 18–19.
209. JF, ll. 994–9, 1054–61; and for a discussion of Fantosme's depiction of the Flemings, Oksanen, *Flanders and the Anglo-Norman World*, 234–41.
210. JF, ll. 1000–1, 'de Deu la grant venjance/Qu'il fist descendre sur Flamens e sur la gent de France'. 'Blessed be God who has destroyed the wicked', noted the Melrose chronicle, 'so that they should not destroy the good!' (Melrose, 40).
211. Torigni, 261. Men remembered too how the saint had struck down Eustace, son of King Stephen, for his depredations against the abbey's lands only twenty years before (Torigni, 176; Gervase, I, 155).
212. *GH*, I, 62; and cf. JF ll. 1086–91.
213. Diceto, I, 378.
214. Even though not actively hostile, so large a force caused considerable damage: the sheriff of Kent and Surrey recorded a default of 40 shillings because of the Flemings' depredations and their seizure of grain (*PR 20 Henry II*, 2).
215. *GH*, I, 62 (now La Haye-Descartes, Indre et Loire, arr. Loches); Boussard, *Le Comté d'Anjou*, 48–9.
216. *GH*, I, 62, and 47. For Preuilly-sur-Claire (Indre et Loire, arr. Loches), see Boussard, *Le Comté d'Anjou*, 11–12; idem, *Le Gouvernement d'Henri II*, 21, 102, 483, 226–7. Peter de Montrabei subsequently appears as one of Henry II's commissioners for the inquiry in 1177 into the respective rights of Henry and Louis in the Auvergne (*Recueil*, II, 61, no. 506).
217. *GH*, I, 62–3. No mention is made of Henry II attacking Saint Maure, the seat of Hugh, one of the leading conspirators in the revolt, and it may well have been an early target once the Young King's defection had become clear. For Saint Maure, Boussard, *Le Comté d'Anjou*, 49–51.
218. *GH*, I, 63.
219. A. Richard, *Histoire des comtes de Poitou, 778–1204*, 2 vols (Paris, 1903) II, 169–73; Boussard, *Le Gouvernement d'Henri II*, 483.
220. Gervase, I, 242; WN, I, 170–1, Torigni, 255–6, Diceto, I, 355, *GH*, I, 42.
221. Gervase, I, 242–3.
222. *Expugnatio*, 120–3; Lucan, *Bellum civile*, I: 1.

223. To Howden, the attack on Henry was treason (*proditio*), and he describes the rebels as 'the wicked authors of treason (*nefandae proditionis auctores*)' (*GH*, I, 42, 47).

224. Melrose, 40.

225. Peter of Blois, *Epistolae*, no. 33 (*PL*, CCVII, cols 109–10).

226. *GH*, I, 52–3.

227. *GH*, I, 45, 47, 'nefanda proditorum rabies'. Newburgh, who drew much from Howden, similarly speaks of 'the unfilial madness (*infilialis vesania*) of the son against his father' (WN, I, 180). For a discussion of such imagery, D. Power, '"La Rage méchante des traiîtres prit feu". Le discours sur la révolte sous les rois Plantagenêts (1144–1224)', *La Trahison au Moyen Âge: de la monstruosité au crime politique (Ve–XVe siècles)*, ed. M. Billoré and M. Soria (Rennes, 2009), 53–65.

228. Diceto, I, 355–66.

229. Diceto, I, 355.

230. Thus, for example, *The Chronicle of Battle Abbey*, 276–7, noted, 'the Lord's martyr, or rather the Lord, for His martyr, seemed to seek vengeance for the innocent blood. For the king, the king's son, rebelled against his father, bent on expelling him from the throne, and many of the magnates sided with him, and helped him'.

231. On these, see J. Crick, 'Geoffrey of Monmouth, Prophecy and History', *JMH*, 18 (1992), 357–71; C. Daniel, 'The Merlin Prophecies: A Propaganda Tool of the XII and XIII Centuries', *Convaincre et persuader: communication et propagande au XII et XIIIe siècles*, ed. M. Aurell (Poitiers, 2007), 211–34; and G. Ashe, 'The Prophecies of Merlin: Their Originality and Importance', *Magistra Doctissima. Essays in Honour of Bonnie Wheeler*, ed. D. Armstrong, A. W. Armstrong and H. Chickering (Kalamazoo, Mich., 2013), 71–9.

232. Guernes, ll. 6128–6130; *Garnier's Becket*, 163. As early as 1155, the potential political sensitivity of the prophecies of Merlin, not least in regard to Welsh resistance to Anglo-Norman domination, had caused the poet Wace to omit them from his *Roman de Rou* (J. Blacker, 'Where Wace Feared to Tread: Latin Commentaries on Merlin's Prophecies in the Reign of Henry II', *Arthuriana*, 6 (1996), 36–52).

233. *GH*, I, 42–3.

234. *Expugnatio*, 124–5. The concluding phrase of this passage, that the father would suffer 'until Scotland bewails the penitence of a pilgrim', was read by Gerald as foretelling the capture of William the Lion in 1174 on the very day Henry II had completed a public act of penance at Becket's shrine. For Gerald's interest in the prophecies and his belief in the existence of a second Merlin, Merlin Ambrosius, *Expugnatio*, 313, n. 161; and R. Bartlett, 'Political Prophecy in Gerald of Wales', *Culture politique des Plantagenêt (1154–1224)*, ed. M. Aurell (Poitiers, 2003), 303–11.

235. *GH*, I, 63–4; Torigni, 262, has Henry II spend Christmas at Bur-le-Roi.

236. Diceto, I, 373, 374; JF, ll. 115–18; *Expugnatio*, 120–1; Eyton, 173; and see S. Isaac, 'Cowardice and Fear Management: The 1173–74 Conflict as a Case Study', *Journal of Medieval Military History*, 4 (2006), 50–64.

237. Diceto, I, 374.

Chapter 9: Invasion

1. Diceto, I, 379.

2. *GH*, I, 45. The counts of Perche had been increasingly drawn into the orbit of Blois during the 1150s and 1160s; see K. Thompson, *Power and Border Lordship in Medieval France: The County of the Perche, c. 1000–1226* (Woodbridge, 2002), 91–6. Rotrou aimed to recover the castles of Moulins and Bonsmoulins, which Henry had taken in 1158 at the time he had confirmed Bellême to Rotrou, and he had joined the war against Henry II in 1167–68 (Roger of Wendover, *The Flowers of History*, ed. H. G. Hewlett, 2 vols, Rolls Series, 1886–1889, I. 47; Torigni, 239; Power, *The Norman Frontier*, 125).

3. Warren, *Henry II*, 132.

4. Torigni, 161–2: *RHF*, XV, 461, 520–2: M. Chibnall, 'Normandy', *The Anarchy of Stephen's Reign*, ed. E. King (Oxford, 1994), 93–115, at 109–10; L. Grant, 'Suger and the Anglo-Norman World', *ANS*, 19 (1997), 51–68, at 63–4; Power, *The Norman Frontier*, 239, 360–1, 395. Earlier, in 1136, Geoffrey himself had struck at Lisieux in his first major campaign of invasion, and had only been prevented from a major success by being wounded and because his army was decimated by dysentry.

5. Torigni, 242–3; Thompson, *Power and Border Lordship*, 96.

6. Torigni, 227; Thompson, *Power and Border Lordship*, 169; Power, *The Norman Frontier*, 350–1.

7. *GH*, I, 45 and n. 14, noting that he also held the castle of 'Muscecuard'; Power, *The Norman Frontier*, 351.

8. F. Neveux, 'La Ville de Sées du haut Moyen Âge à l'époque ducale', *ANS*, 17 (1994), 2145–63; idem, 'L'Urbanisme au Moyen Âge dans quelques villes de Normandie', *L'Architecture normande au Moyen Âge*, ed. M. Baylé (Caen, 1997), I, 271–87, at 274, with a plan of later medieval Sées at 280.

9. Diecto, I, 379.

10. Diceto, I, 379, noted that the townsmen's success was the more remarkable because they were 'without a prince, even without a duke' to lead them. Henry II, however, must have looked to its defences and garrison, appreciating Sées' strategic significance as much as his son did.

11. Torigni, 263; Sassier, *Louis VII*, 455.

12. Torigni, 263; Diceto, I, 381.

13. Torigni, 263.

14. *GH*, I, 64, where Howden notes that the money was raised by a levy on their lands.

15. The castle's strategic importance had been increased by the fact that the defensive role of Norham, the other great border fortress on the lower reaches of the Tweed, as well as that of Durham, had been neutralized by Bishop Hugh of Durham's complicity with the Scots. Hugh's neutrality is advocated by G. V. Scammell, *Hugh du Puiset, Bishop of Durham* (Cambridge, 1956), 36–43, but contemporaries, including Henry II, clearly saw him as a rebel.

16. JF, ll. 1143–50, 1153–4. Jordan strongly implies that they were led by a rebel lord, whom he knew well, but refrained from naming 'because his reputation suffered there'.

17. JF, ll. 1151–62.

18. JF, ll. 1163–84.

19. JF, ll. 1188–90; H. Van Werke, *Een Vlaamse Graaf van Europees formaat: Filips van de Elzas* (Haarlem, 1976), 20–5, who refers to an invasion of England from Scotland by one 'Jordan the Fleming'; Varenbergh, *Relations diplomatiques*, 81–2.

20. JF, ll. 1201–17, 1242–5.

21. JF, ll. 1279–86.

22. JF, ll. 1287–306.

23. JF, ll. 1185–314, notes that Roger commanded 20 knights, but the Pipe Roll only records wages for 10 knights and forty serjeants (*PR 20 Henry II*, 105). It is possible that the knights were accompanied by squires or *valets de guerre*, thereby increasing the actual number of fighting men available.

24. *GH*, I, 64; Diceto, I, 379.

25. JF, ll. 1320–1. Newburgh (WN, I, 182), who records that Mowbray gave his eldest son as a hostage to King William and in return received a pledge of aid, believed that Mowbray only came north to join William after the fall of his Yorkshire castles, but Jordan's testimony is to be preferred here.

26. JF, ll. 1334–41, where Fantosme calls Port's men 'his borderers' (*ses marchiz*). Adam seems to have fled to Scotland, though little is known of his movements. He appears at Roxburgh, granting 'Wibaldingtun', probably Whittington in south-east Herefordshire, to Kelso abbey (*Liber St Marie de Calchou*, no. 357; *RRS*, II, 22, n.19a).

27. WN, I, 180–1; trans. Walsh and Kennedy, 130–1.

28. WN, I, 180, noting that Leicester's vassals, 'as though fired with a desire to avenge their lord . . . gathered to their side a horde of scoundrels (*improbi*)' and commenced raiding.

29. *GH*, I, 64. In 1113, Henry I had granted his brother-in-law David the earldom of Huntingdon by marriage to Matilda, daughter of Earl Waltheof and widow of Simon de Senlis. Though King Stephen initially recognized David's son Henry as earl, hostilities with the Scots led him to grant the earldom of Huntingdon and Northampton to Simon de Senlis II, Maud's son by her first husband, in 1141. Stephen had granted it to Simon de Senlis III in 1156, but Henry II had resumed the honour into his own hands and in 1157 granted the earldom to Malcolm IV; Barrow, *RRS*, I, 10, 105ff.; K. Stringer, 'Simon de Senlis (II), earl of Northampton and earl of Huntingdon (d. 1153), *ODNB*; Stringer, *Earl David*, 19.

30. JF, ll. 1096–106; Stringer, *Earl David*, 13–18, for a detailed discussion of the grant of the Lennox.

31. *GH*, I, 45; Howden, II, 47; *RRS*, I, no. 207; *VCH*, Cambs, II, 388–9; Stringer, *Earl David*, 21.

32. Stringer, *Earl David*, 20, n. 61. The caput of the honour of Huntingdon, however, was at Fotheringhay, but though it too had a significant motte and bailey castle, there is little or no record of its role in the war (ibid., 73)

33. Stringer, *Earl David*, 27.

34. Ralph Niger, *Chronicle*, 176; trans. Anderson, *Early Sources for Scottish History*, II, 280.

35. Its significance is reflected in the amount spent on pay for the garrison, which amounted to £416 7s. 8d. in the fiscal year 1173–74, having risen sharply from the £142 1s. spent the year previously (*PR 19 Henry II*, 32–3; *PR 20 Henry II*, 54–5; Beeler, *Warfare in England*, 174).

36. JF, ll. 1119–31. For Bertram, R. Dace, 'Bertran de Verdun: Royal Service, Land, and Family in the Late Twelfth Century', *Medieval Prosopography*, 20 (1999), 75–93; and M. Hagger, *The Fortunes of a Norman Family; the de Verduns in England, Ireland and Wales, 1066–1316* (Dublin, 2001). A

glimpse of how damaging the raids of the Leicester garrison were is provided by the Pipe Rolls, which show that the royal estates at Rothley and Medbourne were wasted, preventing the collection of revenue until at least two years later (*PR 20 Henry II*, 140, 180).

37. G. Turbutt, *A History of Derbyshire*, vol. 2. *Medieval Derbyshire* (Cardiff, 1999).

38. *GH*, I, 69.

39. A new keep had been built at Nottingham between 1170 and 1172 with work amounting to over £675 (*PR 17 Henry II*, 50–1, 52; *PR 18 Henry II*, 7; Brown, 'Royal Castle-Building in England', 46–7). For plans of the town and castle, *The Victoria History of the County of Northampton*, III, ed. W. Page (London, 1930), plate opposite 31, 32.

40. The extent of depredations at a local level is suggested in a confirmation, 1177 x 1181, by Archbishop Richard of Canterbury of grants made by Richard, bishop of Coventry, to re-endow the lands of his deanery 'que tempore hostilitatis tot fere in nichilum redacta est' (*EEA, II: Canterbury, 1162–1190*, 128 (no. 155)).

41. *GH*, I, 106.

42. *GH*, I, 106.

43. However, the *Chronicle of Hugh Candidus*, ed. W. T. Mellows (Oxford, 1949), 131–2, concludes with a protestation of his innocence, claiming that although he was accused in secret by some of the monks, he was not found guilty by proof or confession, but says that his downfall was due to the 'iram et adquisicionem regis'.

44. For the date, *RRS*, II, 96. William was in Perth on 23 May for the election of Joscelin, bishop of Glasgow.

45. *GH*, I, 65. For Liddell, King, *Castellarium Anglicanum*, I, 88. It is notable that Jordan, who devotes much praise to the Stutevilles, is silent on this episode.

46. *GH*, I, 65; JF, ll. 1327–408.

47. JF, ll. 1409–54.

48. *GH*, I, 65.

49. JF, ll. 1586–9. Glanville, who from 1173 was also sheriff of Lancashire, had been given custody of the honour of Richmond on the death of Duke Conan.

50. JF, ll. 1457–62; *PR 22 Henry II*, 119. As a royal castle, it was under the overall command of Robert de Stuteville (*GH*, I, 65).

51. JF, ll. 1584–5. David I had granted Appleby and the lordship of north Westmorland to his constable Hugh de Moreville, who was also an important tenant of the honour of Huntingdon. After Henry II forced Malcolm to restore the northern counties in 1157, he recognized de Morville's holdings in England, but only on condition that the lordship of Appleby was held by his son, also called Hugh, already a staunch Angevin supporter (K. Stringer, 'Hugh de Moreville (d. 1162)', *ODNB*; R. M. Franklin, 'Hugh de Moreville (d. 1173/4)', *ODNB*). The younger Hugh, however, forfeited the castle and lordship in the wake of his involvement in the murder of Thomas Becket, and it would seem that, in 1174, William the Lion was able to benefit from these recent upheavals, and from the fact that his own constable, Richard de Morville, was Hugh's brother.

52. The Scots then slighted the castle, including the keep (JF, ll. 1483–92, 1506).

53. *PR 14 Henry II*, 169, 170, 173; *PR 18 Henry II*, 66.

54. *GH*, I, 65; *WN*, I, 182. Less plausibly, Fantosme has it that de Vaux only made such an agreement on learning from the justiciar that King Henry intended to cross to England within a fortnight (ll. 1506–22, and ll. 1628–40).

55. *English Episcopal Acta, XXVII, York, 1189–1212*, ed. M. Lovatt (Oxford, 2004), xxix–lvii, provides a valuable survey of Geoffrey's career.

56. Gerald of Wales, *De vita Galfridi archiepiscopi Eboracensis*, in Gerald, *Opera*, IV, 364–5; *GH*, I, 68; Diceto, I, 379. Nevertheless, as late as 1179–80, the justices in eyre could fine Hamo Beler and other men on the Isle 20 marks 'pro fossato levato injuste', while Adam Painel was amerced 2 marks 'de castello de Insula non bene prostrato' (*PR 26 Henry II*, 53).

57. *Vita Galfridi*, 368. For a far less flattering description of Geoffrey, Gervase, I, 520.

58. *Vita Galfridi*, 366–7.

59. *GH*, I, 68. Lincoln's *servitium debitum* was sixty knights, that of York twenty (*EHD*, II, 969).

60. *Vita Galfridi*, 366–7.

61. *GH*, I, 69. By Easter 1173, William de Stuteville had also been entrusted with the custody of Knaresborough castle, which the king had removed from Hugh de Moreville following Becket's murder.

62. *GH*, I, 67, 73, 160; Howden, II, 57. Northallerton was later destroyed on the king's orders in 1176. Geoffrey of Coldingham says it was built by Bishop Hugh and not demolished after 1154 ('De statu ecclesiae Dunhelmensis', in *Historiae Dunelmensis scriptores tres: Gaufridus de Coldingham, Robertus de Graystanes, et Willielmus de Chambre*, ed. J. Raine, Surtees Society, 9 (1839), 12). There

are two castles, however, at Northallerton, of which one may be the new fortification of 1174; King, *Castellarium Anglicanum*, II, 5522 and n. 58.

63. *Vita Galfridi*, 367.
64. Diceto, I, 381, who has the Young King come to Wissant to send off Ralph on 14 July. His dating is clearly confused, for he notes that Ralph landed at Orwell on 15 May and that Norwich fell to them on 1 June. Howden has the Young King come to Gravelines on 24 June to join the main invasion force (*GH*, I 171).
65. Diceto, I, 381, 'milites probatissimos et a Flandrensium multitudine selectos'.
66. Diceto, I, 381; Gervase, I, 247.
67. Ralph Niger, *Chronicle*, 176.
68. Diceto, I, 381; Ralph Niger, *Chronicle*, 176, says that that the city fell 'at the first assault'. Fantosme, ll. 889–91, believed that a traitor from Lorraine had let them in, but he mistakenly places the attack on Norwich in the campaign of 1173, and his information on events in this theatre were clearly limited, as he himself admits (JF, l. 890).
69. JF, ll. 916–24.
70. M. McKisack, 'London and the Succession to the Crown during the Middle Ages', *Studies in Medieval History Presented to F. M. Powicke*, ed. R. W. Hunt, W. A. Pantin and R. Southern (Oxford, 1948), 76–89.
71. *Liber custumarum*, in *Munimenta Gildhallae Londoniensis*, ed. H. T. Riley, 3 vols in 4 (Rolls Series, 1849–62), II, part I, 31–2; J. H. Round, 'The Commune of London', in idem, *The Commune of London and Other Studies* (London, 1899), 219–60; S. Reynolds, 'The Rulers of London in the Twelfth Century', *History*, 57 (1972), 337–57.
72. Similarly, in 1135, the decision of London to back Stephen had been influenced in part by his control of the Boulogne fleet, which played a major role in carrying merchandise to Flanders (Brooke and Keir, *London 800–1216*, 33–4).
73. *PR 19 Henry II*, 186. For the heavy farm, Round, 'Commune of London', 229–34; Brook and Keir, *London 800–1216*, 41, and Henry's grants to individual London guilds, C. Barron, *London in the Later Middle Ages. Government and People, 1200–1500* (Oxford, 2004), 200–1. London's wealth was reflected in the fact that whereas Winchester rendered about £150 annually to the Exchequer for the borough farm, and Lincoln £180, London gave £500, and was also subject to a number of such arbitrary forced loans or *dona* (Brooke and Keir, *London 800–1216*, 41).
74. JF, 1609–12. For the location of Montfichet's castle, *The British Atlas of Historic Towns*, ed. M. D. Lobel, II: *The City of London. From Prehistoric Times to c. 1520* (Oxford, 1989), 81, and map 'City of London, c. 1270'; King, *Castellarium Anglicanum*, I, 271. It lay immediately north of Baynard's Castle, the other baronial fortress within London, which occupied the south-west corner of the old Roman walls.
75. Richard FitzGilbert, 'Strongbow', had fought for Henry II in 1173 in defence of Gisors (*Song of Dermot*, ll. 2864–945), but was back in Ireland in 1174 with Henry's permission, to lead an unsuccessful expedition into Thomond. His cousin, Robert of Montfort-sur-Risle, who held the former Clare honours of Orbec and Bienfaite in Normandy (evidently forfeited by Richard by 1153), is named by Howden among the rebels (*GH*, I, 45).
76. *GH*, I, 71. Ralph of Diss noted that, following the capture of William the Lion and the surrender of the major rebel strongholds in the Midlands in July, both William earl of Gloucester and his son-in-law Richard, earl of Clare, 'who were held in suspicion', hurried to Henry II to profess their loyalty (Diceto, I, 385).
77. Diceto, I, 381.
78. WN, I, 181; Diceto, I, 37. Among the rebels' strongholds still resisting were Champtoceaux and Sablé.
79. Diceto, I, 379–80. Henry entered Maine on 30 April.
80. Diceto, I, 380. For Henry II's position in Poitou, and the castles and resources available to him as duke, see Debord, *La Société laïque dans les pays de La Charente*, 375–83, who also provides a valuable catalogue of the principal castles of the region before 1200 (Appendix I and II, 455–84).
81. *GH*, I, 63; Gillingham, *The Angevin Empire*, 34; Flori, *Eleanor*, 105–6.
82. *Annales de St Aubin*, 38. J. Flori, *Richard the Lionheart. King and Knight* (Paris, 1999), 34–5, suggests that Richard had been active in Poitou from Easter 1173, though Howden believed that he was with the Young King at Drincourt.
83. Debord, *La Société laïque dans les pays de La Charente*, 385–8, and fig. 66.
84. Diceto, I, 380; Gillingham, *Richard I*, 49–50.
85. *GH*, I, 71; Diceto, I, 380. Henry II took Saintes on 11 June.
86. Vigeois, 320.

87. For Maurice, *Recueil, Introduction*, 405–6, and for Henry's regional officials, R. Barton, 'Between the King and the Dominus: The Seneschals of Plantagenet Maine and Anjou', *Les Seigneuries dans l'espace Plantagenêt (c. 1150–c.1250)*, ed. M. Aurell and F. Boutoulle (Bordeaux, 2009), 139–62. After the king's departure, Maurice de Craon pressed home the campaign of suppression, destroying Champtoceaux, Sablé, St Lupus and St Bris near Sablé (*Annales de St Aubin*, 38; Eyton, 183). Henry's chief commanders in Poitou are revealed in his grant to Notre Dame de Saintes; Porteclia, seneschal of Poitou, William Maingot, Hamelin de Mientor, Geoffrey de Taunai, Theobald Chabot, Maurice de Craon and Nivard de Rochefort (*Recueil*, II, no. 465; and ibid., Introduction, 73).
88. Diceto, I, 380, 'opere sumptuoso'; *GH*, I, 71, 'munitionem fortissimam'. Howden dates Henry II's seizure of Ancenis to around 11 June (*GH*, I, 71).
89. *GH*, I, 71.
90. Diceto, I, 381; Torigni, 264.
91. Torigni, 263–4.
92. Torigni, 263. See Power, *The Norman Frontier*, 403–4 and 403, n. 90, for Henry II's gifts of land in England to William Mauvoisin and Enguerrand de Fontaines, seneschal of Ponthieu, in spring 1174.
93. *HWM*, ll. 2263–70.
94. Diceto, I, 381; trans. Hallam, *Plantagenet Chronicles*, 129.
95. Diceto, I, 381–2.
96. *GH*, I, 71–2, noting the date as 'around the Nativity of St John the Baptist' (24 June). It is doubtless this siege castle that is referred to in *PR 20 Henry II*, 63, which notes expenditure 'in operatione novi castelli de Hunted'.
97. *GH*, I, 71.
98. Diceto, I, 384; Lloyd, *A History of Wales*, II, 544. *PR 20 Henry II*, 21, 77, 121 reveal that these Welsh had been supplied with victuals by the sheriffs of Oxfordshire, Herefordshire and Gloucestershire, no doubt in part to limit the possible damage the Welsh might inflict on friendly territory.
99. Henry II had restored to Rhys his son, Hywel 'Sais' (the Englishman), who had long been a hostage, while before leaving for France in 1172, Henry II had made Rhys 'his justice in all Deheubarth': *Brut y Tywysogion (Peniarth)*, 67, 68; Lloyd, *A History of Wales*, II, 543. Dadfydd ap Owain of Gwynedd had also stayed loyal, and in the summer of 1174 – as a reward, or perhaps to secure his loyalty at a time of crisis before July – he received the hand of Henry II's half-sister Emma, the natural daughter of Geoffrey of Anjou, a prestigious match (*GH*, I, 51). See J. Gillingham, 'Henry II, Richard and the Lord Rhys', *Peritia*, 10 (1996), 225–36; and R. Turvey, *The Lord Rhys, Prince of Deheubarth* (Llandysul, 1997).
100. *Brut y Tywysogion (Hergest)*, 222; I. W. Rowlands, "Warriors fit for a Prince": Welsh Troops in Angevin Service, 1154–1216', *Mercenaries and Paid Men. The Mercenary Identity in the Middle Ages*, ed. J. France (Leiden, 2008), 207–30.
101. Howden, II, 61.
102. For Louis' invasion, S. McGlynn, *Blood Cries from Afar. The Forgotten Invasion of England* (Stroud, 2013). It is very likely that Prince Louis was aware of the allies' invasion plans of 1174, and he in turn sent a powerful advance force before the main fleet sailed.
103. *GH*, I, 72.
104. *WN*, I, 181; trans. Walsh and Kennedy, 133.
105. His total force cannot be known with certainty, but his fleet was said to number 37 ships, and, taking as an estimate 100–150 men per ship, this would suggest a force of 3,700–5,500 men (Cheyette, *Ermengard of Narbonne*, 281 and n. 27).
106. Vigeois, 319.
107. The argument of Boussard, 'Les Mercenaires', followed by that of Jones, 'The Generation Gap of 1173–1174', 37 – that Henry II's use of mercenaries in 1173–74 changed the nature of warfare and made defeat of Louis VII's feudal army and those of his allies inevitable – fails to acknowledge the critical role played throughout the war by Flemish and other stipendiary troops, themselves hardly a new phenomenon in Anglo-Norman warfare.
108. Howden, II, 61; Torigni, 264, remarked that he brought 'few, indeed almost none of his Norman barons with him', relying primarily on his mercenaries.
109. *GH*, I, 72; Howden, II, 61; Torigni, 263; *PR 20 Henry II*, 21.
110. *GH*, I, 72; Barlow, *Becket*, 269–71.
111. Torigni, 264; *MTB*, II, 445. For Henry's penance see Barlow, *Becket*, 269–70; T. Keefe, 'Shrine Time. Henry II's Visits to Thomas Becket's Tomb', *Haskins Society Journal*, 11 (2003), 115–22; Vincent, 'Pilgrimages of the Angevin Kings of England', 16.
112. Torigni, 264, placed his beating in the monks' chapter house, the morning after his vigil.

113. Guernes, l. 5920; *Garnier's Becket*, 157.
114. *PR 21 Henry II*, 209, 212.
115. William of Canterbury, 489. William relates how Thomas appeared in a vision to some of them in Thanet, who were anxiously keeping watch and had implored his help, telling them that he would save them from invasion (ibid., 489–90).
116. *GH*, I, 72; JF, ll. 1916–44.
117. *GH*, 1, 67; Howden, II, 63; Scammell, *Hugh du Puiset*, 38–9.
118. *GH*, I, 65.
119. *GH*, I, 65–6; William of Canterbury, 490. This force also contained the knights of the military household of the archbishop of York, led by its constable Randulf de Thilli (*GH*, I, 65–6).
120. JF, ll. 1700–4; *GH*, I, 66; William of Canterbury, 490.
121. William of Canterbury, 490.
122. *GH*, I, 67; WN, I, 183, 'vacare videbatur'.
123. WN, I, 183–4. William of Canterbury, 491, puts the force at over 300.
124. WN, I, 184; William of Canterbury, 491.
125. WN, I, 184–5. William of Canterbury, 491, records as part of the larger miracle of the king's capture the story that although the Scots had earlier intercepted a messenger from William de Vesci to his son, left as castellan in Alnwick, informing him that help would be forthcoming within three days, the Scots had not bothered to read the contents of the letters, and were thus not forwarned.
126. WN, I, 185.
127. William was immediately sent to the comparative safety of Richmond to be closely guarded.
128. *GH*, I, 67–8; Howden, II, 63; WN, I, 186.
129. *GH*, I, 67. He retained Hugh de Bar, however, with his force of knights, whom he dispatched to garrison his castle of Northallerton. One Fulk of Selby was subsequently fined £10 for sending his ship to Flanders, presumably to transport men or materiel for the rebellion (*PR 21 Henry II*, 180; Scammell, *Hugh du Puiset*, 39, n. 3).
130. Melrose, 41.
131. Torigni, 264.
132. WN, I, 185.
133. Guernes, ll. 6060–6065; *Garnier's Becket*, 161; William of Canterbury, 490–1; WN, I, 187–9. Likewise Gerald of Wales cited the prophecy of Merlin, 'Blood shall rise against the man of blood, until Scotland shall weep over the pilgrim's penance' (Gerald, *Opera*, V, 300–1). William's capture was also seen as divine punishment for the Scots' sacrilege in slaying those sheltering in the church at Warkworth (*GH*, I, 66; WN, I, 184–5).
134. M. Penman, 'The Bruce Dynasty, Becket and Scottish Pilgrimage to Canterbury, *c.*1178–1404', *JMH*, 32 (2006), 346–70.
135. *GH*, I, 72.
136. *GH*, I, 72–3.
137. H. Braun, 'Some Notes on Bungay Castle', and idem, 'Bungay Castle: Report on the Excavations', *Proceedings of the Suffolk Institute of Archaeology and Natural History*, 22 (1935/7), 109–99, 212–13.
138. That Henry expected a siege is shown by his summoning of 500 carpenters to Seleham (*PR 20 Henry II*, 38).
139. *GH*, I, 73.
140. WN, I, 191.
141. WN, I, 190.
142. Diceto, I, 386.
143. *GH*, I, 73.
144. *GH*, I, 73.
145. Howden, II, 64.
146. Torigni, 265; William of Canterbury, 491–2; Howden, II, 65.
147. As William of Newburgh, I, 190, noting that 'Rouen is one of the most famous cities of Europe'. For Rouen, see L. Musset, 'Rouen au temps des Francs et sous les ducs', in M. Mollat, ed., *Histoire de Rouen* (Paris, 1979), 31–74; Gauthiez, 'Paris, un Rouen capétien?', 117–36; P. Cailleux, 'Le Développement urbain de la capitale normande entre Plantagenêts et Capétiens', *1204. La Normandie entre Plantagenêts et Capétiens*, 261–74; *Society and Culture in Medieval Rouen, 911–1300*, ed. L. V. Hicks and E. Brenner (Turnhout, 2012).
148. For Duke Henry's confirmation in 1150 of Henry I's grant, *Recueil*, I, no. 14.
149. L. Musset, 'Une aristocratie d'affaires anglo-normande après la conquête', *Études normandes*, 35 (1986), at 10–11; Bates, 'The Rise and Fall of Normandy', 32.
150. Diceto, I, 404.

151. *Chronicon Rotomagensi, RHF,* XVII, 786, 'innumerabili multitudine peditum'. WN, I, 190, similarly notes that Louis invaded the duchy 'cum tremendo exercitu'. In 1144, the count of Flanders alone had brought 1,400 knights with him to the siege (Torigni, 148–9).
152. B. Gauthiez, 'Hypothèses sur la fortification de Rouen au onzième siècle: le donjon de Richard II, et l'enceinte de Guillaume', *ANS,* 14 (1992), 61–76.
153. *Chronicon Rotomagensi,* 785; Torigni, 147–8; D. Crouch, *The Reign of King Stephen, 1135–1154* (Harlow, 2000), 194–5; King, *King Stephen,* 198. So imposing was the great tower at Rouen that it had come to symbolize the power and authority of the Norman dukes, and Geoffrey's rule of the duchy was dated from the day of its capture by him (*Chronicon S. Michaelis in periculo maris, RHF,* XII, 773; Torigni, 148; Crouch, *Reign of King Stephen,* 195, n. 15).
154. Torigni, 209, *s.a.* 1161.
155. *Recueil,* I, no. 14; *GH,* I, 74.
156. WN, I, 190; trans. adapted from Kennedy and Walsh, 145; and see the description of Rouen by Orderic, III, 36–7.
157. Chibnall, *Empress Matilda,* 152 and n. 53. This replaced an earlier bridge, apparently damaged or even broken down in the siege of 1144 and repaired by Geoffrey in 1145 (Torigni, 151).
158. Torigni, 147–8.
159. WN, I, 191; Diceto, I, 386.
160. WN, I, 191–2; trans. Kennedy and Walsh, 147.
161. WN, I, 191–2; trans. Kennedy and Walsh, 147.
162. WN, I, 192.
163. P. Meyer, 'Notice sur la manuscrit II, 6, 24 de la bibliothèque de l'université de Cambridge', *Notices et extraits de la Bibliothèque nationale,* 32/ii (1886), 37–81 at 71; Power, 'Henry, Duke of the Normans', 127–8.
164. WN, I, 192.
165. Newburgh sums up this view by quoting Virgil's *Aeneid,* 'Where an enemy is concerned, who asks whether it is guile or valour? *(Aeneid,* II, l. 390, 'dolus an virtus, quis in hoste requirat?').
166. WN, I, 192–3.
167. WN, I, 193–4.
168. R. Rogers, *Latin Siege Warfare in the Twelfth Century* (Oxford, 1992), 150 and n. 88.
169. *GH,* I, 74.
170. *GH,* I, 74; *PR 20 Henry II,* 135; Lloyd, *A History of Wales,* II, 544, n. 39. The Welsh were probably those earlier engaged in the siege of Tutbury. Henry also brought with him King William and the earls of Leicester and Chester, who were imprisoned first at Caen, then at Falaise (*GH,* I, 74).
171. *GH,* I, 74–5: William of Canterbury, 493.
172. *GH,* I, 75; Torigni, 265; WN, I, 196.
173. *GH,* I, 75.
174. *GH,* I, 75.
175. *GH,* I, 75. In reworking this incident in his *Chronica,* Howden makes the French more timid, stating that they dared not move beyond their tents, and that when some knights of the king of England's household stood on the battlements of the walls (presumably referring to the defensive works of their siege camp), no one dared fight them off (Howden, II, 66).
176. *GH,* I, 75. Howden, II, 66, notes that Malaunay lay between Rouen and the village of Tostes.
177. In this regard, it is surely no coincidence that Jordan Fantosme does not recount the relief of Rouen in any detail but rather ends his poem with the conclusion of hostilities in England, with only the briefest of references to the siege (JF, ll. 2043–5, 2062–5).
178. Torigni, 265; *GH,* I, 76.
179. *GH,* I, 76; Torigni, 265, who remarks, 'In truth, I ascribe that peace to the mother of our Lord Jesus Christ'; Gervase, I, 250; *HWM,* ll. 2321–4 and l. 2321; Vincent, 'Henry III and the Blessed Virgin Mary', 130.
180. *HWM,* ll. 2320–44.
181. *GH,* I, 76–7.
182. *GH,* I, 76.
183. *GH,* I, 76; Howden, II, 66.
184. *GH,* I, 76–7.
185. *HWM,* ll. 2271–7; 'And we knew full well, and saw with our own eyes,' noted the *History of William Marshal,* 'that even the king of France, the supporter of Henry's son, was so greatly displeased with the excessive spendings and outgoings that he was not prepared to commit himself to the same extent as at first, I can tell you.'
186. *HWM,* ll. 2235–62.
187. Though by no means representing the total sum Henry spent in the war, the Pipe Rolls indicate an expenditure in England alone of over £4,000 on castle repair, garrison wages and victualling in

the year 1172–73, which probably represented over 20 per cent of pre-war annual revenue as recorded in the rolls. In 1173–74, the sum was £3,213, two-thirds of which was spent on garrisons (*PR 19 Henry II*, xxiii; Beeler, *Warfare in England*, 179, 183).

188. Evidence of victualling from the Pipe Rolls suggests that sheriffs responsible for providing such supplies were responding to careful and effective central planning (M. Prestwich, 'The Victualling of Castles', *Soldiers, Nobles and Gentlemen. Essays in Honour of Maurice Keen*, ed. P. Coss and C. Tyerman (Woodbridge, 2009), 169–82, at 172; Latimer, 'How to Suppress a Rebellion', 163–77). In the south-east, London, Berkhamsted and Dover appear to have been principal supply depots for castles in the region (Beeler, *Warfare in England*, 178).

189. Beeler, *Warfare in England*, 183; Jones, 'The Generation Gap of 1173–1174', 36.

190. Jones, 'The Generation Gap of 1173–1174', 38–9.

191. Such a pattern of warfare was not uncommon. For instructive parallels in thirteenth-century Germany, see M. Toch, 'The Medieval German City under Siege', *The Medieval City under Siege*, ed. I. A. Corfis and M. Wolfe (Woodbridge, 1995), 35–48, at 40.

192. For the significance of battle as ordeal, G. Duby, *Le Dimanche de Bouvines* (Paris, 1973), trans. C. Tihanyi as *The Legend of Bouvines. War, Religion and Culture in the Middle Ages* (Cambridge, 1990), 110–21.

Chapter 10: A Fragile Peace, 1175–1177

1. *GH*, I, 77.

2. Peter of Blois, 'Dialogus inter regem Henricum secundem et abbatem Bonevallis', ed. R. B. C. Huygens, *Revue Benedictine*, 68 (1958), 87–112, at 98–100; Joliffe, *Angevin Kingship*, 100; Vincent, 'Strange Case of the Missing Biographies', 246; and M. Billoré, 'Idéologie chrétienne et éthique politique à travers le *Dialogus inter regem Henricum secundum et abbatem Bonnevallis* de Peter de Blois', *Convaincre et persuader: communication et propagande aux XIIe et XIIIe siècles*, ed. M. Aurell (Poitiers, 2007), 81–109. For the importance of anger as a political tool, see the studies collected in *Anger's Past. The Social Uses of Emotion in the Middle Ages*, ed. B. H. Rosenwein (Ithaca, NY, and London, 1998), especially G. Althoff, 'Ira Regis. Prolegomena to a History of Royal Anger', 59–74; S. White, 'The Politics of Anger', 127–52; R. Barton, 'A "Zealous Anger" and the Regeneration of Aristocratic Relationships in Eleventh- and Twelfth-Century France', 153–70; and P. Hyams, 'What did Henry III of England Think in Bed and in French about Kingship and Anger?', 92–126. See also the important discussions of anger in D. Bates, 'Anger, Emotion and a Biography of William the Conqueror', *Gender and Historiography: Studies in the Earlier Middle Ages in Honour of Pauline Stafford*, ed. J. L. Nelson, S. Reynolds and S. M. Johns (London, 2012), 21–33; and R. E. Barton, 'Emotions and Power in Orderic Vitalis', *ANS*, 33 (2010), 41–60, at 50–3.

3. *CTB*, II, no. 243, at 1050–1, and n. 10; ibid., no. 244, at 1064–5.

4. *MTB*, VI, 72: Warren, *Henry II*, 183.

5. Aird, *Robert Curthose*, 88–98; Bates, 'Anger, Emotion and a Biography of William the Conqueror', 28–9.

6. Geoffrey Malaterra, *De rebus gestis Rogerii Calabriae et Siciliae comitis et Roberti Guiscardi ducis fratris eius, auctore Gaufredo Malaterra, monacho Benedictino*, ed. E. Pontieri (Rerum Italicarum Scriptores, Bologna, 1927–1928), 78–9 (III: 36).

7. E. Kantorowicz, *Frederick the Second, 1194–1250* (London, 1931), 400–7; D. Abulafia, *Frederick II* (London, 2002), 232–43. In the laws Frederick issued at Mainz in 1235, it was decreed that any son who attempted to seize or harm his father's lands or castles was to suffer permanent disinheritance (ibid., 243).

8. Thus, for example, the great German monarch Otto I was said to have been at a loss as to how to respond when his rebellious son Luidolf submitted to him at Mainz in 953. He finally fell back on blaming the instigators (*fautores*) of the plot, against whom suitable reprisals were taken (Widukind, *Res gestae saxonicae*, ed. P. Hirsch and H. E. Lohmann. *MGH, SS* (Hanover, 1935), III: 18; K. Leyser, *Rule and Conflict in an Early Medieval Society: Ottonian Saxony* (London, 1979), 86 and n.19).

9. For a discussion of this trope, J. T. Rosenthal, 'The King's "Wicked Advisors" and Medieval Baronial Rebellions', *Political Science Quarterly*, 82 (1967), 595–618.

10. *HWM*, ll. 2345–54.

11. Guernes, ll. 6068–80; trans. Short, 173.

12. *Expugnatio*, 122–5; and William of Newburgh, who noted that 'Undoubtedly the clemency of this great prince towards most faithless transgressors and most savage enemies is rightly reckoned worthy of wonder and of praise in this affair' (WN, I, 176; trans. Kennedy and Walsh, 127). Lyttleton called it 'among the noblest acts of clemency that have ever embellished the history of mankind' (G. Lyttleton, *The History of the Life of Henry the Second and of the Age in which Be Lived*, 4 vols (London, 1767), III, 525–6).

13. Wace, *Roman de Rou*, ll. 77–88.
14. Ibid., ll. 74–6.
15. *Recueil*, II, no. 468; *GH*, I, 77–9. Howden notes that the negotiations began on 29 September, and that the treaty was concluded the following day (*GH*, I, 77). Ralph of Diss gives the date of 11 October for the settlement 'between Tours and Amboise', which must refer to the subsequent ratification of the treaty at Falaise (the text given in *Recueil*, II, no. 468). A summary of the main terms was sent by the king 'to his faithful men', presumably some time soon after in October 1174 (*Recueil*, II, no. 469; Diceto, I, 394–5).
16. *GH*, I, 79; *Recueil*, II, no. 469.
17. Torigni, 265.
18. *GH*, I, 77; *Recueil*, II, no. 469; Diceto, I, 395. Similarly, all castles fortified in the king's lands were to be reduced to the condition they were in fifteen days before the war's start.
19. *GH*, I, 78.
20. *GH*, I, 78; *Recueil*, II, no. 469; Diceto, I, 394, 'in voluntate mea sunt'.
21. *GH*, I, 79.
22. *GH*, I, 77.
23. *GH*, I, 77–8.
24. Continuation of Richard of Poitiers, *RHF*, XII, 420; Vincent, 'Henry II and the Poitevins', 122; *PR 19 Henry II*, 94–5.
25. He also was permitted to retain the four royal manors (with an annual value of £114) that he had been granted by King Stephen, apparently in agreement with Henry Plantagenet, back in 1153 (Wareham, 'Hugh (I) Bigod', *ODNB*).
26. *PR 1 John*, 253, records the proffer of 60 marks by Henry Mallory to have full seisin of the lands which his father Ansketil Mallory, the constable of Leicester, 'lost for his service to Henry the Young King, the King's brother'; *Red Book of the Exchequer*, II, ccli, 768–9; Fox, 'Honour and Earldom of Leicester', 390.
27. *PR 26 Henry II*, 105; Fox, 'Honour and Earldom of Leicester', 390. Similarly, the lands of Hugh of Chester appear in the Pipe Rolls from 1174 to 1177.
28. N. Barratt, 'Finance and Economy in the Reign of Henry II', *Henry II. New Interpretations*, 242–56, at 250. Hence, for example, in 1174–75, Hugh de Gundeville, the sheriff of Northamptonshire, rendered account for the lands of Simon FitzPagan and of seven others 'quia receptaverunt inimicos regis' (*PR 21 Henry II*, 44).
29. Diceto, I, 395.
30. Diceto, I, 395.
31. Diceto, I, 404.
32. *Dialogus*, 116–17. Richard here quotes the *Aeneid*, VI: 853. For Richard, J. G. H. Hudson, 'Richard FitzNigel and the "Dialogue of the Exchequer"', *Perceptions of the Past in Twelfth-Century Europe*, ed. P. Magdalino (1992), 75–98.
33. *RHF*, XII, 420; Turner, *Eleanor*, 232; Guernes, ll. 6137–40; trans. Short, 175.
34. Turner, *Eleanor*, 229–39; G. Seabourne, *Imprisoning Medieval Women. The Non-Judicial Confinement and Abduction of Women in England, c. 1170–1509* (London, 2011), 61–2, 69–70, 79.
35. Gervase, I, 256; Flori, *Eleanor*, 118–19; Turner, *Eleanor*, 234–5.
36. For Eleanor's period of captivity, Flori, *Eleanor*, 118–36; Turner, *Eleanor*, 230–55.
37. It is uncertain which these were, but the fact that in 1176 the Young King had his disgraced vice-chancellor Adam de Churchdown imprisoned at Argentan suggests he held control of this fortress (*GH*, I, 122–3; Smith, 'Households', 90).
38. Barratt, 'Finance and Economy', 248–9, confirming the essential veracity of the figures given by J. H. Ramsay, *A History of the Revenues of the Kings of England, 1066–1399*, 2 vols (Oxford, 1925), I, 191. These figures did not, however, represent the king's full revenues, as payments into the Chamber and total royal revenues are unknown. For Normandy, V. Moss, 'Normandy and England in 1180: The Pipe Roll Evidence', *England and Normandy in the Middle Ages*, ed. D. Bates and A. Curry (London, 1994), 185–95; and idem, 'The Norman Fiscal Revolution, 1193–8', in *Crises, Revolutions and Self-Sustained Growth. Essays in European Fiscal History, 1130–1830*, ed. W. M. Ormrod, M. Bonney and R. Bonney (Stamford, 1999), 38–57, at 40–1, noting that by 1198, this sum had risen sharply to 99,000 *livres angevins*.
39. *GH*, I, 78; Diceto, I, 394; *Recueil*, II, no. 468. There are no extant financial records for Aquitaine or Brittany to allow comparison with the actual income granted to Richard and Geoffrey.
40. Everard, *Brittany and the Angevins*, 129.
41. Gervase, I, 243.
42. *GH*, I, 78 'in Andegaviae et in terra quae fuit comitis Andegaviae'.
43. Norgate, *John Lackland*, 6; Neveux, *La Normandie*, 538, 'son Benjamin'.

44. Torigni, 268; Gillingham, *Richard I*, 53–4. The earl was buried at his father Henry I's foundation of Reading abbey (*GH*, I, 105).
45. *GH*, I, 79.
46. *GH*, I, 79.
47. *GH*, I, 79; Gillingham, 'Doing Homage', 75.
48. Diceto, I, 396–7; *Liber Niger de Scaccarii*, ed. T. Hearne, 2 vols (London, 1774), I, 36–40, with eighteen more names on the witness list; *Recueil*, II, nos 471, 471; *Anglo-Scottish Relations, 1174–1328: Some Select Documents*, ed. and trans. E. L. G. Stones (Oxford, 1970), no. 1. The initial agreement made at Falaise was witnessed by Richard and Geoffrey, but not the Young King, though his rights as overlord of the Scots were included in it.
49. *GH*, I, 81; Torigni, 266, and 234, where he notes a great council meeting at Christmas 1168 in the 'new hall'.
50. Diceto, I, 398.
51. *GH*, I, 81.
52. *GH*, I, 81–2.
53. *GH*, I, 81.
54. *GH*, I, 82.
55. *GH*, I, 82, 'et ipse adhuc cereus erat in vitium flecti'; Horace, *Ars poetica*, tr. A. S. Kline (2005), 160–5: 'The beardless youth, free of tutors at last, delights/In horse and hound, and the turf of the sunlit campus,/He's wax malleable for sin, rude to his advisors,/Slow in making provision, lavish with money,/Spirited, passionate, and swift to change his whim'. William of Tyre, Bk 16: 3 similarly cites this verse in relation to Baldwin III's quarrels with his mother Melisende.
56. Diceto, I, 398; Howden, II, 71.
57. Howden, II, 71; *GH*, I, 82.
58. As Leyser, *Rule and Conflict*, 168, n. 1, notes, 'a royal charisma could be tested and rejected'.
59. Smith, '*Acta*', 298, suggests that this act may well have marked the moment from which all the Young King's *acta* became legitimate once more in the eyes of his father.
60. WN, I, 196–7; trans. Kennedy and Walsh, 154–5.
61. *GH*, I, 82–3.
62. *GH*, I, 83.
63. *GH*, I, 83. Nevertheless, it would appear that the count retained at least one charter from the Young King, for at a summit in 1182, Count Philip gave Henry II a 'cartam juvenis regis', and was again quitclaimed of all obligations by young Henry and his brothers (*GH*, I, 286).
64. *GH*, I, 83.
65. *GH*, I, 83.
66. Diceto, I, 399. The chronicler's home town of Diss lay within this theatre of war and may well have suffered in the ravages.
67. *GH*, I, 133.
68. *GH*, I, 83, 84; Diceto, I, 399, has 8 May.
69. Diceto, I, 399.
70. *GH*, I, 84: Diceto, I, 399. For the council and its canons, *GH*, I, 84–91; *Councils and Synods*, II (no. 168), 965–93; and for Richard's election, Gervase, I, 239–42, 243–5, 247.
71. *Councils and Synods*, II, 991; *GH*, I, 89; C. N. L. Brooke, 'Aspects of Marriage Law in the Eleventh and Twelfth Centuries', *Proceedings of the Fifth International Congress of Medieval Canon Law, Salamanca 1976* (Vatican City, 1980), 333–44, at 337 and n. 9.
72. Diceto, I, 399–401. Remarkably, these secular proceedings were not recorded by Howden in either the *Gesta Henrici* or the later *Chronica*.
73. *Recueil*, II, no. 488; Diceto, I, 400–1; trans. in Appleby, *Henry II*, 234–5.
74. Appleby, *Henry II*, 234–5.
75. That his homage could be regarded as having a negative impact on his regal status is strikingly shown by the marginal *signum* which accompanies this letter in one manuscript of Ralph's *Ymagines*, showing two hands offering up a crown (Lambeth Palace Library MS 8. 90v). I am most grateful to Laura Cleaver for drawing this to my attention.
76. JF, ll. 17–22.
77. JF, ll. 931–40.
78. *Recueil, Introduction*, 258–9, together with Henry II's original grant of 1173 x 1174; Smith, '*Acta*', no. 13. The Young King's charter is witnessed by a number of his own household knights, including William Marshal. This also seems the most likely occasion for the Young King's witnessing of a charter of Henry II's to Auger the huntsman, quitclaiming a rent of 26 shillings from the farm of Waltham (*The Early Charters of Waltham Abbey*, ed. R. Ransford (Woodbridge, 1989), no. 282; *Letters and Charters of Henry II*, no. 3138, issued at Westminster, May x November 1175. This is one of the very few extant charters of Henry II to be witnessed by the Young King, who heads the witness list as 'rex Henricus filius meus').

79. Guernes, ll. 6141–55; trans. Short, 175.
80. Gervase, I, 3–29; P. Draper, 'William of Sens and the Original Design of the Choir Termination of Canterbury Cathedral, 1175–1179', *Journal of the Society of Architectural Historians*, 42 (1983), 238–48; P. Kidson, 'Gervase, Becket and William of Sens', *Speculum*, 68 (1993), 969–91; M. F. Hearn, 'Canterbury Cathedral and the Cult of Becket', *Art Bulletin*, 76 (1994), 19–54.
81. Gervase, I, 256: Diceto, I, 399.
82. *GH*, I, 92, 'curiam et festum regium'; *Brut y Tywysogion (Peniarth)*, 70. The Gloucester council probably took place in the royal hall and palace just outside the city, which had long been the site of the Christmas crown-wearings of the late Anglo-Saxon and early Norman kings.
83. Sir William Dugdale, *Monasticon Anglicanum*, ed. J. Caley, H. Ellis and B. Bandinel, 6 vols (London, 1817–1830), IV, 615; Lloyd, *A History of Wales*, II, 547 and n. 55.
84. *GH*, I, 92; *Earldom of Gloucester Charters*, ed. R. B. Patterson (Oxford, 1973); R. B. Patterson, 'William, second earl of Gloucester (d. 1183)', *ODNB*. Although he was the son of Robert of Gloucester, William's relations with Henry had gradually soured after 1154, and the earl found himself increasingly an outsider at court.
85. *PR 21 Henry II*, 88–9; Lloyd, *A History of Wales*, II, 543 and n. 33, 546 and n. 51; and for wider context, Gillingham, 'Henry II, Richard I and the Lord Rhys', 59–68.
86. *GH*, I, 91–3.
87. Diceto, I, 401; *GH*, I, 93.
88. In this context, it is striking that, despite his key role in the suppression of the rebellion in England in 1174, Geoffrey receives no mention in Fantosme's poem.
89. *Dialogus*, 114–15.
90. Norgate, *Angevin Kings*, II, 170.
91. Warren, *Henry II*, 142–3.
92. Smail, 'Latin Syria', 14–15.
93. Lloyd, *A History of Wales*, II, 544.
94. John of Salisbury, *Policraticus*, IV: 4. Thus, for example, after his return from crusade in 1192, Philip Augustus ostentatiously 'never went abroad unless surrounded by an armed guard, contrary to the custom of his ancestors', informing those who wondered at this novel behaviour that he feared for his life from assassins sent by Richard (WN, I, 365–6).
95. Map, 452–3.
96. Suger, *Vie de Louis*, 190, adding that Henry I took to always wearing a sword indoors, and heavily fined his own men if they went out without their own swords; *Gesta regum*, I, 744–5.
97. Thus William of Malmesbury (*Gesta regum*, I, 726–9) records how when leading a force towards Wales in 1114, Henry I had been shot at by an archer – not by a Welshman but, as the king himself had sworn, by one of his own subjects – and had only been saved from the assassin's arrow by the quality of his hauberk.
98. *GH*, I, 93; Howden, II, 78, 79.
99. *Annales de Saint Aubin*, 16; trans. Aurell, *Plantagenet Empire*, 37.
100. Barratt, 'Finance and Economy', 250, 254, noting that the county farm payments brought in only £2,400, though widespread expenditure by royal officials set off against income accounted for another £21,000.
101. *GH*, I, 104.
102. V. Moss, 'The Defence of Normandy, 1193–8', *ANS*, 24 (2001), 145–61, at 150–1. By the time of the earliest surviving Norman Exchequer Rolls, those of 1179–80, loss of ducal revenue was still around 4.25 per cent, and doubtless had been considerably higher in the years immediately after the war. The first accounts for the region of Arques and Dieppe, for example, were not rendered until 1179–80, while that for Verneuil, where payment was made not only for extensive repairs to the castle but for the mills 'burned in the time of war', still showed a shortfall in revenue (ibid.; *Magni rotuli scaccarii Normanniae*, I, 66–8, 72, 84).
103. Diceto, II, 148; *Concilia Rothomagensis provinciae*, ed. G. Bessin, 2 vols in 1 (Rouen, 1717), II, 30–1; Peter of Blois, *Epistolae*, no. 28 (misdated 1172), and 33 (*PL* CCVII, cols 96–8, 109–10); Schluntz, 'Archbishop Rotrou', 130–4.
104. A number of justices had probably already begun a major series of eyres throughout the country to hear both civil and criminal cases: *Pleas before the King and his Justices, 1198–1212*, ed. D. Stenton, 3 vols (Selden Society, 83, 1966), III, lvi–lvii, where it is suggested that the eyres began before the king's return to England in May. Ranulf de Glanville and Hugh de Cressy visited fifteen counties, and Thomas Basset and William de Lanvaley another fourteen, in what appears to have been 'the very first countrywide visitation' by royal justices (P. Brand, '*Multis Vigiliis Excogitatam et Inventam*: Henry II and the Creation of the English Common Law', *Haskins Society Journal*, 2 (1990), 197–222, reprinted in P. Brand, *The Making of the Common Law* (London, 1992), 79–102, at 82–3 and n. 26).

105. *GH*, I, 94. The circumstances of Gilbert's killing are reconstructed in detail by H. Docherty, 'The Murder of Gilbert the Forester', *Haskins Society Journal* 23 (2011), 155–204.

106. *GH*, I, 94, and ibid., 92. It was on this occasion that the Young King witnessed a confirmation by his father of lands and rights to St Mary's cathedral priory, Carlisle (Sir William Dugdale, *Monasticon anglicanum*, ed. J. Caley, H. Ellis and B. Bandinel, 6 vols (London, 1817–1830), VI, 144; *Letters and Charters of Henry II*, no. 3039).

107. *GH*, I, 94. This action was indignantly condemned by J. H. Round 'as a gross breach of faith' (*PR 22 Henry II*, xiii).

108. On the forest law, *Dialogus*, 90–3; Warren, *Henry II*, 390–5.

109. *GH*, I, 97; and for a map of the royal forests, Warren, *Henry II*, 392. Fines were also levied from the citizens of York (*PR 21 Henry II*, 182–3).

110. *GH*, I, 92, 94; Howden, II, 79; Diceto, I, 402; Warren, *Henry II*, 391; Crook, 'The Earliest Exchequer Estreat', 32–4.

111. *PR 22 Henry II*, xxiv. Fines of £100 or 100 marks, however, were not uncommon, and even lesser sums appear considerably heavier than average forest amercements. In Buckinghamshire, for example, four men are amerced £100 and two 100 marks, while in Oxfordshire three were fined 200 marks, and another four £100 each (*PR 22 Henry II*, xxiv, 22–4, 30–3).

112. *GH*, I, 94; *PR 22 Henry II*, 93–7, 112–18; Crook, 'The Earliest Exchequer Estreat', 34, noting that the sum raised by the whole forest eyre amounted to almost £14,644. This was an enormous sum, at a time when annual income recorded on the Pipe Rolls before 1173 was *c*.£21,000. In the financial year of 1176/7, audited revenue gained from the eyres, forest offences and the profits of justice greatly boosted total revenue to £30,000, of which only 14 per cent was receipts from the county farms (Barratt, 'Finance and Economy', 253). Robert of Torigni admitted that by such measures against his barons the king 'defrauded them of a large amount of silver' (Torigni, 267). Fines of £100 or 100 marks were not uncommon, and even lesser sums appear considerably heavier than average forest amercements. In Buckinghamshire, for example, four men are amerced £100 and two 100 marks, while in Oxfordshire, three were fined 200 marks, and another four £100 each (*PR 22 Henry II*, xxiv, 22–4, 30–3).

113. *GH*, I, 95–9; Howden, II, 80–82; Diceto, I, 397.

114. *GH*, I, 96–9. Earl David had remained in Henry's custody as a hostage, presumably since his capitulation in July 1174 at Northampton (Diceto, I, 398).

115. Such at least was the tradition reported by Edward I to Pope Boniface in 1301, when it was noted that these items 'remain and are kept in that church up to the present day' (*Anglo-Scottish Relations*, ed. Stones, 204–5, no. 102).

116. As surety, William had to surrender the castles of Edinburgh, Stirling, Roxburgh, Berwick and Jedburgh (*GH*, I, 97; cf. *PR 21 Henry II*, 16). As Barrow notes, 'It was … the Young King's promise to restore the northern counties that finally brought the king of Scots into the war; but whether, or for how long, young Henry or his successors would have kept these promises is another matter' (*RRS*, II, 7).

117. *De principis*, 156; trans. Stevenson, 137–8. William of Canterbury, 491, drawing on Geoffrey of Monmouth (*Historia Regum Britanniae*, I: xi. c. 7), noted that Henry II, without even setting foot there, had subjugated Scotland in a manner unseen since King Malgo, the fourth to rule after King Arthur.

118. In 1185, he restored to William the honour of Huntingdon 'as honourably and as fully as he had had it before the war', and returned Edinburgh castle so that it could form part of the dower which the king of Scots could bestow on his bride, Ermengard of Beaumont (*GH*, II, 44–5). Other key castles, however, remained in Angevin hands at Henry II's death in 1189 (Warren, *Henry II*, 186–7).

119. *GH*, I, 101–3; Howden, II, 30; Diceto, I, 348; Gervase, I, 235. As Warren, *Henry II*, 201–2, notes, Ruaidhrí does not seem to have performed homage to Henry II but only to have sworn a personal oath of fealty. The Young King neither appears among the witness list of the treaty nor is known to have issued a charter of confirmation.

120. *GH*, I, 104–5; Gervase, I, 256–7.

121. *GH*, I, 107; Diceto, I, 404, 'juxta consilium filii sui regis'. The Young King and his father had held their joint Christmas court at Windsor (*GH*, I, 106).

122. Diceto, I, 404, 'in revenge for the injuries which the lords of these castles had frequently inflicted on the king the father'. He names Huntingdon, Walton, Leicester, Groby, Tutbury, Dudley, Thirsk 'and many others'. For a list of the destroyed castles and evidence from the Pipe Rolls, Beeler, *Warfare in England*, 370, n. 136.

123. *GH*, I, 68–9.

124. *GH*, I, 107; *Pleas before the King and his Justices*, III, lvii–lix. On the significance of this early general eyre, in which seemingly for the first time the justices themselves made the majority of

judgments, rather than as previously simply presiding over sessions in which judgments were reached by those normally attending county or other courts, see P. Brand, '*Multis Vigilis Excogitatam et Inventam*: Henry II and the Creation of the English Common Law', *Haskins Society Journal*, 2 (1990), 197–222, reprinted in P. Brand, *The Making of the Common Law* (London, 1992), 79–102, at 83–4. Young Henry's former *magister*, Hugh de Gundeville, served as one of the justices assigned to the circuit covering the Midland shires of Lincolnshire, Nottinghamshire, Derbyshire, Staffordshire, Warwickshire, Northamptonshire and Leicestershire (Vincent, 'Hugh de Gundeville', 133–4).

125. *GH*, I, 110.
126. *GH*, I, 111.
127. *GH*, I, 110.
128. *GH*, I, 110.
129. *GH*, I, 108–9.
130. *GH*, I, 109–10.
131. *GH*, I, 110, 'quae assisa est per consilium regis filii sui, et hominum suorum per quos ituri sunt comitatus'.
132. *HWM*, ll. 1889–91.
133. King Louis VII had visited St James in 1154, combining this with a diplomatic visit, as his wife Constance was daughter of Alphonso of Castile (Torigni, 182). The monks of St Denis were also fostering close links with Santiago: E. Greenhill, 'Eleanor of Aquitaine, Abbot Suger and Saint-Denis', *Eleanor of Aquitaine: Patron and Politician*, ed. W. W. Kibler (Austin, 1976), 81–113. Philip of Flanders had been to Compostella in 1172, returning in time to play a key role in peace talks between Henry and Louis after the settlement at Avranches (*Expugnatio*, 108–9). In 1177, Henry II himself was to inform King Ferdinand of Leon that he wished to make a pilgrimage to Compostella, and that he had long wished so to do, but though he requested a safe conduct, he never set out (*GH*, I, 157). In the event, no Plantagenet king of England ever visited Compostella, Rome or Jerusalem (Vincent, 'Pilgrimages', 18).
134. *GH*, I, 114.
135. As evidenced by Richard's campaign in January 1177 (*GH*, I, 131–2).
136. *GH*, I, 114.
137. *HWM*, ll. 2395–407.
138. Chrétien de Troyes, *Arthurian Romances*, trans. Kibler, 124–5.
139. *HWM*, ll. 2404–5, 2412–18.
140. *HWM*, ll. 2400–1, and cf. ll. 1889–91.
141. Philippe de Novare, *Les Quatre Âges de l'homme*, ed. M. de Fréville (Paris, 1888), 38–9; trans. Painter, *William Marshal*, 30. In just this way, noted the *History*, the Marshal himself had gained the reputation for prowess that had won him his position as the Young King's tutor in arms by an itinerant life 'in tournaments and war' in 'all the lands where a knight should think of winning renown' (*HWM*, ll. 1884–5, ll. 1516–25, and cf. ll. 1889–904).
142. *History of the Counts of Guines*, ch. 93; trans. Shopkow, 125–6.
143. WN, II, 422: *HWM*, ll. 2409–11.
144. *HWM*, ll. 1531–48.
145. *GH*, I, 114.
146. *GH*, I, 115; *PR 22 Henry II*, 90–1, where Robert Mald receives 56 shillings 'for paying the Queen's maintenance at Winchester'; Turner, *Eleanor*, 237. Joanna may also have been at the Easter court, for in May the Sicilian ambassadors were sent to Winchester to see her (*GH*, I, 116).
147. *GH*, I, 115.
148. Gillingham, *Richard I*, 52–4.
149. *GH*, I, 115; *PR 22 Henry II*, 207, recording the payment of £7 10s. for the esnecca for the Young King's crossing, and a further £7 15s. for the four ships that also crossed with him carrying his household and that of Queen Margaret. Evidently for security, the Young King's treasure was shipped in a separate vessel under the custody of Adam de Yqeboeuf, a reflection of Adam's importance within the Young King's *mesnie*.
150. *HWM*, ll. 2436–49. The *History* here contracts the chronology of April to June 1176, having the Young King sail directly from Dover to Wissant, and omitting his crossing to Barfleur and his journey to the Île-de-France, whence he more probably moved on to Flanders (see *HWM*, III, 72, n. to l. 2438).
151. *HWM*, ll. 2459–60, 67–70.
152. *HWM*, ll. 2471–96. For Ressons and its situation, *HWM*, III, 73, n. to l. 2473.
153. *HWM*, ll. 249–72518.
154. *HWM*, l. 2508.
155. Diceto, I, 407; *GH*, I, 120.

156. *GH*, I, 120.
157. *GH*, I, 121.
158. *Grand Cartulaire de Fontevraud*, ed. J.-M. Bienvenue et al., 2 vols (Poitiers, 2000, 2005), II, no. 830, noting Geoffrey's gift to Fontevraud after his fatal participation 'cum Henrico Juniore, Anglorum rege, filio Henrici regis, adversus comitem Engolismensem in expeditione'. This suggests that part of young Henry's force had been raised from the knight service of Anjou.
159. *GH*, I, 121, 'pravo usus concilio'. L. Clédat, *Du rôle historique de Bertran de Born, 1175–1200* (Paris, 1879), 35, followed by Norgate, *Angevin Kings*, II, 210, suggest Bertran de Born as the probable culprit, though this cannot be substantiated and probably considerably exaggerates Bertran's political importance.
160. Thus Howden had noted how his army in 1176 had been swollen by knights attracted from surrounding regions by the generous wages Richard was offering (*GH*, I, 120).
161. *GH*, I, 121.
162. Smith, '*Acta*', 299–301, and for his chaplains William, Nicholas and John see, for example, ibid., nos 27, 30, 31 and 32.
163. *GH*, I, 122; Diceto, I, 406. For Geoffrey, D. Carpenter, 'The Dignitaries of York Minster in the 1170s: a Reassessment', *Northern History*, 43 (2006), 21–37, at 25–6, 33–4.
164. *GH*, I, 122.
165. *GH*, I, 122. Howden's detailed knowledge of these events is a further reflection of the close ties he had to Archbishop Roger and the clerics in his circle (Gillingham, 'The Travels of Roger of Howden', 74–6). He appears to have been deeply affected by the death of Geoffrey and another York cleric, Robert Magnus, in a shipwreck in 1177, and Adam of Churchdown may also have been known to him. Certainly the Young King's treatment of Adam only served to reinforce Howden's poor opinion of him.
166. *GH*, I, 122–3; Howden, II, 94–8. Though Adam was handed over to Henry II, the king nevertheless had him kept in custody of the abbot of Hyde until he could consult with his council on further action.
167. *GH*, I, 124. On the death of William d'Aubigny, earl of Sussex, he took the castle of Arundel into his hands (*The Complete Peerage*, ed. G. E. Cockayne, 14 vols (London, 1910–1959), I, 235–6; *History of the King's Works*, II, 554). Henry had even carried out similar measures in Ireland; on the death of Strongbow in April 1176, the king immediately sent William FitzAldelin to take all his castles into royal hands (*GH*, I, 125).
168. *GH*, I, 124; and cf. *Chronicle of Battle Abbey*, 174–5. For Ongar, J. H. Round, 'The Honour of Ongar', *Transactions of the Essex Archaeological Society*, new series, vii (1900), 142–52; King, *Castellarium*, I, 146.
169. *GH*, I, 126–7; *PR 22 Henry II*, 179; *PR 23 Henry II*, 29 (Leicester); *PR 23 Henry II*, 144 (Bennington, Hertfordshire). Mountsorrel was taken into the king's hands because a jury ruled that it was part of the royal demesne (*GH*, I, 126–7). Geoffrey de Tourville's castle at Weston Turville, which was dependent on the honour of Leicester, had been destroyed earlier (*PR 20 Henry II*, 82; and for its link to Leicester, Crouch, *Beaumont Twins*, 120, 134–5).
170. *GH*, I, 124. Over an eighteen-month period, Ilchester was given wide powers to reorganize the Exchequer, tax, and enforce assizes. He left in 1177 and his place was taken until 1200 by William FitzRalph (Neveux, *La Normandie*, 542). At some stage, whether earlier or now, Henry had the castles of William of Tancarville demolished (Map, 488–9).
171. Torigni, 272.
172. *GH*, I, 124–5.
173. *GH*, I, 11–20, where Howden notes the departure of the clerical escort after the council at Winchester convened on 15 August, 127; Howden, II, 94–8.
174. *GH*, I, 120. For Joanna's marriage and journey to Sicily, C. Bowie, *The Daughters of Eleanor of Aquitaine* (Turnhout, 2014), 89–94, 131–40.
175. *GH*, I, 131. Geoffrey and John were with their father in England, while Richard held a separate Christmas court at Bordeaux.
176. *GH* I, 127, where Howden notes that Ralph was 'the wealthiest of the barons of the king of England in Berry'. Torigni, 274, with pardonable exaggeration, claimed its worth to be 'equal to the revenue of the duchy of Normandy'. For the lordship of Châteauroux, Boussard, *Le Gouvernement*, 128–32; and for its strategic significance Gillingham, 'Events and Opinions', 58–9; idem, *Richard I*, 56–7.
177. *GH*, I, 127.
178. M. Pacaut, *Louis VII et son royaume* (Paris, 1964), 178–202; Boussard, *Gouvernement*, 128–32; Warren, *Henry II*, 144.
179. *GH*, I, 131–2; Gillingham, *Richard I*, 56.

180. *GH*, I, 132.
181. *GH*, I, 132.
182. *GH*, I, 132.
183. Henry's policy in 1177 was exceptional in its threat of direct aggression against Louis, marking, as Yves Sassier notes, 'une logique de vengeance' ('Reverentia regis', 34–5).
184. *GH*, I, 138.
185. *GH*, I, 133, 136.
186. *GH*, I, 158–9. Henry gave Philip 500 marks, while he supplied a further 500 marks through the Hospitallers to retain a force of knights in defence of the kingdom of Jerusalem (*GH*, I, 133, 158, 159).
187. *GH*, I, 159.
188. Howden, II, 136.
189. *GH*, I, 134–5.
190. *GH*, I, 161.
191. *GH*, I, 154.
192. *GH*, I, 143–4; S. D. Church, 'Roger Bigod (III), second earl of Norfolk (*c.*1143–1221)', *ODNB*.
193. *GH*, I, 160.
194. *GH*, I, 160; Howden, II, 133.
195. *GH*, I, 160–1.
196. *GH*, I, 162.
197. *GH*, I, 167.
198. *GH*, I, 168; Howden, II, 143.
199. Boussard, *Gouvernement*, 523–4; Warren, *Henry II*, 144–5.
200. *Recueil*, II, 61; Warren, *Henry II*, 145, n. 2.
201. *GH*, I, 169.
202. *GH*, I, 168–9.
203. *GH*, I, 175, 177.
204. *GH*, I, 178–9.
205. *GH*, I, 177.
206. Warren, *Henry II*, 145.
207. *GH*, I, 181, 190.
208. *GH*, I, 190.
209. *GH*, I, 190–94. The full text of the treaty, in which the Young King is listed as a witness, is also given by Gerald of Wales in *De principis*, 166–9. The site of the conference was chosen not only because it was on the duchy's south-east frontier with France, but because, earlier that year, on the death of Waleran, son of William Lupellus, Henry II had finally obtained possession of this key stronghold, 'which he had long desired' and which, despite its close ducal associations, neither his father nor his grandfather had held directly (Torigni, 276).
210. *GH*, I, 195; Torigni, 275, who noted that such were the storms at sea that some thirty ships of the wine fleet from Poitou had also been sunk.
211. *GH*, I, 194–5, presumably with the host of Normandy, which Henry II had summoned to muster at Argentan on 9 October (ibid.).
212. *GH*, I, 195–6.
213. *GH*, I, 196.
214. *GH*, I, 196–7.
215. Torigni, 276.

Chapter 11: Apogee

1. *HWM*, ll. 2637–44.
2. In his *Estoire de la guerre sainte*, written in the later 1190s, the poet Ambroise could remember him as 'the young king who jousted with such great vigour (*ki si jostoit a grand desroi*)' (Ambroise, *The History of the Holy War*, ed. and trans. M. Ailes and M. Barber, 2 vols (Woodbridge, 2003), ll. 94–6). Similarly, the *Histoire des ducs de Normandie*, 82, noted, 'Les tornoiements antoit et amoit'.
3. For the tournament and its development, M. Parisse, 'Le Tournoi en France, des origines à la fin du XIIIe siècle', *Das ritterliche Turnier im Mittelalter*, ed. J. Fleckstein (Göttingen, 1985), 175–211; J. Barker, *The Tournament in England, 1100–1400* (Woodbridge, 1986); R. Barber and J. Barker, *Tournaments. Jousts, Chivalry and Pageants in the Middle Ages* (Woodbridge, 1989); Crouch, *Tournament*, which provides the most extensive analysis yet of the organization, operation and social context of twelfth- and thirteenth-century tournaments; and D. Barthélemy, 'Les origines du tournoi chevaleresque', *Agôn: a la compétition, Ve-XIIe siècles*, ed. F. Bougard, R. Le Jan and T. Leinhard (Turnhout, 2012), 112–29.

4. *HWM*, ll. 4971–6. For Anet and Sorel, *HWM*, III, note to line 3889, and for Ressons-sur-Matz, ibid., III, note to line 2473. On the season, Crouch, *Tournament*, 11, 32–5, and for the location of tournaments, ibid., 8, 11, 39–55.

5. Ulrich von Zatzikhoven, *Lanzelet*, cited in K. G. T. Webster, 'The Twelfth-Century Tourney', *Anniversary Papers by Colleagues and Pupils of George Lyman Kitteridge* (Boston and London, 1913), 227–34, at 228.

6. Galbert of Bruges, *The Murder of Charles the Good, Count of Flanders*, trans. J. B. Ross (New York, 1960), 91–2.

7. *Historia Gaufridi*, 83; Crouch, *Tournament*, 166. John's account, however, of Geoffrey's tournament at the head of a Breton contingent against the Normans at Mont St-Michel, supposedly *c*.1128, contains much that is fictitious and literary.

8. Crouch, *Image of Aristocracy*, 135.

9. Gilbert of Mons, cc. 55, 57, 62, 77, 85, 92, 98, 100, 101; *HWM*, ll. 2909–17.

10. O. Verlinden, 'The Fairs of Champagne and Flanders', *Cambridge Economic History of Europe*, ed. M. M. Postan et al., III (Cambridge, 1963), 119–50.

11. *HWM*, ll. 3141–2.

12. Melrose, 37; *HWM*, ll. 1319–41, and ibid., III, note to l. 1324, for King William's presence at a tournament held in 1166 between Saint-Jamme and Valennes, in which the Marshal captured Peter, his chamberlain.

13. WN, II, 422; Barker, *The Tournament*, 7–10; Crouch, *Tournament*, 9–11, 40–1.

14. Suger had even disapproved of Louis VI's individual feats of arms as a knight in war itself as unbecoming the royal majesty (*Vie de Louis VI*, 78–80; Koziol, 'The Problem of Sacrality', 135).

15. Sazzarin, *Roman de Ham*, in *Histoire des ducs de Normandie et des rois d'Angleterre*, ed. F. Michel (Paris, 1840), 216; trans. Crouch, *Tournament*, 199.

16. Diceto, I, 428. Ralph's comments would suggest a qualification to the view that Henry regarded his son's activities merely as 'wasteful and trivial' (Crouch, *Tournament*, 23).

17. M. Keen and J. R. V. Barker, 'The Medieval English Kings and the Tournament', *Das ritterliche Turnier im Mittelalter*, ed. J. Fleckenstein (Göttingen, 1985), 212–28; and for the context of these developments, N. Saul, *For Honour and Fame. Chivalry in England, 1066–1500* (London, 2011).

18. *HWM*, ll. 1201–12. For the organization of such teams, Crouch, *Tournaments*, 72–4, 80, 89.

19. *HWM*, ll. 257–8.

20. *HWM*, ll. 2780–7. For the date, *HWM*, II, 75, note to line 2775.

21. *HWM*, ll. 4481–749. In listing the knights of the Young King's retinue by name according to these regional divisions, it is clear that the author of the *History* was following the layout of the tournament roll he had in front of him.

22. *HGM*, III, 58, n. 4. After the war, Robert held important posts in the duchy, including the farm of the prévôté of Lillebonne between 1175 and 1180, and that of Lyons la Forêt in 1179–80. It may well be for this reason that, though English, Roger appears among the Norman contingent of the Young King's team.

23. Diceto, I, 428.

24. *HWM*, ll. 3381–90. All three of these Flemish lords would go on to play important roles in the service of Richard I.

25. *HWM*, ll. 3583–92. The author of the *History* regrettably did not fulfil his promise that 'one day I shall list them for you and name them, every single one' (ibid., ll. 3591–8).

26. *HWM*, ll. 4489–541.

27. *HWM*, ll. 3197–201, and for the date, *HWM*, III, note to l. 3182; *HWM*, ll. 4557–780. John, the author of the *History*, tells that he drew on an *escrit*, almost certainly a surviving rotulet drawn up for the tournament itself (*HWM*, l. 4539). Crouch, 'Hidden History', 116, suggests this was 'perhaps a souvenir list made up for the participants', but it may equally have been based on a form of muster roll or wage list. That such a roll was preserved in the Marshal's archives perhaps suggests that one of his functions in the Young King's household was to supervise the muster and payment of knights, just as the Marshal of England did (ibid., 116; J. H. Round, *The King's Serjeants and Officers of State with their Coronation Services* (London, 1911), 76–7, 82).

28. For the significance of the emergence of the banneret, D. Crouch, *The Birth of Nobility. Constructing Aristocracy in England and France, 900–1300* (Harlow, 2005), 247–8.

29. *HWM*, ll. 4762–7.

30. As David Crouch, *Tournament*, 24, notes, 'two hundred pounds was the annual income of a moderately wealthy baron, or the amount that the county of Worcester owed the king every year'.

31. *HWM*, ll. 4768–70.

32. *HWM*, ll. 5073–89.

33. *HWM*, ll. 3720–63.

34. *History of the Counts of Guisnes*, ch. 92; trans. Shopkow, 125. This was the (unnamed) nephew of Arnold of Cayeux, who had been appointed principal advisor to Arnold by his father.
35. *HWM*, ll. 3202–8.
36. *HWM*, ll. 2637–50.
37. Gilbert of Mons, c.57; trans. Napran, 57.
38. *HWM*, ll. 2651–66.
39. *GH*, I, 207, quoting Cassiodorus (*Libro I Epistolarum*, XXXIX, and *Variarum libri*, XII, I.50).
40. *HWM*, ll. 2563–636; ll. 3606–59; ll. 5547–53. 'And of course,' notes the *History*, 'was that not bound to be the case? After all, he had the best instructor in arms that there ever was in his time or since' (ll. 3651–5).
41. *HWM*, ll. 5547–53.
42. *HWM*, ll. 3599–615.
43. The Young King's brother Richard would rescind their father's prohibition and from 1194 license tournaments in England 'considering that the French were more expert in battle, from being more trained and instructed', and 'so that from warlike games they [the English] might previously learn the real art and practice of war, and that the French should not insult the English knights as unskilful and uninstructed' (WN, II, 423).
44. *HWM*, ll. 1308, 1210, 2502–3, 3455–520, 3707–14, 4987; III, 64 note to line 1308; Crouch, *Tournament*, 68. Some tournaments, such as the one at Ressons-sur-Matz, might begin directly with the mêlée, for here 'there were no formal contests, there were no preliminaries' (*HWM*, ll. 2502–3).
45. *HWM*, ll. 5513–19.
46. *HWM*, ll. 1304–6; HWM, III, notes to lines 5529 and 1304; Crouch, *Tournament*, 80–1.
47. *HWM*, ll. 1307–8, 'then the companies (*li conrei*) rode forward in tight and ordered formation (*sereement e sanz desrei*)'.
48. *HWM*, ll. 5569–88.
49. *HWM*, ll. 2497–8, 'Li conrei . . . serré et bataillé se tindrent'; and ll. 2499–518.
50. *HWM*, ll. 2736, 'fols est qui trop tost se desrote'.
51. *HWM*, ll. 2801–11.
52. *HWM*, ll. 2815–19.
53. For the importance of keeping a reserve, *HWM*, ll.10, 583–676; Gillingham, *Richard I*, 288.
54. *HWM*, ll. 4823– 906.
55. *HWM*, ll. 2713–29.
56. *HWM*, ll. 4823–6, 4908–26.
57. J. Gillingham, 'War and Chivalry in the History of William Marshal', *Thirteenth Century England II*, ed. P. Coss and S. Lloyd (Woodbridge, 1988), 1–13, reprinted in J. Gillingham, *Richard Coeur de Lion: Kingship, Chivalry and War in the Twelfth Century* (London, 1994), 227–41, especially 231–8.
58. *HWM*, ll. 2719–29.
59. *HWM*, l. 2718, 'a grand proëce a mestier sens'.
60. *HWM*, ll. 2820–45, and for the rule-breaking, *HWM*, III, 75, n. to l. 2801.
61. *HWM*, l. 2750, and *HWM*, III, 74, n. to l. 275.
62. For the arms of William FitzEmpress, *Early Northamptonshire Charters*, 24–5; A. Ailes, 'Heraldry in Twelfth-Century England: The Evidence', *England in the Twelfth Century. Proceedings of the 1988 Harlaxton Symposium*, ed. D. Williams (Woodbridge, 1990), 1–16, at 3, and plate 1; idem, *The Origins of the Royal Arms of England* (Reading, 1982), 64–6. For the possible arms of Henry II, R. Viel, 'Les Armoiries probables d'Henri II d'Angleterre', *Archivum Heraldicum*, 70 (1965), Bulletin 2–3, 19–23; Ailes, *Origins of the Royal Arms*, 54–63; Vincent, 'The Seals of Henry II', at 17–22. Gervase of Tilbury, referring to the Prophecies of Merlin, noted of Henry and his sons: 'You see, then, how from the roaring lion there sprang four cubs, each of which grew into a powerful lion himself, or at least gave evidence of having a similar nature, fostering the hope of future distinction' (*Otia imperialia*, 488–9).
63. Ailes, *Origins of the Royal Arms*, 64–6; idem, 'The Governmental Seals of Richard I', *Seals and their Context in the Middle Ages*, ed. P. R. Schofield (Oxbow, 2015), 101–10. Between 1185 and 1199, however, John's seal as Lord of Ireland and Count of Mortain depicts a shield bearing two lions: A. Ailes, 'The Seal of John as Lord of Ireland and Count of Mortain', *The Coat of Arms*, 117 (1981), 341–50.
64. Crouch, *William Marshal*, 47.
65. At the start of a combat at Eu, for example, William Marshal avoided the lance of his attacker Sir Matthew de Walincourt, and in turn 'dealt him such a violent blow as they met that he knocked him off his horse to the ground', before leading away his horse as a prize (*HWM*, ll. 3215–23).
66. *HWM*, ll. 4856–60.
67. *HWM*, ll. 2509–11: 'there you would have seen many a blow dealt by mace and sword to the head and to the arms'.

68. *HWM*, ll. 3780–92.
69. *HWM*, ll. 3780–805.
70. *GH*, I, 350, 361. He noted, however, that others said he had died of an illness of the bowels (ibid., I, 350).
71. Howden, II, 166–7, trans. H. T. Riley, *The Annals of Roger of Hoveden*, 2 vols (London, 1853), I, 490; Seneca, *Epist*. XIII.
72. *HWM*, III, note to l. 3107; Gillingham, 'Conquering the Barbarians', in idem, *The English in the Twelfth Century*, 50; Crouch, *Tournament*, 142–3.
73. *HWM*, ll. 1438–61.
74. *HWM*, ll. 4899–902. No records for the purchase of the Young King's armour survive, but it was doubtless the best that could be bought. A revealing indication of how costly royal equipment might be is the payment of no less than £16 6s. 8d. for 'the helmet of the king and a belt' for Henry II in 1159 (*PR 5 Henry II*, 2).
75. *HWM*, ll. 4935–70.
76. *HWM*, ll. 1335–41, 'a lui bonement se fia'; ll. 1344–8, 'celui afia prison a render sei en sa prison'; ll. 1351–3.
77. *HWM*, ll. 2840–74.
78. For example, *HWM*, ll. 1436–40, and ll. 1423–61. William is praised for taking Philip de Valognes and another knight captive in 1166 'sanz maufere e sanz mesprisons' (ibid., ll. 1349–50).
79. *HWM*, ll. 1324–38; 2840–56; *HWM*, III, 65 note to line 1332.
80. *HWM*, ll. 4861–98.
81. *HWM*, ll. 2607–18.
82. *HWM*, ll. 2958–9.
83. *HWM*, ll. 2519–40.
84. *HWM*, ll. 2542–1.
85. *HWM*, ll. 2552–62.
86. *HWM*, ll. 2519–62.
87. *HWM*, ll. 2607–12; ll. 5561–5.
88. See, for example, *HWM*, ll. 2615–18; ll. 5561–5. The editors of the *History* suggest this reflects 'what must have been a major contemporary criticism of the Marshal's conduct' (*HWM*, III, 74, n. to l. 2545).
89. *HWM*, ll. 3426–40; ll. 4319–28; ll. 2875–82.
90. At a tournament *c*.1177, the *History* records how even before the fight, in their lodgings, the over-confident French 'had shared out all the equipment and money [from redeeming horses and arms] belonging to the English' (*HWM*, ll. 2600–6).
91. *HWM*, ll. 2933–5 and ll. 1502–11.
92. The *History*, ll. 4235–72, notes a horse worth £40, though the Marshal succeeded in paying on £7 to another knight claiming half of the horse. In 1173, the agreement between Henry II and Count Raymond of Toulouse reckoned a 'dextrarius de pretio' to be worth 10 marks of silver or more (*GH*, I, 36), but often warhorses could cost far more – as much as £50–£100 or above (R. H. C. Davis, *The Medieval Warhorse*, London, 1989, 67).
93. Gilbert of Mons, ch. 131, noted that in 1187, at Châteauroux, Baldwin de Strépy was the only knight in the retinue of Count Baldwin not to have an armoured horse.
94. *HWM*, ll. 1353–60. Horses so taken would then be entrusted to squires, to be kept safely while the knight returned to the fray (*HWM*, ll. 3269–327).
95. Crouch, *Tournament*, 96.
96. *HWM*, ll. 3367–73; ibid, ll. 1367–1372.
97. *HWM*, ll. 3391–424. The *History* describes Roger as 'a brave and doughty man, renowned for feats of arms, venturesome and clever, but inclined to be greedy' (*HWM*, ll. 3382–90). For Roger, also named 'de Gaugy', *HWM*, III, note to l. 3385.
98. Wigain 'li clers de la cuisine', is referred to in *PR 28 Henry II*, 155, as 'Wigan clericus regis filii Regis'; *HGM*, III 43; and *HWM*, III, n. to l. 3417. For such rolls, D. Crouch, ' Hidden History', 115–16, 'the biographer can only be quoting from and describing a little parchment rotulet he had before his eyes'.
99. *HWM*, ll. 3254–366. At Joigny in 1178 or 1179, however, the Marshal generously shared out his booty with those taken prisoner and with those knights who had taken a crusader's vow, while he released many of the knights he himself had captured, and 'for this he was considered a very worthy man' (*HWM*, ll. 3558–62).
100. Crouch, *Tournament*, 24.
101. *HWM*, ll. 3719–843.
102. *HWM*, ll. 3020–36.
103. *HWM*, ll. 3305–8.

104. Aurell, *Plantagenet Empire*, 133–4; Vincent, 'The Court of Henry II', 320, for 'Roland the Farter', who held land by the serjeantry tenure of performing 'a jump, a whistle and a fart' (presumably the humour lay in these actions being simultaneous) annually at the king's Christmas court. For the Easter court at Winchester in 1176, 'the king's bear' was brought from Northampton by the royal bear keeper (*ursarius*) (*PR 22 Henry II*, 29).

105. For valuable overviews and extensive bibliography see M. Aurell, 'Henry II and Arthurian Legend', in *Henry II: New Interpretations*, 362–394, especially 364–6, and for discussion of the wider question of literary patronage at the Angevin court, Gillingham, 'The Cultivation of History, Legend and Courtesy', 25–52.

106. Marie de France, *Lais*, ed. L. Harf-Lancner and K. Warnke (Paris, 1990), Prologue, ll. 44–7. Aurell, 'Henry II and Arthurian Legend', 375, notes, however, that such terms were conventional ones applicable to any monarch.

107. J. F. Benton, 'The Court of Champagne as a Literary Centre', *Speculum*, 36 (1961), 551–91; and A. Putter, 'Knights and Clerics at the Court of Champagne: Chrétien de Troyes' Romances in Context', *Medieval Knighthood V. Papers from the Sixth Strawberry Hill Conference*, ed. S. Church and R. Harvey (Woodbridge), 243–66, at 250–1.

108. R. Lejeune, 'La Date du *Conte du Graal* de Chrétien de Troyes', *Le Moyen Âge*, 60 (1954), 51–79; P. Zunthor, 'Toujours à propos de la date du *Conte du Graal*', *Le Moyen Âge*, 65 (1959), 579–86.

109. L. D. Benson, 'The Tournament in the Romances of Chrétien de Troyes and *L'Histoire de Guillaume le Maréchal*', *Chivalric Literature. Essays on Relations between Literature and Life in the Later Middle Ages*, ed. L. D. Benson and J. Leyerle (Toronto, 1980), 1–24, 147–51.

110. *HWM*, ll. 3041–54.

111. *HWM*, ll. 3466–70, 3524–6.

112. Geoffrey of Monmouth, *Historia regum Brittaniae*, BK IX: 13.

113. Vincent, 'The Court of Henry II', 332.

114. Legge, *Anglo-Norman Literature and its Background*, 81–5.

115. *Wace, The Hagiographical Works*, ed. J. Blacker, G. S. Burgess and A. V. Ogden (Leiden, 2013); Gervase, *Otia imperialia*, xcii.

116. FitzStephen, 99–100. Similarly, before his assumption of the habit at St Denis, the celebrated master of the Paris schools, Peter Abelard (d. 1142), had been noted for his fine clothes, costly horses and impressive retinue, as well as for his 'elegance of manners' (*elegantia morum*) and his courtly bearing, which led him to be referred to as 'palatinus' by his admirers (M. Clanchy, 'Abelard – knight (*miles*), courtier (*palatinus*) and man of war (*vir bellator*)', in *Medieval Knighthood, V*, ed. S. Church and R. Harvey (Woodbridge, 1995), 108–18, at 108–12).

117. JF, ll. 732–4; Ashe, *Fiction and History in England, 1066–1200*, 105–14; and R. Bezzola, *Les Origines et la formation de la littérature courtoise en occident* (Paris, 1944–63), III. Part 1, 198–206.

118. Benoît of St Maure, *Le Roman de Troie*, ed. L. Constans, 6 vols (Paris, 1904–12); Thomas of Kent, *Le Roman d'Alexandre ou Le roman de toute chevalerie*, ed. C. Gaullier-Bougassas and L. Harf-Lancner (Paris, 2003); Alexandre de Paris, *Roman d'Alexandre*, ed. E. Armstrong et al., in *The Medieval French Alexander*, 2 vols (Princeton, NJ, 1937).

119. *Cligès*, in *Arthurian Romances*, trans. Kibler, 123.

120. Joseph of Exeter, *The Illiad of Dares Phrygius*, trans. G. Roberts (Cape Town, 1970), 63–4; W. B. Sedgwick, 'The Bellum Troianum of Joseph of Exeter', *Speculum*, 5 (1930), 49–76; K. Bate, 'Joseph of Exeter [Canterbury], poet (*fl. c.*1180–1194)', *ODNB*. Gerald of Wales similarly regarded the Young King as another Hector (Gerald, *Opera*, V, 193; *De principis*, 173–5).

121. *Cligès*, in *Arthurian Romances*, trans. Kibler, 123.

122. *Epistolae*, no. 57, 76; M. D. Legge, *Anglo-Norman in the Cloisters* (Edinburgh, 1950), 6–9; Rigg, *A History of Anglo-Latin Literature*, 87.

123. Coggeshall, 121–4; Gervase, *Otia imperialia*, xxvii. According to the story Ralph claimed to have heard from Gervase himself, the girl protested that if she lost her virginity she would be eternally damned. As the Cathars claimed that sex and reproduction were inherently evil, Gervase, who was a zealot in his condemnation of heresy, jumped to the conclusion that she too must be a heretic. He was busy engaging with her in theological disputation when Archbishop William of Rheims arrived, with the upshot that the unfortunate girl was burned at the stake.

124. Gervase, *Otia imperialia*, xcii, 14–15.

125. Among its subjects was a discussion of costume, to which Gervase refers when remarking on the tight-fitting clothing worn by the men of Narbonne, similar to fashions of the Spaniards and Gascons (Gervase, *Otia imperialia*, 298–9).

126. Gervase, *Otia imperialia*, 14–15.

127. Wace, *Roman de Rou*, I, part III, ll.5–10.

128. *History of the Counts of Guisnes*, ch. 97; trans. Shopkow, 130.

Chapter 12: Keeping the Balance of Power

1. *De principis*, II: 11; trans. Stevenson, 152–3.
2. For this period, the *History*'s narrative consists largely of a series of tournaments, with little or no reference to wider political events. While on occasion it notes the Young King's absence from tournaments which were attended by the Marshal and other of his household knights, such, for example, as those held at Joigny and Eperon (*HWM*, ll. 3426–40; ll. 4319–28), it rarely states why. An exception is the *History*'s comment that the Young King decided not to join the Marshal at the tournament at Pleurs (Marne, cant. Sézanne) in the spring of 1178, because 'that site was much too far from where the King was for very heavy baggage (*trop grant herneis*) to be moved, so he did not go' (*HWM*, ll. 2875–82; ibid., III, note to line 2879).
3. One manuscript of the *Gesta Henrici* stops in 1177, and it seems likely that Howden was largely absent from the Angevin court during 1178 and 1179 (*GH*, I, xlv). Although he briefly records some of Richard's campaigns in Aquitaine, in a short narrative compressing events between July 1178 and Easter 1179 (*GH*, I, 212–13), his principal interest in the annals of 1178 was the problem of heresy in southern France. As John Gillingham, 'Events and Opinions', 74–5, has suggested, it may well be that Howden accompanied the anti-heresy mission of Henry, abbot of Clairvaux, and other leading clergy to Aquitaine in 1178.
4. Torigni, 277, 286; *Chronique du Bec*, ed. A. A. Porée (Rouen, 1883), 10, 21–2; and for Henry II's grant, *Recueil*, II, no. 534; (*Letters and Charters of Henry II*, no. 183). For the wider architectural context of the rebuilding of Bec, see L. Grant, *Architecture and Society in Normandy, 1120–1270* (New Haven and London, 2005), with a brief discussion of Bec itself at 75–6.
5. Chibnall, *Empress Matilda*, 189–91.
6. Torigni, 277.
7. *Chronique du Bec*, 21–2. Rings were a common token of conveyance. Henry II, for example, made a similar gift of a ring on the altar to mark a grant to the abbey of Le Valasse (Torigni, ed. Delisle, II, 165, n. 2).
8. Smith, '*Acta*', no. 35.
9. He styles himself 'Henricus Dei gratia Rex Anglorum, et dux Normannorum, et comes Andegavorum, Regis Henrici filius', and somewhat unusually refers to Henry II 'of distinguished memory' (*The Cartae Antiquae Rolls 11–20*, ed. J. Conway Davies, Pipe Roll Society, new series, xxxiii, London, 1960, no. 359, and ibid., no. 358, for Henry II's own grant; *The Early Charters of the Augustinian Canons of Waltham Abbey, Essex, 1062–1230*, ed. R. Randsford, Woodbridge, 1989, lxiv and nos 26–8 (calendared); Smith, '*Acta*', 325–6, no. 32, who suggests a probable date for the Young King's charter of September 1180, as opposed to 1177 as suggested by Eyton, 218–19).
10. Smith, '*Acta* ', no. 31.
11. Smith, '*Acta*', no. 19, dated 23 September 1182 x early 1183; M. Billoré, 'Henri le Jeune confirme les privilèges judiciaires de l'abbaye de Fontevraud', *Dans le secret des archives. Justice, ville et culture au Moyen Âge*, ed. M. Billoré and J. Picot (Rennes, 2014), 79–98, which prints the text in full together with a detailed analysis of the nature of these fiscal and judicial rights. I am most grateful to Maité Billoré for sending me a copy of this valuable study.
12. *Recueil, Introduction*, 257; Smith, '*Acta*', no. 29.
13. *GH*, I, 221, 238; Diceto, I, 428.
14. Diceto, I, 428.
15. *GH*, I, 238; Eyton, 225–6. Game from the king's hunt was sent from Bicknore to Winchester, while the sheriff of Worcester accounted for 50 marks for the Young King (*PR 25 Henry II*, 89, 92).
16. *GH*, I, 238, notes that the council was held 'coram rege filio suo'.
17. *GH*, I, 238.
18. *GH*, I, 238–9; *Pleas before the King or His Justices*, III, lxi–lxii.
19. *GH*, I, 207–8; D. M. Stenton, *English Justice between the Norman Conquest and the Great Charter, 1066–1215* (Philadelphia, Pa., 1964), 75–6; R. V. Turner, 'The Origins of Common Pleas and the King's Bench', *American Journal of Legal History*, 21 (1977), 238–54.
20. *The Treatise on the Laws and Customs of the Realm of England commonly called Glanvill*, ed. G. D. G. Hall (London, 1965), c. 26–8; Warren, *Henry II*, 352–4; Hudson, *Formation of the English Common Law*, 134, 203–5; J. Hudson, *The Oxford History of the Laws of England*, II, 871–1216 (Oxford, 2012), 519–20, 527–8, 600–3.
21. *GH*, I, 240. He sailed to Wissant, *c*.22 April (Eyton, 227).
22. As suggested by *HWM*, III, note to l. 3683, and see ibid. for details of the date and location.
23. *GH*, I, 240; Torigni, 282; Rigord, 9–10.
24. Torigni, 282–3; Rigord, 124–7; Sassier, *Louis VII*, 468, 'atteint de l'une de ces peurs quasi pathologiques dont le Philippe Auguste de l'âge adulte sera coutumier'.

25. E. Bournazel and J.-P. Poly, 'Couronne et mouvance: institutions et représentations mentales', *La France de Philippe Auguste. Le temps des mutations*, ed. R. H. Bautier (Paris, 1982), 217–36, at 230; Sassier, *Louis VII*, 468–9.

26. Diceto, I, 433; Torigni, 283; and Herbert of Bosham, who noted that 'it is unheard of for kings of France to cross the sea except perhaps to fight against nations hostile to the Faith' (Bosham, 538). It is striking that Rigord suppresses any mention that Louis crossed to England and of his pilgrimage to Canterbury (Rigord, 124–7).

27. *GH*, I, 240–1; Howden, II, 192–3; Diceto, I, 433; *Expugnatio*, 222–3.

28. *GH*, I, 242–3.

29. A. Cartellieri, *Philipp August. II. König von Frankreich*, 4 vols (Leipzig, 1899–1921), I, 37–41.

30. *GH,* I, 242–3.

31. Certainly the tract *De majoratu et seneschalcia* indicates that functions at royal crown-wearings were among the most important duties of the seneschal of France. It claimed that Fulk V had fulfilled the functions of the seneschal at a crown-wearing by Louis VI at Bourges, while Geoffrey le Bel had done likewise at two of Louis VII's crown-wearings (*RHF*, XII, 92; XV, 439, 602; Bémont, 'Hugues de Clers', 257, n. 4 and 5).

32. Rigord, 126–9.

33. *Récits d'un ménestrel de Reims*, 8 (ch. 15).

34. Howden, II, 194, 'de jure ducatus de Normanniae'.

35. Diceto, 438–9, trans. Hallam, *Plantagenet Chronicles*, 164.

36. Torigni, 287, 'magna exenia in auro et argento, et de venatione Anglicana'.

37. Rigord, 160–3. This incident is not dated by Rigord but it must have occurred before 1183, and the sharp deterioration of relations between Henry II and Philip following young Henry's death and Philip's coronation offers the most plausible occasion for so exceptional a present.

38. Torigni, 287.

39. *HWM*, ll. 4465–71. Gilbert of Mons, ch. 92, notes that Count Baldwin of Hainault attended the coronation at Count Philip's request with eighty knights at his own expense, even though he did not owe homage or allegiance to King Philip.

40. Diceto, II, 5; *GH*, I, 245, puts the crossing in late March.

41. Cartellieri, *Philipp August*, I, 37–67; Baldwin, *Government of Philip Augustus*, 15–16. In so doing he was aided by the absence of Count Henry on a diplomatic mission to Constantinople to escort Louis' daughter Agnes to marry the emperor's son (*GH*, I, 239).

42. Ralph of Diss notes that he had publicly sworn to King Louis 'custodiendo, protegendo, legaliter instruendo' his son (Diceto, II, 8).

43. Gilbert of Mons, ch. 94; trans. Napran, 74, n. 304. Isabella was the daughter of Baldwin, count of Hainault (1171–95) and Margaret, Count Philip's sister.

44. Diceto, II, 5; Baldwin, *Government of Philip Augustus*, 15.

45. *GH*, I, 245–6; Diceto, II, 5. For the coronation prerogatives of the archbishop of Rheims, see E. A. R. Brown, '"Franks, Burgundians and Aquitainians" and the Royal Coronation Ceremony in France', *Transactions of the American Philosophical Society*, 82 (1992), 1–189, at 35, n. 136.

46. Diceto, II, 6; Baldwin, *Government of Philip Augustus*, 16.

47. Diceto, II, 4; *GH*, I, 244.

48. Diceto, I, 5.

49. *GH*, I, 245; Diceto, II, 5. The Young King had sailed from Dover before Easter (20 April), while his father crossed from Portsmouth.

50. GH, I, 246; Howden, II, 196.

51. *De principis*, 188–90; Gilbert of Mons, ch. 95.

52. *GH*, I, 246; Diceto, II, 6.

53. *GH*, I, 246–7.

54. *GH*, I, 247–9; Diceto, II, 6; *Recueil des actes de Philippe Auguste*, ed. H.-F. Delaborde, C. Petit-Dutaillis, J. Boussard and M. Nortier, 5 vols (Paris, 1916–2004), I, no. 7.

55. T. de Hemptinne, 'Aspects des relations de Philippe Auguste avec la Flandre au temps de Philippe d'Alsace', *La France de Philippe Auguste*, ed. Bautier, 255–62.

56. Gilbert of Mons, chs 96, 97, 99. Howden confuses this conflict with the count of Flanders' subsequent hostilities against Raoul de Clermont (*GH*, I, 277; Cartellieri, *Philipp August*, 102, n. 5).

57. *GH*, I, 276–7; Howden, I, 260; *Letters of Arnulf of Lisieux*, 213–15. William had come to Normandy at Henry II's command to reach a settlement of a major ecclesiastical dispute in Scotland regarding the appointment of a new bishop of St Andrews (*GH*, I, 250–1, 263–60).

58. Diceto, II, 7–8.

59. Diceto, II, 7–8.

60. Diceto, II, 8, 'totam Normanniam filii sui regis dispositionem supponeret'; trans. Hallam, *Plantagenet Chronicles*, 166.

61. *GH*, I, 284; Diceto, II, 8; Gilbert of Mons, ch. 99, trans. Napran, 77.
62. Gilbert of Mons, ch. 99. Breteuil was strategically located between Amiens and Beauvais.
63. According to Ralph of Diss, the count of Flanders had also sought the aid of Emperor Frederick to attack the king of France (Diceto, II, 8).
64. Gilbert of Mons, ch. 99; trans. Napran, 78; *GH*, I, 283–4; Diceto, II, 8.
65. Gilbert of Mons, ch. 99.
66. Diceto, II, 9: Gervase, I, 297.
67. Torigni, 300, 'obiit Hunfredus de Bohun, positus in exercitus cum rege Henrico juniore'.
68. Diceto, II, 9.
69. Diceto, II, 9.
70. Diceto, II, 9. The early thirteenth-century *Histoire des ducs*, 82, recalls how the Young King 'mena les Normans à Senslis, quant li cuens de Flandres destruisi la tierre le roi Phelippe de France, ki estoit ses serouges; et, por la paour de lui, se concorda li cuens de Flandres au roi Phelippe de France'. On this text, and for the marked Franco-Norman, rather than Anglo-Norman focus of other versions of the *Chronique de Normandie*, see G. Federenko, 'The Thirteenth-Century *Chronique de Normandie*', *ANS*, 35 (2012), 163–80, at 174–7.
71. Diceto, II, 9–10.
72. Gilbert of Mons, ch. 99.
73. *GH*, I, 284.
74. Gilbert of Mons, ch. 99. He laconically notes only that 'with the lord king of France armed for battle on one side and the count of Flanders on the other, they came to battle (but not by God's will)'. Count Philip was by no means a spent force, as his renewed campaigns in 1182 revealed.
75. Gilbert of Mons, ch. 103.
76. Ibid.; *GH*, I, 284–5; *De principis*, 189–90. The settlement is discussed by E. Van Houts, 'The Warenne View of the Past, 1066–1203', *ANS*, 103–121, at 118–119 (and Appendix II), noting the fact that Henry II's half-brother Hamelin of Warenne was married to Countess Isabelle's grand-daughter Isabelle, and that he may perhaps have played a role in these negotiations.
77. *GH*, I, 283–4. Howden believed that Philip of Flanders also surrendered a charter granted to him in 1173 by the Young King, and again quitclaimed young Henry and his brothers of all the agreements he had made with them during the war (ibid., I, 286).
78. Diceto, II, 10; GH, I, 285, and for the text of the will, Gervase, I, 298–300; *Foedera*, I, 47; *Recueil*, II, no. 612; *Letters and Charters of Henry II*, no. 1260. He may in part have been motivated to do so then because of anxieties about the Channel crossing after a period of rough weather. For a discussion of this will, and for the wider context of Angevin testamentary depositions, see Gillingham, 'At the Deathbeds of the Kings of England', 509–30; and Church, 'King John's Testament', 505–28, especially at 511.
79. Diceto, II, 10; Allen, 'Henry II and the English Coinage', *Henry II. New Interpretations*, 275.
80. Diceto, II, 10. The phenomenon of such enormous post-mortem bequests and the possible reaction of heirs is discussed by E. A. R. Brown, 'Royal Testamentary Acts from Philip Augustus to Philip of Valois', *Herrscher- und Fürstentestamente*, 415–30. Nevertheless, despite the huge bequest, Henry noted that the sum only represented 'a certain part of my money', and in 1189 Richard was said to have inherited more than 100,000 marks in his father's treasuries (Howden, III, 7–8; Gillingham, 'Deathbeds of the Kings of England', 523 and n. 64). Both William Rufus and Robert Curthose are recorded as having honoured the extensive bequests of William the Conqueror after his death in 1087 (Aird, *Robert Curthose*, 104–5).
81. *PR 25 Henry II*, 101; Norgate, *Richard*, 31.
82. Torigni, 296; Everard, *Brittany and the Angevins*, 127–31. Henry still retained the county of Nantes and the honour of Richmond in his own hands. For the date, Torigni, ed. Delisle, II, 104, n. 4.
83. Everard, *Brittany and the Angevins*, 131.
84. As the *Histoire des ducs*, 84, later noted, 'Quant li jouenes rois Henris vivoit, il li aidoit por chou que il voloit avoir la tierre de chà mer'.
85. The Astronomer, *Vita Ludovici*, ch. 4. Similarly, in 855 Charles the Bald had his son Charles the Child crowned king of Aquitaine at Limoges (*Ademari Cabannensis Chronicon*, ed. P. Bourgain (Turnhout 1999)).
86. Vincent, 'Henry II and the Poitevins', 120–4.
87. *GH*, I, 196–7; Howden, II, 147–8.
88. Vigeois, 324; Painter, 'The Lords of Lusignan', 33.
89. Diceto, II, 19.
90. Gillingham, 'Events and Opinions', 62.
91. Gillingham, 'Events and Opinions', 62 and n. 25. Between 1175 and 1183 Richard had faced a major revolt almost every year, save for a brief period between mid 1179 and 1181.

92. In 1181, for example, Richard had ordered the destruction of the walls of Limoges, including the bourg of St Martial (Vigeois, 326). In 1179, Aimar of Limoges, William count of Angoulême and 'many others' left the duchy on pilgrimage, and it is probable that the undertaking of such a journey was part of the terms of peace imposed on them by Richard (Vigeois, 325).
93. Vigeois, 326.
94. *GH*, I, 292: Gillingham, *Richard I*, 66.
95. *De principis*, 247. It is unlikely that many contemporaries in the duchy would have agreed with Kate Norgate that 'his sternness towards the barons who withstood his will was none other than what Gerald represents it to have been – part of a wholesome and necessary discipline' (Norgate, *Richard*, 36–7).
96. Gervase, I, 303, 304–5. As a monk professed at Christ Church, Canterbury, by Archbishop Thomas in 1163, Gervase very probably had contact with young Henry on his pilgrimages to Becket's shrine, which may in part account for the evident esteem in which he held the Young King.
97. For Bertran's career, Padern, 12–33; and Gouiran, vii–lv.
98. 'Tortz et gerras e joi d'amor' (Padern, no. 2), ll. 212–28.
99. 'Miez sirventes vueilh far dels reis amdos' (Padern, no. 38; Gouiran, no. 32), ll. 17–24. This *sirventes* is dated to *c*.1190.
100. 'Pois Ventadorns' (Padern, no. 10; Gouiran, no. 10), ll. 31–2. For the Poitevin nobles' right to settle their quarels by warfare, Howden, III, 255, 'consuetudines et leges Pictaviae ... in quibus consuetum era tab antique, ut magnates causas suas proprias invicem gladiis allegarent'.
101. 'Ges no me desconort' (Padern, no. 17; Gouiran, no. 17), ll. 35–43; 'Pois Ventedorns', ll. 1–30. The lord of Montfort was probably Raymond of Turenne's son-in-law, Bernart du Casnac (Padern, no. 10, note to l. 2).
102. 'Pois Ventedorns', ll. 25–30 and ll. 17–24.
103. Vigeois, 330. The Puy-Saint Front district had developed around the burgeoning pilgrimage church of Saint Front, and lay immediately to the east of the *cité*, the shrunken remainder of the old Gallo-Roman town of Versunna, in which the count's castle was situated.
104. Vigeois, 330.
105. Vigeois, 330–1.
106. Vigeois, 330–1.
107. Vigeois, 318–19; A. Richard, *Histoire des comtes de Poitou, 778–1204*, II, 150–3; Gillingham, *Richard I*, 40. For Sainte Valérie, Bozoky, 'Le Culte des saints', 280–1.
108. D. F. Callahan, 'Eleanor of Aquitaine, the Coronation Rite of the Duke of Aquitaine and the Cult of St Martial of Limoges', *The World of Eleanor of Aquitaine*, ed. M. Bull and C. Léglu (Woodbridge, 2005), 29–36, noting the interpolation of a new *ordo* into an existing text in the late twelfth century, which stipulated that the new duke was not only to receive the ring of St Valerie, but was now to receive a silk mantle, a small crown, a ducal banner, sword and spurs.
109. Vigeois, 331, 'pallium, in cuius ornatu scriptum est, Henricus Rex'.
110. This would explain the comment of Torigni, 305, when describing the Young King's last days in June 1183, that he 'per guerram fere per annum Deum et sanctam ecclesiam et patrem suum offenderat'.
111. Vigeois, 330, records his presence with Henry II and an assembly of nobles at Grandmont on 24 June, the feast of St John. For his proactive support in the revolt, Everard, *Brittany and the Angevins*, 132; Gillingham, *Richard I*, 69. That Young Henry may already have made an alliance with Raymond V of Toulouse can perhaps be inferred from Bertran's comment that 'Count Raymond is honoured here, since he has newly allied himself with the king (*ar ab lo rei s'es novel-lamen afiatz*)' ('Tortz et gerras e joi d'amor', ll. 33–5). In this same *sirventes*, Bertran instructs his messenger Papiol, 'Go quickly to the Young King; tell him too much sleeping doesn't please me' (ibid., ll. 57–9).
112. Vigeois, 331.
113. 'Un sirventes on motz no faill' (Padern, no. 3; Gouiran, no. 16), ll. 36–42.
114. Vigeois, 331.
115. Vigeois, 331.
116. *GH*, I, 287–8; K. Jordan, *Henry the Lion* (Oxford, 1986), 183–4. The couple had left Germany in July 1182.
117. 'Ges de disnar non for'ormais maitis' (Padern, no. 10; Gouiran, no. 2), ll. 7–8.
118. 'Casutz sui en mal de pena' (Padern, no. 9; Gouiran, no. 3), ll. 25–36; W. Kellerman, 'Bertran de Born und Herzogin Matilda von Sachsen', *Études de civilisation médiévale (IXe–XIIe siècles): mélanges offerts à Edmond-René Crozet* (Poitiers, 1974), 447–60. It was at Argentan that Matilda gave birth to a son, whose name is unknown and who probably died young (*GH*, I, 288).

119. He took the Taillefer castle of Blanzac while Oliver, brother of the viscount of Castillon in Perigord, fortified Chalais against the duke (Vigeois, 332; *The Chronicle and Historical Notes of Bernard Itier*, ed. A. W. Lewis (Oxford, 2012), s.a 1182).
120. *GH*, I, 289.
121. *GH*, I, 289, 'pravorum usus consilio'; Howden, II, 266, where this incident is placed earlier in the year, before the peace established between Philip Augustus and Count Philip of Flanders. The *Gesta's* placing near the end of the year seems more likely.
122. *GH*, I, 288–9.
123. Everard, *Brittany and the Angevins,* 131. Henry II may have been withholding Nantes precisely because the combination of this and the rest of Brittany would give Geoffrey a position of great strategic power in relation to the other Angevin continental domains (ibid., 130).
124. Torigni, 302.
125. *GH*, I, 289.
126. *GH*, I, 274–6; Alexander III, *Epistolae, PL* CC, no. 1504. Vigeois, 330, recording Baldwin's resignation from direct rule that year, notes the king had been 'utilis ad rempublicam, armis strenuis, sed leprosus'.
127. *GH*, I, 275–6. Pope Alexander had attempted to kill two birds with one stone by authorizing Count Hugh, the nephew of Bishop Hugh de Puiset, to lead a force of Brabançons against the Muslims in Spain.
128. *Expugnatio,* 200–3; Diceto, II, 33–4.
129. *GH*, I, 78. Few details of Queen Margaret's regular outgoings are known, but it would seem likely that the payment to her in 1174–75 of £30 (or 120 *livres angevins*) for twenty-eight days' expenditure had not been exceptional (*PR 21 Henry II*, 41). If so, Henry II was being equally generous in more than doubling her allowance. By comparison, when in 1181 his natural son Geoffrey finally resigned as bishop elect of Lincoln and was made chancellor, Henry II had assigned him the annual revenue of 500 marks from the revenues of England and 500 marks from those of Normandy (*GH*, I, 272).
130. *GH*, I, 291, 'centum militibus de familia sua, scilicet regis filii sui, redderet servicia sua'.
131. *GH*, I, 291.
132. Duby, 'Youth in Aristocratic Society', 112–22.
133. Diceto, I, p. 428; Vigeois, 331, 334.
134. Such problems were inherent in the *mesnie*: the *History* had noted that William's companions in the household of William de Tancarville had been jealous of the chamberlain's favour towards him (*HWM*, ll. 774–804, 1513–14).
135. Crouch, *William Marshal*, 47.
136. E. Baumgartner, 'Trouvères et losengiers', *CCM*, 25 (1982), 171–8; Crouch, *William Marshal*, 47–8; and Aurell, *Plantagenet Empire*, 60–4, on the rivalries of the court.
137. *HWM*, ll, 6463–7, where this figure is called 'the man who had hatched, pursued and carried out that act of treachery, and was the instigator of all the harm that was done'. He cannot have been Peter FitzGuy, who had served as a seneschal to the Young King before 1177, for he had taken service with Henry II by 1181 (*HWM*, III, 102, note to line 6466; *Recueil, Introduction*, 260, 261).
138. *HWM*, ll. 5221–40; Crouch, *William Marshal*, 48.
139. For this topos in contemporary romances such as *Gui de Warewic* and *Ami et Amile*, see Crouch, *William Marshal*, 49.
140. William of Tyre, Bk XIV, chs 15–18. Charged with treason and challenged to single combat, Hugh not only failed to present himself for wager of battle but fled to the Muslims of Ascalon, with whom he then attacked the kingdom. Though Fulk succeeded in establishing peace, Hugh's subsequent assassination plunged the court into fresh scandal.
141. Angevin tradition had it that in 1000, Fulk Nerra had burned his first wife Elizabeth of Vendôme for infidelity (Norgate, *Angevin Kings*, I, 152).
142. *GH*, I, 99–101; Howden, II, 82–3. The incident is discussed by R. F. Hervey, 'Cross-Channel Gossip in the Twelfth Century', *England and the Continent in the Middle Ages: Studies in Memory of Andrew Martindale,* ed. J. Mitchell (Stamford, 2000), 48–59.
143. *Les Tristan en vers*, ed. C. Payen (Paris, 1974); Chrétien de Troyes, *Lancelot*, ed. E. Choiseul (Geneva, 1999).
144. Crouch, *William Marshal*, 49–50. Yet conversely as Ashe, 'William Marshal, Lancelot and Arthur', 32, suggests, 'the frequency of the trope in literature is almost as likely to have inspired the Marshal's enemies as his biographer; they may indeed have concoted the story because of its inherent pre-existence as a possibility'.
145. Howden's statement that in 1183 Philip received her with honour and provided for her every need hardly suggests her arrival under a cloud of shame and scandal (*GH*, I, 296).

146. *HWM*, ll. 5364–426.
147. *HWM*, ll. 5480–596; ibid., III, note to line 5492.
148. *HWM*, ll. 5491–630.
149. Torigni, 304; *GH*, I, 291; Howden, *Chronica*, II, 273, 'cum filiis et filias et familia multa'; *HWM*, ll. 5693–714, who notes it was proclaimed as far as the Empire. Patterson, 'Great Festivals in the South of France', 215–16, draws a parallel with Frederick Barbarossa's magnificent court at Mainz in 1184, at which he knighted his sons Henry and Frederick. Its exceptional splendour and cost may well have been informed by Henry II's 1182 court, at which Barbarossa's Welf rival was a principal guest, and the desire to surpass it.
150. *HWM*, ll. 5693–843.
151. *HWM*, ll. 5921–60, 6155–70; Crouch, *William Marshal*, 51–2.
152. It is notable that while in 1183 Count Philip did not prevent the Marshal from returning to the Young King, he himself stayed aloof from the war.
153. *HWM*, III, 99 note to line 5693, suggesting the possibility that the *History* may even have been presenting a muddled version of the incident involving Tancarville.
154. Map, 488–91.

Chapter 13: The Brothers' War, 1183

1. 'Ieu chan que.l reys m'en a preguat' (Padern, no. 14; Gouiran, no. 12), ll. 67–72, and 77–8. Bertran's allusion is to Charlemagne's legendary conquest of Muslim Spain.
2. *GH*, I, 292, 'sicut ligio domino suo'.
3. Vigeois, 322.
4. Now Haut-Clairvaux outside the village of Scorbé-Clairvaux (Vienne, cant. Châtellerault), where the fragmentary remains of Richard's keep still commands the countryside. The castle itself was not new, but Richard enlarged and heightened the existing donjon (M.-P. Baudry, *Châteaux 'Romans' en Poitou-Charente* (La Crèche, 2011), 153–4).
5. Norgate, *Richard the Lionheart*, 46 and n. 1. Torigni, 302, believed Clairvaux to be 'de feudo Andegavensi'.
6. Gillingham, *Richard I*, 69 and n. 53. The sensitivity of constructing a castle at Clairvaux is suggested by Torigni's statement that Richard did so secretly (*latenter*) (Torigni, 302).
7. Powicke, *The Loss of Normandy*, 191–2.
8. 'Pois Ventedorns', ll.12–16: 'I think all Angoumois has greater honour in abundance than Sir Carter, who abandoned his cart – he does not have any money, and he does not steal it without fear – for I prize a small fief with honour more than a great empire without it'. For the text of the *razo*, Gouiran, no. 10, 183–5. The unreliability of such *razos* is stressed by Moore, *The Young King*, 36–8, but he is perhaps too ready to follow A. Stimming, *Bertran de Born* (2nd edn, Halle, 1913), in dismissing the *razo*'s explanation here.
9. 'Pois Ventedorns' (Padern, no. 10; Gouiran, no. 10), ll. 33–40.
10. *GH*, I, 291; Diceto, II, 18.
11. *GH*, I, 36.
12. Gillingham, *Richard I*, 70.
13. Diceto, II, 18; *GH*, I, 291–2.
14. *GH*, I, 292. Gervase, I, 303, notably hostile to Richard, noted that he refused homage 'suae confidens tirannidi', despite his father's prayers and commands.
15. Diceto, II, 18–19.
16. Once he himself became his father's principal heir after the Young King's death, however, Richard was to change this view. He refused to contemplate ceding Aquitaine to John in 1184, and as king from 1189 treated his father's lands as an entity to be kept in his own hands.
17. Diceto, II, 18; Norgate, *Richard the Lionheart*, 49.
18. *GH*, I, 294.
19. *GH*, I, 294.
20. *GH*, I, 294–5.
21. *GH*, I, 295.
22. *GH*, I, 295.
23. *GH*, I, 295.
24. *GH*, I, 292.
25. Diceto, II, 19.
26. *HWM*, ll. 6340–5.
27. Vigeois, 332.
28. Vigeois, 332; *GH*, I, 296.

29. *GH*, I, 292.
30. *GH*, I, 293–4, 295; *HWM*, ll. 6384–7, noting that on the Young King's orders Geoffrey had collected 'a bold and powerful company of good knights'. For Geoffrey's ability to raise knights in Brittany, whether directly from tenants of the ducal domains or the levying of the wider obligation of *exercitus* in the duchy as a whole, see Everard, *Brittany and the Angevins*, 106–7, 133.
31. *De principis*, I: 8.
32. *HWM*, ll. 6360–8.
33. Vigeois, 332: 'Pois Ventedorns' (Padern, no. 10; Gouiran, no. 10), ll. 1–2, where Bertran also mentions Guillem de Gourdon as a member of the league.
34. The Lusignans are listed among those whom Bertran de Born calls on for aid, together with Geoffrey de Rancon and Aimery VII, viscount of Thouars ('Pois Ventedorns' (Padern, no. 10; Gouiran, no. 10), ll. 25–30).
35. HWM, ll. 6413, and ll. 6517–6524, where improbably the *History* has Geoffrey praise the Marshal and advise the Young King to recall him to his service.
36. *HWM*, ll. 6356–60.
37. *HWM*, l. 6395, and ll. 6388–92. The only one of the Young King's household knights to be mentioned by name in reference to the muster at Limoges and the ensuing siege is the Flemish knight, Roger de Jouy (*HWM*, l. 6414, and for this knight, *HWM*, III, 78–9, note to l. 3385). Gerald of Wales similarly notes that young Henry was aided by 'the flower of the young knights of France (*electa Gallice milicie iuventute*)' (*Expugnatio*, 196–7).
38. For the *routiers*, see above, 165–6, 169–70, 193, 202, and for an important recent analysis of these bands and their impact, see J. France, 'Capuchins as Crusaders: Southern Gaul in the Twelfth Century', *Reading Medieval Studies*, 36 (2010), 77–93; idem, 'People against Mercenaries: The Capuchins in Southern Gaul', *Journal of Medieval Military History*, 8 (2010), 1–22; and idem, 'Mercenaries and Capuchins in Southern France', *Shipping, Trade and Crusade in the Medieval Mediterranean. Studies in Honour of John Pryor*, ed. R. Gurtwagen and E. Jeffreys (Aldershot, 2012), 289–315.
39. Map, 118–19.
40. France, 'Mercenaries and Capuchins', 293–5.
41. C. Devic and J.-J. Vaissete, *Histoire générale de Languedoc*, ed. A Molinier et al. (16 vols, Toulouse, 1872–1904), 1878, VIII, 341.
42. Cheyette, *Ermengard of Narbonne*, 277.
43. Rigord, 166–7; Cheyette, *Ermengard of Narbonne*, 279, who also suggests that the 'Asperes' and 'Pailer' mentioned by Vigeois were bands drawn from Aspres and Pallars in the Pyrenees; P. Contamine, *War in the Middle Ages* (Oxford, 1984), 244; France, 'Mercenaries and Capuchins', 290–1.
44. Map, 118–19, who counted among their number 'men banished for sedition, false clerics, runaway monks, all those who have forsaken God'. *Chronicon universale anonymi Laudunensis (1154–1219)*, ed. A. Cartellieri and W. Stechele (Leipzig and Paris, 1929), 37, lists bands 'Rutariorum, Arragonensium, Basculorum, Brabancionum et aliorum conducticiorum'. Map, 328, gives a still fuller range, noting the operation in Aquitaine of 'primo Basculi, postmodum Teuthonici Flandrenses et, ut rustice loquar, Brabansons, Hannuyers, Asperes, Pailer, Navar, Turlau, Vales, Roma, Coterel, Catalans, Aragones'. They were also known by other generic terms, 'Coterellis', 'Triaverdinis' or 'Rutharii' (C. J. Hefele, *Histoire des Conciles*, ed. H. Leclerq, 9 vols, Hildesheim, 1973, 5:2 1106–8). For a discussion of these terms, France, 'Mercenaries and Capuchins', 290–1.
45. Torigni, 282, for example, noted how in 1179, when Richard had disbanded his army after the fall of Taillebourg and his defeat of the Poitevin rebels, a force of 'Basques, Navarrese and Brabanters' sacked and burned Bordeaux.
46. Vigeois, 334. On the black reputation of these forces for atrocities, Strickland, *War and Chivalry*, 297–302.
47. Map, 118–19.
48. Diceto, I, 407, describing the Brabançons in the pay of the count of Angoulême in 1176.
49. Vigeois, 323; Diceto, I, 407.
50. *Histoire des Conciles*, 5: 2, 1106–8.
51. These measures were detailed by the archbishop of Narbonne in a letter to his suffragans sent shortly after his return from the Lateran Council; Devic and Vaissete, *Histoire générale de Languedoc*, VIII, 341; Cheyette, *Ermengard of Narbonne*, 277.
52. *GH*, I, 293.
53. Vigeois, 332.
54. Vigeois, 332.
55. *GH*, I, 293.
56. Howden, II, 274.

57. *GH*, I, 293.

58. *GH*, I, 296; Vigeois, 332.

59. Vigeois, 333. On the topography of medieval Limoges, see B. Barrière, 'Une agglomération double (XIe–XIIe siècles)', *Histoire de Limoges*, ed. L. Pérouas (Toulouse, 1989), 61–82; and idem, 'The Limousin and Limoges in the Twelfth and Thirteenth Century', *Enamels of Limoges, 1100–1350*, ed. J. P. O'Neil (Metropolitan Museum of Art, New York, 1996), 22–32.

60. Vigeois, 332.

61. *GH*, I, 296. For the events at Limoges and the ensuing campaign between February and June 1183, we are almost wholly reliant on the testimony of Geoffrey of Vigeois and of Roger of Howden. Their narratives are often vague, fragmented and sometimes contradictory. Howden may have been in the Limousin for part of this period, but it is evident that during the final stages of the Young King's struggle with his father he was away on royal business, and that the reports he received from those with the king were rumours or allegations about the Young King's supposed conduct rather than careful reportage. Similarly, much depends on the dating of the relevant poems of Bertran de Born, but their chronology is at best tentative. The resulting difficulty even in reconstructing the sequence of events is reflected in the differing narratives provided by Norgate, *Richard the Lionheart,* and Gillingham, *Richard I.* What follows here differs in places from both, but can only be equally tentative. That given in F. Marvaud, *Histoire des vicomtes et de la vicomté de Limoges*, 2 vols (Paris, 1873), I, 239–60, is confused and unreliable.

62. Vigeois, 332; *GH*, I, 296.

63. *GH*, I, 296

64. Vigeois, 332, who calls it a 'castrum'.

65. Vigeois, 332.

66. Vigeois, 332, who notes of Henry II that the inhabitants of the Château 'irritaverunt eum graviter, idcirco noluit consolari leviter'.

67. *GH*, I, 296.

68. Vigeois, 332–3,'propugnacula ac defensacula lignea multiplicia super muros'.

69. Vigeois, 333. He adds, ironically, 'and had they not been prevented by an enemy of the king, the burgesses would have shaved the beard of the great bishop St Augustine [i.e destroyed the outer buildings of the monastery of St Augustine's] with the same razor as with St Martin's.'

70. Vigeois, 333.

71. Sancho's toponym appears in two forms, that of Séranne, an upland region in the Hérault (Norgate, *Richard the Lionheart*, 53), or as Savannac, a village also in the Hérault (*RHF*, XVIII, 214; Cheyette, *Ermengard of Narbonne*, 282).

72. Vigeois, 333, noting that this was on 13 February.

73. Vigeois, 333.

74. Vigeois, 333, 334, dating the attack on Brive to 27 February.

75. 'Pois Ventedorns', ll. 41–6.

76. Vigeois, 334; France, 'Mercenaries and Capuchins', 3 and n. 13, who renders this as 'sleepers on straw'; Cheyette, *Ermengard of Narbonne*, 279–80.

77. Vigeois, 334.

78. Vigeois, 334, who places these events 'during the days of Lent', and dates the sack of Brantôme to 26 February. In 1183, Lent began on 13 February, with Easter Day falling on 17 April.

79. Vigeois, 334.

80. *HWM*, ll. 6371–82; Vigeois, 334.

81. Vigeois, 334–5. Henry, however, appears to have returned briefly to Poitiers, where he is found on 3 March (*Recueil*, II, no. 639).

82. *GH*, I, 297.

83. *GH*, I, 297, calls the lands so ravaged 'terra regis', but these were presumably those of the duke, or of Richard and Henry's supporters.

84. *Expugnatio*, 196–7; *Topographica Hibernica*, 200; *De principis*, 176, 178; Gillingham, *Richard I*, 68; 'Rassa, tant creis e mont'e poia' (Padern, no. 13; Gouiran, no. 1), l.1 and Padern, no. 13, note to line 1. To Howden, he was 'the son of treason *(filius proditionis)*' (*GH*, I, 297).

85. Everard, *Brittany and the Angevins*, 135.

86. 'D'un sirventes no.m cal farloignor ganda' (Padern, no. 11; Gouiran, no. 11), ll. 33–6.

87. In a *sirventes* composed shortly after the Young King's death, but before the final suppression of the rebellion in Aquitaine, he notes, 'If Count Geoffrey doesn't go away [from the Limousin] he will have both Poitou and Gascony – even though he doesn't know how to please the ladies' – 'Seignur en coms, a blasmar' (Padern, no. 16; Gouiran, no. 19), ll. 49–51.

88. According to William of Newburgh, Geoffrey later tried to obtain Anjou from Henry II, but when Richard refused to countenance this, Geoffrey went over to Philip Augustus, who 'busied himself in the matter' (WN, I, 235). One way in which he did so was by granting Geoffrey the seneschalship of France, 'which pertains to Anjou' (*De principis*, 176). Geoffrey's claims to Anjou may also in part explain the alacrity with which the Angevin baronage supported the claim of Arthur and Constance against that of John in 1199 on the death of Richard.
89. *GH*, I, 297.
90. *GH*, I, 297, 'ut ex post facto apparuit'.
91. 'D'un sirventes no.m cal farloignor ganda', ll. 1–8.
92. Ibid., ll. 9–24; Padern, no. 11, notes to lines 12 and 13. The tower of Mirmanda was part of the castle in Orange, stormed by William in the chanson *Prise d'Orange*, part of the larger cycle, the *Geste de Guillaume d'Orange*. See D. Boutet, *Le Cycle de Guillaume d'Orange, anthologie* (Paris, 1996); and P. E. Bennett, *The Cycle of Guillaume d'Orange or Garin de Monglane: a Critical Bibliography* (Woodbridge, 2004).
93. 'D'un sirventes no.m cal farloignor ganda', ll. 25–32.
94. *GH*, I, 297.
95. *GH*, I, 297.
96. Map, 282–3.
97. Gillingham, *Richard I*, 67, suggests that his actions 'bear the marks of a man tormented by uncertainty and doubt'.
98. *GH*, I, 298.
99. *GH*, I, 298.
100. *GH*, I, 298–9.
101. John Gillingham has plausibly suggested that Howden had been sent from the Limousin to England as one of Henry II's messengers to order the chapter of Lincoln to elect Walter of Coutances to the bishopric, which would also explain his knowledge of the Young King's attempt to contest Walter's election. Howden may have attended the ecclesiastical assembly at Caen on 26 May, or at least had access to good information about it (Gillingham, 'Events and Opinions', 79–81).
102. Vigeois, 335, who also notes how the body of St Julian and other saints taken from the destroyed abbey of St Martin's were translated to St Martial's.
103. Vigeois, 335.
104. *HWM*, ll. 6459–512, 6513–606.
105. *PR 29 Henry II*, 148–9.
106. Vigeois, 335. Henry II also ordered the confiscation of any lands Geoffrey held in England.
107. Vigeois, 335.
108. *Commemoratio Abbatum Basilice S. Marcialis*, in *Chroniques de Saint-Martial de Limoges*, ed. H. Duples-Agier (Paris, 1874), 14, 'ad instar palacii regalis'; Callahan, 'Eleanor of Aquitaine, the Coronation Rite of the Duke of Aquitaine and the Cult of St Martial of Limoges', 35. By the early thirteenth century, it controlled some 84 dependent houses. See C. de Lasteyrie, *L'Abbaye de Saint-Martial de Limoges* (Paris, 1901).
109. Vigeois, 335–6; *The Chronicle of Bernard Itier*, 52–5, gives the total as 52 marks of gold and 103 of silver.
110. Vigeois, 335–6; *The Chronicle of Bernard Itier*, 226–7.
111. Vigeois, 335–6. Roger of Howden believed that it was Count Geoffrey who, under the guise of a truce to speak with his brother, had plundered the shrine of St Martial, and that the sum taken, 'according to the estimate of good men', was 52 marks of gold and 27 marks of silver (*GH*, I, 299).
112. 'Ieu chan que.l reys m'en a preguat' (Padern, no. 14; Gouiran, no. 12), ll. 9–12.
113. *GH*, I, 294. Queen Eleanor had remained under comfortable house arrest, and the troubles of 1183 do not seem to have adversely affected the conditions of her confinement (Turner, *Eleanor*, 243).
114. *PR 29 Henry II*, 40, 153–4. Allowances were paid from these monies for the upkeep of Earl Robert and his family; the countess and her daughter received 3 shillings a day for food and clothing. Leicester's lands were restored a year later (*PR 30 Henry II*, xxiv).
115. *PR 29 Henry II*, 121.
116. *GH*, I, 294.
117. *PR 29 Henry II*, xxiii, 19, 20, 118, 119, 138, 160.
118. 'Ieu chan que.l reys m'en a preguat', ll. 37–42.
119. *GH*, I, 299 and n. 2. As Howden had stated clearly that Walter was elected 'per mandatum regis', Stubbs' suggestion is surely correct that a word in Howden's subsequent text was missing, and that it should read 'Quod cum regi *filio* nunciatum esset [i.e Coutances' election], respondit quod non permitteret illum esse episcopum in regno suo qui sine ejus consensus et voluntate electus fuit'.

Walter was subsequently consecrated at Angers, 'in the chapel of the lord king and in his presence', by Archbishop Richard of Canterbury (Torigni, 305).
120. Map, 280–1.
121. 'Ieu chan que.l reys m'en a preguat', ll. 31–6. According to Wace, *Roman de Rou*, ll. 3925–6, 'Valie!' was the war cry of the Angevins.
122. M. Prestwich, *Armies and Warfare in the Middle Ages: The English Experience* (New Haven, Conn., and London, 1996), 128–9.
123. Peter of Blois, *Epistolae*, letter 69, col. 214: 'Et unde haec proditoriae factionis iniquitas, ut Andegavensis exercitus, tanquam transfuga et desertor domininum suum in acie hostilitibus cuneis fugiendo exponeret?'
124. Vigeois, 336, who notes, without further explanation, that Henry II left Limoges after Easter. The king's movements, however, are difficult to trace, reflecting the absence from his court of Roger of Howden, who gives no information about Henry II's actions between Easter and the death of the Young King on 11 June.
125. Vigeois, 336.
126. Vigeois, 336.
127. Vigeois, 336. For Henry II's patronage of the abbey, Hallam, 'Henry II, Richard I and the Order of Grandmont', 165–86; Hutchison, *The Hermit Monks of Grandmont*, 57–62; J. Martin and L. E. M. Walker, 'At the Feet of St Stephen Muret: Henry II and the Order of Grandmont *redivivus*', *JMH*, 16 (1990), 1–12.
128. Vigeois, 336.
129. Thus, for example, John, count of Eu (1140–70), had extorted treasure from his abbey of Le Tréport to meet the heavy costs of the 1166 campaign, when Eu was invaded by the counts of Flanders, Boulogne and Ponthieu (*Cartulaire de l'abbaye de St-Michel de Tréport*, ed. P. Laffleur de Kermaingant (Paris, 1880), 63–4; *HWM*, III, 62, note to line 827).
130. Vigeois, 336; and for Raymond's involvement, 'Pois Ventedorns', l. 2.
131. 'Ieu chan que.l reys m'en a preguat', ll. 61–6. Padern, no. 14, note to line 63, reads 'Champagne' as an allusion to French mercenaries sent by King Philip, but there seems no reason why it could not refer to the assistance of the count of Champagne himself.
132. 'Pois Ventedorns', ll. 17–24.
133. Map, 280–1.
134. *HWM*, ll. 6607–64. It is more than unlikely, however, that King Henry gave the Marshal letters patent giving him 'absolute leave to fight him, set fire to his property and do all within his power to do' (ibid., ll. 6657–64).
135. *HWM*, ll. 6669–76; *CDF*, I, no. 35; Torigni, ed. Delisle, II, 121, n. 1; Delville, *Tombeaux de la cathédrale de Rouen*, 162.
136. *GH*, I, 300; Howden, II, 278.
137. Peter of Blois, *Epistolae*, no. 47 (wrongly dated 1174) (*PL*, CCVII, cols 157–41).
138. *GH*, I, 303.
139. Vigeois, 336.
140. Mason, 'Rocamadour in Quercy', 39–54.
141. Vigeois, 336; Howden, II, 278. The Young King is also said to have taken Durendal, Roland's famous sword, which, legend had it, had been miraculously transported to Rocamadour from the battlefield at Roncesvalles where Roland had fallen (Norgate, *Angevin Kings*, II, 226–7, followed by E. Mason, 'The Hero's Invincible Weapon: an Aspect of Angevin Propaganda', *The Ideals and Practice of Medieval Knighthood*, III, ed. C. Harper-Bill and R. Hervey, 121–37, at 126–7). Durendal is not, however, mentioned by Howden in either the *Gesta* or the *Chronica*, nor by Vigeois, and there seems no contemporary authority for the story. For Durendal, G. J. Brault, *The Song of Roland. An Analytical Edition*, 2 vols (University Park, Pa., and London, 1978), I, 252–3.
142. *GH*, I, 301–2.
143. *GH*, I, 300.
144. *GH*, I, 300; Howden, II, 278.
145. Vigeois, 338.

Chapter 14: *Vir Sanctus*

1. *Anthology of Troubadour Lyric Poetry*, ed. A. R. Press (Edinburgh, 1971), 24–5 (no. 6).
2. M. Evans, *The Death of Kings. Royal Deaths in Medieval England* (London, 2006), 105–15, gives a valuable discussion of the Young King's death, which is also used as a case study of the problems of constructing 'la vie affective' by H. Vollrath, 'Aliénor d'Aquitaine et ses enfants: une relation affective', *Plantagenêts et Capétiens: confrontations et héritages*, ed. M. Aurell and N.-Y. Tonnerre (Brepols, 2006), 113–23, at 119–23.

3. *GH*, I, 300.
4. *Magistri Thomae Agnelli, Wellensis archidiaconi, Sermo de morte et sepulture Henrici regis junioris* (hereafter *De morte*), in *Radulphi de Coggeshall Chronicon Anglicanum*, ed. J. Stevenson (Rolls Series, London, 1875), 265–6; Howden, I, lxvii; Vigeois, 337–8; *CDF*, I, no. 37. On his own deathbed in 1189, Henry II is said to have given his natural son Geoffrey a 'very fine golden ring with a leopard, which he greatly treasured (*annulum aureum optimum cum pantera, quam valde carum habebat*)', and which he had originally intended to send to his son-in-law, Alfonso of Castile (Gerald, *De vita Gaufridi*, 371).
5. Torigni, 306; Evans, *The Death of Kings*, 109.
6. Torigni, 306; *GH*, I, 301.
7. *GH*, I, 300.
8. Torigni, 305; Vigeois, 336, 'justo Dei judicio percussus'; WN, I, 233, noting that 'by the judgment of God' he was attacked by a fever, 'the avenger of both his faithless acts'.
9. Map, 280–1.
10. This tympanum is illustrated in J. Evans, *Art in Medieval France, 987–1498* (London, 1948), plate 248, where it is given a mid-twelfth-century date. Bishop Hugh of Lincoln was said to have drawn the attention of the newly crowned King John to the figures of the damned on the tympanum of Fontevraud abbey as a warning to rule justly (Adam of Eynsham, *The Life of St Hugh of Lincoln*, ed. D. Farmer, 2 vols (Oxford, 1961–1962), II, 140–1, and for wider context, A. Musson, 'Controlling Human Behaviour? The Last Judgment in Late Medieval Art and Architecture', *Theorizing Legal Personhood in Late Medieval England*, ed. A. D. Boboc (Leiden, 2015), 166–91).
11. *HWM*, ll. 6884. For approaches to death and the *ars moriendi* see D. Crouch, 'The Troubled Deathbeds of Henry I's Servants: Death, Confession and Secular Conduct in the Twelfth Century', *Albion*, 34 (2002), 24–36; and idem, 'The Culture of Death in the Anglo-Norman World', *Anglo-Norman Political Culture and the Twelfth-Century Renaissance*, ed. C. W. Hollister (Woodbridge, 1997), 157–80.
12. Howden, II, 278–9. The Angevin chroniclers were anxious to stress that he had performed penance in the presence of, and been shriven by, men of suitable piety. Thus, for example, Ralph Niger, *Chronicle*, 93, noted that he died 'sub testimonio sanctorum virorum, in sancta devotione', and Torigni, 305, recorded his absolution 'a quodam sanctissimo episcopo et multis aliis'.
13. Vigeois, 337.
14. Howden, II, 279.
15. Howden, II, 279; Vigeois, 336–7. Examination of the tomb of the Young King's sister Eleanor at the Castilian royal mausoleum at Las Huelgas revealed that a number of richly decorated cushions had been placed at her feet and her head (M. Gómez-Moreno, *El Pantéon Real de las Huelgas de Burgos* (Madrid, 1946), 27, 68, 87–8).
16. Evans, *The Death of Kings*, 110.
17. William of Malmesbury, *Gesta regum*, I, 438–9, who has Fulk cry, 'Reject not, O Lord, Thy piteous servant Fulk, Thy perjurer, Thy renegade. Accept a penitent soul, Lord Jesus Christ'. For the context of Fulk's contrition, see B. Bachrach, 'The Pilgrimages of Fulk Nerra, count of the Angevins, 987–1040', *Religion, Culture and Society in the Early Middle Ages* (Studies in Medieval Culture, xxiii, Kalamazoo, Mich., 1987), 205–17.
18. Suger, *Vie de Louis*, 284.
19. *De morte*, 266–7. Nevertheless, when young Henry respectfully bowed to the wishes of clergy, the ring could not be removed, a sign of divine recognition of his father's forgiveness (ibid., 267).
20. *HWM*, ll. 6891–2, 'son testament qu'il fist bien e menbreement'. The *History*, l. 6968, again refers to the Young King's 'testement', including his bequests and instructions as to his burial.
21. Howden, II, 279. The future Louis VII had promised his elder brother Philip that he would complete his unfulfilled vow to go on pilgrimage to Jerusalem, a pledge which it was claimed was among the chief reasons that Louis went on crusade; Odo of Deuil, *De profectione Ludovici VII in Orientem*, ed. and trans. V. G. Berry (1948), 6–7; Pacaut, *Louis VII*, 47.
22. *HWM*, ll. 6891–905.
23. Vigeois, 337.
24. Vigeois, 338.
25. Torigni, 307.
26. William de Mandeville, for example, who died in Normandy and whose body could not be transported back to his family foundation at Walden because of the danger of winter storms, had his heart sent there, but his body was buried at the abbey of Mortemer (*Foundation of Walden*, 84, n. 64). For the division of the corpse, see E. A. R. Brown, 'Death and the Human Body in the Later Middle Ages: Boniface VIII and Legislation on the Division of the Corpse', *Viator*, 12 (1981), 221–70; D. Westerhof, *Death and the Noble Body in Medieval England* (Woodbridge, 2008); and I. Warntjes, 'Programmatic Double Burial (Body and Heart) of the European High Nobility,

*c.*1200–1400. Its Origin, Geography, and Functions', *Death at Court,* ed. K. H. Spiess and I. Warntjes (Wiesbaden 2012), 197–259.

27. Rouen, Archives départementales de la Seine-Maritime, G 3569 (3); *CDF,* I, no. 38; and above, ch. 2, n. 162; Howden, I, lxvii; Vigeois, 338; *HWM,* ll. 69671–73.

28. Bodleian MS Laud Misc. 71, f. 118v.

29. *HWM,* ll. 6912–15.

30. Howden, II, 279.

31. *GH,* I, 300, 'quod unicuique quod promeruerat, servitia sua solveret'.

32. *GH,* I, 301; Diceto, II, 19.

33. Diceto, II, 19. For Anglo-Norman prejudice against the inhabitants of Aquitaine reflected in Ralph's comment, Gillingham, 'Events and Opinions', 58–65.

34. Diceto, II, 20.

35. Vigeois, 338.

36. Howden, II, 367; *De principis,* III: 28.

37. Vigeois, 338; and for Theobald, E. Kartusch, *Das Kardinalskollegium in der Zeit von 1181–1227* (Wien, 1948), no. 105.

38. Vigeois, 338; *GH,* I, 300: Howden, II, 280. Howden believed that the Young King's *familiares* had buried his entrails and brain at Martel, but Vigeois' better-informed testimony is to be preferred.

39. Diceto, II, 20; Vigeois, 338; *Gesta,* I, 300, 303; Howden, II, 280. A very similar process is recorded on the death of Earl Geoffrey de Mandeville in 1166, when his attendants 'immediately removed the entrails and brain from the corpse and buried them reverently in a consecrated place, with gifts of alms. When salt had been put over all the rest of the body, including the heart, and it had been wrapped in the finest hide, they carefully sewed it up and enclosed it securely in a casket made of fir wood, and having wrapped this in an embroidered cloth, they put it on a wagon', drawn by horses (*Foundation of Walden,* 38–9).

40. Vigeois, 338.

41. Vigeois, 338; *GH,* I, 301.

42. *HWM,* ll. 7044–6, 'for he loved him beyond all others'.

43. Peter of Blois, *Epistolae,* no. 2 (*PL,* CCII, cols 3–6).

44. *GH,* I, 302–3; Vigeois, 338; *HWM,* ll. 7047–9, 'but the king was of such disposition that nobody could perceive for a moment any change to his countenance'.

45. *GH,* I, 302–3.

46. Vigeois, 337. Though no details of the rout of Raymond survive, the poet Ambroise deemed it important enough to be recounted as one of Richard's God-given victories by a royal chaplain in 1192 during the Third Crusade (*Estoire de la Guerre Sainte,* ll. 9609–14). Bertran de Born's antipathy to Alfonso was reflected in two biting *sirventes* possibly written in 1183, 'Pois lo gens terminitz floritz' and 'Qan vei pels vergegiers despleiar' (Padern, nos 21 and 22; Gouiran, nos 23, 24). Cf. L. E. Kastner, 'Bertran de Born's Sirventes against King Alphonso of Aragon', *Modern Philology,* 34 (1937), 225–48.

47. 'Ges no me desconort' (Padern, no. 17; Gouiran, no. 17), ll. 1–75; Vigeois, 337; Norgate, *Richard the Lionheart,* 40–56; Gillingham, *Richard I,* 66–76.

48. Vigeois, 339. The Capuchins are discussed in detail by France, 'People against Mercenaries', 13–22, and idem, 'Mercenaries and Capuchins', 295–312.

49. *GH,* I, 304.

50. *GH,* I, 303.

51. Map, 280–1. Howden also noted 'defuncto ita rege filio, omnia in pace facta sunt' (*GH,* I, 304).

52. Diceto, II, 19.

53. *Biographies des troubadours: textes provençaux des XIII et XIVe siècles,* ed. J. Boutière and A.-H. Shulz (2nd edn, Paris, 1974), 92, 107–8; Gouiran, I, 3–4 (Vida, II); Clédat, *Bertran de Born,* 57–8; Norgate, *Angevin Kings,* II, 231.

54. *HWM,* ll. 7063–155. For the wider context of the incident with Sancho, see D. Crouch, 'William Marshal and the Mercenariat', *Mercenaries and Paid Men: The Mercenary Identity in the Middle Ages,* ed. J. France (Leiden, 2008), 15–32.

55. *HWM,* ll. 7239–58; Crouch, *William Marshal,* 55–6.

56. *GH,* I, 303; Torigni, 163. Geoffrey's tomb, which may well have had an effigy, was situated before the altar of the Crucifix, in front of the second main pillar of the nave, to which the famous enamel plaque was attached (D. Christophe, 'La Plaque de Geoffroy Plantagenêt dans la cathédrale du Mans', *Hortus Artium Medievalium,* 10 (2004), 75–80).

57. *GH,* I, 303; Diceto, II, 20.

58. Such hijacking did not stand in isolation. *The Foundation of Walden,* 38–41, for example, records how in 1166 the mother of Earl Geoffrey de Mandeville appropriated his body from his chosen burial site at Walden in favour of her own foundation of Chicksands, so that 'she might ever afterwards have all her son's relatives and closest friends to assist in the promotion of her monastery'.

59. *GH*, I, 303–4.

60. *CDF*, I, nos 35–8, and above, 35, n. 150. The testimony of Bishop Bertran is given in Howden, I, lxvii.

61. *De morte*, 269–72; Eyton, 251; P. B. Gams, *Series episcoporum ecclesiae catholicae* (Regensburg, 1873), 614; D. Spear, 'Les Doyens du chapitre cathédrale de Rouen, durant la période ducale', *Annales de Normandie*, 33 (1983), 91–119, at 102–3; *Fasti ecclesiae Gallicanae, 2, Diocèse de Rouen*, ed. V. Tabbagh (Turnhout, 1998), 77. Robert's efforts on this mission may perhaps have been closely linked to his attempts to secure election to the archbishopric of Rouen as successor to Rotrou. Among those who accompanied the Young King's body from Le Mans to Rouen was Ivo, arch-deacon of Rouen (*De morte*, 269); Eyton, 251. For context, D. Spear, 'Les Chanoines de la cathéd-rale de Rouen pendant la period ducale', *Annales de Normandie*, 41 (1991), 135–76.

62. Diceto, II, 230, 'on the north side'; *HWM*, ll. 7157–72.

63. Torigni, 306. Cf. L. Musset, 'Les Sépultures des souverains normands: un aspect de l'idéologie du pouvoir', *Autour du pouvoir ducal normand, Xe–XIIe siècles*, ed. L. Musset, J.-M. Bouvris and J.-M. Maillefer (Cahiers des Annales de Normandie, 17, Caen, 1985), 19–44.

64. Schlicht, *La Cathédrale de Rouen vers 1300*, 347–55. Choosing to break with traditional Capetian practice of burial in St Denis, Louis was interred as his own foundation of Cistercians at Barbeau (Fleury), where his widow Adela of Champagne had a full-sized effigy of the king erected over his tomb (A. Erlande-Brandenburg, *Le Roi est mort. Etudes sur les funérailles, les sépultures et les tombeaux des rois de France jusqu'à la fin du XIII siècle* (Geneva, 1975), 75–7, 87–8, 161–2; 111–12, Hallam, 'Royal Burial', 369; E. A. R. Brown, 'Burying and Unburying the Kings of France', in idem, *The Monarchy of Capetian France and Royal Ceremonial* (London, 1991), 243–4, fig. 1). The tomb of Henry the Liberal (d. 1181), at the collegiate church of Saint-Etienne de Troyes, was commissioned by his widow Marie de France, the daughter of Eleanor of Aquitaine and Louis VII, and depicted him lying with his hands joined in prayer, and wearing a cap similar to that depicted on the tomb of Geoffrey Plantagenet in the enamel funerary plaque at Le Mans (A.F. Arnaud, *Voyage archéologique et pittoresque dans le département de l'Aube* (Troyes, 1837), II, pl. 14, and M. Bur, 'Les Comtes de Champagne et la "Normanitas": sémiologie d'un tombeau', *ANS* (1980), 22–32, at 22.

65. Schlicht, *La Cathédrale de Rouen vers 1300*, 347–55, with a discussion of the different dating of the effigy, as well as illustrations of the tombs and of Gagnières' drawing of the Young King's effigy. Following its mutilation, the effigy remained long buried in the sanctuary, only to suffer an unsym-pathetic restoration following its rediscovery in 1866, including of the missing head, forearms, part of the feet and the lion on which young Henry's feet rested. It was moved to its present position in the south ambulatory of the choir only in 1956 following extensive repairs to the cathedral after the damage suffered in World War Two, while the near-contemporary effigy of Richard (marking his heart-burial in the cathedral in 1199) was placed opposite in the north ambulatory (ibid.). For the discovery of the Young King's effigy, J. B. D. Cochet, 'Découverte du tombeau et de la statue de Henri Court-Mantel [*sic*] dans le choeur de la cathédrale de Rouen', *Bulletin de la Commission des antiquités de la Seine-Inférieure*, 1 (1867–1869), 93–102.

66. *Thomas Agnellus, Sermonis de diversis*, Bodleian MS Laud Misc. 71; R. Sharpe, *A Handlist of Latin Writers of Great Britain and Ireland before 1540* (Brepols, 1997, revised 2001), 639. For his kinship with Reginald, *English Episcopal Acta, X. Bath and Wells, 1061–1205*, ed. F. M. R. Ramsay (Oxford, 1995), no. 91.

67. He subsequently also obtained a canonry at Tournai (*MTB*, VII, no. 699: Duggan, *Thomas Becket*, 183). He was well connected, and may have been related to the Henry d'Earley who, with his wife and two sons, was drowned in a shipwreck while crossing with the king back from Normandy to England in March 1170 (*GH*, I, 4), where Henry is described as 'nobilissimus baronum Angliae'; Howden, II, 3–4). More certainly, he was a kinsman of Bishop Reginald, while his nephew William of Earley founded Buckland priory (*Fasti ecclesiae Anglicanae, 1066–1300*, ed. J. Le Neve, compiled by D. E. Greenway (London, 1968), VII, 31–5, 'Archdeacons of Wells').

68. Crouch, *William Marshal*, 51, n. 16; N.Vincent, 'Patronage, Politics and Piety in the Charters of Eleanor', *Plantagenêts et Capétiens*, 17–60, at 43; Turner, *Eleanor*, 244. The sermon is partly printed in Thomas Agnellus, *De morte et sepultura Henrici regis Anglie junioris* in *Radulphi de Coggeshall Chronicon Anglicanum*, ed. J. Stevenson (Rolls Series, London, 1875), 265–73, but considerable sections are omitted from the original text in Bodleian MS Laud Misc. 71, and the Young King's death is misdated to 1182.

69. WN, I, 234.

70. *HWM*, ll. 18, 468–18, 496. For a discussion of the light which the lengthy deathbed scene given in the *History* throws on late twelfth-century attitudes to death, see G. Duby, *Guillame le Maréchal ou le meilleur chevalier du monde* (Paris, 1984), 1–34; Crouch, *William Marshal*, 207–16.

71. *De morte*, 266, 267, 268.

72. *De morte*, 266–7.

73. *De morte*, 267, 'Huic ergo non debet martyrii Gloria denegari, qui tantarum persecutionum violentia vitam finivit vice gladii'.
74. *De morte*, 272–3; trans. Flori, *Eleanor*, 126. Thomas here quotes from 1 Corinthians 2:9.
75. Evans, *The Death of Kings*, 111; Matthew 8:1–4; 9:20–22.
76. *De morte*, 267. As Aurell, *Plantagenet Empire*, 114, notes, young Henry's posthumous healing of such illnesses was closely analogous to the royal 'touching' for scrofula.
77. *De morte*, 267–8.
78. *De morte*, 268.
79. *De morte*, 268; and for the shaft of light as a common hagiographical topos, Evans, *Death of Kings*, 111.
80. WN, I, 234.
81. *De morte*, 272, where the removed 'cerea signorum monimenta' may refer to ex-votos or wax effigies of afflicted limbs or bodies commonly left at such shrines by those seeking a cure (E. Duffy, *The Stripping of the Altars. Traditional Religion in England, 1400–1580*, 2nd edn, New Haven, Conn., and London, 2005, 197–9).
82. J. C. Russell, 'The Canonization of Opposition to the King in Angevin England', *Haskins Anniversary Essays*, ed. C. H. Taylor and J. L. La Monte (Boston, 1929), 279–90, reprinted idem, *Twelfth-Century Studies* (New York, 1978), 248–60.
83. Crouch, *William Marshal*, 50.
84. 'Si tuit li doil e-il plor e-il marrimen' (Gouiran, no. 14), ll. 33–40; *Anthology of Troubadour Lyric Poetry*, ed. Press, 170–1.
85. *Charters of Duchess Constance*, no. Ge7, and Plate 1; Bibliothèque Municipale de la ville de Rouen, Y.44 (Cartulary of Rouen), f. 58r. The grant was made 'by the advice of the canons of the church of Rouen', and with the consent of his wife, Constance, who also issued her own confirmation of the grant (*Charters of Duchess Constance*, 47, no. C4).
86. Cartulary of Rouen, f. 73r–v; *CDF*, I, no. 4; D. Crouch, 'The Origins of Chantries: Some Further Anglo-Norman Evidence', *JMH*, 27 (2001), 159–80, at 172. Margaret also expressed her intention to provide another endowment when she had greater resources.
87. Hawise was also a widow, for her husband Earl William had died in Henry II's custody, having been one of those arrested as a result of the Old King's reaction to the outbreak of the Young King's war in Aquitaine (Patterson, 'William, second earl of Gloucester'); and for Hawise herself, S. M. Johns, *Noblewomen, Aristocracy and Power in the Twelfth-Century Anglo-Norman Realm* (Manchester, 2003), 81–3.
88. Cartulary of Rouen, ff. 32–3; *CDF*, I, no. 46. Richard confirmed the grant the same day. It was also confirmed by Geoffrey Plantagenet, as archbishop elect of York, by Clement III and by the papal legate, John of Anagni, in 1189 (Cartulary of Rouen, f. 26; *Papsturkunden in Frankreich. II. Normandie*, ed. Ramackers, Göttingen, 1937, 387–8, no. 294; *CDF*, I, nos 48, 49 and 50; *English Episcopal Acta*, XXVII: *York,* nos 58 and 59).
89. Crouch, 'The Origins of Chantries', 172–3, 177–9; S. Marritt, 'Secular Cathedrals and the Anglo-Norman Aristocracy', *Cathedrals, Communities and Conflict in the Anglo-Norman World*, ed. P. Dalton, C. Innsley and L. Wilkinson (Woodbridge, 2011), 151–68, at 154.
90. Cartulary of Rouen, ff. 32–3; *CDF*, I, no. 46. Among the witnesses to Richard's confirmation issued the same day were two of the Young King's former associates, William Marshal and William de St John (Cartulary of Rouen, ff. 32–3; *CDF*, I, no. 47). As king, John's grant to his monastery of Beaulieu in 1205 was given for the souls of his father Henry, his brothers Henry and Richard, and his mother Eleanor, though it is notable that Geoffrey of Brittany is not mentioned (*The Cartae Antiquae Rolls 1–10*, ed. L. Landon (Pipe Roll Society, new series xvii, London, 1939)).
91. Vincent, 'Patronage, Politics and Piety', 42–3.
92. *CDF*, no. 1101; J. Martindale, 'Eleanor of Aquitaine', *Richard Coeur de Lion in History and Myth*, ed. J. Nelson (London, 1992), 17–50, at 17–18. For Eleanor's commemoration of the Young King, see also *The Early Charters of the Canons of Waltham Abbey*, ed. R. Ransford (Woodbridge, 1989), no. 297.
93. Gillingham, '*Stupor mundi*', 402, 404–6.
94. Gillingham, '*Stupor mundi*', 402, 'ante magnum altare versus meridiem ex opposite tumbe Henrici regis tercii fatris sui'; and *Annales de Wintonia*, in *AM*, II, 71.
95. Crouch, *William Marshal*, 66 and n. 16. The cartulary of Rouen also records among the abbey's precious vestments a 'chasuble of William Marshal', as well as others given by Henry's sister Matilda of Saxony (Cartulary of Rouen Cathedral, f. 26). When these were donated is unknown, but it is possible that they were intended for the priests assigned to the chantries for the Young King.
96. N. Vincent, *Norman Charters from English Sources: Antiquaries, Archives and the Rediscovery of the Anglo-Norman Past* (Pipe Roll Society, new series 59, London, 2013), no. 7, 'pro salute anime domini mei Henrici minoris regis'.

97. *English Episcopal Acta, VI: Norwich, 1070–1214*, ed. C. Harper-Bill (Oxford, 1990), Appendix I, 364, no. 68, dated 1183 x 1200 and attested by John, bishop of Norwich, who dedicated the chapel; and ibid., no. 63, 'pro salute anime tue [i.e John Lestrange] et tuorum et domini Regis Henrici junioris et Alienor regine et filiorum'. An inspeximus dated 10 April 1204 of Walter of Coutances as archbishop of Rouen, of donations to the abbey of Foucarmont in the diocese of Rouen, lists: 'Item. Pro anima Henrici Regis Anglorum Junioris decimam denariorum ministerii sui de Fulcardi monte' (de Gray Birch, 'On the Seals of King Henry the Second, and of his son the so-called Henry the Third', 336–7).

98. G. Gyorffy, 'Thomas à Becket and Hungary', *Hungarian Studies in English*, 4 (1969), 45–52; K. B. Slocum, 'Angevin Marriage Diplomacy and the Early Dissemination of the Cult of Thomas Becket', *Medieval Perspectives*, 14 (1999), 214–28 at 222; Bowie, *The Daughters of Henry II and Eleanor*, 167–8. On Margaret's marriage, *GH*, I, 346, 360; Rigord, 216–19; Z. J. Kosztolnyik, *From Colman the Learned to Béla III (1095–1196): Hungarian Domestic Policies and their Impact upon Foreign Affairs* (East European Monographs, Boulder, Colo., 1987), 212–14; and J. Laszlovsky, 'Nicholaus Clericus: a Hungarian Student at Oxford University in the Twelfth Century', *JMH*, 14 (1988), 217–31. Ralph Niger, *Chronicle*, 93, refers to Béla as 'gloriosus rex'.

99. *GH*, I, 304.

100. *GH*, I, 305; Turner, *Eleanor*, 245.

101. *GH*, I, 304–5.

102. *GH*, I, 306. It was not, however, until 1186 that Margaret issued a charter stating the final terms of the *compositio* which she had agreed with Henry II and King Philip, by which she quitclaimed her rights in return for an annuity of the considerably higher sum of 2,700 *livres angevins* to be guaranteed by the Hospitallers and Templars and paid through the latter at Paris (*The New Palaeographical Society: Facsimiles of Ancient Manuscripts*, ed. E. Maunde Thompson et al., 2 vols (London 1903–12), I, plate 123; *Recueil*, no. 660 and *Atlas*, plate xxv; *CDF*, nos 372–94). A. Sandy, 'The Financial Importance of the London Temple in the Thirteenth Century', *Essays in Medieval History Presented to T. F. Tout*, ed. A. G. Little and F. M. Powicke (Manchester, 1925), 151.

103. *GH*, I, 306.

104. Following the death of King Béla in 1196, Margaret, unlike young Henry, was able to fulfil her own vow to undertake a pilgrimage to the Holy Land. On arriving at Acre with a company of knights, she was welcomed by her nephew, Henry of Champagne, the ruler of the Latin kingdom of Jerusalem, but died shortly thereafter, and was buried in the cathedral at Tyre (Howden, IV, 14, 32; *La Continuation de Guillaume de Tyr (1184–1187)*, ed. M. R. Morgan (1184–97), Paris, 1982, c.183). During the Third Crusade, she had given a magnificent tent to Emperor Frederick Barbarossa as he was passing through the lands of his ally King Béla (*The Crusade of Frederick Barbarossa*, ed. and trans. G. Loud, Aldershot, 2013, 58).

105. Gillingham, 'Doing Homage', 77–80. I am grateful to John Gillingham for discussion of this point.

106. *GH*, I, 306.

107. *GH*, I, 306; Howden, II, 284.

108. Howden, II, 345; Diceto, II, 55; William le Breton, *Philippide*, in *Oeuvres de Rigord et de Guillaume le Breton*, ed. F. Delaborde, 2 vols (Paris, 1882), II, 70–1; L. Diggelmann, 'Hewing the Ancient Elm: Anger, Arboricide, and Medieval Kingship', *Journal of Medieval and Early Modern Studies*, 40 (2010), 249–72.

109. *GH*, I, 308.

110. Gillingham, *Richard I*, 76–9. John lacked the deeply felt support the barons of Aquitaine had given to the young Henry and was no match in the field for Richard, while Bertran de Born also suggests that many of the Aquitanian nobles had lost confidence in Geoffrey, whom they regarded as having abandoned them in 1183 to gain better terms for himself ('Qan la novella flors par el vergan', ll. 33–40).

111. 'Qan la novella flors par el vergan', ll. 33–40.

112. Gervase, I, 436; Howden, II, 355.

113. *De principis*.

114. Gillingham, *Richard I*, 94–100.

115. Samuel Daniel, *The Collection of the History of England* (London, revised edn, 1634), 92.

116. R. C. Strong, *Henry, Prince of Wales, and England's Lost Renaissance* (London, 1986); *The Lost Prince. The Life and Death of Henry Stuart*, ed. C. MacLeod (London, 2012).

117. Daniel, *Collection of the History of England*, 92.

118. Fawtier, *Capetian Kings*, 49.

119. Daniel, *Collection of the History of England*, 92.

120. Plassmann, 'The King and his Sons', 165.

121. JF, l. 152.
122. Daniel, *Collection of the History of England*, 102.
123. Gillingham, 'Problems of Integration', 116.
124. 'Mon chan fenis ab dol et ab maltraire', ll. 4–9.
125. 'Mon chan fenis ab dol et ab maltraire', ll. 61–5.
126. As Gerald of Wales commented, 'he was surrounded by an army so select and fully equipped as in our own days or before was never seen nor heard of to have followed one leader' (*De principis*, II: 10).
127. 'Si tuit l idol e.hl plor e.lh marrimen' (Gouiran, no. 14), ll. 29–32 (*Anthology of Troubadour Lyric Poetry*, ed. Press, 170–1).
128. 'Mon chan fenis ab dol et ab maltraire', ll. 43–56.
129. Gervase, *Otia imperialia*, 486–7.

Bibliography

Manuscript Sources

London, Lambeth Palace Library, MS 96
Oxford, Bodleian MS Laud Misc. 71
Rouen, Bibliothèque Municipale de la ville de Rouen, Y.44.

Printed Primary Sources

Actus pontificum Cenomannis in urbe degentium, ed. G. Busson and A. Lédru (Le Mans, 1902)
Adam of Eynsham, *The Life of St Hugh of Lincoln*, ed. D. Farmer, 2 vols (Oxford, 1961–1962)
Ademari Cabannensis Chronicon, ed. P. Bourgain (Turnhout, 1999)
Aelred of Rievaulx: The Historical Works, ed. M. L. Dutton and trans. J. P. Freeland (Kalamazoo, Mich., 2005)
Ailred of Rievaulx, *Genealogia regum Anglorum, Patrologia Latina*, cxcv, cols 711–38
Alcuini epistolae, ed. E. Dümmler, *MGH, Epistolae Karolini Aevi*, II (Berlin, 1895)
Alexander III, 'Epistolae et privilegia', *Patrologia Latina*, CC
Alexandre de Paris, *Roman d'Alexandre*, ed. E. Armstrong et al., *The Medieval French Alexander*, 2 vols (Princeton, NJ, 1937)
Ambroise, *Estoire de la guerre sainte*, ed. and trans. M. Marber and M. Ailes, 2 vols (Woodbridge, 2003)
The Anglo-Saxon Chronicle. A Collaborative Edition, ed. D. Dumville and S. Keynes (Cambridge, 1983), vol. 7. *MS E*, ed. S. Irvine (Cambridge, 2004)
—— *Two of the Saxon Chronicles Parallel*, ed. C. Plummer, 2 vols (Oxford, 1892)
Anglo-Scottish Relations, 1174–1328: Some Select Documents, ed. and trans. E. L. G. Stones (Oxford, 1970)
Annales Cestrensis (Chester Annals), ed. R. C. Christie (Lancashire and Cheshire Record Society, vol. 14, 1886)
Annales monastici, ed. H. R. Luard, 5 vols (Rolls Series, London, 1864–1869)
Annales Radingenses, in *Ungedruckte Anglo-Normanische Geschichtsquellen*, ed. F. Lieberman (Strasbourg, 1879)
Annales regni Francorum, 741–829, ed. F. Kurze, *MGH, SRG*, VI (Hanover, 1895)
Annales sancti Albini Andegavensis, in *Recueil d'annales angevines et vendômoises*, ed. L. Halphen (Paris, 1903)
Annals and Memorials of St Edmund's Abbey, ed. T. Arnold, 2 vols (Rolls Series, London, 1890)
Annals of the Reigns of Malcolm IV and William, Kings of Scotland, AD 1153–1214, ed. A. C. Lawrie (Glasgow, 1910)
Anonimi Laudenensis chronicon universale, ed. A. Cartellieri and W. Stechele (Leipzig and Paris, 1909)
Anthology of Troubadour Lyric Poetry, ed. A. R. Press (Edinburgh, 1971)
Arnulf of Lisieux, *The Letters of Arnulf of Lisieux*, ed. F. Barlow (Camden Society, 3rd series, lxi, 1939)
—— *The Letter Collections of Arnulf of Lisieux*, ed. C. P. Schriber (Lampeter, 1997)
The Astronomer, *Vita Hludowici imperatoris*, ed. E. Tremp, *MGH, SRG*, 44 (Hanover, 1995)
Benoît of St Maure, *Le Roman de Troie*, ed. L. Constans, 6 vols (Paris, 1904–1912)
Bernard Itier, *The Chronicle and Historical Notes of Bernard Itier*, ed. and trans. A. W. Lewis (Oxford, 2012)

Bertran de Born, *Poésies complètes de Bertran de Born*, ed. A. Thomas (Toulouse, 1888)
—— *L'Amour et la guerre. L'oeuvre de Bertran de Born*, ed. and trans. G. Gouiran, 2 vols (Aix-en-Provence, 1985)
—— *The Poems of the Troubadour Bertran de Born*, ed. and trans. W. D. Padern, T. Sankovitch and P. Stablein (Berkeley, 1986)
Biographies des troubadours: textes provençaux des XIII et XIVe siècles, ed. J. Boutière and A.-H. Shutz (2nd edn, Paris, 1974)
The Book of the Foundation of Walden Monastery, ed. and trans. D. Greenway and L. Watkiss (Oxford, 1999)
Brut y Tywysogion: Peniarth MS 20, ed. and trans. T. Jones (Cardiff, 1941)
Brut y Tywysogion: Red Book of Hergest Version, ed. and trans. T. Jones (Cardiff, 1955)
Calendar of Charter Rolls, 6 vols (Public Record Office, 1903–1927)
Calendar of Documents Preserved in France, 918–1208, ed. J. H. Round (London, 1899)
Calendar of Documents Relating to Scotland Preserved in Her Majesty's Public Record Office, ed. J. Bain, 5 vols (Edinburgh, 1881–1886)
The Cartae Antiquae Rolls 1–10, ed. L. Landon (Pipe Roll Society, new series, xvii, London, 1939)
The Cartae Antiquae Rolls 11–20, ed. J. Conway Davies (Pipe Roll Society, new series, xxxiii, London, 1960)
Cartulaire de l'abbaye de St-Michel de Tréport, ed. P. Laffleur de Kermaingant (Paris, 1880)
Cartularium monasterii beatae Mariae Caritatis Andegavensis, ed. P. Marchegay (Angers, 1854)
Cartularium monasterii de Ramesia, ed. W. H. Hart and P. A. Lyons, 3 vols (Rolls Series, 1884–1893)
Cartulary of the Monastery of St Frideswide, ed. S. R. Wigram, 2 vols (Oxford Historical Society, xxviii, xxxi, 1895–1896)
The Cartulary of St John's, Colchester, ed. S. Miller (Roxburghe Club, 1897)
Charters of the Anglo-Norman Earls of Chester, c. 1071–1237, ed. G. Barraclough (Lancashire and Cheshire Record Society, cxxvi, 1988)
The Charters of Duchess Constance of Brittany and her Family, 1171–1221, ed. J. Everard and M. Jones (Boydell, 1999)
Charters of the Honour of Mowbray, 1107–1191, ed. D. E. Greenway (London, 1972)
The Charters of King David I: The Written Acts of David I King of Scots, 1124–53, and of his son Henry Earl of Northumberland, 1139–52, ed. G. W. S. Barrow (Woodbridge, 1999)
Chrétien de Troyes, *Arthurian Romances*, trans. W. W. Kibler (London, 1991)
—— *Lancelot*, ed. E. Choiseul (Geneva, 1999)
Chronica de gestis consulum Andegavorum, in *Chroniques des comtes d'Anjou et des seigneurs d'Ambroise*, ed. L. Halphen and R. Poupardin (Paris, 1913)
The Chronicle of Battle Abbey, ed. and trans. E. Searle (Oxford, 1980)
The Chronicle of Hugh Candidus, ed. W. T. Mellows (Oxford, 1949)
The Chronicle of Melrose Abbey: a Stratographic Edition, Volume I, ed. D. Broun and J. Harrison (Woodbridge, 2007)
Chronicles of the Reigns of Stephen, Henry II and Richard I, ed. R. Howlett, 4 vols (Rolls Series, London, 1884–1889)
Chronicle of Richard of Devizes, ed. and trans. J. T. Appleby (London, 1963)
Chronicon monasterii de Abingdon, ed. J. Stevenson, 2 vols (Rolls Series, 1858)
Chronicon Rotomagensi, RHF, XVII.
Chronicon Turonense magnum, in *Recueil des chroniques de Touraine*, ed. A. Salmon (Tours, 1854)
Chronicon universale anonymi Laudunensis (1154–1219), ed. A. Cartellieri and W. Stechele (Leipzig and Paris, 1929)
La Chronique de Giselbert de Mons, ed. L. Vanderkindere (Brussels, 1904)
Chronique du Bec, ed. A. A. Porée (Rouen, 1883)
Chroniques des comtes d'Anjou et des seigneurs d'Ambroise, ed. L. Halphen and R. Poupardin (Paris, 1913)
The Church Historians of England, trans. J. Stevenson, 8 vols (London, 1853–1858)
Commemoratio Abbatum Basilice S. Marcialis, in *Chroniques de Saint-Martial de Limoges*, ed. H. Duples-Agier (Paris, 1874)
Concilia Rotomagensis provinciae, ed. G. Bessin, 2 vols in 1 (Rouen, 1717)
Continuatio Beccensis, in *Chronicles of the Reigns of Stephen, Henry II and Richard I*, ed. R. H. Howlett, 4 vols (Rolls Series, London, 1885), IV, 317–27
The Correspondence of Thomas Becket, Archbishop of Canterbury, 1162–1170, ed. and trans. A. J. Duggan, 2 vols (Oxford, 2000)
Councils and Synods, with other Documents Relating to the English Church, I. AD 871–1204, ed. D. Whitelock, M. Brett and C. N. L. Brooke, 2 vols (Oxford, 1981)
The Crusade of Frederick Barbarossa, ed. and trans. G. Loud (Aldershot, 2013)
Le Cycle de Guillaume d'Orange, Anthologie, ed. D. Boutet (Paris, 1996)

Dante, *The Divine Comedy, I: Inferno*, ed. and trans. J. D. Sinclair (Oxford, 1939)

The Deeds of the Normans in Ireland: La Geste des Engleis en Yrlande, ed. E. Mullally (Dublin, 2002)

Dialogus de Scaccario and the Constitutio Domus Regis, ed. and trans. E. Amt and S. Church (Oxford, 2007)

Diplomatic Documents Preserved in the Public Record Office, I (1101–1272), ed. P. Chaplais (London, 1964)

Dugdale, *Monasticon Anglicanum*, ed. J. Caley, H. Ellis and B. Bandinel, 6 vols (London, 1817–1830)

The Earldom of Chester and its Charters, ed. A. T. Thacker (Chester Archaeological Society, vol. 71 (Chester, 1991)

Earldom of Gloucester Charters, ed. R. B. Patterson (Oxford, 1973)

The Early Charters of the Augustinian Canons of Waltham Abbey, 1062–1230, ed. R. Ransford (Woodbridge, 1989)

Early Sources for Scottish History, ed. A. O. Anderson, 2 vols (Edinburgh, 1922; reprinted Stamford, 1990)

Early Yorkshire Charters, ed. W. Farrer and C. T. Clay, 12 vols (Edinburgh, 1914–1965)

English Coronation Records, ed. L. G. Wickham Legg (London, 1901)

English Episcopal Acta, I: Lincoln, 1067–1185, ed. D. M. Smith (Oxford, 1980)

English Episcopal Acta, II: Canterbury, 1162–1190, ed. C. R. Cheney and B. E. A. Jones (Oxford, 1986)

English Episcopal Acta, VI: Norwich, 1070–1214, ed. C. Harper-Bill (Oxford, 1990)

English Episcopal Acta X: Bath and Wells, 1061–1205, ed. F. M. R. Ramsay (Oxford, 1995)

English Episcopal Acta, XX: York, 1154–1181, ed. M. Lovatt (Oxford, 2000)

English Episcopal Acta, XXVII: York, 1189–1212, ed. M. Lovatt (Oxford, 2004)

English Episcopal Acta, XXXI: Ely, 1109–1197, ed. N. Karn (Oxford, 2005)

English Historical Documents, II, 1042–1189, ed. and trans. D. C. Douglas (2nd edn, Oxford, 1961)

English Lawsuits from William I to Richard I, ed. R. C. Van Caenegem, 2 vols (London, 1990–1991)

Etienne de Fougères, *Le Livre des manières*, ed. J. T. E. Thomas (Paris and Louvain, 2013)

Facsimiles of Early Charters from Northamptonshire, ed. F. M. Stenton (Northampton Record Society, 4, Northampton, 1930)

Facsimiles of Early Charters in Oxford Muniment Rooms, ed. H. E. Salter (Oxford, 1929)

Falconis Beneventi Chronicon, in *Cronistie scrittori sincroni napoletani*, ed. G. Del Re, 2 vols (Naples, 1845; reprinted Aalen, 1975), I, and trans. G. Loud and T. Wiedemann, *The History of the Tyrants of Sicily by 'Hugo Falcandus', 1154–69* (Manchester, 1998)

Fasti ecclesiae Anglicanae, 1066–1300, ed. J. Le Neve, compiled by D. E. Greenway (London, 1968–)

Florentii Wigorniensis monachi chronicon ex chronicis, ed. B. Thorpe, 2 vols (London, 1848–1849)

Fulbert of Chartres, *Letters and Poems*, ed. F. Behrends (Oxford, 1976)

Galbert of Bruges, *The Murder of Charles the Good, Count of Flanders*, trans. J. B. Ross (New York, 1960)

Geffrei Gaimar, *Estoire des Engleis*, ed. and trans. I. Short (Oxford, 2009)

Geoffrey Malaterra, *De rebus gestis Rogerii Calabriae et Siciliae comitis et Roberti Guiscardi ducis fratris eius, auctore Gaufredo Malaterra, monacho Benedictino*, ed. E. Pontieri (*Rerum Italicarum Scriptores*, Bologna, 1927–1928)

Geoffrey of Monmouth, *The Historia Regum Brittaniae of Geoffrey of Monmouth, V. Gesta Regum Britanniae*, ed. and trans. N. Wright (Cambridge, 1991)

Geoffrey of Vigeois, *Chronica*, ed. P. Labbe, *Novae Bibliothecae manuscriptorum et librorum rerum Aquitanicarum*, 2 vols (Paris, 1657)

Gerald of Wales, *Giraldi Cambrensis opera*, ed. J. S. Brewer, F. Dimock and G. Warner, 8 vols (Rolls Series, London, 1861–1891)

—— *Expugnatio Hibernica: The Conquest of Ireland, by Giraldus Cambrensis*, ed. and trans. A. B. Scott and F. X. Martin (Dublin, 1978)

—— *The History and Topography of Ireland*, trans. J. O'Meara (London, 1982)

Gervase of Canterbury, *The Historical Works of Gervase of Canterbury*, ed. W. Stubbs, 2 vols (Rolls Series, London, 1879–1880)

Gervase of Tilbury, *Otia imperialia*, ed. and trans. S. E. Banks and J. W. Binns (Oxford, 2002)

The Gesta Normannorum Ducum of William of Jumièges, Orderic Vitalis and Robert of Torigni, ed. and trans. E. M. C. van Houts, 2 vols (Oxford, 1992–1995)

Gesta regis Henrici secundi Benedicti abbatis: The Chronicle of the Reigns of Henry II and Richard I, AD 1169–1192, ed. W. Stubbs, 2 vols (Rolls Series, London, 1867)

Gesta Stephani, ed. and trans. K. R. Potter and R. H. C. Davis (Oxford 1976, reprinted 2004)

Gilbert Foliot, *The Letters and Charters of Gilbert Foliot*, ed. A. Morey and C. N. L. Brooke (Cambridge, 1967)

Gilbert of Mons, *La Chronique de Giselbert de Mons*, ed. L. Vanderkindere (Brussels, 1904), trans. L. Napran, *Gilbert of Mons, Chronicle of Hainault* (Woodbridge, 2005)

Glavill, *The Treatise on the Laws and Customs of the Realm of England commonly called Glanvill*, ed. G. D. G. Hall (London, 1965).

Grand cartulaire de Fontevraud, ed. J.-M. Bienvenue, R. Favreau and G. Pon, 2 vols (Poitiers, 2000, 2005)

Guernes, *La Vie de Saint Thomas le Martyr par Guernes de Pont-Sainte-Maxence: poème historique du XIIe siècle (1172–1174)*, ed. E. Wahlberg (Lund, 1922), trans. I. Short, *A Life of Thomas Becket in Verse* (Toronto, 2013)

—— *Garnier's Becket*, trans. J. Shirley (Chichester, 1975)

Henry of Huntingdon, *Historia Anglorum*, ed. D. Greenway (Oxford, 1996)

Herbert of Bosham, *Vita Sancti Thomae archiepiscopi et martyris, auctore Herberto de Boseham*, and *Excerpta ex Herberti de Bosham Libro Melorum* in *Materials for the History of Thomas Becket, Archbishop of Canterbury*, ed. J. C. Robertson and J. B. Sheppard, 7 vols (Rolls Series, London, 1875–1885), III, 155–534, and 535–54

L'Histoire de Guillaume le Maréchal, comte de Striguil et de Pembroke, régent d'Angleterre de 1216 à 1219: poème français, ed. P. Meyer, 3 vols (Société de l'Histoire de France, Paris, 1891–1901)

Histoire des conciles, ed. C. J. Hefele and H. Leclerq, 9 vols (Hildesheim, 1973)

Histoire des ducs de Normandie et des rois d'Angleterre, ed. F. Michel (Paris, 1840)

Historia Ecclesiae Abbendonensis, ed. J. Hudson, 2 vols (Oxford, 2002, 2007)

Historia gloriosi Ludovici VII, ed. A. Molinier (Paris, 1887)

Historiae Anglicanae scriptores decem, ed. Sir Roger Twysden (London, 1652)

Historiae Dunelmensis scriptores tres: Gaufridus de Coldingham, Robertus de Graystanes, et Willielmus de Chambre, ed. J. Raine (Surtees Society, 9, 1839)

Hugh the Chanter, *The History of the Church of York, 1066–1127*, ed. and trans. C. Johnson (London, 1961)

Ibn al-Athir, *The Chronicle of Ibn al-Athir for the Crusading Period from al-Kamil fi'l-ta'rikh. Part 2. The Years 541–589/1146–1193: The Age of Nur al-Din and Saladin*, trans. D. S. Richards (Aldershot, 2007)

Jocelin of Brakelond, *Chronica Jocelini de Brakelonda*, ed. J. G. Rokewood (Camden Society, London, 1840)

—— *Chronicle of Jocelin of Brakelond*, ed. H. E. Butler, London, 1949

John of Hexham, *Historia*, in *Symeonis monachi Opera Omnia*, ed. T. Howlett, 2 vols (Rolls Series, London, 1882–1885), II

John of Salisbury, *Policraticus*, ed. C. C. J. Webb, 2 vols (Oxford, 1909)

—— *The Historia pontificalis of John of Salisbury*, ed. and trans. M. Chibnall (London, 1956)

—— *The Statesman's Book of John of Salisbury*, trans. J. Dickinson (New York, 1963)

John of Worcester, *The Chronicle of John of Worcester*, ed. R. R. Darlington and P. McGurk, 3 vols (Oxford, 1995–)

Jordan Fantosme's Chronicle, ed. and trans. R. C. Johnston (1981)

Joseph of Exeter, *The Illiad of Dares Phrygius*, trans. G. Roberts (Cape Town, 1970)

Lamberti Ardensis historia comitum Ghisnensium, ed. J. Heller, *MGH, Scriptores*, 24, trans. L. Shopkow, *The History of the Counts of Guines and Lords of Ardres* (Pennsylvania, 2001)

Landon, L., *The Itinerary of Richard I* (Pipe Roll Society, new series, xiii, London, 1935)

Layamon, *Brut*, ed. G. L. Brook and R. F. Leslie, 2 vols (Early English Text Society, 1963, 1978)

Libelli de lite imperatorum et pontificum, ed. E. Bernheim et al., 3 vols, *MGH* (Berlin, 1892–1897)

Liber custumarum, in *Munimenta Gildhallae Londoniensis*, ed. H. T. Riley, 3 vols in 4 (Rolls Series, 1849–1862)

Liber pontificalis, ed. L. Duchesne, 3 vols (2nd edn, Paris, 1955–1957)

Liber S. Marie de Calchou. Registrum cartarum abbacie Tironensis de Kelso, ed. C. Innes, 2 vols (Edinburgh, 1846)

The Life and Death of Thomas Becket, ed. and trans G. Greenaway (London, 1961)

The Life of Edward who Rests at Westminster, ed. F. Barlow (revised edn, Oxford, 1992)

The Life and Letters of Thomas à Becket, trans. J. A. Giles, 2 vols (London, 1846)

The Lives of Thomas Becket, trans. M. Staunton (Manchester, 2001)

Magni rotuli scaccarii Normanniae sub regibus Angliae, ed. T. Stapleton, 2 vols (London, 1840–1844)

Marie de France, *Lais*, ed. L. Harf-Lancner and K. Warnke (Paris, 1990)

Materials for the History of Thomas Becket, Archbishop of Canterbury (MTB), ed. J. C. Robertson and J. B. Sheppard, 7 vols (Rolls Series, London, 1875–1885)

Matthew Paris, *Matthaei Parisiensis monachi sancti Albani, historia Anglorum*, ed. F. Madden, 3 vols (Rolls Series, London, 1865–1869)

—— *Matthaei Parisiensis monachi sancti Albani, Chronica majora*, ed. H. R. Luard, 7 vols (Rolls Series, London, 1872–83)

Magni Rotuli Scaccarii Normanniae sub regibus Angliae, ed. T. Stapleton, 2 vols (London, 1840–1844)

The Melrose Chronicle, ed. A. O. Anderson and M. O. Anderson (London, 1936)

The Memoranda Roll for the Michaelmas Term of the First Year of the Reign of King John (1199–1200),
    ed. H. G. Richardson (Pipe Roll Society, 59, new series, xxi, 1943)
Memorials of the Church of SS Peter and Wilfrid, ed. J. T. Fowler, 3 vols (Surtees Society, 1882–1888)
Memorials of St Edmund's Abbey, ed. T. Arnold, 3 vols (Rolls Series, London, 1890–1896)
Nécrologie-Obituaire de la cathédrale du Mans, ed. G. Busson and A. Ledru (1906)
The New Palaeographical Society: Facsimiles of Ancient Manuscripts, ed. E. Maunde Thompson and
    others, first series, 2 vols (London, 1903–1912)
Il Novellino, ed. A. Conte (Rome, 2001)
Odo of Deuil, *De profectione Ludovici VII in Orientem*, ed. and trans. V. G. Berry (1948)
De oorkonden van de graven van Vlaanderen (Juli 1128–17 Januari 1168), ed. T. de Hemptinne and
    A. Verhulst (Brussels, 1988)
*De oorkonden der graven van Vlaanderen (Juli 1168–September 1191), II. Uitgave Band II. Regering Filips
    van der Elzas (Eerste Deel, 1168–1177)*, ed. T. de Hemptinne and A. Verhulst (Brussels, 2001)
Orderic Vitalis, *The Ecclesiastical History of Orderic Vitalis*, ed. M. Chibnall, 6 vols (Oxford, 1969–1980)
Ordinances des roys de France de la troisième race, 21 vols (Paris, 1723, reprinted Farnborough, 1967–1968)
Ottonis episcopi Frisingensis chronica sive historia de duabus civitatibus, ed. A. Hofmeister, (*MGH, SRG*),
    45 (1912).
Papsturkunden für Kirchen im Heiligen Lande, ed. R. Hiestand (Göttingen, 1985)
Papsturkunden in Frankreich. II. Normandie, ed. J. Ramackers (Göttingen, 1937)
Peter of Blois, *Epistolae, Patrologia Latina*, CCVII
—— 'Dialogus inter regem Henricum secundem ed abbatem Bonevallis', ed. R. B. C. Huygens, *Revue
    Bénédictine*, 68 (1958), 87–112
Philippe de Novare, *Les Quatre Ages de l'homme*, ed. M. de Fréville (Paris, 1888)
The Pipe Rolls, *The Great Rolls of the Pipe for the Second, Third and Fourth Years of the Reign of Henry II,
    1155–1158*, ed. J. Hunter (Record Commission, 1844)
—— *The Great Rolls of the Pipe of the Reign of Henry the Second*, 5th to 34th years, 30 vols (Pipe Roll
    Society, 1884–1925)
The Plantagenet Chronicles, ed. and trans. E. Hallam (London, 1995)
Pleas before the King and his Justices, 1198–1212, ed. D. Stenton, 3 vols (Selden Society, 83, 1966)
Radulphi de Coggeshall Chronicon Anglicanum, ed. J. Stevenson (Rolls Series, London, 1875)
Radulphi Nigri Chronica, ed. R. Anstruther (London, 1851)
Ralph of Diss, *Opera Historica: The Historical Works of Master Ralph de Diceto, Dean of London*, ed.
    W. Stubbs, 2 vols (Rolls Series, London, 1876)
Reading Abbey Cartularies, ed. B. R. Kemp, 2 vols (London, 1986–1987)
Récits d'un ménestrel de Reims au treizième siècle, ed. N. de Wailly (Société de l'Histoire de France, Paris,
    1876)
Recueil d'annales angevines et vendômoises, ed. L. Halphen (Paris, 1903)
Recueil des actes de Henri II, ed. L. Delisle and E. Berger, 4 vols (Paris, 1909–1917)
Recueil des actes de Lothaire and Louis V, ed. L. Halphen and F. Lot (Paris, 1908)
Recueil des actes de Louis VI roi de France (1108–1137), ed. R-H. Bautier and J. Dufour, 3 vols (Paris,
    1992–1993)
Recueil des actes de Philippe Ier, roi de France (1059–1108), ed. M. Prou (Paris, 1908)
Recueil des actes de Philippe Auguste, ed. H.-F. Delaborde, C. Petit-Dutaillis, J. Boussard and M. Nortier,
    5 vols (Paris, 1916–2004)
Recueil des chroniques de Touraine, ed. A. Salmon (Tours, 1854)
The Red Book of the Exchequer, ed. H. Hall, 3 vols (London, Rolls Series, 1896)
Regesta Regni Hierosolymitani, ed. R. Röhricht (Innsbruck, 1893)
*Regesta regum Anglo-Normannorum, 1066–1154, III, Regesta regis Stephani ac Mathildis imperatricis et
    Gaufridi et Henrici ducis normannorum, 1135–1154*, ed. H. A. Cronne and R. H. C. Davis (Oxford,
    1968)
Regesta Regum Scottorum, I. The Acts of Malcolm IV, King of Scots, 1153–1165, ed. G. W. S. Barrow
    (Edinburgh, 1960)
Regesta Regum Scottorum, II. The Acts of William I, King of Scots, 1165–1214, ed. G. W. S. Barrow with
    W. W. L. Scott (Edinburgh, 1971)
Reginaldi monachi Dunelmensis libellus de admirandis beati Cuthberti, ed. J. Raine (Surtees Society, 1835)
Ricardi de Cirencestria speculum historiale de gestis regum Angliae, ed. J. A. B. Mayor, 2 vols (London,
    1869)
Richer of Saint-Rémi, *Histories*, ed. and trans. J. Lake, 2 vols (Cambridge, Mass., and London, 2011)
Rigord, *Histoire de Philippe Auguste*, ed. É. Charpentier, G. Pon and Y. Chauvin (Paris, 2006)
Robert of Torigni, *Chronique de Robert de Torigni*, ed. L. Delisle, 2 vols (Rouen, 1872–1873)
—— *The Chronicle of Robert of Torigni*, in *Chronicles of the Reigns of Stephen, Henry II and Richard*, ed. R.
    Howlett, 4 vols (Rolls Series, London, 1884–1889), IV

Roger of Howden, *The Annals of Roger of Hoveden*, trans. H. T. Riley, 2 vols (London, 1853)

—— *Chronica magistri Rogeri de Hoveden*, ed. W. Stubbs, 4 vols (Rolls Series, London, 1868–1871)

Roger of Wendover, *The Flowers of History*, ed. H. G. Hewlett, 3 vols (Rolls Series, London, 1886–1889)

Romualdi Salernitani Chronicon, ed. C. A. Garufi (Rerum Italicarum Scriptores, Città dei Castello, 1935)

Sazzarin, *Roman de Ham*, in *Histoire des ducs de Normandie et des rois d'Angleterre*, ed. F. Michel (Paris, 1840)

Select Charters and other Illustrations of English Constitutional History from the Earliest Times to the Reign of Edward the First, ed. W. Stubbs (Oxford, 9th edn, 1946)

The Song of Dermot and the Earl, ed. G. H. Orpen (Oxford, 1892)

The Song of Roland. An Analytical Edition, ed. G. J. Brault, 2 vols (University Park, Pa., and London, 1978)

Stephen of Rouen, *Draco Normannicus*, in *Chronicles of the Reigns of Stephen, Henry II and Richard I*, ed. R. Howlett, 4 vols (Rolls Series, London, 1884–1889), II, 589–782

Stevenson, J., *The Church Historians of England*, 8 vols (London, 1853–1858)

Suger, *Vie de Louis VI le Gros*, ed. H. Waquet (Paris, 1964); trans. R. Cusimano and J. H. Moorhead, *The Deeds of Louis the Fat* (Washington, DC, 1992)

Thomas Agnellus, *De morte et sepultura Henrici Regis Anglie Junioris*, in *Radulphi de Coggeshall Chronicon Anglicanum*, ed. J. Stevenson (Rolls Series, London, 1875), 265–273

Thomas of Kent, *Le Roman d'Alexandre ou Le roman de toute chevalerie*, ed. C. Gaullier-Bougassas and L. Harf-Lancner (Paris, 2003)

Thómas Saga Erkibyskups, ed. and trans. E. Magnusson, 2 vols (Rolls Series, London, 1875–1883)

Les Tristan en vers, ed. C. Payen (Paris, 1974)

van Caenegem, R. C., ed., *English Lawsuits from William I to Richard I*, 2 vols (London, 1990–1991)

La Vie d'Édouard le Confesseur, ed. O. Södergard (Uppsala, 1948)

Vitae B. Petri Abricensis et B. Hamonis monachorum coenobii Saviniacensis, ed. E. P. Sauvage, *Analecta Bollandiana*, II (1883), 500–560

Wace, *Wace's Roman de Brut. A History of the British Text and Translation*, ed. and trans. J. Weiss (Exeter, revised edn, 2002)

—— *Wace's Roman de Rou*, trans. G. S. Burgess, with the text of A. J. Holden and notes by G. S. Burgess and E. M. C. van Houts (St Helier, Jersey, 2002)

—— *The Hagiographical Works*, ed. J. Blacker, G. S. Burgess and A. V. Ogden (Leiden, 2013)

Walter Daniel, *The Life of Aelred of Rievaulx by Walter Daniel*, ed. F. M. Powicke (London, 1950)

Walter Map, *De Nugis Curialium*, ed. and trans. M. R. James, revised by C. N. L. Brooke and R. A. B. Mynors (Oxford, 1983)

The Warenne (Hyde) Chronicle, ed. and trans. E. M. C. van Houts and R. C. Love (Oxford, 2013)

Widukind of Corvey, *Res Gestae Saxonicae*, ed. P. Hirsch and H. E. Lohmann. *MGH, SS* (Hanover, 1935)

William le Breton, *Gesta Philippi Augusti*, in *Oeuvres de Rigord et de Guillaume le Breton*, ed. F. Delaborde, 2 vols (Paris, 1882)

William of Canterbury, *Miraculorum gloriosi martyris Thomae Cantuariensis archiepiscopi*, in *Materials for the History of Thomas Becket, Archbishop of Canterbury*, ed. J. C. Robertson and J. B. Sheppard, 7 vols (Rolls Series, London, 1875–1885), I

William of Conches, *Opera omnia*, I. *Dragmaticon philosophiae*, ed. I. Ronca (Corpus Christianorum Continuatio mediaevalis, 152: Turnhout, 1997); *A Dialogue on Natural Philosophy*, trans. I. Ronca and M. Curr (Notre Dame, Indi., 1997)

William FitzStephen, *Vita sancti Thomae Cantuarensis archiepiscopi et martyris*, in *Materials for the History of Thomas Becket, Archbishop of Canterbury*, ed. J. C. Robertson, 7 vols (Rolls Series, London, 1875–1885), III, 1–154

William of Malmesbury, *Historia novella*, ed. E. King and trans. K. Potter (2nd edn, Oxford, 1998)

—— *Gesta regum Anglorum*, ed. R. A. B. Mynors, R. M. Thompson and M. Winterbottom, 2 vols (Oxford, 1998–1999)

William of Newburgh, *Guilielmi Neubrigensis historia . . . libris quinque*, ed. T. Hearne, III (Oxford, 1719)

—— *Historia rerum Anglicarum*, in *Chronicles of the Reigns of Stephen, Henry II and Richard I*, ed. R. Howlett, 4 vols (Rolls Series, London, 1884–1889), I and II

—— *The History of English Affairs, Book II*, ed. and trans. P. G. Walsh and M. J. Kennedy (Oxford, 2007)

William of Tyre, *Chronique*, ed. R. B. C. Huygens, 2 vols (Corpus Christianorum, Continuatio medievalis 63–63a, Turnhout, 1986), trans. E. A. Babcock and A. C. Krey, *A History of Deeds Done beyond the Sea*, 2 vols (New York, 1976)

—— *La Continuation de Guillaume de Tyr (1184–1187)*, ed. M. R. Morgan (1184–1197) (Paris, 1982)

Secondary Works

Abulafia, D. H., *Frederick II* (London, 2002)
—— 'Robert of Selby [Salesby] (*fl.* 1137–1151), administrator', *ODNB*
Ailes, A., 'The Seal of John as Lord of Ireland and Count of Mortain', *The Coat of Arms*, 117 (1981), 341–50
—— *The Origins of the Royal Arms of England* (Reading, 1982)
—— 'Heraldry in Twelfth-Century England: The Evidence', *England in the Twelfth Century. Proceedings of the 1988 Harlaxton Symposium*, ed. D. Williams (Woodbridge, 1990), 1–16
—— 'The Governmental Seals of Richard I', *Seals and their Context in the Middle Ages*, ed. P. R. Schofield (Oxbow, 2015), 101–10
Aird, W. M., 'Frustrated Masculinity: The Relationship between William the Conqueror and his Eldest Son', in *Masculinity in Medieval Europe*, ed. D. M. Hadley (Harlow, 1999), 39–70
—— *Robert Curthose, Duke of Normandy (c. 1050–1134)* (Woodbridge, 2008)
Alexander, J. W., 'New Evidence on the Palatinate of Chester', *EHR*, 85 (1970), 717–27
—— 'The Alleged Palatinates of Norman England', *Speculum*, 56 (1981), 17–27
Allen, M., 'Henry II and the English Coinage', in *Henry II. New Interpretations*, ed. C. Harper-Bill and N. Vincent (Woodbridge, 2007), 257–77
Almond, R., *Medieval Hunting* (Stroud, 2003)
Althoff, G., 'Ira Regis. Prolegomena to a History of Royal Anger', *Anger's Past. The Social Uses of Emotion in the Middle Ages*, ed. B. H. Rosenwein (Ithaca, NY, and London, 1998), 59–74
—— *Heinrich IV* (Darmstadt, 2006).
Amt, E., 'Richard de Lucy, Henry II's Justiciar', *Medieval Prosopography*, 9 (1988), 61–87
The Accession of Henry II in England: Royal Government Restored, 1149–1159 (Woodbridge, 1993)
—— 'William FitzEmpress (1136–1164)', *ODNB*
Anderson, C. B., 'Wace's *Roman de Rou* and Henry II's Court: Character and Power', *Romance Quarterly*, 47 (2000), 67–82
Appleby, J. T., *Henry II, the Vanquished King* (London, 1962)
Archer, T. A., revised E. Hallam, 'Rosamund Clifford [*called* Fair Rosamund] (*b.* before 1140?, *d.* 1175/6)', *ODNB*
Arnaud, A. F., *Voyage archéologique et pittoresque dans le département de l'Aube* (Troyes, 1837)
Arrignon, C., Debiès, M.-H., and Palazzo, E., *Cinquante années d'études médiévales: à la confluence de nos disciplines. Actes du Colloque organisé à l'occasion du cinquantenaire du CESCM, Poitiers, 1–14 septembre 2003* (Turnhout, 2005)
Asbridge, T., *The Greatest Knight* (London, 2015)
Ashe, G., 'The Prophecies of Merlin: Their Originality and Importance', in *Magistra Doctissima. Essays in Honour of Bonnie Wheeler*, ed. D. Armstrong, A. W. Armstrong and H. Chickering (Kalamazoo, Mich., 2013), 71–9
Ashe, L., *Fiction and History in England, 1066–1200* (Cambridge, 2007)
—— 'William Marshal, Lancelot and Arthur: Chivalry and Kingship', *ANS*, 30 (2008), 19–40
Aubrun, M., 'Le Prieur Geoffroy du Vigeois et sa chronique', *Revue Mabillon*, 58 (1974), 313–25
Aurell, M., ed., *La Cour Plantagenêt (1154–1204). Actes du Colloque tenu à Thouars du 30 Avril au 2 mai 1999*, (Poitiers, 2000)
—— 'Aux origines de la légende noire d'Aliénor d'Aquitaine', in *Royautés imaginaires (XIIe–XIVe siècles)*, ed. A-H. Allirot, G. Lecuppre and L. Scordia (Turnhout, 2005), 89–102
—— *L'Empire des Plantagenêt, 1154–1254* (Paris, 2003), trans. D. Crouch, *The Plantagenet Empire* (Harlow, 2007)
—— 'Henry II and Arthurian Legend', *Henry II: New Interpretations*, ed. C. Harper-Bill and N. Vincent (woodbidge, 2007), 362–94
—— *La Légende du Roi Arthur 550–1250* (Mesnil-sur-l'Estrée, 2007)
—— *Le Chevalier lettré: savoir et conduite de l'aristocratie au XII et XIIIe siècles* (Paris, 2011)
Aurell, M. and Tonnerre, N.-Y., eds, *Plantagenêts et Capétiens: confrontations et héritages* (Brepols, 2006)
Bachrach, B. S., 'Henry II and the Angevin Tradition of Family Hostility', *Albion*, 16 (1984), 111–30
—— 'The Pilgrimages of Fulk Nerra, count of the Angevins, 987–1040', in *Religion, Culture and Society in the Early Middle Ages* (Studies in Medieval Culture, xxiii, Kalamazoo, Mich., 1987), 205–17
—— 'L'Art de guerre angevin', *Plantagenêts et Capétiens: confrontations et héritages*, ed. M. Aurell and N. Y. Tonnerre (Brépols, 2006), 267–84
Backhouse, J. and De Hamel, C., *The Becket Leaves* (London, 1988)
Bak, J., ed., *Coronations: Medieval and Early Modern Monarchic Ritual* (Berkeley, 1990)
Baldwin, J., 'Qu'est-ce les Capétiens ont appris des Plantagenêts?', *CCM*, 29 (1986), 3–8
The Government of Philip Augustus (Berkeley, 1986)

Barber, R., *Henry Plantagenet: a Biography* (Woodbridge, 1964)

Barber, R. and Barker, J., *Tournaments. Jousts, Chivalry and Pageants in the Middle Ages* (Woodbridge, 1989)

Barker, J., *The Tournament in England, 1100–1400* (Woodbridge, 1986)

Barlow, F., 'The English, Norman and French Councils Called to Deal with the Papal Schism of 1159', *EHR*, 51 (1936), 264–8

—— 'The King's Evil', *EHR*, 95 (1980), 3–27

—— *William Rufus* (London, 1983)

—— *Thomas Becket* (London, 1986)

—— 'Herbert of Bosham (d. *c*.1194)', *ODNB*

Barraclough, G., *The Earldom and County Palatinate of Chester* (Oxford, 1984)

Barrière, B., 'Une agglomération double (XIe–XIIe siècles), in *Histoire de Limoges*, ed. L. Pérouas (Toulouse, 1989), 61–82

—— 'The Limousin and Limoges in the Twelfth and Thirteenth Centuries', in *Enamels of Limoges, 1100–1350*, ed. J. P. O'Neil (Metropolitan Museum of Art, New York, 1996), 22–32

Barron, C., *London in the Later Middle Ages. Government and People, 1200–1500* (Oxford, 2004)

Barrow, G. W. S., 'The Reign of William the Lion, king of Scotland', *Historical Studies*, 7 (1969), 21–44, reprinted in G. W. S. Barrow, *Scotland and its Neighbours in the Middle Ages* (London: Hambledon, 1992), 67–90

—— 'The Scots and the North of England', *The Anarchy of King Stephen's Reign*, ed. E. King (Oxford, 1994), 231–53

—— 'King David I, Earl Henry and Cumbria', *Transactions of the Cumberland and Westmorland Antiquarian and Archaeological Society*, new series, 49 (1999), 117–22.

Barthélemy, D., *La Chevalerie: de la Germanie antique à la France du xiie siècle* (Paris, 2007)

—— 'Les origines du tournoi chevaleresque', *Agôn: le compétition, Ve–XIIe siècles*, ed. F. Bougard, R. Le Jan and T. Leinhard (Turnhout, 2012), 112–29

Bartlett, R., *England under the Norman and Angevin Kings, 1075–1225* (Oxford, 2000)

—— 'Political Prophecy in Gerald of Wales', *Culture politique des Plantagenêt (1154–1224)*, ed. M. Aurell (Poitiers, 2003), 303–11

—— *Gerald of Wales, 1146–1223* (Oxford, 1982), republished as *Gerald of Wales. A Voice of the Middle Ages* (Stroud, 2006)

Barton, R. E., 'A "Zealous Anger" and the Regeneration of Aristocratic Relationships in Eleventh- and Twelfth-Century France', *Anger's Past. The Social Uses of Emotion in the Middle Ages*, ed. B. H. Rosenwein (Ithaca, NY, and London, 1998), 153–70

—— 'Between the King and the Dominus; the Seneschals of Plantagenet Maine and Anjou', *Les Seigneuries dans l'espace Plantagenêt (c. 1150–c.1250)*, ed. M. Aurell and F. Boutoulle (Bordeaux, 2009), 139–62

—— 'Emotions and Power in *Orderic Vitalis*', *ANS*, 33 (2010), 41–60

Bate, K., 'Joseph of Exeter [Canterbury], poet (*fl. c*.1180–1194)', *ODNB*

Bates, D., 'The Rise and Fall of Normandy, *c*.911 to 1204', *England and Normandy in the Middle Ages*, ed. D. Bates and A. Curry (London, 1994), 19–35

—— 'The Prosopographical Study of Anglo-Norman Royal Charters', *Family Trees and the Roots of Politics: The Prosopography of Britain and France from the Tenth to the Twelfth Century*, ed. K. S. B. Keats-Rohan (Woodbridge, 1997), 89–102

—— 'The Conqueror's Adolescence', *ANS*, 35 (2002), 1–18

—— *Writing Medieval Biography, 750–1250: Essays in Honour of Professor Frank Barlow*, ed. D. Bates, J. Crick and S. Hamilton (Woodbridge, 2006)

—— 'Anger, Emotion and a Biography of William the Conqueror', *Gender and Historiography: Studies in the Earlier Middle Ages in Honour of Pauline Stafford*, ed. J. L. Nelson, S. Reynolds and S. M. Johns (London, 2012), 21–33

Bateson, M. et al., *Records of the Borough of Leicester*, 7 vols (London, 1899–1974)

Baudry, M.-P., *Châteaux 'Romans' en Poitou-Charente* (La Crèche, 2011)

Baume, A., 'Le Document et le terrain: la trace du système défensif normand au XIIe siècle', *1204: La Normandie entre Plantagenêts et Capétiens*, ed. A.-M. Flambard-Héricher and V. Gazeau (Caen, 2007), 93–112

Baumgartner, E., 'Trouvères et losengiers', *CCM*, 25 (1982), 171–8

Bautier, R.-H., ed., *La France de Philippe Auguste. Le temps des mutations* (Paris, 1982)

—— '"Empire Plantagenêt" ou "Espace Plantagenêt". Y eut-il une civilisation du monde Plantagenêt?', *Cahiers de civilisation médiévale*, 29 (1986), 139–47

Becker, P. A., 'Jordan Fantosme, la guerre d'Écosse, 1173–4', *Zeitschrift für romanische Philologie*, 64 (1944), 449–556

Bedos-Rezak, B., 'Signes et insignes du pouvoir royal et seigneurial au Moyen Âge: le témoignage des sceaux', in *Les Pouvoirs de commandement jusqu'en 1610 (actes du 105e Congrès national des sociétés savants, Caen, 1980* (Paris, 1984), 47–62

—— 'Suger and the Symbolism of Royal Power: The Seal of Louis VII', *Abbot Suger and St Denis. A Symposium*, ed. P. L. Gerson (New York, 1986), 95–103

—— 'Women, Seals and Power in Medieval France, 1150–1350', *Women and Power in the Middle Ages*, ed. M. Erhler and M. Kowalaski (Athens, Ga, 1988), 61–82

Beeler, J., 'Castles and Strategy in Norman and Early Angevin England', *Speculum*, 31 (1956), 581–601 *Warfare in England, 1066–1189* (Ithaca, NY, 1966)

Bémont, C., 'Hugues de Clers et le De Senescalcia Franciae', *Études d'histoire au Moyen Âge dediées à Gabriel Monod* (Paris, 1896), 253–60.

Benjamin, R., 'A Forty Years War: Toulouse and the Plantagenets, 1156–1196', *Bulletin of the Institute for Historical Research*, 61 (1988), 270–85

Bennett, M., 'Poetry as History? The *Roman de Rou* of Wace as a Source for the Norman Conquest', *ANS*, 5 (1985), 21–39

—— 'Wace and Warfare', *ANS*, 11 (1988), 37–57

—— 'Military Masculinity in England and Northern France, c.1150–c.1225', in *Masculinity in Medieval Europe*, ed. D. M. Hadley (London, 1999), 85–8

—— 'The Uses and Abuses of Wace's Roman de Rou', in *Maistre Wace: A Celebration. Proceedings of the International Colloquium held in Jersey, 10–12 September 2004*, ed. G. S. Burgess and J. Weiss (Société Jersaise, 2006), 31–40

Bennett, P., 'La Chronique de Jordan Fantosme', *CCM*, 40 (1997), 35–56

—— *The Cycle of Guillaume d'Orange or Garin de Monglane: a Critical Bibliography* (Woodbridge, 2004)

Benson, L. D., 'The Tournament in the Romances of Chrétien de Troyes and *L'Histoire de Guillaume le Maréchal*', *Chivalric Literature. Essays on Relations between Literature and Life in the Later Middle Ages*, ed. L. D. Benson and J. Leyerle (Toronto, 1980), 1–24, 147–51

Benton, J. F. 'The Court of Champagne as a Literary Centre', *Speculum*, 36 (1961), 551–91

Bethell, D., 'The Making of a Twelfth-Century Relic Collection', *Popular Belief and Practice*, ed. G. J. Cumming and D. Baker (Studies in Church History, 8, Cambridge, 1972), 61–71

Bezzola, R. R., *La Cour d'Angleterre comme centre littéraire sous les rois Angevins (1154–1199)* (Paris, 1963)

Biancalana, J., '"For Want of Justice": The Legal Reforms of Henry II', *Columbia Law Review*, 88 (1988), 433–536

Biddle, M., 'Seasonal Festivals and Residence: Winchester, Westminster and Gloucester in the Tenth to Twelfth Centuries', *ANS*, 8 (1985), 51–72

Biddle, M. and Clayre, B., *Winchester Castle and the Great Hall* (Winchester, 1983)

—— 'Idéologie chrétienne et éthique politique à travers le *Dialogus inter regem Henricum secundum et abbatem Bonnevallis* de Peter de Blois', *Convaincre et Persuader: communication et propagande aux XIIe et XIIIe siècles*, ed. M. Aurell (Poitiers, 2007), 81–109

Billoré, M. 'Y a-t-il une "oppression des Plantagenêtsh sur l'aristocratie à la veille de 1204?', *Plantagenêts et Capétiens, confrontations et he'ritages*, ed. M. Aurell and N.-Y. Tonnerre (Brépols, 2006), 145–61

—— 'Henri le Jeune confirme les privilèges judiciaires de l'abbaye de Fontevraud', *Dans le secret des archives. Justice, ville et culture au Moyen Âge*, ed. M. Billoré and J. Picot (Rennes, 2014), 79–98

—— *De gré ou de force. L'aristocratie normande et ses ducs (1150–1259)* (Rennes, 2014)

Birch, W. de Gray, 'On the Seals of King Henry the Second, and of his Son the so-called Henry the Third', *Transactions of the Royal Society of Literature of the United Kingdom*, second series, no. xi (1878), 301–37

—— *Catalogue of Seals in the Department of Manuscripts in the British Museum*, 6 vols (London, 1887–1900)

—— *Seals* (London, 1907)

Bisson, T. M., *The Medieval Crown of Aragon* (Oxford, 1986)

—— *The Crisis of the Twelfth Century: Power, Lordship and the Origins of European Government* (Princeton, 2009)

Blacker, J., 'Oez veraie estoire; History as Mediation in Jordan Fantosme's Chronicle', *The Formation of Culture in Medieval Britain*, ed. F. H. M. Le Saux (Lampeter, 1995), 27–35

—— 'Where Wace Feared to Tread: Latin Commentaries on Merlin's Prophecies in the Reign of Henry II', *Arthuriana*, 6 (1996), 36–52

Bloch, M., *Les Rois thaumaturges* (Strasbourg, 1924), trans. J. E. Anderson as *The Royal Touch: Sacred Monarchy and Scrofula in England and France* (London, 1973)

Boase, T. S. R., 'Fontevrault and the Plantagenets', *Journal of the British Archaeological Society*, 3rd series, 34 (1971), 1–10

Bony, P., 'L'Image du pouvoir seigneurial dans les sceaux: codification des signes de la puissance, de la fin du XIe au début du XIIIe siècle dans les pays d'oïl', *117e Congrès national des sociétés savantes, Clermont Ferrand, 1992. Histoire médiévale et philologie* (Paris, 1993), 489–523

Boorman, J., 'The Sheriffs of Henry II and the Significance of 1170', *Law and Government in Medieval England and Normandy. Essays in Honour of Sir James Holt*, ed. G. Garnet and J. Hudson (Cambridge, 1994), 255–75

—— 'Hugh de Gundeville', *ODNB*

'Ralph FitzStephen (d. 1202)', *ODNB*

Bouchard, C. B., 'Eleanor's Divorce from Louis VII: The Uses of Consanguinity', *Eleanor of Aquitaine. Lord and Lady*, ed. B. Wheeler and J. C. Parsons (New York, 2003), 223–36

Bournazel, E., *Le Gouvernement capétien, 1108–1180* (Paris, 1975)

Bournazel, E. and Poly, J.-P., 'Couronne et mouvance: institutions et représentations mentales', *La France de Philippe Auguste. Le temps des mutations*, ed. R. H. Bautier (Paris, 1982), 217–36

Boussard, J., *Le Comté d'Anjou sous Henri Plantagenet et ses fils (1151–1204)* (Paris, 1938)

—— 'Les Mercenaires au XIIe siècle: Henri II Plantagenêt et les origines de l'armée de métier', *Bibliothèque de l'École des Chartes*, 106 (1945–6), 189–224

—— *Le Gouvernement d'Henri II Plantagenêt* (Paris, 1956)

—— 'Philippe Auguste et les Plantagenêts', *La France de Philippe Auguste. Le temps des mutations*, ed. R.-H. Bautier (Paris, 1982), 263–87

Bowie, C. M., *The Daughters of Henry II and Eleanor of Aquitaine* (Turnhout, 2014)

Bozoky, E., 'Le Culte des saints et des reliques dans la politique des premiers rois Plantagenêts', *La Cour Plantagenêt (1154–1204)*, ed. M. Aurell (Poitiers, 2000), 277–91

—— 'The Sanctity and Canonization of Edward the Confessor', *Edward the Confessor. The Man and the Legend*, ed. R. Mortimer (Woodbridge, 2009), 173–86

Bradbury, J., 'Fulk le Réchin and the Origin of the Plantagenets', *Studies in Medieval History Presented to R. Allen Brown*, ed. C. Harper-Bill, C. Holdsworth and J. Nelson (Woodbridge, 1989), 27–42

—— 'Geoffrey V of Anjou, Count and Knight', *The Ideals and Practice of Medieval Knighthood*, III, ed. C. Harper-Bill and R. Harvey (Boydell, 1990), 21–38

—— *Philip Augustus, King of France, 1180–1223* (London, 1998)

Brand, P., '*Multis Vigilis Excogitatam et Inventam*: Henry II and the Creation of the English Common Law', *Haskins Society Journal*, 2 (1990), 197–222, reprinted in P. Brand, *The Making of the Common Law* (London, 1992), 79–102

—— 'Henry II and the Creation of the English Common Law', *Henry II: New Interpretations*, ed. C. Harper-Bill and N. Vincent (Woodbridge, 2007), 215–32

Brand'honneur, M., 'Seigneurs et réseaux de chevaliers du nord-est du Rennais sous Henri Plantagenêt', *Noblesses de l'espace Plantagenêt*, ed. M. Aurell (Poitiers, 2001), 165–84

Braun, H., 'Bungay Castle: Report on the Excavations', *Proceedings of the Suffolk Institute of Archaeology and Natural History*, 22 (1935/37), 109–99, 212–13

—— 'Some Notes on Bungay Castle', *Proceedings of the Suffolk Institute of Archaeology*, xxii (1947), 109–19

Brooke, C. N. L., 'Aspects of Marriage Law in the Eleventh and Twelfth Centuries', *Proceedings of the Fifth International Congress of Medieval Canon Law, Salamanca 1976* (Vatican City, 1980), 333–44

—— 'The Marriage of Henry II and Eleanor of Aquitaine', *The Historian*, 20 (1988), 3–8

—— *The Medieval Idea of Marriage* (Oxford, 1989)

Brooke, C. N. L., with Keir, G., *London 800–1216: The Shaping of the City* (London, 1975)

Brooke, Z. N., 'The Register of Master David of London, and the Part he played in the Becket Crisis', *Essays in History Presented to Reginald Lane Poole*, ed. H. W. C. Davis (Oxford, 1927), 227–45

Broughton, B. B., *The Legends of King Richard I Coeur de Lion* (The Hague and Paris, 1966)

Broun, D., 'Britain and the Beginnings of Scotland', *Journal of the British Academy*, 3 (2015), 107–37

Brown, A. E., ed., *The Growth of Leicester* (Leicester, 1970)

Brown, E. A. R., 'Death and the Human Body in the Later Middle Ages: Boniface VIII and Legislation on the Division of the Corpse', *Viator*, 12 (1981), 221–70

—— 'La Notion de la légitimité et la prophétie à la cour de Philippe Auguste', *La France de Philippe Auguste*, ed. R. H. Bautier (Paris, 1982), 77–111

—— '"Franks, Burgundians and Aquitainians" and the Royal Coronation Ceremony in France', *Transactions of the American Philosophical Society*, 82 (1992), 1–189

—— 'Royal Testamentary Acts from Philip Augustus to Philip of Valois', *Herrscher- und Fürstentestemente im Westeuropäische Mittelalter*, ed. B. Kasten (Cologne, Weimar and Vienna, 2008), 415–30

Brown, R. A., 'Framlingham Castle and Bigod 1154–1216', *Proceedings of the Suffolk Institute of Natural History and Archaeology*, 25 (1950), 127–48, and reprinted in *Castles, Conquest and Charters* (Woodbridge, 1989)

—— *English Castles* (London, 1976)

—— 'Royal Castle-Building in England, 1154–1216', *EHR*, 70 (1955), 353–98, and reprinted in Brown *Castles, Conquest and Charters* (Woodbridge, 1989)

——'A List of Castles, 1154–1216', *EHR*, 74 (1959), 249–80, and reprinted in Brown, *Castles, Conquest and Charters* (Woodbridge, 1989)

—— *Castles from the Air* (Cambridge, 1989)

—— *Castles, Conquest and Charters* (Woodbridge, 1989)

Brown, R. A., Colvin, H. M. and Taylor, A. J., *The History of the King's Works. The Middle Ages*, 2 vols (London, 1963)

Bruckmann, J., 'The Ordines of the Third Recension of the Medieval English Coronation Ordo', *Essays in Medieval English History Presented to Bertie Wilkinson*, ed. T. A. Sandquist and M. R. Powicke (Toronto, 1969), 99–115

Brundage, J. A., 'The Canon Law of Divorce in the Mid-Twelfth Century: Louis VII c. Eleanor of Aquitaine', *Eleanor of Aquitaine. Lord and Lady*, ed. B. wheeler and S. C. Parsons (New York, 2003), 213–22

Buc, P., 'David's Adultery with Bathsheba and the Healing Power of Capetian Kings', *Viator*, 24 (1993), 101–20

Bull, M., *The Miracles of Our Lady at Rocamadour* (Woodbridge, 1999)

Bullough, V. L., 'On Being a Male in the Middle Ages', *Medieval Masculinities: Regarding Men in the Middle Ages*, ed. C. A. Lees (Minneapolis, 1994), 31–43

Bur, M., 'Les Comtes de Champagne et la "Normanitas": sémiologie d'un tombeau', *ANS*, 3 (1980), 22–32

Caille, J., 'Ermengarde, vicomtesse de Narbonne (1127/29–1196/97), une grande figure féminine du Midi aristocratique', *La Femme dans l'histoire et la société médiévale, 66th Congress of the Federation Historique du Languedoc-Roussillon* (Narbonne, 1994), 9–50

Cailleux, P., 'Le Développement urbain de la capitale normande entre Plantagenêts et Capetiens', *1204. La Normandie entre Plantagenêts et Capétiens*, ed. A. Flambard-Héricher and V. Gazeau (Caen, 2007), 261–74

Callahan, D. F., 'Eleanor of Aquitaine, the Coronation Rite of the Duke of Aquitaine and the Cult of Saint Martial of Limoges', *The World of Eleanor of Aquitaine*, ed. M. Bull and C. Léglu (Woodbridge, 2005), 29–36

Cantor, N., *Church, Kingship and Lay Investiture in England, 1089–1135* (New York, 1969)

Carpenter, D., *The Minority of Henry III* (London, 1990)

—— *The Struggle for Mastery: Britain 1066–1284* (London, 2003)

—— 'The Dignitaries of York Minster in the 1170s: a Reassessment', *Northern History*, 43 (2006), 21–37

Cartellieri, A., *Philipp II August, König von Frankreich*, 4 vols (Leipzig, 1899–1921)

Cathcart-King, D. J., 'The Fight at Coleshill', *Welsh Historical Review*, 2 (1965), 367–73

—— *Castellarium anglicanum*, 2 vols (London, 1983)

Chartrou, J., *L'Anjou de 1109 à 1151: Foulques de Jérusalem et Geoffroi Plantagenêt* (Paris, 1928)

Chauou, A., *L'Idéologie Plantagenêt. Royauté arthurienne et monarchie politique dans l'espace Plantagenêt (XIIe–XIIIe siècles)* (Rennes, 2001)

Cheney, C. R., 'A Monastic Letter of Fraternity to Eleanor of Aquitaine', *EHR*, 51 (1936), 488–93

Cheney, M. G., 'The Recognition of Pope Alexander III: Some Neglected Evidence', *EHR*, 84 (1969), 474–97

—— *Roger Bishop of Worcester, 1164–1179* (Oxford, 1980)

Cheyette, F. L., *Ermengard of Narbonne and the World of the Troubadours* (Ithaca, NY, 2001)

Chibnall, M., *The Empress Matilda. Queen Consort, Queen Mother and Lady of the English* (Oxford, 1991)

—— 'Charters of the Empress', *Law and Government in Medieval England and Normandy*, ed. J. Hudson and G. Garnett (Cambridge, 1994), 276–98

—— 'Normandy', *The Anarchy of Stephen's Reign*, ed. E. King (Oxford, 1994), 93–115

—— 'L'Avènement au pouvoir d'Henri II', *CCM*, 37 (1994), 41–8

—— 'The Empress Matilda and her Sons', *Medieval Mothering*, ed. J. C. Parsons and B. Wheeler (New York and London, 1996), 279–94

Christie, N., Creighton, O., Edgeworth, M. and Hamerow, H., *Transforming Townscapes. From Burgh to Borough: The Archaeology of Wallingford, 800–1400* (Society for Medieval Archaeology, 2013)

Christophe, D., 'La Plaque de Geoffroy Plantagenêt dans la cathédrale du Mans', *Hortus Artium Medievalium*, 10 (2004), 74–80

Church, S. D., 'Roger Bigod (III), second earl of Norfolk (c.1143–1221)', *ODNB*

—— 'King John's Testament and the Last Days of his Reign', *EHR*, 125 (2010), 505–28

—— *King John: England, Magna Carta and the Making of a Tyrant* (London, 2015)

Clanchy, M., *From Memory to Written Record. England 1066–1307* (2nd edn, Oxford, 1993)
—— 'Abelard – Knight (*Miles*), Courtier (*Palatinus*) and Man of War (*Vir Bellator*)', *Medieval Knighthood V: Papers from the Sixth Strawberry Hill Conference, 1994*, ed. S. Church and R. Harvey (Woodbridge, 1995), 101–18
Clédat, L., *Du rôle historique de Bertran de Born, 1175–1200* (Paris, 1879)
Cochet, J. B. D., 'Découverte du tombeau et de la statue de Henri Court-Mantel dans le choeur de la cathédrale de Rouen', *Bulletin de la Commission des antiquités de la Seine-Inférieure*, 1 (1867–1869), 93–102
Colvin, H. M. et al., *The History of the King's Works*, 8 vols (London, HMSO, 1963–1982)
Contamine, P., *War in the Middle Ages* (Oxford, 1984)
Cook, B. J., '*En monnaie aiant cours*: The Monetary System of the Angevin Empire', *Coins and History in the North Sea World, c.500–c.1250: Essays in Honour of Marion Archibald*, ed. B. J. Cook and G. Williams (Leiden, 2006), 617–86
Corner, D., 'The Earliest Surviving Manuscripts of Roger of Howden's *Chronicle*', *EHR*, 98 (1983), 297–310
—— 'The *Gesta regis Henrici secundi* and *Chronica* of Roger, parson of Howden', *Bulletin of the Institute of Historical Research*, 56 (1983), 26–44
Cownie, E., 'Adam de Port (*fl.* 1161–1174)', *ODNB*
Cox, E. L., *The Eagles of Savoy. The House of Savoy in Thirteenth Century Europe* (Princeton, NJ, 1974)
Crick, J., 'Geoffrey of Monmouth, Prophecy and History', *Journal of Medieval History*, 18 (1992), 357–71
Crook, D., 'The Earliest Exchequer Estreat and the Forest Eyres of Henry II and Thomas fitzBernard, 1175–80', *Records, Administration and Aristocratic Society in the Anglo-Norman Realm. Papers Commemorating the 800th Anniversary of King John's Loss of Normandy*, ed. N. Vincent (Woodbridge, 2009), 29–44
Crossland, J., *William Marshal: The Last Great Feudal Baron* (London, 1962)
Crouch, D., *The Beaumont Twins. The Roots and Branches of Power in the Twelfth Century* (Cambridge, 1985)
—— *The Image of Aristocracy in Britain, 1000–1300* (London, 1992)
—— 'The Hidden History of the Twelfth Century', *Haskins Society Journal*, 5 (1993), 111–30
—— 'Normans and Anglo-Normans: a Divided Aristocracy?'. *England and Normandy in the Middle Ages*, ed. D. Bates and A. Curry (London, 1994), 51–67
—— 'The Culture of Death in the Anglo-Norman World', *Anglo-Norman Political Culture and the Twelfth-Century Renaissance*, ed. C. W. Hollister (Woodbridge, 1997), 157–80
—— *The Reign of King Stephen, 1135–1154* (Harlow, 2000)
—— 'The Origins of Chantries: Some Further Anglo-Norman Evidence', *JMH*, 27 (2001), 159–80
—— 'The Troubled Deathbeds of Henry I's Servants: Death, Confession and Secular Conduct in the Twelfth Century', *Albion*, 34 (2002), 24–36
—— *William Marshal. Knighthood, War and Chivalry, 1147–1219* (2nd edn, London, 2002)
—— *The Birth of Nobility. Constructing Aristocracy in England and France, 900–1300* (Harlow, 2005)
—— *Tournament* (London, 2005)
—— 'Writing a Biography in the Thirteenth Century: The Construction and Composition of the History of William Marshal', *Writing Medieval Biography*, 221–35
—— 'Biography as Propaganda in the *History of William Marshal*', *Convaincre et persuader: communication et propagande aux XII et XIIIe siècles*, ed. M. Aurell (Poitiers, 2007), 503–12
—— 'William Marshal and the Mercenariat', *Mercenaries and Paid Men: The Mercenary Identity in the Middle Ages*, ed. J. France (Leiden, 2008), 15–32
—— 'The Court of Henry II of England in the 1180s, and the Office of King of Arms', *The Coat of Arms: The Journal of the Heraldry Society*, 3rd series, 5 (2010), pt 2, 47–55
—— 'The *Roman des Franceis* of Andrew de Coutances: Significance, Text and Translation', *Normandy and its Neighbours, 900–1250. Essays for David Bates*, ed. D. Crouch and K. Thompson (Turnhout, 2011), 175–98
—— 'Reginald, earl of Cornwall (d. 1175)', *ODNB*
—— 'Robert [Robert de Beaumont], second earl of Leicester (1104–1168)', *ODNB*
—— 'Robert de Breteuil, [Robert ès Blanchmains, Robert the Whitehanded, Robert de Beaumont], third earl of Leicester (*c.*1130–1190)', *ODNB*
—— 'Robert de Breteuil, fourth earl of Leicester', *ODNB*
Csendes, P., *Heinrich VI* (Darmstadt, 1993)
Cummins, J., *The Hound and the Hawk. The Art of Medieval Hunting* (London, 1988)
Dace, R., 'Bertran de Verdun: Royal Service, Land, and Family in the Late Twelfth Century', *Medieval Prosopography*, 20 (1999), 75–93

Dalton, P., 'Aiming at the Impossible: Ranulf II Earl of Chester and Lincolnshire in the Reign of King
     Stephen', *The Earldom of Chester and its Charters*, details 109–36
'William le Gros, count of Aumale and earl of York (*c.*1110–1179)', *ODNB*
Damian-Grint, P., 'Truth, Trust and Evidence in the Anglo-Norman Estoire', *ANS*, 18 (1995), 63–78
'Benoît de Sainte-Maure et l'idéologie Plantagenêt', *Plantagenêts et Capétiens: confrontations et héritages*,
     ed. M. Aurell and N.-Y. Tonnerre (Brépols, 2006), 413–28
The New Historians of the Twelfth Century (Woodbridge, 1999)
Daniel, C., 'The Merlin Prophecies: a Propaganda Tool of the XII and XIII Centuries', *Convaincre et
     persuader: communication et propagande au XII et XIIIe siècles*, ed. M. Aurell (Poitiers, 2007), 211–34
Daniel, S., *The Collection of the History of England* (London, revised edn, 1634)
D'Arcy Boulton, J., 'Classic Knighthood as a Nobiliary Dignity: The Knighting of Counts and Kings'
     Sons in England, 1066–1272', *Medieval Knighthood. Papers from the Sixth Strawberry Hill Conference,
     1994*, ed. S. D. Church and R. E. Harvey (Woodbridge, 1995), 41–100
Dauzier, M., *Le Mythe de Bertran de Born du Moyen Âge à nos jours* (Paris, 1986)
David, C. W., *Robert Curthose, Duke of Normandy* (Cambridge, Mass., 1920)
Davis, R. H. C., *The Medieval Warhorse* (London, 1989)
DeAragon, R. C., 'The Child-Bride, the Earl and the Pope: The Marital Fortunes of Agnes of Essex',
     Haskins Society Journal, 17 (2007), 200–16
Debord, A., *La Société laique dans les pays de La Charente. X–XIIe siècles* (Paris, 1984)
de Hemptinne, T., 'Aspects des relations de Philippe Auguste avec la Flandre au temps de Philippe
     d'Alsace', *La France de Philippe Auguste. Le temps des mutations*, ed. R. H. Bautier (Paris, 1982),
     255–62
Delisle, L., 'Sur la date de l'association de Philippe, fils de Louis le Gros, au government du royaume',
     Journal des savants (1898), 736–40
Delville, A., *Tombeaux de la cathédrale de Rouen* (Rouen, 1833)
Dette, C., 'Kinder und Jungendliche in der Adelsgesellschaft des frühen Mittelalters', *Archiv für
     Kulturgeschichte*, 76 (1994), 1–34
Devic, C. and Vaissete, J.-J., *Histoire générale de Languedoc,* ed. A. Molinier *et al.*, 16 vols (Toulouse,
     1872–1904)
Dhondt, J., 'Élection et hérédité sous les Carolingiens et les premiers Capétiens', *Revue belge de philol-
     ogie et d'histoire*, 18 (1939), 913–53
'Les Relations entre la France et la Normandie sous Henri Ier', *Normannia*, 12 (1939), 465–86
Diggelmann, L., 'Marriage as a Tactical Response: Henry II and the Royal Wedding of 1160', *EHR*,
     119 (2004), 954–64
—— 'Hewing the Ancient Elm: Anger, Arboricide, and Medieval Kingship', *Journal of Medieval and
     Early Modern Studies*, 40 (2010), 249–72
Ditmas, M. R., 'The Curtana or Sword of Mercy', *Journal of the British Archaeological Association*, 3rd
     series, 29 (1966), 122–33
Docherty, H., 'Robert de Vaux and Roger de Stuteville, Sheriffs of Cumberland and Northumberland,
     1170–1185', *ANS*, 28 (2005), 65–102
—— 'The Murder of Gilbert the Forester', *Haskins Society Journal*, 23 (2011), 155–204
Dor, J., 'Langues françaises et anglaises, et multilinguisme à l'époque d'Henri II Plantagenêt', *CCM*, 29,
     61–72
Draper, P., 'William of Sens and the Original Design of the Choir Termination of Canterbury
     Cathedral, 1175–1179', *Journal of the Society of Architectural Historians*, 42 (1983), 238–48
Duby, G., *Le Dimanche de Bouvines* (Paris, 1973), trans. C. Tihanyi as *The Legend of Bouvines. War,
     Religion and Culture in the Middle Ages* (Cambridge, 1990)
—— 'Youth in Aristocratic Society', in G. Duby, *The Chivalrous Society*, trans. C. Postan (London,
     1977), 112–22
—— *Medieval Marriage* (Baltimore, 1979)
—— *Guillaume le Maréchal, ou le meilleur chevalier du monde* (Paris, 1984)
Duggan, A., 'The Coronation of the Young King in 1170', *Studies in Church History*, 2, ed.
     G. J. Cumming (London, 1968), 165–78
—— 'Ralph de Diceto, Henry II and Becket', *Authority and Power. Studies in Medieval History
     Presented to Walter Ullman*, ed. B. Tierney and P. Linehan (Cambridge, 1980), 59–81
—— 'The Cult of St Thomas Becket in the Thirteenth Century', *St Thomas Cantilupe, Bishop of
     Hereford. Essays in his Honour*, ed. M. Jancey (Hereford, 1982), 21–44
—— 'Geoffrey Ridel (d. 1189), administrator and bishop of Ely', *ODNB*
—— 'Diplomacy, Status and Conscience: Henry II's Penance for Becket's Murder', *Forschungen zur
     Reichs-, Papst- und Landesgeschichte: Peter Herde zum 65. Geburtstag*, ed. K. Borchardt and E. Bunz
     (Stuttgart, 1998), 265–90, reprinted in A. Duggan, *Thomas Becket: Friends, Networks, Texts and Cult*
     (Aldershot, 2007), 265–90

—— 'Ne in dubium: The Official Record of Henry II's Reconciliation at Avranches, 21 May 1172', EHR, 115 (2000), 643–58, reprinted in A. Duggan, Thomas Becket: Friends, Networks, Texts and Cult (Aldershot, 2007), 643–58

Thomas Becket (London, 2004)

—— 'The Price of Loyalty: The Fate of Thomas Becket's Learned Household', Thomas Becket: Friends, Networks, Texts (Aldershot, 2007), 1–18

—— Thomas Becket: Friends, Networks, Texts and Cult (Aldershot, 2007)

Duggan, C., 'The Becket Dispute and Criminous Clerks', Bulletin of the Institute for Historical Research, xxxv (1962), 1–28

—— 'Richard of Ilchester, Royal Servant and Bishop', TRHS, 5th series, 16 (1966), 1–21

Dunbabin, J., France in the Making, 843–1180 (Oxford, 2000)

—— 'Henry II and Louis VII', Henry II. New Interpretations, 47–62

Duncan, A. A. M., Scotland. The Making of the Kingdom (Edinburgh, 1975)

—— The Kingship of the Scots, 842–1292: Succession and Independence (Edinburgh, 2002)

Dutton, K., 'Ad erudiendum tradidit: The Upbringing of Angevin Comital Children', Anglo-Norman Studies, 32 (2010), 24–39

—— 'The Personnel of Comital Administration in Greater Anjou, 1129–1151', Haskins Society Journal, 23 (2011), 125–54

—— 'The Assertion of Identity, Authority and Legitimacy: Angevin Religious Patronage in the County of Maine, 1110–1151', Monasteries on the Borders of Medieval Europe: Conflict and Cultural Interaction, ed. E. Jamroziak and K. Stöber (Turnhout, 2014), 211–36

Dutton, M. L., 'Aelred Historian: Two Portraits in Plantagenet Myth', Cistercian Studies Quarterly, 20 (1993), 113–44

Eaglen, R. J., The Abbey and Mint of Bury St Edmunds to 1279 (British Numismatic Society Special Publication, no. 5; London, Spink, 2006)

Eales, R., 'Local Loyalties in Norman England: Kent in Stephen's Reign', ANS, 8 (1985), 88–108

—— 'William of Ypres, styled count of Flanders (d. 1164/5)', ODNB

Edwards, J. G., 'Henry II and the Fight at Coleshill: Some Further Reflections', Welsh Historical Review, 3 (1967), 253–61

Evans, J., Art in Medieval France, 987–1498 (London, 1948)

Evans, M., The Death of Kings. Royal Deaths in Medieval England (London, 2006)

Everard, J., Brittany and the Angevins. Province and Empire, 1158–1203 (Cambridge, 2000)

—— 'Lands and Loyalties in Plantagenet Brittany', Noblesses de l'espace Plantagenêt (1154–1224), ed. M. Aurell (Poitiers, 2001), 185–97

—— 'Wace: The Historical Backround: Jersey in the Twelfth Century', Maistre Wace: A Celebration. Proceedings of the International Colloquium held in Jersey, 10–12 September 2004, ed. G. S. Burgess and J. Weiss (Société Jersaise, 2006), 1–16

Evergates, T., Feudal Society in the Baillage of Troyes under the Counts of Champagne, 1152–1284 (London, 1975)

Fawtier, R., The Capetian Kings of France. Monarchy and Nation, 987–1328 (London, 1960)

Federenko, G., 'The Thirteenth-Century Chronique de Normandie', ANS, 35 (2012), 163–80

Flahiff, G. B., 'Ralph Niger: an Introduction to his Life and Works', Mediaeval Studies, 2 (1940), 104–26

Flanagan, M. T., 'Strongbow, Henry II and Anglo-Norman Intervention in Ireland', War and Government in the Middle Ages. Essays in Honour of J. O. Prestwich, ed. J. Gillingham and J. C. Holt (Woodbridge, 1984), 62–77

—— Irish Society, Anglo-Norman Settlers, Angevin Kingship: Interactions in Ireland in the Late Twelfth Century (Oxford, 1989)

—— 'Henry II, the Council of Cashel and the Irish Bishops', Peritia, 10 (1996), 184–211

—— 'Household Favourites: Angevin Royal Agents in Ireland under Henry II and John', Seanchas. Studies in Early and Medieval Irish History and Literature in Honour of Francis J. Byrne, ed. A. R. Smith (Dublin, 2005), 357–80

—— 'William fiz Aldelin [William Fitzaldhelm], (d. before 1198), administrator', ODNB

Fliche, A., Le Règne de Philippe Ier, roi de France (1060–1108) (Paris, 1912)

Flori, J., L'Idéologie du glaive: le préhistoire de la chevalerie (Geneva, 1984)

—— 'Chevalerie et liturgie', Le Moyen Âge, 4e série, 23 (1978), 247–78, 409–42

—— L'Essor de la chevalerie, XI–XIIe siècles (Geneva, 1986)

—— Richard Coeur de Lion: roi-chevalier (Paris, 1999), trans. J. Birrell, Richard the Lionheart: King and Knight (Edinburgh, 2006)

—— Aelinor d'Aquitaine. La reine insoumise (Paris, 2004), trans. O. Classe, Eleanor of Aquitaine, Queen and Rebel (Edinburgh, 2007)

Folz, R., La Souvenir et la légende de Charlemagne dans l'empire germanique médiéval (Paris, 1950)

Foreville, R., *L'Église et la royauté sous Henri II Plantagenêt (1154–1189)* (Paris, 1943)
—— 'Le Sacre des rois anglo-normands et angevins et le serment du sacre (XIe–XIIe siècles)', *Proceedings of the Battle Conference on Anglo-Norman Studies*, 1 (1978), 49–62
Forey, A., 'Henry II's Crusading Penances for Becket's Murder', *Crusades*, 7 (2008), 153–64
Fowler, G. H., 'Henry FitzHenry at Woodstock', *EHR*, 39 (1924), 240–41
Fox, L., *Leicester Castle* (Leicester, 1944)
France, J., *Western Warfare in the Age of the Crusades, 1000–1300* (London, 1999)
—— ed., *Mercenaries and Paid Men. The Mercenary Identity in the Middle Ages* (Leiden, 2008)
—— 'Capuchins as Crusaders; Southern Gaul in the Twelfth Century', *Reading Medieval Studies*, 36 (2010), 77–93
—— 'People against Mercenaries: The Capuchins in Southern Gaul', *Journal of Medieval Military History*, 8 (2010), 1–22
—— 'Mercenaries and Capuchins in Southern France', *Shipping, Trade and Crusade in the Medieval Mediterranean. Studies in Honour of John Pryor*, ed. R. Gurtwagen and E. Jeffreys (Aldershot, 2012), 289–315
Franklin, R. M., 'Hugh de Moreville (d. 1173/4)', *ODNB*
Funck-Bretano, F., *The Middle Ages* (London, 1922)
Gaborit-Chopin, D., 'Le Trésor au temps de Suger', *Le Trésor de St Denis, les dossiers d'archéologie*, 158 (1991)
Garnett, G., 'The Third Recension of the English Coronation Ordo: The Manuscripts', *Haskins Society Journal*, 11 (1998), 43–71
—— *Conquered England: Kingship, Succession and Tenure, 1066–1166* (Oxford, 2007)
—— 'Robert Curthose – the Duke who Lost his Trousers', *ANS*, 35 (2012), 213–44
Gathagan, L., 'The Trappings of Power: The Coronation of Matilda of Flanders', *Haskins Society Journal*, 13 (2000), 21–39
Gauthiez, B., 'Hypothèses sur la fortification de Rouen au onzième siècle: le donjon de Richard II, et l'enceinte de Guillaume', *Anglo-Norman Studies*, 14 (1992), 61–76
—— 'Paris, un Rouen capétien? Développements comparés de Rouen et de Paris sous les règnes de Henri II et Philippe Auguste', *ANS*, 16 (1993), 117–36
Geary, P., *Living with the Dead in the Middle Ages* (London, 1994)
Gem, R. D. H., 'The Romanesque Rebuilding of Westminster Abbey', *Proceedings of the Battle Conference on Anglo-Norman Studies*, 3 (1980), 33–60
Géraud, H., 'Les *Routiers* au XIIe siècle', *Bibliothèque de l'École des Chartes*, 3 (1841–1842), 125–47
'Mercadier: les *Routiers* au XIIIe siècle', *Bibliothèque de l'École des Chartes*, 3 (1841–1842), 417–43
Gillingham, J., 'Some Legends of Richard the Lionheart: Their Development and Influence', *Riccardo Cuor di Leone nella storia e nella leggenda, Accademia Nazionale dei Lincei, problemi attuali di scienza e di cultura*, 253 (1981), 35–50, and reprinted in Gillingham, *Richard Coeur de Lion*, 181–92
—— 'War and Chivalry in the History of William Marshal', *Thirteenth Century England II*, ed. P. Coss and S. Lloyd (Woodbridge, 1988), 1–13, reprinted in Gillingham, *Richard Coeur de Lion*, 227–41
—— 'Love, Marriage and Politics in the Twelfth Century', *Forum for Modern Language Studies*, 25 (1989), 292–303, reprinted in Gillingham, *Richard Coeur de Lion*, 243–55
—— 'The Context and Purposes of Geoffrey of Monmouth's *History of the Kings of Britain*', *ANS*, 13 (1991), 99–118, reprinted in Gillingham, *The English in the Twelfth Century*, 19–40
—— 'The English Invasion of Ireland', *Representing Ireland: Literature and the Origins of Conflict, 1534–1660*, ed. B. Bradshaw, A. Hadfield and W. Maley (Cambridge, 1993), 24–42, reprinted in Gillingham, *The English in the Twelfth Century*, 145–60
—— *Richard Coeur de Lion: Kingship, Chivalry and War in the Twelfth Century* (London 1994)
—— 'Henry II, Richard I and the Lord Rhys', *Peritia*, 10 (1996), 225–36, reprinted in Gillingham, *The English in the Twelfth Century*, 59–68
—— 'The Travels of Roger of Howden and his View of the Irish, Scots and Welsh', *ANS*, 20 (1997), 151–70, reprinted in Gillingham, *The English in the Twelfth Century*, 69–91
—— *Richard I* (London and New Haven, Conn., 1999)
—— *The English in the Twelfth Century: Imperialism, National Identity and Political Values* (Woodbridge, 2000)
—— 'Royal Newsletters, Forgeries and English Historians: Some Links between Court and History in the Reign of Richard I', *La Cour Plantagenêt (1154–1204)*, ed. M. Aurell (Poitiers, 2000), 71–86
—— *The Angevin Empire* (2nd edn, London, 2001)
—— 'From *Civilitas* to Civility: Codes of Manners in Medieval and Early Modern England', *TRHS*, (2002), 267–89
—— 'Two Yorkshire Historians Compared: Roger of Howden and William of Newburgh', *Haskins Society Journal*, 12 (2002), 15–37

—— 'Events and Opinions: Norman and English Views of Aquitaine, *c*.1152–*c*.1204', *The World of Eleanor of Aquitaine: Literature and Society in Southern France between the Eleventh and Thirteenth Centuries*, ed. M. Bull and C. Léglu (Woodbridge, 2005), 57–81

—— 'Problems of Integration within the Lands Ruled by the Norman and Angevin Kings of England', *Fragen der politischen Integration im mittelalterlichen Europa*, ed. W. Maleczek (Ostfildern, 2005), 85–135

—— '*Stupor Mundi*: 1204 et un obituaire de Richard Coeur de Lion depuis longtemps tombé dans l'oubli', *Plantagenêts et Capétiens*, 397–412

—— 'The Cultivation of History, Legend and Courtesy at the Court of Henry II', *Writers of the Reign of Henry II: Twelve Essays*, ed. R. Kennedy and S. Meecham-Jones (New York, 2006), 25–52

—— 'Writing the Biography of Roger of Howden, King's Clerk and Chronicler', *Writing Medieval Biography, 750–1250: Essays in Honour of Professor Frank Barlow*, ed. D. Bates, J. Crick and S. Hamilton (Woodbridge, 2006), 207–20

—— 'Doing Homage to the King of France', *Henry II: New Interpretations*, ed. C. Harper-Bill and N. Vincent (Woodbridge, 2007), 63–84

—— 'At the Deathbeds of the Kings of England', *Herrscher- und Fürstentestemente im westeuropäische Mittelalter*, ed. B. Kasten (Cologne, Weimar and Vienna, 2008), 509–30

—— 'The Meeting of the Kings of France and England, 1066–1204', *Normandy and its Neighbours, 900–1250. Essays for David Bates*, ed. D. Crouch and K. Thompson (Turnhout, 2011), 17–42

—— 'Coeur de Lion in Captivity', *Quaestiones medii aevi novae*, 18 (2013), 59–83

Gilmour, D., 'Bekesbourne and the King's Esnecca, 1110–1445', *Archaeologia Cantiana*, 132 (2012), 315–27

Gómez-Moreno, M., *El Panteon Real de las Huelgas de Burgos* (Madrid, 1946)

Goodrich, M., 'Bartholemeus Anglicus on Child-rearing', *History of Childhood Quarterly/Journal of Psychohistory*, 3 (1975), 75–84

Görich, K., 'Verletzte Ehre. König Richard der Löwenherz als gefangener Kaiser Heinrichs VI', *Historisches Jahrbuch*, 123 (2003), 65–91

—— *Friedrich Barbarossa. Eine Biographie* (Munich, 2011)

Gouiran, G., 'Bertran de Born, troubadour de la violence?', *La Violence dans le monde médiéval* (Aix-en-Provence, 1994), 237–51

Grandsen A., *Historical Writing in England*, 2 vols (London, 1974, 1982)

Grant, L., 'Suger and the Anglo-Norman World', *ANS*, 19 (1997), 51–68

—— *Abbot Suger of St Denis* (Harlow, 1998)

—— *Architecture and Society in Normandy, 1120–1270* (New Haven, Conn., and London, 2005)

Green, J., 'Lords of the Norman Vexin', *War and Government in the Middle Ages*, ed. J. Gillingham and J. C. Holt (Woodbridge, 1984), 47–63

—— 'Anglo-Scottish Relations, 1066–1174', *England and Her Neighbours, 1066–1453* M. Jones and M. Vale (London: Hambledon, 1989), 53–72

—— 'Aristocratic Loyalties on the Northern Frontier of England, circa 1100–1174', *England in the Twelfth Century: Proceedings of the 1988 Harlaxton Symposium*, ed. D. Williams (Woodbridge, 1990), 83–100

—— *The Aristocracy of Norman England* (Cambridge, 1997)

—— 'Fécamp et les rois anglo-normands', *Tabularia. Sources écrites de la Normandie médiévale*, 2 (2002) 9–18

Henry I: King of England and Duke of Normandy (Cambridge, 2006)

—— 'Henry I and the Origins of the Court Culture of the Plantagenets', *Plantagenêts et Capétiens: coufrontations et héritages*, ed. M. Aurell and N.-Y. Tonnerre (Brépols, 2006), 485–96

Greenhill, E., 'Eleanor of Aquitaine, Abbot Suger and Saint-Denis', *Eleanor of Aquitaine: Patron and Politician*, ed. W. W. Kibler (Austin, 1976), 81–113

Grundmann, H., 'Rotten und Brabazonen. Söldner-heere in 12. Jahrhundert', *Deutsches Archiv für die Erforschung des Mittelalters*, 5 (1942), 419–92

Guillot, O., *Le Comte d'Anjou et son entourage au XIe siècle*, 2 vols (Paris, 1972)

Gyorffy, G., 'Thomas à Becket and Hungary', *Hungarian Studies in English*, 4 (1969), 45–52

Hackett, W. M., 'Knights and Knighthood in *Girart de Roussillon*', *Ideals and Practice of Medieval Knighthood*, II, ed. C. Harper-Bill and R. Harvey (Woodbridge, 1988), 40–5

Hagger, M., *The Fortunes of a Norman Family; the de Verduns in England, Ireland and Wales, 1066–1316* (Dublin, 2001)

Hallam, E., 'Henry II, Richard I and the Order of Grandmont', *JMH*, 1 (1975), 165–86

—— 'Royal Burial and the Cult of Kingship in France and England, 1060–1330', *JMH*, 8 (1982), 339–80

—— 'Henry [Henry the Young King] (1155–1183), Prince', *ODNB*

Halphen, L., *Le Comté d'Anjou au xième siècle* (Paris, 1906)

—— 'Les Entrevues des rois Louis VII et Henri II durant l'exil de Thomas Becket en France', in Halphen., *A travers l'histoire du Moyen Âge* (Paris, 1950), 266–74

Hamilton, B., 'Women in the Crusader States: The Queens of Jerusalem, 1100–1190', *Medieval Women*, ed. D. Baker (Ecclesiastical History Society, 1978), 143–74

—— 'Prester John and the Three Kings of Cologne', *Studies in Medieval History presented to R. H. C. Davis*, ed. H. Mayr-Harting and R. I. Moore (London, 1985), 177–91

—— *The Leper King and his Heirs. Baldwin IV and the Crusader Kingdom of Jerusalem* (Cambridge, 2000)

—— 'Ralph (d. 1174), administrator and Bishop of Bethlehem', *ODNB*, 45, 871–2

Harris, I., 'Stephen of Rouen's *Draco Normannicus*: a Norman Epic', *The Epic in History*, ed. L. S. Davidson, S. N. Mukherjee and Z. Zlatar (Sydney, 1994), 112–24

Haskins, C. H., *Norman Institutions* (Cambridge, Mass., 1918)

Hearn, M. F., 'Canterbury Cathedral and the Cult of Becket', *Art Bulletin*, 76 (1994), 19–54

Hervey, R. F., 'Cross-Channel Gossip in the Twelfth Century', *England and the Continent in the Middle Ages: Studies in Memory of Andrew Martindale*, ed. J. Mitchell (Stamford, 2000), 48–59

Hicks, L. V. and Brenner, E., *Society and Culture in Medieval Rouen, 911–1300* (Turnhout, 2012)

Hodgson, C. E., *Jung Heinrich, König von England, Sohn König Heinrichs II* (Jena, 1906)

Hollister, C. W., 'Normandy, France and the Anglo-Norman Regnum', *Speculum*, 51 (1976), 202–42, reprinted in Hollister, *Monarchy, Magnates and Institutions in the Anglo-Norman World* (London, 1986), 17–57

—— *Henry I*, ed. A. C. Frost (London and New Haven, Conn., 2001)

Hollister, C. W. and Keefe, T. K., 'The Making of the Angevin Empire', *Journal of British Studies*, 12 (1973) 3–19

Holt, J. C., 'Politics and Property in Early Medieval England', *Past and Present*, 57 (1972), 3–52, reprinted in Holt, *Colonial England, 1066–1215* (London, 1997), 113–60

—— 'Feudal Society and the Family in Early Medieval England, II: Notions of Patrimony', *TRHS*, 5th series, 33 (1983), 193–220, reprinted in *Holt Colonial England*, 197–222

—— 'The Acta of Henry II and Richard I of England, 1154–1189: The Archive and its Historical Implications', *Fotographische Sammlungen Mittelältischer Urkunden in Europa*, ed. P. Rück (Sigmaringen, 1989), 137–40

—— '1153: The Treaty of Winchester', *The Anarchy of Stephen's Reign*, ed. E. King (Oxford, 1994), 291–316

—— 'The Writs of Henry II', *Proceedings of the British Academy*, 89 (1996), 47–64

—— *Magna Carta* (Cambridge, 3rd edn, 2015)

Holt, J. C. and Mortimer, R., *Acta of Henry II and Richard I* (List and Index Society, Special Series, 21, Gateshead, 1986)

Hosler, J., 'Henry II's Military Campaigns in Wales, 1157–1165', *Journal of Medieval Military History*, 2 (2004), 53–71

—— 'The Brief Military Career of Thomas Becket', *Haskins Society Journal*, 15 (2006), 88–100

—— *Henry II. A Medieval Soldier at War, 1147–1189* (Leiden, 2007)

—— 'Revisiting Mercenaries under Henry Fitz Empress', *Mercenaries and Paid Men: The Mercenary Identity in the Middle Ages*, ed. J. France (Leiden, 2008), 33–42

Houth, E., *Les Comtes de Meulan, ix–xiii siècles*, Mémoires de la société historique et archéologique de Pontoise, du Val d'Oise et du Vexin, vol. 70 (Pontoise, 1981)

Hudson, J. G. H., 'Richard FitzNigel and the "Dialogue of the Exchequer"', *Perceptions of the Past in Twelfth-Century Europe*, ed. P. Magdalino (1992), 75–98

—— *The Formation of the English Common Law* (Harlow, 1996)

—— *The Oxford History of the Laws of England*, II, *871–1216* (Oxford, 2012)

—— 'Ilchester, Richard of', *ODNB*

Huffman, J. P., *The Social Politics of Medieval Diplomacy. Anglo-German Relations, 1066–1307* (Ann Arbor, Mich., 2000)

Hutchison, C. A., *The Hermit Monks of Grandmont* (Kalamazoo, Mich., 1989)

Hutton, W. H., *Thomas Becket* (Cambridge, 1926)

Hyams, P., 'What Did Henry III of England Think in Bed and in French about Kingship and Anger?', *Anger's Past. The Social Uses of Emotion in the Middle Ages*, ed. B. H. Rosenwein (Ithaca, NY, and London, 1998), 92–126

Innes, M., '"A Place of Discipline": Carolingian Courts and Aristocratic Youth', *Court Culture in the Early Middle Ages. Proceedings of the First Alcuin Conference*, ed. C. Cubitt (Turnhout, 2003), 59–76

Isaac, S., 'The Problem with Mercenaries', *The Circle of War in the Middle Ages: Essays on Medieval Military and Naval History*, ed. D. J. Kagay and L. J. Villalon (Woodbridge, 1999), 101–10

—— 'Cowardice and Fear Management: The 1173–74 Conflict as a Case Study', *Journal of Medieval Military History*, 4 (2006), 50–64

Jaeger, C. S., *The Origins of Courtliness. Civilizing Trends and the Formation of Courtly Ideals, 939–1210* (Philadelphia, Pa., 1985)

Jarnut, J., 'Die Frühmittelalterliche Jagd unter rechts- und sozialgeschichtlichen Aspekten', *L'uomo di fronte al mondo animale nell'alto medioevo* (XXXI Settimana, Spoleto, 1985), 765–98

John, E., *Orbis Britanniae* (Leicester, 1966)

Johns, S. M., *Noblewomen, Aristocracy and Power in the Twelfth-Century Anglo-Norman Realm* (Manchester, 2003)

Johnston, R. C., 'The Historicity of Jordan Fantosme's *Chronicle*', *JMH*, 2 (1976), 159–68

Joliffe, J. E. A., *Angevin Kingship* (London, 1955)

Jones, L., 'From Anglorum Basileus to Norman Saint: The Transformation of Edward the Confessor', *Haskins Society Journal*, 12 (2002), 99–120

Jones, M., 'Geoffrey, duke of Brittany (1158–1186)', *ODNB*

Jones, T. M., 'The Generation Gap of 1173–1174: The War of the Two Henries', *Albion*, 5 (1973), 24–40

—— *War of the Generations. The Revolt of 1173–4* (University Microfilms International for the Medieval Text Association, Ann Arbor, Mich., 1980)

Jordan, K., *Henry the Lion* (Oxford, 1986)

Kantorowicz, E. H., *Frederick the Second, 1194–1250* (London, 1931)

—— *Laudes Regiae: a Study in Liturgical Acclamations and Medieval Ruler Worship* (Berkeley and Los Angeles, 1946)

Kaeuper, R. W., *Chivalry and Violence* (Oxford, 2001)

—— 'William Marshal, Lancelot and the Issue of Chivalric Identity', *Essays in Medieval Studies*, 22 (2005), 1–19

Kastner, L. E., 'Bertran de Born's Sirventes against King Alphonso of Aragon', *Modern Philology*, 34 (1937), 225–48

Kealey, E. J., *Roger of Salisbury, Viceroy of England* (Berkeley and London, 1972)

Keefe, T. K., 'Geoffrey Plantagenet's Will and the Angevin Succession', *Albion*, 6 (1975), 226–74

—— *Feudal Assessments and the Political Community under Henry II and his Sons* (Berkeley, Los Angeles and London, 1983)

—— 'Place Date Distribution of Royal Charters and the Historical Geography of Patronage Strategies at the Court of Henry II Plantagenet', *Haskins Society Journal*, 1 (1990), 179–88

—— 'Shrine Time. Henry II's Visits to Thomas Becket's Tomb', *Haskins Society Journal*, 11 (2003), 115–22

—— 'William [William of Blois], earl of Surrey [Earl Warenne] (c.1135–1159)', *ODNB*

—— 'Henry II (1133–1189), King of England, duke of Normandy and of Aquitaine, and count of Anjou', *ODNB*

Keen, M., *Chivalry* (New York and London, 1984)

—— *Nobles, Knights and Men-at-Arms in the Middle Ages* (London, 1996)

Keen, M. with Barker, J. R. V., 'The Medieval English Kings and the Tournament', *Das ritterliche Turnier im Mittelalter zu einer vergleichenden Formen und Verhaltensgeschichte des Rittertums*, ed. J. Fleckenstein (Göttingen, 1985), 212–28; reprinted in M. Keen, *Nobles, Knights and Men-at-Arms in the Middle Ages* (London, 1996), 83–100

Keenan-Kedar, N., 'Alienor d'Aquitaine conduite en captivité. Les peintures murales commémoratives de Sainte Radegonde de Chinon', *CCM*, 41 (1998), 317–30

Kellerman, W., 'Bertran de Born und Herzogin Matilda von Sachsen', *Études de civilisation médiévale (IXe–XIIe siècles): mélanges offerts à Edmond-René Crozet* (Poitiers, 1974), 447–60

Kelly, S. E., 'Offa (d. 797), king of the Mercians', *ODNB*

Kemp, B., 'The Miracles of the Hand of St James', *Berkshire Archaeological Journal*, 65 (1970), 1–19

Kidson, P., 'Gervase, Becket and William of Sens', *Speculum*, 68 (1993), 969–91

King, D. J. C., *Castellarium Anglicanum*, 2 vols (Milwood, NY, 1983)

King, E., *Medieval England, 1066–1485* (Oxford, 1988)

—— 'The Accession of Henry II', *Henry II. New Interpretations*, 24–46

—— *King Stephen* (London, 2010)

—— 'Henry of Winchester: The Bishop, the City and the Wider World', *Anglo-Norman Studies*, 37 (2014), 1–23

—— 'Eustace (c.1129–1153), count of Boulogne', *ODNB*

—— 'Henry of Blois (c.1093–1171), bishop of Winchester', *ODNB*

—— 'William Peverel (b. c.1090, d. after 1155), baron', *ODNB*

Kingsford, C. L., 'Some Political Poems of the Twelfth Century', *EHR*, 5 (1890), 311–26

Kleinast, W., *Deutschland und Frankreich in der Kaiserzeit*, 3 vols (Stuttgart, 1974–1975)

Knowles, D., *Thomas Becket* (London, 1970)

Kosztolnyik, Z. J., *From Colman the Learned to Béla III (1095–1196): Hungarian Domestic Policies and their Impact upon Foreign Affairs* (Boulder, colo., 1987), 212–14

Koziol, G., 'England, France and the Problem of Sacrality in Twelfth-Century Ritual', *Cultures of Power, Lordship, Status and Process in Twelfth-Century Europe*, ed. T. Bisson (Philaelphia, Pa., 1995), 124–48

Krüger, K. H., 'Herrschaftsnachfolge als Vater–Sohn-Konflikt', *Frühmittelalterliche Studien*, 36 (2002), 225–40

Kuhl, E., 'Time and Identity in Stephen of Rouen's *Draco Normannicus*', *JMH*, 40 (2014), 421–34

Landon, L., *The Itinerary of Richard I* (Pipe Roll Society, new series, xiii, London, 1935)

de Lasteyrie, C., *L'Abbaye de Saint-Martial de Limoges* (Paris, 1901)

Laszlovsky, J., 'Nicholaus Clericus: a Hungarian Student at Oxford University in the Twelfth Century', *JMH*, 14 (1988), 217–31

Latimer, P., 'Henry II's Campaigns against the Welsh, 1165', *Welsh History Review*, 14 (1989), 523–35

—— 'How to Suppress a Rebellion: England, 1173–74', *Rulership and Rebellion in the Anglo-Norman World, c. 1066–c. 1216. Essays in Honour of Professor Edmund King*, ed. P. Dalton and D. Luscombe (Farnham, 2015), 163–77

Lawyer, J. E., 'Ailred of Rievaulx's Life of Edward the Confessor: A Medieval Idea of Kingship', *Fides et Historia*, 31 (1999), 45–65

Legge, D. M., 'The Inauguration of Alexander III', *Proceedings of the Society of Antiquaries of Scotland*, 80 (1945–1946), 77–80

—— *Anglo-Norman in the Cloisters* (Edinburgh, 1950)

—— *Anglo-Norman Literature and its Background* (Oxford, 1963)

Le Goff, J., 'The Symbolic Ritual of Vassalage', in Le Goff, *Time, Work and Culture* (Chicago, 1980), 237–87

Le Jan, J., 'Apprentissages militaires, rites de passage, et remises d'armes au haut Moyen Âge', *Éducation, apprentisages, initiation au Moyen Âge. Actes du premier colloque international de Montpellier, Cahiers du CRISIMANO*, 1 (1993), 214–22

Lejeune, R., 'La Date du *Conte du Graal* de Chrétien de Troyes', *Le Moyen Âge*, 60 (1954), 51–79

Lemarignier, J.-F., *Recherches sur l'hommage en marche et les frontières féodales* (Lille, 1945)

Le Patourel, J. H., 'The Norman Conquest, 1066, 1106, 1154', *Proceedings of the Battle Conference on Anglo-Norman Studies*, 1 (1978), 103–20, 216–20

—— 'Le Gouvernement de Henri II Plantagenêt et la mer de la Manche', *Recueil d'études offerts au Doyen M. de Bouärd* (Annales de Normandie extra, Caen, 1982), II, 323–33

—— 'Henri II Plantagenêt et la Bretagne', *Mémoires de la Société d'Histoire et d'Archéologie de la Bretagne*, 58 (1981), 99–116; reprinted in Le Patourel, *Feudal Empires: Norman and Plantagenet* (London, 1984), 1–17

—— 'The Plantagenet Dominions', in Le Patourel, *Feudal Empires: Norman and Plantagenet* (London, 1984), 289–308

—— 'Angevin Successions and the Angevin Empire', in Le Patourel, *Feudal Empire: Norman and Plantagenet* (London, 1984), 1–17

Le Saux, F. H. M., *A Companion to Wace* (Cambridge, 2005)

Lemoine Descourtieux, A., 'Les Pouvoirs sur la frontière de l'Avre (XIe–XIIIe siècle), Eure: du pouvoir seigneurial au pouvoir ducal, puis à l'autonomie urbaine', *Les Lieux de pouvoir au Moyen Âge en Normandie et sur ses marges*, ed. M.-M. Flambard-Héricher (Tables Rondes du CRAHM, 2. Caen, 2006), 101–18

—— *La Frontière normande de l'Avre. De la fondation de la Normandie à sa réunion au domaine royal (911–1204)* (Mont-Saint-Aignan, 2011)

Levison, W., *England and the Continent in the Eighth Century* (Oxford, 1946)

Lewis, A. W., 'Anticipatory Association of the Heir in Early Capetian France', *AHR*, 83 (1978), 906–27

—— *Royal Succession in Capetian France: Studies on Familial Order and the State* (Cambridge, Mass., and London, 1981)

—— 'The Birth and Childhood of King John: Some Revisions', *Eleanor of Aquitaine, Lord and Lady*, ed. B. Wheeler and J. C. Palsons (New York, 2003), 159–75

Lewis, S., *The Art of Matthew Paris in the Chronica Majora* (Berkeley, 1987)

Leyser, K., 'Frederick Barbarossa, Henry II and the Hand of St James', *EHR*, 90 (1975), 481–506

—— *Rule and Conflict in an Early Medieval Society: Ottonian Saxony* (London, 1979)

—— 'Ritual, Ceremony and Gesture: Ottonian Germany', in Leyser, *Communications and Power in Medieval Europe. The Carolingian and Ottonian Centuries*, ed. T. Reuter (London, 1994), 189–213

Lieberman, M., 'A New Approach to the Knighting Ritual', *Speculum*, 90 (1015), 391–423

Lindemann, R. H. F., 'The English Esnecca in Northern European Sources', *Mariner's Mirror*, 74 (1988), 75–82

Lloyd, J. E., *A History of Wales from the Earliest Times to the Edwardian Conquest*, 2 vols (London, 1911)

Lobel, M. D., *The Borough of Bury St Edmund's* (Oxford, 1935)

—— *The British Atlas of Historic Towns*, ed. M. D. Lobel, II. *The City of London. From Prehistoric Times to c.1520* (Oxford, 1989)

Lodge, A., 'Literature and History in the *Chronicle* of Jordan Fantosme', *French Studies*, 44 (1992), 257–70

Lovatt, M. 'Geoffrey (1151?–1212)', *ODNB*

—— 'Archbishop Geoffrey of York: a Problem in Anglo-French Maternity', *Records, Administration and Aristocratic Society in the Anglo-Norman Realm*, ed. N. Vincent (Woodbridge, 2009), 91–124

Luchaire, A., *Études sur les actes de Louis VII* (Paris, 1885)

—— *Louis VI le Gros. Annales de sa vie et de son règne (1081–1137)* (Paris, 1890)

—— 'Hugues de Clers et le "De senescalcia Franciae"', *Mélanges d'histoire du Moyen Âge*, I, in *Bibliothèque de la Faculté des lettres de Paris*, III, 1897)

—— *Social France at the Time of Philip Augustus* (New York, 1912)

Luckhardt, J., and Niehoff, F., eds, *Heinrich der Löwe und seine Zeit. Herrschaft und Repräsentation der Welfen*, 1125–1235, 3 vols (Munich, 1995)

Lutan, S., 'L'Iconographie royale de Saint-Martin de Candes', *Alienor d'Aquitaine* (303: Arts, Recherches et Creation, Nantes, 2004), 108–17

Luxford, J. M., 'The Tomb of King Henry I in Reading Abbey: New Evidence Concerning its Appearance and the Date of its Effigy', *Reading Medieval Studies*, 30 (2004), 15–31

Lyon, J. R., 'Fathers and Sons: Preparing Noble Youths to be Lords in Twelfth-Century Germany', *JMH*, 34 (2008), 291–310

Lyttleton, G., *The History of the Life of Henry the Second and of the Age in which he Lived*, 4 vols (London, 1767)

McCarthy, M. R., Summerson, H. R. T. and Annis, R. G., *Carlisle Castle. A Survey and Documentary History* (Historic Buildings and Monuments Commission, London, 1990)

McCracken, P. 'Scandalizing Desire: Eleanor of Aquitaine and the Chroniclers', *Eleanor of Aquitaine. Lord and Lady*, ed. B. Wheeler and J. C. Parsons (New York, 2003), 247–64

Macdonald, I., 'The Chronicle of Jordan Fantosme: Manuscripts, Author and Versification', *Studies in Medieval French presented to Alfred Ewart* (1961), 242–58

Macé, L., *Les Comtes de Toulouse et leur entourage, XIIe–XIIIe siècles. Rivalités, alliances et jeux de pouvoir* (Toulouse, 2000)

McGlynn, S., *Blood Cries from Afar. The Forgotten Invasion of England* (Stroud, 2013)

McKisack, M., 'London and the Succession to the Crown during the Middle Ages', *Studies in Medieval History presented to F. M. Powicke*, ed. R. W. Hunt, W. A. Pantin and R. Southern (Oxford, 1948), 76–89

MacLeod, C., *The Lost Prince. The Life and Death of Henry Stuart* (London, 2012)

Maitland, F. W., 'Henry II and the Criminous Clerks', *EHR*, 7 (1892), 224–34

Marritt, S., 'Secular Cathedrals and the Anglo-Norman Aristocracy', *Cathedrals, Communities and Conflict in the Anglo-Norman World*, ed. P. Dalton, C. Innsley and L. Wilkinson (Woodbridge, 2011), 151–68

Martin, E., 'Haughley Castle', *Proceedings of the Suffolk Institute of Archaeology and History*, 42 (2012), 543–9

Martin, J. and Walker, L. E. M., 'At the Feet of St Stephen Muret: Henry II and the Order of Grandmont *Redivivus*', *JMH*, 16 (1990), 1–12

Martindale, J., '"*Cavalaria et Orgueill*". Duke William IX and the Historian', *Ideals and Practice of Medieval Knighthood, II. Papers from the Third Strawberry Hill Conference*, ed. C. Harper-Bill and R. Harvey (Woodbridge, 1988), 87–116

—— '"An Unfinished Business": Angevin Politics and the Siege of Toulouse, 1159', *ANS*, 23 (2000), 115–54

—— 'Secular Propaganda and Aristocratic Values: The Autobiographies of Count Fulk le Réchin of Anjou and William of Poitou, duke of Aquitaine', *Writing Medieval Biography. Essays in Honour of Frank Barlow*, ed. D. Bates, J. Crick and S. Hamilton (Woodbridge, 2006), 143–59

Marvaud, F., *Histoire des vicomtes et de la vicomté de Limoges*, 2 vols (Paris, 1873)

Mason, E., 'Rocamadour in Quercy above all other Churches: The Healing of Henry II', *The Church and Healing*, ed. W. J. Sheils (Studies in Church History, 19, 1982), 39–54

—— 'The Hero's Invincible Weapon: an Aspect of Angevin Propaganda', *The Ideals and Practice of Medieval Knighthood, III. Papers from the Fourth Strawberry Hill Conference, 1988*, ed. C. Harper-Bill and R. Harvey (Woodbridge, 1990), 121–37

—— '"The Site of King-Making and Consecration": Westminster Abbey and the Crown in the Eleventh and Twelfth Centuries', *The Church and Sovereignty*, ed. D. Wood (Oxford, 1991), 57–76

Mason, J. F. A., 'William [William Aetheling, William Adelinus, William Adelingus] (1103–1120)', *ODNB*

Matthew, D., *The Norman Kingdom of Sicily* (Cambridge, 1992)

Mayr-Harting, M., 'Henry II and the Papacy, 1170–1189', *Journal of Ecclesiastical History*, 16 (1965), 39–53

Ménager, L. R., 'L'Institution monarchique dans les états normands d'Italie', *CCM*, 2 (1959), 303–31, 445–68

Mesqui, J. and Toussaint, P., 'Le Château de Gisors aux XIIe et XIIIe siècles', *Archéologie médiévale*, 20 (1990), 253–317

Meyer, P., 'Notice sur la manuscrit II, 6, 24 de la bibliothèque de l'université de Cambridge', *Notices et extraits de la Bibliothèque nationale*, 32/ii (1886), 37–81

Michel, F., 'Deux années du règne de Henri II (1173–1174)', *Revue anglo-française*, 2ème série, 2 (Paris, 1841), 5–44

Mitchell, S. K., *Taxation in Medieval England* (New Haven, Conn., 1951)

Mooers, S. L. 'Backers and Stabbers: Problems of Loyalty in Robert Curthose's Entourage', *Journal of British Studies*, 21 (1981), 1–17

Moore, O. H., *The Young King Henry Plantagenet 1155–1183 in History, Literature and Tradition* (Columbus, Ohio, 1925)

Morey, A. and Brooke, C. N. L., *Gilbert Foliot and his Letters* (Cambridge, 1965)

Moss, V., 'Normandy and England in 1180: The Pipe Roll Evidence', *England and Normandy in the Middle Ages*, ed. D. Bates and A. Curry (London, 1994), 185–95

—— 'The Norman Fiscal Revolution, 1193–8', *Crises, Revolutions and Self-Sustained Growth. Essays in European Fiscal History, 1130–1830*, ed. W. M. Ormrod, M. Bonney and R. Bonney (Stamford, 1999), 38–57

—— 'The Defence of Normandy, 1193–8', *ANS*, 24 (2001), 145–61

Muntz, P., *Frederick Barbarossa* (Ithaca, NY, 1969)

Musset, L., 'Rouen au temps des Francs et sous les ducs', in M. Mollat, ed., *Histoire de Rouen* (Paris, 1979), 31–74

—— 'Les Sépultures des souverains normands: un aspect de l'idéologie du pouvoir', *Autour du pouvoir ducal normand, X–XIIe siècles*, ed. L. Musset, J.-M. Bouvris and J.-M. Maillefer (Cahiers des Annales de Normandie, 17, Caen, 1985), 19–44

'Un Empire à cheval sur la mer: les périls de la mer dans l'État anglo-normand d'après les chartes, les chroniques et les miracles', *Les Hommes et la mer dans l'Europe du Nord-Ouest de l'Antiquité à nos jours*, ed. A. Lottin, J.-C. Hoquet and S. Lebecq (Villeneuve d'Ascq, 1986), 413–24

—— 'Une Aristocratie d'affaires anglo-normande après la conquête', *Études normandes*, 35 (1986),

Musson, A., 'Controlling Human Behaviour? The Last Judgement in Late Medieval Art and Architecture', *Theorizing Legal Personhood in Late Medieval England*, ed. A. D. Boboc (Leiden, 2015), 166–91

Nelson, J. L., 'The Rites of the Conqueror', *The Proceedings of the Battle Conference on Anglo-Norman Studies*, 4 (1982 for 1981), 117–32, 210–21, and reprinted in J. Nelson, *Politics and Ritual in Early Medieval Europe* (1986), 375–401

—— 'Carolingian Royal Ritual', *Rituals of Royalty. Power and Ceremonial in Traditional Societies*, ed. D. Cannadine and S. Price (Cambridge, 1987), 137–80

—— 'Early Medieval Rites of Queen-making and the Shaping of Medieval Queenship', *Queens and Queenship in Medieval Europe*, ed. A. J. Duggan (Woodbridge, 1997), 301–15

Neveux, F., 'La Ville de Sées du haut Moyen Âge à l'époque ducale', *ANS*, 17 (1994), 2145–63

—— 'L'Urbanisme au Moyen Âge dans quelques villes de Normandie', *L'Architecture normande au Moyen Âge*, ed. M. Baylé (Caen, 1997), I, 271–87

—— *La Normandie des ducs aux rois, Xe–XIIe siècle* (Rennes, 1998)

Nichols, D., *Medieval Flanders* (London, 1992)

Nip, R., 'The Political Relations between England and Flanders, 1066–1128', *ANS*, 21 (1998), 145–67

Nolan, K., 'The Queen's Choice: Eleanor of Aquitaine and the Tombs at Fontevraud', *Eleanor of Aquitaine. Lord and Lady*, ed. B. Wheeler and J. C. Parsons (New York, 2003), 377–405

Norgate, K., *England under the Angevin Kings*, 2 vols (London, 1887)

—— *John Lackland* (London, 1902)

—— *The Minority of Henry III* (London, 1912)

—— *Richard the Lionheart* (London, 1924)

Ohnesorge, W., 'Das Mitkaisertum in der abendländischen Geschichte des früheren Mittelalters', *Zeitschrift der Savigny-Stiftung für Rechtsgeschichte*, 67 (1950), 309–35; and reprinted in Ohnesorge, *Abendland und Byzanz* (Darmstadt, 1963)

—— 'Die Idee der Mitregentschaft bei den Sachsenherrschern', *Mitteilungen des Österreichischen Staatsarchivs*, 25 (1972), 539–48, reprinted in Ohnesorge, *Ost-Rom und der Western* (Darmstadt, 1983), 117–27

Oksanen, E., 'The Anglo-Flemish Treatises and Flemish Soldiers in England, 1101–1163', *Mercenaries and Paid Men. The Mercenary Identity in the Middle Ages*, ed. J. France (Leiden, 2008), 261–74

—— *Flanders and the Anglo-Norman World, 1066–1216* (Cambridge, 2012)

Oppitz-Trotman, G., 'Penance, Mercy and Saintly Authority in the Miracles of St Thomas Becket', *Studies in Church History*, 47 (2011), 136–47

Opll, F., *Friedrich Barbarossa* (Darmstadt, 1990)

Oram, R., *David I. The King who Made Scotland* (Stroud, 2004)

Orme, N., *From Childhood to Chivalry; the Education of English Kings and the Aristocracy, 1066–1530* (London, 1984)

Orpen, G. H., *Ireland under the Normans, 1169–1333*, 4 vols (Oxford, 1911–20)

Ostrogorsky, G., 'Das Mitkaisertum im mittelalterlichen Byzanz', *Doppelprinzipat und Reichsteilung im Imperium Romanum*, ed. E. Kornemann (Leipzig and Berlin, 1930), 166–78

Owen, D. D. R., *Eleanor of Aquitaine. Queen and Legend* (Oxford, 1993)

—— *William the Lion, 1143–1214: Kingship and Culture* (East Linton, 1997)

Painter, S., *William Marshal: Knight-Errant, Baron and Regent of England* (Baltimore, Md., 1933)

Parisse, M., 'Le Tournoi en France, des origines à la fin du XIIIe siècle', *Das Ritterliche Tournier im Mittelalter*, ed. J. Fleckstein (Göttingen, 1985), 175–211

Paterson, L. M., 'Knights and the Concept of Knighthood in Twelfth-Century Occitan Epic', *Forum of Modern Language Studies*, 17 (1981), 117–30

—— 'Great Court Festivals in Southern France and Catalonia in the Twelfth and Thirteenth Centuries', *Medium Aevum*, 51 (1982), 213–21

—— *The World of the Troubadours. Medieval Occitan Society, c. 1100–c. 1300* (Cambridge, 1993)

Patterson, R. B., 'William, second earl of Gloucester (d. 1183)', *ODNB*

Peltzer, J., 'Henry II and the Norman Bishops', *EHR*, 119 (2004), 1202–29

Penman, M., 'The Bruce Dynasty, Becket and Scottish Pilgrimage to Canterbury, c.1178–1404', *JMH*, 32 (2006), 346–70

Pfister, C., *Études sur le règne de Robert le Pieux, (996–1031)* (Paris, 1885)

Phair, R. W., 'William Longespée, Ralph Bigod and Countess Ida', *American Genealogist*, 77 (2002), 279–81

Plassmann, A., 'The King and his Sons: Henry II's and Frederick Barbarossa's Succession Strategies Compared', *ANS*, 36 (2013), 149–66

Poole, A. L., 'Henry Plantagenet's Early Visits to England', *EHR*, 47 (1932), 447–51

Power, D., 'Of What did the Angevin Frontier of Normandy Comprise?', *ANS*, 17 (1994), 181–202

—— 'King John and the Norman Aristocracy', *King John. New Interpretations*, ed. S. D. Church (Woodbridge, 1999), 117–36

—— 'Angevin Normandy', *A Companion to the Anglo-Norman World*, ed. C. Harper-Bill and E. M. C. van Houts (Woodbridge, 2003), 63–85

—— *The Norman Frontier in the Twelfth and Early Thirteenth Centuries* (Cambridge, 2004)

—— 'Les Châteaux de la Normandie: défenses Plantagenêts ou résidences aristocratiques?', *Cinquante années d'études médiévales: à la confluences de nos disciplines: Actes du Colloque organisé à l'occasion de cinquentenaire du CESCM, Poitiers, 1–4 septembre 2003*, ed. C. Arrignon *et al.* (Turnhout, 2005), 149–64

—— 'Henry, Duke of the Normans (1149/50–1189)', *Henry II. New Interpretations*, 85–128

—— '"La Rage méchante des traîtres prit feu". Le discours sur la révolte sous les rois Plantagenêts (1144–1224)', *La Trahison au Moyen Âge. De la monstruosité au crime politique (Ve–XVe siècles)*, ed. M. Billoré and M. Soria (Presses universitaires de Rennes, 2009), 53–65

Powicke, F. M., 'The Honour of Mortain in the Norman *Infeudationes Militium* of 1172', *EHR*, 26 (1911), 89–93

—— *The Loss of Normandy, 1189–1204* (Manchester, 1913; 2nd edn, Manchester and New York, 1961)

Prentout, H., *De l'origine de la formule 'Dei gratia' dans les chartes d'Henri II* (Caen, 1926)

Prestwich, J. O., *The Place of War in English History, 1066–1214* (Woodbridge, 2004)

Prestwich, M., *Armies and Warfare in the Middle Ages: The English Experience* (New Haven, Conn., and London, 1996)

—— 'The Victualling of Castles', *Soldiers, Nobles and Gentlemen. Essays in Honour of Maurice Keen*, ed. P. Coss and C. Tyerman (Woodbridge, 2009), 169–82

Previté Orton, C. W., *The Early History of the House of Savoy (1000–1233)* (Cambridge, 1912)

Puccetti, V. L., *Un fantasma letterario. Il «Re Giovane» del Novellino* (Bologna, 2008)

Putter, A., 'Knights and Clerics at the Court of Champagne: Chrétien de Troyes' Romances in Context', *Medieval Knighthood V. Papers from the Sixth Strawberry Hill Conference*, ed. S. Church and R. Harvey (Woodbridge), 243–66

Radford, L. B., *Thomas of London before his Consecration* (Cambridge, 1984)

Ramsay, J. H., *A History of the Revenues of the Kings of England, 1066–1399*, 2 vols (Oxford, 1925)

Rector, G., '"Faites le mien désir": Studious Persuasion and Baronial Desire in Jordan Fantosme's Chronicle', *JMH*, 34 (2008), 311–46

Reed, P. C., 'Countess Ida, Mother of William Longespée, Illegitimate Son of Henry II', *American Genealogist*, 77 (2002), 137–49

Renoux, A., *Fécamp. Du palais ducal aux palais de Dieu* (Paris, 1991)

Reynolds, S., 'The Rulers of London in the Twelfth Century', *History*, 57 (1972), 337–57

Richard, A., *Histoire des comtes de Poitou, 778–1204*, 2 vols (Paris, 1903)

Richardson, H. G., 'The English Coronation Oath', *TRHS*, 4th series, 23 (1941), 129–58

—— 'The English Coronation Oath', *Speculum*, 24 (1949), 44–75

—— 'The Coronation in Medieval England: The Evolution of the Office and the Oath', *Traditio*, 16 (1960) 111–202

Rigg, A. G., *A History of Anglo-Latin Literature, 1066–1422* (Oxford, 1992)

Roacher, J., *Rocamadour et son pèlerinage: étude historique et archéologique*, 2 vols (Toulouse, 1979)

Robinson, I. S., *Henry IV of Germany, 1056–1106* (Cambridge, 1999)

Rogers, R., *Latin Siege Warfare in the Twelfth Century* (Oxford, 1992)

Rosenthal, J. T., 'The King's "Wicked Advisors" and Medieval Baronial Rebellions', *Political Science Quarterly*, 82 (1967), 595–618

Rosenwein, B. H., ed., *Anger's Past: The Social Uses of an Emotion in the Middle Ages* (Ithaca, NY, and London, 1998)

Ross, B., 'Audi Thoma . . . Henriciani Nota: A French Scholar Appeals to Thomas Becket?', *EHR*, 89 (1974), 333–8

Round, J. H., 'The Commune of London', in Round, *The Commune of London and Other Studies* (London, 1899), 219–60

—— 'The Inquest of the Sheriffs (1170)', in Round, *The Commune of London* (London, 1899), 125–36

—— 'The Families of St John and of Port', *The Genealogist*, new series, 16 (1899–1900), 1–13

—— 'The Honour of Ongar', *Transactions of the Essex Archaeological Society*, new series, vii (1900), 142–52

—— *Studies in Peerage and Family History* (London, 1901)

—— 'The Early Charters of St John's Abbey, Colchester', *EHR*, 16 (1901), 721–30

—— 'The Counts of Boulogne as English Lords', *Studies in Peerage and Family History* (London, 1901), 147–81

—— 'A Glimpse of the Young King's Court (1170)', in Round, *Feudal England* (London, 1909), 503–8

—— *The King's Serjeants and Officers of State* (London, 1911)

Rowe, J. G., 'Alexander III and the Jerusalem Crusade. An Overview of Problems and Failures', *Crusaders and Muslims in Twelfth-Century Syria*, ed. M. Shatzmiller (Leiden, 1992), 118–23

Rowlands, I. W., '"Warriors fit for a Prince": Welsh Troops in Angevin Service, 1154–1216', *Mercenaries and Paid Men. The Mercenary Identity in the Middle Ages*, ed. J. France (Leiden, 2008), 207–30

Russell, J. C., 'The Canonization of Opposition to the King in Angevin England', *Haskins Anniversary Essays*, ed. C. H. Taylor and J. L. La Monte (Boston, 1929), 279–90, reprinted in Russell, *Twelfth-Century Studies* (New York, 1978), 248–60

Saltman, A., *Theobald. Archbishop of Canterbury* (London, 1956)

Sandford, F., *A Genealogical History of the Kings of England and Monarchs of Great Britain* (London, 1677)

Sandy, A., 'The Financial Importance of the London Temple in the Thirteenth Century', *Essays in Medieval History Presented to T. F. Tout*, ed. A. G. Little and F. M. Powicke (Manchester, 1925), 147–62

Sassier, Y., *Louis VII* (Paris, 1991)

—— '*Reverentia Regis*; Henri II face à Louis VII', *1204. La Normandie entre Plantagenêts et Capetiens*, ed. A.-M. Flambard-Héricher and V. Gazeau (Caen, 2007), 23–35

Saul, N., *For Honour and Fame. Chivalry in England, 1066–1500* (London, 2011)

Scaglioni, A., *Knights at Court. Courtliness, Chivalry and Courtesy from Ottonian Germany to the Italian Renaissance* (Berkeley, Los Angeles and Oxford, 1991)

Scammell, G. V., *Hugh du Puiset, Bishop of Durham* (Cambridge, 1956)

Schlicht, M., *La Cathédrale de Rouen vers 1300* (Caen, 2005)

Schlight, J., *Monarchs and Mercenaries* (New York, 1968)

Schmidt, U., *Königswahl und Thronfolge im 12. Jahrhundert* (Cologne, Weimar and Vienna, 1987)

Scholz, B. W., 'The Canonization of Edward the Confessor', *Speculum*, 36 (1961), 38–49

Schramm, P. E., *A History of the English Coronation* (Oxford, 1937)

—— *Herrschaftszeichen und Staatssymbolik*, 4 vols (Stuttgart, 1954–1978)

Schröder, S., *Macht und Gabe: Materielle Kultur am Hof Heinrichs II. Von England* (Husum, 2004)

Scott, W. W., 'Malcolm IV', *ODNB*

Seabourne, G., *Imprisoning Medieval Women. The Non-Judicial Confinement and Abduction of Women in England, c.1170–1509* (London, 2011)

Sedgwick, W. B., 'The Bellum Troianum of Joseph of Exeter', *Speculum*, 5 (1930), 49–76

Seipel, W, ed., *A Brief Guide to the Kunsthistorisches Museum, II: Masterpieces of the Secular Treasury* (Vienna, 2008)

Sharpe, R., *A Handlist of Latin Writers of Great Britain and Ireland before 1540* (Turnhout, 1997, revised 2001)

Slade, C. F., 'Wallingford Castle in the Reign of Stephen', *Berkshire Archaeological Journal*, 58 (1960), 33–43

Slocum, K. B., 'Angevin Marriage Diplomacy and the Early Dissemination of the Cult of Thomas Becket', *Medieval Perspectives*, 14 (1999), 214–28

Smail, R. C., 'Latin Syria and the West, 1149–1187', *TRHS*, 5th series, 19 (1969), 1–20

Smalley, B., *The Becket Conflict and the Schools* (Totowa, NJ, 1973)

Smith, R. J., 'Henry II's Heir: The *Acta* and Seal of Henry the Young King, 1170–1183', *EHR*, 116 (2001), 297–326

Spear, D., 'The Norman Empire and the Secular Clergy, 1066–1204', *Journal of British Studies*, 21 (1982), 1–10

—— 'Les Doyens du chapitre cathédrale de Rouen, durant la période ducale', *Annales de Normandie*, 33 (1983), 91–119

—— 'Les Chanoines de la cathédrale de Rouen pendant la période ducale', *Annales de Normandie*, 41 (1991), 135–76

—— 'Power, Patronage and Personality in the Norman Cathedral Chapters, 911–1204', *ANS*, 20 (1998), 205–21

Staunton, M., 'Thomas Becket's Conversion', *ANS*, 21 (1998), 193–211

—— *Thomas Becket and his Biographers* (Woodbridge, 2006)

Stenton, D. M., *English Justice between the Norman Conquest and the Great Charter, 1066–1215* (Philadelphia, Pa., 1964)

Stenton, F. M., *Anglo-Saxon England* (3rd edn, Oxford, 1989)

Stevens, S. D., *Music in Honour of St Thomas* (Sevenoaks, 1975)

Stevenson, A., 'The Flemish Dimension of the Auld Alliance', *Scotland and the Low Countries, 1124–1994*, ed. G. Simpson (East Linton, 1996), 28–42

Stimming, A., *Bertran de Born* (2nd edn, Halle, 1913)

Stocker, D., *St Mary's Guildhall, Lincoln* (London, 1991)

Storelli, X., 'La Figure d'Absalon dans la famille royale anglo-normande (XIe–XXIIe siècles)', *La Parenté déchirée: les luttes intrafamiliales au Moyen Âge*, ed. M. Aurell (Turnhout, 2010), 321–41

Strickland, M. J., 'Arms and the Men: War, Loyalty and Lordship in Jordan Fantosme's Chronicle', *Medieval Knighthood, IV: Papers from the Fifth Strawberry Hill Conference 1990*, ed. C. Harper-Bill and R. Harvey (1992), 187–22

—— *War and Chivalry. The Conduct and Perception of War in England and Normandy, 1066–1217* (Cambridge, 1996)

—— 'On the Instruction of a Prince. The Upbringing of Henry, the Young King', *Henry II. New Interpretations*, ed. C. Harper-Bill and N. Vincent (Woodbridge, 2007), 184–214

—— 'Henry I and the Battle of the Two Kings: Brémule, 1119', *Normandy and its Neighbours, 900–1250: Essays for David Bates*, ed. D. Crouch and K. Thompson (Turnhout, 2011), 77–116

—— 'William Longespée [Lungespée] (I), third earl of Salisbury', *ODNB*

Stringer, K. J., *Earl David of Huntingdon, 1152–1219: a Study in Anglo-Scottish History* (Edinburgh, 1985)

—— 'State-building in Twelfth-Century Britain: David I, King of Scots, and Northern England', *Government, Religion and Society in Northern England, 1000–1700*, ed. J. C. Appleby and P. Dalton (Stroud, 1997), 40–62

—— 'Simon de Senlis (II), earl of Northampton and earl of Huntingdon (d. 1153)', *ODNB*

—— 'Hugh de Moreville (d. 1162)', *ODNB*

Strong, R. C., *Henry, Prince of Wales, and England's Lost Renaissance* (1986)

Coronation. A History of Kingship and the British Monarchy (London, 2005)

Stubbs, W., *Seventeen Lectures on the Study of Medieval and Modern History* (3rd edn, Oxford, 1900)

Suggett, H., 'An Anglo-Norman Return to the Inquest of Sheriffs', *Bulletin of the John Rylands Library*, 27 (1942–43), 179–81

Swietek, F. R., 'King Henry II and Savigny', *Cîteaux*, 38 (1987), 14–23

Tabuteau, E. Z., 'The Role of Law in the Succession to Normandy and England', *Haskins Society Journal*, 3 (1991), 141–69

Tait, J., 'A New Fragment of the Inquest of Sheriffs (1170)', *EHR*, 39 (1924), 80–3

Tanner, H. A., *Families, Friends and Allies: Boulogne and Politics in Northern France and England, c. 879–1160* (Leiden, 2004)

Teske, G., 'Ein unerkanntes Zeugnis zum Sturz des Bischofs Arnulf von Lisieux?', *Francia* 16 (1989), 185–206

Thacker, A.T., 'The Earls and their Earldom', *The Earldom of Chester and its Charters*, ed. A. T. Thacker (Chester Archaeological Society, vol. 71, Chester, 1991), 7–22

—— 'The Cult of King Harold at Chester', *The Middle Ages in the North West*, ed. T. Scott and P. Starkey (Oxford, 1995), 155–76

Thompson, J. W., *The Literacy of the Laity in the Middle Ages* (Berkeley and Los Angeles, 1939)

Thompson, K. H., 'The Lords of Laigle: Ambition and Insecurity on the Borders of Normandy', *ANS*, 18 (1996), 177–99

—— 'Lords, Castellans, Constables and Dowagers: The Rape of Pevensey from the Eleventh to the Thirteenth Century', *Sussex Archaeological Collections*, cxxxv (1997), 213–14

—— *Power and Border Lordship in Medieval France: The County of Perche, c. 1000–1226* (Woodbridge, 2002)

—— 'Affairs of State: The Illegitimate Children of Henry I', *JMH*, 2 (2003), 129–51

—— 'L'Héritier et le remplaçant: le rôle du frère puîné dans la politique anglo-normande (1066–1204)', *Tinchebray, 1106–2006. Actes du colloque de Tinchebray (28–30 septembre 2006)*, ed. V. Gazeau and J. Green (Caen, 2009), 93–100.

Thompson, P. A., 'An Anonymous Verse Life of Thomas Becket', *Mittellateinisches Jahrbuch*, 20 (1985), 147–54

Toch, M., 'The Medieval German City under Siege', *The Medieval City under Siege*, ed. I. A. Corfis and M. Wolfe (Woodbridge, 1995), 35–48

Tout, T. F., 'Hugh, fifth earl of Chester', revised T. K. Keefe, *ODNB*

Trexler, R. C., *The Journey of the Magi: Meanings in History of a Christian Story* (Princeton, NJ, 1997)

Trio, P., 'Vlaanderen in de twaalfde eew: een hoogtepunt in de geschiedenis van het graafschap', *Thomas Becket in Vlaanderen. Waarheid of Legende?* (Kortrjk, 2000), 17–36

Truax, J. A., 'Anglo-Norman Women at War: Valiant Soldiers, Prudent Strategists or Charismatic Leaders?', *The Circle of War in the Middle Ages*, ed. D. J. Kagay and L. J. Villalon (Woodbridge, 1999), 111–26

Turbutt, G., *A History of Derbyshire*, vol 2: *Medieval Derbyshire* (Cardiff, 1999)

Türk, E., *Nugae Curialium. Le règne d'Henri II Plantagenêt (1145–1189) et l'éthique politique* (Geneva, 1977)

—— *Pierre de Blois. Ambitions et remords sous les Plantegenêts* (Turnhout, 2006)

Turner, R. V., 'The Origins of Common Pleas and the King's Bench', *American Journal of Legal History*, 21 (1977), 238–54

—— 'The Miles Literatus in Twelfth- and Thirteenth-Century England: How Rare a Phenomenon?', *American Historical Review*, 83 (1978), 928–45

—— 'Richard Barre and Michael Belet: Two Angevin Civil Servants', *Medieval Prosopography*, 6 (1985), 25–49

—— 'Eleanor of Aquitaine and her Children: an Inquiry into Medieval Family Attachment', *JMH*, 14 (1988)

—— 'The Children of Anglo-Norman Royalty and their Upbringing', *Medieval Prosopography*, 11 (1990), 17–52

—— 'Changing Perceptions of the New Administrative Class in Anglo-Norman and Angevin England: The Curiales and their Conservative Critics', *Journal of British Studies*, 29 (1990), 93–117

—— 'The Problem of Survival for the Angevin Empire: Henry II's and his Sons' Vision Compared to Late Twelfth-Century Realities', *American Historical Review*, 100 (1995), 78–95

—— 'The Households of the Sons of Henry II', *La Cour Plantagenêt (1154–1204). Actes du Colloque tenu à Thouars du 30 avril au 2 mai 1999*, ed. M. Aurell (Poitiers, 2000), 49–62

—— 'Eleanor of Aquitaine, Twelfth-Century English Chroniclers and her "Black Legend"', *Nottingham Medieval Studies*, 52 (2008), 17–42

—— *Eleanor of Aquitaine* (New Haven, Conn., and London, 2009)

—— 'Walter de Coutances (d. 1207), administrator and archbishop of Rouen', *ODNB*

Turvey, R., *The Lord Rhys, Prince of Deheubarth* (Llandysul, 1997)

Tyerman, C., *England and the Crusades, 1095–1588* (Chicago, 1988)

Ullmann, W., *Growth of Papal Government* (London, 1955)

Urry, W., *Thomas Becket. His Last Days* (Stroud, 1999)

Van Eickels, K., *Vom inszenierten Konsens zum systematisierten Konflikt: Die englische–französischen Beziehungen und ihre Wahrnehmung und der Wende vom Hoch- zum Spätmittelalter* (Stuttgart, 2002)

—— 'L'Hommage des rois anglais et de leurs héritiers aux rois français au XIIe siècle: subordination imposée ou reconnaissance souhaitée?', *Plantagenêts et Capétiens: confrontations et héritoges*, ed. M. Aurell and N.-Y. Tonnerre (Tarnhout, 2006) 377–85

Van Houts, E. M. C., 'Nuns and Goldsmiths: The Foundation and Early Benefactors of Saint Radegund's Priory, Cambridge', *Church and City, 1000–1500. Essays in Honour of Christopher Brooke*, ed. D. Abulafia, M. Franklin and M. Rubin (Cambridge, 1992), 59–79

—— 'Le Roi et son historien: Henri II Plantagenêt et Robert de Torigni, abbé du Mont-Saint-Michel', *CCM*, 37 (1994), 115–18

—— 'The Anglo-Flemish Treaty of 1101', *ANS*, 21 (1998), 169–74

—— *Memory and Gender in Medieval Europe, 900–1200* (Houndmills, 1999)

'The Warenne View of the Past, 1066–1203', *ANS*, 103–121

Van Werke, H, *Een Vlaamse Graaf van Europees formaat: Filips van de Elzas* (Haarlem, 1976)

Varenbergh, E., *Histoire de relations diplomatiques entre le comté de Flandre et l'Angleterre au Moyen Âge* (Brussels, 1874)

Verbruggen, J. F., *The Art of Warfare in Western Europe during the Middle Ages* (2nd edn, Woodbridge, 1997)

Verhulst, A. E., 'Note sur une charte de Thierry d'Alsace, comte de Flandre, pour l'abbaye de Fontevrault (21 avril 1157)', *Études de civilisation médiévale (IXe–XIIe siècles): mélanges offerts à Edmond-René Labande* (Poitiers, 1974), 711–19

Verlinden, C., *Robert I le Frison* (Antwerp and Paris, 1935)

Verlinden, O., 'The Fairs of Champagne and Flanders', *Cambridge Economic History of Europe*, III ed. M. M. Postan et al. (Cambridge, 1963), 119–50

Viel, R., 'Les Armoiries probables d'Henri II d'Angleterre', *Archivum Heraldicum*, 70 (1965), Bulletin 2–3, 19–23

Vincent, N., *Acta of Henry II and Richard I. Part Two* (List and Index Society, Special Series, 27, Kew, 1996)

—— 'William Marshal, King Henry II and the Honour of Châteauroux', *Archives*, 35 (2000), 1–15

—— 'King Henry II and the Poitevins', *La Cour Plantagenêt*, ed. M. Aurell (Poitiers, 2000), 103–35

—— 'Les Normands de l'entourage d'Henri II Plantagenêt', *La Normandie et l'Angleterre au Moyen Âge*, ed. M. Bouet and V. Gazeau (Caen, 2003), 75–88

—— 'The Murderers of Thomas Becket', *Bischofsmord im Mittelalter*, ed. N. Fryde and D. Reitz (Göttingen, 2003), 211–72

—— *Becket's Murderers* (The Friends of Canterbury Cathedral and the William Urry Memorial Trust, 2004)

—— 'Henry III and the Blessed Virgin Mary', *The Church and Mary*, ed. R. Swanson (Boydell, 2004), 126–46

—— 'Patronage, Politics and Piety in the Charters of Eleanor of Aquitaine', *Plantagenêts et Capétiens*, 17–60

—— 'The Strange Case of the Missing Biographies: The Lives of the Plantagenet Kings of England, 1154–1272', *Writing Medieval Biography, 750–1250. Essays in Honour of Professor Frank Barlow*, ed. D. Bates, J. Cric and S. Hamilton (Woodbridge, 2006) 237–58

—— 'The Court of Henry II', *Henry II. New Interpretations*, ed. C. Harper-Bill and N. Vincent (Woodbridge, 2007), 278–34

—— 'Did Henry II Have a Policy towards the Earls?', *War, Government and Aristocracy in the British Isles, c.1150–1500. Essays in Honour of Michael Prestwich*, ed. C. Given-Wilson, A. Kettle and L. Scales (Woodbridge, 2008), 1–26

—— ed., *Records, Administration and Aristocratic Society in the Anglo-Norman Realm. Papers Commemorating the 800th Anniversary of King John's Loss of Normandy* (Woodbridge, 2009)

—— 'Hugh de Gundeville (fl. 1147–81)', *Records, Administration and Aristocratic Society in the Anglo-Norman Realm. Papers Commemorating the 800th Anniversary of King John's Loss of Normandy*, ed. N. Vincent (Woodbridge, 2009), 125–52

—— 'The Pilgrimages of the Angevin Kings of England', *Pilgrimage. The English Experience from Becket to Bunyon*, ed. C. Morris and P. Roberts (Cambridge, 2010), 20–28

—— 'William of Canterbury and Benedict of Peterborough: The Manuscripts, Date and Context of the Becket Miracle Collections', *Hagiographie, idéologie et politique au Moyen Âge en Occident, Hagiologia*, 8 (2012), 347–87

—— *Norman Charters from English Sources: Antiquaries, Archives and the Rediscovery of the Anglo-Norman Past* (Pipe Roll Society, new series 59, London, 2013)

—— 'The Seals of Henry II and his Court', *Seals and their Context in the Middle Ages*, ed. P. Schofield (Oxford, 2015), 7–34

Vollrath, H., 'The Kiss of Peace', *Peace Treaties and International Law in European History*, ed. R. Lesaffer (Cambridge, 2004), 162–83.

—— 'Alénor d'Aquitaine et ses enfants: une relation affective', *Plantagenêts et Capétiens*, 113–23

Vones-Liebenstein, U., '*Vir uxorious*? Barbarossas Verhältnis zur Comitissa Burgundiae in Umkrieg des Friedens von Venedig', *Stauferreich im Wandel. Ordnungsvorstellungen und Politik in Zeit Friedrich Barbarossas*, ed. S. Weinfurter, Mittelalter Forschungen, 9 (Stuttgart, 2002), 189–219

—— 'Aliénor d'Aquitaine, Henri le Jeune et la révolte de 1173: un prélude à la confrontation entre Plantagenêts et Capetiéns?', *Plantagenêts et Capétiens*, 75–93

Voyer, C., 'Les Plantagenêts et la chapelle de Sainte-Radegonde de Chinon: en débat', *Alienor d'Aquitaine* (303. Arts, recherché, et créations, 2004), 187–93

Wallace-Hadrill, J. M., *Early Germanic Kingship in England and on the Continent* (Oxford, 1971)

Wareham, A., 'The Motives and Politics of the Bigod Family, c.1066–1177', *ANS*, 17 (1994), 223–42

—— 'Hugh (I) Bigod, first earl of Norfolk (d. 1176/1177) magnate', *ODNB*

Warntjes, I., 'Programmatic Double Burial (Body and Heart) of the European High Nobility, c.1200–1400. Its Origin, Geography, and Functions', *Death at Court*, ed. K. H. Spiess and I. Warntjes (Wiesbaden, 2012), 197–259

Warren, W. L., *King John* (London, 2nd edn, 1978)

—— *The Governance of Norman and Angevin England* (London, 1987)

—— 'Biography and the Medieval Historian', *Medieval Historical Writing in the Christian and Islamic Worlds*, ed. D. O. Morgan (London, 1982), 5–18

—— *Henry II* (2nd edn, London and New Haven, Conn., 2000)

Webster, K. G. T., 'The Twelfth-Century Tourney', *Anniversary Papers by Colleagues and Pupils of George Lyman Kitteridge* (Boston and London, 1913), 227–34

Weiler, B., 'Knighting, Homage, and the Meaning of Ritual: The Kings of England their Neighbors in the Thirteenth Century', *Viator*, 37 (2006), 275–300

—— 'Suitability and Right: Imperial Succession and the Norms of Politics in Early Staufen Germany', *Making and Breaking the Rules of Succession in Medieval Europe, c.1000– c.1600*, ed. F. Lachaud and M. Penman (Turnhout, 2008), 71–86

—— 'Kings and Sons: Princely Rebellions and the Structures of Revolt in Western Europe, c.1170–c.1280', *Historical Research*, 82 (2009), 17–40

Westerhof, D., *Death and the Noble Body in Medieval England* (Woodbridge, 2008)

Wethered, F. T., *St Mary's Hurley in the Middle Ages* (London, 1898)

Wheeler, B. and Parsons, J. C., *Eleanor of Aquitaine. Lord and Lady* (New York, 2003)

Whetham, D., *Just Wars and Moral Victories: Surprise, Deception and the Normative Framework of European War in the Later Middle Ages* (Leiden, 2009)

White, G. H., 'The Constitutio Domus Regis and the King's Sport', *Antiquaries Journal*, 30 (1950), 52–6

White, G. J., *Restoration and Reform, 1153–1165. Recovery from Civil War in England* (Cambridge, 2000)

White, S., 'The Politics of Anger', *Anger's Past. The Social Uses of Emotion in the Middle Ages*, ed. B. H. Rosenwein (Ithaca, NY, and London, 1998), 127–52

Wood, C. T., 'Fontevraud, Dynasticism and Eleanor of Aquitaine', *Eleanor of Aquitaine. Lord and Lady*, ed. B. Wheeler and J. C. Parsons (New York, 2003) 407–22

Wyton, A. B., *The Great Seals of England from the Earliest Period to the Present Time* (London, 1887)

Zunthor, P., 'Toujours à propos de la date du *Conte du Graal*', *Le Moyen Âge*, 65 (1959), 579–86

Unpublished Theses

Dutton, K., 'Geoffrey, Count of Anjou and Duke of Normandy, 1129–151' (unpublished PhD thesis, University of Glasgow, 2011)

Schlunz, T. P., 'Archbishop Rotrou of Rouen (1164–1183): A Career Churchman in the Twelfth Century' (PhD thesis, University of Illinois at Urbana-Champaign, 1973)

Smith, R., 'The Royal Family in the Reign of Henry II' (Master of Arts Thesis, University of Nottingham, 1961)

Index